Equal Pay

Employment Law Handbook

August 2011

IDS

THOMSON REUTERS

Equal Pay

Employment Law Handbook

Previous edition 2008

Incomes Data Services Ltd
Finsbury Tower, 103-105 Bunhill Row, London EC1Y 8LZ
Tel: 0845 077 2911 Fax: 020 7393 8081
Website: www.incomesdata.co.uk

ISBN 978 0 414 02987 3

IDS Employment Law Handbook, 'Equal Pay', is published by Incomes Data Services Limited (Registered in England & Wales, Company No 913794. Registered Office and address for service: 100 Avenue Road, London NW3 3PF).

The information contained in this journal in not intended to be a substitute for specific legal advice and readers should obtain advice from a qualified adviser in relation to individual transactions or matters.

No natural forests were destroyed to make this product: only farmed timber was used and re-planted.

A CIP catalogue record for this book is available from the British Library.

Typeset by DC Graphic Design, Swanley Village, Kent BR8 7PA
Printed by St Austell Printing Co, 41 Truro Road, St Austell, Cornwall PL25 5JE

Contents

Abbreviations

Courts

ECJ	European Court of Justice
ECHR	European Court of Human Rights
PC	Privy Council
SC	Supreme Court
HL	House of Lords
CA	Court of Appeal
Ct Sess	Court of Session
NICA	Northern Ireland Court of Appeal
QBD	Queen's Bench Division
Div Ct	(Queen's Bench) Divisional Court
KBD	King's Bench Division
ChD	Chancery Division
NIRC	National Industrial Relations Court
EAT	Employment Appeal Tribunal
ET	Employment Tribunal

Case references

AC	Law Reports, Appeal Cases
All ER	All England Law Reports
Ch	Law Reports, Chancery Division
CMLR	Common Market Law Reports
COET	Employment Tribunal folio number
EAT	Employment Appeal Tribunal unreported case number
ECR	European Case Reports
ET	Employment Tribunal unreported case number
EWCA	Court of Appeal unreported case number
ICR	Industrial Cases Reports
IRLR	Industrial Relations Law Reports
ITR	Industrial Tribunal Reports
KB	Law Reports, King's Bench Division
QB	Law Reports, Queen's Bench Division
SCOET	Scottish Employment Tribunal folio number
TLR	Times Law Reports
WLR	Weekly Law Reports

Legislation

DDA	Disability Discrimination Act 1995
EA	Employment Act 2002
EqA	Equality Act 2010
EqA 2006	Equality Act 2006
EqPA	Equal Pay Act 1970
ERA	Employment Rights Act 1996
ETA	Employment Tribunals Act 1996
RRA	Race Relations Act 1976
SDA	Sex Discrimination Act 1975
TULR(C)A	Trade Union and Labour Relations (Consolidation) Act 1992

Statutory references, unless otherwise stated, are to the Equality Act 2010

Introduction

The United Kingdom has had sex equality legislation in place since 1975, when the Sex Discrimination Act 1975 (SDA) was enacted and the provisions of the Equal Pay Act 1970 (EqPA) came into force. For 25 years, these Acts, together with the relevant EU measures, formed a single code dealing with gender discrimination. The distinction between the two is discussed in Chapter 1 under 'UK gender equality legislation' but, briefly, the EqPA was aimed primarily at discriminatory terms in an employment contract while the SDA covered discrimination in the formation, variation and termination of such a contract, together with harassment. Both the SDA and EqPA were repealed on 1 October 2010 and replaced by the Equality Act 2010 (EqA). The new Act houses all the discrimination provisions in domestic law under one roof. However, the distinction between the areas covered by the EqPA and the SDA persists, as they are governed by separate provisions within the EqA. This Handbook is concerned with contractual 'equal pay', while the concept of 'equal treatment' is dealt with in IDS Employment Law Handbook, 'Sex Discrimination' (2008).

The term 'equal pay' can be misleading, as the statutory provisions are not merely concerned with gender equality in 'pay', but with gender equality in *all* contractual terms. Indeed, Chapter 3 of Part 5 of the EqA – which contains the substantive provisions previously governed by the EqPA – is entitled 'Equality of Terms' rather than 'Equal Pay'. However, given that this area of law has been known as 'equal pay' law for so long – and the term is still used in European legislative measures – we have retained the original terminology in this Handbook.

Like the EqPA, the provisions in Chapter 3 of Part 5 of the EqA operate by implying into the contracts of all employees a 'sex equality clause', which acts to modify an employee's contract to ensure that none of its terms are less favourable than those of a comparable employee of the opposite sex. The sex equality clause will not take effect, however, if the employer can demonstrate that the differential between a claimant and her comparator is due to a 'material factor' other than the difference in sex.

Impact of European law. No discussion of UK equal pay law would be possible without extensive reference to European law – in particular, to Article 157 of the Treaty on the Functioning of the European Union (previously Article 141, and before that Article 119, of the EC Treaty), in which the EU right to equal pay for equal work is enshrined. Given that the EqA is the means by which this right is implemented in the United Kingdom, courts and tribunals must always have Article 157 in mind when considering equal pay issues.

Article 157 is a very short provision, and the simplicity of its terminology has left it to the European Court of Justice (ECJ) to define the limits within which the principle of equal pay should be applied. Unfortunately, this has proved a rather piecemeal process as, at various points over the years, high-profile ECJ decisions have altered our understanding of central concepts such as who might amount to a valid comparator for equal pay purposes, and the workings of the employer's 'genuine material factor defence'. The upshot is that equal pay law is very much a moving target, which at times makes it extremely confusing.

Explosion of equal pay claims. Not only are equal pay claims often extremely complicated, both legally and factually, they are also numerous. In 2008, both Acas and the Tribunals Service published figures indicating that the unthinkable had happened – equal pay had surpassed unfair dismissal to become the most common ground of complaint before employment tribunals. In subsequent years unfair dismissal reclaimed its crown, but the number of equal pay claims remains high, in part as a result of the fact that local government and the health sector have been conducting large-scale job evaluation and regrading initiatives, termed 'single status' and 'Agenda for Change' respectively. Although one of the driving forces behind these exercises was the elimination of sex bias in pay, they – together with the increasing involvement of 'no win, no fee' solicitors and confirmation from the courts that employees are entitled to claim up to six years' arrears of pay – have in fact generated a swathe of equal pay litigation, based on both past and present pay practices. This has placed increasing pressure on the tribunal system, employers and unions alike, and has brought equal pay to the forefront of most employment practitioners' minds.

Male and female claimants. For linguistic ease, the language of the EqPA was couched in terms of the complainant being a woman and, in practice, this was – and still is – normally the case. But this did not mean that only women were entitled to bring proceedings – the rights contained therein applied equally to men. Unlike its predecessor, the EqA takes a gender-neutral approach to drafting, referring to a 'person' where the EqPA would have referred to a woman. However, in this Handbook we have adopted the same language as the EqPA in this regard, so that references to a complainant in the abstract generally refer to a woman. But it should be borne in mind that in every case (except where the context otherwise makes clear) the principles under discussion apply equally to male complainants.

Scheme of the Handbook

The scheme of the Handbook is as follows:

- Chapter 1 outlines the history of equal pay law. It also considers the considerable impact of European law in this area and explains the background to the current public sector equal pay litigation

- Chapter 2 covers the general scope of the equal pay provisions in the EqA and discusses the crucial mechanism by which equal pay is secured under the Act – namely, the contractual 'sex equality clause'

- Chapter 3 is concerned with the items of remuneration and other benefits that are regarded as 'pay' for the purposes of the EqA and the relevant European legal measures

- Chapter 4 contains an analysis of the nature of the comparison that has to be made in order to secure equal pay under the EqA

- Chapters 5, 6 and 7 discuss the three bases on which a claimant can claim equal pay with a comparator of the opposite sex – namely, being employed on 'like work', 'work rated as equivalent' under a job evaluation study, or 'work of equal value'. Chapter 7 includes details of the special tribunal procedure that applies to equal value claims

- Chapter 8 contains an extensive discussion of the 'material factor defence' by which employers can seek to escape liability under the EqA by showing that the pay differential between the claimant and her comparator is due to non-discriminatory factors

- Chapter 9 discusses the means by which the right to equal pay can be enforced and the extent to which arrears of remuneration can be recovered

- Chapter 10 takes a practical look at the features of pay systems that are particularly susceptible to discrimination and considers the steps that can be taken to eliminate such discrimination

- Chapter 11 examines the 'victimisation' provisions that afford special protection to individuals who take action under or in relation to the EqA.

The law is stated as at 1 July 2011. This Handbook completely replaces IDS Employment Law Handbook, 'Equal Pay' (2008), which should now be discarded.

1 Law in context

In June 1888, during a speech entitled 'Female Labour', members of the Fabian **1.1** Society were horrified to learn of the squalid pay and conditions of women working at the Bryant and May match factory in East London. The following day, Annie Besant interviewed some of the 'match girls' and discovered that they were working 14 hours a day for a wage of less than five shillings a week. Even then, they did not always receive their full wage because of a system of fines for offences that included talking, dropping matches and going to the lavatory without permission. On 23 June 1888, Besant wrote a newspaper article about the way the match girls were being treated. The company reacted by attempting to force their workers to sign a statement that they were content with their working conditions. When a group of women refused to sign, the organisers of the group were sacked. Immediately, 1,400 of the women went on strike. Such was the hue and cry from prominent reformers (including Catherine Booth of the Salvation Army and George Bernard Shaw) that, after three weeks, the company agreed to re-employ the dismissed women and bring an end to the system of fines. The women accepted the terms and returned in triumph.

The 1888 Bryant and May dispute was the first strike by unorganised workers to gain national publicity. It led the same year to the Trades Union Congress passing a resolution in favour of the principle of equal pay for women. However, it was a long time before governments were persuaded that it was necessary or desirable to use legislation to achieve equality between the sexes. Women's contribution to the war effort in 1914–18 brought about one, albeit limited, early legislative intervention: the Sex Disqualification (Removal) Act 1919. That Act provided that a person could not be disqualified by sex or marriage from exercising any public function, holding any civil or judicial office or post, entering any civil profession or vocation, or being admitted to any incorporated society. The 1919 Act, however, did not protect women from discrimination once they had entered an office or profession.

1

1.2 In 1955 the Conservative Government agreed, through the Civil Service National Whitley Council, to introduce equal pay for 'like work' in the non-industrial Civil Service. Similar arrangements were subsequently negotiated by trade unions in local government, the nationalised industries and the health service. However, a TUC survey in 1960 concluded that, for the most part, collective bargaining had failed to extend equal pay beyond the public sector – see 'TUC Annual Report 1961'.

At the same time, international trends were encouraging governments to give more attention to the promotion of equal pay and equal opportunities at work. In 1951 the International Labour Organisation (ILO) passed its Convention 100. This provided that 'each member shall, by means appropriate to the methods in operation for determining rates of remuneration, promote equal, in so far as is consistent with such methods, ensure the application to all workers of the principle of equal remuneration for men and women workers for work of equal value'. The United Kingdom was an ILO member, as well as a signatory to the UN Declaration of Human Rights and the European Convention on Human Rights, not to mention aspiring, from the 1950s, to join the European Common Market. In these circumstances, it is not surprising that, over time, British politicians grew more receptive to the idea of protecting the rights of women at work through statutory intervention.

1.3 In 1964 the Labour Party's general election campaign included the so-called 'Charter of Rights for all employees', one of which was 'the right to equal pay for equal work'. After much discussion and delay, this formed the basis of the Equal Pay Act 1970 (EqPA). A subsequent Labour government then pushed through the Sex Discrimination Act 1975 (SDA). These measures came into force together on 29 December 1975 (and remained in force until 1 October 2010, when they, along with almost every other piece of domestic anti-discrimination legislation, including the aforementioned Sex Disqualification (Removal) Act 1919, were replaced by a single statute, the Equality Act 2010 (EqA)).

It was confidently predicted in 1975 that women's pay would rapidly move towards full equalisation with men's. But that has not happened. As we shall see below, the disparity between men's and women's hourly and weekly earnings, though halved since the coming into force of the EqPA, continues to be substantial. In order to understand the context in which the equal pay law operates, it is crucial to appreciate not only the extent of the so-called 'gender pay-gap', but also the complex reasons why, despite legislative efforts, the gap stubbornly persists. No less important are the wider economic and social implications of women receiving lower pay than men.

1.4 This chapter therefore begins by exploring the gender pay gap – what it is and why it matters. We then look at the reasons for the substantial growth in public sector equal pay claims over the last five years, before considering the scope of the current UK gender equality legislation. Equal pay also has a European dimension and the final sections of this chapter focus on the relationship between domestic and European law, setting out the specific EU measures aimed at tackling inequality of pay. As the remaining chapters of this Handbook are devoted to an exploration of these measures in detail, the intention in this chapter is simply to provide context and give readers an overview of the relevant legislative framework.

The gender pay gap   1.5

In 1950, women accounted for 30 per cent of the total labour force. By 1980, that proportion had grown to 40 per cent. Over the last quarter century there has been a further marked increase in the number of women entering the labour market, with women now consistently accounting for approximately half the workforce – the 2010 figures show that the UK workforce consisted of 12.7 million men and 12.3 million women. For all that, there remains a huge difference in the patterns of male and female employment. The most significant concerns part-time working. The Office of National Statistics (ONS) Annual Survey of Hours and Earnings (ASHE) for 2010 shows that 42.3 per cent of the jobs occupied by women are part time (defined as 30 hours or fewer per week). This compares to just 11.7 per cent for men. Clearly, the main reason for this is that women still tend to be the primary carer in their families. Whereas 38 per cent of women with dependent children work part time, the equivalent figure for men is just 4 per cent. This, as we shall see, has a dramatic impact on the pay gap between the sexes.

Extent of the pay gap   1.6
What is clear from the ONS's ASHE for 2010 is that women represent a powerful force in the labour market. When, however, the focus turns to the pay they receive, the statistics reveal a persistent and substantial discrepancy compared with men.

Prior to the enactment of the EqPA, many private companies and public organisations had separate pay scales for men and women. Such were the stark differentials in 1970 that the government of the day agreed to delay the implementation of the EqPA's provisions to give employers time to phase in the necessary changes to their pay structures and collective agreements to achieve formal equality for male and female employees doing 'like work'; hence the reason why an Act passed in 1970 only came into force on 29 December 1975. Across the intervening five-year period, the difference in average earnings between men and women fell from 37 to 30 per cent. Over time, this discrepancy has been further reduced, but at a slow pace. The latest figures derived from the ONS's ASHE reveal that, as at April 2010, the average full-time man in the UK earned £16.25 per hour, whereas the female equivalent earned just £13.73.

This gives a headline gender pay gap of 15.5 per cent. Expressed another way, the average woman receives only 84 pence for every £1 earned by the average man.

1.7 There is also a significant gender pay gap for part-time employees. The 2010 figures showed that the average part-time man earned £12.06 per hour whereas the female equivalent earned £10.64. This comprises a gender pay gap of 11.7 per cent. The *overall* comparison of the earnings of both full- and part-time men and women shows a pay gap of 19.3 per cent

The figures for 2010 represent a small reduction in the size of the pay gap compared with the corresponding figures for the preceding year (down from 16.4 per cent for full-timers, 11.8 per cent for part-timers and 20.1 per cent overall). The trend, therefore, continues to be towards a narrowing of the pay gap, but only by agonisingly small degrees year-on-year. Judged by the rate of progress achieved in the 36 years since the enactment of the EqPA, it will take many more decades before the average female full-time employee will achieve pay parity with an equivalent male full-timer.

1.8 It should be pointed out that these headline gender pay gap percentages are based on the internationally recognised standard using the mean figures for average earnings. Traditionally, the gender pay gap is calculated on the basis of gross hourly earnings excluding overtime as published by the ONS, with women's mean pay expressed as a percentage of men's mean pay. The gender gap is then expressed as the difference between this and 100 per cent. This was the method used in the United Kingdom's official earnings survey figures until 2004, when the ONS announced that its preferred measure had changed to a comparison of median hourly earnings, excluding overtime, for full-time men and women. The median is the midpoint of the earnings distribution. The ONS said it preferred this measure because, unlike the mean, it is not distorted by extreme values – i.e. by comparatively few employees earning disproportionately large or small amounts. On the median measure, the gender pay gap for full-time employees in 2010 was 10.2 per cent, down from 12.2 per cent in 2009.

There has been some controversy over the ONS's changed basis for the pay gap calculation. In particular, it is widely contended that there is every reason to prefer the mean measure when it comes to analysing gender inequality in pay precisely because the extreme values are highly relevant. In any graph depicting the salary distributions of men and women according to occupation, it will be seen that many more women than men are clustered in the jobs at the lower end of the salary range and there are many more men than women at the higher end. The median fails to take this into account and so under-represents the scale of the gender pay gap. The mean figures for earnings continue to be adopted by, among others, the European Commission when calculating comparative figures for the gender pay gap across the European Union and by the ILO for the purposes of monitoring its Conventions on equality.

Influence of occupation, sector and educational attainment. The fact that **1.9** the headline annual figures – howsoever calculated – take into account *all* occupations disguises the fact that in some occupations the gender pay gap is much greater than the average. Conversely, there are some where the pay gap between the sexes is very small, and even a few where women earn, on average, more than men. According to a survey covering 240 occupations conducted by the GMB union in 2007, there are 23 occupations in which pay equality between men and women has now been fully achieved. These include ambulance staff, kitchen and catering assistants, train drivers and social workers. But clearly these are the exception to the rule. The ONS's ASHE for 2010 includes median pay gap figures based on hourly earnings in nine broad occupational sectors, all of which show a gender pay gap. The highest gap of 31.4 per cent was for skilled trades occupations, but there were also high gaps for managerial and senior officials (22.3 per cent) and process, plant and machine operatives (22.2 per cent). The lowest gaps were for professional (1.6 per cent) and associate professional and technical roles (4.9 per cent).

One relatively 'good news' story was highlighted by the Low Pay Commission in its 2008 Annual Report. The Commission observed that, since the introduction of the national minimum wage in 1999, there has been a marked reduction in the differentials between the lowest paid male and female workers. The gap between men's and women's hourly pay among the bottom 20 per cent of earners stood at 10.5 per cent in 1998 but had fallen to 3.8 per cent by 2007. Around two thirds of the jobs that were covered by the increase in the minimum wage in October 2007 were held by women. That women should benefit in this way will come as no surprise, as they are disproportionately represented in the low-paying sectors of the economy. According to the ONS's statistics, 55 per cent of employees working in low-paying sectors are female, with some occupations such as nursery nurses, care assistants, office workers in administrative and secretarial roles, and hairdressers being overwhelmingly so.

As a general rule, the gender pay gap is more of a problem in the private sector **1.10** than in the public sector. For full-time employees, the pay gap for median hourly earnings is 10 per cent in the public sector, but 19.8 per cent in the private sector. The figures for part-time workers show a different story, with a 20.6 per cent gap in the public sector, but a negative pay gap (meaning women earn more than men) of 2 per cent in the private sector. The figures combining part- and full-time median hourly earnings show a gap of 19.2 per cent in the public sector and 27.5 per cent in the private sector. This is partly because, owing to the prevalence of women in the public sector, there is relatively less gender segregation and the opportunities for promotion and attaining senior positions are relatively evenly spread. Nearly two thirds of the public sector workforce comprises women, compared with two fifths of the private sector. Women's greater tendency to work in the public sector is part of the reason why there is a significant gender pay gap among graduates, according to research carried out by Gender Equality Network (part of the Economic and Social Research Council) in 2008. Using data from a study of more than 3,000 graduates who gained their first degrees in 1995, the research found that young women, even at an early stage in their careers, do not appear to have achieved equal earnings with their male peers and that the gender pay gap continues to increase as their careers develop. Few of these women had children, so the impact of family formation and childcare responsibilities on their career patterns could not be the main reason for this significant gap in pay. Examining a number of factors that might be influencing this pattern, including hours of work, sector of the labour market, and the degree subject studied, the research found that, seven years after graduation, more than half of the female graduates in full-time employment were employed in the public or not-for-profit sector, compared with only one third of male graduates.

As public sector earnings are approximately 10 per cent lower than private sector earnings, this suggests that women may be 'trading off' high earnings in their career for other conditions of employment, such as job security, family-friendly policies and job satisfaction. Detailed qualitative interviews disclosed that men were more likely to value high financial rewards, whereas women were more likely to put a high value on doing socially useful work. The research concluded that the Government's current emphasis on persuading organisations of the advantages they gain from retaining well-qualified women may not be enough to narrow the gender pay gap. The research also raises questions about how roles are valued in society and the nature of the tasks that attract high salaries.

1.11 **Geographical and age differentials.** The 2010 ASHE figures include a breakdown of median hourly earnings by region, demonstrating the extent to which the pay gap varies across the country. The figures for all employees (both full- and part-time) show that the South East had the widest pay gap (24.9 per cent), followed by the East Midlands (22.5 per cent). The lowest pay gap was in Northern Ireland (10.2 per cent) – perhaps attributable to the high rate of public sector employment there – followed by Scotland and London (both 17.2 per cent). Note, however, that ASHE only includes regional pay gaps based on median hourly earnings excluding overtime. It seems fair to assume that the pay gap for London would be higher when calculated on the basis of mean hourly earnings, since the financial services industry has a large number of high-earning men.

The pay of women across all age groups is undermined by inequality. But the size of the gap reaches its peak for both full- and part-time female workers in their 40s. The gap is at its narrowest for the younger age groups (0.5 per cent in the case of 16- and 17-year olds, 3.4 per cent in the case of 18–21 year-olds and 3.7 per cent in the case of 22–29 year-olds). It then widens in the 30–39 age band to 14.6 per cent, reaching its high point of 27.4 per cent in the 40–49 age group as women's pay declines and men's continues to grow. These latter two age groups coincide with a very high rate of full-time working for men (over 95 per cent) and a significant rise in part-time working for women. The gender pay gap remains at 27.4 per cent for the 50–59 age group and falls to 19.5 per cent for the 60+ age group.

Clearly, these figures are testimony to the effect that career breaks have on women. Such breaks affect women's level of work experience, which in turn can impact on their pay rates. On returning to the labour market, women often elect to work part time to accommodate the continuing demands of being a primary carer. Even though the pay gap tends to narrow again in a woman's later working life, the considerable detrimental effect on pay and career prospects caused by the earlier move away from full-time employment means that many women carry a legacy of pay inequality throughout the remainder of their working lives. **1.12**

Occupational segregation and related factors **1.13**
It is clear from the discussion above that the headline gender pay gap figures mask the true extent to which women experience inequality in certain sections of the labour market. However, it is rarely the case nowadays that pay inequality is the result of deliberate and overt discrimination. The major causes of pay discrimination tend to be the result of indirect discrimination based on a combination of some or all of the following factors:

- the ingrained notion of the man as principal breadwinner, resulting in the view (underpinned by collective bargaining) that it is socially necessary to ensure that male full-time employees receive a 'family wage'

- the existence of pay structures that disadvantage women because of the greater burden on them of childcare and other domestic responsibilities

- women's segregation into relatively low-paying, predominantly 'female' occupations

- segregation of men and women within the workplace into different types of job – 'female' and 'male' labour – and historical pay bargaining agreements that allow salary structures to reflect the relative negotiating power of groups of predominantly male and female employees

- women's lower positions within internal grading systems and other occupational hierarchies

- the depression of women's pay in women's workplaces and occupations caused by employers' access to cheap, part-time female labour

- the lower incidence of union organisation or other representation in women's workplaces and women's relative lack of bargaining power

• the greater competitive pressure on employers in markets dealing with the products of 'women's labour'.

1.14 Although all these factors contribute to the general explanation for pay inequality, not all feature in every workplace where women are shown to receive lower pay. Nor are the remedies for tackling pay discrimination under the EqA and European Community law equipped to counter every cause of the gender pay gap. Indeed, some factors may not be discriminatory at all. In an analysis of the ASHE pay statistics, 'Modelling the gender pay gap in the UK: 1998 to 2006', an ONS statistician concluded that as much as two thirds of the gender pay gap was attributable to 'unobservable factors'. Of the observable factors, the Report accepted that age, occupation, industry and sector variables all have a significant impact on earnings for men and women. In particular, women's wages are more dispersed by region than men's – supporting theories of reduced female labour mobility resulting in lower earnings in all regions other than London.

More orthodox views generally attribute the pay gap to a combination of three main causes:

• gender segregation in the labour market

• the impact of caring responsibilities

• discrimination.

1.15 Regarding the first of these, official statistics show that more than half of employed women work in just ten occupational groups and that in each of these women predominate in terms of numbers. The fact that some occupations (and to a lesser extent industries) are dominated by women and that the relevant jobs tend to be lower paid are clearly significant factors in explaining the gender pay gap. But other more tentative factors may be at work to explain why women are drawn to particular types of job. Evidence suggests that the seeds of segregation can be sewn during the early years of an individual's life – influenced by gender-stereotyped early environments, the attitudes of parents, teachers and career advisers, etc. Although these influences are hard to measure, their impact cannot be discounted.

To the extent that occupational segregation causes a general undervaluing of so-called 'women's work', the legal remedies currently available do not, with one exception, extend to allowing women to compare themselves with male comparators employed by other employers in different occupations. The exception is where there is shown to be a 'single source' responsible for the pay differences between employees employed by different employers within the same 'service' – see Chapter 4 under '"Same employment" or "single source"'.

1.16 The sole equal pay remedy intended to penetrate job labels and tackle the issue of job segregation is a claim based on 'equal value' – see Chapter 7, 'Work of equal value'. The concept behind an equal value claim is that a woman should be able to compare herself to a man undertaking entirely different work for the same employer on the basis that her work is of equal value to his and that she is accordingly entitled to the same level of remuneration as him. When this remedy was introduced in 1984 the expectation was that deeply held stereotypes and entrenched inequalities within pay structures would be unearthed and dealt with. However, whatever success individual claimants may have had in this regard, no one would seriously claim that the equal value option has been an unqualified triumph. The complexity of the process; the fact that any pre-existing job evaluation study is binding unless proven to be discriminatory; and the fact that an independent expert's report into the comparative value of the female claimant's and male comparator's jobs can lead to protracted arguments and challenge by the parties, have all conspired to undermine the efficacy of equal pay law as it stands at present in overcoming the problems caused by patterns of occupational segregation.

Why does the pay gap matter?   1.17
Injustice is always a good reason for addressing a legal or social problem. And it is undoubtedly unjust that so many of the women who make up half the United Kingdom's working population should suffer discrimination – albeit for complex and multilayered reasons – with regard to their terms and conditions. The former Equal Opportunities Commission estimated that, on the basis of the 2007 gender pay gap, an average woman working full time would lose £330,000 (or £210,000 after deductions for income tax and NI Contributions) over the course of her working life compared with an equivalent man.

But there are wider economic and social consequences to the gender pay gap – there are inefficiency costs associated with undervaluing women's work. To cope with the competing demands of being the primary carer and the need to contribute to the family income, women often elect to work part time. But much part-time work is characterised (especially in the private sector) by low pay and low skills, meaning that women's skills and experience are underused. Switching to part-time work often involves occupational downgrading, with studies showing, for example, that 44 per cent of professional women who downgrade when converting to part-time work move into jobs where the average employee even lacks 'A' levels. The long hours associated with high quality full-time work often trap women into accepting part-time employment well below their potential. As the United Kingdom's modern economy often bemoans a chronic skills shortage, it is reasonable to assume that the failure to utilise women's skills and experience has a substantial economic cost.

Finally, compelling evidence suggests that inequality caused by the gender pay   1.18
gap extends beyond women's working lives. A report commissioned by the Department of Work and Pensions in 2005, 'Women and pensions: the evidence', cited statistics showing that in 2004 only 23 per cent of women aged

9

60 were in receipt of a full basic State pension. 2.2 million women were not making sufficient NI contributions to be entitled to a State pension at all. However, the most dramatic discrepancy between men and women was the extent to which they had access to occupational pension benefits during retirement. A combination of being disproportionately concentrated in occupations where no workplace pension was on offer and lower earnings levels in jobs that did attract pensions meant that, on average, women received between £50 and £100 a week less by way of private pension income than men of an equivalent age.

1.19 Growth in public sector claims

In its Annual Report for 2007/08, the conciliation service Acas announced that the number of equal pay claims received in 2007/08 was 58,513 – up from 27,497 the previous year. This meant that, for the first time in its history, the number of equal pay complaints received by Acas for conciliation exceeded the number of unfair dismissal complaints. The official statistics of the Employment Tribunal Service tell a similar story. Covering the period from April 2006 to March 2007, the figures show that the number of tribunal applications leapt by 155 per cent on the previous year to a record-breaking 44,013 equal pay claims. This was more than two-and-a-half times the number of such claims lodged in 2005/06, and even that number was double the figure for the preceding year. The numbers peaked in 2008/09, when 62,700 equal pay claims were received, before dropping to 45,700 in 2009/10 and then to 37,400 in 2009/10.

This surge in the number of equal pay claims can largely be accounted for by the multiple claims being brought against local authorities and the NHS following the introduction of new job evaluation schemes aimed at combating decades of unequal pay (discussed under 'Local government "single status" litigation' below). It has placed a massive strain not only on the tribunal system but also on the budgets of local authorities and other public sector employers. The size of the equal pay settlements already reached by these employers is astonishing. But what is of even greater concern is the scale of compensation that remains to be paid once claims in the pipeline have been satisfied. Small wonder that newspaper headlines, even before the current budget cuts, spoke of a crisis in local government funding. All this has given urgency to the calls for reform of equal pay law.

1.20 Local government 'single status' litigation

In 1997 public service trade unions and local authority employers entered into a national collective agreement, known as 'the Green Book', which sets out a single pay structure applicable to all local authority employees. This so-called 'single status agreement' covers the pay and conditions for 1.4 million employees ranging from architects and lawyers to cleaners and school meals staff. Prior to

10

the introduction of the single status agreement, the terms and conditions of local authority employees were governed by different collective agreements that were nationally negotiated and reviewed. These were known as 'the White Book' in the case of manual workers, 'the Purple Book' in the case of administrative, professional, technical and clerical workers (APTC), and the 'Red Book' in the case of skilled craft workers.

The principal aim of the new single status agreement was to unify the terms and bargaining structures applicable to the White Book manual workers and Purple Book white collar workers and to this end it provided for all manual and APTC jobs to be graded on the same scales. Crucially, the agreement expressly recognised the need to ensure that the new arrangements complied with equal pay law. One of the fundamental purposes of the agreement was to remove the inequalities of pay that had crept into local government employment as a result of the various bargaining arrangements that had applied to different occupational groups. It was a key requirement that, under the Green Book, there was to be equality of pay for men and women doing equally rated work. For that reason, new job evaluation studies (JESs) were to be conducted locally under procedures involving panels of employer and employee representatives. Once the JESs were completed and the Green Book implemented, the work of any employee on a particular scale would be rated as equivalent to any other employee on that scale, regardless of the nature of their work. This made it inevitable that a great deal of negotiation needed to take place before any individual local authority would be ready for transition to the Green Book.

1.21 Initially, no timetable was specified for completion of the negotiations and no deadline set for implementation. Councils were faced with the task of negotiating local pay structures in a context of cash shortages due to budget constraints imposed by successive governments and progress in implementing single status was therefore very slow. In October 2003 the Local Government Pay Commission identified equal pay as the main issue concerning local authorities. In an effort to address the slow progress in implementing single status, a 2004 national agreement imposed a timetable for the completion and implementation of new pay structures over a three-year period. Local pay and grading reviews were to be completed by April 2006 with full implementation expected by 31 March 2007. Local authorities were to propose a timetable for regular pay audits and conduct an equality impact assessment of changes to pay and grading under single status.

Unfortunately, only 34 per cent of councils had completed pay reviews and/or implemented outcomes by the 31 March 2007 deadline, although according to research conducted by Local Government Employers (LGE), that figure had increased to 47 per cent by the beginning of 2008. In addition, a further 40 per cent had reviews under way. It was particularly unfortunate from the councils' point of view that, with effect from 19 July 2003, the EqPA had been amended to provide that a claimant would, if successful, be entitled to any arrears of pay that she should have received (as a result of the successful claim) going back for a period of up to six years from the date on which tribunal proceedings were commenced – see the discussion in Chapter 9 under 'Remedies – arrears of remuneration'. This had the consequence that, often acting on advice from union representatives, many female employees who had become frustrated by the slow (and in some cases non-existent) progress in securing implementation of the Green Book revisions started to file equal pay claims in large numbers in order to force the issue with their employers and secure their position with regard to backdated pay. At the same time, many other potential claimants found that the official line being taken by their union was to hold off taking legal action while grading reviews were still under way.

1.22 Attracted by the possibility of securing six-year back-payments for large numbers of potential clients, no win, no fee solicitors leapt into the void and encouraged many women to bring claims notwithstanding their unions' equivocations. This has caused considerable tension – not to say hostility – between the private solicitors' firms on the one hand, and the unions and local authorities on the other. Whereas the former contend they are representing the interests of numerous individual claimants who have suffered long-term pay discrimination, the latter argue that employees' interests are better served by securing negotiated settlements based on a fully considered restructuring of grades and pay rates that takes everyone's interests into account.

1.23 **Prohibitive cost of implementing agreements.** According to LGE, councils in England and Wales face a total bill of at least £2.8 billion for dealing with the fall-out from these equal pay issues. Of this sum, around half (£1.49 billion) is accounted for by pay increases resulting from the conferment of new grades after job evaluation and the introduction of a new pay structure. The remainder is made up of back pay (estimated at £0.99 billion), and protected pay (£0.35 billion) paid – usually over two or three years – to protect the salaries of those who find their grading reduced after job evaluation. The concern is that the final total cost could significantly increase given the number of claims involved. Although the Government has offered some additional capitalisation to local authorities to help them meet the eye-watering costs of implementing the single status agreement, there is widespread concern that the sums on offer are nowhere near enough to deal with the problem.

1.24 **Legal implications for employers and unions**

The vast sums of money required to meet the demands of single status is not the only troublesome feature of the equal pay litigation so far as unions and employers are concerned. The extent to which it is lawful for locally negotiated agreements to include protection for the salaries of male workers downgraded following revised job evaluation has itself become the focus of litigation. In July 2008 the Court of Appeal ruled in Redcar and Cleveland Borough Council v

Bainbridge and ors and another case; Middlesbrough Borough Council v Surtees and ors 2009 ICR 133, CA, that temporary pay protection arrangements offered only to those employees who, following the implementation of a JES, would thereby suffer a drop in pay were unlawful as they perpetuated historical indirect sex discrimination. Although the phasing out of pay discrimination by 'cushioning the blow' of sudden pay cuts could, in the Court's view, be a legitimate objective, the arrangements in the particular cases were not objectively justified as the employers had given no thought to mitigating their continuing discriminatory effect. This ruling is discussed in greater detail in Chapter 8, 'Material factor defence', under 'Specific material factors – pay protection'.

Another major headache (in this case specifically for trade unions) was caused by the Court of Appeal's ruling in GMB v Allen and ors 2008 ICR 1407, CA, that a trade union had been guilty of indirect sex discrimination in achieving low-level settlements in respect of female members' equal pay claims against a council as part of its negotiated 'single status' deal. The union had been seeking to strike a balance between three competing objectives: representing its female members who wished to pursue equal pay claims relating to pay inequalities pre-dating the introduction of the revised pay structure; ensuring pay protection for those members whose pay would otherwise be reduced owing to the results of the JES; and improving and ensuring equal pay in the future for all its members. Mindful of the prohibitively large payouts facing the employer – Middlesbrough Metropolitan Borough Council – the union decided to focus on the interests of those seeking protected pay and on its ideal of achieving pay equality for the future, at the cost of maximising the back-pay claims of its female members.

1.25 In line with this policy, the GMB advised some of its members to settle their equal pay claims against the council for approximately 25 per cent of their potential value on the basis that this would avoid lengthy legal proceedings and, in view of the sums involved, possible job losses. Some members who initially accepted the union's advice became disenchanted with the settlement after taking advice from no win, no fee solicitors. They, along with others who had never acceded to the union's position in the first place, brought tribunal claims under the SDA, contending that the union's position had adversely affected female members. The union defended these claims on the ground that any indirect sex discrimination was justified because it had been pursuing the aim of achieving equality with as little collateral damage as possible. In approving the employment tribunal's decision to reject the union's argument, the Court of Appeal held that the methods used by the union to persuade the female members to settle their claims had not been a proportionate means of achieving a legitimate aim.

13

1.26 NHS 'Agenda for Change'

The cases discussed above show what a minefield equal pay law has become for employers and unions struggling to deal with historical and deeply entrenched discrimination in pay structures. Similar issues are afflicting the changes being made to NHS pay structures as the result of the Agenda for Change (AfC) initiative. This, like the Green Book agreement in local government, has entailed a huge programme of job evaluation and harmonisation of terms and conditions, with the aim of achieving a new pay structure that is equal pay proof. But because the focus has been on delivering equal pay for work of equal value in the here and now rather than tackling historical discrimination, unions have advised many of the huge number of female employees employed in the NHS that they have a legal right to back pay if they can prove they earned less than men in comparable jobs. In the light of the ruling in the Allen case (above), they are clearly right to do so. Following the implementation of AfC, many thousands of equal pay claims have been lodged by claimants represented both by Unison and by no win, no fee lawyers. All this mirrors the pattern described above in respect of local government.

1.27 UK gender equality legislation

Until very recently, the principal sex discrimination statutes in the United Kingdom were the Equal Pay Act 1970 (EqPA) and the Sex Discrimination Act 1975 (SDA), both of which came into force on 29 December 1975. The EqPA was concerned with *contractual* sex discrimination, i.e. less favourable treatment of women compared to men (or vice versa) in the terms of employment – despite its name, the Act was never limited to equality in pay. It achieved its purpose by providing that every contract of employment was deemed to include a 'sex equality clause' which modified any contractual term that was less favourable than the equivalent term enjoyed by an actual comparator of the opposite sex doing equal work so as to be no less favourable. However, an employer had a defence to an equal pay claim if it could show that the difference in 'pay' between the claimant and the comparator was genuinely due to a material factor that was not itself the difference of sex.

While the EqPA was wide enough to cover any contractual term, including, but not limited to, those relating to pay, it did not offer a remedy for sex discrimination that was not rooted in the contract of employment. So, for example, an employer's refusal to recruit or promote a woman because of her sex was not covered, as it was not a contractual matter. Such discrimination was left to the SDA, which outlawed any less favourable treatment on the ground of sex in the formation, operation, variation and termination of the employment relationship. In contrast to the EqPA, unequal treatment falling within the scope of the SDA could be proved either by reference to an actual comparator, or by consideration of how a hypothetical comparator would have been treated.

The distinction between discrimination in contractual terms and discrimination **1.28** in all other work-related matters was not without criticism, particularly as statutes such as the Race Relations Act 1976 covered both forms of discrimination and allowed both to be established by way of reference to a hypothetical comparator. Nevertheless, the separation of the EqPA and the SDA lasted until both Acts were repealed and replaced by the Equality Act 2010 in October 2010.

Equality Act 2010 1.29

The Equality Act 2010 (EqA), which repealed and replaced both the EqPA and the SDA on 1 October 2010, is a vast statute, extending to 218 sections and 28 schedules. It was introduced in order to harmonise UK discrimination law that was, up to that point, spread across 35 Acts of Parliament and 52 statutory instruments. However, harmonisation does have its limits, and one of the key decisions made by the Government of the time was to retain the distinction between sex discrimination in contractual terms and sex discrimination in all other work-related matters. The former was the purview of the EqPA and is now governed by Chapter 3 of Part 5 of the EqA, which is entitled 'Equality of Terms' (this Chapter also includes provisions relating to gender equality in pension schemes, formerly found in Ss.62–64 of the Pensions Act 1995). Sex discrimination in all other work-related matters, formerly dealt with by the SDA, is now governed by the general discrimination provisions contained in Part 2 (read with Chapter 1 of Part 5) of the 2010 Act. The distinction between equal pay claims and other claims of sex discrimination has also been maintained in respect of time limits – see Chapter 9 under 'Time limits' for more details.

Indeed, despite calls for fundamental reform, the changes in respect of what can still be termed 'equal pay law' have been minimal – the provisions of the EqPA, as interpreted by three decades of case law, have effectively been transplanted wholesale into the EqA, albeit using different wording on occasion. Thus, a claimant must still point to an actual, as opposed to hypothetical, comparator of the opposite sex who is doing like work, work of equal value or work rated as equivalent (S.65 EqA). A 'sex equality clause' operates to modify any contractual term which is less favourable than that of the comparator (S.66). The sex equality clause will not apply, however, if the employer shows that the difference in pay is due to a material factor, reliance on which does not involve either direct sex discrimination or unjustified indirect sex discrimination (S.69).

However, although the Government shied away from many proposals for **1.30** reform – hypothetical comparators, mandatory equal pay audits, and representative actions to name but a few – there are some new equal pay provisions in the EqA. One example is S.78, which concerns mandatory reporting of gender pay gap information (see below under 'Gender pay reporting'). But while all other provisions in Chapter 3 of Part 5 came into

15

force on 1 October 2010, S.78 has yet to receive a commencement date and, given the change of Government that took place shortly after the Act received Royal Assent, may never come into force. Another new provision is S.77, which is designed to promote greater transparency in pay systems by outlawing so-called 'pay secrecy clauses'. However, as we explain in Chapter 9 under 'Pay secrecy clauses', the usefulness of this provision to claimants has been doubted in many quarters.

Note that while the EqA has not heralded a substantial overhaul of the law pertaining to equal pay, the rewording of some aspects of the EqPA potentially has some seemingly unintended consequences of substance. These are highlighted in the relevant chapters of this Handbook.

1.31 **Application to Northern Ireland.** Note that the equal pay and discrimination in employment provisions in the EqA apply to England, Wales and Scotland, but not to Northern Ireland – S.217 EqA. The Equal Pay Act (Northern Ireland) 1970 remains in force, as does the Sex Discrimination (Northern Ireland) Order 1976 SI 1976/1042. Given that the EqA retains the distinction between equal pay and sex discrimination, it seems likely that, despite the differences in statutory language, Northern Ireland case law will continue to be relevant in England, Wales and Scotland, and vice versa. This is all the more so given the strong influence of EU law in this area – see under 'European Union law' and 'EU gender equality measures' below.

1.32 **Equal pay or sex discrimination?**
As explained above, there was a distinction between discrimination to which the SDA applied and discrimination to which the EqPA applied and an employee seeking to complain of sex discrimination in employment could not normally choose which Act to rely on when bringing a claim. This was an important restriction, since the fact that the SDA permitted a hypothetical comparison meant it was generally easier to establish sex discrimination under that Act than under the EqPA. Furthermore, a claimant relying on the SDA (as opposed to the EqPA) did not have to establish that he or she was employed on equal work (i.e. like work, work rated as equivalent under a job evaluation study or work of equal value) with that of the comparator.

To ensure that a claimant brought his or her claim under the correct Act, S.6(6) SDA stated that S.6(2) SDA (which rendered it unlawful for an employer to discriminate against an employee in the way it afforded access to benefits, facilities or services) did 'not apply to benefits consisting of the payment of money when the provision of those benefits is regulated by the [employee's] contract of employment'. So, any contractual term relating to pay could not be the subject of a complaint under the SDA and the EqPA was the only avenue of redress open to the claimant. This meant that he or she would have to point to an actual comparator of the opposite sex doing equal work and being paid

16

more. In the absence of such a comparator, there would be no redress, even if there was good evidence for concluding that there was a link between pay and gender, and that an employee of the opposite sex, doing the same job, would have been paid more.

In this way, the SDA expressly excluded contractual pay claims, regardless of **1.33** whether the claimant was able to bring a claim under the EqA (although the SDA could apply to complaints regarding non-contractual pay, such as a discretionary bonus). It also excluded non-pay claims rooted in the contract of employment, provided that a claim could be brought under the EqPA. S.8(5) SDA stated that 'an act does not contravene S.6(2) if: (a) it contravenes a term modified or included by virtue of an equality clause, or (b) it would contravene such a term but for the fact that the equality clause is prevented from operating by S.1(3) of the EqPA'. The combined effect of these provisions, as summarised by the EAT in Peake v Automotive Products Ltd 1977 ICR 480, EAT, was that only the EqPA could apply to less favourable treatment relating to the payment of money regulated by a term in the contract of employment, and to any other matter regulated by the contract of employment if the equality clause applied, i.e. if there was a valid comparator. In the absence of a valid comparator, a complaint about a non-money matter in the contract could be made under the SDA, in the same way as a complaint about a matter not regulated by the contract.

Equal pay/sex discrimination demarcation under the EqA. The demarcation **1.34** between sex discrimination claims and equal pay claims has been maintained in much the same form in the EqA (albeit with one important difference noted below). Different parts of the Act govern the two different types of claim: Chapter 3 of Part 5 covers contractual terms by providing for the insertion of a 'sex equality clause' (equivalent to the 'equality clause' formerly inserted by the EqPA), while Part 2 (read with Chapter 1 of Part 5) covers sex discrimination in employment generally (equivalent to the scope of the former SDA).

The division between the two regimes is enforced by Ss.70 and 71 EqA. S.70(1) provides that S.39(2) – which prohibits discrimination in terms of employment, among other things – has no effect in relation to a term that is modified or included by virtue of a sex equality clause, or that would be so modified were it not for a successful 'material factor' defence under S.69 EqA. (A similar exclusion applies in relation to Ss.49(6) and 50(6), which cover discrimination against office-holders.) Furthermore, neither the inclusion of a less favourable term (compared with that of an actual comparator doing equal work) in the employee's terms, or the failure to include in the employee's terms a term equal to that enjoyed by such a comparator, is to be treated as sex discrimination under Part 2 – S.70(2). This replicates what used to be S.8(5) of the SDA, with the same effect, i.e. if all the elements for an equal pay claim are there (equal work, actual comparator, etc), then the claimant cannot choose to bring a sex discrimination claim instead – it is the 'equal pay' route or nothing. If the claim is defeated by the employer's 'material factor' defence, there will be no prospect of a sex discrimination claim in the alternative.

1.35 The specific exclusion of contractual pay claims from the sex discrimination legislation by virtue of S.6(6) SDA is replicated by S.71(1) EqA. This states that S.39(2) does not apply to a term of a person's work that relates to pay but in relation to which a sex equality clause has 'no effect'. Thus, the default position – as previously – is that pay claims are excluded from the sex discrimination provisions, regardless of whether the elements of an equal pay claim are present. However, S.71(2) goes on to note that this exclusion applies 'except in so far as treatment of the person amounts to a contravention of [S.39(2)] by virtue of S.13 [direct discrimination] or 14 [dual discrimination]'. This represents a key difference between the position set out in S.71 EqA and the position under the old law as set out in S.6(6) SDA as it specifically allows for a claim of sex discrimination in pay to be brought under the sex discrimination provisions in limited circumstances. The significance of this is that sex discrimination in pay may, for the first time, be established on the basis of a hypothetical comparison. We examine the scope and implications of this new provision in Chapter 4, 'Comparators', under 'Hypothetical comparators'.

1.36 **Claiming under both the 'equal pay' and 'discrimination' provisions of the EqA.** Under the antecedent legislation, there was no procedural objection to a claim alleging breaches of both the EqPA and the SDA. Indeed, employment tribunal statistics suggest that upwards of 20,000 equal pay claims registered in 2006/07 also included an allegation of sex discrimination. Of these, many if not most would have been alleging distinct and separate grounds for discrimination (or 'causes of action'), some of which would have been governed by the EqPA and some by the SDA. However, some of the 20,000 cases would have framed separate equal pay and sex discrimination claims by way of alternative in circumstances where it was unclear which of the two Acts applied. Such a case could arise where, for example, a claimant sought to argue that the denial of a bonus was discriminatory. There might be some doubt – as in Hoyland v Asda Stores Ltd 2006 IRLR 468, Ct Sess (Inner House) – whether the bonus in question was regulated by the contract of employment, and until that issue had been determined it would remain unclear which cause of action applied. In such circumstances, it would be sensible to plead both in the alternative.

The situation remains unchanged under the EqA and it is expected that many claimants will bring claims under both Chapters 1 and 3 of Part 5 of the EqA. However, as was the position under the antecedent legislation, different time limits apply to the discrimination and equal pay claims – see Chapter 9 under 'Time limits'.

Gender pay reporting
1.37

The Equality and Human Rights Commission (EHRC), among others, has long called for the introduction of mandatory equal pay audits, to make employers address pay discrimination outside the context of equal pay claims by exposing inequalities. The Equality Act 2010 does not go so far as to require full equal pay audits but, as an initial tentative step towards greater transparency, does lay down a basic mechanism for highlighting indicators of unequal pay.

Section 78 EqA allows regulations to be made requiring employers to publish pay information 'for the purpose of showing whether... there are differences in the pay of male and female employees'. Such regulations, which would apply to employers with 250 or more employees, would prescribe the factors by reference to which such differences are to be measured and a failure to comply would either be treated as a summary offence, punishable by a fine of up to £5,000, or be subject to an enforcement procedure set down in the regulations themselves. Government departments, the armed forces, and public authorities identified in Schedule 19 for the purposes of the public sector equality duties are exempted. However, the public sector equality duties are likely to impose more onerous requirements with regard to transparency on public sector employers. For more detail, see IDS Employment Law Guide, 'The Equality Act 2010' (2010), Chapter 7.

No regulations have yet been made under S.78 and it is uncertain whether this provision will ever be given effect. Although it is not stated in the 2010 Act, the Labour Government which introduced the Act made it clear that it would not use the power in S.78 before April 2013. The Government's aim was for employers to publish such information on a voluntary basis, and it only intended to exercise the statutory power if sufficient progress on reporting had not been made. The Coalition Government formed in May 2010 has taken the similar view that a voluntary approach should be the first step. In its 'Equality Strategy – Building a Fairer Britain' (published in December 2010) the Coalition Government stated: 'We will... work with business and others to develop a voluntary scheme for gender pay reporting in the private and voluntary sector which will be available to all private and voluntary sector businesses, but particularly those with 150 or more employees. We expect and want the voluntary approach to work. This will give better information and is more likely to drive successful change. We will annually review the numbers of companies releasing information, and its quality, under the voluntary approach to assess whether this approach is successful and take a view over time whether alternatives are required, including using a mandatory approach through S.78 of the Equality Act 2010. While we work with business and others to ensure the voluntary approach is successful, we will not commence, amend or repeal S.78.'
1.38

1.39 ## Codes of Practice

Under S.14 of the Equality Act 2006 (EqA 2006), the EHRC has the power to issue Codes of Practice in connection with any matter addressed by the Equality Act 2010. Under S.15(4)(b) EqA 2006, an employment tribunal hearing a sex discrimination or equal pay case is obliged to take into account any provision in a Code that appears relevant to the proceedings before it. On 11 October 2010 the EHRC produced two Codes which are relevant to the matters addressed in this Handbook:

- *Code of Practice on Equal Pay.* This Code draws on case law to give guidance in relation to the equal pay provisions in the EqA 2010. It also covers equal pay review, identifies discriminatory elements in pay systems and provides guidance on drawing up an equal pay policy

- *Code of Practice on Employment.* This covers the discrimination provisions in the EqA, including victimisation, that can arise in connection with an equal pay claim.

The above Codes were issued in October 2010, but were technically in draft form until 6 April 2011, when they were formally brought into force by the Equality Act 2010 Codes of Practice (Services, Public Functions and Associations, Employment, and Equal Pay) Order 2011 SI 2011/857.

(Note that Northern Ireland has its own equivalent Codes of Practice – 'Removing sex bias from recruitment and selection – a Code of Practice' and the 'Code of Practice on equal pay'.)

1.40 ## European Union law

No treatment of equal pay law would be complete, or indeed possible, without some reference to European Union (EU) law and the rules that govern its relationship with UK legislation. In the wake of the Lisbon Treaty (which came into force on 1 December 2009), two treaties form the principal sources of EU law: the Treaty on the Functioning of the European Union (TFEU) (which started life as the Treaty of Rome), and the Treaty on European Union (TEU) (which is often referred to as the Maastricht Treaty). These are supplemented by a large number of Directives and Regulations that govern specific areas over which the EU has legislative competence, e.g. equality between men and women.

1.41 ### Relationship between EU law and UK law
To understand the effect of European measures relating to equal pay, it is first necessary to understand how EU law interacts with UK law. The starting point is the European Communities Act 1972, which came into force on 1 January 1973, the date on which the United Kingdom joined the European Union (then

known as the European Communities). At that point, the United Kingdom ceded its sovereignty over certain areas, including sex equality, to the Community, and courts and tribunals became bound by the principle, established by the European Court of Justice (ECJ) in Van Gend en Loos v Nederlandse Administratie der Belastingen 1963 ECR 1, ECJ, that EU law has supremacy over domestic law. This supremacy is underlined by S.3(2) of the 1972 Act, which requires courts and tribunals to have regard to the European Treaties, European legislation and decisions of the ECJ in deciding cases before them. The 1972 Act also provided an enabling power, still frequently used, for the introduction of Regulations necessary for the implementation of further developments in EU law – S.2.

The EqA is, among other things, the legislative instrument by which the United Kingdom implements into domestic law the right to equal pay contained in Article 157 of the TFEU. Thus, tribunals and courts applying and interpreting the Act must do so by reference to the equal treatment provisions of the TFEU, the legislation made under them (e.g. EU Directives), and the case law of the ECJ. As will become clear in the rest of this chapter and throughout this Handbook, the application of ECJ case law to the provisions of the EqPA (that are now found in the EqA) has been behind some of the most significant upheavals in UK equal pay law, and has been critical to ensuring that individuals benefit from the full extent of their rights under EU law.

Direct effect
1.42

According to the ECJ in Van Gend en Loos v Nederlandse Administratie der Belastingen 1963 ECR 1, ECJ, the TFEU is not to be treated simply as an instrument governing relations between Member States. Rather, in those areas where the Community has legislative competence (such as sex equality), the TFEU and the Directives made under it are capable of conferring upon individuals substantive rights whose existence owes nothing to national laws. Where an individual enjoys such directly conferred EU rights, he or she can rely on them in domestic proceedings, and the court or tribunal hearing those proceedings will be obliged (because of the supremacy of EU law) to disapply any national provision that conflicts with those rights. Where, in domestic proceedings, an individual is entitled to rely directly upon a provision of EU law in this way, that provision is said to have 'direct effect' in relation to that individual.

Conditions for direct effect. Not every provision of European law is intended 1.43 to confer rights on individuals, however. For one thing, some classes of EU legislation – e.g. Recommendations – are intended to provide voluntary guidance rather than create binding rights and obligations.

Secondly, it is important to understand that even where a provision is contained in a measure which EU law treats as legally binding – a Treaty Article, for

21

instance, or a Directive – it will not necessarily have direct effect. In Van Gend en Loos v Nederlandse Administratie der Belastingen (above) the ECJ explained that a provision of EC law will be capable of direct effect only where it is clear and precise; is unconditional and unqualified; and is not subject to the need for further implementing measures by Member States. Many Articles of the TFEU and the TEU are no more than statements of general principle and cannot have been intended to confer specific rights on individuals. Similarly, a quick glance at the recast EU Equal Treatment Directive (No.2006/54) (see under 'EU gender equality measures' below) will disclose several Articles that do no more than introduce, exhort or explain in a general way.

1.44 **How direct effect works.** In Biggs v Somerset County Council 1995 ICR 811, EAT, the Appeal Tribunal adopted what came to be known as the 'conservative' interpretation of direct effect. That case concerned a claim for an unfair dismissal that had occurred some 18 years before. B, the claimant, had not applied to a tribunal when she was first dismissed because the unfair dismissal legislation then in force expressly excluded employees who, like her, had worked below a specified weekly hours threshold. She changed her mind in 1994 after the House of Lords (in R v Secretary of State for Employment ex parte EOC and anor 1994 ICR 317, HL) declared the hours threshold to be in breach of the principle of equal pay for equal work now enshrined in Article 157 of the TFEU (then Article 119 of the EC Treaty). An important aspect of B's case was her submission that she was entitled to rely on Article 157 as a 'free-standing' right, separate from her domestic claim for unfair dismissal. The advantage of relying on a separate EU cause of action, from B's perspective, was that this might not be subject to the same three-month time limit as the unfair dismissal claim.

However, the EAT rejected the existence of a separate EU cause of action outright. It stated that a tribunal's jurisdiction is limited to that granted to it by specific measures of national legislation. Although a tribunal is bound to apply relevant EU law 'within its jurisdiction', it has no jurisdiction to hear and determine disputes about EU law generally. The EAT was not prepared to accept that such jurisdiction could be inferred from the European Communities Act 1972.

1.45 In the EAT's view, the more radical approach previously adopted by the Scottish EAT in Secretary of State for Scotland and anor v Wright and anor 1991 IRLR 187, EAT – where a claim for redundancy payments was allowed to proceed even though it relied on Article 157 and the Equal Treatment Directive (No.76/207) (now incorporated into the recast EU Equal Treatment Directive) – was based on a false legal premise. Directly effective EU rights do not create a separate cause of action, unconnected with the domestic legal framework. Rather, they allow a tribunal to disapply incompatible provisions of domestic law within its jurisdiction. Accordingly, an application to a tribunal must

22

always be based on the relevant domestic statutory cause of action – even if the applicant intends that the tribunal should disapply some provision of that cause of action on the ground of its incompatibility with his or her EU rights. Once the incompatible provision has been disapplied, the application will proceed on the basis of the modified statutory cause of action.

The Court of Appeal approved the EAT's approach in the Biggs case (see Biggs v Somerset County Council 1996 ICR 364, CA) and it has been followed in several cases since – see, for example, Staffordshire County Council v Barber 1996 ICR 379, CA; Secretary of State for Employment v Mann and ors 1997 ICR 209, CA; and Barry v Midland Bank plc 1997 ICR 192, EAT. However, more recent decisions have cast doubt on whether this line of authority is strictly correct. Notably, the European Court's judgment in Impact v Minister for Agriculture and Food and ors 2008 IRLR 552, ECJ, suggests that domestic tribunals might acquire jurisdiction to hear claims based on the direct effect of EU law without such jurisdiction being expressly granted by legislation. There, Irish civil servants sought to rely on the direct effect of provisions of the EU Fixed-term Work Directive (No.1999/70) based on facts occurring after the deadline for transposition of the Directive had passed in July 2001 but before the implementing provisions of Irish law came into force in July 2003. They brought their complaints before a Rights Commissioner, whose jurisdiction was established under the domestic provisions from July 2003 but who enjoyed no express jurisdiction to hear claims based directly on the Directive. The employer challenged the Rights Commissioner's jurisdiction to hear claims based on facts occurring before 2003 and, after an appeal to the Labour Court, a reference was made to the ECJ.

The ECJ held that a specialised court (such as, in this instance, the Rights **1.46** Commissioner) which is granted jurisdiction in matters relating to transposing legislation must also have jurisdiction to hear claims arising directly from the Directive thereby transposed, in respect of the period between the deadline for transposing the Directive and the date on which the transposing legislation entered into force. This is so provided it is established that the obligation on the claimant to bring before an ordinary court, at the same time, a separate claim based directly on the Directive would involve procedural disadvantages liable to render the exercise of the rights conferred on him or her by EU law excessively difficult.

Applying the reasoning adopted by the ECJ in the Impact ruling, it is arguable that a claimant wishing to rely directly on the effect of Article 157 should be able to do so in the employment tribunal even though, under the EqA, no express provision is made for an Article 157 claim to be heard there. This may seem like an academic distinction, given that Article 157 and Chapter 3 of Part 5 of the EqA cover roughly the same ground. However, as is highlighted elsewhere in this Handbook, there are instances where the right to equal pay under the EU Treaty is wider than that expressly provided for under the EqA. It is therefore important for a claimant to know how and where his or her directly effective rights under the TFEU can be enforced. This issue is addressed more fully in Chapter 9 under 'Jurisdiction of tribunals – Article 157 claims'.

1.47 **'Horizontal' and 'vertical' direct effect.** Over the years, a distinction has grown up in the jurisprudence of the ECJ between so-called 'horizontal' and 'vertical' direct effect. Where a provision of EU law has 'horizontal' direct effect, it can be relied upon by an individual in proceedings against another individual. Where a provision has 'vertical' direct effect, it can only be relied upon by an individual in proceedings against a Member State.

An Article of the TFEU which is found to be capable of conferring rights on an individual under the test established by the ECJ in Van Gend en Loos v Nederlandse Administratie der Belastingen 1963 ECR 1, ECJ (see above), will have both 'horizontal' and 'vertical' direct effect – i.e. it can be relied upon by an individual in proceedings against either a Member State or another individual. Article 157 is a classic example of this.

1.48 Like a Treaty Article, a provision contained in an EU Directive will be capable of direct effect if it is clear and precise, unconditional and unqualified, and is not subject to the need for further implementing measures by Member States – Van Duyn v Home Office 1975 Ch 358, ECJ. It is a further condition that a provision in a Directive capable of direct effect will not in fact be directly effective until the deadline for Member States to implement the Directive has passed. However, provisions in a Directive can only have 'vertical', not 'horizontal', direct effect – i.e. they can be relied upon by an individual in proceedings against a Member State but not against another individual. This is because (unlike Treaty Articles) Directives are binding only on Member States and consequently the justification for 'vertical' direct effect – that Member States should not benefit from their own default in implementing a Directive – does not apply to private employers (see Marshall v Southampton and South West Hampshire Area Health Authority (Teaching) 1986 ICR 335, ECJ). Perhaps by way of compensation, the courts have adopted a reasonably broad view of what constitutes 'the State' for the purposes of 'vertical' direct effect. It is not restricted simply to the Crown, government departments and local government, etc, but encompasses any organisation that can be said to be an 'emanation of the State'. The ECJ has held that it is for the national courts to determine whether a particular body constitutes an emanation of the State, but added that 'a body, whatever its legal form, which has been made responsible, pursuant to a measure adopted by the State, for providing a public service under the control of the State and has for that purpose special powers beyond those which result from the normal rules applicable in relations between individuals is included among the bodies against which the provisions of a Directive capable of having direct effect may be relied upon' – Foster and ors v British Gas plc 1991 ICR 84, ECJ.

Indirect effect   1.49
Along with supremacy and direct effect, the third key concept pertinent to the applicability of EU law is 'indirect effect'. The ECJ has explained the principle of indirect effect in the following terms: '[I]n applying national law and in particular a national law specifically introduced to implement [an EU measure], national courts are required to interpret domestic law in the light of the wording and purpose of the Directive' – Von Colson and Kamann v Land Nordrhein-Westfalen 1984 ECR 1891, ECJ. The European Communities Act 1972 contains a requirement to much the same effect.

The usefulness of indirect effect in an employment law context lies in the fact that it applies regardless of whether the party sued is an emanation of the State or an individual. Consequently, it may be relied upon by private sector employees who, as we have explained above, are unable to rely on the direct effect of Directives that have not been properly implemented into national law. An illustration of the principle of indirect effect in action is provided by the EAT's decision in Chessington World of Adventures Ltd v Reed 1998 ICR 97, EAT. In that case the Appeal Tribunal was prepared to interpret the concept of discrimination 'on grounds of sex' broadly in order to bring discrimination against transsexuals within it, and thus reconcile the SDA with the Equal Treatment Directive.

Courts and tribunals should be prepared to go quite far in their attempt to **1.50** reconcile national legislation with EU law. The obligation is not limited to domestic law specifically designed to implement the Community measure in question – Webb v EMO Air Cargo (UK) Ltd 1993 ICR 175, HL, following Marleasing SA v La Comercial Internacional de Alimentacion SA 1992 1 CMLR 305, ECJ. The courts have even shown themselves ready to insert words into provisions of domestic legislation where this has been necessary to achieve compatibility. For example, the Court of Appeal read words into the 'work rated as equivalent' provisions of the EqPA so as to allow a claim that should, as a matter of EU law, have been possible – Redcar and Cleveland Borough Council v Bainbridge and ors (No.1) 2008 ICR 238, CA (for further details, see Chapter 6 under 'Claimant's job must be rated equal or greater in value'). The EAT also felt justified in ignoring words in S.6(4A) of the Sex Discrimination Act 1986 where it was necessary to do so in order to give full effect to the Equal Treatment Directive – Unison and anor v Brennan and ors 2008 ICR 955, EAT.

However, the principle of indirect effect does not impose an absolute duty on courts and tribunals to interpret domestic law in accordance with EU law, merely a duty to do this 'so far as possible' – Marleasing SA v La Comercial

25

Internacional de Alimentacion SA (above). According to the House of Lords, where national law is clear and capable of only one meaning, it must not be distorted to make it comply with an EU Directive that has a different meaning – Webb v EMO Air Cargo UK Ltd (No.2) 1995 ICR 1021, HL.

1.51 Suing the State

In Francovich and ors v Italian Republic 1995 ICR 722, ECJ, the European Court established the principle that an individual citizen may be entitled to sue his or her government for damages resulting from its failure to implement an EU Directive. This is of great importance because the limitations on the principles of direct and indirect effect (see above) mean that for some private sector employees a 'Francovich-style' claim against the State will be their only means of redress. However, the ECJ has made it clear that the remedy is not restricted to individuals in respect of whom a Directive has no direct effect. As a result, public sector employees may be able to choose between relying directly on a Directive or making a 'Francovich-style' claim – (1) Brasserie du Pêcheur SA v Federal Republic of Germany (2) R v Secretary of State for Transport ex parte Factortame Ltd and ors 1996 IRLR 267, ECJ.

It must be said that a Francovich-style claim in respect of equal pay is an unlikely prospect. Although, as noted under 'Direct effect – how direct effect works' above, there remains some judicial disagreement over the means by which an equal pay claimant can rely directly on EU law, courts and tribunals generally manage to give effect to the full extent of Article 157 and the recast Equal Treatment Directive in equal pay claims. This is particularly so given the special treatment of the Directive in terms of its direct effect – see below, under 'Equal Pay Directive'.

1.52 EU gender equality measures

Article 3(3) of the TEU establishes that equality between men and women is one of the fundamental principles of EU law. However, only Article 157 of the TFEU actually provides a (horizontally and vertically) directly effective right – that of 'equal pay for male and female workers for equal work or work of equal value'. Although para (3) of Article 157 refers to the principle of equal treatment between men and women, it does not go so far as to confer on individuals a right to equal treatment – it merely provides a specific legal basis for the adoption of further measures to ensure the application of the principle of equal treatment. Thus there is a significant difference between, on the one hand, the regime for asserting the right to equal treatment in matters of pay and, on the other, the regime for asserting the right to equal treatment in employment generally. As noted above, in matters of pay, claimants will look to Article 157 as interpreted by ECJ case law in order to put their claim under the EqA as favourably as possible. In matters of sex discrimination in employment generally, by contrast, claimants will rely on the ECJ's interpretation of the various Equal Treatment Directives when claiming under the discrimination provisions in the EqA.

Below, we outline the provisions of EU law that govern the principle of equal treatment as it applies to pay. Equal treatment in employment generally is covered in depth in IDS Employment Law Handbook, 'Sex Discrimination' (2008).

Article 157   1.53

Article 157 of the TFEU (formerly Article 141, and before that Article 119, of the EC Treaty) enshrines the elimination of unequal pay between men and women as one of the fundamental aims of the European Union. It was included by the original drafters of the Treaty of Rome because it was thought necessary to ensure that Member States did not exploit women as a source of cheap labour in order to obtain a competitive advantage and thereby distort the functioning of the common market.

Article 157 is in very simple terms – its key provisions are contained within the first two paragraphs as set out below:

'1. Each Member State shall ensure that the principle of equal pay for male and female workers for equal work or work of equal value is applied.

2. For the purpose of this Article, 'pay' means the ordinary basic or minimum wage or salary and any other consideration, whether in cash or in kind, which the worker receives directly or indirectly, in respect of his employment, from his employer.

Equal pay without discrimination based on sex means –

(a) that pay for the same work at piece rates shall be calculated on the basis of the same unit of measurement;

(b) that pay for work at time rates shall be the same for the same job.'

However, if Article 157 leaves the reader with the impression that equal pay is   1.54
a relatively simple concept in theory, 50 years of judicial interpretation indicates that applying it is anything but. The simplicity of the terminology used by Article 157 has meant that it has been left to the ECJ to define the limits within which the principle of equal pay is to be applied, which has meant that understanding of key concepts has advanced piecemeal.

Some of the ECJ's more significant decisions on the scope of Article 157 include:

• that access to occupational pension schemes is within the concept of equal pay, meaning that exclusion of certain categories of worker may be unlawful

27

if it disproportionately disadvantages one sex over another – Bilka-Kaufhaus GmbH v Weber von Hartz 1987 ICR 110, ECJ

- that a woman seeking to establish unequal pay can compare herself with the predecessor in her job, but not with a hypothetical man – Macarthys Ltd v Smith 1980 ICR 672, ECJ; Coloroll Pension Trustees Ltd v Russell and ors 1995 ICR 179, ECJ

- that unequal pay can be established by comparison between a man and a woman doing equal work or work of equal value within the same establishment or service where a 'single source' is responsible for setting pay levels – Lawrence and ors v Regent Office Care Ltd and ors 2003 ICR 1092, ECJ.

1.55 In general terms, Article 157 applies to all the remuneration an employee receives from her employer, including contractual benefits, gratuitous and discretionary benefits and benefits that the employer is required to provide by statute. In this respect, Article 157 goes wider than the equal pay provisions in Chapter 3 of Part 5 of the EqA, which are confined to contractual remuneration. However, in another respect Article 157 is narrower because it does not encompass discrimination in contractual matters other than pay.

The 'single source' test established by the ECJ in Lawrence (above) highlighted another disparity between the UK gender equality legislation and Article 157, in that the EqPA and its successor provisions in the EqA restrict equal pay comparisons to those in common employment. These discrepancies are discussed in detail in this Handbook as and when they become relevant.

1.56 Equal Pay Directives

The first EU Directive concerning equal pay was Council Directive No.75/117 on the application of the principle of equal pay for men and women (the Equal Pay Directive), which came into force in February 1975. This Directive was consolidated into the recast EU Equal Treatment Directive (No.2006/54) (the recast Directive) with effect from 15 August 2009 (considered further below), but bears some consideration here. The Equal Pay Directive was implemented to facilitate the practical application of the principle of equal pay enshrined in what is now Article 157. It was not (and nor are its successor provisions in the recast Directive) intended to alter in any way the content or scope of the principle as set out in the Treaty and elucidated by the case law of the ECJ – Jenkins v Kingsgate (Clothing Productions) Ltd 1981 ICR 592, ECJ.

Like Article 157, the essential provisions of the Equal Treatment Directive were in relatively simple terms. Article 1 provided:

'The principle of equal pay for men and women outlined in Article [157] of the Treaty, hereinafter called "principle of equal pay", means, for the same work or for work to which equal value is attributed, the elimination of all discrimination on grounds of sex with regard to all aspects and conditions of remuneration.

In particular, where a job classification system is used for determining pay, it must be based on the same criteria for both men and women and so drawn up as to exclude any discrimination on grounds of sex.'

A similar but not identical provision can be found in Article 4 of the recast Directive.

1.57 The Directive therefore elaborated on the basic principle of equal pay now set down in Article 157. Although, as noted above, the Directive was not intended to alter the scope or content of Article 157, it did have a profound effect on the way it was to be enforced in the United Kingdom. In Commission of the European Communities v United Kingdom of Great Britain and Northern Ireland 1982 ICR 578, ECJ, the European Court ruled that the United Kingdom had failed to fulfil its Treaty obligations, as set out by the Directive, with regard to facilitating an equal pay claim based on work of equal value. The UK Government had argued that the 'work rated as equivalent' provisions contained in S.1(2)(b) and (5) EqPA allowed a woman's claim to be based on the value of her work and that UK law therefore complied with the Directive. The ECJ disagreed – in its view, by making the right to equal pay for work of equal value dependent upon the existence of a job evaluation study (JES), which could only be carried out with the consent and cooperation of the employer, the United Kingdom effectively denied individuals the right to bring a claim where no such study had been carried out. This fell short of the obligations imposed by the Directive, which require that a woman is entitled to claim equal pay for work of equal value whether or not a JES had been undertaken. As a result, the Government enacted the Equal Pay (Amendment) Regulations 1983 SI 1983/1794 to introduce equal value provisions into the EqPA from 1 January 1984 – these provisions, now contained in the EqPA, are explained in Chapter 7, 'Work of equal value'.

Recast Equal Treatment Directive

1.58 Until recently, in addition to the Equal Pay Directive, there were six different Directives dealing with gender equality:

- No.76/207 on equal treatment for men and women as regards access to employment (the Equal Treatment Directive)

- No.2002/73, amending Directive No.76/207, on equal treatment for men and women as regards employment, vocational training and promotion and working conditions

- No.86/378 on equal treatment for men and women in occupational social security schemes

- No.96/97, amending Directive No.86/378, on the implementation of the principle of equal treatment for men and women in occupational social security schemes

- No.97/80 on the burden of proof in cases of discrimination based on sex (the Burden of Proof Directive)

- No.98/52 on the extension of Directive No.97/80 to the United Kingdom.

1.59 However, in 2006 the European Parliament and the Council of Ministers consolidated all seven measures, together with relevant case law from the ECJ, into the recast EU Equal Treatment Directive (No.2006/54) (the recast Directive), which relates to 'the implementation of the principle of equal opportunities and equal treatment of men and women in matters of employment and occupation'. The new Directive came into force on 15 August 2006 and had to be implemented by Member States by 15 August 2008, although in most cases the measures were already implemented in order to comply with the original Directives. The seven consolidated Directives were repealed with effect from 15 August 2009, and references to those Directives elsewhere in EU legislation are now to be read as a reference to the relevant part of the recast Directive.

The recast Directive is a consolidating measure rather than an extension or expansion of the principles of equal treatment, and has therefore had no impact on the scope of European equal pay law. It does, however, incorporate certain principles derived from case law that may not have been explicit in the existing Directives. For example, the Preamble notes that it is now established that, in certain circumstances, the principle of equal pay is not limited to situations in which men and women work for the same employer. There are also specific provisions covering the right to equal benefits under occupational pension schemes, taking account of ECJ case law in this regard.

1.60 Given that the recast Directive is not intended to make substantive changes to equal pay law, it is unnecessary to set out its provisions in any great detail. What follows is a brief description of the key provisions governing the scope and application of the principle of equal pay. For details of the recast Directive's application to equal treatment in employment generally, see IDS Employment Law Handbook, 'Sex Discrimination' (2008).

Note that the European Commission was obliged to conduct a review of the recast Directive by 15 February 2011 and, if appropriate, propose any amendments it deems necessary. At the time of writing (May 2011) no such amendments had been proposed.

1.61 **Definitions.** Article 2(1) of the recast Directive contains key definitions that were previously contained in the amended Equal Treatment Directive. So far as equal pay is concerned, only the first two of these definitions are worth setting out:

- *direct discrimination*: where one person is treated less favourably on the ground of sex than another is, has been or would be treated in a comparable situation

- *indirect discrimination*: where an apparently neutral provision, criterion or practice would put persons of one sex at a particular disadvantage compared with persons of the other sex, unless that provision, criterion or practice is objectively justified by a legitimate aim, and the means of achieving that aim are appropriate and necessary.

Article 2(2) states that discrimination includes any less favourable treatment of a woman related to pregnancy or maternity leave, among other things.

Equal pay. Article 1 of the Equal Pay Directive is re-enacted in Article 4 of the **1.62** recast Directive, with a slight rewording. It provides:

> 'For the same work or for work to which equal value is attributed, direct and indirect discrimination on grounds of sex with regard to all aspects and conditions of remuneration shall be eliminated.
>
> In particular, where a job classification system is used for determining pay, it shall be based on the same criteria for both men and women and so drawn up as to exclude any discrimination on grounds of sex.'

Thus the principle of equal pay expressly includes the elimination of both direct and indirect discrimination, as defined by Article 2 (above).

The recast Directive restates the obligations on Member States aimed at **1.63** ensuring the effective application of the principle of equal pay that were previously contained in the Equal Pay Directive. These obligations include:

- providing a means of legal redress – Article 17(1) (formerly Article 2 of the Equal Treatment Directive)

- abolishing any pay discrimination arising from laws, regulations or administrative provisions – Article 23(a) (formerly Article 3 of the Equal Treatment Directive)

- providing that terms contrary to the principle of equal pay in collective agreements, wage scales, wage agreements or individual contracts may be amended or declared null and void – Article 23(b) (formerly Article 4 of the Equal Treatment Directive)

- protecting employees from dismissal based on their enforcement of the right to equal pay – Article 24 (formerly Article 5 of the Equal Treatment Directive).

Retroactive effect. Chapter 2 of Title II of the recast Directive, which contains **1.64** Articles 5–13, incorporates the provisions of Directive No.86/378 on equal treatment for men and women in occupational social security schemes. Article

31

12 of the recast Directive sets out how the principle of equal pay is to apply to the calculation of benefits under such schemes. In this regard, it incorporates the ECJ's decision in Barber v Guardian Royal Exchange Assurance Group 1990 ICR 616, ECJ, where the Court applied a temporal limitation so that claimants seeking equal treatment retrospectively cannot have periods of service before 17 May 1990, the date of judgment, taken into account, except in limited circumstances. For details, see Chapter 3 under 'Occupational pensions'.

1.65 **Remedies and enforcement.** Chapter 1 of Title III of the recast Directive (Articles 17 and 18) imposes obligations on EU Member States to put in place adequate judicial procedures for the enforcement of obligations under the Directive. Article 17 establishes that such procedures should not be limited in their application to persons who are still in the relationship in which the discrimination occurred, and should instead be available to all persons who consider themselves wronged by a failure to apply the principle of equal treatment. Para 3 of Article 17 goes on to state that this shall be without prejudice to national rules regarding time limits. Article 18 deals with the question of compensation, requiring Member States to introduce measures necessary to ensure that victims of sex discrimination are able to gain 'real and effective' compensation that reflects the loss and damage sustained and is both dissuasive and proportionate.

1.66 **Burden of proof.** The burden of proof provisions originally contained in the Burden of Proof Directive can now be found in Article 19 of the recast Directive. This provision states that, where a complainant who considers that the principle of equal treatment has not been applied to him or her establishes facts from which it may be presumed that there has been direct or indirect discrimination, it shall be for the respondent to prove that there has been no breach of that principle. This Article applies equally to complaints under Article 157 TFEU – Article 19(4).

1.67 **Equality bodies.** Article 20 places an obligation on Member States to create a body (or bodies) for the promotion, analysis, monitoring and support of equal treatment of all persons. Such bodies can – as is the case with the Equality and Human Rights Commission in the United Kingdom – be the national body with the responsibility for safeguarding human rights or individual rights. Their competences should include providing assistance to victims of discrimination in pursuing claims, conducting surveys concerning discrimination, and publishing reports and recommendations.

1.68 **Victimisation.** Article 24 requires measures to be put in place to protect employees, and employees' representatives, from dismissal or other adverse treatment by the employer as a reaction to a complaint aimed at enforcing compliance with the principle of equal treatment. In the United Kingdom, such protection now exists in Ss.27 and 39(3) and (4) EqA, and was previously covered by the victimisation provisions in the SDA.

Direct or indirect effect. As previously explained under 'European Union law 1.69 – direct effect' above, while EU Treaty Articles can have both vertical and horizontal direct effect (i.e. they can be enforced directly against both the State and private individuals), EU Directives generally only have vertical direct effect, meaning that they can only be relied upon directly against the State. In proceedings between private individuals, Directives can normally only be relied upon *indirectly*, i.e. the court must interpret applicable rules of law to conform with the Directive, so far as it is possible to do so. However, it has been acknowledged that the Equal Pay Directive was a special case, and the same must also be true of the provisions now found in the recast Directive. Given that that Directive is not intended to alter the scope of Article 157, it should be read together with that Article. This was the view of Mr Justice Elias, President of the EAT, when he undertook an extensive examination of the application of the European provisions to equal pay disputes in Villalba v Merrill Lynch and Co Inc and ors 2007 ICR 469, EAT. He concluded that 'the reach of the Directive is not limited by the principle that Directives are not horizontally effective; it is equidistant with Article [157] itself, and that has been held to have direct effect'.

2 Right to equal pay

How do equal pay claims work?

Who is covered?

The sex equality clause

Permissible discrimination

Occupational pension schemes

Maternity

In this chapter we focus on the scheme of the equal pay provisions contained in **2.1** Chapter 3 of Part 5 of the Equality Act 2010 (EqA) – as interpreted in the light of EU law (for which see Chapter 1) – and how they take effect. We begin by explaining how equal pay claims, which are notoriously complex, are supposed to work. We then look in more detail at the various groups of workers who are protected by the Act's provisions; at the 'sex equality clause', the mechanism by which the EqA achieves equal pay; at the limited circumstances in which pay discrimination is expressly permitted; at the application of the principle of equal pay to occupational pension schemes; and at the particular protection now afforded to women on maternity leave.

How do equal pay claims work?   2.2

In general terms, the equal pay provisions in the EqA make it unlawful for an employer to discriminate between men and women in relation to the terms of their contracts of employment. The reach of equal pay law is therefore wider than simply terms and conditions related strictly to 'pay'. The Act achieves its objective by implying a 'sex equality clause' into every employee's contract of employment, enabling an employee to bring a tribunal claim where he or she is treated less favourably than a comparable employee of the opposite sex in relation to a contractual term. A 'sex equality clause' is defined in S.66(2) as a provision that has the following effect:

- 'if a term of A's [the claimant] is less favourable to A than a corresponding term of B's [the comparator of the opposite sex] is to B, A's term is modified so as not to be less favourable

- if A does not have a term which corresponds to a term of B's that benefits B, A's terms are modified so as to include such a term'.

This covers the most common instances of unequal pay – where the claimant's basic pay is lower than that of her comparator, and where the claimant is not

35

entitled to a bonus or some other remuneration to which her comparator is contractually entitled for doing equal work. In the former case, the sex equality clause operates to amend the term setting basic pay so that it is equal to that of the comparator; in the latter, the sex equality clause operates to insert a term entitling the claimant to the same bonus arrangement or remunerative benefit.

2.3 The language of S.66 EqA is gender-neutral. This marks a departure from the language used in the EqPA, which was couched in terms of the complainant being a woman comparing her terms to those of a man, and then included a provision making it clear that a man could compare his terms to those of a woman (S.1(13)). For ease of use, throughout this Handbook we have maintained the semantic approach taken in the EqPA, so that references to a complainant in the abstract generally refer to a woman. However, in every case (except where the context otherwise makes clear), the principles under discussion apply equally to male complainants.

Below, we consider the two general types of equal pay claim that can be brought in tribunals: individual claims and collective claims.

2.4 Individual equal pay claims

As we shall see throughout this Handbook, courts and tribunals have struggled for over 30 years to decide how, exactly, individual equal pay claims are supposed to proceed. In this section, we cut through the agonised reasoning that case law has produced, and attempt to provide a relatively straightforward formula to be followed.

An equal pay claim can be thought of as a tennis match, with the ball being bashed from one player to the other. At various stages of the litigation the ball will move from the employee's to the employer's side of the court, and vice versa, leaving one party or the other to meet a particular legal and evidential burden. So, the claimant first has to 'serve', by establishing an appropriate comparator with regard to her equal pay claim; that is, a man in the same employment as her (for which see Chapter 4) whose contractual terms (for which see Chapter 3) are more favourable than hers. She must also show that she is employed on:

- 'like work' with her comparator (see Chapter 5)

- 'work rated as equivalent' to his under a job evaluation study (see Chapter 6), or

- 'work of equal value' to his (see Chapter 7).

2.5 If the claimant succeeds in this task, the employer must 'return serve' by showing that the difference in pay between the claimant and the comparator can be explained by reference to a 'material factor' which does not involve treating the claimant less favourably than the comparator because of her sex.

In the absence of a material factor, the claim must succeed. Conversely, proof of a material factor means the employer has successfully returned serve back to the employee. At this stage, if the claim is to progress, the employee will need to produce evidence, in the form of statistics or otherwise, that the material factor relied upon by the employer is tainted by indirect sex discrimination. If she can do this, the ball will return to the employer, who must then satisfy the tribunal that reliance on the material factor in question can be 'objectively justified' as a necessary means of achieving a legitimate aim. If the employer shows justification, the claim will fail; if the employer does not, the claim will succeed. The complex matters of the material factor defence, the circumstances in which a material factor might be gender-tainted, and how objective justification can be demonstrated are discussed at length in Chapter 8.

Unfortunately, each stage of the process explained above can be extremely convoluted – particularly where multiple claimants and comparators are involved – meaning that many equal pay claims take a very long time to be resolved and can be extremely costly to litigate.

Collective dimension to claims for equal pay 2.6

Section 145(1) EqA provides that 'a term of a collective agreement is void in so far as it constitutes, promotes or provides for treatment of a description prohibited by this Act'. An employee, or potential employee, who is, or would be, subject to such a term may apply to an employment tribunal for a declaration that the term is void – S.146.

A tribunal's powers under S.146 are fairly limited, in that it can only declare the offending term void and cannot modify or amend it. It is therefore questionable whether that section complies with EU law and, in particular, Article 23(b) of the recast EU Equal Treatment Directive (No.2006/54) (formerly Article 4 of the EU Equal Pay Directive (No.75/117)), which stipulates that: 'Member States shall take the necessary measures to ensure that... provisions contrary to the principle of equal treatment in individual or collective contracts of agreements... shall be, or may be, declared null and void or are amended.'

The problem is that victims of pay discrimination usually want their pay to be 2.7 increased to the same level as the advantaged group, rather than have the advantaged group's pay reduced to the level of their own. To do this, tribunals need to be able to amend discriminatory terms, rather than merely declare them null and void. It is possible to read Article 23(b) as giving Member States the choice between providing for a power to declare terms null and void and providing for a power of amendment. However, the European Court of Justice (ECJ) made it clear in Kowalska v Freie und Hansestadt Hamburg 1992 ICR 29, ECJ, and Nimz v Freie und Hansestadt Hamburg 1991 IRLR 222, ECJ, that Article 119 of the Treaty of Rome (now Article 157 of the Treaty on the

37

Functioning of the European Union (TFEU)) – which enshrines the principle of equal pay for equal work – entitles a national court to set aside the indirectly discriminatory provisions of a collective agreement and, in so doing, to ensure that the members of the disadvantaged group are treated in the same way and have the same system and benefits applied to them as members of the advantaged group. In other words, a power of amendment is required for the tribunal to be able to give full effect to the right to equal pay.

A counter-argument to the contention that S.146 EqA is in breach of Article 23(b) of the recast Equal Treatment Directive is that, since the terms relating to pay contained within non-legally binding collective agreements are usually incorporated into the binding contracts of individual employees, any discriminatory terms in such collective agreements can be dealt with under the EqA's mechanism for individual enforcement. This, as we shall see under 'The sex equality clause' below, provides for the modification of a woman's contract in the event that her comparator's contract contains a more advantageous term. However, this argument appears to have been rejected by the European Court in Commission of the European Communities v United Kingdom of Great Britain and Northern Ireland 1984 ICR 192, ECJ. There, the argument was used to defend proceedings brought by the Commission against the United Kingdom for its failure to implement Article 4 of the EU Equal Treatment Directive (No.76/207). The ECJ ruled: 'The United Kingdom's argument to the effect that the non-binding character of collective agreements removes them from the field of application of [the Equal Treatment] Directive cannot be accepted, even if account is taken of the United Kingdom's observation that individual contracts of employment entered into within the framework of a collective agreement are rendered void by S.77 [Sex Discrimination Act 1975 (SDA)]... [Article 4 of] the Directive... covers all collective agreements without distinction as to the nature of the legal effects which they do or do not produce... The need to ensure that the Directive is completely effective therefore requires that any clauses in such agreements which are incompatible with the obligations imposed by the Directive upon the Member States may be rendered inoperative, eliminated or amended by appropriate means.' Although this particular case concerned Article 4 of the Equal Treatment Directive, as opposed to the similarly worded Article 4 of the Equal Pay Directive (now Article 23(b) of the recast Equal Treatment Directive), we would suggest that the ECJ would apply the same reasoning in a case considering the application of Ss.145 and 146 EqA.

2.8 ## Who is covered?

Section 64(1) EqA provides that the right to equal pay applies to a person who is 'employed' or who holds 'a personal or public office'. Below, we consider the definition of employment contained in S.83(2) EqA. As we shall see, this definition is relatively broad, and covers similar (if not identical) ground to that of 'worker', which determines who has the right to equal pay under Article 157 TFEU. We then look at the position of overseas claimants before examining the special provisions that apply to office holders and members of the armed forces.

'Employment' under the EqA   2.9

The definition of 'employment' in the EqA is wider than that contained in the Employment Rights Act 1996, which, for the purposes of unfair dismissal and various other statutory rights, limits the concept of 'employment' to employment under a 'contract of employment'. In contrast, the EqA covers:

- employment under a contract of employment, a contract of apprenticeship or a contract personally to do work – S.83(2)(a)

- Crown employment – S.83(2)(b)

- employment as a relevant member of the House of Commons staff – S.83(2)(c)

- employment as a relevant member of the House of Lords staff – S.83(2)(d).

This definition, which applies to all discrimination claims brought under Part 5 of the EqA ('work'), is similar in form to that which appeared in S.1(6) EqPA, albeit that the new definition refers to 'a contract personally to do work' whereas the old one referred to 'a contract personally to execute any work or labour'. In addition, Crown employment and employment as a relevant member of House of Commons or House of Lords staff now fall within the general definition of employment, rather than being brought within the scope of equal pay law by separate provisions, as was the case under the EqPA.

Contractual relationship. It goes without saying that there must be a contract   2.10 of some sort in order for S.83(2)(a) to be satisfied. An example of a case in which a claimant could not establish the requisite contractual relationship is Ealing, Hammersmith and Hounslow Family Health Services Authority v Shukla 1993 ICR 710, EAT, a sex discrimination case. There, S applied for a job as a general practitioner. He started proceedings under the SDA when the FHSA failed to appoint him. The employment tribunal made a preliminary ruling that it had jurisdiction to hear S's claim. This was wrong, the EAT held, because the relationship between a GP and the FHSA was based on statutory provisions rather than contract.

The Shukla decision was relied upon by the EAT in North Essex Health Authority (now known as Essex Strategic Health Authority) v David-John 2004 ICR 112, EAT, a race discrimination case. There, the EAT held that while the arrangement with the Health Authority imposed a number of obligations on a GP in relation to the patients on his or her list, those obligations were statutory rather than contractual. Accordingly, a GP's race discrimination claim could not proceed. (Note that the EAT went on to state that if it was wrong,

39

and there was a contract between the GP and the Health Authority, the requirement that it be a contract for personal performance was not met because the GP was not required personally to treat the patients.)

2.11 **Personal service.** In order to fall within the definition of 'employment' in S.83(2)(a), the worker concerned must personally carry out the work or labour. In Mirror Group Newspapers Ltd v Gunning 1986 ICR 145, CA, a sex discrimination case, the Court of Appeal emphasised that this means the contract must have as its 'dominant purpose' the execution of personal work or labour. Personal responsibility for the carrying out and efficiency of the work is not itself sufficient. There, the dominant purpose of the contract was simply the regular and efficient distribution of newspapers, and there was no evidence that the contractor was obliged personally to engage in the operation of the distribution agreement. Accordingly, the contract was not one for personal service within the scope of the discrimination legislation. Similarly, in Patterson v Legal Services Commission 2004 ICR 312, CA, a race discrimination case, the Court of Appeal held that a solicitor was not seeking 'employment' with the Legal Services Commission when she applied for a legal aid franchise because, although she was a sole practitioner, she was not obliged to carry out the work under the contract personally. The Court also appeared to endorse the EAT's decision in Inland Revenue Commissioners and ors v Post Office Ltd 2003 ICR 546, EAT, that an *option* to carry out work personally did not make the personal carrying out of the work the dominant purpose of the contract, even though the parties might have expected the person concerned to perform the work personally.

The fact that an individual does not actually perform *all* of the work personally does not necessarily preclude the 'dominant purpose' test from being met. So long as the contracting party performs the essential part of the work, he or she is free to assign or delegate other aspects to another person. For example, a solicitor may delegate some of the legal work on a case to an assistant and rely on a secretary to carry out ancillary tasks, like typing and posting letters and other documents – Kelly and anor v Northern Ireland Housing Executive 1998 ICR 828, HL. (Note that in Patterson v Legal Services Commission (above) the Court of Appeal's conclusion that the solicitor applying for a legal aid franchise was not obliged to carry out the work personally was not arrived at on the basis that she could delegate some of the work, but on the ground that the contract would not have imposed obligations on her to do the legal aid work in question personally in the first place, and would have provided that she was entitled to instruct 'approved representatives' to carry it out.)

2.12 The question of whether the fact that an individual can provide a replacement prevents a finding that the contract's dominant purpose is to carry out the work personally has generated a good deal of case law. For example, in Robinson v Highswan Associates t/a The Republic Nightclub and ors EAT 1020/01 the

EAT held that a self-employed DJ who worked at a nightclub every Monday but could, if he was unable to appear, send a suitable replacement to do the work was in 'employment' for the purposes of the Race Relations Act 1976. Referring to Byrne Brothers (Formwork) Ltd v Baird and ors 2002 ICR 667, EAT, in which the Appeal Tribunal held that a term in a contract giving a limited power to provide a substitute did not prevent four self-employed carpenters who normally carried out the work themselves from falling within the definition of 'worker' in the Working Time Regulations 1998 SI 1998/1833, the EAT held that, notwithstanding the DJ's limited ability to provide a substitute, the dominant purpose of the arrangement was for him to provide his music services.

It appears from these cases that the right to provide a replacement must be limited in some way if it is not to prevent a finding of personal service. For example, it may be restricted to where the individual is unable to perform the work personally for some reason (e.g. ill health); or it may be that the replacement must be suitable or that the approval of the other party to the proposed replacement must be sought. A blanket right to provide a substitute is unlikely to be seen as consistent with a requirement of personal service. This was the situation in Hawkins v Darken t/a Sawridgeworth Motorcycles 2004 EWCA Civ 1755, CA, where the Court of Appeal reinstated the decision of an employment tribunal (which had been overturned by the EAT) that a self-employed van driver who could employ somebody else to undertake his deliveries had failed to show that the dominant purpose of the contract was the personal performance of the work, meaning that he was not employed by the company for the purposes of the Disability Discrimination Act 1995.

Illegal contracts. An individual might be prevented from asserting his or her **2.13** contractual or statutory employment rights – including those under the EqA – where his or her employment contract is 'tainted with illegality'. Illegality cases are not always very clear cut. Several concern individuals who are designated (wrongly) as self-employed rather than employees, potentially amounting to a fraud on HM Revenue and Customs. The relevant question for present purposes is: when will the doctrine of illegality apply in such circumstances to prevent a woman claiming equal pay?

The leading authority on illegality and the right to claim unfair dismissal is the joined cases of Enfield Technical Services v Payne; Grace v BF Components Ltd 2008 ICR 30, CA. In the first case, P began working for ETS Ltd in 1998 under what was termed a sub-contractor's contract. This contained an undertaking that P would work exclusively for ETS Ltd, but would receive no sickness or holiday pay. When ETS Ltd dispensed with P's services and he brought a claim of unfair dismissal, the employment tribunal agreed that his contract was one of employment, and rejected ETS Ltd's argument that incorrectly representing P to HMRC as self-employed rendered the contract void for illegality. In the second case, G began working for BFC Ltd in June 2002 after responding to an advertisement requiring services to be provided on a self-employed basis. He was paid a daily rate, for which he invoiced BFC Ltd, and received no sickness or holiday pay. G worked only for BFC Ltd during this time, and paid his own tax and national insurance contributions. Soon after G started, BFC Ltd offered him a permanent contract with an annual salary but he refused, preferring to maintain his self-employed status. In August 2003, however, BFC Ltd told G that it was liable for his tax and NI contributions, as he was to all intents and purposes an employee, and insisted he sign an employment contract or be dismissed. G eventually agreed and signed a contract on 18 September 2003. His employment was terminated on 12 January 2004 and he also brought an unfair dismissal claim. In order to establish the requisite one year's continuous employment, G argued that his arrangements with BFC Ltd before September 2003 amounted to employment. The tribunal found on the facts that until September 2003 the parties had represented to HMRC that G was self-employed when he was in fact an employee. He was therefore engaged under an illegal contract, which could not be relied upon to establish continuity of employment.

2.14 On appeal, the EAT heard both cases together. In its view, it would be absurd if a contract should be deemed illegal simply because the parties had wrongly, but in good faith, thought it fell into one legal category when in fact it fell into another. The EAT thought that where a worker claims self-employed status knowing that it is unsustainable on the facts, that might amount to unlawful misrepresentation. However, it is not the mischaracterisation of the legal status – which happened in P's and G's cases – that is unlawful, but the implicit misrepresentation of the underlying facts. The EAT therefore held that in neither case was there illegality. The Court of Appeal upheld that decision. Lord Justice Pill, giving the leading judgment, considered that the EAT had been correct to treat misrepresentation of facts as an essential element of a finding of illegality. It is not enough that the arrangements have the effect of depriving HMRC of tax to which it was in law entitled. There must be some attempt to conceal the true facts of the relationship before a contract is rendered illegal for the purposes of a doctrine rooted in public policy.

That, then, is the position so far as unfair dismissal is concerned. Unfortunately, the position with regard to sex (and other) discrimination claims is a little more complicated, as borne out by the Court of Appeal's decision in Hall v Woolston Hall Leisure Ltd 2001 ICR 99, CA. There, the Court began by identifying three circumstances in which a contract might be unenforceable for illegality: first, where the contract was entered into with the intention that an illegal act be committed; secondly, where the contract was prohibited by statute; and thirdly, where the contract, though lawfully made, is illegally performed, and the 'employee actively participates in the illegal performance'. So far, so uncontroversial.

However, the Court went on to observe that the fact that an employee's contract **2.15** is tainted with illegality does not necessarily disqualify him or her from bringing a sex discrimination claim. A sex discrimination claim, it pointed out, is not founded upon, and does not seek to enforce, obligations arising from the contract of employment. The Court of Appeal proceeded to hold that in discrimination cases there is therefore an additional requirement if an employer's illegality defence is to succeed. That is, there must be a causal link between the employee's claim and the illegality in question. The Court stated that: '[T]he correct approach of a tribunal in a sex discrimination case should be to consider whether the applicant's claim arises out of or is so clearly connected or inextricably bound up or linked with the illegal conduct of the applicant that the court could not permit the applicant to recover compensation without appearing to condone that conduct.' Turning to the facts of the case, the Court held that there had been no causal link between H's acquiescence in the unlawful failure by the employer to deduct tax and national insurance, and her sex discrimination claim. The illegality in question consisted only of the employer's manner of paying wages, and the duty to pay tax and national insurance rested on the employer. Furthermore, H had not actively participated in the illegality, and the Court could see nothing that showed H guilty of any unlawful conduct. Lord Justice Peter Gibson stated that '[H's] acquiescence in the employer's conduct, which is the highest her involvement in the illegality can be put, no doubt reflects the reality that she could not compel the employer to change its conduct. That acquiescence is in no way causally linked with her sex discrimination claim.' Accordingly, H was entitled to compensation for her financial loss following her dismissal for pregnancy, which was unlawful under the SDA (and remains unlawful under the EqA).

So, which test applies where an employer attempts to have an equal pay claim set aside because of a possible fraud on the Revenue? Is it simply the standard misrepresentation test espoused in Enfield Technical Services v Payne; Grace v BF Components Ltd (above) in respect of unfair dismissal; or need the illegality be inextricably linked to the equal pay claim itself, as in the discrimination test set out in Hall v Woolston Hall Leisure Ltd (above)? The answer is not entirely clear. On balance, we suggest that there is a crucial difference between discrimination claims and equal pay claims, meaning that the standard Enfield test should apply. One of the reasons why the Court of Appeal in Hall decided that illegality is not in itself sufficient to defeat a discrimination claim was that such a claim is not necessarily founded upon the contract of employment. However, as we shall explain under 'The sex equality clause' below, equal pay claims are indisputably founded upon the contract of employment; they are concerned with inequality in contractual terms, and equal pay is achieved by virtue of the sex equality clause implied into every contract of employment by

S.66 EqA. That said, we are not aware of any reported instance of an equal pay claim being defeated on the basis of illegality, and so this theory has not been tested in the courts.

2.16 Turning from Revenue fraud cases, other illegality cases are less problematic, whichever test applies. This is particularly so where the claimant is responsible for the illegality with which the contract is tainted. For example, in Vakante v Addey and Stanhope School (No.2) 2005 ICR 231, CA (a race discrimination case), V, a Croatian national, sought asylum in the United Kingdom. He obtained a post as a trainee teacher at a school, having stated that his asylum claim was pending but falsely indicating that he did not need a work permit. At no point did he apply for permission to work. He was subsequently dismissed from his post and brought a claim of race discrimination. Applying the formula advanced in Hall v Woolston Hall Leisure Ltd (above), the Court of Appeal held that V was solely responsible for his illegal conduct in working for the school and creating an unlawful situation, on which he then had to rely in order to establish that there was a duty not to discriminate against him. V's complaints of discriminatory treatment were so inextricably bound up with his illegal conduct in obtaining and continuing employment with the school that, if the tribunal were to permit him to recover compensation, it would appear to condone his illegal conduct. He had therefore disqualified himself from pursuing his claim.

By contrast, where the employee is less culpable in the illegality, a tribunal will be less likely to deprive him or her of his or her employment rights. In San Ling Chinese Medicine Centre v Lian Wei Ji EAT 0370/09, for example, the employer sought to prevent a former employee's claim of unfair dismissal, among other claims, from proceeding on the ground of illegality because she was in breach of immigration rules. L's employer had successfully applied for a work permit on her behalf, stating that her yearly salary would be £18,000, but L later signed a contract agreeing to a salary of only £15,000. The EAT rejected the employer's contention that L's working for a lower salary than specified in her work permit application amounted to knowing participation in illegality. The tribunal had accepted L's evidence that she had been pressured into agreeing the lower rate of salary, under threat of her employment being terminated and the consequent loss of her right to work in the United Kingdom. The EAT therefore held that L's claim could proceed.

For a more detailed consideration of illegality in employment contracts see IDS Employment Law Handbook, 'Contracts of Employment' (2009), Chapter 4, under 'Illegality'.

2.17 **Crown employment.** The EqA applies to the Crown and to Crown employment in the same way as it applies to private employers. This is because the statutory definition of 'employment' in S.83(2) EqA extends to 'Crown employment' – S.83(2)(b). S.83(9) provides that 'Crown employment' has the meaning given in S.191 of the Employment Rights Act 1996 (ERA), which is 'employment under or for the purposes of a government department or any officer or body exercising on behalf of the Crown functions conferred by a statutory provision'.

House of Commons and House of Lords staff. The EqA applies to House of Commons and House of Lords staff in the same way as it applies to private employees – S.83(2)(c) and (d). **2.18**

Section 83(5) provides that a 'relevant member of the House of Commons staff' has the meaning given in S.195 ERA, i.e. any person 'who was appointed by the House of Commons Commission or is employed in the refreshment department, or who is a member of the Speaker's personal staff' – S.195(5) ERA. Normally, the House of Commons Commission is the employer of staff appointed by the Commission, and the Speaker is the employer of his or her personal staff and of any person employed in the refreshment department and not appointed by the Commission – S.83(5)(a) EqA and S.195(6) ERA. Alternatively, the House of Commons Commission or the Speaker may designate a person to be treated as the employer of any description of staff (other than the Speaker's personal staff) – S.83(5)(b) EqA and S.195(7) ERA.

Section 83(6) EqA provides that a 'relevant member of the House of Lords staff' has the meaning given in S.194 ERA, i.e. 'any person who is employed under a contract of employment with the Corporate Officer of the House of Lords' – S.194(6) ERA.

'Workers' under Article 157
2.19
As mentioned in the introduction to this section, Article 157 TFEU (formerly Article 141 of the EC Treaty) is concerned with equal pay for 'workers', whereas the EqA covers individuals who are in 'employment'. At first glance, the word 'worker' would seem to cover a wider category of individuals than simply 'employees'. If this were so, then the EqA would not implement EU law fully. However, as noted under 'Employment under the EqA', above, the EqA's definition of 'employment' is fairly wide and, as a result, most individuals who are 'workers' under Article 157 will also be in 'employment' for EqA purposes.

Given the lack of controversy in this area to date, we do not intend to explore the meaning of 'worker' in Article 157 (which is not, in fact, defined in the TFEU) in any great depth. For the sake of completeness, though, we shall set out the ECJ's thoughts on the matter, as expressed in Allonby v Accrington and Rossendale College and ors 2004 ICR 1328, ECJ:

- the principle of equal pay forms part of the foundations of the EU. In the circumstances, the term 'worker' used in Article 157 (then Article 141 of the EC Treaty) cannot be defined by reference to the legislation of the Member States, but has an EU meaning. It cannot be interpreted restrictively

45

- for Article 157 purposes, a 'worker' is a person who 'performs services for and under the direction of another person in return for which he receives remuneration'

- the authors of the Treaty did not intend that the term 'worker' should include independent service providers 'who are not in a relationship of subordination with the person who receives the services'

- however, the fact that a person is formally classified as self-employed by national law does not exclude the possibility that he or she must be classified as a 'worker' within the meaning of Article 157. He or she will have such 'worker' status if his or her 'independence is merely notional, thereby disguising an employment relationship within the meaning of that article'

- provided that a person is a 'worker' within the meaning of Article 157, 'the nature of his legal relationship with the other party to the employment relationship is of no consequence in regard to the application of that article'.

2.20 Although the definitions of 'employment' in the EqA and 'worker' for the purposes of Article 157 are similar, we would not suggest that they are identical. Therefore, equal pay claimants who are struggling to show that they are in 'employment' under the Act should consider also arguing that they are 'workers' under Article 157. If they can show that they fall within either definition, their claims will be allowed to proceed.

2.21 Overseas claimants

The EqPA only applied to individuals employed at establishments in Great Britain – S.1(1). The EqA, however, is silent as to its territorial scope. According to the Explanatory Notes to the Act, the decision to leave territorial restrictions out of the EqA follows the precedent of the ERA, leaving it to employment tribunals to determine whether the Act applies – para 15. (S.196 ERA, which stipulated that many provisions of the ERA did not apply to an employee who 'ordinarily works outside Great Britain', was repealed by the Employment Relations Act 1999.)

If the territorial scope of the ERA is to be taken as a reference point for the territorial scope of the EqA, the test laid down by the House of Lords in Lawson v Serco Ltd and other cases 2006 ICR 250, HL, will be relevant. This is the leading authority on determining territorial jurisdiction in respect of claims of unfair dismissal under the ERA following the repeal of S.196. In that case, their Lordships held that the right not to be unfairly dismissed under S.94 ERA applies to employees employed in Great Britain at the time of dismissal. This means that peripatetic employees – who include, for example, airline pilots and international management consultants and salesmen – are able to claim unfair dismissal if they are based in Great Britain at the time they are dismissed.

Their Lordships also acknowledged two other exceptional categories of **2.22** employee who will be able to claim unfair dismissal even though they are not employed in Great Britain at the relevant time, provided their employment has strong enough connections with Great Britain and British employment law. One category covers expatriate employees, such as foreign correspondents on British newspapers, who live and work in a foreign country but who nevertheless remain permanent employees of the newspaper. The second is that of expatriate employees of a British employer who work within a British enclave in a foreign country. Thus, a civilian who worked on a British military base in Germany and a security supervisor working for a British company at a Royal Air Force base in the South Atlantic were both entitled to bring claims under the ERA. Lord Hoffmann emphasised that whether an employee was employed in Great Britain (or, in the case of a peripatetic employee, was based there) must be decided according to the factual position at the time of the dismissal, rather than according to where the employee could be employed under the terms of the contract of employment.

Given that the EqA is following the precedent of the ERA in leaving the question of the statute's geographical reach to tribunals to determine, it makes sense for tribunals to apply the Lawson v Serco test to fill the gap. However, a straight application of that test would result in a more restrictive scope of the right to equal pay than that which pertained under the EqPA. The meaning of employment 'at an establishment in Great Britain', for the purpose of S.1 EqPA, was governed by S.10 SDA. This had the effect that an employee would be regarded as working at an establishment in Great Britain in two situations:

- where the employee worked wholly or partly in Great Britain – S.10(1). This would apply even if the employee was based outside Great Britain, provided that he or she actually worked partly inside Great Britain

- where the employee worked wholly outside Great Britain, but the following three conditions were satisfied. First, the employer had a place of business at an establishment in Great Britain. Secondly, the employee's work was for the purposes of the business carried on at that establishment. And thirdly, the employee was ordinarily resident in Great Britain either at the time when the employment was applied for or offered, or at any time during the course of the employment – S.10(1A).

On the face of it, the Lawson v Serco test is narrower in scope than these **2.23** provisions. For instance, it excludes those recruited in Britain for a British business but who work outside Great Britain, unless they fall within the exceptions set out by the House of Lords as discussed above. Consequently, some employees who were previously covered by the EqPA are potentially excluded from the protection of the EqA.

However, it seems unlikely that Lawson v Serco – if it is to be applied to equal pay cases – will be applied so rigidly as to exclude claims that would have been allowed to proceed under the EqPA. Indeed, current authority on the territorial reach of domestic discrimination legislation indicates a much more flexible approach. In Ministry of Defence v Wallis 2011 EWCA Civ 231, CA, the Court of Appeal held that a woman working in Belgium, who could not, on a literal reading, satisfy S.10 SDA, could nonetheless bring a claim of sex discrimination before an employment tribunal. (S.10 SDA governed the geographical application of the prohibition on sex discrimination in employment generally, as well as the right to claim equal pay.) W had moved to Belgium when her husband, a member of the British armed forces, was posted to NATO headquarters there. She secured employment with the MoD in the British section of international schools linked to the NATO headquarters. It was MoD policy actively to seek to employ the dependants of serving military staff for the good morale of the armed forces. The terms and conditions of employment reserved for such dependants were expressly governed by English law.

2.24 These facts did not satisfy the conditions that S.10 SDA placed on work done wholly outside Great Britain – W did not work for the purposes of an establishment in Great Britain; nor was she ordinarily resident in Great Britain at any relevant time. But the Court of Appeal decided that this should not present a barrier to the effective vindication of W's rights under EU law. It accepted that W had a directly enforceable right under the recast EU Equal Treatment Directive (No.2006/54) to protection from discrimination and held that a tribunal should disapply any provision of national law, such as S.10 SDA, that posed an obstacle to the effective enforcement of that right, or at least interpret it purposively so that the obstacle is overcome. The Court rejected the MoD's submission that a Member State, in giving effect to Directive rights, is obliged to provide a remedy only to those working within its territory, as defined by national law. It did not consider that W's rights would be 'effectively' protected if she were obliged to lodge her claim in Belgium, particularly when her related unfair dismissal claim was allowed to proceed in the employment tribunal.

Thus, even the generous territorial jurisdiction provisions of the SDA had to be disapplied where a claimant with a close connection to Great Britain was prevented from bringing a claim. And given that this result flowed from obligations under EU law, the repeal of the SDA should not affect the legal position. Even if tribunals do apply Lawson v Serco to equal pay claims, this should lead to the same result. The Court of Appeal in Duncombe v Secretary of State for Children, Schools and Families and another case 2010 ICR 815, CA, held that the Lawson test ought to be modified in its application to UK law where necessary to give effect to directly effective rights derived from EU law. (Note that this case was appealed to the Supreme Court on a separate point –

see Duncombe v Secretary of State for Children, Schools and Families and another case 2010 ICR 495, SC.)

Ships, hovercraft and aircraft. Although the EqA is silent as to its territorial   2.25
scope, it enables the Government to make regulations specifying the extent to which Part 5 of the Act (which includes the law on equality of terms) applies to work on ships and hovercraft and to seafarers generally – S.81. For the purposes of this section, it does not matter whether the employment arises or the work is carried out within or outside the United Kingdom, meaning that the regulations may make provision for work on ships outside Great Britain.

Draft regulations – the Equality Act 2010 (Work on Ships and Hovercraft) Regulations 2011 – have been laid before Parliament. Until they take effect, the Equality Act 2010 (Commencement No.4, Savings, Consequential, Transitional, Transitory and Incidental Provisions and Revocation) Order 2010 SI 2010/2317 has, with one exception, preserved the position under the previous legislation. Articles 10 and 11 of the Order set out detailed transitory provisions relating to ships and hovercraft. Article 11(1) – in conjunction with Schedule 3 to the Order – 'saves', despite their repeal or revocation, most of the substantive provisions in antecedent legislation that applied to work on ships and hovercraft and to seafarers. This includes S.10 SDA, which extended the scope of the EqPA to employment on board a British-registered ship, hovercraft or aircraft. The one exception applies to work on board British-registered aircraft, which is not covered by the Order. This presumably means that tribunals' territorial jurisdiction in respect of such work will be determined in the normal way by applying the test set out in Lawson v Serco Ltd and other cases (above), as modified by EU obligations.

Offshore workers. The EqA also allows for an Order in Council to be made   2.26
extending specified provisions of Part 5 of the Act to individuals and corporate bodies working offshore – S.82. Such an Order – the Equality Act 2010 (Offshore Work) Order 2010 SI 2010/1835 – was laid before Parliament on 28 July 2010 and came into force along with the Equality Act on 1 October. Article 2 provides that the entirety of Part 5 of the EqA applies to offshore work unless it takes place in the Northern Irish Area as defined by the Civil Jurisdiction (Offshore Activities) Order 1987 SI 1987/2197, or concerns a ship in the course of navigation or one that is fishing or dredging (which excludes the excavation of the sea-bed or its subsoil in the course of pipe laying).

Offshore work is defined by S.82(3) EqA as activities in the territorial sea adjacent to the United Kingdom, activities mentioned in S.11(2) of the Petroleum Act 1998 in waters within subsection (8)(b) or (c) of that section, or activities mentioned in S.87(1)(a) and (b) of the Energy Act 2004. Employment tribunals have jurisdiction to hear claims in relation to the first two – Article 3; claims relating to S.87(1) of the Energy Act must be brought in the High Court or Court of Session – Article 4.

49

2.27 **Office holders**
Section 64(1)(b) EqA specifically provides that the principle of equal pay for equal work applies to a person holding a 'personal or public office'. S.83(8) states that 'personal or public office' is to be construed in accordance with Ss.49–52. These sections establish, among other things, that a 'public office' is an office or post to which appointment is made by a member of the executive, or on the recommendation or subject to the approval of a member of the executive, or on the recommendation or subject to the approval of the House of Commons, the House of Lords, the National Assembly for Wales or the Scottish Parliament – S.50(2). A 'personal office' is an office or post to which a person is appointed to discharge a function personally under the direction of another person, and in respect of which an appointed person is entitled to remuneration – S.49(2). Schedule 6 to the Act, which has effect by virtue of S.52(9), sets out various offices that are *excluded* from these definitions, such as parliamentary, local government and political party offices.

2.28 **Armed forces personnel**
Part 5 of the Equality Act 2010, which includes the provisions on equality of terms outlined in this chapter, applies to service in the armed forces as it does to employment generally – S.83(3). This means that armed forces personnel can claim equal pay. However, an employment tribunal does not have jurisdiction to determine a claim relating to a time when the claimant was serving as a member of the armed forces *unless* the person has made a service complaint under the existing procedure, or a complaint under the old service redress procedures, and the complaint has not been withdrawn – Ss.121 and 127(6) and (7) EqA. The EAT in Molaudi v Ministry of Defence EAT 0463/10, considering a similar procedural requirement under the old Race Relations Act 1976, held that a service complaint lodged out of time would not suffice to permit the complainant to later bring a tribunal claim. A service complaint, in this context, means one that is capable of being considered substantively. Tribunal procedure in armed forces equal pay claims is considered further in Chapter 9 under 'Jurisdiction of tribunals – jurisdiction in respect of the armed forces'.

2.29 **The sex equality clause**

As mentioned above, the EqA achieves its purpose by implying an 'equality clause' into every contract of employment – S.66. The effect of this is that where a woman is employed on

- like work
- work that has been rated as equivalent under a job evaluation study, or
- work of equal value

50

with a man in the 'same employment', then, provided her employer has no 'material factor' defence (see Chapter 8), she has the right to have her contract modified so that none of her terms are less favourable than his. This may be done by amending an existing term of her contract so that it corresponds to that in the contract of her male comparator (S.66(2)(a)), or by inserting a new term into her contract where such a term is included in the man's contract but not in hers (S.66(2)(b)).

Less favourable treatment only

2.30

In order for the sex equality clause to operate, at least one aspect of the woman's contract must be less favourable than that of a comparable man. This point is neatly illustrated by the case of Pointon v University of Sussex 1979 IRLR 119, CA. There, P was engaged as a lecturer at the University of Sussex. She was placed on point 5 of the salary scale and paid £4,403 per annum. A younger man was then appointed as a lecturer in the same subject, also on point 5 of the salary scale, but at a salary of only £4,190. Although P was receiving a slightly higher salary than her male colleague, she claimed that she was entitled under the EqPA to be placed at least four grades higher than him (and thus receive an even higher salary) on the basis of her superior qualifications (she had a PhD), her experience, and the fact that she was older. The Court of Appeal held that P's claim could not be sustained because there was no term in her contract that was less favourable than the equivalent term in her comparator's contract. She could not claim that she was getting less pay because she was, in fact, already getting more. Nor could she claim that her grading per se was less favourable because both she and her comparator were on the same grade. Moreover, P's argument that she should have been graded higher because she was older had no merit because 'the age wage norm' – whereby, under the normal arrangements in the university, the older a person was the more points he or she got for the purposes of ascertaining the appropriate grade – was not a contractual term. It was merely an internal system for guidance and did not form any part of the official appointing procedure.

Difference must be because of sex

2.31

Even where it can be shown that a claimant is employed on like work, work rated as equivalent or work of equal value with her comparator, it is important to recognise that the EqA is only concerned to remove inequalities in the contract between the claimant and her comparator if such inequalities are attributable to sex discrimination. If there are non-discriminatory reasons to pay the comparator more, then the sex equality clause will not operate to modify the claimant's contract to bring it into line with his. In this sense, by showing that the criteria of equal work and a difference in pay are satisfied, the claimant sets up a rebuttable presumption that the difference is attributable to sex. It is then for the employer to offer the real, non-discriminatory explanation, if there is one, by showing, under S.69 EqA, that there is a material factor other then sex which satisfactorily explains why the claimant is paid less or receives unequal treatment in respect of her contractual terms (see Chapter 8 for full details).

2.32 Term-by-term comparison

The sex equality clause operates in respect of each individual term of the contract: it does not treat all the terms relating to pay as generic. This was made clear by the House of Lords in Hayward v Cammell Laird Shipbuilders Ltd 1988 ICR 464, HL, where it rejected the employer's argument that any less favourable terms in a claimant's contract could be counter-balanced by other more favourable terms. H had contended that she was entitled to equal pay, for work of equal value, with three male comparators. The employer argued that although the term in her contract relating to pay was clearly less favourable than the corresponding term in the men's contracts, if the contracts were considered as a whole then she was treated at least as favourably as they were. This was because some of her terms were more favourable than similar terms in the men's contracts and these balanced out the pay inequality of which she complained. The employer's contention on this point succeeded before the tribunal, the EAT and the Court of Appeal. The House of Lords, however, took a different view.

The case turned on the construction of S.1(2)(c) EqPA (now Ss.65 and 66 EqA, read together), which stated that if 'any term of the woman's contract is or becomes less favourable to the woman than a term of a similar kind in the contract under which [the] man is employed, that term of the woman's contract shall be treated as so modified as not to be less favourable'. Their Lordships had to determine what was meant by the word 'term' in this subsection. In their view, it referred to a distinct provision or part of a contract that has sufficient content to make it possible to compare it, from the point of view of the benefits it confers, with a similar provision or part in another contract. Thus, they concluded, a woman was entitled under the EqPA not to be treated less favourably than a man under *each individual provision* of her contract, regardless of whether her contract as a whole could be said to be not less favourable than his. Provisions relating to pay, holiday entitlement, bonuses, sickness benefits, company car, etc, could not be lumped together as one term called 'pay', simply because they provided the total remuneration package for the job. So, provided that the woman could show that she was employed on equal work with her comparator, she had the right to have each separate term equalised with his.

2.33 The decision of the House of Lords in Hayward is consistent with the ECJ's subsequent ruling in Barber v Guardian Royal Exchange Assurance Group 1990 ICR 616, ECJ, where it stated that genuine transparency of pay structures, permitting an effective review of payments by reference to the principle of equality, can only be possible if 'the principle of equal pay applies to each of the elements of remuneration granted to men and women'.

What is a 'term'? The simple answer given by the House of Lords in Hayward **2.34** gives rise to more complex questions when we consider what should be treated as a distinct 'term' for the purpose of the term-by-term comparison. The Court of Appeal in Degnan and ors v Redcar and Cleveland Borough Council 2005 IRLR 615, CA, had to answer this question with regard to basic pay and attendance allowances. There, the four female claimants were paid an hourly rate and received no other payment. They brought claims for equal pay citing comparators who received the same basic hourly rate but also two other monetary benefits; namely, a fixed bonus (of between 33 and 40 per cent, depending on the comparator's job), and a weekly attendance allowance (of between £13.91 and £34.88). Payment of the attendance allowance was dependent on the worker attending work, but not on him necessarily remaining at work throughout the shift. If the worker failed to attend for authorised reasons – for example, on account of notified sickness – he would lose his allowance for that day. If there was unauthorised absence for any one day in the week, the attendance allowance was lost for the whole week. The claimants sought equal pay in respect of both the bonus payments and attendance allowances, and the question arose whether these elements in the comparators' pay package were separate and distinct, or part of a single term dealing with basic pay. If the bonuses and attendance allowances were distinct, the claimants would effectively be entitled to 'cherry-pick', choosing the most advantageous comparator in respect of each. An employment tribunal concluded that the fixed bonuses were part of basic pay, but that the attendance allowance was a distinct and separate term.

The Council appealed to the EAT, which turned to Hayward v Cammell Laird Shipbuilders Ltd (above) for guidance. It noted that the particular terms at issue in Hayward concerned paid meal breaks, paid holiday and sickness benefits. It was therefore apparent that the subject of the comparison in Hayward comprised terms extending well beyond monetary pay. The EAT thought that the propositions to be derived from the House of Lords' decision included that, in comparing a term of a claimant's contract with any similar term of a comparator's contract, it is impermissible to lump together the whole of the contractual or other benefits under a general term relating to 'pay'. A 'term' in this context, said the EAT, means 'a term making a comparable provision for the same subject matter'; thus, claimants' and comparators' contracts must be analysed to discern which are separate and distinct terms or parts of the contract, and which make comparable provision for the same subject matter. The EAT accepted – as the parties had conceded – that the provision for a fixed bonus was not a separate and distinct term or part of the comparators' contracts, but was part of the same term that provided for the payment of the hourly rate. The EAT went on to hold that the attendance allowance also formed part of the same term, because it related to the same subject matter – namely, the monetary payment for performance of the contract

53

by attending and working during normal working hours. The fact that the allowance could be paid to a man who left work soon after he arrived for the day did not detract from its connection to payment for normal working hours; nor did the fact that employees lost the attendance allowance for the whole of the week if one day's absence was unauthorised.

2.35 The female workers appealed to the Court of Appeal, which upheld the EAT's decision. The Court rejected the claimants' submission that the EAT had offended the principles laid down by the House of Lords in Hayward by 'lumping together' different terms. Nor was the EAT's classification of the term in question – 'provision for monetary payment for the performance of the contract during normal working hours' – flawed. It was not 'manufactured' (i.e. artificial), but a realistic classification based on careful analysis. The Court also noted that the EAT's decision had the desirable result of facilitating equalisation, as intended by the EqPA, instead of giving the women a higher rate of total monetary pay than any single male comparator. It therefore dismissed the appeal.

The Degnan case was concerned with fixed bonuses, which were found to be a component of a single pay term. The question arises whether other types of bonus would be similarly regarded. In our view, if the bonus in question is performance-related it is more likely to be treated as a separate term. Support for this can be gleaned from the remarks of Lord Goff in Hayward, where he said: 'If a contract contains provisions relating to (1) basic pay, (2) benefits in kind such as the use of a car, (3) cash bonuses, and (4) sickness benefits, it would never occur to me to lump all these together as one "term" of the contract, simply because they can all together be considered as providing for the total "remuneration" for the services to be performed under the contract. In truth, these would include a number of different terms.' The reference to 'cash bonuses' suggests that some types of bonus payments should be considered separate terms from basic pay.

2.36 Indeed, the effect of Degnan would appear to be fairly limited, following the EAT's decision in Brownbill and ors v St Helens and Knowsley Hospital NHS Trust 2010 ICR 1383, EAT. There, an employment tribunal, applying Degnan, found that clauses providing for enhanced pay for working unsocial hours during the normal working week should be treated as part of a single contractual term dealing with basic pay. However, on appeal, the EAT held that Degnan turned on its own facts: the claimants in that case had conceded that the fixed bonus was part of basic pay and the Court had decided that the attendance allowance was a benefit paid merely for turning up to work and so was inseparable from basic pay. Here, by contrast, the terms provided for enhanced rates contingent upon the work being done at unsocial hours, even though they were part of the claimants' normal working hours. They were not, therefore, part of the same term relating to basic pay. Furthermore, the tribunal had found the right to an unsocial-hours premium to be a distinct contractual term, with sufficient content that it could be compared separately. In the EAT's view, Degnan did not lay down a general principle that a broad, overall approach should be taken when comparing terms relating to remuneration for normal working hours. Such a conclusion would be wholly inconsistent with the clear wording of the EqPA (now EqA) and the House of Lords' decision in Hayward.

'Leap-frogging'. The decision in Hayward v Cammell Laird Shipbuilders Ltd **2.37** (above) gave rise to some concern about 'leap-frogging' – whereby a woman could claim equality in respect of a more advantageous term in a comparable man's contract, and he could claim equality in respect of a more advantageous term in her contract. In this context, employers gloomily predicted that the costs of eliminating discrimination in their pay practices would begin to spiral out of control. As it happens, the anticipated spate of leap-frogging claims did not arrive.

Nonetheless, it is worth posing the question of whether the material factor defence under S.69 EqA (for which see Chapter 8) could be used to prevent any attempt at leap-frogging. The House of Lords declined to give a conclusive opinion about this in the Hayward case because the employer failed to raise a material factor defence. However, Lord Mackay tentatively expressed a view that S.1(3) EqPA (the predecessor to S.69 EqA) would not permit an employer to defend an equal pay claim on the basis that there were other terms in the claimant's contract that were more favourable than the corresponding terms in her comparator's contract. Lord Goff, on the other hand, expressed the opposite view. We would suggest that, in the light of the ECJ's decision in the Barber case to the effect that the principle of equality applies to each individual element of the pay package, Lord Mackay's approach seems the right one.

However, in Leverton v Clwyd County Council 1989 ICR 33, HL, the House **2.38** of Lords noted that sometimes different holiday entitlements are taken into account when assessing employees' basic pay, and suggested that, in such circumstances, a difference in pay between a claimant and comparator might be accounted for in terms of their respective holiday entitlements. In Leverton, the claimant (a nursery nurse) worked 32.5 hours a week and was entitled to 70 days' annual leave. Meanwhile, her comparators worked between 37 and 39 hours a week and were entitled to 20 days' holiday (plus increments after five years' service). A pro rata calculation of notional hourly income yielded figures of £4.42 for the claimant and £4.40 for the comparator. On this basis, the House of Lords ruled that a 'causal connection' existed between the differences in hours of work and holiday entitlement between a female school nursery nurse and her comparators such as to constitute a genuine material factor justifying the pay differential between them. Their Lordships held that, as a general rule, where a woman's and a man's regular annual working hours, unaffected by any significant additional hours of work, can be translated into a

55

notional hourly rate of pay that yields no significant difference between them, it is a legitimate if not a necessary inference that the difference in their annual salary is both due to, and justified by, the difference in the hours they work in the course of a year and has nothing to do with the difference of sex.

2.39 **'Piggyback' claims.** It is self-evident that a man may not claim equal pay directly with another man (or a woman with another woman). However, it is possible for a man to 'piggyback' on a female colleague's claim (that cites a different man as a comparator) so that, if she succeeds, he may then claim equal pay with her. This was confirmed by the EAT in Hartlepool Borough Council v Llewellyn and ors and other cases 2009 ICR 1426, EAT. There, male employees doing the same work as female equal pay claimants brought contingent claims on the basis that, if the female claimants were successful in establishing equal pay with their male comparators, then the male employees would be entitled to the same pay by comparison with the female claimants. The EAT explained that a man is entitled to the benefit of a contractual term enjoyed by a female comparator, even if the female comparator herself has only acquired the benefit of that term as a result of the operation of the sex equality clause, as the clause does not distinguish between terms deriving from agreement and terms inserted or modified by statute. Moreover, the male claimants would be entitled to arrears of pay for the full period in respect of which their female comparators are awarded arrears. The arrears awarded to the female comparators represented pay, albeit paid late, and only as a result of their bringing a tribunal claim. That being so, it was hard for the EAT to see any principled reason why that pay should be excluded from consideration in deciding whether the male claimant has received equal pay with the female comparator.

The EAT refused to accept that, because such claims only arise as and when a tribunal makes an award in favour of the female comparators, they are necessarily premature if brought at the same time as the women's claims. There are obvious conveniences in contingent piggyback claims being included in the proceedings from the start, even though it may be appropriate as a matter of case management to put them, or aspects of them, on the back-burner pending determination of the primary claims. Even if such claims are technically premature in the sense that a cause of action has not yet arisen, employment tribunals are empowered under what is now S.127(3) EqA to entertain claims for declaratory relief where a dispute arises 'about the effect of an equality clause or rule', and that would give a sufficient jurisdictional foundation for making contingent claims pending the point at which they may mature into claims for substantial relief.

2.40 **Effect of the sex equality clause**
When a sex equality clause operates, its effect is to vary the claimant's contract so that it ceases to be less favourable than her comparator's. In essence, the term constituting less favourable treatment has to be struck out of the claimant's

contract and the better term (as contained in the comparator's contract) substituted in its place. If the claimant's contract does not contain any term equivalent to her comparator's, then the sex equality clause operates to import such a term.

Removal of less favourable treatment. It is important to note that the effect of the operation of a sex equality clause is not necessarily to achieve absolute parity between the claimant's and comparator's contractual terms. It is rather to eradicate the less favourable treatment. If, for example, a woman is claiming equality in terms of basic rates of pay, but for non-discriminatory reasons the comparator's pay also includes some additional element, then even if the claimant is employed on equal work with her comparator, she is only entitled to the same basic rate of pay and not to the additional element. In Electrolux Ltd v Hutchinson and ors 1977 ICR 252, EAT, Mr Justice Phillips posited the following example: if men and women work alongside one another doing the same tasks but the men receive a special Sunday-working premium because they (unlike the women) are required to work a Sunday shift once every three weeks, the mere fact that women do not work on a Sunday will not usually prevent their being regarded as employed on like work with the men. If the fact that the men work on Sundays is reflected in their pay packets not just in the form of an additional allowance but in higher basic rates, the sex equality clause in the women's contracts would operate to entitle them to the same basic rates as the men. However, the men's and women's actual pay would still not be equal in amount, since the men would continue to be entitled to the Sunday working premiums. But the less favourable treatment in respect of the women's basic rates would have been eliminated.

2.41

A similar approach was adopted by the ECJ with regard to the scope of Article 157 TFEU. In Stadt Lengerich v Helmig and five other cases 1996 ICR 35, ECJ, collective agreements provided for overtime payments to be payable to employees working beyond 'the normal working time' specified in the agreements. However, normal working time was defined in terms of full-time working. This meant that even if part-time workers worked beyond their normal working hours, they would not receive extra pay until they had exceeded the equivalent of a full-time employee's hours. The part-time employees alleged that the terms on which overtime payments were made were indirectly discriminatory and thus contrary to Article 157. The ECJ rejected that argument. Acknowledging that it would be a breach of Article 157 if the overall pay of full-time employees was higher than that of part-time employees in respect of the same number of hours worked, the Court ruled that in this case there was no unequal pay as between full- and part-time employees because their overall pay was the same for the number of hours worked. A part-time employee whose contractual hours were 18 per week received, if he or she worked 19 hours per week, the same overall pay as a full-time employee who worked 19 hours in a particular week. Similarly, part-time employees also

57

received the same overall pay as full-time employees if they worked more than the normal working hours specified by the collective agreement, because on doing so they became entitled to overtime supplements.

2.42 **Upgrade, not downgrade.** Where the sex equality clause operates, the consequence is that the claimant's terms are brought into line with the more advantageous terms of the comparator's contract. The effect is not to downgrade the comparator's terms to bring them into line with the claimant's less advantageous terms. This is made clear by the way in which the EqA defines the sex equality clause. Under S.66 it is the claimant's contract that has to be modified to ensure that it is not less favourable than the comparator's, not the other way round.

2.43 **Equal, not higher pay.** We noted under 'Less favourable treatment only' above that the sex equality clause will not operate unless an aspect of the woman's contract is less favourable than that of a comparable man. In Evesham v North Hertfordshire Health Authority and anor 2000 ICR 612, CA, the Court of Appeal considered the slightly different question of whether it is possible, where a claimant does manage to show less favourable treatment, for the operation of the sex equality clause to result in her being entitled to a *more* favourable term than that of her 'equal' comparator.

That case involved E, a female speech therapist who had been employed by the Authority since 1983. By 1987, E was employed on pay scale Code ST46, on a salary of £14,592. At that point, she brought an equal pay claim, citing M, a top grade clinical psychologist, as her male comparator. M, who had been employed for less than a year, was on pay scale SD61, and his annual salary in 1987 was £22,667. On his pay scale, M would receive in the succeeding years four annual increments of £719, £1,134, £1,045, and £1,059, so that by the end of the fifth year his salary would rise to £26,624. E established before the employment tribunal that her work was of equal value to that of M, and succeeded in her equal pay claim. At a subsequent remedies hearing, the tribunal held that E's contract should be modified so that she would be paid on the clinical psychologists' pay scale at the same point on that scale as M had reached; she should receive the same salary as her comparator, and should progress up that scale at the same rate as him.

2.44 E appealed against the tribunal's decision on remedy, arguing that the fact that her work had been found to be of equal value to that of M meant that she was entitled to be paid on the pay scale for clinical psychologists of M's grade. But she should not enter that pay scale on the bottom rung, as M had done in 1987 because he was newly in post, but at the level commensurate with her five years' service; i.e. she should have the benefit of four annual increments, meaning that her salary in 1987 should have been £26,624. However, the EAT, and thereafter the Court of Appeal, upheld the tribunal's decision. The Court of Appeal noted that E had established that she was employed on work of equal value to that of one particular comparator – M – and not with all district clinical psychologists employed on M's grade. Although the annual increment was related to length of service and not performance, E's greater length of service and experience clearly played a significant part in establishing that she was doing work of equal value to that of her comparator. Were she to enter the comparator's pay scale at a higher incremental level at the relevant date – the date of her claim – then she would receive pay at a level in excess of that received by her comparator with whom she had established equal value, and commensurate with the pay scale of somebody with whom she had not established equal value. The Court went on to say that neither the obligation to modify terms in E's contract nor the obligation to include in her contract a term found in the comparator's contract required the employer to modify or include a term so that the term in E's contract became more favourable than the term in M's. All that had to be achieved was equality of treatment of the claimant and the particular comparator she had chosen.

Note that even if it had been the case that the claimant's work was of superior value to that of the comparator, it would not follow that she would be entitled to be placed on the comparator's pay scale at a higher grade than him. In order for that to happen, she would have to have identified a comparator who allegedly did work of equal value to hers (i.e. a person who was actually employed at the point of the pay scale on which she contended she should have been placed having regard to the value of her job and her level of qualifications and experience).

Right to new pay rate remains even if comparator leaves. It seems that, once **2.45** conditions are ripe for the sex equality clause to take effect, a claimant becomes entitled, as a matter of right, to a comparator's more advantageous terms. She does not lose that entitlement even if she ceases to be able to meet the conditions under the EqA by which she 'secured' the entitlement in the first place – for example, if the comparator leaves his employment and there is no longer any other comparable man at the same establishment. The case of Sorbie and ors v Trust Houses Forte Hotels Ltd 1977 ICR 55, EAT, illustrates this point. There, waitresses in a restaurant claimed equal pay with a waiter who was employed on like work until 5 January 1976, when he was promoted to the position of 'banqueting supervisor'. A tribunal found that they were entitled to the higher pay rate for days worked between 29 December 1975 (the date when the EqPA came into force) and 5 January 1976. But after that date (being the date when the waiter was promoted) the claimants had no continuing entitlement to the higher rates because there was no longer a comparable man engaged on like work. The EAT allowed the appeal, reasoning that once the equality clause had taken effect, the claimants' contracts remained modified. Only if something else happened – such as a further contractual agreement between the parties, a further collective agreement or a further statutory modification by reason of a subsequent operation of the sex equality clause – would their contractual pay rates be varied.

2.46 **Does the sex equality clause amend the contract in the absence of a claim?**
In Sodexo Ltd v Gutridge and ors 2009 ICR 1486, CA, the Court of Appeal
was principally concerned with the time limit for bringing an equal pay claim
following a transfer of employment to which the Transfer of Undertakings
(Protection of Employment) Regulations 1981 SI 1981/1794 (TUPE) applied
(now replaced by the Transfer of Undertakings (Protection of Employment)
Regulations 2006 SI 2006/246). However, that question required it also to
consider at what point in time the sex equality clause operates to amend a
woman's contract, and whether that can happen even before an equal pay claim
has established that the conditions necessary to trigger the clause are in place.

G was one of a number of cleaners and domestic staff employed by North Tees
and Hartlepool NHS Foundation Trust until 1 July 2001, on which date they
transferred under TUPE to S Ltd. Over five years later, in December 2006, G
and several of her colleagues brought equal pay claims against S Ltd. They
based their claims on a comparison, not with any of S Ltd's employees, but
with maintenance workers who had been employed by the Trust at the same
time as them but who had not transferred. The claimants did not argue that
they should receive the benefit of any improvements in terms offered to those
comparators after the transfer (comparisons with men employed by a different
employer are not generally permissible – see Chapter 4 under '"Same
employment" or "single source"'). Rather, they argued that the equality clause
had taken effect, prior to the transfer, to confer upon them enhanced contractual
rights, i.e. those enjoyed by the male maintenance workers. Since TUPE
automatically transferred all the Trust's liabilities under the employees'
contracts to S Ltd, that company thereby became obliged to honour the
'enhanced' terms – regardless of the fact that, in the absence of successful equal
pay claims, S Ltd had no way of knowing that such enhancement was required
by the sex equality clause.

2.47 An employment judge at a pre-hearing review allowed the claims to proceed.
He agreed with the claimants that – presuming that there had, in fact, been
unequal pay before the transfer – the sex equality clause had the effect of
substituting more favourable terms and conditions of employment into the
claimants' contracts; that these terms were then protected by TUPE; and that S
Ltd could be liable for its ongoing failure to pay the claimants accordingly. On
appeal, the EAT essentially upheld the tribunal's decision on this point,
accepting the claimants' submission 'that the equality clause does not simply
hover over the employment relationship between an employer and employee; it
bites once the conditions for its application are met'. In other words, the sex
equality clause can take effect without the need for a tribunal determination
with regard to unequal pay. Referring to Sorbie and ors v Trust Houses Forte
Hotels Ltd (above), Mr Justice Elias, then President of the EAT, said: '[A]
woman cannot continue to compare herself with the man once he ceases to be
a comparator, but she does not lose such enhanced rights as have already been

60

incorporated into her contract. Those rights are by then crystallised and she remains entitled to enforce them as a term of the contract. It would be wholly at odds with the purposes of the equal pay legislation if the woman could receive the male rate only whilst the male was employed on equal work.' So, the claimants could enforce their claims against S Ltd 'in so far as they relate to the failure by the transferee to honour their contracts'.

When the case reached the Court of Appeal, the principal issue was when the time limit for G's claim began to run. However, the Court unanimously rejected S Ltd's argument that the claimants' right to equal pay had not survived the transfer because the equality clause operated only during the period when the claimant and comparator were in the same employment. The claimants were seeking to rely on a right that had crystallised while they were in the same employment as their male comparators and which continued to be their right until validly terminated or varied. That right was not terminated on transfer, but was transferred to S Ltd under TUPE.

So, the Sodexo case suggests that the sex equality clause, inserted into **2.48** employment contracts by S.66 EqA, operates to amend an employee's contract *regardless of whether an equal pay claim is actually brought*. Of course, employees' ability to enforce the right to equal pay is restricted by time limits – typically, a claim must be brought in the employment tribunal within six months of the end of employment. However, claimants who are out of time under the tribunal regime may be able to recover damages in the county court or the High Court – see Abdulla and ors v Birmingham City Council 2011 IRLR 309, QBD, discussed in Chapter 9 under 'Jurisdiction of tribunals – choice of forum'. There is also more detailed discussion in Chapter 9 of the general enforcement issues arising from the Sodexo case – see under 'Time limits'.

Permissible discrimination   2.49

There are three situations where an employer can continue to discriminate between men and women with regard to pay without breaking the law. The first two exceptions, now contained in Schedule 7 to the EqA but formerly found in S.6(1)(a) and (b) EqPA, provide that a sex equality clause shall *not* operate in relation to any contractual terms:

• affected by compliance with the laws regulating the employment of women or the appointment of women to public offices – para 1, Sch 7. This provision is of diminishing importance since the SDA 1986 repealed many of the statutory provisions that specifically 'protected' women and further repeals were enacted by the Employment Act 1989. The exclusion operated to prevent men asserting the sex equality clause in order to claim the same protection as was afforded to women under special legislation

- affording special treatment to women in connection with pregnancy or childbirth – para 2, Sch 7. This provision applies only to special treatment, which probably means more favourable treatment, given to women in this respect. Therefore, for example, a man cannot claim that he should be accorded the same treatment vis-à-vis paternity leave as a woman receives in respect of maternity leave. (Further maternity issues are discussed below under 'Maternity').

2.50 The third exception, which used to be in S.6(1B) EqPA but is now found in S.66(3) EqA, provides that a sex equality clause can modify a term relating to a woman's membership of or rights under an occupational pension scheme only in so far as a sex equality rule would have effect in relation to the term. A sex equality rule is implied into occupational pension schemes and imposes an obligation on pension trustees to ensure equal treatment under the scheme – see 'Occupational pension schemes' below. As the Explanatory Notes to the 2010 Act states, S.66(3) is designed 'to ensure that the provisions relating to equality of terms at work and the provisions governing pension schemes in Ss.67 and 68 operate effectively together so that action can be taken against an employer as it could against a trustee, to ensure, for example that a defence that operates in relation to one, will operate in relation to the other' – para 224.

2.51 Occupational pension schemes

During the early 1990s, it became apparent that EU law, in particular what is now Article 157 TFEU as interpreted by the ECJ in Barber v Guardian Royal Exchange Assurance Group 1990 ICR 616, ECJ, required the elimination of sex discrimination from the rules and contract terms relating to access to occupational pension scheme membership and the contributions and benefits payable in respect of such membership. The UK Government's response to this development was contained in Ss.62–64 of the Pensions Act 1995, which imposed an equality obligation on pension trustees by requiring any occupational pension scheme that did not contain an 'equal treatment rule' to be treated as including one. These provisions were repealed by the EqA and replaced by Ss.67–69 of that Act.

By virtue of S.67(1), a 'sex equality rule' is implied into any occupational pension scheme that does not already include one. Like a sex equality clause, this has the effect that if a relevant term of the scheme is less favourable to an employee than it is to a comparator of the opposite sex doing equal work, then the offending term is modified so as not to be less favourable – S.67(2)(a). Similarly, any term that confers a discretion capable of being exercised in a way that would be less favourable to the employee than to the comparator is modified so as to prevent the exercise of the discretion in that way – S.67(2)(b). The rule covers the terms on which people become members of the scheme or on which members are treated, and any discretions the exercise of which is capable of affecting the way in which people become members of the scheme or the way in which members are treated – S.67(3) and (4). The equal treatment rule also has effect in respect of benefits under the scheme for members' dependants – S.67(5) and (6).

Where a scheme's effects on a person differ according to that person's family, **2.52** marital or civil partnership status, a comparison of the effect on persons of the opposite sex must be with persons who have the same status – S.67(7).

Note that the 'material factor defence' applies to pension schemes in much the same way as it applies to employment – see Chapter 8. So, if the pension trustees or managers show that a relevant difference in treatment between men and women is because of a material factor which is not the difference of sex, then the equality rule will not take effect – S.69(4).

The equality rule is limited in its retroactive scope. In so far as the rule relates **2.53** to *access* to an occupational scheme, its effect is limited by S.67(9) to pensionable service from 8 April 1976. This is the date of the European Court's judgment in Defrenne v Sabena 1976 ICR 547, ECJ, establishing that Article 157 has direct effect. The rule's effect on the *treatment of members* of an occupational pension scheme is limited in time by S.67(10) to pensionable service from 17 May 1990, being the date on which the European Court held in Barber v Guardian Royal Exchange Assurance Group 1990 ICR 616, ECJ, that occupational pension schemes fell within the scope of Article 157.

Remedying unequal treatment
2.54

It is not always a simple matter to remedy unequal treatment in pension schemes. While an employer has absolute discretion over terms of employment, and so can be expected to put right any pay discrimination once proved, pension scheme trustees and managers are limited by the deeds of the scheme. Accordingly, S.68 EqA provides for 'sex equality alterations' to be made to an occupational scheme, which are defined in S.68(5) as 'such alterations... as may be required to secure conformity with a sex equality rule'.

In substance, S.68 permits trustees or managers to make, by resolution, alterations to the scheme to ensure compliance with the sex equality rule where they otherwise lack the power to do so – S.68(1). In addition, trustees and managers may make sex equality alterations even where they do have the power under the scheme to make changes but where the procedure for exercising it is liable to be unduly complex or protracted, or involves obtaining consents which cannot be obtained or which can be obtained only with undue delay or difficulty – S.68(2). In this latter regard, the Explanatory Notes give the example of a large scheme requiring consultation with all members before an amendment to the rules may be made. If such consultation is impracticable because some deferred members cannot be traced, then the trustees may make the necessary alterations by relying on the power in S.68 – see para 235. There is apparently no obligation to achieve such compliance with the complex or protracted rules as is practicable. So, in the example given in the Explanatory Notes, the trustees would not be obliged to undertake consultation with those members who cannot be traced.

2.55 By virtue of S.68(4) EqA, any sex equality alterations to a scheme may have retroactive effect – meaning that they can be applied in respect of the rules of and benefits payable under the scheme from a date prior to the making of the alteration.

2.56 **Exceptions**

Many occupational pension schemes mirror the rules governing access to state retirement benefits, which treat men and women differently with regard to the age at which they become entitled to such benefits. To accommodate this, the EqA, like the Pensions Act 1995 before it, expressly permits some disparate treatment linked to state retirement provision.

The exceptions to the application of the sex equality rule are set out in Part 2 of Schedule 7 to the EqA. Para 4 of that Schedule allows payments of different amounts for comparable men and women, in prescribed circumstances, if the difference is attributable to differences in the retirement benefits to which men and women are entitled or would be entitled under the state pension provisions set out at Ss.43–55 of the Social Security Contributions and Benefits Act 1992.

2.57 In addition, para 5 provides that applying prescribed actuarial factors that differ for men and women to the calculation of employer contributions or to the determination of benefits is a permissible difference in treatment.

These exceptions only apply in such circumstances as are prescribed by regulations or where prescribed actuarial factors have been used. The relevant regulations are the Equality Act 2010 (Sex Equality Rule) (Exceptions) Regulations 2010 SI 2010/2132, which prescribe circumstances/factors previously prescribed under the Pensions Act 1995.

2.58 # Maternity

As discussed below, the scope for bringing equal pay claims relating to a period of maternity leave is limited, in that a woman is not entitled in this period to receive pay equal to a comparable man who remains at work. However, the EqA does provide some protection for women on maternity leave in relation to pay increases and the payment of bonuses.

2.59 **No entitlement to full pay during maternity leave**

The right to equal pay is partially suspended while a woman is on maternity leave. Although the EqA, like the EqPA, is silent on the issue, the basic rule is that a woman is not entitled, during this period, to receive pay equal to a comparable man who remains at work. This derives from the decision in Gillespie and ors v Northern Health and Social Services Board and ors 1996 ICR 498, ECJ, where the European Court made it clear that a woman cannot rely upon equal pay legislation to claim full pay during maternity leave. In the Court's view, women taking maternity leave are in a special position which requires them to be afforded special protection, but which is not comparable either with that of a man or with that of a woman actually at work. In this regard, neither Article 157 TFEU nor the recast EU Equal Treatment Directive (No.2006/54) requires that a woman should continue to be paid full pay during maternity leave. Nor do those instruments set out any specific criteria to determine the amount of benefit that should be paid during maternity leave.

The ECJ's decision in Abdoulaye and ors v Régie Nationale des Usines Renault SA 2001 ICR 527, ECJ, shows that the reasoning underpinning the Gillespie ruling – that women on maternity leave are in a 'special position' – can cut both ways. In Abdoulaye several male employees claimed equal pay with women who received a lump-sum maternity allowance. They complained that their employer's refusal to pay an equivalent allowance to fathers was contrary to Article 157. The employer, relying on Gillespie, responded that the male and female employees were not in a comparable position. The lump-sum payments were designed to offset the occupational disadvantages, inherent in maternity leave, that affect female workers. The ECJ agreed that, in circumstances where one-off maternity payments were, in fact, designed for such a purpose, men were not in a comparable position and therefore could not claim entitlement under Article 157 to an equivalent lump-sum allowance. It accepted the employer's premise that women who take maternity leave may, in practice, face disadvantages in the workplace, including non-promotion and denial of performance-related salary increases either during the leave period or on their return to work. (This accords with the thrust of para 2 of Schedule 7 to the EqA, which is discussed under 'Permissible discrimination' above.)

Maternity equality clause 2.60

While women on maternity leave are not entitled to full pay, the EqA does provide some protection in respect of certain aspects of pay. This is done by means of a 'maternity equality clause', which is implied into the terms of a woman's work by virtue of S.73(1) and has the effect referred to in S.74 – see 'Effect of maternity equality clause' below. While the EqPA did not create a specific 'maternity equality clause', it achieved the same effect by specifically applying the general equality clause (see S.1(2)(d)–(f) and (5A)). Those provisions were introduced by the Employment Equality (Sex Discrimination) Regulations 2005 SI 2005/2467 to ensure compliance with Article 157 TFEU, as interpreted by the ECJ in Alabaster v Woolwich plc and anor 2005 ICR 695, ECJ. That case made it clear that, regardless of whether a woman can point to an appropriate male comparator, she is entitled to have included in the calculation of her statutory maternity pay a pay rise awarded to her after the end of the period used for calculating the earnings-related element of her statutory maternity pay but before the end of her maternity leave.

2.61   **Effect of maternity equality clause.** The main purpose of the maternity equality clause set out in S.74 is to enshrine a woman's right to benefit from pay rises in the calculation of her contractual maternity pay, subject to certain conditions. It provides that if a woman's terms of employment provide for her maternity-related pay to be calculated by reference to her pay at a particular point (S.74(1)), and her pay increases, or would have increased had she not been on maternity leave, after that point (S.74(2)), then the term that provides for the woman's pay to be calculated at a certain time is modified to provide for that increase (S.74(5)). This is unless the terms of employment already provide for her maternity-related pay to be subject to such an increase (S.74(4)), or the woman's maternity-related pay is 'what her pay would have been had she not been on maternity leave, or the difference between the amount of statutory maternity pay to which she is entitled and what her pay would have been had she not been on maternity leave' (S.74(3)). In the latter case, pay rises during maternity leave would be taken into account in any event without the contract expressly providing for it.

Note that 'maternity-related pay' for these purposes means the pay that a woman is entitled to as a result of being pregnant or in respect of times when she is on maternity leave, other than statutory maternity pay – S.74(9). The definition of 'maternity-related pay' that used to apply under S.1(2) EqPA expressly included pay by way of bonus but this has been left out of the definition in the 2010 Act. However, nothing in the consultation on the Act, the Explanatory Notes or the Equality and Human Rights Commission's 'Code of Practice on Equal Pay' (2010) suggests that any narrowing of the definition of 'pay' was intended in this regard. Indeed, the Explanatory Notes state that S.74 is designed to replicate the effect of provisions previously found in the EqPA – para 256. In any event, European and domestic case law indicating that bonuses amount to 'pay' should continue to apply under the EqA.

2.62   In addition to the maternity-related pay provisions contained in S.74(1)–(5), S.74(6) and (7) EqA state that a woman shall receive the following contractual payments if they would have been given to her had she not been on maternity leave:

- pay (including pay by way of bonus) in respect of times before the woman is on maternity leave
- pay by way of bonus in respect of times when she is on compulsory maternity leave (i.e. the two weeks immediately following the birth – S.213(3))

- pay by way of bonus in respect of times after the end of the protected period (being the end of statutory maternity leave – S.74(10)).

So, any contractual bonus due in respect of any of the periods mentioned above **2.63** must still be given. However, nothing in this section obliges the employer to treat a woman who is absent on maternity leave (other than compulsory maternity leave) as working for the purpose of calculating entitlement to a contractual bonus.

Finally, S.74(8) EqA provides that the maternity equality clause will apply to ensure that a woman's pay upon her return to work after maternity leave will be subject to 'an increase to which it would have been subject had she not been on maternity leave'. In other words, the taking of maternity leave may not be used by the employer as justification for witholding a pay rise.

Exclusion of maternity and pregnancy discrimination. In the same way that **2.64** Ss.70 and 71 make the equal pay provisions of the EqA the proper avenue of redress for complaints of sex discrimination in relation to contractual terms, so S.76 makes the maternity equality clause the proper avenue for complaints of maternity or pregnancy discrimination in relation to contractual terms. S.76(1) and (1A) provide that the 'relevant maternity and pregnancy discrimination provision' has no effect in relation to a term of a woman's work that is modified by a maternity equality clause, or that relates to pay but in relation to which a maternity equality clause has no effect. The relevant provision in this regard is S.39(2), which prohibits discrimination in terms of employment, among other things (or S.49(6) or S.50(6) when the claim relates to a personal or public office). Furthermore, S.76(2) provides that the inclusion in a woman's contract of a term that requires modification by the sex equality clause does not constitute maternity and pregnancy discrimination.

Maternity and pensions   2.65

As we have seen, although a woman on maternity leave has no right under the equal pay legislation to receive full pay, she is entitled to certain protections in relation to her pay while absent from work. A woman on maternity leave also benefits from protection in relation to her rights under an occupational pension scheme. The protection is given effect by S.75 EqA, which provides for the deemed inclusion of a 'maternity equality rule' in an occupational pension scheme. In brief, the rule has the effect that any term of the scheme, or any discretion capable of being exercised under it, that purports to treat a woman differently in respect of time when she is on maternity leave compared with time when she is not, is modified so that both periods fall to be treated in the same way – S.75(3) and (4). Any term or discretion relating to membership of the scheme, accrual of rights or determination of benefits payable under the scheme falls within the scope of the maternity equality rule – S.75(5) and (6).

It is made clear by S.75(7) that the rule does not require the woman's contributions to the scheme in respect of the time when she is on maternity leave to be determined other than by reference to the amount she is paid during that time. Thus, while there is a requirement under the general rule to treat a woman on maternity leave as if she were not on maternity leave (and so on full pay) for the purpose of pension contributions, she may not be required to continue making the contributions she would have otherwise made. It is unclear whether the employer must make up the woman's contributions in this respect. The Department for Work and Pensions' view on para 5(2) of Schedule 5 to the Social Security Act 1989, which made similar provision to S.75(7) EqA, was that the employer was not obliged to make up the shortfall. However, the Explanatory Notes to the new Act state that 'a woman who is paid while on maternity leave *will be entitled to accrue rights in a scheme as though she were paid her usual salary* but she will only be required to make contributions based on her actual pay' (our emphasis) – para 264. Given that the full accrual of rights, at least under a defined contribution scheme, depends on full contributions from employer and employee, it would seem that the employer is expected to foot the bill for what would be the woman's normal contributions during paid maternity leave. However, this view has not been tested in the courts and so the point remains unclear.

2.66 It is at least clear that, once a woman's right to maternity pay has expired, the employer is not obliged to make payments on her behalf. S.75(9)(a) EqA provides that the equal treatment rule does not apply to the accrual of rights under the scheme with regard to time when the woman is on additional maternity leave (i.e. the second six months of maternity leave) but is not being paid by her employer. The reference to being 'paid by her employer' includes a reference to the receipt of statutory maternity pay (S.75(10)) and so it will usually only be in the last three months of maternity leave, when the right to statutory pay is exhausted, that this rule will take effect.

Note that some aspects of the maternity equality rule have limited effect with regard to past periods of maternity leave. The rule does not apply for any purpose (not just to the accrual of rights, which is covered by S.75(9)(a) above) to a period of additional maternity leave (i.e. the second six months of statutory maternity leave), during which the woman is not being paid, in respect of which the expected week of childbirth began before 5 October 2008 – S.75(9)(b). This reflects the fact that the right to equal treatment applied differently to ordinary maternity leave (the first six months) and additional maternity leave before that date. Furthermore, the rule does not apply to a period of ordinary maternity leave, during which the woman is not being paid, in respect of which the expected week of childbirth began before 6 April 2003 – S.75(8). This was the date of earlier substantial changes to the maternity leave and pay regime.

3 The concept of 'pay'

As we explain in Chapter 1 under 'UK gender equality legislation', the equal **3.1** pay provisions formerly found in the Equal Pay Act 1970 (EqPA) and now contained in Chapter 3 of Part 5 of the Equality Act 2010 (EqA) are concerned with gender equality in contractual terms generally, not just those terms relating to remuneration. Nevertheless, the concept of 'pay' is of paramount importance, particularly as Article 157 of the Treaty on the Functioning of the European Union (TFEU) (formerly Article 141 of the EC Treaty) enshrines the principle of 'equal *pay* for male and female workers for equal work or work of equal value' (our stress).

The Collins English Dictionary defines 'pay' simply as 'money given in return for work or services; a salary or wage'. However, as we explain in this chapter, both European and domestic equal pay law cover much more than this. Below, we look at how the courts (and the European Court of Justice (ECJ) in particular) have given a broad interpretation to the concept of 'pay' when considering the scope of Article 157. Doing so has enabled them to apply the principle of equal pay for equal work to a wide range of employment-related payments and benefits – such as, for example, occupational pensions, unfair dismissal compensation and severance payments.

3.2 Definitions

The principle of 'equal pay for equal work' derives from Article 157 TFEU. This was initially transposed into domestic law by way of the EqPA, which has since been repealed and replaced by the EqA. But despite the fact that the EqA and Article 157 adhere to the same underlying principle, the definitions of 'pay' contained within them are significantly different. We outline the differences and their consequences below.

3.3 Equality Act 2010

Despite the word 'pay' in the EqPA's title, the Act actually applied to *all contractual terms* under which a person was employed 'whether concerned with pay or not'. This broad scope is now reflected in the wording of the EqA, where the term 'equal pay' and references to 'pay' have been dropped. Instead, Chapter 3 of Part 5 is headed 'Equality of terms', reflecting the fact that although most equal pay claims concern 'pay' terms (salary, commission, contractual bonus payments, etc), tribunals can and do hear complaints about discriminatory 'non-pay' terms as well – e.g. terms covering contractual holiday entitlement, guaranteed overtime working and privileged access to sporting and social facilities.

To fall within the scope of the equal pay provisions, the pay, benefit or facility in question must be part of, or regulated by, the employee's contract of employment. This flows inevitably from the fact that the provisions operate via the medium of the contractual 'sex equality clause' (see Chapter 2 under 'Sex equality clause'), rather than through a general prohibition against discrimination. Where an employee alleges that she has suffered discrimination in relation to *non-contractual* remuneration or benefits – an ex gratia bonus, for example – a claim should be brought under S.39(2)(b) EqA (previously S.6(2) of the Sex Discrimination Act 1975 (SDA)), which prohibits an employer from discriminating in the way it affords '[an employee] access, or by not affording [an employee] access, to opportunities for promotion, transfer or training or for receiving any other benefit, facility or service'.

3.4 Before the enactment of the EqA, claimants had to ensure that they brought their claim under the correct Act, since the SDA and the EqPA covered mutually exclusive grounds: the EqPA did not cover non-contractual benefits, while the SDA did 'not apply to benefits consisting of the payment of money when the provision of those benefits [was] regulated by the woman's contract of employment'. Given that the provisions covering discrimination and equal pay now reside in the same statute, claimants no longer need to establish which Act applies. However, the two jurisdictions remain mutually exclusive (see Chapter 1 under 'UK gender equality legislation – equal pay or sex discrimination'), so the need to frame allegations of unfair treatment on the ground of sex under the right provision remains. If a claimant attempts to rely on the wrong set of provisions, her claim will fail – a fact neatly demonstrated by the case of Hoyland v Asda Stores Ltd 2006 IRLR 468, Ct Sess (Inner House) (see under 'Bonuses' below). There, an employee's SDA claim in respect of a bonus scheme was rejected on the basis that it fell outside the scope of that Act, in that it was regulated by the employee's contract of employment. It followed that the claim should instead have been brought under the EqPA.

Article 157 of the Treaty on the Functioning of the European Union

3.5

Article 157 TFEU requires that men and women in all Member States should receive 'equal pay for equal work'. 'Pay' is defined for these purposes as 'the ordinary basic or minimum wage or salary and any other consideration, whether in cash or in kind, which the worker receives, directly or indirectly, in respect of his employment from his employer'. The same definition applies, by implication, to provisions formerly found in the EU Equal Pay Directive (No.75/117) and now incorporated into the recast EU Equal Treatment Directive (No.2006/54). The content of this Directive, and its relationship with Article 157 and UK sex equality law, is discussed in Chapter 1 under 'EU gender equality measures'. As the Directive adds nothing new to the definition of 'pay', we refer only to Article 157 throughout the rest of this chapter.

The scope of Article 157 is in some ways more restrictive than that of the equal pay provisions in Chapter 3 of Part 5 of the EqA. Most obviously, the Article 157 definition excludes 'non-pay' contractual terms, such as holiday entitlement. It follows that a claimant will only be able to rely directly upon Article 157 – which she might wish to do if, for example, her choice of comparator falls outside the EqA (for which see Chapter 4) – to bring a claim in respect of terms relating to actual payment of some sort. Where a person alleges gender inequality in employment outside the realm of 'pay' (as defined), the relevant measure of EU law is not Article 157 but the recast EU Equal Treatment Directive (No.2006/54), details of which are given in Chapter 1 under 'EU gender equality measures'.

Nevertheless, the courts – led by the ECJ – have construed the definition of 'pay' in Article 157 relatively widely. It has been applied not only to remuneration (basic salary, overtime pay, sales commission, etc) but also to all other payments or benefits that a worker may receive from the employer on account of his or her employment, whether received during the employment or after it has been terminated – Garland v British Rail Engineering Ltd 1982 ICR 420, ECJ. In this way, Article 157 has been held to cover automatic pay increases, sickness and maternity pay, certain fringe benefits, severance and redundancy payments, training allowances and occupational pensions.

3.6

Furthermore, Article 157 is broader than the equal pay provisions in the EqA in one significant respect: it covers both contractual *and* non-contractual rights, meaning that a discretionary bonus or ex gratia payment made by the employer to the worker will constitute 'pay' for the purposes of Article 157 but will not be covered by the equality of terms provisions in Chapter 3 of Part 5 of the EqA. Instead, such non-contractual benefits must be dealt with under the discrimination provisions contained in Chapter 1 of Part 5 of the Act.

3.7 Why is the Article 157 definition important? In most cases, the Article 157 definition of 'pay' will be irrelevant, since claimants can normally rely on the domestic sex equality laws – i.e. the EqA – to offer the same protection as that available under European law. On some occasions, however, individuals who claim to have suffered discrimination may find that they can obtain no redress, or only inadequate redress, under domestic law. In such cases, the claimants may ask domestic tribunals to give effect to the European legislation. In this regard, it will often be advantageous for claimants to show that there has been a breach of the principle of equal pay (under Article 157) as opposed to a breach of the principle of equal treatment (under the recast Equal Treatment Directive). This is because, unlike the Directive, Article 157 has both 'vertical' and 'horizontal' direct effect, meaning that all employees – in both the public and the private sector – can seek to rely directly on its provisions in domestic proceedings. For a fuller discussion of how Article 157 impacts on UK law, see Chapter 1 under 'European Union law – relationship between EU law and UK law', and Chapter 9 under 'Jurisdiction of tribunals – Article 157 claims'.

3.8 Wages

Looking at the wages, or salary, received by an employee for work performed is the most obvious starting point when considering what falls within 'pay' for the purposes of bringing an equal pay claim under the EqA and Article 157.

Article 157 specifically states that 'pay' includes 'the ordinary basic or minimum wage or salary... which the worker receives... in respect of his employment from his employer'. There is no requirement that 'pay' in this respect must be a fixed amount. The ECJ has held that the principle of equal pay for equal work under Article 157 applies to piece-work pay schemes, where pay depends entirely or in large measure on the individual output of each worker. For example, in Specialarbejderforbundet i Danmark v Dansk Industri (acting for Royal Copenhagen A/S) 1996 ICR 51, ECJ, the European Court held that a scheme that consisted of a fixed element, paid as a basic hourly wage, and a variable element, paid by reference to the number of items produced, fell within the concept of 'pay' under Article 157.

Bonuses and share options 3.9

Since the equal pay provisions in the EqA are concerned with all contractual terms, a contractual bonus scheme will be covered. Bonus schemes that are genuinely discretionary, however, will not be covered, as the provisions do not impact upon non-contractual benefits. Any complaint relating to a disparity of treatment in relation to a non-contractual scheme would have to be made on the basis of less favourable treatment under the discrimination provisions in the EqA.

However, the mere fact that a bonus scheme is described as 'discretionary' does not mean that it is a foregone conclusion that it will fall outside the scope of the equal pay provisions. In Hoyland v Asda Stores Ltd 2006 IRLR 468, Ct Sess (Inner House), an employee's SDA claim in respect of a 'discretionary' bonus scheme was rejected on the basis that it should have been brought under the EqPA. Looking at the bonus scheme in detail – the bonus had not been withheld from anyone who satisfied the stipulated qualifying requirements and its amount was not, in reality, discretionary – it was clear that the bonus payment was, in fact, an entitlement that arose out of the contract of employment and was regulated by it. Given that the bonus was categorised as a contractual benefit, the claimant fell foul of S.6(6) SDA, which stated that the SDA 'does not apply to benefits consisting of the payment of money when the provision of those benefits is regulated by the woman's contract of employment'.

However, a different conclusion was reached in Hosso v European Credit 3.10 Management Ltd EAT 0475/09, which concerned the allocation of share options. There, the claimant brought a claim under the EqPA regarding the difference in the allocation of share options paid to her and those paid to her male comparator. The EAT noted that the scheme in question had not been referred to or incorporated into the claimant's contract, nor had any later amendment been made to that contract referring to the scheme. Furthermore, the EAT took the view that the scheme was genuinely discretionary as to the number of shares, if any, to be allocated. It followed that the share scheme was 'wholly different' to the bonus scheme in Hoyland, where both bonus entitlement and allocation were predetermined by the scheme rules. Since the share scheme was not 'regulated' by the claimant's contract of employment, the EAT concluded that the claim should have been brought under the SDA, not the EqPA.

As both these cases illustrate, it is not always obvious whether a payment is contractual or not. If there is any doubt as to which regime applies, it is advisable for a claimant to plead sex discrimination and equal pay in the alternative and ensure that the claim is lodged within the least favourable time limit (for details of the time limits that apply in equal pay claims, see Chapter 9 under 'Time limits'; for details of the time limits that apply in discrimination

73

cases, see IDS Employment Law Handbook, 'Disability Discrimination' (2010), Chapter 9, under 'Time limits'.

3.11 For the purposes of European Union law, both contractual and non-contractual bonuses are covered by Article 157. This was reiterated by the European Court in Lewen v Denda 2000 ICR 648, ECJ, where the Court stated that Article 157 covers all consideration paid to a worker in respect of his or her employment by the employer, whether immediate or future and whether paid under a contract of employment, by virtue of legislative provisions, or on a voluntary basis. The reason why an employer pays a benefit is of little importance in this respect, provided that the benefit is granted in connection with employment. As a result, a voluntary Christmas bonus that was paid to employees did constitute 'pay' under Article 157 even though it was an incentive for future work or loyalty to the undertaking rather than for work already performed.

3.12 Pay increases/merit pay

Automatic increases in the level of someone's pay – e.g. as part of a career progression system based strictly on seniority – will constitute 'pay' for the purposes of Article 157, and are therefore covered by the principle of 'equal pay for equal work'. The distinction between equal 'pay' (under Article 157) and equal 'treatment' (under the recast Equal Treatment Directive) in this context is illustrated by the following cases:

- **Nimz v Freie und Hansestadt Hamburg** 1991 IRLR 222, ECJ: a collective agreement provided that N, as a part-timer, had to work for 12 years before being upgraded in the salary hierarchy. Full-timers, by contrast, were promoted after only six years. Because progression was virtually automatic under this system, the ECJ was prepared to treat the salary increase as 'pay' within the meaning of Article 157

- **Hall and anor v Revenue Commissioners and anor** 1999 ICR 48, ECJ: H and S worked for the Irish Civil Service in a job-share arrangement, each working exactly half the time of a full-time employee. They moved one point up the incremental pay scale with each year of service, and were paid pro rata to the hours worked, according to the point they had reached on the scale. When they subsequently changed to full-time employment, their position on the incremental pay scale was adjusted due to a rule that one year's job-sharing service was reckonable for the purposes of the pay scale as six months' full-time service. As a result, both H and S were downgraded. For example, H, who had reached the ninth point on the incremental pay scale, was placed on the eighth point when she began full-time employment. Applying the decision in Nimz (above), the ECJ held that the claimants' regrading fell within the concept of 'pay' as defined by Article 157 because both automatically suffered a reduction in pay when their employment relationship converted into a full-time arrangement

- **Gerster v Freistaat Bayern** 1998 ICR 327, ECJ: as a part-timer, G took longer to acquire the required seniority for promotion and a pay increase than if she had worked full time. However, length of service only determined G's eligibility for promotion. Unlike the claimant's case in Nimz (above), where promotion was automatic, management made the final decision on whether to promote each eligible employee by assessing that person on his or her merits. For the ECJ, the introduction of an element of managerial discretion transformed matters. G's real complaint was about inequality in career advancement: in effect, a breach of the principle of 'equal treatment', not of 'equal pay'.

On the domestic front, the question of whether pay progression arrangements **3.13** fall to be covered by the equal pay provisions rather than the discrimination provisions of the EqA depends on whether those arrangements are contractual. In Home Office v Bailey and ors 2005 IRLR 757, EAT, the claimants and their 'equal' male comparators were subject to different contractual pay progression systems: progression for the claimants was dependent on performance rating, whereas that for the male comparators involved guaranteed pay increments. The EAT held that a tribunal had been fully entitled under the EqPA to modify the claimants' less favourable terms in this regard.

Where, however, a claimant's pay progression complaint is linked to the employer's failure to promote her to a more senior role, this will fall within S.39(2) EqA (discrimination in employment) rather than the equal pay provisions. Discriminatory promotion practices are considered in more detail in IDS Employment Law Handbook, 'Sex Discrimination' (2008).

Sick pay

3.14

Any sick pay that a worker receives under the terms of his or her employment contract, or a collective agreement, will be 'pay' for the purposes of Article 157. The same is true of statutory sick pay, following the ECJ's ruling that Article 157 applied to the German equivalent of statutory sick pay – Rinner-Kühn v FWW Spezial-Gebäudereinigung GmbH and Co KG 1989 IRLR 493, ECJ. Although the obligation on employers to make these payments derives from statute, employees can be said to receive them by virtue of the employment relationship and, for that reason, the qualifying conditions for 'pay' will have been met.

3.15 Maternity pay

As with sick pay above, maternity pay – whether statutory or contractual – will fall within the scope of Article 157. That was made clear in Gillespie and ors v Northern Health and Social Services Board and ors 1996 ICR 498, ECJ, where the ECJ explained that, since the benefit paid by an employer under legislation or collective agreements to a woman on maternity leave is based on the employment relationship, it constitutes 'pay' within the meaning of Article 157.

However, it by no means follows from this that a woman on maternity leave is entitled to the same pay as a comparable man in the same employment doing the same work (or work rated as equivalent or of equal value) as her. According to the European Court in Gillespie, this is due to the fact that women taking maternity leave are 'in a special position which requires them to be afforded special protection, but which is not comparable either with that of a man or with that of a woman actually at work'. Consequently, neither Article 157 nor the recast Equal Treatment Directive could be relied upon to give women the right to continue to receive full pay during maternity leave. Nor do these instruments set out any specific criteria to determine the amount of benefit that should be paid during maternity leave. As a result, the claimants' claim that they had been discriminated against on the ground of their sex when they received half-pay during most of their maternity leave had to be rejected.

3.16 Nevertheless, the equal pay provisions in the EqA do provide some protection for women on maternity leave in relation to pay increases, bonuses and pensions. The relevant provisions – Ss.72–76 EqA (formerly S.1(2)(d)–(f) EqPA) – were introduced by the Employment Equality (Sex Discrimination) Regulations 2005 SI 2005/2467 to ensure compliance with Article 157 following the ECJ's ruling in Alabaster v Woolwich plc and anor 2005 ICR 695, ECJ. Ss.72–76 EqA are examined in Chapter 2 under 'Maternity'.

3.17 Fringe benefits

So long as a benefit is referable to the employment relationship it will fall within the meaning of 'pay' contained in Article 157. In Garland v British Rail Engineering Ltd 1982 ICR 420, ECJ, the European Court had to consider the travel facilities granted to retired rail workers. Reiterating the words of what was then Article 141 of the EC Treaty, it ruled that the concept of 'pay' encompassed any consideration, whether in cash or in kind, whether immediate or future, provided that the worker receives it, albeit indirectly, in respect of his or her employment from the employer. Therefore it did not matter that the facilities in question were in the nature of a concession which ex-employees had no legal or contractual right to receive or that they were payable after employment had ended.

76

However, in Lommers v Minister van Landbouw, Natuurbeheer en Visserij 2002 IRLR 430, ECJ, the European Court held that a scheme under which a public employer made subsidised nursery places available to employees did not fall within the concept of 'pay' under Article 157. Instead, the scheme was to be regarded as a 'working condition' within the meaning of what was then the EU Equal Treatment Directive No.76/207 (now part of the recast Equal Treatment Directive), in that it facilitated the exercise of the occupational activity of the employees concerned.

That said, where the employee's contract of employment specifically provides **3.18** for the provision of child-care facilities, that term will be covered by the equal pay provisions in the EqA (if not Article 157) as a benefit conferred on the employee under his or her contract of employment. The same will apply to other fringe benefits that employees are entitled to under their contracts, such as a company car, gym membership, etc.

Allowances   3.19

The ECJ has held that an allowance paid to employees to compensate them for their loss of earnings while away on a training course constitutes 'pay' within the meaning of Article 157 – Arbeiterwohlfahrt der Stadt Berlin eV v Bötel 1992 IRLR 423, ECJ, and Kuratorium für Dialyse und Nierentransplantation eV v Lewark 1996 IRLR 637, ECJ. Both cases concerned payments made to members of staff workplace committees (women who worked part time) who had attended training courses related to their committee duties. When compensation for attending the courses was limited to their (part-time) contractual working hours, even though they had attended on a full-time basis, they complained to their employers. Although these payments did not arise from the contract of employment, the ECJ accepted that they were 'pay' because they derived ultimately from the employment relationship.

However, the EAT in Manor Bakeries Ltd v Nazir 1996 IRLR 604, EAT, subsequently declined to follow the decision in Bötel in the context of an allowance paid to employees attending a trade union conference, finding that the ECJ's decision was distinguishable. The Nazir case involved two delegates to the annual conference of the Bakers' Union. Their employer paid both a sum equivalent to the earnings they would have received if they had been at work. This meant that although the conference lasted four full working days, N, a part-timer (and a woman) who worked four-and-a-half hours a day, was paid less than her full-time male colleague. The EAT rejected N's equal pay claim. It considered that, under Article 157, 'pay' had to be in relation to 'work', and the ECJ's decision in Bötel was based on the fact that participation in training by staff committee members amounted to 'work'. By contrast, participation in a trade union conference could not be said to be 'work' and, therefore, the allowance given to N and her colleague did not qualify as 'pay'.

3.20 This decision created an apparent incongruity between UK and European law in relation to allowances that must be paid to part-time workers. However, given the decision of a differently constituted EAT in 1999, it is now widely accepted that the decision in Nazir should no longer be regarded as good law. The facts in Davies v Neath Port Talbot County Borough Council 1999 ICR 1132, EAT, were as follows. D, who worked part time for the Council's meals-on-wheels service, was a GMB union health and safety representative. In that capacity she asked the Council if she could attend two full-time training courses run by the GMB, one from 20–24 May 1996; the other from 24–28 June 1996. On both occasions the Council reluctantly agreed to allow her to attend but, instead of paying her an allowance calculated by reference to the hours that she actually spent attending the courses, it only paid her an allowance equivalent to the contractual wage she received for working part time. D complained to an employment tribunal that she was entitled to a higher allowance on the basis of her right to equal pay for equal work. The tribunal applied the decision in Nazir and dismissed her claim, finding that attending the training courses could not be regarded as 'work' for the purposes of Article 157, which meant that the allowance received by her was not 'pay' within the meaning of that Article.

On appeal, the EAT overturned the tribunal's decision, holding that the tribunal had erred in applying the decision in Nazir. What it should have done was follow the ECJ's decision in Arbeiterwohlfahrt der Stadt Berlin eV v Bötel (above), which set out the correct question for the purpose of determining whether an allowance paid to an employee for attendance at a training course constitutes 'pay' within the meaning of Article 157: did the employee attend the course 'by reason of the existence of the employment relationship'? Asking itself the correct question, the EAT held that attending a training course organised by a recognised trade union was related to the employment relationship and the safeguarding of staff interests. Attendance at such training courses was therefore 'work' within the meaning of Article 157 because that attendance is by reason of the existence of an employment relationship. It followed that D was entitled, on the basis of the right to equal pay for equal work, to receive an allowance calculated by reference to the actual time she spent attending the courses.

3.21 In the light of this decision and the European decisions upon which it is based, it seems highly unlikely that tribunals will follow the Nazir decision. The rule now is simply that where a part-time worker takes time off for training or any other comparable reason arising out of the employment relationship, the employer must expect to compensate that person in respect of any time spent training, or doing any comparable activity, in full. It will in all likelihood be in breach of the right to equal pay and thus discriminatory to pay part-time workers merely their contractual entitlement.

Apart from ensuring consistent application of the principle of 'equal pay for equal work' when it comes to allowances, Davies v Neath Port Talbot County Borough Council (above) should also be welcomed for another reason: it firmly puts the focus back on the employment relationship. At first sight, asking whether the claimant was doing 'work' for which she was entitled to be paid the same as a comparable man in the same employment – as the EAT did in Nazir – seemed an attractive and logical approach to equal pay. However, as the EAT said in Davies, whether or not the time off was for 'work' is an irrelevance within the context of affording equal pay to men and women. Employment contracts often envisage circumstances where a worker receives pay but does no work in respect of that pay. Holiday pay, sick pay and maternity pay are but three examples. It is the relationship that is important here, not the work done under that relationship. The question of the work to which that pay relates arises in connection with whether a woman and her comparator are engaged on equal work. The danger of the EAT's reasoning in Nazir was that such payments were potentially excluded from the rigours of scrutiny by reference to the principles of equality. On the basis of that logic, employers could have had a policy whereby all men attending union conferences were paid twice their weekly pay and women were paid nothing, and this could not be challenged under equal pay law.

So, the payment in question simply needs to arise by reason of the employment **3.22** relationship – and does not require work actually to be carried out – to constitute 'pay' under Article 157. Another case demonstrating this is Hlozek v Roche Austria GmbH 2004 1 ECR I-11491, ECJ, which concerned a bridging allowance paid to employees who, upon termination of the employment relationship, had reached the age of 55 (for men) or 50 (for women) and were not yet entitled to a pension. The ECJ held that the allowance, which originated from a collective agreement, was paid 'by reason of the employment relationship which existed' between the employer and workers who were dismissed as a result of a restructuring, and thus constituted 'pay' for the purposes of Article 157 – regardless of the fact that it was paid after termination of the employment relationship and provided for payment of the allowance without the workers being required to perform any work.

Redundancy and severance payments **3.23**

In accordance with its broad interpretation of Article 157 in Garland v British Rail Engineering Ltd 1982 ICR 420, ECJ (see 'Fringe benefits' above), the European Court has ruled conclusively that redundancy payments constitute 'pay', despite the fact that workers receive them at the end of their employment. The ECJ characterised such payments as a form of deferred pay to which the worker is entitled by reason of his or her employment but which is paid on termination of the employment relationship with a view to enabling him or

adjust to the new circumstances arising from such termination – Barber
.ardian Royal Exchange Assurance Group 1990 ICR 616, ECJ. This
.ies whether the worker's right to receive the payment derives from a
.ntractual term, from some provision in a collective agreement, or from
.atute, because in each case the worker is entitled to receive the benefit in
question from his or her employer by reason of the existence of the employment
relationship – see also, for example, Hammersmith and Queen Charlotte's
Special Health Authority v Cato 1988 ICR 132, EAT. The same principle
applies to severance payments made upon termination of the employment
relationship for any other reason – see, for example, Kowalska v Freie und
Hansestadt Hamburg 1992 ICR 29, ECJ, for a decision regarding severance
payments made upon retirement.

In fact, the ECJ went even further in Commission of the European Communities
v Kingdom of Belgium 1993 IRLR 404, ECJ, holding that certain benefits paid
in addition to a severance payment upon termination of the employment
relationship fell within the concept of 'pay' under Article 157. That case
concerned a rule under Belgian law which provided that workers aged 60 and
over who were made redundant had the right to an additional monthly payment
from their last employer, provided they were entitled to unemployment benefit.
The European Commission sought a ruling from the ECJ as to whether this law
infringed the equal pay principle, as women ceased to be eligible for
unemployment benefit at the age of 60 under Belgian law (in contrast with
men, who were eligible until the age of 65), which meant that they were
precluded from ever receiving the additional payment. The ECJ held that the
additional payment was not a social security benefit, as contended for by the
Belgian Government, but came within the concept of 'pay' for the purposes of
Article 157, as the payment was the responsibility of the last employer, was due
by reason of the employment relationship that existed between the parties, and
had its origins in an agreement between the social partners. The Belgian law
was thus incompatible with Article 157.

3.24 **Pay in lieu of notice**
There is, as yet, no conclusive authority on whether payments in lieu of notice
also constitute 'pay' for the purposes of Article 157. The Court of Appeal was
prepared to accept the employee's argument in Clark v Secretary of State for
Employment 1997 ICR 64, CA, that the concept of 'pay' might encompass
statutory notice payments made by the Secretary of State in the event of an
employer's insolvency under S.182 of the Employment Rights Act 1996. But
this concession was obiter (i.e. without binding force) at best, since the Court
ultimately found against the employee on other grounds and itself described
what it had said about the applicability of Article 157 as only 'provisional'.
Nevertheless, it is difficult to identify any meaningful way in which notice pay
can be said to differ from redundancy pay and other severance payments and

we submit that the EAT in the Clark case had been correct to conclude that payments in lieu of notice (including the statutory payments made by the Secretary of State) do constitute 'pay' within Article 157 – see Clark v Secretary of State for Employment 1995 ICR 673, EAT.

Unfair dismissal compensation 3.25

Unfair dismissal compensation constitutes 'pay' for the purposes of Article 157. However, it took some time for this position to be established. In Mediguard Services Ltd v Thame 1994 ICR 751, EAT, the Appeal Tribunal stated that the compensatory award was indistinguishable, in all material respects, from a statutory redundancy payment (see 'Redundancy and severance payments' above) and that it must therefore fall within the definition of 'pay' as well. In the EAT's opinion, this conclusion was unavoidable, meaning that it was not necessary to ask the ECJ to give a ruling on the matter.

The House of Lords in R v Secretary of State for Employment ex parte Seymour-Smith and anor 1999 ICR 447, HL, on the other hand, was less sure of this and decided to refer the issue to the ECJ. The ECJ confirmed that unfair dismissal compensation falls within the definition of 'pay' in Article 157, as it is designed to give an employee what he or she would have earned if the employer had not unlawfully terminated the employment relationship. This is not the case, however, with the conditions determining eligibility for reinstatement or re-engagement. Since these are concerned with 'working conditions' or the right to take up employment rather than 'pay', they fall within the scope of the recast Equal Treatment Directive rather than Article 157.

Occupational pensions 3.26

Occupational pension schemes have long raised issues of sex discrimination because of the different retiring ages and life expectancies of men and women, and the traditional exclusion of part-timers from participation (most part-timers being women). For a long time, it was generally believed that people who alleged that they had been discriminated against in regard to pension benefits and/or membership of a scheme had no effective legal remedy. This was due to the fact that death and retirement benefits were originally expressly excluded from the protection of the EqPA and the SDA, and because the general understanding of European law was that occupational pension schemes fell within the realm of social security rather than 'pay'. The ECJ ruled in Defrenne v Belgian State 1971 ECR 445, ECJ, that payments under social security schemes could not be 'pay' for the purposes of Article 157.

This all changed with a number of ECJ rulings on occupational pension schemes – described below – which placed many aspects of these schemes firmly within the scope of Article 157 and the principle of 'equal pay for equal work'. In

81

Bestuur van het Algemeen Burgerlijk Pensioenfonds v Beune 1995 IRLR 103, ECJ, for example, the ECJ held that the decisive criterion to be applied when determining whether a pension scheme falls within the scope of Article 157 is whether the pension is paid to the worker by reason of his or her employment relationship with the former employer. Since occupational pension schemes are, by definition, inextricably linked with employment, it would appear that Article 157 covers them all.

3.27 The revolution in the way European law treated occupational pension schemes had a knock-on effect in the United Kingdom. In 1995 Parliament enacted the Pensions Act 1995, which amended both the EqPA and the SDA to cover almost all occupational pension schemes. The 1995 Act also introduced an 'equal treatment rule' into all such schemes which required the scheme trustees to observe the principle of equal treatment in respect of the scheme. The relevant provisions in the 1995 Act were repealed by the EqA in 2010 and replaced by Ss.67 and 68 of that Act, which insert a 'sex equality rule' into all schemes – see further Chapter 2 under 'Occupational pensions'.

In what follows we consider the important cases in this area. However, it should by no means be treated as a comprehensive review of pension equality issues, which is outside the scope of this Handbook.

3.28 Note that in this section we refer to two main types of occupational pension scheme. These are: final salary schemes, in which the ex-employee receives a pension related to his or her salary immediately before retirement; and money purchase schemes, where the level of pension is determined by the amount of contributions paid into the pension fund by the ex-employee and/or his or her employer throughout the period of employment.

3.29 Access to membership
Historically, many occupational pension schemes limited participation to full-time workers, who tend to be men, and excluded part-timers, who tend to be women. However, in Bilka-Kaufhaus GmbH v Weber von Hartz 1987 ICR 110, ECJ, the European Court ruled that occupational pensions were 'pay' within the meaning of Article 157 and that a worker's entitlement to join an occupational pension scheme fell within the scope of the right to 'equal pay for equal work' – see further Dietz v Stichting Thuiszorg Rotterdam 1996 IRLR 692, ECJ. As a result, where the exclusion of part-time employees from a scheme has a disparate adverse impact on women (for which, see Chapter 8 under 'Taint of sex discrimination'), it will contravene Article 157 unless the employer can establish that the exclusion is objectively justified by factors unrelated to any discrimination on the ground of sex (for which, see Chapter 8 under 'Showing objective justification').

The application of the principle of 'equal pay for equal work' in the context of occupational pension scheme membership was considered further in Preston and ors v Wolverhampton Healthcare NHS Trust and ors (No.3) 2004 ICR 993, EAT – a case in which the EAT dealt with a number of issues arising from equal pay claims brought by some 60,000 employees who had been denied access to occupational pension schemes because of their part-time status. The Appeal Tribunal held that, subject to objective justification, the mere exclusion of an employee from scheme membership on the basis of part-time status amounted to a breach of the equality clause. This was so regardless of whether the employee in question would have joined the relevant scheme had she been eligible to do so. The EAT went on to say, however, that there is no breach of the equal pay provisions where pension scheme membership is compulsory for full-time staff and optional for part-time staff. In its view, what mattered was the right to scheme membership. Indeed, voluntary membership of a pension scheme could be a positive advantage for part-time employees, since they could elect not to become members if they were unable to afford contributions.

A current or former part-time employee discriminated against with regard to **3.30** access to scheme membership is entitled to have the benefits of which he or she has been deprived calculated on the basis of all periods of pensionable service since 8 April 1976 (the date on which the ECJ first ruled in Defrenne v Sabena 1976 ICR 547, ECJ, that Article 157 has direct effect), or the commencement of the employee's employment, whichever is later – Preston and ors v Wolverhampton Healthcare NHS Trust and ors (No.2) 2001 ICR 217, HL.

Note that part-time workers may also rely on the Part-time Workers (Less Favourable Treatment) Regulations 2000 SI 2000/1551 to ensure parity of treatment with full-time workers with regard to access to an occupational pension scheme.

Benefits   3.31
The decision in Bilka-Kaufhaus GmbH v Weber von Hartz 1987 ICR 110, ECJ, principally concerned access to occupational pension schemes. The main authority regarding the applicability of Article 157 to the level of pension benefits is Barber v Guardian Royal Exchange Assurance Group 1990 ICR 616, ECJ. In that case the ECJ confirmed that pensions paid under an occupational pension scheme are 'pay' for the purposes of Article 157 and are therefore subject to the principle of 'equal pay for equal work'. However, having regard to the serious financial implications which its decision represented for pension scheme funding, the Court imposed a temporal limitation on claims: individuals cannot rely on the direct effect of Article 157 to claim equality in the level of pension benefits payable in respect of periods of service up to and including the date of the ruling in Barber, namely 17 May 1990. This temporal limitation does not apply to workers who had by 17 May 1990 initiated legal proceedings or equivalent claims, and nor does it apply where a member of an occupational pension scheme has been denied access to a particular benefit, since this is tantamount to a denial of access to membership

83

of the scheme itself and should be treated as such (see above) – Dietz v Stichting Thuiszorg Rotterdam 1996 IRLR 692, ECJ; Magorrian and anor v Eastern Health and Social Services Board and anor 1998 ICR 979, ECJ.

3.32 **The impact of the Barber temporal limitation.** Equal pay claims contesting the level of pension benefit payable to an employee are subject to the temporal limitation imposed by Barber. The practical implications of this are best illustrated by way of an example. In Quirk v Burton Hospitals NHS Trust and anor 2002 ICR 602, CA, Q, a male nurse, was employed by Burton Hospitals NHS Trust and was a member of the NHS Pension Scheme. Under the relevant regulations governing his pension at the time, he was allowed to retire at 55 but had to wait until he turned 60 before he could receive his pension. Female nurses, on the other hand, could take early retirement at 55 with an immediate pension. Following the ECJ's ruling in Barber, the National Health Service Pension Scheme Regulations 1995 SI 1995/300 were brought in to enable both male and female nurses to retire at 55 with an immediate pension. However, because of the temporal limitation imposed by Barber, the Regulations provided that a man's benefits on early retirement would be calculated by reference to his pensionable service from 17 May 1990 – the date of the Barber judgment – whereas a woman's benefits on early retirement took into account all of her pensionable service. Q brought a tribunal claim, arguing that he had suffered discrimination contrary to Article 157 in respect of his pension rights. His case, he submitted, was an 'access' case, meaning that the whole of his pension should be calculated by reference to the principle of equal pay.

The Court of Appeal disagreed. It reiterated the distinction, established under ECJ case law, between claims relating to the calculation of benefits under a pension scheme ('level of benefits' cases) and those relating to the right to join or be fully admitted to a pension scheme ('access' cases), with the temporal limitation set out in Barber applying to the former but not to the latter. In the instant case, Q's complaint did not concern the right to belong to a pension scheme, and nor did it relate to denial of access to a special scheme or a special part of the scheme. It related to the fact that, unlike a female member of the scheme, if Q retired at 55 his pensionable service would be calculated so as not to take into account his years of pensionable service prior to 17 May 1990. This characterised the case as a level of benefits case to which the temporal limitation applied. It followed that Q had not been discriminated against contrary to Article 157. The disparity of treatment that existed by virtue of the NHS Pension Scheme Regulations was permissible because of the temporal limitation set out by the ECJ in Barber. The Court's judgment thus reiterates that age-related sex discrimination in the context of pension benefits is contrary to Article 157 only in respect of its effect in relation to employment after 17 May 1990.

3.33 The Court of Appeal went on to give some useful guidance on how to determine whether the temporal limitation applies in a particular case. In its view, the short question that should be asked is whether the discrimination complained of involves the application of a condition based on age that varies according to sex. This, it thought, was a better way of ascertaining whether the temporal limitation applied than to ask whether it was an 'access' or a 'level of benefits' case. In Q's situation the temporal limitation clearly applied: the discrimination men suffered in the period prior to 17 May 1990 when taking retirement was an age-related discrimination. However, leaving aside the ECJ case law, the Court thought that there may be a more direct route to the same result. Q claimed that his pension was discriminatory in that it differed from that of a female comparator because she received an amount calculated by reference to the whole of her service, including service prior to 17 May 1990. However, by virtue of Protocol No.2 to the Treaty on European Union ('the Barber Protocol') (now Protocol No.33 of the consolidated versions of the Treaty on European Union and the Treaty on the Functioning of the European Union), which enshrines the temporal limitation set out in Barber, that part of a woman's pension which relates to service prior to 17 May 1990 is not to be regarded as 'pay' for the purposes of Article 157. Accordingly, the failure of the pension scheme to take into account the male employee's years of pensionable service prior to 17 May 1990 did not give rise to discrimination because, with the application of the Barber Protocol, the pay of the female comparator was deemed to be the same as his.

Equalisation of pension benefits post-Barber. One of the consequences of the 3.34 ECJ's decision in Barber, and its decision to postpone the impact until after 17 May 1990, is that there is no requirement on employers to ensure equal treatment of men and women in relation to the accrual of pension benefits prior to the date of judgment in that case. Beyond that date, however, both male and female members of occupational pension schemes have to be treated the same.

Equalisation during 'Barber window'. In practice, changes to pension scheme 3.35 rules to ensure equal treatment of men and women in the accrual of benefits could not occur overnight. Nevertheless, following the Barber decision employers were obliged to prevent discrimination in the short term, even before an 'equalisation amendment' to the scheme was introduced. Case law has demonstrated that in the period between the Barber decision and the introduction of the equalisation amendment – a period known as the 'Barber window' – male members' benefits under the scheme had to be 'levelled up', so that they were entitled to be treated as if their retirement age were the same as that of female members. An illustration:

- **Harland and Wolff Pension Trustees Ltd v Aon Consulting Financial Services Ltd** 2007 ICR 429, ChD: the employer operated a pension scheme that provided for a retirement age of 63 for men and 60 for women. The rules of the scheme explicitly permitted amendments designed to reduce the level of benefits payable to members, and also allowed such amendments to

85

take effect retrospectively. In the light of the Barber decision, on 7 September 1993 the employer executed a new deed and rules, which equalised the retirement age of men and woman at 63, to have retrospective effect from 17 May 1990. Thus, the level of women's benefits was reduced, or 'levelled down', compared to the men's. The High Court held that levelling down pension benefits by adopting a common retirement age of 63 for men and women in respect of the period between 17 May 1990 and 7 September 1993 – i.e. during the 'Barber window' – contravened the EU principle of equal pay. It was not permissible to achieve equality during this period by levelling down the benefits of the advantaged sex. Accordingly, the disadvantaged male members of the pension scheme were entitled – for the purposes of the 'Barber window' period – to have their benefits levelled up to match those of the advantaged female members.

3.36 **Equalisation from date of rule amendment.** Whereas benefits had to be 'levelled up' during the Barber window, once an equalisation amendment to the scheme rules takes effect there is no requirement as to how the employer ensures equal treatment between men and women. Accordingly, employers have been entitled to achieve equalisation in the accrual of benefits for pension purposes by reducing the benefits of the group of employees that was previously favoured – Coloroll Pension Trustees Ltd v Russell and ors 1995 ICR 179, ECJ, and Smith and ors v Avdel Systems Ltd 1995 ICR 596, ECJ.

3.37 **Survivors' entitlements to pension benefits.** The concept of 'pay' is not restricted to pension benefits that the employee receives directly. In Ten Oever v Stichting Bedrijfspensioenfonds voor het Glazenwassers-en Schoonmaakbedrijf 1995 ICR 74, ECJ, the European Court ruled that a survivor's pension – paid to a widow, for example – falls within the scope of Article 157. This is because such a benefit, although it is not paid to the employee but to his or her survivor, is an advantage that derives from membership of the scheme which the employee enjoys by reason of the employment relationship. Note that the temporal limitation imposed by the ECJ in Barber (see above) will also apply in cases involving survivors' benefits.

3.38 **Public sector pension schemes**
Public sector workers in the United Kingdom are normally members of the statutory scheme applicable to the class of workers to which they belong rather than members of an occupational pension scheme specific to the department, school, hospital trust or authority that employs them. For some time it was unclear whether benefits under such public sector pension schemes could amount to 'pay' for the purposes of Article 157, or whether such schemes would be categorised as social security schemes, taking them outside the equal pay regime. To clarify, in Defrenne v Belgian State 1971 ECR 445, ECJ, the European Court stated that social security schemes or benefits are directly governed by legislation without any element of agreement within the

undertaking or the occupational branch concerned and are obligatorily applicable to general categories of workers.

Now, however, ECJ case law has firmly established that a pension scheme for public sector workers falls within the scope of the principle of equal pay if the benefits payable under the scheme are paid to the worker by reason of his or her employment relationship with the public employer, notwithstanding the fact that such a scheme forms part of a general statutory scheme. So, in Bestuur van het Algemeen Burgerlijk Pensioenfonds v Beune 1995 IRLR 103, ECJ (the first in a line of authorities on this issue) the ECJ held that benefits paid under the Dutch Civil Service pension scheme fell within the Article 157 definition of 'pay'. As we have already explained, in that case the ECJ asserted that the one decisive criterion to be applied when determining whether a pension scheme falls within the scope of Article 157 is whether the pension is paid to the worker by reason of his or her employment relationship with the former employer. Applying this broad 'employment-related' test to the Dutch scheme, the ECJ ruled that where a statutory pension scheme concerns only a particular category of worker, is directly related to the period of service and pays an amount calculated by reference to the employee's last salary, the pension paid by the public employer is entirely comparable to that paid by a private employer to his or her former employees and therefore comes within the scope of the Article 157 definition of 'pay'.

In light of this, a domestic decision – Griffin v London Pensions Fund Authority **3.39** 1993 ICR 564, EAT – should be approached with caution. There, the EAT – in a decision that pre-dates the ECJ's ruling in Beune – concluded that a pension paid under the Local Government Pension Scheme Regulations 1997 SI 1997/1612 fell just outside the definition of 'pay' in Article 157. This was because the statutory regulations governing the scheme were exhaustive, leaving no discretion to an individual employer, and the scheme itself applied to a 'general category' of workers (i.e. local government employees). As the ECJ subsequently confirmed in Beune, a pension scheme can fall within the EU concept of 'pay' notwithstanding the fact that it forms part of a general statutory scheme. Furthermore, the ECJ's acceptance of the entire Dutch Civil Service in that case as a 'particular category' of worker suggests that the EAT in Griffin was wrong to describe local authority employees as a 'general category' of worker.

Additional voluntary contributions
3.40
Prior to April 2006, there was a legal obligation on all UK occupational pension schemes to offer their members the opportunity to acquire extra benefits by making additional voluntary contributions (AVCs). While this requirement was removed by S.267(1) of the Pensions Act 2004, many schemes still offer this facility.

The general rule is that pension benefits will constitute 'pay' for the purposes of Article 157 irrespective of whether they are paid for by employers' or employees' contributions. However, benefits derived from AVCs are the exception to this rule. The ECJ has ruled that Article 157 will not apply to AVCs or to the benefits financed by them – Coloroll Pension Trustees Ltd v Russell and ors 1995 ICR 179, ECJ. According to the ECJ, the AVCs are made on a purely voluntary basis and the pension scheme merely provides an administrative framework.

3.41 Discriminatory actuarial assumptions

Article 157 requires that the contributions paid by employees into an occupational pension scheme must be the same for men and women – Coloroll Pension Trustees Ltd v Russell and ors (above). By contrast, employers' contributions into final salary schemes will generally be higher for female employees than for male employees. This is because of the actuarial factors that are used to determine how much money is required to fund the scheme; namely, the fact that women live on average longer than men and that the cost of providing a retirement pension for a woman will therefore be greater.

These actuarial factors ensure that comparable men and women receive the same pension on retirement. However, they may lead to disparities where the employee leaves early. In Neath v Hugh Steeper Ltd 1995 ICR 158, ECJ, N was made redundant and had the choice between waiting for his pension – with the option to convert part into a capital lump sum payable immediately – and transferring his acquired pension rights to another scheme. As a result of the inequality in his employer's contributions, the transfer value of N's pension and the value of the lump sum option were lower than the values which a woman in the same circumstances would have received. N claimed that he was being discriminated against in his pension options contrary to Article 157. A tribunal referred the question of the applicability of Article 157 to the ECJ. The European Court ruled that the transfer benefit and lump sum option which N alleged were discriminatory did not constitute 'pay' within the meaning of Article 157. It explained its decision on the basis that, in a final salary pension scheme, the consideration which the employee receives consists of the payment of a periodic pension. The funding arrangements chosen by the employer to secure the payment of the pension are not part of this, and therefore remain outside the scope of Article 157. This distinction, the ECJ concluded, necessarily extended to those benefits whose value can be determined only by reference to the funding arrangements chosen, i.e. the benefits in issue in N's case.

3.42 In Coloroll Pension Trustees Ltd v Russell and ors (above), the ECJ held that it was permissible to apply sex-based actuarial assumptions even though this resulted in men who opted for early retirement receiving a lower pension than comparable women and in lower reversionary pensions being paid to men's wives than would have been paid to women's husbands in circumstances where

88

members offered to surrender part of their annual pensions. The basis for this was that any inequality in the amounts of such benefits arising from the use of actuarial factors in the funding of the scheme was not caught by Article 157.

It is important to note that both the Neath and Coloroll decisions concerned benefits payable under final salary schemes. It is not clear if similar reasoning would be applied to money purchase schemes.

4 Comparators

Apart from the rarely utilised right to challenge discriminatory terms of **4.1** collective agreements under S.146 of the Equality Act 2010 (EqA) (as to which see Chapter 2 under 'How do equal pay claims work? – collective dimension to claims for equal pay'), the only recourse that a woman has in respect of pay discrimination is to individually lodge a claim under the EqA. Generally speaking, such a claim can only progress if she can establish a disparity between her contractual terms and those of an appropriate male comparator.

A number of requirements must be satisfied for a comparator to be a valid comparator. In this chapter, we expand upon the following points:

- S.64(1) EqA requires that a comparator be of the opposite sex to the claimant

- a comparator must be employed 'in the same employment' as the claimant. This, according to S.79 EqA, means that the individuals concerned must be employed by the same employer or associated employers at the same establishment, or at different establishments at which common terms and conditions of employment are observed either generally or for employees of the relevant classes. Note, however, that decisions of the European Court of Justice (ECJ) have established that Article 157 of the Treaty on the Functioning of the European Union (TFEU), which enshrines the right to equal pay for equal work at EU level, is less restrictive than the EqA in this regard. In essence, Article 157 allows claims to be brought where there is a 'single source' responsible for and capable of rectifying a pay disparity between a man and a woman. Given this, some claimants have attempted to use Article 157 to modify or displace the overly restrictive 'same employment' requirement of S.79 EqA

- an equal pay claim requires a flesh-and-blood comparator. In other words, it is not sufficient to point to a hypothetical male comparator and ask the tribunal to consider whether the claimant's contractual terms and conditions would have been different to his had he been employed. (The limited but potentially significant exception to this, provided for by S.71(2) EqA, is also explored)

- European case law has established that a comparator need not be in the same employment at the same time as the claimant, and that it is open to a woman to compare her pay with that of a male predecessor. In the EAT's view, however, a comparison with a male successor is not permitted

- in certain limited circumstances, the EqA burden on a woman to point to a male comparator might have to be set aside in order to give effect to Article 157. For example, according to the European Court of Justice, national rules with regard to pay can be set aside simply on the basis of a statistical analysis that demonstrates an adverse disparate impact on one sex as compared to the other.

4.2 Note that S.65 EqA also requires a claimant to be employed on 'like work', 'work rated as equivalent' or 'work of equal value' to that of her chosen male comparator if her claim is to proceed. We look at these three alternatives in Chapters 5, 6 and 7 respectively.

4.3 **Opposite sex**

In order to show unequal treatment for equal pay purposes, a claimant has to point to a comparator of the opposite sex. This requirement is evident from S.64 EqA, which states that the provisions in Ss.66–70 (which cover the sex equality clause in employment contracts, the sex equality rule in pension schemes, the material factor defence, and the demarcation between equal pay and sex discrimination) will only apply where:

- a person (A) is employed on work that is equal to the work that a comparator of the opposite sex (B) does; or

- a person (A) holding a personal or public office does work that is equal to the work that a comparator of the opposite sex (B) does.

4.4 In most cases, the requirement for a comparator to be of the opposite sex is a non-issue. However, in Collins v Wilkin Chapman Ltd EAT 945/93 the question arose whether a claimant could claim equal pay with a comparator who physically appeared to be of the opposite sex, but who biologically was of the same sex. In that case, a female word-processing operator employed by a firm of solicitors claimed to be doing work of equal value to that of an ostensibly male colleague who was paid more than her. Unknown to her (and indeed to her employer at the time of the comparator's recruitment), the comparator was suffering from 'gender dysphoria syndrome', which meant that he was, in fact, biologically female. An employment tribunal dismissed the claimant's equal pay complaint on the ground that the comparator was not of the opposite sex.

In upholding that decision, the EAT rejected the claimant's contention that what is now Article 157 TFEU should be interpreted as permitting a person to claim equal pay by reference to a comparator who is perceived to be of the opposite sex. Gender, as a matter of law, was determined at birth, and the TFEU did not require any other view of the matter to be taken.

At the time of the Collins decision, the EAT's reasoning seemed to apply to any situation where a claimant seeks equal pay with a pre- or post-operative transsexual. However, things have moved on significantly since then. In Goodwin v United Kingdom 2002 IRLR 664, ECtHR, the European Court of Human Rights held that the refusal of English law to recognise a male-to-female transsexual as legally female was a breach of her rights under the European Convention on Human Rights. This ruling was taken on board in the sex discrimination case of Chief Constable of West Yorkshire Police v A and anor (No. 2) 2004 ICR 806, HL, in which their Lordships held that, since EU law demands that a transsexual employee must be recognised in his or her reassigned gender for the purpose of carrying out his or her duties, statutory rules with regard to the searching of suspects by police had to be interpreted as applying to the claimant in her reassigned gender unless there were strong policy reasons to prevent this.

Furthermore, on 4 April 2005 the Gender Recognition Act 2004 (GRA) came **4.5** into force, enabling transsexual people (provided they satisfy certain conditions) to have their acquired gender legally recognised. A transsexual can apply to the 'Gender Recognition Panel', which must grant such recognition if the individual in question:

- has or has had gender dysphoria
- has lived in the acquired gender throughout the preceding two years
- intends to continue to live in the acquired gender until death, and
- complies with various evidential requirements imposed by and under S.3 GRA.

Clearly, the Goodwin and West Yorkshire police cases, as well as the GRA, have implications for the issue of equal pay comparators, and the value of the Collins decision as a precedent must be in doubt, since the observation therein that gender, as a matter of law, is determined at birth is no longer strictly accurate.

On the topic of gender reassignment, note that the discrimination provisions in **4.6** the EqA protect individuals from pay discrimination because of *gender reassignment*, as this is a protected characteristic provided for in S.4. While S.70 EqA operates to exclude claims of pay discrimination because of sex from the remit of the discrimination provisions and provides that such matters will be exclusively covered by the equal pay provisions in Chapter 3 of Part 5 of the

Act, this provision does not apply where the protected characteristic at issue is gender reassignment. So, if a transsexual person is receiving less pay than a comparable non-transsexual person in the same job, he or she should bring a discrimination claim under S.39(2)(a) EqA, which prohibits an employer from discriminating against an employee as to his or her terms of employment.

4.7 'Same employment' or 'single source'

Although the statutory language in the EqA does not refer to a claimant and her comparator being employed in the 'same employment' in the same way as S.1(2) EqPA previously did, the substantive requirement for claimant and comparator to be in the same employment remains by virtue of S.79 EqA. That provision largely recreates S.1(6) EqPA, which formerly stated that 'men shall be treated as in the same employment with a woman if they are men employed by her employer or any associated employer at the same establishment or at establishments in Great Britain which include that one and at which common terms and conditions of employment are observed either generally or for employees of the relevant classes'. S.79 effectively splits this definition in two, while also removing the territorial requirement that the establishments in question must be in Great Britain (see further Chapter 2, under 'Who is covered?'). As a result, there are two situations in which a woman will be regarded as being in the same employment as a man, namely:

- where the claimant and her comparator are employed by the same employer or an associated employer at the same establishment – S.79(3), or

- where the claimant and her comparator are employed at different establishments belonging to the same employer or an associated employer at which 'common terms' of employment are observed – S.79(4).

4.8 These two alternatives are considered in detail below. Before we turn to these, however, we should reiterate the point made in the introduction to this chapter that EU law takes a less restrictive view than the EqA with regard to comparators. Unlike the EqA, Article 157 TFEU does not require the claimant and her chosen comparator to be in common employment in order for an equal pay claim to proceed. Rather, it allows such a claim where the man and woman are employed 'in the same establishment or service' and the pay disparity in question is attributable to a 'single source'; that is, where there is one body that is both responsible for the inequality and which has the power to restore equal treatment – Article 157, as interpreted by the ECJ in Lawrence and ors v Regent Office Care Ltd and ors 2003 ICR 1092, ECJ. As we shall see under '"Single source" responsible for pay' below, this raises the possibility of claimants being able to use Article 157 to modify or displace the restrictive provisions in the EqA in this regard. For a general examination of how Article 157 impacts upon domestic law, see Chapter 1 under 'European Union law'.

Same employment at same establishment   4.9

The comparator requirements in S.79 EqA present few problems where the claimant(s) and comparator(s) concerned are employed at the same workplace (that is, presupposing that there is no dispute over the basic applicability of the EqA to the particular workplace – a topic discussed in Chapter 2 under 'Who is covered?'). Here, so long as the claimant is employed by the same employer as her comparator, she will be entitled to compare her terms with his. This was stressed in Lawson and ors v Britfish Ltd 1988 ICR 726, EAT, in which the Appeal Tribunal overturned an employment tribunal's decision that it could not hear a complaint under the EqPA where, although the claimant and her comparators were employed at the same establishment, they did not enjoy common terms and conditions. The EAT properly confirmed that, once it is found that the claimant and the comparator are employed at the same establishment, the issue of whether there are common terms and conditions does not arise.

Furthermore, it is clear from the wording of S.79(3)(a) that a woman may compare herself with a man employed by an associated employer at the same establishment, even though the two employers do not apply common terms and conditions of employment to employees in the same classes as the claimant and her comparator. The definition of 'associated employer' for these purposes is discussed below, under 'Associated employers'.

In City of Edinburgh Council v Wilkinson and ors 2010 IRLR 756, EAT, the   4.10
Appeal Tribunal widened the definition of 'establishment' – in the context of the requirement in S.1(6) EqPA that the claimant and comparator be employed at the same establishment or at different establishments at which common terms apply (now re-enacted in S.79 EqA) – potentially to the extent that commonality of terms and conditions will rarely be an issue. The EAT considered an entire Council to be a single establishment, so that claimants working in schools, hostels, libraries and social work could compare themselves to gardeners, grave-diggers and refuse collectors. It ruled that while an 'establishment' requires a clear identity, it might be unduly restrictive to confine this to a single geographic location. In the absence of a finding that the individual locations were individual subsets of the Council's operation, the EAT held the Council to be a single establishment for the purposes of the EqPA.

It seems certain that a similarly inclusive approach will apply to the concept of 'establishment' under the EqA, as S.79(3) and (4) impose the identical requirement that the claimant and comparator be employed either at the same establishment or at different establishments at which common terms apply. Moreover, it is notable that the rationale underpinning the EAT's decision in the City of Edinburgh case has now been incorporated into the EHRC Code of Practice on Equal Pay, which at para 53 states: 'The definition of establishment

95

is not restricted to a single physical location. For example, a woman may claim equal pay with a man doing equal work employed by the same Council but working in a different geographic location.'

4.11 Same employment at different establishments

The second, broader category of 'same employment' that could be distilled from S.1(6) EqPA was the situation where claimant and comparator were employed by the same employer but at different establishments. The situation was rather clumsily defined by S.1(6) as prevailing where the claimant and comparator work 'at establishments… which include [the one at which the claimant is employed] and at which common terms and conditions of employment are observed either generally or for employees of the relevant classes'. S.79(4) EqA defines this same category with a little more clarity. It provides that 'same employment' is satisfied where:

- 'B is employed by A's employer or an associate of A's employer,

- B works at an establishment other than the one at which A works, and

- common terms apply at the establishments (either generally or as between A and B).'

4.12 The effect of S.79(4) EqA is broadly similar to that of the 'different establishment' part of S.1(6) EqPA. The essence of S.1(6) has been preserved: namely, that if claimant and comparator are employed at different establishments, the claimant must clear the extra hurdle of showing that 'common terms and conditions' apply if an employment tribunal is to be satisfied that they are in the same employment. The House of Lords in British Coal Corporation v Smith and ors 1996 ICR 515, HL, considered the meaning of 'common terms and conditions' in the context of S.1(6) EqPA. Their Lordships indicated that this does not mean identical terms, or the same terms with only de minimis variations. Rather, on a broad basis, the terms must be substantially comparable. The use of the same words, without further definition, in S.79(4) means that this same test should still apply under the Equality Act 2010.

The question that then arises is: between whose terms of employment must this commonality be shown? As seen above, S.1(6) EqPA previously required the claimant to show that common terms applied either 'generally' or 'for employees of the relevant classes'. The first option has been transposed in identical form to the EqA – the third limb of S.79(4) EqA allows the claimant to rely on a comparator who works for the same employer at a different establishment if common terms apply 'generally'. According to Lord Slynn in British Coal, who was considering the word within the context of S.1(6) EqPA, this means that common terms apply to all or most workers.

4.13 Interestingly, however, the former second option under S.1(6) EqPA of showing that common terms apply 'for employees of the relevant classes' does not reappear in S.79 EqA. In its place, the third limb of S.79(4) gives the claimant the option of showing that common terms apply 'as between A and B', i.e. as between claimant and comparator. This small change of wording creates a potentially substantive difference in the test for common employment where the claimant and comparator work at different establishments. In British Coal, the House of Lords had interpreted the 'relevant classes' aspect of the S.1(6) EqPA test to mean common terms and conditions within those relevant classes – the claimants would not have to show common terms as between them and their comparators. In other words, the claimants and those doing the same work at different establishments had to be on common terms; and the comparators and those doing the same work at different establishments (and at the claimant's establishment, if any) had to be on common terms; but no commonality was required between those two sets of terms. Furthermore, if there were no employees of the comparator's class employed at the claimant's establishment, then the employment tribunal would have to consider whether, if the comparator were to be employed in the same establishment as the claimant, he or she would be employed on similar terms and conditions to those under which he or she was employed at the different establishment. If not, then the comparison would be invalid.

By replacing the requirement of commonality of terms for the 'relevant classes' with a requirement of commonality as between claimant and comparator, S.79(4) has the effect that a situation highlighted by the British Coal analysis is no longer covered by the new law – namely, where common terms apply in respect of the claimant's work at all establishments, and common terms apply in respect of the comparator's work at all establishments, but there is no commonality of terms as between those two sets of terms. If there is no commonality between the terms enjoyed by the claimant and those enjoyed by the comparator – and there is no commonality 'generally', as outlined above – then S.79(4) cannot apply. This change of wording was not highlighted in any of the consultations on the Equality Bill, the Parliamentary debates, or in the Explanatory Notes. It is therefore impossible to tell whether it reflects an intention to restrict the circumstances in which comparison may be made, or if it is merely a result of infelicitous drafting. Nevertheless, on the straight wording of the Act, at least, the scope for showing 'same employment' where claimant and comparator are employed at different establishments has been narrowed.

However, all the foregoing may be limited in impact, as case law developments **4.14** under the EqPA around the time the EqA was passed mean that the need to show common terms may have greatly diminished in importance. In City of Edinburgh Council v Wilkinson and ors 2010 IRLR 756, EAT (considered under 'Same employment at same establishment' above), the EAT adopted a wide definition of 'establishment' under which an entire local authority was regarded as one establishment. Since the wording of S.1(6) EqPA at issue in the Wilkinson case was practically identical to that in S.79(3) and (4) EqA, courts and tribunals are bound to interpret the new provisions in the same way, thus making the situation in which a claimant would have to show common terms and conditions very rare.

4.15 **Same collective agreement.** In Leverton v Clwyd County Council 1989 ICR 33, HL, the House of Lords held that where a claimant and her chosen comparators (who worked at different establishments) were employed by the same local authority under terms and conditions set by the appropriate National Joint Council (NJC), she was to be regarded as employed on 'common terms and conditions' with them, and hence in the 'same employment' as them within the meaning of S.1(6) EqPA (now S.79 EqA). This was so regardless of the fact that significant differences existed between the employees' hours of work and holiday entitlements.

The Leverton case concerned a nursery nurse who claimed that she was entitled to equal pay for work of equal value with male clerical staff employed at different establishments within the Council. Both she and her comparators were employed under the conditions of service of the NJC for Local Authorities' Administrative, Professional, Technical and Clerical Services (the 'Purple Book'). However, she enjoyed shorter hours and longer holidays. The tribunal, the EAT and the Court of Appeal (by a majority) all decided that the claim could not succeed, as the differences in hours and holidays meant that the claimant and her comparators could not be described as being in the 'same employment' within the meaning of the EqPA.

4.16 The House of Lords disagreed. In its view, Parliament's purpose in drafting the legislation could not have been to require a woman to show that her terms and conditions of employment are identical to those of a comparator. Rather, the correct approach is to take a broad look at the terms and conditions for all employees or for relevant groups of employees. This involves a comparison of the terms and conditions applicable to a wide range of employees whose individual terms may vary significantly. Applying this approach to the facts, Lord Bridge stated that: 'Terms and conditions of employment governed by the same collective agreement seem to me to represent the paradigm, though not necessarily the only example, of the common terms and conditions of employment contemplated by the subsection.' Their Lordships went on to hold that, since both the claimant and her comparators were employed under the terms of the Purple Book, they were employed on 'common terms and conditions', and the differences in hours and holidays did not, therefore, prevent their being regarded as employed in the 'same employment'.

Accordingly, where the general terms and conditions at different establishments belonging to the same employer or an associated employer are governed by the same collective agreement (or any other similar type of device whereby general conditions are standardised), we suggest that women may claim that they are in the 'same employment' with men at that other establishment, even if their individual terms vary.

A slightly different, and more complex, issue arose in South Tyneside **4.17** Metropolitan Borough Council v Anderson and ors 2007 ICR 1581, CA. There, the claimants worked as school support staff – typically cooks or cleaners – in South Tyneside community schools. Each was employed by the local authority, STC, and was paid according to her grade at a rate set by a collective agreement – known as the 'White Book' – which applied to a wide range of local authority employees. None of the men with whom the claimants sought to compare themselves – a group including drivers, a street cleaner, a painter, a refuse collector and a foreman – worked in schools. However, these men were employed by STC on the same White Book terms and conditions as the claimants. An employment tribunal agreed with the claimants that they were in the 'same employment' as their comparators within the meaning of S.1(6) EqPA (now S.79 EqA). The EAT upheld the tribunal's decision in this regard, and the local authority appealed to the Court of Appeal. It accepted that those claimants who were employed directly by the local authority were employed on 'common terms and conditions' with their male comparators. Thus, it confined its appeal to those claimants who were employed on the recommendation of school governors, pointing out that Reg 15 of the School Staffing (England) Regulations 2003 SI 2003/1963 (which have since been repealed) gave the governing body of each community school discretion to determine the terms and conditions of employment of each of those claimants. This meant that if, in a hypothetical scenario, one of the male comparators were to be employed at a school where a claimant worked, there would be no certainty that he and the claimant would share 'common terms and conditions'.

The Court of Appeal rejected the local authority's argument. The fact that a male comparator would never be required to work at a claimant's school on account of the nature of his work did not mean that the claimant was required to establish that, if a comparator were to be employed at the claimant's school, he and she would be employed on common terms and conditions. It was sufficient that the claimant and the comparator were in fact employed by the same employer, albeit in different establishments, on similar terms and conditions. Thus, the equal pay claims could proceed. The Court of Appeal went on to comment that even if it had decided against the claimants on this point, it would, in any event, have allowed the equal pay claims to proceed on the basis that a claimant's terms and conditions and those of a male comparator hypothetically employed at her school would be broadly similar because he would be placed on the same pay grade as her. The margin of discretion which the local authority sought to vest in the school governors under Reg 15 of the 2003 Regulations was largely illusory. The Court considered it both 'legally and factually fanciful' to suppose that the school governors could select and bind the local authority to an inappropriate grade for a new member of staff.

There will ordinarily be a known pay grade for school support staff, departure from which by the governors would be both unrealistic and arguably perverse.

4.18 Note that the position of the claimants in the Anderson case can be contrasted with that of the claimants in Dolphin and ors v Hartlepool Borough Council and ors and another case EAT 0559/05. In Dolphin, female support staff working in voluntary-aided schools who were actually employed by the governing bodies of those schools (rather than by Hartlepool Borough Council) could not use the EqPA to claim pay equal to that of men who were employed by that Council, as they did not share common employment.

4.19 **'Broadly similar' terms.** One issue that remained unclear after the House of Lords' decision in Leverton v Clwyd County Council 1989 ICR 33, HL, was whether a woman could compare herself with comparators employed at different establishments whose terms and conditions were governed by a different collective agreement than hers. As previously mentioned, the principal reason why their Lordships found in the claimant's favour on the 'common terms and conditions' point in Leverton was that she and her comparators were all white collar workers covered by the same Purple Book agreement. But what if her chosen comparator had been a manual employee of the Council covered by a different agreement negotiated by a different union? So long as he shared the claimant's workplace there would be no problem, since in cases where the claimant and her comparator are employed at the same establishment there is no need for them to be employed on common terms and conditions (see under 'Employed at same establishment' above). However, if he worked for the same employer as the claimant (or an associated employer of her employer) but at a different workplace, it is arguable that some of Lord Bridge's comments in Leverton could serve to defeat the woman's claim for equal pay. In Lord Bridge's view, the terms and conditions had to be applicable 'to all the employees at the relevant establishments, or to a particular class or classes of employees to which both the woman and the men belong'. On one reading of these remarks, Lord Bridge could be assumed to mean that both the comparator at his workplace and the claimant at her workplace have to be employed on similar terms and conditions deriving from the same collective agreement.

If such a meaning were to be ascribed to Lord Bridge's remarks then it would be in contrast to the dissenting opinion of Lord Justice May in the Court of Appeal (1988 IRLR 239, CA) in Leverton. May LJ (whose judgment was expressly approved by the House of Lords, including Lord Bridge) indicated that emphasis was to be placed on the terms and conditions of each group of relevant employees. In other words, so long as, for example, nursery nurses are or would be employed on the same terms and conditions at whichever establishment they were based, and so long as the same applies to the comparators chosen by such a nurse in a claim for equal pay, then under the broad construction of S.1(6) both groups would be regarded as employed on 'common terms and conditions' for the purposes of the subsection. A comparison or commonality of terms between the claimant and her comparators would not be necessary. Given the House of Lords' approval of May LJ's judgment and the fact that Lord Bridge was at pains to point out that situations where the same collective agreement operates across different bargaining groups are the paradigm but not sole example of where common terms and conditions will be taken to apply, it seems reasonable to conclude that Lord Bridge did not mean to imply that a claimant and her comparator have to be subject to the same collective terms if they are to be regarded as employed on common terms and conditions albeit at different workplaces.

The House of Lords had a further opportunity to consider the question of what **4.20** is meant by 'common terms and conditions' in the context of a cross-establishment comparison in British Coal Corporation v Smith and ors 1996 ICR 515, HL. There, women employed by British Coal as canteen workers and cleaners sought to claim equal pay with surface mineworkers and clerical workers also employed by British Coal but at different establishments. A tribunal accepted the women's contention that they were employed in the 'same employment' as their comparators, even though each of the classes of employee to which the comparators belonged was subjected to separate bargaining agreements and different pay structures. The case was appealed, eventually, to the House of Lords, which rejected British Coal's argument that S.1(6) EqPA required the claimants and their comparators to be employed on the same terms. Their Lordships held that if a man in the comparator's class is not actually employed at the claimant's establishment, then the claimant has to show that the terms and conditions on which such a man would be employed at her establishment are broadly similar to her own. The purpose of the requirement to show 'common terms and conditions' was to ensure that the terms and conditions of the comparator and the claimant (where employed at different establishments) are sufficiently similar for a fair comparison to be made. Consequently, for a comparator to be regarded as being in the 'same employment' as a claimant, it was sufficient that the terms and conditions of employees of the comparator's class at both his and the claimant's establishments are (or would be) broadly similar. They do not have to be identical.

The decision in the British Coal case appears to establish that it is not necessary for the claimant employed at one establishment and her comparator employed by the same employer at a different establishment to be subject to the same collective agreement in order to be regarded as employed on 'common terms and conditions'. In this respect, Lord Slynn (with whose speech the other Law Lords agreed) observed: '[I]t seems to me that when dealing with the comparison of terms and conditions, the relevant classes having been established, [the employment tribunal in the instant case] clearly adopted a broad commonsense approach which seems to me to have been in accordance with the speech of Lord Bridge of Harwich [in the Leverton case]. On this basis it concluded that

101

surface mineworkers were governed by a nationally negotiated agreement which sets basic and overtime rates of pay, sick pay, holidays and other similar matters... They also found that canteen workers were all in the same employment because their terms were governed by national agreements... If, as I consider, the terms and conditions do not have to be identical, but on a broad basis to be substantially comparable, then it seems to me that the [employment] tribunal did not err in law in the way it directed itself and there was clearly material on which it could base its finding that the claimants and their comparators were in the same employment.'

4.21 The British Coal case has been considered by two decisions of the EAT in Scotland. The first was Dumfries and Galloway Council v North and ors 2009 ICR 1363, EAT. There the claimants – classroom assistants, learning assistants and nursery nurses employed by the Council in its schools under terms contained in a collective agreement known as the Blue Book – sought to compare themselves with men employed as road workers, groundsmen, refuse collectors, refuse lorry drivers and a leisure attendant. The male comparators' terms were governed by a separate collective agreement, known as the Green Book. The claimants were all based at schools and worked under the management and direction of the head teacher, who also had an element of discretion regarding the choice of employees to work at his or her school. Anyone employed in a school had to first go through a vetting procedure, carried out by the government agency Disclosure Scotland in order to check their criminal conviction history and any appropriate non-conviction information. By contrast, the comparators worked at a variety of depots and council sites, and only the groundsmen, road workers and refuse workers did any of their work at schools, and in any event were not subject to the control or discretion of the head teacher. Only the leisure attendant and some of the groundsmen were subject to a vetting procedure.

An employment tribunal, relying on the British Coal decision, found that the claimants and their comparators were employed in the 'same employment'. The Council appealed to the EAT, where Lady Smith, having examined the Leverton and British Coal decisions, concluded that in light of those cases, a woman is not prevented from using a male comparator at another establishment just because there are no men employed in his class at her own establishment. She can use that comparator provided she can show that he would, if he were to be employed at her establishment, be employed on terms and conditions broadly similar to his existing ones. Consequently, Lady Smith accepted that British Coal allows a tribunal to carry out a hypothetical exercise. However, the issue before Lady Smith was whether such an exercise could be based on an assumption of facts that would never occur, since there was no evidence in the instant case that the comparators would ever be employed to carry out their jobs in the claimants' schools.

Lady Smith concluded that it is necessary to show that there is a 'real possibility' **4.22** of the comparator being employed at the same establishment as the claimant in the job – or a broadly similar one – that he carries out at the other establishment. The claimant must then show that the terms and conditions on which he would be employed at her establishment would be broadly similar to those on which he is currently employed. In the instant case, the tribunal's conclusion that the comparators were in the same employment was not supported by the fact that they undertook work – such as refuse collection – that was necessary for the school's operation; nor did it follow that because a small number of the schools had swimming pools they would employ leisure attendants. Even if it had been possible for the comparators to be employed at the Council's schools, there would still have to be findings of fact to support a conclusion that they would have been employed on terms and conditions that were broadly similar to their existing ones. Lady Smith found that the absence of the need to satisfy the Disclosure Scotland check procedure for all but a minority of the comparators, and the lack of management and direction by the head teacher, were important factors that militated against the conclusion that the claimants and their comparators were employed on broadly similar terms and conditions. Accordingly, she upheld the Council's appeal and substituted a finding that the claimants and their comparators were not in the same employment.

The Dumfries case was not, however, the end of the matter, as Lady Smith revisited her opinion in the later case of City of Edinburgh Council v Wilkinson 2010 IRLR 756, EAT (also considered under 'Same employment at same establishment' above). In that case the claimants – predominantly women employed at a range of Council departments in a range of posts, including jobs in schools, hostels, libraries and social work – sought to compare their pay with manual workers employed at a single Council department. The employment judge found that the claimants and comparators were employed on common terms and conditions, but went on to find that even if they were not, the claimants could show that they were in the same employment on the basis that both groups were employed on common terms and conditions respectively even though it was not inconceivable that the male comparators might be assigned to work at a location where one of the claimants worked.

On appeal, the Council argued that the employment judge had been wrong to **4.23** embark on this hypothetical exercise as there was no 'real possibility' of a male comparator ever being transferred to the claimants' establishment to carry out his job. However, Lady Smith concluded that, although the application of the British Coal hypothesis requires a 'factual substratum', she had been wrong in her analysis of the issue in the Dumfries case. Requiring the claimant to show a 'real possibility' was too restrictive an interpretation of S.1(6) EqPA, which could undermine the principle of equal pay in Article 157 TFEU. Instead, provided it could be shown that the comparators – regardless of the establishments at which they work – are always employed on common terms and conditions, it would be legitimate to assume that they would be employed on those terms and conditions if taken on to work at the claimants' establishment, with the result that the men and the women are to be regarded as being in the same employment. In Lady Smith's view, circumstances where the comparators are always employed under the same collective agreement would be the paradigm application of the hypothetical exercise sanctioned in British Coal.

Lady Smith's latter interpretation of the British Coal case in Wilkinson was subsequently approved by the Court of Session (Inner House) when it heard an appeal in the Dumfries case – North and ors v Dumfries and Galloway Council 2011 IRLR 239, Ct Sess (Inner House). The Court stated that the 'real possibility' test that was identified and subsequently disowned by Lady Smith 'would undoubtedly place an additional burden upon an equal pay claimant. In our view, that additional burden should not be so imposed, partly because such a test is not articulated in statute or precedent, and partly for the policy reasons set out by Lady Smith in Wilkinson.'

4.24 The test applied by the House of Lords in the Leverton and British Coal cases, as interpreted by the EAT in Wilkinson and the Court of Session in the Dumfries case, for showing common terms and conditions across different establishments undoubtedly assists women to overcome the major hurdle of identifying an appropriate male comparator. Of course, identifying such a comparator does not necessarily mean that the equal pay claims will ultimately succeed. Indeed, the employers in the Leverton and British Coal cases were able to thwart the women's claims by successfully making out a 'material factor' defence, showing that the differences in pay between the claimants and their comparators were due to genuine, non-sex-based reasons. Details of how such a defence can be mounted can be found in Chapter 8.

4.25 **Work not done at an establishment.** The EqA does not define 'establishment' (and nor did the EqPA) and so this concept is only limited by the small amount of case law that has built up on it. However, the EqA does introduce a new test for deciding at which establishment employees are to be taken to work. S.80(3) provides: 'If work is not done at an establishment, it is to be treated as done at the establishment with which it has the closest connection.' Despite this being an entirely new provision – nothing similar existed in the EqPA – it was not highlighted in any of the consultations on the Equality Bill, nor is it mentioned in the Explanatory Notes or the Code of Practice. Accordingly, it is not clear what perceived flaw in the pre-EqA regime this clarification is designed to address. As we have seen above, plenty of case law under the EqPA has considered whether employees at different establishments could be the subject of an equal pay comparison, but in no reported case was the fact of any employee's employment at a particular establishment in dispute. If this issue does arise, tribunals are likely to look to other legislation using similar wording in different contexts. For example, S.10 SDA (not replicated in the EqA) used to apply the same test to decide whether an employee was employed 'at an establishment in Great Britain', which was crucial to the issue of whether the claimant was within that Act's geographical scope. However, no case law examined the meaning of 'close connection' in any detail. We would suggest that, given the recent authority for interpreting 'establishment' broadly, the question of 'close connection' to an establishment will rarely pose problems for claimants. The issue is most likely to arise in the context of mobile workers, such as travelling salesmen and -women. It might be open to an employer defending an equal pay claim in this context to argue that different areas of the country amounted to separate establishments and that the claimant and the comparator were employed at different ones. But it would be open to a tribunal to find – following the direction in City of Edinburgh Council v Wilkinson 2010 IRLR 756, EAT (discussed above), that 'establishment' is not necessarily the same thing as geographical location – that there was just one establishment at which all were employed. Claimants might also deploy the 'single source' argument to convince the tribunal that, notwithstanding employment at different establishments, there is a single source responsible for the pay differential with the power to remedy it – see under '"Single source" responsible for pay' below for more details.

Associated employers

4.26

In order for either of the comparative scenarios in S.79 EqA to apply (see the previous section), the claimant and her chosen comparator must be employed by the same employer or by an associated employer. S.79(9) stipulates that two employers are associated 'if (a) one is a company of which the other (directly or indirectly) has control or (b) both are companies of which a third person (directly or indirectly) has control'. This is the same definition that applies in the context of proving continuity of employment under the Employment Rights Act 1996.

In Hasley v Fair Employment Agency 1989 IRLR 106, NICA, the Northern Ireland Court of Appeal decided that statutory bodies corporate were not 'companies' within the meaning of the Equal Pay Act (Northern Ireland) 1970 (which contains similar wording to S.79 EqA) – and hence were not 'associated employers'. Thus a female office administrator employed by the Fair Employment Agency was precluded from claiming equal pay with a male administrator employed by the Equal Opportunities Commission for Northern Ireland since both were statutory bodies rather than companies.

However, in Scullard v Knowles and anor 1996 ICR 399, EAT, the Appeal Tribunal observed that, whereas the definition of associated employers under what is now S.79(9) EqA excludes a comparison between the contractual terms of employees employed by employers that are not companies, Article 157 TFEU envisages a wider class of potential comparators. This was made clear by the

4.27

ECJ's decisions in Defrenne v Sabena 1976 ICR 547, ECJ, and Macarthys Ltd v Smith 1980 ICR 672, ECJ, where, as the EAT noted in the Scullard case, it was held that Article 157 covered 'cases in which men and women receive unequal pay for equal work which is carried out in the *same establishment or service*, whether private or public' (our stress). The Defrenne case drew no distinction between work carried out in the same establishment or service for limited companies and work carried out for other employers, whether incorporated or not. The EAT concluded that, in so far as the comparison that could be made under Article 157 was broader than the statutory definition of 'associated employer' allows, the latter was displaced by the wider definition in Article 157.

Since the Scullard case, there have been a number of significant ECJ decisions with regard to when 'cross-employer' comparisons might be permitted under Article 157. It is to these that we now turn.

4.28 'Single source' responsible for pay

We noted under 'Associated employers' above that in Defrenne v Sabena 1976 ICR 547, ECJ, and Macarthys Ltd v Smith 1980 ICR 672, ECJ, the European Court ruled that Article 157 TFEU envisages equal pay comparisons to be made with persons employed in the 'same service or establishment as the claimant'. Whereas the word 'establishment' appeared to focus on the place where work is carried out – mirroring the test under S.79 EqA that we have already discussed – the word 'service' seemed to relate more to the nature of the employment. It was thus arguable that 'service' covers an organisation of different employers who together provide a unified local or national service; and that, unlike the EqA, Article 157 envisaged cross-employment comparisons for equal pay purposes in such circumstances.

In Lawrence and ors v Regent Office Care Ltd and ors 2003 ICR 1092, ECJ, the extent to which such comparisons are allowed under EU law was clarified to some extent. According to the European Court, Article 157 allows a comparison to be made between employees of different employers, so long as it can be shown that any pay differential can be attributed to a 'single source'; that is, where there is a single body responsible for the inequality and that body has the power to restore equal treatment. The upshot is that an employee can rely directly on Article 157, or use that Article as an aid to the interpretation of the domestic equal pay provisions, to argue that her pay should be equal to that of men who are not, on the face of it, valid comparators under S.79 EqA.

4.29 As the post-Lawrence case law demonstrates, the question of when this 'single source' test will be satisfied is not a simple one to answer. We now turn to the relevant cases in detail before attempting to draw some conclusions.

The Lawrence case. We start with the ECJ's comments in Lawrence, a case **4.30**
involving school dinner ladies whose jobs with North Yorkshire County
Council had been contracted out. Prior to the contracting-out exercise, their
jobs had been rated as equivalent to those of male staff employed by the Council
in other service areas, such as refuse collecting and gardening. The dinner ladies
argued that, although they were no longer employed by the Council, they could
still claim equal pay with these men.

An employment tribunal dismissed the women's claims on the ground that, in
order for there to be discrimination in pay between men and women, the person
who discriminates has to be in control of both the women's and the comparators'
wages. That was not the case here as, following the contracting out of the
school meals and cleaning services, the claimants ceased to be employed by the
Council and became employed by the private contracting companies. The EAT
rejected the appeal, whereupon the employees appealed to the Court of Appeal.
That Court decided to stay proceedings and to refer the following question to
the ECJ: is Article 157 directly applicable in the circumstances of this case so
that it can be relied upon by the employees in national proceedings to enable
them to compare their pay with that of men in the employment of the North
Yorkshire County Council who were performing work of equal value?

In its ruling on that question, the ECJ confirmed that there is nothing in the **4.31**
wording of Article 157 to suggest that the applicability of that provision is
limited to situations in which men and women work for the same employer.
However, where the differences identified in the pay conditions of workers
performing equal work or work of equal value cannot be attributed to a 'single
source', there is no single body which is responsible for the inequality and
which can restore equal treatment. Such a situation does not come within the
scope of Article 157, and the work and the pay of such workers cannot be
compared on the basis of that provision. It followed, therefore, that the
claimants in Lawrence were unable to compare the pay terms and conditions
applicable to their employment with the private contractors with those of the
male comparators who continued to work for the Council.

Post-Lawrence case law. The Article 157 'single source' test set out in Lawrence **4.32**
can, theoretically at least, be useful to claimants whose equal pay claims would
otherwise fail under the EqA at the 'in the same employment' stage. However,
the case law since Lawrence has demonstrated that the 'single source' hurdle is
itself a formidable one for claimants to surmount. The following two cases help
illustrate this point:

• **Allonby v Accrington and Rossendale College and ors** 2004 ICR 1328,
ECJ: between 1990 and 1996 A, a lecturer, was employed part time by
a college, ARC. A's contract was terminated with effect from 29 August
1996 and she was offered re-engagement with ARC through ELS, a limited
company operating as an employment business. She registered with ELS on

107

a self-employed basis and her pay became a proportion of the fee agreed between ELS and ARC. Her income fell and she lost a series of benefits ranging from sick pay to access to a defined career structure. She brought an equal pay claim against ELS, arguing that, for equal pay purposes, her pay could be compared to that of J, a male teacher employed by ARC, who enjoyed the additional benefits of being a college employee. An employment tribunal rejected this argument, and A's appeal to the EAT was unsuccessful on this point. A appealed once more, and the Court of Appeal agreed with the tribunal that the EqPA did not allow A to compare herself with J because he was not 'employed by her employer or any associated employer at the same establishment' as required by S.1(6) EqPA. Whereas both individuals worked at the same establishment, they had different employers – in A's case ELS, and in J's case ARC. The Court decided, however, that it was necessary to refer the case to the ECJ for a ruling on whether the EqPA was in this respect incompatible with Article 157. The European Court concluded that a woman in A's position – whose contract of employment with the college for which she works is not renewed but who is immediately made available to provide the same services to her previous employer through an employment business – is not entitled to rely on Article 157 to bring an equal pay claim against the employment business, using as a basis for comparison the remuneration received by a man still employed by the college. It was clear on the facts that the male comparator chosen by A was paid by the college under conditions determined by the college, whereas the employment agency agreed with A the level of pay that she would receive for each assignment. The fact that the level of pay received by A was influenced by the amount the college paid the agency was not a sufficient basis for concluding that the college and the agency constituted a 'single source' to which the differences between the claimant's pay and those of her comparator could be attributed. Accordingly, A's equal pay claim failed

- **Dolphin and ors v Hartlepool Borough Council and ors and another case** EAT 0559/05: female support staff working in voluntary-aided schools, and employed by the governing bodies of those schools, attempted to claim pay equal to that of male workers employed at different establishments by the Council. An employment tribunal, however, rejected their claims, concluding that the claimants had not been able to establish that they were in the same service as their comparators by virtue of there being a single source responsible for the inequalities in pay. On appeal, the EAT upheld the tribunal's decision. Although on the evidence the governing bodies and the Council applied the same pay scales and remuneration to their employees, the voluntary-aided schools at which the claimants worked were run by their governing bodies as separate entities and operated autonomously in terms of engaging staff as an employer and being responsible for staff terms and conditions. Accordingly, the claimants were unable to establish that the local authority was the 'single source' responsible for setting the terms and conditions of employment of which complaint was made and thus able to restore equality.

Even where a claimant can demonstrate common employment with her **4.33** comparator (but cannot fulfil the 'same employment' test of S.79 EqA as she works at a different establishment to her comparator and does not enjoy broadly similar conditions), the Article 157 'single source' test will not necessarily be satisfied. In Department for Environment, Food and Rural Affairs v Robertson and ors 2005 ICR 750, CA, civil servants in one government department wished to compare their pay with civil servants in another. They could not rely upon the EqPA since they did not fulfil the restrictive 'same employment' test set out in S.1(6) of that Act (now recreated in S.79 EqA). They therefore attempted to rely on Article 157. The question for the Court of Appeal was whether there was a 'single source' responsible for Civil Service pay, meaning that the claimants' comparators were valid for Article 157 purposes. The Court held that there was no such source, meaning that the claims must fail. In its view, the fact that the civil servants shared common employment (in the sense that all civil servants are employed by the Crown) was not enough to satisfy the 'single source' test where their pay levels were set by different government departments. Furthermore, it was not enough that, despite having delegated pay-setting responsibility to individual departments, the Crown theoretically retained power to intervene and remedy pay inequalities. Given that responsibility for negotiating terms and conditions had been delegated by the Crown to individual government departments, there was no single source to which differences in pay could be attributed. Nor could it be accepted that the Crown continued to be the body responsible for the differences because it retained the power to regulate civil servants' pay even after delegation, or alternatively because it could revoke the delegation of pay bargaining at any time. Neither of these theoretical legal possibilities made the Crown the body responsible for the pay difference of which the claimants complained.

The Court of Appeal's decision in the DEFRA case influenced a differently constituted Court in Armstrong and ors v Newcastle upon Tyne Hospital Trust 2006 IRLR 124, CA. Prior to 1985, the Newcastle Health Authority (NHA) made bonus payments both to its 'domestic ancillary' workers, most of whom were female, and to its porters, most of whom were male. In that year, the domestic work was put out to tender, and an in-house tender was accepted. As a result of the tendering process, the domestic staff lost their right to bonuses, whereas bonus payments to porters continued. The domestic staff and the porters remained in the NHA's employ until 1991, when responsibility for the Authority's four hospitals was divided between two new hospital trusts, the Royal Victoria Infirmary (RVI) and the Freeman. In 1998, the RVI and the Freeman merged, becoming the Newcastle upon Tyne NHS Hospital Trust (the NHT). In 2001 a group of female domestic workers brought equal pay

109

claims against the NHT. They argued that their work was of equal value to that of male porters working at the RVI, who continued to receive the bonus payments to which the domestic workers were no longer entitled. A preliminary issue arose before the employment tribunal as to whether those claimants who were not employed at the RVI could, for equal pay purposes, compare their pay with that of male staff working at that hospital. The tribunal concluded that the RVI staff and the non-RVI staff were not 'in the same employment' as defined by S.1(6) EqPA (now S.79 EqA), since they worked at different establishments at which common terms and conditions were not observed. Notwithstanding the merger of the RVI and Freeman Trusts, said the tribunal, the bonus agreements adopted at various hospitals were subject to collective negotiation on a departmental basis. Nor, the tribunal continued, did the claims fall within Article 157. The bonus schemes at the different hospitals constituted 'essentially different employment regimes', and it could not be said that the difference in pay between the non-RVI domestic ancillary staff and the RVI porters was attributable to a 'single source' within the meaning of the ECJ's decision in Lawrence.

4.34 Having failed on appeal before the EAT, the claimants appealed further to the Court of Appeal, arguing that the NHT had decided to assume responsibility for harmonising rates of basic pay and some other terms for ancillary staff at its various hospitals. It had also stopped the bonus scheme altogether for new starters. Its intervention in this regard showed that it could have entered into negotiations to remove the difference in pay between the non-RVI domestic staff and the RVI porters if it had so wished. In these circumstances, the claimants argued, the NHT was, for the purposes of Article 157, a 'single source' responsible for the difference in pay between them and the RVI porters. The Court of Appeal rejected this argument, and dismissed the equal pay claims. It was established in the DEFRA case (above) that, in order to constitute a single source for the purposes of Article 157, the claimants had to show not only that they had the same employer as their comparators, but also that the employer was the body responsible for setting the terms of both groups of employees. Although the employer in the instant case had taken some part in the negotiations at departmental level, and there was some evidence of harmonisation of terms and conditions, the employment tribunal had been entitled to find that the employer had not assumed responsibility for the terms and conditions of all the employees for the purposes of the DEFRA test.

Thus far, the case law does not provide much comfort for prospective claimants. So are there any circumstances in which Article 157 might assist someone who cannot fall within the 'same employment' test of the EqA? Perhaps an example can be found in the following Court of Session case, which in fact preceded Lawrence by a matter of a few months:

- **South Ayrshire Council v Morton** 2002 ICR 956, Ct Sess (Inner House): around 600 primary school head teachers in Scotland claimed equal pay with secondary school head teachers. In a test case, an employment tribunal had to consider whether M, a female primary school head, could compare herself with a male teacher who worked for a different local authority. M conceded that the two education authorities in question were not 'associated employers' within the meaning of S.1(6) EqPA. However, she argued that S.1(6) was incompatible with Article 157 and that, owing to that Article, she should be allowed to rely upon a comparator employed by a different local authority. The tribunal noted that the salary scales of primary and secondary school teachers in Scotland at the relevant time were set by the Scottish Joint Negotiating Committee (SJNC), a quasi-autonomous body set up by the Education (Scotland) Act 1980 under the general control of the Secretary of State. Furthermore, although each education authority was autonomous as regards its own employees, this formal autonomy was to a large extent abridged by the SJNC, and there was in practice very little scope for an individual authority to vary a teacher's salary. The tribunal then turned to the ECJ's decision in Defrenne v Sabena (discussed above), noting that Article 157 allows a woman to nominate a comparator employed by a different employer if she and the comparator are employed 'in the same establishment or service'. Applying the facts of the case to this wording, the tribunal concluded that education authorities have a 'sufficient community of interest for the whole structure of education to be regarded as a "service"'. Accordingly, given the scope of Article 157, M was entitled to compare herself with a man employed by a different education authority. SAC appealed unsuccessfully to the EAT and the Court of Session. In the Court's view, it was logical and reasonable to suggest that in a uniform statutory regime governing pay and conditions in the public sector of education, comparisons may be made across the boundaries of the authorities that are obliged to give effect to it.

Although, as stated above, the South Ayrshire case was decided some months **4.35** before the ECJ's ruling in Lawrence from which the 'single source' test derives, in our view it provides a good illustration of the concept of a 'single source'. The situation where teachers employed by different local authorities have their salary rates set by the same national collective agreement seems to fall squarely within the ECJ's notion of pay conditions deriving from a single source in respect of which a single body – in this case, the joint negotiating body responsible for collective agreement – can take the necessary steps to eradicate any inequality of treatment.

According to the EAT in Beddoes and ors v Birmingham City Council and other cases EAT 0037–43/10 and others, it will be extremely rare (if ever) for Article 157's 'single source' test to be less generous than the 'same employment' test that applies under domestic law. However, the Appeal Tribunal considered

111

in that case that even if the highly unusual situation arose where only the 'same employment' test was satisfied, that would be sufficient for equal pay purposes under UK law. In doing so, it approved the EAT's earlier decision in North Cumbria Acute Hospitals NHS Trust v Potter and ors 2009 IRLR 176 EAT, which held that there is no requirement to establish a 'single source' on top of the requirements set out in S.1(6) EqPA. The claimants in the Beddoes case were employed by the Council at different schools in non-teaching roles – mainly as catering staff and cleaners. The Council argued that, when construing and applying the concept of 'same employment' for the purpose of S.1(2) EqPA, the single source test set out in Lawrence (above) applied. However, it further contended that in the instant case there was no single source because, although the claimants were formally employed by the local authority, the governing body of a school could by virtue of Reg 15 of the School Staffing (England) Regulations 2003 SI 2003/1963 (which have since been repealed) require the local authority to take on employees on terms that the authority did not consider appropriate. This meant that it was the governors of the individual schools, not the Council itself, who had the ultimate authority to set terms and conditions.

4.36 Rejecting the Council's contention, the EAT held that the theoretical discretion accorded by Reg 15 of the 2003 Regulations did not preclude the Council from being the single source of the claimants' and comparators' terms and conditions. In so holding, it ruled that the Court of Appeal's (obiter) reasoning on the effect of the 2003 Regulations in South Tyneside Metropolitan Borough Council v Anderson and ors 2007 ICR 1581, CA (see under 'Same employment at different establishments – same collective agreement' above), although not on the 'single source' issue, was directly applicable. If the idea of the governors binding the Council to 'an inappropriate grade' is 'legally and factually fanciful', it could not be relied on to support the contention that the governors, rather than the Council, were the true 'source' of the claimants' terms and conditions.

The EAT went on to say that, even if the Council's 'single source' argument had been upheld, its appeal would still have failed. The Council had conceded that the claimants and comparators were employed by it in the 'same establishment' as that phrase has traditionally been construed under UK case law – see under 'Same employment at same establishment' and 'Same employment at different establishments' above. In the EAT's view, it involved no departure from EU law if the concept of 'same employment' in S.1(2) EqPA is construed naturally, so that all employees of the same employer are available as comparators for equal pay purposes, provided they satisfy the establishment criterion. In the words of the EAT's President, Mr Justice Underhill: 'The most that can be said is that, in certain highly unusual cases, the 1970 Act may be more generous in the comparisons that it permits than EU law; but that is not objectionable in principle.' There is no reason to suppose that Underhill P's observation will not apply with equal force to the relevant provisions of the EqA.

Post-TUPE comparisons

4.37

Under Reg 4(1) of the Transfer of Undertakings (Protection of Employment) Regulations 2006 SI 2006/246 (TUPE), when a 'relevant transfer' takes place – essentially, when there is a sale of a business or a change of service provider – the transfer will not operate to terminate the employment contract of any person employed by the transferor in the transferring entity. Rather, any such contract will have effect after the transfer as if originally made between the employee and the transferee. Furthermore, under Reg 4(2), all the transferor's rights, powers, duties and liabilities under or in connection with any such contract will transfer to the transferee. For full details, see IDS Employment Law Handbook, 'Transfer of Undertakings' (2011), Chapters 3 and 4.

What, then, is the effect of TUPE on equal pay claims? In King and anor v Tees Valley Leisure Ltd ET Case No.2500814/05 K was employed by a council until her employment was transferred to TVL Ltd. She sought to claim that her right to equal pay with a comparator employed by the council was a right that transferred under what is now Reg 4(2) of TUPE. An employment tribunal dismissed K's claim. It pointed out that a comparator for equal pay purposes must be employed by the same or an associated employer. The right to equality with someone in the same employment does not equate to a right to be compared with someone who, because of a TUPE transfer, is no longer in the same employment at the time when the comparison is made.

That this is the accepted position in most TUPE cases was confirmed by Mr Justice Elias, President of the EAT, in Sodexo Ltd v Gutridge and ors 2009 ICR 70, EAT. We should point out that the claimants in that case, who had transferred under TUPE, did not, in fact, seek to argue that they were entitled to make post-transfer, cross-employer comparisons. It is interesting, nevertheless, to note Elias P's thoughts on this issue. He stated: '[I]t was conceded that [the claimants] could not, with respect to the period after the transfer, continue to receive the benefit of any improvements in the terms and conditions afforded to the [transferor's employees]. The equality clause could not continue to operate with respect to employees of the transferor once claimant and comparator were employed by a different employer. Comparison across employers is exceptionally possible [see under '"Single source" responsible for pay' above]. The claimants concede that this is not the case here.'

4.38

The Sodexo case, which progressed to the Court of Appeal as Sodexo Ltd v Gutridge 2009 ICR 1486, CA, was not, however, full of good news for transferees so far as pay claims go, as we shall explain. The case concerned G, who was one of a number of cleaners and domestic staff employed by North Tees and Hartlepool NHS Trust until 1 July 2001. On that date, these employees transferred to S Ltd under TUPE. Over five years later, in December 2006, G and several of her colleagues brought pay claims against S Ltd. Their argument was as follows:

- for a period of time up to the transfer on 1 July 2001, the Trust was in breach of its obligations under the EqPA, as it paid the female claimants less than male maintenance employees who were engaged on equal work

- given this, the sex equality clause had the effect, prior to the transfer, of substituting more favourable terms and conditions of employment into the claimants' contracts of employment, awarding them pay equal to that of their male comparators. The clause 'bit' as soon as unequal pay existed; there was no need for a legal ruling to be obtained against the transferor in order for it to take effect

- the effect of TUPE was that the claimants automatically transferred to S Ltd on 1 July 2001, together with the more favourable terms and conditions derived from the application of the sex equality clause

- by failing to honour those more favourable terms (albeit as a result of its ignorance as to their existence) the transferee committed an ongoing breach of contract.

4.39 At a pre-hearing review, S Ltd argued that the claims were misconceived. The employment tribunal, the EAT and the Court of Appeal, however, agreed with the essence of the claimants' logic – that rights under a sex equality clause survive a TUPE-transfer – and allowed their claims to proceed. The substantive issues – for example, whether there was, in fact, unequal pay during the course of the claimants' employment with the Trust; and, if so, whether a genuine material factor unrelated to sex could account for any such pay differential – had still to be determined by the tribunal. This placed S Ltd in the unenviable position of having to defend a potential pay inequality that it did not create, in order to disprove a potential breach of contract that it did not know that it might be committing.

The upshot is that transferees may, as a matter of law, be held liable in respect of pay discrimination for which a transferor was responsible, even where that discrimination does not come to light until a long time after the transfer. This is clearly an issue for lawyers to consider when drawing up warranties and indemnities in a TUPE context. There was some saving grace for transferees, however, since a majority of the Court of Appeal considered that the time limit for bringing such a claim is six months from the date of transfer rather than six months from the date of the ending of the claimant's employment with the transferee – see Chapter 9 under 'Time limits – effect of TUPE'. The Sodexo case is also considered in Chapter 2 under 'The sex equality clause'.

4.40 Overseas comparators
Unlike the EqPA, S.1(6) of which only permitted a comparison between a man and a woman if they were employed 'at the same establishment or at establishments in Great Britain which include that one and at which common

terms and conditions of employment are observed', the EqA does not place any territorial limitation on the right to claim equal pay or on the identity of a comparator. As we saw in Chapter 2 under 'Who is covered? – overseas claimants', it will be for the courts to determine whether the EqA applies, most likely by reference to the House of Lords' decision in Lawson v Serco Ltd and other cases 2006 ICR 250, HL.

In addition to some overseas comparators now potentially being permitted by the EqA, a claimant can also arguably rely on Article 157 in order to attempt such a comparison. In fact, in Villalba v Merrill Lynch and Co and ors ET Case Nos.2302467 and 2305203/03 an employment tribunal allowed a claimant to do exactly that. The tribunal noted that Article 157 contains no geographical constraints. Given this, and the fact that the employer was 'a worldwide organisation that considers its discretionary pay awards... on a worldwide basis', the tribunal deemed the territorial constraint then imposed by the wording of S.1(6) EqPA to be inappropriate in the circumstances. Thus, it allowed the claimant to seek (albeit, in the event, unsuccessfully) pay equal to that of male colleagues in the United States. Although the tribunal's finding on this point does not amount to binding precedent – and was not a matter on appeal when the case subsequently progressed to the EAT and Court of Appeal – it stands as encouragement to claimants wishing to compare their pay to that of overseas colleagues.

Hypothetical comparators 4.41

As we saw in Chapter 1, 'Law in context', the equal pay provisions in the Equality Act 2010, like those in the Equal Pay Act 1970 before them, do not admit the possibility of 'hypothetical' comparators. In Coloroll Pension Trustees Ltd v Russell and ors 1995 ICR 179, ECJ, the European Court suggested that the same is true of Article 157 of the Treaty on the Functioning of the European Union. The Court took the view that a woman cannot claim pay to which she could be entitled if she belonged to the other sex 'in the absence, now or in the past' of a male comparator.

Interestingly, the recast EU Equal Treatment Directive (No.2006/54) states that direct discrimination occurs 'where one person is treated less favourably on grounds of sex than another is, has been or *would be* treated in a comparable situation' (our emphasis) – Article 2(1)(a). Then, at Article 4, the recast Directive requires such direct discrimination to be eliminated with regard to 'to all aspects and conditions of remuneration'. Arguably, all this means that, in a roundabout way, the concept of a hypothetical comparator has found its way into the European equal pay regime. However, the argument that the Directive requires UK equal pay law to provide for a hypothetical comparison was put to, and rejected by, the EAT in Walton Centre for Neurology and Neuro Surgery NHS

115

Trust v Bewley 2008 ICR 1047, EAT, when considering the provisions under the EqPA. Mr Justice Elias, then President of the EAT, acknowledged that 'there are cogent arguments which can be advanced in favour of permitting hypothetical comparisons in equal pay cases. The justification for refusing hypothetical comparisons with respect to pay but permitting it for other forms of discriminatory conduct is not self-evident. Moreover, it may be said that even if no precise assessments can be made, if there is evidence pointing to discrimination, a rough and ready remedy is better than none at all.' Nevertheless, in Elias P's view, the argument that the Directive had transformed the scope of legitimate equal pay comparisons is difficult to sustain since, among other things, 'the Directive cannot expand the scope or effect of an article of the Treaty... It is well established that the Directive and Article [157] are to be read together and that the former does not alter the scope or content of the principle of equal pay; but merely assists in its application.' (Note that Elias P was considering the terms of the amended Equal Treatment Directive (No.76/207) and its cross-reference to the Equal Pay Directive (No.75/117), both of which were incorporated into the recast Equal Treatment Directive (No.2006/54) with effect from 15 August 2009. However, the same definition of direct discrimination that was found in Article 2(2) of the original Equal Treatment Directive appears in Article 2(1)(a) of the recast Directive.)

4.42 Given this, it was certainly the case under the EqPA that a woman who believed she was being paid poorly because of her gender but could not point to a flesh-and-blood male comparator had no legal remedy. And, on the face of the basic equal pay provisions of the EqA so far discussed, it might seem that that position remains unchanged. S.70 EqA provides the equal pay provisions with exclusive jurisdiction where contractual terms are concerned, and within that jurisdiction hypothetical comparators are not allowed (see Chapter 1 under 'UK gender equality legislation' for details). Following public consultation on the Equality Bill, the previous Government, in the Green Paper 'A Framework for Fairness: Proposals for a Single Equality Bill for Great Britain' (June 2007), stuck to the view that the equal pay regime in this country should, for a combination of practical and legal reasons, continue to require actual as opposed to hypothetical comparators. One of the Government's specific concerns was that allowing hypothetical comparators might lead to 'perverse results'. For example, a male gardener could potentially claim the same pay as a caretaker (also male) on the grounds that the work was of equal value, by citing a hypothetical female caretaker as an example. There was a risk that equal pay law could thereby be turned into a 'fair pay for equal work law', potentially bringing about a large number of claims which would have nothing to do with gender inequality, and possibly even producing results that tend to increase the gender pay gap.

Presumably, the previous Government's policy to continue with the status quo as regards the requirement for an actual comparator, and the lack of any desire to adopt changes on the part of the Coalition Government that came to power in May 2010, is indicative of a Government stance that the unavailability of a hypothetical comparator in equal pay claims is not incompatible with European law as it currently stands. However, one very significant change to the position under the EqA compared with that under the EqPA is that the new Act does contain a special provision – S.71(2) – allowing for the use of hypothetical comparators in a narrow type of gender pay discrimination claim. This is discussed in detail in the following section, but suffice to say here that this provision may well come to the aid of a claimant who is unable to bring an equal pay claim solely because of the inability to point to an actual comparator.

Section 71(2) EqA claims   4.43
As we saw in Chapter 1 under 'UK gender equality legislation – equal pay or sex discrimination?', Ss.70 and 71 EqA continue the demarcation that existed in the EqPA and SDA between sex discrimination in contractual terms (which falls under the equal pay provisions in Chapter 3 of Part 5) and sex discrimination in the way those terms are applied (which falls under the discrimination provisions in Chapter 1 of Part 5). However, S.71 bears further scrutiny, because it clearly entails a change in the law from the position that existed under the EqPA. This provision states that where a contractual term relates to pay, but a sex equality clause or rule has no effect, the prohibition of discrimination by an employer against his employee provided for in S.39(2) has no effect, except in so far as the treatment of the employee amounts to either direct discrimination under S.13 or dual discrimination under S.14 – S.71(2). (Note that S.14 EqA, which defines combined (or 'dual') discrimination, has yet to be brought into force, and the Government's 'Plan for Growth' that accompanied the 2011 Budget statement indicates that it will not come into force during the current Parliament. For the time being, therefore, S.71(2) only applies in respect of *direct* sex discrimination.)

So, what circumstances will be covered by S.71(2)? The Explanatory Notes emphasise that the provision can only apply where the sex equality clause provided for in S.66 does not operate. This is most likely to be the case where the claimant is unable to point to a flesh-and-blood comparator doing equal work, but has some other evidence that direct sex discrimination is influencing her pay. The Notes provide the following example: 'An employer tells a female employee "I would pay you more if you were a man" or tells a black female employee "I would pay you more if you were a white man". In the absence of any male comparator the woman cannot bring a claim for breach of an equality clause but she can bring a claim of direct sex discrimination or dual discrimination (combining sex and race) against the employer.'

Based on the actual wording of S.71, we take the view that its potential may go   4.44
far wider than the limited example given in the Explanatory Notes and Code.

117

Provided that direct sex discrimination can be established to explain a pay differential, it is possible to conceive of S.71 being used to found a remedy under the sex discrimination provision of S.39(2) EqA in respect of claims for which there was previously no remedy simply because they did not fit within the current equal pay framework. Four examples spring to mind:

4.45 **Size of pay differential.** The need for an actual comparator under the existing equal pay mechanism means that the claimant is restricted as to the amount that he or she can claim to be being underpaid. A claimant can point to the highest paid person of the opposite sex doing equal work and establish the right to be paid the same. He or she can not, however, point to a comparator doing work of greater value and argue that the actual pay differential is not justified by the difference in value between the jobs. Such a claim might, though, be brought under S.71(2). For example, if an equal value claim is defeated by a finding that the proposed comparator does work of greater value, but only slightly greater, the claimant might instead pursue a pay discrimination claim on the basis that that slightly greater value is being disproportionately rewarded. Similarly, a woman employed on a job rated at the top end of one pay grade might point to a man employed in a job at the bottom end of the next grade up, and argue that the difference in pay does not accurately reflect the small difference in duties. In either case, the claimant would need to convince the tribunal that there was a discriminatory reason behind the disproportionate weighting. In considering such claims, tribunals ought to bear in mind the Government's caveat that the legislation is concerned with equal pay, not fair pay.

4.46 **Better pay than comparator rated lower.** For the same reasons that an employee could not complain about disproportionate pay differentials under the EqPA, nor could an employee claim on the basis of a lack of a difference in pay. For example, imagine that A, a woman who is the only employee in a grade two role, is paid the same as B, a man employed on grade one. Under the contractual mechanism of the EqPA, there is no case to answer in the absence of a better-paid employee also on grade two. Under S.71(2), in contrast, it should be possible for A to argue that B's being paid the same for less work is prima facie evidence of direct sex discrimination, calling for an explanation from the employer.

4.47 **Comparison with a successor.** The level of pay of a successor in employment might constitute relevant evidence of direct discrimination. As we will see below under 'Predecessors and successors – successors', the EAT in Walton Centre for Neurology and Neuro Surgery NHS Trust v Bewley 2008 ICR 1047, EAT, rejected the argument that a woman could claim equal pay with an otherwise valid comparator in respect of a period during which she was employed but the comparator was not yet in the same employment. In so holding, the EAT rejected the notion that a woman may compare herself, under the EqPA, with a better-paid man who replaces her in her job. It considered that such a claim is precluded for the same reasons that preclude hypothetical comparators.

Now that the requirement of an actual comparator may be dispensed with in certain circumstances, it may well be possible for pay discrimination arguments based on successor comparators to be resurrected. So, a woman who leaves employment and discovers that her male replacement is paid £10,000 more for exactly the same work will have at least a prima facie case of sex discrimination, which S.71(2) will allow her to bring. Of course, there may well be good, non-discriminatory reasons for the increase in salary – it may be, for example, that the employer has recently discovered that the role was underpaid in accordance with the market rate, and so resolved to remedy the imbalance for the incoming employee, regardless of sex. However, these are potentially adequate explanations for apparent discrimination, which a fact-finding tribunal is well placed to consider in the context of a direct discrimination claim.

Right comparator, wrong workplace. As noted above under '"Same **4.48** employment" or "single source"', for an equal pay claim to get off the ground, the claimant and the comparator must be employed by the same employer, as broadly defined. Where the 'same employment' test is not satisfied, employees might instead claim pay discrimination under S.71 using their would-be comparators as relevant evidence. Thus, where a local council pays different rates at different locations that are autonomous enough to be considered separate establishments, an equal pay claim would not be permitted across the separate locations. However, a S.71 pay discrimination claim might succeed if employees doing one job at one location could establish a discriminatory reason why employees doing different but equally valuable jobs at a different location are paid more. For example, a tribunal might accept an argument that the employer views one type of work as 'women's work' and so pays a lower rate.

It should be borne in mind, when considering all four of the scenarios discussed above, that any application of S.71 allows (indeed requires) a claim relating to pay to proceed by way of a sex discrimination complaint rather than an equal pay claim. The possibilities discussed make sense only once the relative freedoms and advantages of a sex discrimination complaint are factored in. These include the availability of hypothetical comparisons, the application of the burden of proof rules – including the obligation to infer discrimination in the absence of a clear explanation for apparent discriminatory treatment – in cases of direct discrimination, and the fact that tribunals will not necessarily be hidebound by the rule against considering 'fair' or 'proportionate' pay (as opposed to 'equal' pay) when it comes to establishing whether the treatment meted out to the claimant is any way tainted by discrimination.

4.49 Predecessors and successors

The language of the EqPA suggested that the scope of comparison was limited to someone of the opposite sex employed contemporaneously with the claimant. However, European case law (considered in detail below under 'Predecessors') established that for the purposes of Article 157 TFEU, a claimant can compare herself with a male predecessor. The more problematic question of whether a claimant may claim equal pay with her successor was answered in the negative by the EAT, but has never been put to the European Court of Justice. In a departure from the approach taken under the EqPA and a recognition of the effect of case law, S.64(2) EqA provides that the work of a claimant and her comparator do not have to be done contemporaneously. However, it seems unlikely that this actually heralds any change in the substance of the law in this regard: paragraph 234 of the Explanatory Notes to the EqA state that S.64 is intended to clarify but does not 'widen the existing provisions on who a person can use as a comparator for the purpose of a claim for breach of an equality clause or rule'.

4.50 Predecessors

In Macarthys Ltd v Smith 1980 ICR 672, ECJ, the European Court ruled that the principle of equal pay for equal work in Article 157 TFEU is not confined to situations where men and women are contemporaneously doing equal work. Accordingly, the claimant in this case could compare herself to a predecessor in the job – a man she had been recruited to replace four months previously, and who had received a higher salary than her.

The female claimant in question was employed as a warehouse manager on £50 per week. The previous manager, a man, had been paid £60 per week. On her claim under the EqPA, both the employment tribunal and the EAT found that the claimant was entitled to compare herself to her predecessor, but the majority of the Court of Appeal decided that, on its true construction, that Act only covered situations where the woman and the man were employed contemporaneously. However, the Court referred the case to the ECJ for a decision on whether the woman's situation was covered by European legislation and, in particular, Article 157. The ECJ ruled that there is no requirement for contemporaneous employment under European law: the principle of equal pay under what is now Article 157 applies whether the woman is employed at the same time or subsequently to the man with whom she wishes to compare herself. In the light of the ECJ's conclusion, the Court of Appeal held that the claimant could claim equal pay with her predecessor.

4.51
As we have seen above, S.64(2) EqA now expressly provides that a comparator's work does not need to be contemporaneous with that of the claimant. However, the principle that a predecessor can be named as a comparator under domestic equal pay law was well established long before the EqA. A tribunal example:

- **Leacock v Association of MBAs** ET Case No.2204564/03: L began working for the Association as assistant database administrator. When U, the database administrator, left, L took over his job but received a lower salary. U had been appointed in 2000 on a salary of £18,000 per annum, yet in 2002 L was paid only £16,000 for performing the same role. In the summer of 2003 the Association sought advice on salaries from independent consultants and was advised that database administrators such as L earned between £18,000 and £22,000. At that point, L's salary was increased to £17,430. L brought an equal pay claim, naming U as her comparator, and the tribunal upheld her claim.

In theory, there is no limit to how far into the past a claimant may delve to find **4.52** a predecessor who was more highly paid. Although there is a six-year limitation on the amount of back pay that can be awarded, there is no such limitation on the period over which a comparison may be made. In Kells v Pilkington plc 2002 IRLR 693, EAT, the EAT held that the six-year limitation period on claiming damages with regard to equal pay (for which, see Chapter 9 in the section on 'Remedies' under 'Arrears of remuneration – no limit on period of comparison') does not prevent an employee from bringing a claim comparing her pay to that of a predecessor in employment who had been employed more than six years previously. In addition, the EAT made the interesting point that a woman can bring an equal pay claim even where she is paid more than her male predecessor was, as long as her predecessor had been on a higher pay scale or grade at the time he was employed to do a similar job. As the EAT observed, however, the evidential problems of showing that a comparator is relevant increase the further back one goes, and, in addition, the employer might find it easier in such circumstances to point to differentiating factors giving rise to a material factor defence (for which, see Chapter 8).

A final important point to make is that in Walton Centre for Neurology and Neuro Surgery NHS Trust v Bewley 2008 ICR 1047, EAT, the Appeal Tribunal took the view that, although a woman is entitled to bring an equal pay claim in respect of a more highly paid male predecessor, such a comparison is limited to the terms and conditions enjoyed by the predecessor at the termination of his employment. Attempting to ascertain the pay rises that the predecessor would have received if he had remained in the respondent's employ would be far too speculative an exercise. In the words of Mr Justice Elias, 'the comparison is limited to what he was in fact paid at the time of the termination of [the predecessor's] contract. In other words, no authority has suggested that the comparison with the predecessor could legitimately take account of likely pay increases which the predecessor would have secured had he remained employed.'

Successors

4.53

For some time, it was thought that a claimant could point to a successor comparator. In Diocese of Hallam Trustee v Connaughton 1996 ICR 860, EAT, the EAT held that a female employee was entitled to claim equal pay with a more highly paid male successor to her post. The EAT relied upon Article 157 TFEU and the interpretation given to it by the ECJ in Macarthys Ltd v Smith 1980 ICR 672, ECJ (considered above under 'Predecessors'), to overcome the fact that, on its face, the EqPA limited the scope of the comparison to men who are employed contemporaneously with a claimant. Where the comparator was the claimant's immediate successor, the EAT was satisfied that the scope of Article 157 was such to allow the claimant 'to advance a case to the effect that the male successor's contract was so proximate to her own as to render him an effective comparator, as effective as if "actual"'. However, the EAT warned that although there was nothing to prevent a claimant from comparing herself to a male successor, in practice the task of proving entitlement to equal pay inevitably becomes more difficult if the comparator is not in current employment with the claimant. The task for tribunals in such cases would be to determine, first, whether the claimant's and comparator's jobs comprise like work or work of equal value, and then whether there is a genuine material factor that causes the disparity in pay.

However, the possibility of an equal pay claimant pointing to a successor comparator was expressly rejected by the EAT in Walton Centre for Neurology and Neuro Surgery NHS Trust v Bewley 2008 ICR 1047, EAT. The claim in that case was brought by B, who had been employed by the Trust as a senior health care/nursing assistant. Her job was evaluated under a job evaluation study (JES) at band 3 with effect from 1 October 2004. On 23 June 2006 B presented an equal pay claim before the employment tribunal, seeking up to six years' back pay. B identified three male comparators: D, the Performance and Governance assistant, and H and T, who were both IT helpdesk officers. She submitted that, prior to 1 October 2004, her work had been of equal value to that of her male comparators and that, after that date, the comparators' work had been rated as equivalent to hers under the JES. Before the tribunal, an issue arose as to the extent to which the three men were valid comparators, as they had commenced employment with the Trust after B – D had begun work on 1 April 2004; H on 28 February 2005; and T on 28 July 2005.

4.54 The employment tribunal accepted that a legitimate comparison could be made with regard to the period during which the comparators were in contemporaneous employment with B. However, it was in dispute as to whether a comparison could be made for the purposes of the earlier period, when B was employed but the comparators were not. Given this, the tribunal was asked to determine whether 'successors' can be relied on as comparators for the purpose of an equal pay claim. As the EqPA only envisaged comparison with someone employed at the same time as the claimant (a state of affairs that has been carried through to the equal pay provisions in the EqA), the real issue for the tribunal was whether Article 157, as interpreted in the case law of the ECJ, permits a comparison with a successor. The employment judge, relying on the

Diocese of Hallam case discussed above, found that it does. B could therefore rely on the identified comparators for the purpose of her equal pay claim, including in respect of the period when the comparators had not yet commenced employment with the Trust. On appeal, however, Mr Justice Elias, then President of the EAT, concluded that the tribunal's decision could not stand because the reasoning in Diocese of Hallam was 'fundamentally defective'. The EAT in that case had mistakenly relied on a passage contained in the ECJ's judgment in Macarthys Ltd v Smith (above), which related to the argument that the European Commission had put to the ECJ (and was in fact rejected) and not to the ECJ's decision itself. As a result, the Diocese of Hallam case had been decided 'per incuriam' (i.e. by mistake) and was 'not an authority that can be relied upon in any way'.

Mr Justice Elias stated that European case law has established that comparisons for the purpose of equal pay claims are confined to parallels that may be drawn on the basis of concrete appraisals of the work actually performed by employees of different sexes within the same establishment or service. In his view, a comparison with a successor would not enable such a concrete appraisal. He remarked: 'In my judgment the exercise of comparing with a successor is too hypothetical. The comparison requires asking what would have happened in the past, as opposed to the question in Macarthys, which is what did happen in the past. The exercise reconstructs virtual rather than actual history; it asks how events would have progressed had things been otherwise.' Two problems in particular were illustrative of the speculative nature of this type of comparison. The first was the unsafe assumption that if the male successor was receiving higher pay, then he would have done so in the past (i.e. when the claimant was employed, but he was not). The second was the potentially flawed premise that the 'current' pay differential would have existed in the past at the same level.

In summary, then, the EAT held that Article 157 does not allow a female **4.55** employee to claim equal pay with a more highly paid male successor to a job. Such a comparison, which would involve making speculative assumptions about what the man would have earned had he been employed at the same time as the claimant, is akin to a hypothetical comparison, which is not permitted under European law (see above under 'Hypothetical comparators'). As a final thought, Elias P commented that in future a 'somewhat broader comparison' may be acceptable but, in his view, that was a matter for the ECJ to decide, and not the national court.

Note that an equal pay claim based on a comparison with a successor is not ruled out by the wording of the EqA, S.64(2) of which provides that the work of the comparator and the claimant does not have to be contemporaneous. However, the fact that the Bewley case (above) hinged on the scope of Article 157 rather than on the terms of the EqPA means that it remains binding on tribunals applying the EqA. That said, where a claimant is unable to claim equal pay with a successor via the medium of the sex equality clause, there may be the possibility that he or she could rely on the special provision of S.71(2) EqA to bring a sex discrimination claim instead – see under 'Hypothetical comparators – S.71(2) claims' above.

4.56 Comparator requirement set aside

We saw under 'Hypothetical comparators' above that, in Coloroll Pension Trustees Ltd v Russell and ors 1995 ICR 179, ECJ, the European Court took the view that a woman cannot, under Article 157 TFEU, claim pay to which she could be entitled if she belonged to the other sex 'in the absence, now or in the past' of a male comparator. However, there have been some decisions that have departed from this general rule. In recent years, courts have suggested that in certain narrow circumstances the requirement to point to a comparator – whether actual or hypothetical – will be set aside altogether for Article 157 purposes, as discussed below.

4.57 Indirectly discriminatory statutory provisions

In Allonby v Accrington and Rossendale College and ors 2004 ICR 1328, ECJ, the claimant was denied membership of the Teachers' Superannuation Scheme because statutory rules governing the scheme limited membership to individuals with contracts of employment. She argued that the relevant rules should be set aside under Article 157 TFEU as being indirectly discriminatory against women. On this, the ECJ ruled that if a worker seeks to challenge the discriminatory effect of a pension scheme rule derived from national law, there is no need for her to point to a male comparator. The rule can be set aside on the basis of a statistical analysis that demonstrates an adverse disparate impact on one sex compared to the other. In other words, a 'pure' indirect discrimination argument might be advanced under Article 157 where national legislation is the source of the inequality, without the need to show a comparator. The ECJ appeared – though its logic was not particularly clear here – to draw a distinction between cases where national legislation is at issue, and cases relating to occupational pension schemes whose rules are not contained in legislation. It cited its previous decision in Coloroll Pension Trustees Ltd v Russell and ors (above) as authority for the proposition that, in relation to a company occupational pension scheme rule, a worker cannot claim equal pay in the absence of an actual comparator.

4.58 Women claiming benefit of pay awards during maternity leave

A second situation in which the courts have disapplied the rule that an equal pay claimant must be able to point to an opposite sex comparator is where the claim relates to enforcement of a general pay increase that has not been extended to a woman on maternity leave. This exception derives from the Court of Appeal's decision in Alabaster v Barclays Bank plc (formerly Woolwich plc) and anor 2005 ICR 1246, CA. In that case the claimant issued employment tribunal proceedings against her employer in relation to the calculation of her Statutory Maternity Pay ('SMP'). She argued that the employer's failure to take into account a pay rise that came into effect before her maternity leave, but after the period used to calculate her SMP, amounted to a breach of the EqPA and Article 157 TFEU. Noting that the EqPA required a male comparator with whom a woman's pay can be compared (as does the EqA), the tribunal held that the claim must fail, owing to the fact that no such comparator is available in relation to a woman's pay entitlement during maternity leave. The tribunal observed that the correct route by which the claimant should have enforced her right was a claim of unlawful deduction from wages contrary to S.13 of the Employment Rights Act 1996 – a claim that she was out of time to pursue.

Following an unsuccessful appeal to the EAT, the Court of Appeal decided to refer the issue to the ECJ. The European Court ruled that, under Article 157, any pay rise awarded to a woman after the beginning of the SMP calculation period and before the end of her maternity leave must be taken into account for SMP purposes. The case then came back before the Court of Appeal, with the claimant asserting that, as a result of the ECJ's decision, she should be entitled to a remedy. The Court agreed. It held that in order to ensure that the claimant had an effective remedy in national law for rights during maternity leave that were guaranteed by EU law, it was appropriate to disapply those parts of S.1 EqPA that imposed the requirement for a male comparator. In that way, the claimant could succeed in her claim for pay discrimination in respect of her maternity pay entitlement. Although she could have enforced her right by bringing a claim under the unlawful deductions provisions of the ERA, that route did not satisfy EU principles of equality, equivalence and effectiveness. There were significant differences between the ERA and EqPA regimes which could not be objectively justified and which would have left a woman in the claimant's position significantly disadvantaged in comparison with anyone else with an equal pay complaint.

4.59 Note that, following the Alabaster case, new S.1(2)(d)–(f) were added to the EqPA, expressly providing that women on maternity leave need not point to a male comparator in order to bring equal pay claims in certain circumstances. These provisions have been recreated in Ss.72–76 EqA – see Chapter 2 under 'Maternity' for details.

Choosing a comparator
4.60

Subject to the requirements set out in the foregoing sections of this chapter (and to the requirement to show 'like work', 'work rated as equivalent' or 'work of equal value', discussed in Chapters 5, 6 and 7), a woman claiming equal pay is entitled to select the comparator of her choice. It is not for the employment tribunal or the employer to usurp the claimant's right and responsibility to make that choice.

In Ainsworth v Glass Tubes and Components Ltd 1977 ICR 347, EAT, a claimant wanted to claim equal pay with a man working alongside her on the ground that they were both employed on 'like work'. The man was an inspector whose job was to examine manufactured glass products for defects, after which he passed them on to the claimant, who re-examined them. The employment tribunal took the view that it had the right to choose the comparator, and decided to substitute a different man who was working as an inspector at a different time on a different grade. In overturning the tribunal's decision, the EAT made it clear that tribunals cannot substitute their own choice for the person nominated by the claimant. The EAT's decision was subsequently cited with approval by the Court of Appeal in Pickstone and ors v Freemans plc 1987 ICR 867, CA (whose own decision was upheld on appeal to the House of Lords (1988 ICR 697)).

4.61 Effect of a 'token' man paid the same as the claimant

What happens if a woman wishes to claim equal pay with a man on the basis that their work is of equal value but the employer is able to point to a man working alongside her who is employed on work equal to hers and is paid the same as her? Is the woman's freedom to choose the comparator circumscribed in this situation? The question arose directly for consideration in Pickstone and ors v Freemans plc 1988 ICR 697, HL. The House of Lords was adamant that the EqPA had to be interpreted in such a way as to ensure that a woman was not precluded from claiming equal pay with a comparator employed on work of 'equal value' to hers merely because she and another comparator were employed on 'like work'. No doubt, the same would now apply to the EqA.

4.62 Comparator does not have to be representative

In Thomas and ors v National Coal Board 1987 ICR 757, EAT, the Appeal Tribunal took the logic of the House of Lords in Pickstone and ors v Freemans plc (above) a step further, and held that, where the chosen comparator is a member of a group of employees who perform the same work, there is no need for the woman to show that he is fairly representative of that group. In the Thomas case, a group of women claimed equal pay with a single man who was an 'odd man out' in a protected position. The NCB argued that in such circumstances any comparator should be representative of a group rather than be a particular individual holding a unique position. The EAT rejected this argument. The legislation referred to 'a man', not a 'representative man'.

In McPherson v Rathgael Centre for Children and Young People and anor 1991 IRLR 206, NICA, the Northern Ireland Court of Appeal expressed some doubt as to whether an anomalous comparator could be used by a claimant. However, as the issue was not raised before the tribunal, the Court did not have to decide it. In practice, the Court's concern about whether a woman should be entitled to choose an atypical comparator can be dealt with under the 'material factor' defence available to the employer. If the chosen comparator's contractual terms are better than the claimant's because of some anomaly (e.g. because his pay has been 'red-circled' or because of an administrative mistake), then so long as the employer can show that the disparity between the claimant's and comparator's entitlements is due to that anomaly (rather than the sex of the persons concerned) he will succeed in justifying the difference. The material factor defence is considered in detail in Chapter 8.

Multiple comparators

4.63

In theory, there is nothing to stop a claimant choosing several comparators with whom to compare her work. The EqA certainly does not expressly forbid this any more than the EqPA did. In fact, particularly in claims based on equal value, it is a sensible course for claimants to advance a range of different comparators, since the very question of whether a particular job undertaken by a man is of equal value entails a deal of speculation on the part of the claimant at the time when the claim is lodged. This is because she will not at that time have the benefit of an analytical job evaluation study on which to base her assertion of parity and nor, of course, will she be relying upon simply identifying a man who is doing exactly the same work as herself. Since the issue of equal value will only be determined once the claim is under way, a claimant who names more than one comparator increases her prospects of success. Indeed, in many of the well-publicised equal value cases, different comparators were named. For example, in Hayward v Cammell Laird Shipbuilders Ltd 1988 ICR 464, HL, a canteen cook employed in the cafeteria of a shipbuilding company claimed equal pay with men working as painters, insulation engineers and joiners. Similarly, in Enderby v Frenchay Health Authority and anor 1994 ICR 112, ECJ, senior NHS speech therapists named male senior pharmacists and clinical psychologists as their comparators.

Note that, in the Hayward case, the House of Lords held that a woman is entitled to be treated no less favourably than a man in respect of each individual term of her contract, regardless of whether her contract as a whole could be said to be no less favourable than his. We discuss this and its consequences in Chapter 2 under 'The sex equality clause – term-by-term comparison'. This, of course, is another reason why a claimant might point to multiple comparators – because it might be possible for her to 'cherry pick', choosing the most advantageous appropriate male comparator in respect of each of her contractual elements.

127

4.64 However, just because claimants have the right to name more than one comparator does not mean that they can be incautious in exercising that right. In Leverton v Clwyd County Council 1989 ICR 33, HL, Lord Bridge alerted tribunals to possible abuse of the equal value procedure by claimants who cast their net too widely across a range of comparators. He gave the example of a woman who claims equal pay with two men, A (who earns £x) and B (who earns £2x). In his Lordship's view, the woman could hardly complain if the tribunal concluded that her claim of equality with A itself demonstrated that there were no reasonable grounds for her claim of equality with B. Similarly, although, as mentioned in the introduction to this section, it is not generally for the tribunal to usurp a claimant's right to choose her comparator(s), it might be reasonable in some circumstances for the tribunal – as part of its case management directions – to select the most relevant individual comparator from within the class of employees named by the claimant. For example, in Vaughan v Kraft Foods Ltd ET Case No.15688/78 a woman claimed equal pay with a class of about 20 male production supervisors. The tribunal hearing her claim decided that it would be excessively burdensome to examine the case against all the men in the class. It therefore selected three men who seemed most obviously relevant to the woman's claim.

Before moving on, we should highlight a procedural issue concerning multiple comparators that arose in Bainbridge and ors v Redcar and Cleveland Borough Council (No.2) 2007 IRLR 494, EAT. There, the majority of the EAT held that a claimant who has pursued an equal pay claim to judgment in respect of a particular period of time may later seek to run another equal pay claim in relation to the same pay period, but with a different comparator. The second claim would not be prevented from proceeding by the legal rule of 'res judicata', which requires that an action should only be tried once. In the EAT's view, an employer's obligation under the EqPA (now EqA) to pay A the same as B could be distinguished from its obligation under the Act to pay A the same as C.

4.65 **Claimant will be limited to comparator's pay**
In Evesham v North Hertfordshire Health Authority and anor and other cases 2000 ICR 612, CA, the question arose whether a claimant's equal pay entitlement is determined by the precise pay terms of her named comparator or by those of the highest paid employee employed on the same salary range as him. E, a female speech therapist, was employed on pay scale Code ST46, at a salary of £14,592. She brought an equal pay claim, citing M, a top grade clinical psychologist, as her male comparator. M, who had been employed for less than a year, was on pay scale SD61, and his annual salary in 1987 was £22,667. On his pay scale, M would receive in the succeeding years four annual increments of £719, £1,134, £1,045, and £1,059, so that by the end of the fifth year his salary would rise to £26,624. E established before the employment tribunal that her work was of equal value to that of M, and succeeded in her

equal pay claim. At a subsequent remedies hearing, the tribunal held that E's contract should be modified so that she would be paid on the clinical psychologists' pay scale at the same point on that scale as M had reached; she should receive the same salary as her comparator, and should progress up that scale at the same rate as him.

E appealed against the tribunal's decision on remedy, arguing that the fact that her work had been found to be of equal value to that of M meant that she was entitled to be paid on the pay scale for clinical psychologists of M's grade. But she should not enter that pay scale on the bottom rung, as M had done in 1987 because he was newly in post, but at the level commensurate with her five years' service; i.e. she should have the benefit of four annual increments, meaning that her salary in 1987 should have been £26,624. Rejecting E's contention, the EAT, and thereafter the Court of Appeal, upheld the tribunal's decision. The Court of Appeal noted that E had established that she was employed on work of equal value to that of one particular comparator – M – and not with all clinical psychologists employed on M's grade. Although the annual increment was related to length of service and not performance, E's greater length of service and experience clearly played a significant part in establishing that she was doing work of equal value to that of her comparator. Were she to enter the comparator's pay scale at a higher incremental level at the relevant date – the date of her claim – then she would receive pay at a level in excess of that received by her comparator with whom she had established equal value, and commensurate with the pay scale of somebody with whom she had not established equal value.

4.66 The lesson to be drawn from the Court of Appeal's decision is that, having identified a comparator, the claimant's flag was thereafter firmly fixed to its mast, in the sense that the issue of whether she was entitled to equal pay had to be determined solely by reference to the comparator she had chosen and to no other. So the claimant's success was limited because she chose such a junior comparator. In hindsight, she might have been well served to have also identified more senior comparators, or at least men who were more experienced in their jobs and were accordingly placed at a higher point on their pay scale. Of course, it would by no means have been guaranteed that the tribunal would have found E's work to be of equal value to that of such senior clinical psychologists and pharmacists.

Contingent claims

4.67 As discussed under '"Same employment" or "single source"' above, the case of South Ayrshire Council v Morton 2002 ICR 956, Ct Sess (Inner House), concerned female primary school head teachers who, owing to Article 157 TFEU, were able to compare themselves with male secondary school head teachers who worked for a different local authority. Some months later, a different aspect of this litigation also reached the Court of Session – South Ayrshire Council v Milligan 2003 IRLR 153, Ct Sess (Inner House). This concerned M, a male primary school teacher seeking to pursue an equal pay claim. Unlike his female colleagues, he was unable to identify a secondary school head teacher as a comparator, because none of the secondary school head teachers in the area were female. Accordingly, M decided to identify one of the female primary school claimants as a comparator, on the ground that, in the event that her equal pay claim was successful, her terms and conditions of employment would become more favourable than his.

The Court of Session, having considered the Court of Appeal's decision in Preston and ors v Wolverhampton Healthcare NHS Trust and ors and another case 1997 ICR 899, CA, in which similar claims were allowed, concluded that the employment tribunal had not erred in allowing the man's claim to proceed on this contingent basis: the tribunal had been entitled to order a stay of the proceedings in the man's claim pending the outcome of the female comparator's claim. To prevent the claimant from having the opportunity to bring a contingent claim in such circumstances would be to deny him true equality of pay, in breach of Article 157. This was because he would not be able to lodge a claim until after the comparator's claim had been decided, and would therefore suffer real prejudice in terms of back pay under the two-year limitation that was placed on arrears of pay by the EqPA at the time in question.

4.68 Note that the Equal Pay 1970 (Amendment) Regulations 2003 SI 2003/1656 extended the period for claiming arrears of equal pay to up to six years before the date the proceedings are instituted in England and Wales, and up to five years in Scotland, and these time limits have been retained under the EqA – see Chapter 9 under 'Time limits' for details. This does not mean that men will no longer wish to present the kind of contingent claim that was the subject of the Milligan case above – particularly given the length of time that equal pay litigation can take – but it might mean that the need to do so is not quite so pressing.

The circumstances in which a claimant may bring a contingent – sometimes called a 'piggyback' – equal pay claim were given further consideration by the EAT in Hartlepool Borough Council v Llewellyn and ors and three other cases 2009 ICR 1426, EAT. In confirming that such contingent claims are permissible, the EAT explained that a man is entitled to the benefit of a contractual term enjoyed by a female comparator, even if the female comparator herself has only acquired the benefit of that term as a result of the operation of the sex equality clause provided for in what is now S.66 EqA, as the legislation does not distinguish between terms deriving from agreement and terms inserted or modified by statute. Moreover, male claimants would be entitled to arrears of pay for the full period in respect of which their female comparators are awarded arrears. An award of arrears under the EqPA or EqA represents pay, albeit paid late and only as a result of the claimant bringing a tribunal claim. That being so, the EAT said it was hard to discern any principled reason why that pay should be excluded from consideration in deciding whether a male claimant has received equal pay with a female comparator.

The EAT did not accept that such 'piggyback' claims were necessarily premature **4.69** because the claim only arises as and when a tribunal makes an award in favour of the female comparators. On the contrary, the Appeal Tribunal saw 'obvious' conveniences in male contingent claims being included in the proceedings from the start, even though it may be appropriate as a matter of case management to put them, or aspects of them, on the back burner pending determination of the primary claims. Even if such claims are technically premature in the sense of whether a cause of action has arisen, employment tribunals are empowered under what is now S.127(3) EqA to entertain claims for declaratory relief where a dispute arises 'about the effect of an equality clause or rule', and that would give a sufficient jurisdictional foundation for making contingent claims pending the point at which they may mature into claims for substantive relief.

Use of questionnaire procedure
4.70
One of the most difficult issues for employees attempting to identify an appropriate comparator arises from the secrecy that operates in relation to many organisations' pay structures. Given this, the Employment Act 2002 inserted a new S.7B into the EqPA applying the 'questionnaire' procedure used by applicants in sex, race and disability discrimination claims to equal pay claims. The questionnaire procedure enables employees and workers who believe they may be receiving unequal pay related to their gender to seek to establish the key facts in order to, in the words of S.7B(2), 'decide whether to institute proceedings and… to formulate and present [their cases] in the most effective manner'. The questionnaire procedure continues to apply under the Equality Act 2010 by virtue of S.138 EqA, which makes it clear that it governs both discrimination and equal pay claims.

In accordance with S.138(2) the Minister has prescribed forms, contained in the Equality Act 2010 (Obtaining Information) Order 2010 SI 2010/2194 (the Order), by which a complainant can question the employer on any matter that is or may be relevant to an equal pay claim and by which the employer can, if he so wishes, reply to the questions. The standard questions on the prescribed form essentially ask the employer whether he agrees that the complainant has received less pay than her named comparator(s) (if there are any such comparators named); if unequal pay is being paid, to provide the reasons why; and whether he agrees that the complainant is employed on work equal to that of the comparator(s). The form also allows the complainant to ask additional relevant questions – for example, about who potential comparators might be, and about the workings of the employer's pay systems.

4.71 Where the questions are served before a complaint has been made to an employment tribunal, then the questions must be served before the day on which the complaint is lodged at the tribunal. If the questions are served after the complaint has been lodged, then it must be served within 21 days beginning on the day the complaint was made, unless the tribunal allows for them to be served within a further period of time after application by the employee – Article 4 of the Order. If the employer fails to respond to the questionnaire within eight weeks, or answers the questions in an evasive or equivocal fashion, a tribunal may draw an inference from this – S.138(4). We discuss the questionnaire procedure more fully – in particular, the difficulties an employer can face when the information requested might be considered confidential – in Chapter 9 under 'Statutory questionnaire procedure'.

4.72 Disclosure

As we saw under 'Use of questionnaire procedure' above, the statutory questionnaire process does not require an employer to release pay information to a prospective equal pay complainant. Once a claim has been made, however, an employment tribunal can order an employer to do so under the 'disclosure' provisions of rule 10 of Schedule 1 to the Employment Tribunals (Constitution and Rules of Procedure) Regulations 2004 SI 2004/1861.

Full details of how rule 10 works can be found in IDS Employment Law Handbook, 'Employment Tribunal Practice and Procedure' (2006), Chapter 6. For present purposes, the following points are worth noting:

- an order for disclosure may be made by an employment judge on his or her own initiative or upon application by a party to the tribunal – rule 10(d). Increasingly, tribunals make orders for appropriate disclosure as part of case management directions given at a case management discussion. If such orders are not given, or a party wishes to go beyond the scope of the disclosure ordered by the tribunal, then an application for disclosure will not usually be acceded to unless or until the party has unsuccessfully sought disclosure from the other side on a voluntary basis. Therefore, before applying to the tribunal for disclosure, a party should first send a letter to the other side requesting copies of the specified documents and any others upon which that party will rely at the hearing. Where appropriate, such a request can be incorporated into a letter requesting additional information in respect of the employer's ET3

- in National Probation Service (Teesside) v Devon EAT 0419/05 the EAT confirmed that the correct approach for an employment judge to take when dealing with the disclosure of a supposedly confidential document is to weigh up the conflicting interests of the parties and decide whether disclosure is necessary for a fair trial of the action

- matters of confidentiality alone will not prevent a disclosure order, although confidentiality is an issue which an employment judge can take on board when exercising his or her discretion as to whether disclosure should be ordered. If disclosure is necessary for the fair disposal of the proceedings, however, it must be ordered, notwithstanding confidentiality. Before deciding upon making an order in these circumstances, tribunals should inspect the relevant documents and consider whether justice can be done by special measures such as 'covering up' identifiably confidential features – Science Research Council v Nassé 1979 ICR 921, HL.

To what extent, then, can the disclosure process assist equal pay complainants **4.73** to identify and choose appropriate comparators? Usually, by the time that a claimant brings an equal pay complaint she will be expected to have already made her choices in this regard. Ideally, she will identify the comparators when raising a grievance with her employer (the raising of a grievance is currently a prerequisite for bringing an equal pay claim – see under 'Identifying comparators at the grievance stage' above); and will also identify them on her claim form. However, where the employer has failed to provide pay information either under the questionnaire procedure or during the grievance process, the claimant might decide to frame her claim in more general terms, and then seek an order for disclosure of the relevant information.

In Clwyd County Council v Leverton 1987 ICR 158, EAT, the Appeal Tribunal held that, so long as there is a prima facie case that the claimant's contractual terms are less favourable than those of comparable male employees, she can use the disclosure process to obtain disclosure of documents that will enable her to identify the appropriate comparators. The EAT cautioned tribunals not to grant disclosure merely to facilitate 'fishing expeditions' on the part of claimants. However, it held that the claimant 'has grounds for launching her [claim], and when requested to give the names of her comparators, it was entirely legitimate for her to say that she needed discovery in order to get the relevant names'.

Note that the disclosure process might be used by a claimant not only to identify **4.74** appropriate comparators, but also to obtain information that might show that an employer's pay system is tainted by indirect sex discrimination and thus falls to be objectively justified. We discuss the use of disclosure in this regard in Chapter 8 under 'Taint of sex discrimination'.

5 Like work

In Chapter 4 we consider a number of hurdles a claimant must jump in order **5.1** to point to an appropriate comparator under the equal pay provisions in the Equality Act 2010 (EqA) (or Article 157 of the Treaty on the Functioning of the European Union (TFEU)). In addition to these, the claimant must also establish that the work she does is equal to that of her chosen comparator. There are three ways she can do this. She can show that she and the comparator are employed on:

- like work (S.65(1)(a) EqA)

- work rated as equivalent (S.65(1)(b)), or

- work of equal value (S.65(1)(c)).

In this chapter we consider the issues involved in determining whether the work in question is 'like work'. The two alternatives are dealt with in Chapters 6 and 7 respectively.

Meaning of 'like work'   5.2

Section 65(2) EqA states that 'A's work is like B's work if (a) A's work and B's work are the same or broadly similar, and (b) such differences as there are between their work are not of practical importance in relation to the terms of their work'. S.65(3) goes on to state that, for the purposes of the comparison in S.65(2), 'it is necessary to have regard to (a) the frequency with which differences between their work occur in practice, and (b) the nature and extent of the differences'.

There are two significant parts to this definition, which we shall look at in more detail below:

- the claimant's (A's) work must be the same or, if not the same, 'broadly similar' to that of her comparator (B); and

- the difference (if any) between the work A does and the work B does must not be of 'practical importance' in relation to the terms and conditions of employment.

5.3 Employment tribunals must consider these two parts separately when deciding whether a woman is employed on 'like work' with a man – Waddington v Leicester Council for Voluntary Service 1977 ICR 266, EAT. This was also stressed in Baker and ors v Rochdale Health Authority EAT 295/91, where the EAT took the opportunity to restate the two stages involved in a 'like work' claim and remind tribunals that they must be considered in sequential order. The first question is whether the claimant and her comparator are employed on work that is the same or of a broadly similar nature. If so, the second question is whether there are any differences between the tasks that the claimant does and the tasks her comparator does, and, if there are such differences, whether they are of practical importance in relation to the terms and conditions of service. It is for the claimant to prove that she does the same work or work of a broadly similar nature, but the evidential burden of showing 'differences of practical importance' rests on the employer – Shields v E Coomes (Holdings) Ltd 1978 ICR 1159, CA.

Note that the statutory provisions do not permit a woman to claim that her work is, say, 75 per cent like her comparator's so that she is entitled to 75 per cent of his pay. If the claimant is not employed on 'like work', then it is irrelevant that her comparator is paid more than her, even if he is paid more than the difference in their work can reasonably justify – Maidment and Hardacre v Cooper and Co (Birmingham) Ltd 1978 IRLR 462, EAT.

5.4 Same or broadly similar work

So, the initial focus in a 'like work' claim is on the nature of the work being done by the claimant and the comparator, and whether this is the same or broadly similar – S.65(2)(a) EqA. This is a question of fact for the employment tribunal.

As the wording suggests, it is not necessary that the two jobs under comparison be identical; the work only needs to be 'broadly similar'. This allows for the comparison of jobs which, on the face of things, appear to be somewhat different. In Dance and ors v Dorothy Perkins Ltd 1978 ICR 760, EAT, Mr Justice Kilner Brown stated: 'We feel that it is vitally important to reiterate… that it is no part of [a] tribunal's duty to get involved in fiddling detail or pernickety examination of differences which set against the broad picture fade into insignificance.'

5.5 In deciding whether work is broadly similar, the EAT has warned tribunals against attaching too much significance to insubstantial differences. In Capper Pass Ltd v Lawton 1977 ICR 83, EAT, Mr Justice Phillips stated: '[T]he definition requires the… tribunal to bring to the solution of the question, whether work is of a broadly similar nature, a broad judgment. Because, in such cases, there will be such differences of one sort or another it would be possible in almost every case, by too pedantic an approach, to say that the work was not of a like nature despite the similarity of what was done and the similar kinds of skill and knowledge required to do it. That would be wrong. The intention... is clearly that the... tribunal should not be required to undertake too minute an examination, or be constrained to find that work is not like work merely because of insubstantial differences.' The correct approach therefore involves a general consideration of both the work done by the woman and her comparator and the knowledge and skill required to do it. In the Capper Pass case, the EAT upheld a tribunal's finding that a female cook, who was in sole charge of preparing a choice of three lunches daily for 10–20 directors and their guests, was employed on 'like work' with two assistant chefs who helped prepare 350 canteen meals daily in two sittings at breakfast, lunch and tea.

The comparison of jobs must take into account the whole job, however. The EAT has made it clear that any duties that the man and the woman do *not* have in common cannot generally be excluded from consideration – Maidment and Hardacre v Cooper and Co (Birmingham) Ltd 1978 IRLR 462, EAT (where the male comparator had storekeeping duties over and above those of the claimant, which meant the work was not broadly similar). Similarly, a woman cannot 'hive off' some parts of her work and claim equality in respect of the balance of similar duties that remain. The EAT in Maidment did accept, however, that there could be special circumstances where it would be right to exclude a part of a job from comparison, where it is 'in effect separate and distinct'. It gave the example of two cleaners (male and female), doing identical work during the week but where the man came in on Saturdays to cut the grass. Such special circumstances existed in Doncaster Education Authority v Gill EAT 568/89 where the EAT upheld a tribunal's decision that housemaster duties and vocational training carried out by a schoolteacher were separate and severable from the main part of his work, which could be considered 'like work' with that of the claimant once those duties were excluded from the comparison. The tribunal had, in line with the Maidment decision, addressed the question of whether the housemaster and vocational training work were separate and distinct, and had been entitled to reach the conclusion that they were. The EAT finished by noting: 'It is no doubt only an unusual case that will raise such question of severability successfully on the part of the employee, and it will no doubt also only be in a small minority of such exceptional cases that it would not be possible to sever both the activities and the remuneration.'

Despite the established guidance, identifying whether there is like work is not **5.6** always a straightforward task for a tribunal. An example:

- **Stacey and anor v Widney UK Ltd** ET Case Nos.1301823 and 1302961/08: the two claimants worked solely in a sales administrative function and compared their work with B and S. In relation to S, the tribunal found, albeit by a majority, that the claimants were not engaged on 'broadly similar' work. Although there was overlap in functions – i.e. all three of them handled sales orders from customers – the nature of S's job was primarily to arrange for the production of the ordered stock. This finding depended on the majority of the tribunal accepting the employer's submission that production planning accounted for a substantial part of S's job – perhaps, as the employer suggested, as much as 70 per cent. (The dissenting member preferred the claimants' contention that S was not actually undertaking any production planning work because he had been under-performing in his role.) The majority acknowledged that there was doubt over the extent to which S was actually involved in production planning, but stated that they had not heard sufficient evidence on the extent to which S was or was not performing his job.

5.7 Differences of practical importance

Once it is shown that, in general terms, the work is of a broadly similar nature, the tribunal must go on to consider the details of the claimant's and comparator's jobs and enquire whether any differences between them are of 'practical importance in relation to terms and conditions of employment'. Tribunals are guided to some extent by S.65(3). This provides that when comparing job differences, tribunals should consider:

• the frequency or otherwise with which any such differences occur in practice, and

• the nature and extent of the differences.

The Equality and Human Rights Commission's 'Code of Practice on Equal Pay' notes in this regard that differences such as additional duties, levels of responsibility, skills, the time at which the work is done, qualifications, training and physical effort could all be of practical importance – para 36.

5.8 The emphasis at this stage is not so much on the nature of the jobs done by the claimant and her comparator but on the differences (if any) in the tasks and duties that they respectively perform. In Adamson and Hatchett Ltd v Cartlidge EAT 126/77 the EAT held that tribunals must look closely at the detail to decide if there are any differences in the work actually done, how large those differences are and how often they operate. To help determine the existence or otherwise of such differences, the employer must provide the tribunal with a sufficiently detailed analysis of the jobs in question.

To assist in determining whether differences between the claimant's and the comparator's jobs are of 'practical importance', the EAT suggested in British Leyland Ltd v Powell 1978 IRLR 57, EAT, that tribunals might ask themselves whether the differences are such as would put the two employments into

138

different categories or grades under a job evaluation study (for which, see Chapter 6). In that case both the claimant and comparator were drivers for a catering company. The only difference between their respective duties was that the claimant, who worked for the catering section, was not permitted to drive outside the employer's premises as a result of a union demarcation agreement, whereas the comparator, who was employed by the transport section, was required to drive out on the public highway. The EAT upheld the tribunal's decision that this difference was not of such practical importance as would cause the claimant and comparator to be placed on different grades in an evaluation study. Accordingly, the claimant was held to be employed on 'like work' with her comparator and so entitled to equal pay with him.

Further guidance along these lines was given by the EAT in Capper Pass Ltd v 5.9 Allan 1980 ICR 194, EAT, where it ruled that if there are differences between jobs that justify differences in grading, those differences will prevent the two jobs from being regarded as 'like work'. In that case the EAT held that a tribunal was wrong to hold that a female canteen assistant graded 1 and a male canteen attendant graded 3 were employed on 'like work', having accepted that the differential was justified because the man handled larger sums of money than the woman and accordingly had more responsibility. Such a finding, said the EAT, constituted a difference of practical importance between their work, which was accordingly not 'like work' for the purposes of the equal pay provisions.

In establishing what the differences are between the claimant's and comparator's jobs, it is important that the tribunal concentrates mainly on the work that is actually undertaken, rather than on how a job description or contract of employment describes the job and the duties entailed in it. This is well illustrated by the Court of Appeal's decision in Shields v E Coomes (Holdings) Ltd 1978 ICR 1159, CA. In that case the employer owned 90 betting shops. In each of 81 of these shops it employed two female counterhands. In the other nine, located in areas where customers might be troublesome, it employed one female counterhand and one male counterhand. The claimant was one of the women employed at one of these nine shops. She was paid 87 per cent of the man's salary. With regard to her claim for equal pay based on 'like work', the Court of Appeal decided that she and her comparator were engaged on broadly similar work, so the case turned on whether the differences between their respective duties were of practical importance. In the Court's view, the performance of the man's 'security function' did not constitute a difference of practical importance warranting a higher rate of pay. Both employees did the same job and both had to deal with unpleasant customers, each doing so in their own particular way. S.1(4) EqPA (now S.65(2) and (3) EqA) required a comparison to be made between the things that the man and the woman actually did in their jobs and the frequency with which they were done, rather than between the things they could be required to do under their contracts but which were not, in fact, done.

5.10   It is clear from the decision in the Shields case that what the contract of employment requires a person to do in terms of tasks and duties is irrelevant except to the extent that those tasks and duties are actually performed in practice. Similar reasoning was applied by the EAT in Electrolux Ltd v Hutchinson and ors 1977 ICR 252, EAT, when upholding a tribunal's decision that simply because men (but not women) were obliged under their contracts to accept transfers to different jobs, to work compulsory overtime and to work Sunday and night shifts, this did not mean that the differences between the men's and women's work was of practical importance. In the words of Mr Justice Phillips, 'where men and women are in fact doing apparently like work, inasmuch as their work is of the same or a broadly similar nature, it is not a relevant difference for the purpose of S.1(4) that the men as a term of their contracts of employment are, while the women are not, obliged to be available to do additional different duties. For such a difference to be relevant, in our judgment, it must be shown that as well as being obliged to do additional, different duties the men in fact do so to some significant extent.'

The amount of time that the comparator spends on different tasks alleged to be of practical importance may be highly relevant. For example, in Crook v Dexter Paints Ltd COET 2089/166 the claimant was employed alongside two men as a laboratory assistant. She claimed that she was entitled to equal pay as she was employed on 'like work' but her employer alleged that the two men were expected to do shop-floor work as and when required, while the claimant was not. The tribunal found that one man had greater responsibility and so was not employed on 'like work'. However, the other man – who appeared to spend 12 per cent of his working time on shop-floor duties – was on 'like work'. The tribunal was of the view that if he had spent half of his working time on the shop floor, then this would have made his job different, but 12 per cent could be disregarded in the comparison. Similarly, in Redland Roof Tiles Ltd v Harper 1977 ICR 349, EAT, a man and a woman were both employed as clerks and the only difference between their jobs was that, for two periods of five weeks in a three-year period, the man had deputised for a transport supervisor while the latter was on leave. The EAT held that a tribunal was entitled to conclude that the infrequency with which the task arose meant that it was not of practical importance.

5.11   Examples of differences of practical importance
The following are some examples of the sorts of differences that are often claimed to be of 'practical importance' such as to preclude men and women who do broadly similar work from being regarded as employed on 'like work'.

5.12   Differing or additional duties. As mentioned above, a mere contractual obligation on a comparator to do additional duties will be insufficient to constitute a difference of practical importance. The relevant consideration here is the frequency with which he performs those additional duties in practice –

Electrolux Ltd v Hutchinson and ors 1977 ICR 252, EAT. It is only if the comparator actually carries out additional duties that a tribunal should consider whether they constitute differences of practical importance between the two jobs.

One case in which differing and additional duties amounted to differences of practical importance was that of Morgan v Middlesbrough Borough Council 2005 EWCA Civ 1432, CA. There, AM, a primary school administrator, claimed equal pay with M, a secondary school administrator. A tribunal accepted that AM's and M's work was 'broadly similar' – the two employees carried out similar jobs, albeit AM's was at a primary school with relatively few pupils, while M worked at a secondary school with larger numbers. However, the tribunal went on to conclude that AM was not employed on 'like work' to M, as there were differences of practical importance between their roles. The crucial difference, as found by the tribunal, was that AM, as the sole administrator in a small primary school, had to carry out routine tasks – such as sitting on reception, typing and collecting dinner money – of the kind that involved her being on duty at the school throughout the day during term time; whereas M had a more strategic and managerial role in a much larger school, spending time on financial matters that were less term-time related and more apt to year-round work. On appeal, the EAT (by a majority) overturned the tribunal's decision, believing that the tribunal had placed too much emphasis on the different hours that AM and M worked, which should not (as we shall see below) determine whether the work itself is similar or different. The Court of Appeal, however, reinstated the tribunal's conclusion. Given the various differences that the tribunal had identified, it had been entitled to find that AM and M had not been employed on 'like work' for the purposes of S.1(4) EqPA (now S.65(2) and (3) EqA). AM's claim thus failed without the Council being called upon to explain the pay differential between her and her comparator.

Similarly, in Stacey and anor v Widney UK Ltd ET Case Nos.1301823 and **5.13** 1302961/08 the employer succeeded in showing that certain differences between the claimants' and the comparator's work meant that they were not employed on 'like work'. There, the claimants handled sales for windows and blinds and one of their comparators, B, dealt with sales for slides. While many aspects of their work were identical – and certainly of a broadly similar nature – the tribunal found that there were two differences of practical importance between the jobs that meant that the claimants and B were not doing 'like work'. First, B was required to provide technical solutions to problems which, if incorrect, could result in damage to property or persons and expose the employer to liability. Secondly, from time to time B offered bespoke quotations to customers, which were more demanding than the claimants' work. Given B's technical skills and additional responsibilities, the claimants' 'like work' claims failed.

5.14 **Time when work is carried out/flexibility.** The time when work is carried out will not, without more, be regarded as a difference of practical importance for the purposes of S.65(2) and (3) EqA. In Dugdale and ors v Kraft Foods Ltd 1977 ICR 48, EAT, women quality control inspectors who worked day shifts were found to be entitled to the same basic pay or day-shift premium as their male counterparts, who were also obliged to work nights and some Sundays (for which they were given special shift premiums). The EAT held that the time at which the work was carried out should be disregarded for the purposes of determining whether the claimants and their comparators were employed on 'like work'.

Similar reasoning was applied by the EAT in National Coal Board v Sherwin and anor 1978 ICR 700, EAT, where claimants working as canteen workers on the day shift claimed equal pay for doing 'like work' with a male comparator working exclusively on a night shift. The different times at which the claimants and their comparator worked did not, in the EAT's view, amount to a difference of practical importance and they were therefore to be regarded as employed on 'like work'. Curiously, however, in a case several years later involving the very same male comparator, the EAT upheld a tribunal's decision that the fact that the man worked by himself exclusively on nights constituted an additional responsibility such as to constitute a difference of practical importance for the purposes of what was then S.1(4) EqPA – Thomas and ors v National Coal Board 1987 ICR 757, EAT. In reaching that conclusion, the tribunal had been influenced by the evidence of the claimants that they were reluctant to work alone at night because of perceived risk. Explaining the difference in the outcome of these two decisions is not easy. The only possible explanation would seem to be that in the Sherwin case the EAT was merely concerned to hold that the time at which work is performed is not a relevant consideration when determining whether a difference in job duties is of practical importance. In Thomas, on the other hand, the EAT was responding to a particular argument not raised in the earlier case that the comparator's greater responsibility in working alone at night was something that was properly reflected in the terms and conditions of his employment.

5.15 Flexibility in a man's work but not in a woman's will not often, we suggest, amount to a difference of practical importance. Two cases (both decided under the EqPA):

- **Hatch v Wadham Stringer Commercials (Ashford) Ltd** ET Case No.40171/77: a female driver claimed parity of pay with male drivers who worked slightly longer hours, drove larger vehicles and did regular weekend overtime. The employer argued that the fact that the claimant's job was fixed in content, while the men were prepared to change routes, etc, meant that they were not engaged on 'like work'. The tribunal disagreed. Following Dugdale and ors v Kraft Foods Ltd (above), it held that the weekend work should be ignored. Furthermore, the lack of flexibility was the result of a management decision not to ask the claimant to do certain things. Her contract did not prevent her from being more flexible and she was quite prepared to undertake the same tasks as the men

- **Blackburn and Manley v Chief Constable of West Midlands Police** ET Case No.1305651/03 and others: the female claimants were police officers who worked part time because of their childcare responsibilities. They claimed that, owing to their unavailability for 24/7 working, they were being denied equal pay for equal work with full-time police constables who were in receipt of 'Special Priority Payments'. As a preliminary issue, a tribunal held that the claimants were employed on 'like work' with their comparators, meaning that their equal pay claims could proceed. The overarching practicality of police work was that, whatever the time of night or day, officers could never know what to expect or what levels of risk to personal safety might be encountered. On the evidence, the tribunal concluded that 'there is nothing of a substantive nature which we were told occurs with such frequency or severity that that principle is displaced by one which proclaims that the unexpected is significantly more likely to happen or risks increased after 10 pm such that a difference arises of practical importance to a night duty officer's pay and conditions'.

It is important to note that although differences with regard to flexibility or **5.16** time worked might not prevent a claimant being employed on 'like work' with her comparator, this does not mean that such issues are irrelevant for the purposes of an equal pay claim. Far from it. Once a claimant has established that she is employed on 'like work' to that of her higher-paid comparator, the employer then has an opportunity to defend the equal pay claim by establishing that the difference in pay can be explained by a material factor that is not the difference in sex (S.69 EqA)) – and, in some cases, flexibility can amount to such a factor. Indeed, when the Blackburn case discussed above reached the EAT (Chief Constable of West Midlands Police v Blackburn and anor 2008 ICR 505, EAT), the employer was successful in arguing that the difference in pay was due to a genuine material factor – the bonus scheme in question was designed to reward police officers who were available to work at night, and the claimants were not so available. Moreover, although this factor had a disparate adverse impact on women, it was objectively justified as an appropriate and necessary means of achieving the legitimate aim of rewarding unsocial-hours working. Hence the equal pay claims were dismissed, despite the fact that the claimants and their comparators were employed on 'like work' (upheld by the Court of Appeal: Blackburn and anor v Chief Constable of West Midlands Police 2009 IRLR 135, CA). For a full explanation as to how the 'material factor defence' works, see Chapter 8.

5.17 **Responsibilities.** If a man exercises greater responsibility than a woman, that may amount to a difference of practical importance. In Eaton Ltd v Nuttall 1977 ICR 272, EAT, the Appeal Tribunal overturned a tribunal's decision that a female scheduler was engaged on 'like work' with a male scheduler. The tribunal had not, in the EAT's view, fully taken into account the degree of responsibility involved in the two jobs in that a mistake by the claimant would in no way be as costly as a mistake by her male comparator.

In Waddington v Leicester Council for Voluntary Service 1977 ICR 266, EAT, the Appeal Tribunal held that an obligation to supervise, to take responsibility or to control was properly to be taken into account when considering whether the differences between the duties of a female community worker charged with setting up an adventure playground and those of a male playgroup leader were of practical importance. Greater responsibility was also a consideration that led a tribunal to conclude that a male canteen worker working alone at night was not employed on 'like work' with female canteen workers working during the day – Thomas and ors v National Coal Board (above).

5.18 On the other hand, the different responsibilities of W and her male comparator were not sufficient to defeat her 'like work' claim in Walker and anor v Coldwater Seafood (UK) Ltd ET Case Nos.1803252 and 1803265/02. There, the claimants, who worked in 'quality assurance of raw material', cited as a comparator a male employee who did the same work except that he had an additional contractual duty of rejecting or accepting incoming fish. He also stood in for the Raw Material Manager for some ten weeks of the year. The tribunal concluded that, despite these differences, W and her comparator were employed on 'like work' within the meaning of S.1(4). In practice, although the man had an additional written responsibility, he could telephone, e-mail or transmit photographs if he wanted advice on whether fish should be accepted or rejected. It was only on rare occasions that he would have to make a decision alone. Bearing in mind the advances in communications, even when the comparator was deputising for his manager it was unlikely that he would be out of touch with his immediate superior for long.

Similarly, in Payne v Brindley Twist Tafft and James, Solicitors ET Case No.1300092/08 the tribunal concluded that there were no practical differences between the role carried out by the claimant and by M, her comparator. M was held out to be Head of Department, but when he left the claimant effectively took over his role despite being relatively inexperienced. Although the claimant had not been involved in strategic planning to the same extent as M had been and had only supervised other employees on an informal basis, the tribunal still found that they had been employed on 'like work'. However, it went on to hold that since M had been employed on a higher salary because of his post-qualification experience and his salary was further increased because of his success in building up the department, there was a material factor justifying the difference in pay.

Greater geographical responsibility alone is unlikely to defeat a 'like work' **5.19** claim. In Iqbal v Birmingham City Council ET Case No.1303214/07 I was employed by the Council to give benefit advice to tenants living in the Erdington area of Birmingham. M, her comparator, also worked as a welfare adviser, although he dealt with referrals from occupational therapists and covered the whole city. The tribunal found that I and M were engaged on broadly similar work and that there were no substantial differences between their roles: the posts did not materially differ in terms of the demands made on I and M and the level of experience and knowledge that was required of them. In so finding, the tribunal specifically rejected the argument that M's responsibilities were greater because he covered a wider geographical area. In any event, I also worked city-wide when colleagues were on leave or off sick. Nor did it accept that I required more supervision than M. Both were expected to work independently, and the fact that I may have been subject to closer supervision because of her performance was irrelevant to the issue of whether the two were doing 'like work'.

Similarly, in Cope v 3G Food Service Ltd ET Case No.2411801/09 the tribunal found that a female regional manager was employed on like work with a male manager of a different region despite the fact that he was responsible for more depots and more staff. The employer contended that the claimant was not engaged on 'like work' with her comparator, T, because, among other things, he had responsibility for a wider geographical area and therefore had to travel more to visit the depots and staff. The tribunal rejected this argument, finding that the fact that T had to travel further to carry out his work and was therefore away more often did not amount to a difference in his work compared to the claimant, given that her job also involved some element of travel. Nor did the fact that T recruited by interviewing on his own and had conducted a redundancy consultation exercise alone, whereas the claimant had assistance in both instances, amount to a difference in what they did. Both were responsible for recruiting staff and conducting redundancy meetings. The tribunal noted that the only difference was that on one occasion, T stood in for the Managing Director and delivered his presentation at a national meeting, but this, in its view, was not sufficient to amount to a practical difference in their roles.

Skills. Skill levels were an important consideration in Brodie and anor v **5.20** Startrite Engineering Co Ltd 1976 IRLR 101, ET, where a tribunal held that a male and female drill operator working alongside one another were not employed on 'like work' because the man was able to select the appropriate jig and drill, set his own machine, sharpen the drills and carry out minor repairs in such a way as to enable him to carry out his job on his own without the assistance of the charge-hand.

145

A similar decision was reached in Falconer v Campbell Lee Computer Services Ltd EAT 0045/04, where the EAT upheld a tribunal's decision that there was a difference of practical importance between the computer work done by F and that done by her chosen comparator, as the comparator's work was frequently more complex and required a greater understanding of client applications. F's 'like-work' claim was therefore rejected.

5.21 **Qualifications and training.** European case law suggests that professional qualifications and training might, in certain circumstances, have an impact on the 'like work' test. The key case in this regard is Angestelltenbetriebsrat v Wiener Gebietskrankenkasse 2000 ICR 1134, ECJ. There, the two groups of workers were all employed as psychotherapists by the Vienna Area Health Fund. The first group – which included the claimants – comprised those who had trained first as graduate psychologists; and the second group – including the higher-paid male comparators – comprised those who had first completed their general practitioner training as doctors. The Staff Committee at the Health Fund applied to the national court for a declaration that the psychotherapists with a degree in psychology should be classified in the same salary category as doctors employed as psychotherapists. The national court decided to refer the case to the ECJ, asking whether it could be said that the two types of psychotherapist were employed on the 'same work' for the purposes of what is now Article 157 TFEU, in which the right to equal pay for equal work is enshrined at European level (see Chapter 1 under 'EU gender equality measures').

The ECJ stated that although the psychologists and doctors employed as psychotherapists performed seemingly identical activities, in treating their patients they drew upon knowledge and skills acquired in very different disciplines, with the expertise of psychologists being grounded in the study of psychology and that of doctors in the study of medicine. Furthermore, the national court had emphasised that, even though the doctors and psychologists both performed psychotherapy, the doctors were also qualified to perform other tasks in a field that was not open to the latter. The ECJ went on to conclude that where two groups of employees ostensibly do the same job, but are recruited to do that work on the basis of different training and qualifications and can be asked to do different tasks as a result of that training, they are not employed on the 'same work' for the purposes of the right to claim equal pay in accordance with Article 157.

5.22 The exact scope of this decision is difficult to judge. It would appear to suggest that employees who have a different training route may not be doing the 'same work' – and this would probably apply to comparable 'like work' cases under the EqA in the United Kingdom. However, there is always the possibility, both under EU law and UK law, that employees in this situation would be entitled to claim that their work is of *equal value* to that of their comparators (see Chapter 7)

– subject to the employer's establishing a defence that the difference in pay is objectively justified by factors other than the difference of sex (see Chapter 8).

Physical effort. Where a man does work that requires physical strength and which a woman is unable to do, the woman is not employed on 'like work' within the meaning of S.65(2) EqA. However, employers must not simply assume that all women are incapable of doing heavier work: they should assess each woman individually, taking into account her physique and their experience of what other women doing that job have been able to do – Noble and ors v David Gold and Son (Holdings) Ltd 1980 ICR 543, CA. **5.23**

The frequency with which greater strength is required may be relevant. In Bolton and ors v Fry's Diecastings Ltd ET Case Nos.21387–89/86 a tribunal, having considered the infrequency with which extra strength was required and the proportion of men actually required to exercise it, rejected an employer's argument that the differences in physical strength between the male and female employees constituted a difference of practical importance.

Claimant doing more work than comparator. The fact that a woman does more work than her male comparator cannot, perhaps unsurprisingly, be used to argue that she does not do 'like work' for the purposes of S.65(2) EqA. This was confirmed by the EAT in SITA (UK) Ltd v Hope EAT 0787/04. In that case, H was employed by S Ltd as deputy to D, its Group Purchasing Manager. When D moved to another role, H was promoted to take his place. However, her salary was not increased and she brought a 'like work' claim. Before the tribunal, the employer argued that H and D had not been employed on like work, since D, when in post, had a deputy, whereas H did not; and H, in fact, did more work than D had done. The tribunal rejected the employer's argument in this regard, and its decision was upheld by the EAT. The EAT stated that on any purposive construction of the provisions that were then found in the EqPA, 'the fact that a promoted woman undertakes more duties than her male predecessor cannot result in a conclusion that the two are not undertaking like work in order to justify her being paid less'. To hold otherwise would defeat the purpose of the principle of equal pay for men and women outlined in Article 157 TFEU, which is to outlaw discriminatory practices that primarily disadvantage women. **5.24**

Pleading 'like', 'equivalent' and 'equal value' work **5.25**

A woman seeking parity of pay with someone whose work is not the same as hers – i.e. their work is not 'like work' – must use one of the other routes for enforcing equal pay. In other words, she must claim on the basis of her work having been rated as equivalent to her comparator's under a job evaluation study in accordance with S.65(4) EqA or by using the special procedure to prove an equal value claim for the purposes of S.65(6).

In Cornes v Schreiber Furniture Ltd ET Case No.34648/95 an employment tribunal reached the rather surprising conclusion that a claimant was not entitled to claim equal pay on the alternative bases of 'like work' and 'equal value'. In the tribunal's view, such claims are mutually exclusive and should not be heard together, even when they are framed in the alternative. In so holding, the tribunal relied upon the language of S.1(2)(c) EqPA, which stated that the equality clause would operate 'where a woman is employed on work which, *not being work in relation to which paragraph (a) or (b) above applies*, is, in terms of the demands made on her... of equal value to that of a man in the same employment' (our stress). (The equivalent provision in S.65(6) EqA states that a claimant's work is to be regarded as of equal value to her comparators 'if it is (a) neither like B's work nor rated as equivalent to B's work, but (b) nevertheless equal to B's work in terms of the demands made on A by reference to factors such as effort, skill and decision-making'.)

5.26 With respect to the tribunal in the Cornes case, this conclusion cannot be right. While it is clear from the wording of S.1(2)(c) EqPA that it is not possible for a woman to succeed in both a 'like work' and an 'equal value' claim in respect of the same male comparator, there is no reason why a woman should not put her case for equal pay on the basis that if her work is shown not to be 'like work' then it is nonetheless of equal value. This is precisely what happened in Weston v Martin-Baker (Engineering) Ltd ET Case No.14314/84 where the claimant sought equal pay on the alternative bases. The tribunal in that case considered it best to hear her claim for 'like work' first. Having upheld that claim, it did not then have to embark on the lengthy process of considering her claim for equal pay for doing work of 'equal value'. However, it confirmed that had it reached a different conclusion on the 'like work' issue, it would have allowed the 'equal value' claim to be pursued. This approach was affirmed in Redcar and Cleveland Borough Council v Bainbridge and ors 2008 ICR 238, CA, where Lord Justice Kay made it clear that a tribunal is obliged to consider the 'like work' claim first.

We shall give the final word on this issue to Lord Justice Mummery. In a further appeal in the Redcar case – reported as Redcar and Cleveland Borough Council v Bainbridge and ors and another case; Middlesbrough Borough Council v Surtees and ors 2009 ICR 133, CA – he stated: 'There is nothing explicit or implicit in the legislation which requires a claimant to make an irrevocable choice as to one of the three different ways of putting an equal pay claim. The claimants have the right to put their claim in all three of the different ways formulated in the 1970 Act.' No doubt, the same will now apply under the EqA.

6 Work rated as equivalent

What is job evaluation?

Job evaluation – general legal requirements

Discrimination in the evaluation exercise

Alternative claims

The second way in which a woman can claim equal pay under the Equality Act **6.1** 2010 (EqA) is to show that she is paid less than a man in the same employment who is employed on work that has been 'rated as equivalent' (RAE) to hers under a job evaluation study (JES) – S.65(1)(b) EqA. As with the other two grounds on which equal pay can be claimed ('like work' and 'work of equal value' – see Chapters 5 and 7 respectively), the mechanism for doing this is the enforcement of a 'sex equality clause' implied into the contract of employment – see Chapter 2 in the section on 'The sex equality clause'. It is perhaps worth emphasising that if the woman pursues the RAE route she does not need to show that she is employed on 'like work'. However, there is nothing to prevent her from claiming in the alternative – see further Chapter 5 under 'Pleading "like", "equivalent" and "equal value" work'.

(Note that job evaluation can also be used by employers to ward off equal pay claims. This is because a JES can be relied on by an employer to block a woman's equal value claim if her job has been given a different rating to that of her male comparator under a valid JES – S.131(5) and (6) EqA. This is dealt with in detail in Chapter 7 under 'Stage 1 equal value hearing – conclusive job evaluation studies'.)

Since a JES is a necessary prerequisite for work to be RAE, it is first necessary **6.2** to explain briefly what job evaluation actually is. We will then examine the conditions that must be satisfied before a JES can be used to support (or indeed defend) an equal pay claim, before considering the scope for discrimination in the evaluation exercise and how this can be dealt with. Finally, we summarise the other options open to a claimant who is unable to rely on a JES to support her equal pay claim.

What is job evaluation?   6.3

Job evaluation is a way of systematically assessing the relative value of different jobs. In essence, jobs that have been given an equal value under a JES will be RAE for the purposes of the EqA. However, as noted by Lord Russell in O'Brien and ors v Sim-Chem Ltd 1980 ICR 573, HL, 'job evaluation studies with a

— **149**

view to pinpointing equivalents and differences are not confined to the [EqA]: they are in more general use in industry in an attempt to achieve a broadly sound pay structure'. The main purpose of a JES, therefore, is to establish a fair and rational basis for organising pay differentials across a range of jobs. Although traditionally they may have been used primarily to rationalise and reinforce previous job hierarchies and, as such, would consolidate any in-built discrimination, they are now generally used as a tool for moving towards equal pay for work of equal value and tend to be less discriminatory and more gender neutral. Indeed, a discriminatory JES would not be valid for EqA purposes – see under 'Discrimination in the evaluation exercise' below.

6.4   It should be noted that there is no legal obligation on employers to conduct a JES. However, their use has been encouraged by bodies such as Acas and the Equality and Human Rights Commission (EHRC) and they are seen as a way of protecting employers from future equal pay claims or at least making their pay systems more defensible should any equal pay claim be brought against them. Although there is no legal obligation to carry out job evaluation, once a JES has been completed it is binding, and a woman whose work has been RAE under it is entitled to rely upon the results of the JES to gain equal pay. Similarly, an employer can rely on it to defend a 'work of equal value claim' – see Chapter 7 under 'Stage 1 equal value hearing – conclusive job evaluation studies'.

Job evaluation tends to be carried out by larger employers who have the requisite time and resources and who are generally more susceptible to equal pay claims. Indeed, in recent years it has been used extensively in the NHS, higher education and local government sectors to underpin new pay structures designed to provide equal pay via so-called 'single status' agreements. The irony is that, far from protecting employers, this large-scale job evaluation has in fact contributed to a proliferation of equal pay claims in these sectors – see Chapter 1 under 'Growth in public sector claims' for more details.

6.5   **Different methods of job evaluation**
The five main methods of job evaluation used in practice are set out in an appendix to the EAT's judgment in Eaton Ltd v Nuttall 1977 ICR 272, EAT. They are:

- *Points assessment*. This is the most common form of JES. Each job, or a range of representative benchmark jobs, is analysed under a number of different factors or job characteristics such as knowledge, communication and physical skills. Often general factors are further subdivided and weighted, so that, for example, greater or lesser weight is given to particular skills or physical attributes such as strength. Different points are attached to the different factors according to a predetermined scale and each job is thereafter ranked or graded according to the total number of points awarded. The value of each job can then be compared

150

- *Factor comparison.* This technique is now rarely used. It is similar to a points assessment system, being based on an assessment of factors, but no points are allocated. Several benchmark jobs are selected on the basis that their rates of pay are considered to be 'fair'. These jobs are then broken down in terms of specific factors, with a proportion of the wage for the job attributed to each. Total wages are then calculated for all the remaining jobs by adding together the rate of pay for each factor. Points assessment is more common than this method because the use of points enables a larger number of jobs to be ranked at one time

- *Job ranking.* This is perhaps the most straightforward means of job evaluation. Unlike the methods described above, each job is considered as a whole (instead of being broken down into factors). They are ranked in relation to each other on a 'felt fair' basis, which means that, in essence, the rank order reflects the job evaluators' notion of what it ought to be. A ranking table on the basis of grades is then drawn up and each job ascribed to a particular grade. The appropriate level of pay for the job is determined accordingly. However, while this may be a relatively easy task to perform where there are only a small number of jobs involved, it becomes more difficult when a large number of jobs must be taken into consideration

- *Paired comparison.* This is similar to job ranking but involves an element of points scoring. Each job is paired in turn with every other job and awarded points (0, 1 or 2) on the basis of their relative importance, with 0 representing less importance, 1 representing equal importance and 2 representing greater importance. Points for each job are then added up and a ranking order produced according to each total. Again, this system is really only appropriate for evaluating a small number of jobs

- *Job classification.* A grading structure is devised first and jobs are slotted into it after a summary of each job has been prepared and comparisons made on a 'whole job' basis. Individual employees are then placed within the appropriate grade. This approach can help employees understand why their job fits into a particular grade and can be useful for establishing a new company structure. However, it tends to be a fairly inflexible method of job evaluation and is not appropriate for assessing complex jobs that cannot be fitted neatly into one grade.

Of the above methods of job evaluation, only the first two involve breaking the **6.6** jobs down into component factors. These are termed 'analytical' evaluations. Other evaluation methods (like the third to fifth method outlined above) simply compare jobs as a whole without breaking them down into component factors. These are regarded as 'non-analytical' methods. Non-analytical job evaluations tend to be relatively cheap and easy to operate and may therefore be particularly attractive to smaller companies wishing to update or implement new pay and grading systems.

Of course, an analytical job evaluation does eventually build up a rating for the whole job but it does so on the basis of the value ascribed to its component factors. The factors that are generally used in job evaluation projects can be divided into four broad categories: inputs (what jobholders are required to contribute); processes (how jobs are done); accountabilities (for whom the jobholder is responsible); and impact (the job's overall influence on the organisation). Typical factors include knowledge; qualifications; communication; physical skills and demands; business impact; leadership; team-working; decision-making; contacts and networking; customer focus; environment and working conditions; autonomy; interpersonal skills; accountability and responsibility; planning and organising; problem-solving and innovation; emotional demands; analysis; and judgment and initiative.

6.7 The EAT in Eaton v Nuttall (above) recognised the distinction between analytical and non-analytical studies but made no judgement as to which type of evaluation was preferable for the purposes of what was then the EqPA and now would be the EqA. However, this distinction has since become crucial because, as we discuss in the section on 'Job evaluation' under 'General requirements – analytical v non analytical evaluations' below, subsequent case law has confirmed that only 'analytical' job evaluation studies will satisfy the requirements of the EqA.

6.8 Job evaluation – general legal requirements

The EqA itself is fairly brief in its treatment of job evaluation studies and, perhaps surprisingly, does not specify the requirements a JES must satisfy in order to support (or defend) an equal pay claim. S.65(4) simply states that A's work is rated as equivalent to B's work if a job evaluation study:

- gives an equal value to A's job and B's job in terms of the demands made on a worker – S.65(4)(a), or

- would give an equal value to A's job and B's job in those terms were the evaluation not made on a sex-specific system – S.65(4)(b).

(A sex specific system for the purposes of S.65(4)(b) EqA is one which, for the purposes of one or more of the demands made on a worker, sets values for men different from those it sets for women – S.65(5). These provisions are analysed under 'Discrimination in the evaluation exercise' below.)

6.9 Some further explanation of what amounts to a JES is provided by S.80(5) EqA. This states: 'A job evaluation study is a study undertaken with a view to evaluating, in terms of the demands made on a person by reference to factors such as effort, skill and decision-making, the jobs to be done (a) by some or all of the workers in an undertaking or group of undertakings, or (b) in the case of the armed forces, by some or all of the members of the armed forces.'

Given the minimal guidance provided by Ss.65(4) and 80(5), it is perhaps unsurprising that the courts have adopted a somewhat purposive approach over the years and it is now well established that a JES must satisfy a number of requirements before it can be used in equal pay claims. The Equality and Human Rights Commission's Statutory Code of Practice on Equal Pay (the Code of Practice) reflects this case law when it states: 'To be valid, a job evaluation study must:

- encompass both the woman's job and her comparator's

- be thorough in its analysis and capable of impartial application

- take into account factors connected only with the requirements of the job rather than the person doing the job (so, for example, how well someone is doing the job is not relevant), and

- be analytical in assessing the component parts of particular jobs, rather than their overall content on a 'whole job' basis.' – para 41.

6.10 These requirements – which reflect the decided case law under the equivalent provisions of the EqPA – are considered below. Before doing this, however, we briefly consider who bears the burden of proving that a JES meets the requirements.

Burden of proof

6.11 In essence, the person who is seeking to rely on the JES in an equal pay claim has the burden of proving that it satisfies the requirements of the EqA – Bromley and ors v H and J Quick Ltd 1988 ICR 623, CA (see under '"Thorough in analysis" and "capable of impartial application"' below). So, where a claimant is attempting to use a JES to support her claim that she is employed on work RAE, the burden of proving that it meets the EqA requirements lies with her (see England v Bromley London Borough Council 1978 ICR 1, EAT).

On the other hand, if the employer wishes to use a JES to show that the work of the woman and her comparator have been given different values in order to block an equal value claim, it is for the employer to show that the JES satisfies the statutory requirements (see Chapter 7 under 'Stage 1 equal value hearing – conclusive job evaluation studies').

'Thorough in analysis' and 'capable of impartial application'

6.12 In Eaton Ltd v Nuttall 1977 ICR 272, EAT, Mr Justice Phillips held that the equal pay provisions can only apply in respect of what he termed a 'valid' JES, meaning one that is

- 'thorough in analysis', and

- 'capable of impartial application'.

He expanded on this by saying that 'it should be possible by applying the study to arrive at the position of a particular employee at a particular point in a particular salary grade without taking other matters into account except those unconnected with the nature of the work. It will be in order to take into account such matters as merit or seniority, etc, but any matters concerning the work (e.g. responsibility) one would expect to find taken care of in the evaluation study. One which does not satisfy that test, and requires the management to make a subjective judgment concerning the nature of the work before the employee can be fitted into the appropriate place in the appropriate salary grade, would seem to us not to be a valid study for the purpose of [what is now S.65(4) EqA].' Phillips J made the point that it would be wrong not to take responsibility into account but that this should be dealt with as a demand factor under the JES itself (it being connected to the nature of the work).

6.13 It would seem, therefore, that any factor relating to the work itself, such as responsibility, organisation and physical demands, must form part of the job evaluation. These factors will then be awarded points under the JES. However, any factors unconnected with the work and more personal to the individual employee – such as merit and seniority – can be taken into account at a later stage when the points awarded under the JES are actually converted into grades.

In the more recent case of Diageo plc v Thomson EATS 0064/03, Mr Justice Burton, then President of the EAT, expressly endorsed the 'very helpful' test set out by Phillips J in Eaton v Nuttall, observing that it had 'stood the test of time' and was 'to be welcomed'. Burton J stated that when applying the test it was necessary to analyse whether the particular JES had any defects and then, in relation to each defect, conclude whether, individually or collectively, it caused the study not to be thorough in analysis or incapable of impartial application or both. It would be wrong to simply ask whether the JES looked like a good study or whether it had defects in it. There could be a suggestion of defects in almost every study. However, only defects that caused the study not to be thorough in analysis or incapable of impartial application would render the JES invalid. Mathematical errors or faulty reasoning would of themselves go to show that the study is not thorough in its analysis.

6.14 The EAT in the Diageo case went on to hold that the employment tribunal had been correct to find that a JES carried out by one trained evaluator acting alone did not meet the first part of the Nuttall test owing to the fact that it was insufficiently rigorous. In Diageo, D Ltd decided to replace the well-established Hay Evaluation Scheme, which it had used for some 20 years, with its own JES. However, before the new scheme was in place it carried out a job evaluation exercise that was not subject to the Hay Scheme and which was conducted without a job evaluation panel and by only one trained evaluator. The EAT held that the tribunal was entitled to conclude that these defects, together with the absence of the audit reports or continuing monitoring provided by the Hay

154

system and the lack of rationale sheets which normally form part of that system, meant that the JES was not sufficiently thorough in its analysis and was, therefore, invalid, notwithstanding that no particular calculations or rationale could be shown to be in error. However, the EAT emphasised that it was not the case that every JES had to be the equivalent of a Hay study and it would clearly be unhelpful for the courts ever to refer to one particular kind of study as the only or best way of setting about job evaluation. The problem here was that D Ltd had run down the methodology of compliance with its own Hay Scheme before introducing any new scheme, and was doing its best, with the assistance of only one trained evaluator, to hold the fort.

The Nuttall test was also applied in Hartley and ors v Northumbria Healthcare NHS Foundation Trust and ors ET Case No.2507033/07, a significant case for public sector employees in which the validity of the JES underpinning 'Agenda for Change' (the modernised pay structure implemented across the NHS in October 2004) came under detailed scrutiny. The JES had used nine pay bands and 16 factors for job weighting, including knowledge, training and experience; organisational skills; and responsibilities for patient care. There were three ways of evaluating jobs. The preferred option was to match a particular job against a suitable national profile. For this purpose, some variation on a factor-by-factor analysis between the job to be matched and the national profile was permitted. If there was no suitable match, the job was evaluated at local level in accordance with detailed guidance. In the remaining cases, a mixture of the two approaches was used. Approximately 1.2 million jobs were evaluated under the JES. Following the roll-out of the new pay system, some women challenged the validity of the JES with the intention of claiming equal value with men who had been placed higher than them in the grading scale under the JES.

Applying Nuttall, the employment tribunal found that the employer had to **6.15** show that the following criteria had been satisfied:

- the study must provide for jobs to be evaluated by reference to specific demand factors. This was an absolute requirement

- in relation to any particular evaluation, there could not be a material departure from the provisions of the agreed study. Where there was found to be such a departure, which was a question of fact, this invalidated the study for the purposes of the particular evaluation, but not the study as a whole

- the study had to be designed so as to be capable of impartial application, which meant that persons implementing it must be able to do so without making subjective judgments

- the study also had to be designed so that evaluations carried out in accordance with it must be capable of being carried out thoroughly and rigorously.

6.16 With these principles in mind, the tribunal found that the JES was fully compliant with S.1(5) EqPA – now re-enacted in S.65(4) and (5) EqA. Even though jobs were matched against national profiles, it was an analytical JES because the matching was done on a factor-by-factor – as opposed to a whole job – basis. Furthermore, it had been acceptable to use composites of existing jobs, generic profiles for new jobs and a single job as being representative of a whole cluster of jobs for the purpose of carrying out the evaluation exercise. In addition, neither the changes subsequently made to the profiles and to the guidance for those carrying out evaluation exercises, nor the use of three different evaluation methods, invalidated the study: the JES's core elements – i.e. the 16 factor headings and the scoring system for each factor – did not change and the outcome would have been the same whatever evaluation method was used. Indeed, the tribunal stressed that, to be valid, a JES might well need to be able to evolve in order to meet changing circumstances.

The ruling in the Hartley case – although not binding – suggests that NHS employers can rely on Agenda for Change to defend work rated as equivalent claims brought for periods after 1 October 2004.

6.17 **'Objective'.** In Bromley and ors v H and J Quick Ltd 1988 ICR 623, CA, the Court of Appeal found that the approach of English law, as set out in Eaton v Nuttall (above), appeared to be in line with the European approach set out in Rummler v Dato-Druck GmbH 1987 ICR 774, ECJ, in which the ECJ held that it is necessary for a JES to be 'objective'.

In Rummler, a local Labour Court in Germany requested guidance from the ECJ on whether the EU Equal Pay Directive (No.75/117) (now replaced by the recast EU Equal Treatment Directive (No.2006/54)) permitted the use of physical effort as a criterion for job evaluation; and, if so, whether it was possible to take into account the extent to which women would find the work more physically demanding. In the ECJ's view, 'the principle of equal pay requires essentially that the nature of the work to be carried out be considered objectively... Where a job classification system is used in determining remuneration, that system must be based on criteria which do not differ according to whether the work is carried out by a man or by a woman and must not be organised, as a whole, in such a manner that it has the practical effect of discriminating generally against workers of one sex.' The ECJ went on to say, however, that a JES is not discriminatory simply because some of its criteria make reference to attributes more characteristic of men – e.g. muscular effort – provided they correspond to the requirements of the job. Indeed, if muscular effort does correspond to the requirements of the job, it cannot be ignored as a factor under the JES. Further, the value given to a male-oriented factor could not be weighted in favour of women to take account of the fact that it was harder for them to perform. However, in order for the JES as a whole to be non-discriminatory, it must also include criteria that recognise the

156

skills for which women have a particular aptitude – e.g. manual dexterity – provided they also correspond to the requirements of the job.

Although the Court of Appeal in Bromley v Quick endorsed the tests set out in **6.18** Eaton v Nuttall and Rummler it recognised that 'within measure there may be subjective elements in an objective process' and that every job evaluation will 'inevitably at some stage involve value judgments which are inherently to some extent subjective'. This echoes the oft-quoted comment made in Arnold v Beecham Group Ltd 1982 ICR 744, EAT (considered under 'When is a JES "complete"?' below) that job evaluation is 'not an exact science'. This is because there are no universally accepted external criteria available for measuring how much of a factor or quality is involved in a particular job or for measuring what relative weight ought to be attached to the factors or qualities involved. But the Court in Bromley held that where there are subjective elements, care has to be taken to ensure that discrimination is not inadvertently let in. The way in which this can best be done is discussed under 'Discrimination in the evaluation exercise' below.

Analytical versus non-analytical evaluations   6.19

In Bromley and ors v H and J Quick Ltd 1988 ICR 623, CA, the Court of Appeal interpreted S.1(5) EqPA (now recast in Ss.65(4) and 80(5) EqA) to mean that a JES had to be 'analytical', as opposed to 'non-analytical' (see above). This was perhaps not surprising in light of the decision in Eaton Ltd v Nuttall 1977 ICR 272, EAT (also discussed above) that job evaluation studies have to be 'thorough in analysis' and 'capable of impartial application'.

In the Bromley case, some of the employer's female employees claimed that they were being paid less than men who, they argued, were doing work of equal value. The employer engaged a management consultancy to carry out a JES. The study involved ranking 23 benchmark jobs in order of value by means of paired comparisons. These comparisons had been prepared on the basis of selected 'demand factors', such as skills, responsibility and physical and mental demands. Once the benchmark jobs had been ranked in order, the remaining jobs covered by the JES (including those of the complainants and their comparators) were slotted in. This was done on a 'whole job' basis, i.e. each job 'slotted in' was compared with each of the others in terms of their overall content and not by reference to the selected factors. 12 female employees brought claims for equal pay for work of equal value against the employer. Their jobs had been given a lower value than those of their male comparators under the JES. However, they argued that the JES did not bar their claim as it did not satisfy the requirements of S.1(5) EqPA. The case eventually reached the Court of Appeal, which held that, in order to be valid, a JES must have been undertaken on an 'analytical' basis with each job being evaluated in terms of the demands made on the worker under various headings, such as skill, effort

157

and decision-making. Evaluation on a 'whole job' basis, with jobs being assessed in terms of their overall content, is not sufficient.

It is clear that the Court of Appeal's decision was based in part on the widely perceived (and justifiable) view that 'whole job' comparisons are prone merely to replicate the status quo and to perpetuate any discriminatory assumptions built into the evaluation. They are therefore unlikely to meet the criteria of being 'objective' or 'capable of impartial application'. Under such non-analytical methods of job evaluation, no attempt is made to analyse why one order of ranking jobs is felt to be fairer than any other or why one job is felt to be more important than another. Such systems tend automatically to reinforce traditional views about the worth of men's jobs relative to women's. An analytical evaluation, on the other hand, is less dependent upon subjective assessments and the results are more transparent. However, in Dibro Ltd v Hore and ors 1990 ICR 370, EAT, the Appeal Tribunal made the point that even carrying out an analytical job evaluation was not an exact science, stating that 'there will always be a number of subjective issues and in the end it is always the decision of the tribunal and not the opinion of an expert which is relevant'.

6.20 **Benchmark jobs.** The Court in Bromley v Quick (above) was divided on whether all compared jobs need to be evaluated analytically or whether it is sufficient to analyse a range of benchmark jobs. Lord Justice Dillon seems to have inclined to the view that all jobs should be evaluated analytically, but Lord Justice Woolf thought that this would place an immense burden on many employers and that the selection of representative benchmark jobs was permissible provided the jobs were not materially different from the jobs they were chosen to represent. Current thinking would seem to support Woolf LJ's view. For example, the EAT in Paterson and ors v London Borough of Islington and ors EAT 0347/03 impliedly endorsed the use of benchmark jobs for the purposes of job evaluation. In that case, the JES comprised 37 national benchmark jobs against which all other jobs under the JES were evaluated. Although the EAT found against the employer because of the way the JES was carried out, it did not criticise the use of benchmark jobs.

6.21 **JES must cover claimant and comparator**
A JES need not cover all the employees employed in the undertaking to be valid under the EqA. In this regard, S.80(5) EqA states that a JES may evaluate the jobs of 'some or all of the workers in an undertaking or group of undertakings'. However, as the following case makes clear, a JES is only binding in respect of the employees in the undertaking, or group of undertakings, actually covered by the evaluation:

- **McAuley and ors v Eastern Health and Social Services Board** 1991 IRLR 467, NICA: the Board attempted to use a JES in respect of national health ancillary workers in Great Britain to block a claim for equal value by similar workers employed by the NHS in Northern Ireland. The Northern Ireland Court of Appeal held that the JES was not binding on the workers in Northern Ireland, even though there was a policy of maintaining parity of remuneration between health service workers in Great Britain and Northern Ireland. The JES had not been undertaken in respect of employees employed by Northern Irish health boards, nor was there any evidence that the management and trade unions which had agreed to undertake the study in Great Britain intended that it would evaluate jobs done by employees in Northern Ireland.

Therefore, if a woman wishes to rely upon a JES for the purposes of an equal pay claim, she must show that *both* she and her male comparator are actually covered by it. Moreover, the woman and her comparator must be evaluated under the *same* study. This is not always obvious. In Paterson and ors v London Borough of Islington and ors EAT 0347/03 the EAT held that the claimants' and comparator's jobs were not evaluated under a single study because the way in which the comparator's job was assessed involved a material departure from the JES – see further under 'Challenging the results of a JES' below.

Claimant's job must be rated equal or greater in value   6.22
Section 65(4) EqA, in keeping with the prior approach taken in S.1(5) EqPA, seems on its face to require nothing more (or less) than that equivalent values should have been ascribed to the man's and woman's jobs. However, as we shall see below, the courts have adopted a broader approach.

In Murphy and ors v Bord Telecom Eireann 1988 ICR 445, ECJ, the European Court held in the context of an 'equal value' claim that the EU principle of equal pay for equal work extends to claims for equal pay for work of higher value. In other words, a woman doing work of greater value than a man but being paid less than him can claim equal pay. The ECJ noted that 'to adopt a contrary interpretation would be tantamount to rendering the principle of equal pay ineffective and nugatory', as it would allow an employer to avoid paying equal pay by the simple expedient of giving more onerous duties to members of one sex and then paying them less. The EAT in SITA (UK) Ltd v Hope EAT 0787/04 took a similar line in the context of a 'like work' claim, holding that the fact that a woman does more work than her male comparator cannot be used to argue that she did not do 'like work' for the purposes of what is now S.65(2) EqA (see Chapter 5 in the section on 'Differences of practical importance' under 'Examples of differences of practical importance – claimant doing more work than comparator' for an analysis of this decision).

In Redcar and Cleveland Borough Council v Bainbridge and ors (No.1) 2008   6.23
ICR 238, CA, the Court of Appeal considered this issue in the context of RAE claims. The Court had to determine whether female claimants could compare

159

themselves with men who, following a JES, had been placed on a lower grade. The JES (which was embodied in the 'White Book', a collective agreement which applied to a wide range of local authority employees at the time) had placed jobs in six grades. Road sweepers – predominantly men – were on the lowest grade (grade 1). Female catering and care workers, who were on higher grades (grades 2, 3, 4 or 5), were paid less than those men. They argued that they should be allowed to compare themselves with the male road sweepers, even though the JES had rated their jobs more highly than – rather than equivalent to – the men's.

The Council, by contrast, argued that the ECJ's decision in Murphy related only to equal value claims and that the EAT's decision in SITA applied solely to 'like work' claims. Hence, no authority governed the situation where a woman's work was rated more highly than a man's by a JES for the purposes of a claim under what was S.1(2)(b) EqPA and is now S.65(1)(b) EqA. Next, the Council drew attention to the wording of the EqPA itself. S.1(5) stated that a woman is employed on 'work rated as equivalent' to that of a man 'if, but only if, her job and their job have been given an equal value' by the JES. It argued that this should be read literally, so as to exclude a S.1(2)(b) claim based on a JES that rated a woman's work more highly, since the two jobs had not been given an equal value. In so arguing, the Council contended that S.1(2)(b) should be regarded as a purely domestic law concept, rather than as a way of establishing work of equal value for the purposes of what is now Article 157 of the Treaty on the Functioning of the European Union (TFEU) and the EU Equal Pay Directive (now the recast EU Equal Treatment Directive (No.2006/54)). In other words, the ECJ's decision in Murphy regarding the Directive need have no effect in this case.

6.24 The Court of Appeal rejected all of the Council's arguments, holding that 'claims under S.1(2)(b) and S.1(2)(c) [EqPA] are two different and mutually exclusive ways of securing equal pay for work of equal value'. Thus, in the Court of Appeal's view, the case fell squarely within the principle established by the ECJ in Murphy. This left the question of whether the relevant provisions of the EqPA could be interpreted as being in accordance with EU law. The Court of Appeal noted that it is well established that a 'purposive' interpretation – that is, an interpretation of domestic provisions in line with the purpose of EU law – should be adopted in these circumstances, and that this can include reading words into a statute. The solution decided on by the Court of Appeal was that S.1(5) EqPA should be read as including the words italicised below: 'A woman is to be regarded as employed on work rated as equivalent with that of any man if, but only if, her job and their job have been given an equal value *or her job has been given a higher value.*' Furthermore, the Court continued, a later reference in S.1(5) to the situation where a woman's job would have been given an equal value but for discrimination in a JES could be similarly interpreted – see 'Discrimination in the evaluation exercise' below.

Somewhat surprisingly, the words that the Court of Appeal considered should be read into S.1(5) EqPA have not been included in S.65(4)(a) or (b) EqA, which simply refer to a study which 'gives an equal value' or 'would give an equal value'. However, the EHRC Code of Practice on Equal Pay reflects the Court's decision when it states 'A woman may also bring a claim of equal pay where her job is rated higher than that of a comparator under a job evaluation scheme but she is paid less. However, this will not entitle her, if an equality clause applies, to better terms than those her comparator has' – para 45. Nor is a woman whose job is given a slightly lower value, but whose pay is considerably less, entitled to claim a percentage of the difference in pay to reflect the true difference in the values of their jobs.

When is a JES 'complete'?

6.25

It has become well established that a JES must have been completed before it can be relied on. Unfortunately, there has been some confusion as to the point at which a JES can be regarded as 'complete'. The earliest possible point would be when the JES has calculated the overall scores for each job. The latest would be when those points are converted into grades or bands. There is also the issue of whether the results of a JES must have been accepted by both the employer and the employees before it can be said to be complete.

Acceptance of JES by employer and employee representatives. In practice, 6.26 the decision to commission a JES is almost always taken jointly by the employer and the employee representatives, since it is very difficult to conduct a proper evaluation without the cooperation of both sides. In Arnold v Beecham Group Ltd 1982 ICR 744, EAT, the Appeal Tribunal held that this need for cooperation meant that acceptance of the results of a JES by both the employer and employee representatives was a precondition of it being regarded as valid and complete. In that case the union and employer were negotiating a JES. They eventually agreed grade boundaries and the employer notified the employees of their interim grades and their right to appeal. When some of the staff raised objections to the scheme the union informed the company of this and sought to renegotiate. A number of meetings followed in which it transpired that neither side was particularly happy with the JES. As a result, the JES was not implemented and a wage settlement was reached instead. One of the employees who had been placed into a higher grade by the JES brought an RAE claim under S.1(2)(b) EqPA (now S.64(1)(b) EqA). The EAT held that a claimant's right to equal pay under S.1(2)(b) was dependent upon the existence of a complete JES for the purposes of S.1(5) EqPA (now Ss.65(4) and 80(5) EqA) and that a JES would not be complete 'unless and until those whose relationship is to be regulated by it have accepted it as a study'. This was because 'jobs vary greatly and it is difficult to find any formula which in all circumstances will properly evaluate the content of the job. However carefully a study is undertaken and conducted there is always a substantial risk that the results may offend common sense, and be unacceptable to those whose relationship it is designed to regulate.' In reaching this conclusion, the EAT overruled Greene v Broxtowe District Council 1977 ICR 241, EAT (considered under 'Challenging the results of a JES' below), in which another division of the EAT held that an employment tribunal was bound to act upon the results of a JES, even though the parties involved did not accept its conclusions.

The EAT in the Arnold v Beecham case (above) took a relatively broad view of what constitutes 'acceptance' in this context, holding that the union and employer had, in fact, accepted the validity of the JES because they had agreed grade boundaries and had sent notification to the employees telling them their interim grading and inviting appeals. Nevertheless, this decision would appear to mean that a JES will not be complete until its results have been accepted and that a claimant will be unable to claim equal pay under S.65(1)(b) EqA even though a JES may have put her on the same grade as a better-paid man if either party to the study (or a representative of either party, e.g. a trade union) refuses to accept the study. The problem with this approach is that it makes the question of the validity of a JES dependent upon whether the parties are happy with its results. An employer may decide not to endorse a JES if he wishes to maintain pay differentials between jobs that have been shown to be equal in value. Conversely, employees and their representatives may withhold their approval of the results on the basis that jobs they believed to be of equal value have been shown to be unequal. This attitude is unlikely to be acceptable to tribunals. It could perhaps be argued that Arnold v Beecham is aimed at the situation where both employers and employees disagree with the conclusions of the JES and that it does not deal with the situation where only one side rejects the study. However, we suggest that judgment about the validity of a JES should properly be left with the tribunal – not the parties – and that acceptance should not, therefore, be a relevant consideration at all. Nevertheless, until there is concrete authority on the point, the law remains uncertain.

6.27 **Implementation of JES.** If a JES is carried through to its conclusion, the final stage will be its implementation, whereby the mathematical scores awarded to each of the jobs are converted into salary grades or bands. However, not all job evaluation studies are actually implemented and the question therefore arises whether a JES that has not been implemented is nevertheless complete and binding for the purposes of the legislation. S.66(4) EqA is relevant in this regard. This stipulates that where a woman claims equal pay on the basis of her work being rated as equivalent to that of a male comparator, a reference in S.66(2) EqA (which provides for the modification or insertion of contractual terms by way of a sex equality clause) to a term 'includes a reference to such terms (if any) as have not been determined by the rating of the work (as well as those that have)'. This is a departure from the language of the equivalent provision in S.1(2)(b) EqPA, which simply stated that where a woman's work had been RAE by a JES the equality clause in her contract would operate in respect of 'any term... determined by the rating of the work'. The latter words have caused some difficulties for the courts when deciding whether or not implementation of a JES is necessary, as demonstrated by the following case:

- **O'Brien and ors v Sim-Chem Ltd** 1980 ICR 573, HL: a JES had been agreed between the employer and the employees and the employees were informed of their new job grades and the salary range for each. However, because of the Government pay policy at that time, the results of the JES were never implemented. Subsequently, three female employees whose jobs had been given an equal rating under the study with those done by men, but who had continued to be paid less than them, brought RAE claims under S.1(2)(b) EqPA (now re-enacted, with some modification of the statutory language, as S.65(1)(b) and (4) EqA). The Court of Appeal held that their claims could not succeed because the terms of the women's contracts and the men's contracts were not being 'determined by the rating of the work' as required by S.1(2)(b) EqPA: the results of the JES had not been implemented and therefore the pay of the workforce was not being determined by reference to the JES rating. The House of Lords, however, overruled that decision and held that, once a JES has been undertaken and has rated a woman's job as being of equal value with that of a man, a comparison of their respective terms and conditions can then be made for the purposes of S.(1)(2)(b) EqPA. It could not be right that the equality clause could not operate unless and until the study had been implemented because the clear intention of the equal pay legislation was that the equality clause should bite immediately discrimination was detected. The women therefore succeeded and the pay terms in their contracts were modified so as to be not less favourable than those of their male comparators. In reaching its decision, the House of Lords stated that job evaluation studies exist outside the confines of the EqPA, their general purpose being to achieve broadly sound pay structures rather than to determine contract terms for the purposes of the EqPA. Their Lordships admitted that they could see no obvious meaning for the words 'determined by the rating of the work' in the context of an equivalent value claim. At most they indicated that the very outcome of being given an equivalent job rating under a JES was to show the term to be less favourable. However, the House of Lords went so far as to say that the words themselves should be 'jettison[ed]... as making no contribution to the manifest intention of Parliament'.

The House of Lords' decision seems manifestly sensible, since otherwise a **6.28** woman would be unable to take advantage of a JES if the employer simply refused to implement it. Furthermore, the statutory language in S.65(4) EqA seems intended to address the criticism of the words 'determined by the rating of the work' in S.1(2)(b) EqPA, with paragraph 225 of the Explanatory Notes to the 2010 Act explaining that 'where a job evaluation study has rated the work of an employee and comparator as equivalent, the equality clause will give the employee the benefit of all of the comparator's terms, including those which have not been determined by the rating of the work'. This appears to mean that a woman can claim equality of contractual terms once a rating under a JES is decided upon, rather than having to wait until such time as the JES is implemented. Nevertheless, there remains uncertainty, since, if Arnold v Beecham Group Ltd 1982 ICR 744, EAT (discussed above) is correct, it would appear that if an employer refuses to accept a JES a woman cannot then rely on it. This distinction between implementation and acceptance appears somewhat perplexing. However, Arnold v Beecham is not without its critics and it did overrule an earlier EAT decision (Greene v Broxtowe District Council 1977 ICR 241, EAT) which held that acceptance of a JES was not necessary. There may be some benefit for claimants, in cases where a JES has been undertaken but not implemented or accepted by the employer, to plead that the work is equal on the basis of *both* S.65(1)(b) and (c) – i.e. by claiming that the work was rated as equivalent, but arguing in the alternative that it is of equal value and using the result of the unimplemented JES as evidence of such equal value.

6.29 Can a JES be retroactive?

In Redcar and Cleveland Borough Council v Bainbridge and ors and another case; Middlesbrough Borough Council v Surtees and ors 2009 ICR 133, CA, the Court of Appeal confirmed that a claimant may not rely on a comparator doing work RAE in respect of a period before that rating became effective. In that case some of the claimants lodged claims in respect of comparators with whom they were RAE under the Green Book (the 'single status' agreement), seeking back pay in respect of periods before the Green Book was implemented. The claimants argued that since successful 'like work' and 'equal value' claims could be backdated for up to six years prior to the date the claim was instituted, there was no logic in a successful RAE claim being denied corresponding retroactive effect and being treated as the 'odd one out' among the three forms of equal pay claims. They further argued that if RAE claims could not be backdated, claimants would probably have to claim the additional backdated relief by way of the more expensive and time-consuming 'equal value' route. To confer retroactive effect on RAE claims would reduce numerous separate equal value or like work complaints by separate employees as they could instead be joined together as multiple RAE claims.

However, the Court of Appeal confirmed that a JES does not have retroactive effect. It noted that the statutory language then contained in the EqPA and now found in S.65(1)(b) and (4) EqA looks to the present and to the future but not to the past. In addition, the fact that jobs have been given an equal value under a JES means they can then 'be regarded as... rated as equivalent'. It does not mean that they are to be regarded as actually having equal value for the purposes of S.65(1)(c) EqA (although it might be useful evidence of this).

In the Court's view, the argument for retroactive effect overlooked the fact that **6.30** job evaluation schemes have no force whatsoever before they are agreed and that bands and brackets can and do change from one JES to another. Furthermore, it would mean that RAE cases would actually be treated differently from like work and equal value cases. A successful claimant is entitled to backdate compensation by up to six years provided she has proved that she was employed in 'like work' or 'work of equal value' or 'work RAE' (whichever is applicable) during those six years. However, it would be illogical to treat jobs as RAE if there had been no previous rating at all or they had been rated under a different JES during that six-year period.

Claimants may nevertheless be able to rely on a JES as evidence that they were doing work of equal value to that of their comparator prior to the date of the JES. In Hovell v Ashford and St Peter's Hospital NHS Trust 2009 ICR 1545, CA, the Court of Appeal held that where jobs had been rated as equivalent in a JES, albeit with different scores, an employment tribunal could make a finding of equal value in respect of the period before the JES was implemented, on the assumption that there had been no change in the work done by the claimant and her comparator during the relevant period prior to the JES's implementation. However, the JES was not conclusive evidence of equal value before that date.

Interpreting the results of a JES   6.31
The interpretation of the results of job evaluation studies by employment tribunals plays an important part in claims under S.65(1)(b) EqA. The approach that a tribunal should take is influenced by the factor of whether or not the JES has actually been implemented.

Where JES has been implemented. Where a JES has been implemented, the **6.32** question arises as to how to interpret its results for the purposes of the EqA: should regard be had to actual points awarded under the JES before implementation or to the grades or bands (which cover a range of points) into which the jobs have been placed following implementation? The distinction becomes crucial where, for example, the claimant's job scores less than her comparator's under the JES but upon conversion of points the jobs are placed into the same grade. This happened in Springboard Sunderland Trust v Robson 1992 ICR 554, EAT, where the claimant's job had scored 410 points and her comparator's had scored 428. However, when the scores were converted, they fell into the same salary grade, which covered points between 410 and 449. The EAT upheld a majority tribunal decision that the claimant was employed on work RAE within the meaning of what was then S.1(5) EqPA (now Ss.65(4) and 80(5) EqA). In so holding, it confirmed that when determining whether jobs are RAE, it is necessary to have regard to the full results of the JES, including the allocation to grade or scale at the end of the evaluation process.

165

6.33 **Where JES has not been implemented.** If the JES does not involve the translation of job scores into salary grades (i.e. it has not been implemented), the scores themselves will be used to determine whether the jobs are RAE. In Home Office v Bailey and ors 2005 IRLR 757, EAT, two of the claimants covered by a JES were given slightly lower overall scores than their comparators. The difference was very small – one claimant received just 1.32 less than her comparator and the other received only two points less. The JES was not completed in that, although the jobs were scored, pay-banding did not follow and therefore salaries were not adjusted. The Home Office conceded that those claimants who had received scores equal to or higher than their male comparators were engaged on work RAE. However, the two claimants who had received slightly lower scores sought to argue that their work had also been RAE. The employment tribunal agreed, taking the view that based on the expert evidence it had received as to the lack of precise mathematical calculation in a job evaluation exercise, a degree of tolerance was necessary when interpreting JES results and, therefore, slightly lower scores did not necessarily indicate a lack of equality. The tribunal concluded that the difference in the scores in these cases was insignificant and that both jobs were RAE.

The EAT overturned this part of the tribunal's judgment, holding that S.1(5) EqPA was very precise in stating that work is RAE 'if, but only if' the claimant's and comparator's jobs have been given an equal value under a JES. (Note that S.65(4) EqA now drops the 'but only if' wording, but still requires that the JES give equal value to the job of the claimant and comparator.) In the present case the JES terminated at the point-scoring stage; it did not proceed to pay-banding. It was inappropriate to consider where pay bands might have fallen had the JES been completed. Given that this was a complete JES (as a result of the Home Office's concession) entitling the vast majority of claimants to claim that their work was RAE, it could not be right to alter that approach in the case of claimants who scored less than their chosen comparators under that study and introduce extraneous expert evidence to found the proposition that the study had given the respective jobs an equal value. The EAT seemed to attach some significance to the fact that the Home Office had conceded that claimants who had received scores equal to or higher than their male comparators were engaged on work RAE, intimating that this concession rendered the JES complete. However, we suggest that as it is the tribunal which is the final arbiter of whether or not a JES is valid, the Home Office's concession should not be seen as crucial to the EAT's decision.

6.34 Thus, it appears that if a JES concludes with points scored, that will be a complete study and job value will be assessed by reference to those points. However, if the JES proceeds to implementation, it is then necessary to have regard to the full results of the scheme, including the final allocation of grades. This could produce harsh results for claimants who are relying on an unimplemented JES. If a claimant receives only a few points less than her comparator under a JES, it could well be that they would have been allocated to the same grade had their points been converted. However, the EAT in Home Office v Bailey appears to rule out the possibility of considering where pay bands might have fallen had a job evaluation study been implemented.

Challenging the results of a JES   6.35

Where a woman's work has been given a lower rating than that of her comparator under a JES she may be able to challenge the results under the provisions of the study itself. A procedure is often provided whereby individuals who feel that their job has been given too low a value are able to contest that value. The usual practice is for a formal committee to hear the complaint and explain fully the basis of the assessment. If the employee is still not satisfied, then most organisations provide that the complaint may be taken up through the formal grievance procedure, perhaps with the assistance of a union representative. It is important that any appeal committee is trained both in job evaluation and in the avoidance of sex bias.

Tribunals are not permitted to go behind the results of a JES or substitute their own assessments of the respective value of the claimant's and comparator's jobs in the absence of discrimination or of a clear and fundamental mistake in the evaluation process – Greene v Broxtowe District Council 1977 ICR 241, EAT. If the employee exhausts any internal procedure but still feels aggrieved by the low value given to her job, she is left with two limited options. Either she can seek to show that the JES has been tainted by discrimination and that, but for that discrimination, her job would have been rated as equivalent in value to her comparator's job (see under 'Discrimination in the evaluation exercise' below), or she can seek to claim equal pay on one of the alternative bases for so doing, although in practice this second option is likely to be of limited use (see under 'Alternative claims' below).

Clear error or fundamental mistake. According to the EAT in Greene v 6.36
Broxtowe District Council (above), the results of a JES can be challenged where there is a fundamental error in the study or a plain error on the face of the record. The EAT in Arnold v Beecham Group Ltd 1982 ICR 744, EAT (discussed under 'When is a JES complete?' above) cast some doubt on this proposition but in Diageo plc v Thomson EATS 0064/03 the EAT stated that mathematical errors or faulty reasoning would of themselves go to show that a study is not thorough in its analysis (and is therefore invalid). And the following case confirmed that it is possible to challenge the results of a JES if the method of evaluation involves a material departure from the JES rules:

- **Paterson and ors v London Borough of Islington and ors** EAT 0347/03: the claimants sought to argue that their work had been RAE with that of a named male comparator under a JES known as the 'National Joint Council for Local Authorities Scheme'. Under that scheme there were 37 national benchmark jobs against which all other jobs under the JES had to be evaluated before being placed in the rank order. The claimants' jobs had been evaluated against four benchmark jobs. The comparator job, that of assistant caretaker, had been assessed against three benchmark jobs but also against a fourth job which was not one of the benchmark jobs. In fact, it was a jobbing assistant post, which had only been evaluated locally (unlike the benchmark jobs, which had been evaluated nationally). The employment tribunal held that the claimants were employed on work RAE with L. It noted that the scores of the jobbing assistant post were broadly in line with the other three comparator posts. It also found that the National Scheme was intended to be a 'living structure' to which jobs were added at local level from time to time. The EAT, by a majority, overturned the tribunal's finding, holding that for the purposes of S.1(5) EqPA, the evaluation of the claimants' jobs and that of the comparator assistant caretaker had to be carried out under a particular 'study' and that must mean the same study. Otherwise, different jobs might be evaluated by reference to different criteria. The National Scheme was not mandatory in the sense that local authorities were bound to adopt it. However, if it was adopted, it had to be applied uniformly and according to its terms. Otherwise, the job evaluations carried out under it could not be said to be carried out as a single 'study'. The evaluation of the assistant caretaker post was assessed by reference to a non-national job. This involved a clear departure from the Scheme. However, not every such departure would compel a conclusion that the relevant evaluation was not carried out under the study – only a material departure would. The question to be asked was, 'did the method the panel adopted for the evaluation of the assistant caretaker post involve a material departure from the Scheme such that it could not be said that the evaluation was carried out under that Scheme?' The EAT was divided over whether the departure in this case was material. The minority favoured the view that the use of the jobbing assistant post did not involve a material departure: it was only one of four comparisons used in the exercise, and was itself a job which had earlier been locally evaluated under the Scheme. The majority preferred the view that it did involve a material departure, which could not be dismissed as minimal or trivial. It involved the deliberate inclusion of an impermissible comparator post, which by its very inclusion must have been regarded as material for the purposes of the assessment. In the majority's view, therefore, it could not be said that the evaluation of the assistant caretaker post was carried out under the Scheme or under the same 'study' as that under which the evaluation of the claimants' posts were carried out.

6.37 The above case is unusual in that it was the employer who wished to challenge the results of a JES in order to prevent the three claimants from relying on it in an RAE claim. In most cases, it will be the employee who is challenging the results of a JES that gives her job a lower value than that of her comparator in order to prevent it blocking an equal value claim under S.65(1)(c) EqA (see Chapter 7 under 'Step 1 equal value hearing – conclusive job evaluation studies').

Where the results of a JES are successfully challenged on the ground that there has been a fundamental error in the evaluation process, it seems that the requirements of Ss.65(4) and 80(5) EqA will not have been met and that the study cannot therefore be relied upon to found an RAE claim under S.65(1)(b). In these circumstances, the woman would have to claim equal pay on one of the alternative bases for so doing (i.e. 'like work' or 'work of equal value') – see Chapters 5 and 7 respectively.

Discrimination in the evaluation exercise 6.38

To recap, a woman is entitled to equal pay where she is paid less than a man in the same employment who is employed on work RAE to hers. S.65(4) EqA states that a woman (A) will be regarded as being employed on work RAE with that of a man (B) 'if a job evaluation study… gives an equal value to A's job and B's job in terms of the demands made on a worker'.

The second limb of S.65(4) then goes on to provide that a woman will also be regarded as being employed on work RAE as a man in the same employment if a JES *'would give an equal value* to A's job and B's job in those terms were the evaluation not made on a sex-specific system' (our stress). A system is sex-specific if, for the purposes of one or more of the demands made on a worker, it sets values for men different from those it sets for women – S.65(5). This appears to mean that if the evaluation system has treated men and women differently under any of the headings (or criteria) by which jobs have been assessed, the woman is entitled to equal pay if she can show that, had equal treatment been respected, her job would have been RAE.

Section 65(4)(b) therefore enables a claimant to challenge the results of a JES 6.39 where there is overt or blatant discrimination in the values ascribed to the same factor depending upon whether the job is carried out by a man or a woman. It does not, however, appear to cover more subtle forms of discrimination. In particular, it does not appear to provide scope for a claimant to challenge a JES on the ground that it undervalues or fails to take account of the types of skills primarily associated with women.

However, as discussed under 'Job evaluation – general requirements' above, the courts have held that in order for a JES to be valid in the first place, it must be 'capable of impartial application' and 'objective'. This would arguably cover indirect discrimination and could, therefore, be said to bring indirect discrimination within the scope of S.65(4)(b) EqA by the back door. There is certainly a need for indirectly discriminatory features contained in job evaluation systems to be susceptible to challenge since, in practice, it is precisely

169

this kind of discrimination (rather than overt or direct discrimination) that is likely to taint such systems. The evidence suggests that job evaluation studies in the past have often undervalued qualities inherent in work traditionally undertaken by women (e.g. caring and manual dexterity), either by leaving such qualities entirely out of account or by giving greater weight to features that characterise work traditionally carried out by men. But, as we saw above, the ECJ has made it clear that in order for a JES as a whole to be objective and non-discriminatory, it must recognise the skills for which women have a particular aptitude (as well as the skills for which men have a particular aptitude) provided they correspond to the requirements of the job – see Rummler v Dato-Druck GmbH 1987 ICR 774, ECJ.

6.40 Guidance from the EHRC in its publication 'Equal Pay and the Equality Act 2010'; the EU Commission in its 'Code of practice on the implementation of equal pay for work of equal value for women and men' (COM (96) 336); and Acas in its advice booklet, 'Job evaluation: considerations and risks' (September 2010) all provide useful guidance on how discrimination in the context of job evaluation can be avoided. Some of the salient points include:

- fair job evaluation may require a change in traditional assumptions about the value attributable to work carried out predominantly by one sex or the other. The importance allocated to a job is often influenced by social stereotypes as well as individual prejudice

- different job titles may be given to the same or similar jobs according to the gender of the persons who predominantly carry them out (e.g. women in certain jobs tend to be called 'cooks', 'seamstresses', 'shop assistants', 'typing supervisors', 'secretaries' and 'operators'; whereas men doing similar jobs are called 'chefs', 'tailors', 'salesmen', 'office managers', 'administrators' and 'technicians'). Such descriptions may denote differing perceptions of status and worth and in that way have an effect on the value ascribed to the tasks and skill levels required to carry out such jobs

- job descriptions should be constant in format irrespective of the sex of the person carrying out the job in question

- factors that are more likely to be present in female jobs may not be identified by the JES and therefore not valued at all – e.g. caring skills and responsibilities, human relations skills, organisational skills and responsibilities, manual dexterity and coordination. Categorising jobs by reference to light or heavy work or weighting different factors without taking account of other elements in female work impacts adversely on women. Extreme weight should not be given to any factor that is exclusively found in jobs predominantly done by one sex or the other. However, the factors should reflect the real value of the job rather than be a balancing act and, therefore, only relevant factors should be included

170

- classifying work by reference to formal qualifications can have an adverse impact on women because often the kinds of practical qualifications and skills that many women gain are frequently not identified as qualities to be counted positively. For example, nurturing, cleaning and caring skills are often assumed to be an integral part of certain kinds of job and are taken for granted without such qualities receiving their recognition and reward

- where a JES uses benchmark jobs (i.e. those considered to be typical of a grade or group of jobs), they should represent the spread of work done in the organisation as a whole and include a representative sample of female jobs to ensure that the JES takes full account of qualities and elements found in jobs done predominantly by women

- if the JES is an 'off the peg' scheme (i.e. supplied by an external consultant) as opposed to a scheme developed 'in house', the employer should, in addition to checking the way in which the scheme is implemented, ensure that the external consultant has reviewed it in accordance with the above guidance

- job evaluation carried out by only one or two people (e.g. line manager, personnel officer) can result in biased outcomes. This risk is reduced through evaluation by a panel whose members should ideally be representative of the main areas of work and gender composition of the work groups being evaluated, and be trained in equality issues and the avoidance of sex bias

- it is good practice to maintain detailed evaluation records for a number of reasons. For example, it allows the reasons for evaluations to be explained to jobholders and provides information to appeal panel members on what information was taken into account in the initial evaluation

- any appeals against individual job evaluations must be kept separate from the company grievance procedure and should ideally be carried out by an appeals committee which is representative of the workforce and trained in equality issues and the avoidance of sex bias

- there should be regular maintenance and periodic reviews of job evaluation schemes to ensure that regrading or changes in the grading structure are consistent and non-discriminatory and to enable reassessments to be made in the light of the creation of new types of job and changes to the content of existing jobs.

Alternative claims
6.41

If an employee feels aggrieved by the low value given to her job under a non-discriminatory JES, she will be unable to bring an RAE claim under S.65(1)(b) EqA and her only option will be to claim equal pay on one of the alternative bases for so doing (i.e. 'like work' or 'work of equal value'). In practice, however, the 'like work' route is likely to be closed off given that, by virtue of the JES having shown her job to be of unequal value to her comparator's, it is likely that differences of practical importance will have been identified that will make proving that the claimant is employed on 'like work' almost impossible. And as for making an equal value claim, S.131(6) EqA precludes an employment tribunal from entertaining such a claim where the results of a prior non-discriminatory JES have determined that the claimant's and comparator's jobs are not of equal value (see under 'Equal value claims' below). The claimant's only option in such circumstances would be to find a different comparator whose job has not been subject to evaluation under the JES.

As noted in Chapter 5 under 'Pleading "like", "equivalent" and "equal value" work', although it is not possible for a woman to succeed in a 'like work', 'equal value' and RAE claim in respect of the same male comparator over the same time period, she has the right to plead her claim in the alternative. This means she can plead her case on the basis that if her work is shown not to be RAE, it is nonetheless of equal value or alternatively it is nonetheless 'like work'.

6.42 Equal value claims

The most effective way for an employer to block an equal value claim is to point to an existing JES that rates the work of the claimant and the named comparator as being of unequal value. S.131(5) and (6) EqA provide that, where a JES ascribes different values to the work of a claimant and her male comparator, an employment tribunal will be obliged to determine that the jobs are not of equal value. However, this is subject to the proviso that the tribunal must have no reasonable grounds for suspecting that the evaluation contained in the study was either based on a system which discriminates because of sex, or is 'otherwise unreliable' – S.131(6)(a) and (b) EqA. These provisions were formerly contained in S.2A(2A)(a) and (b) EqPA. S.131(7) EqA adds that a system discriminates because of sex for the purposes of S.131(6)(a) if a difference (or coincidence) between values that the system sets on different demands is not justifiable regardless of the sex of the person on whom the demands are made. In other words, equal regard must be had to factors favouring men (e.g. physical effort) and those favouring women (e.g. mental effort) and any difference between the values set by the system on the different demands would have to be objectively justified. S.131(7) essentially replicates old provision S.2A(3) EqPA.

Section 2A(3) came under scrutiny in Ivanoff v City West Housing Trust Ltd ET Case No.2404804/08. There the employer successfully relied on a JES to block an equal value claim. I's and her comparator's jobs were evaluated under a JES (I achieved 354 points and her comparator 397), and thereafter were subjected to a process of moderation (which resulted in I's score being increased to 397 and the comparator's to 469). I was unhappy with her score and another job evaluation interview was carried out. This time, I's raw score was 466, which was then moderated down to 417. I submitted that the JES should not be relied upon because it had been made on a system that discriminated on the ground of sex under S.2A(2A)(a), her main submission being that the process of moderation was indirectly discriminatory because it disproportionately favoured men over women. The employment tribunal did not agree, finding that there was no evidence that the moderation, and the scheme itself, were tainted by sex discrimination. In particular, the moderator, who was not an employee of the respondent, did not deliberately manipulate the scores at the moderation stage to increase the points gap between I and her comparator.

On the face of it, the scope for challenging a JES that is used to block an equal **6.43** value claim on the ground that it is discriminatory is wider than the scope for challenging a JES under S.65(4)(b) EqA on the ground that, but for the taint of direct discrimination, the claimant's work would have been rated as equivalent under a JES. This is because the equal value provisions are not limited to direct or overt discrimination (see Chapter 7 under 'Stage 1 equal value hearing – conclusive job evaluation studies') whereas S.65(4) (when read with S.65(5)) appears to simply prohibit direct discrimination – see under 'Discrimination in the evaluation exercise' above. However, as noted above, the courts have effectively incorporated indirect discrimination into S.65(4) by the back door by requiring that job evaluation studies be 'capable of impartial application' and 'objective'.

The claimant may also challenge a JES used by the employer to block an equal value claim on the ground that it is 'otherwise unreliable'. This is a slight simplification from the wording that existed under the EqPA – 'otherwise unsuitable to be relied upon'. In Hartley and ors v Northumbria Healthcare NHS Foundation Trust and ors, (see above) the tribunal noted that a challenge to a JES under S.2A(2A)(a) (now found at S.131(6)(a) EqA) is confined to any discrimination that may be obtained in the demand factors and weighting of the JES. In contrast, allegations of discrimination in relation to other factors – e.g. in the instant case, the guidance – is considered under S.2A(2A)(b) (currently in S.131(6)(b) EqA). It noted that such challenges, which focus on a particular evaluation as opposed to the evaluation system as a whole, should be confined to cases where there are reasonable grounds for suspecting direct discrimination or an act of omission motivated by bad faith or an improper motive. The tribunal proceeded to find that there were no reasons for not relying on the JES. There was no evidence that national profiles had been designed, or subsequently altered, so as to benefit employees in predominantly male job groups at the expense of predominantly female job groups. Nor did the Department of Health or the trade unions exert influence that achieved inappropriately higher banding for any predominantly male, or indeed female, job groups. Similarly the guidance had not been amended to attain discriminatory and unjustified objectives.

6.44 It is also arguable that 'otherwise unreliable' covers, for example, forms of discrimination other than sex discrimination such as race discrimination – see further Chapter 7 under 'Stage 1 equal value hearing – conclusive job evaluation studies'.

7 Work of equal value

Before 1984 the Equal Pay Act 1970 (EqPA) only provided for equal pay in two **7.1** situations – where the employees in question were employed on 'like work' or where they were employed on 'work rated as equivalent' under a job evaluation study (JES) (see Chapters 5 and 6 respectively). However, from 1 January 1984 the EqPA was amended by the Equal Pay (Amendment) Regulations 1983 SI 1983/1794 to additionally cover work of 'equal value', and these three methods of establishing equal work have been re-enacted in S.65 of the Equality Act 2010 (EqA). S.65(1)(c) and (6) EqA allows a woman to claim equal pay with a man in the same employment, even though their work is of a totally different nature and there is no JES relating to their work, provided that the claimant's and comparator's jobs can be shown to be of equal value.

Nature of an 'equal value' claim. The Equal Pay (Amendment) Regulations **7.2** 1983 were introduced after the European Court of Justice (ECJ) ruled in Commission of the European Communities v United Kingdom of Great Britain and Northern Ireland 1982 ICR 578, ECJ, that the United Kingdom had failed to fulfil its obligations under European law to ensure that women received equal pay for work of equal value. Article 157 of the Treaty on the Functioning of the European Union (then Article 119 of the EEC Treaty) provides that men and women are entitled to equal pay for equal work. The recast EU Equal Treatment Directive (No.2006/54) (which incorporates the provisions formerly found in the EU Equal Pay Directive (No.75/117)) defines equal pay as remuneration without sex discrimination 'for the same work or for work to which equal value is attributed'. The UK Government had argued that the 'work rated as equivalent' provision contained in S.1(2)(b) and (5) EqPA (now S.65(1)(b) and (4) EqA) allowed a woman's claim to be based on the value of her work and that UK law therefore complied with the Directive. The ECJ disagreed. In its view, by making the right to equal pay for work of equal value dependent upon the existence of a JES, which could only be carried out with the consent and cooperation of the employer, the United Kingdom effectively denied individuals the right to bring a claim where no

175

such study had been carried out. This fell short of the European provisions, which entitle a woman to claim equal pay for work of equal value whether or not a JES had been undertaken.

The right to equal pay for work of equal value entitles a woman to equal pay where she can show that, in terms of the demands made on her – for instance, under such headings as effort, skill and decision-making – the work she does is of equal value to that of a man in the same employment – S.65(6) EqA. In essence, what a woman is doing when she claims that her work is of equal value to that of a comparable man is contending that the work she does is of the same worth to the employer as that done by the man, and that she should therefore be paid the same as him. It is apparent from this that before any claim can get off the ground, the claimant must be able to point to a suitable male comparator. The issues that arise when selecting a comparator are the same as in claims for equal pay based on 'like work' or 'work rated as equivalent' and are discussed in detail in Chapter 4. As with all equal pay claims, the mechanism by which the right to equal pay is enforced is the sex equality clause that is expressly or impliedly contained in all employees' contracts of employment – see Chapter 2 under 'The sex equality clause'.

7.3 The potential scope of an equal value claim is something that many people have difficulty in comprehending, since the comparison is not between two employees on the same or even similar work, but between two (or more) jobs that may be entirely different. Often the only thing that the claimant and the comparator have in common is the identity of their employer (or associated employer). Sometimes, of course, the comparisons are between two jobs that have some kind of relationship with one another; for example, a female purchase ledger supervisor comparing herself with a male export documentation clerk, or the head of personnel at a college of education comparing herself with the head of finance. In many other cases, however, the compared jobs are entirely different. For instance, in one of the first cases to be brought under S.1(2)(c) EqPA (now S.65(1)(c) and (6) EqA) a canteen assistant was successful in proving that she did work of equal value to that of a painter, a joiner and an insulation engineer – Hayward v Cammell Laird Shipbuilders Ltd 1988 ICR 464, HL. Other claims have been based on comparisons between a secretary and a joiner, a cook and a thermal insulation engineer, and canteen workers and surface mineworkers.

7.4 **Complexity of equal value procedure.** The rules applicable to equal value claims in England, Wales and Scotland are set out in Schedule 6 to the Employment Tribunals (Constitution and Rules of Procedure) Regulations 2004 SI 2004/1861 ('the Tribunal Regulations'). That Schedule is entitled the 'Employment Tribunals (Equal Value) Rules of Procedure' ('the Equal Value Rules of Procedure'). Virtually identical rules apply to claims in Northern Ireland.

176

The Equal Value Rules of Procedure only apply to equal value claims and are complex and time-consuming, despite having undergone significant changes in recent years intended to make them more user-friendly. In British Coal Corporation v Smith and ors 1996 ICR 515, HL, where female canteen workers and cleaners sought to compare themselves with surface mineworkers, Lord Slynn remarked: 'These appeals illustrate once again the difficult questions which can arise where claims are made that workers are not being accorded equal pay in accordance with the Equal Pay Act 1970, as amended. That these particular proceedings have taken such an extraordinary amount of time is, however, much to be regretted since many of the claims were lodged over ten years ago in respect of employment undertaken prior to and current at that time. It is clear that it defeats an essential purpose of the legislation if employees cannot enforce within a reasonable time such rights (if any) as they have to remedy inequality of remuneration.' The claims in that case, which began in 1985, were eventually settled in 2001.

7.5 The most recent changes to the Rules were introduced on 1 October 2004 by the Employment Tribunals (Constitution and Rules of Procedure) (Amendment) Regulations 2004 SI 2004/2351 ('the Amendment Regulations'), which added a new Schedule 6 to the Tribunal Regulations, setting out a tighter regime for tribunal procedure in equal value cases, both in terms of case management and in the use of expert evidence. In the Regulatory Impact Assessment, published with the Amendment Regulations, the Government expressed the aim of the changes as follows: 'The purpose of reforming the way in which Employment Tribunals deal with equal value cases is to make the system work more effectively and to tackle lengthy delays, especially in the large-scale and more complex cases. The aim is to enable the key facts to be established more quickly and help the Tribunals determine whether jobs are of equal value. This in turn should also encourage the earlier settlement of more cases.' The new rules thus aimed to reduce the delays associated with equal value claims and make them easier to manage by introducing timetables, requiring the early exchange of information, making more effective use of independent experts, and restricting the use of other expert evidence. In addition, the Amendment Regulations set down an indicative timetable for equal value cases, envisaging claims not involving an independent expert to take no more than 25 weeks, and for claims involving an independent expert to conclude within 37 weeks of the claim being issued.

More than six years after the introduction of the new rules, it seems that the indicative timetable bears little relation to the actual experience of many involved in equal value litigation. A survey conducted by the Equal Opportunities Review (EOR, Issue 186, March 2009) found that many cases get held up at the fact-finding stage. Whereas previously the independent expert interviewed the claimant and comparator to establish the facts on which to assess equal value, now the relevant facts are determined by the tribunal before the

177

independent expert prepares a report – see under 'Stage 2 equal value hearing' below. The EOR survey found that the lawyers now tend to draw up job descriptions for the claimant and comparator, which are then disputed by the other side. The survey also found that, according to independent experts and lawyers, this adversarial approach to the fact-finding procedure meant that in multiple public sector claims it is not uncommon for it to take up to four years for the facts to be agreed.

7.6 The new procedural rules go hand in hand with changes made to the EqPA itself by the Equal Pay Act 1970 (Amendment) Regulations 2004 SI 2004/2352 ('the EqPA Regulations'), which also came into effect on 1 October 2004. The detail of these changes, together with those made by the Amendment Regulations, will be considered at the appropriate points in this chapter. All references to specific rules (e.g. rule 4) in this chapter are to the Equal Value Rules of Procedure contained in Schedule 6 to the Tribunals Regulations, unless otherwise stated.

7.7 Scope of 'equal value'

As we have seen in the preceding chapters, in order to bring an equal pay claim under the EqA, a woman must identify an appropriate male comparator in the 'same employment' (as defined in S.79) whose work is equal to hers, but who enjoys more favourable contractual terms (see Chapter 4). S.65 provides for three means by which a woman can establish that her work is equal to that of her male comparator: 'like work' (see Chapter 5); 'work rated as equivalent' (see Chapter 6); and 'work of equal value'. S.65(6) provides that A's work is of equal value to B's work if it is '(a) neither like B's work nor rated as equivalent to B's work, but (b) nevertheless equal to B's work in terms of the demands made on A by reference to factors such as effort, skill and decision-making'.

7.8 When are different jobs of 'equal value'?

As we will see below, the question of whether the claimant's and the comparator's jobs are of 'equal value' for the purpose of the EqA is ultimately a decision for the tribunal to make, with or without the assistance of an independent expert. But how value is attached to the respective jobs is crucial in understanding this type of claim. S.65(6)(b) gives some indication as to the factors that may come into play when making such an assessment: whether a woman's work is of equal value to that of a man in the same employment requires the tribunal to look at the demands made on the woman 'by reference to factors such as effort, skill and decision-making'.

In Brunnhofer v Bank der österreichischen Postsparkasse AG 2001 IRLR 571, ECJ – a case known primarily for its ruling on the justification of pay differentials and therefore discussed in Chapter 8 under 'Introductory issues – objective justification not always required' – the ECJ made valuable comments on how

178

to assess the respective values of two different jobs. It stated that the term 'work of equal value' in (what is now) Article 157 of the Treaty on the Functioning of the European Union and Article 1 of the Equal Pay Directive is entirely qualitative in character and is concerned exclusively with the nature of the work actually performed. In order to determine whether employees perform work of equal value, it is thus necessary to ascertain whether, taking account of factors such as the nature of the work, the training requirements and the working conditions, those persons can be considered to be in a comparable situation. Turning to the facts of the case, which concerned two bank employees in Austria, the Court expressed its doubts as to whether it would consider the claimant to be doing work of equal value to that of her chosen male comparator. Although that was ultimately a decision for the national court to make, the ECJ noted that the comparator was responsible for dealing with important customers and had authority to enter into binding commitments, whereas the claimant had less contact with clients and no authority to enter into commitments directly binding on her employer. The Court further added that the fact that both employees were classified in the same job category under a collective agreement applicable to their employment was not of itself a sufficient factor to conclude that they performed work of equal value.

Measures of equal value
7.9

Although it is ultimately the tribunal's decision whether two jobs are of equal value, it will be led to a great extent by expert evidence – either from the independent expert appointed under the equal value procedure, or from experts instructed (with the tribunal's permission) by the parties. Experts vary in the ways in which they measure equal value. Most adopt a points-based system, identifying factors – such as experience, knowledge, initiative, physical effort, communication skills, etc – and awarding points for each factor, or for elements grouped under a factor heading. However, not only are there a variety of ways in which a job can be divided into factors, and groups of factors, there is also a range of approaches to determining an appropriate score for each factor – some experts have the same number of levels (or available points) for each factor, others allow more levels for some factors, according to the nature of the job. While the former universal approach has the advantage of greater simplicity, the latter approach may allow the expert to tease out the subtleties of the job in question, but there is always the danger that the greater the number of factors and range of levels available for each, the higher the risk of introducing subjective or discriminatory elements into the evaluation.

An alternative way of measuring equal value is the 'greater, equal, lesser' (GEL) method. This approach also breaks the jobs down into factors but, instead of awarding points for each, simply asks whether the comparator's job places a greater, equal or lesser demand on the employee, with regard to each factor, than that of the claimant. The GEL approach may be used as a check on a

179

points-based appraisal system, or as the primary analysis on which the tribunal bases its decision. An example:

- **Bradley v Chesterfield Royal Hospital NHS Trust** ET Case No.2503944/07: the claimant was employed as a cancer pathway facilitator, reviewing and updating electronic databases of patients' treatment details in order to keep checks on the hospital's attainment of cancer treatment targets. She sought to compare herself to a semi-skilled maintenance worker. The independent expert adopted a GEL system using five headings – knowledge and skill components, responsibilities, mental activities, communication activities, and work circumstances – which between them comprised 27 job elements. The tribunal reviewed the comparator's scoring for each of the 27 job elements and decided that the job demands were less on the claimant with regard to nine of the elements, greater in respect of another nine, and equal with regard to the remaining nine. It therefore concluded that equal value was established.

7.10 Must the work be of precisely equal value?

When the equal value provisions were first introduced, it was unclear whether the value of the man's work and the value of the woman's work had to correspond exactly in order for a claim to be brought. Early decisions were divided on this issue. In Wells and ors v F Smales and Son (Fish Merchants) Ltd ET Case Nos.10701–15/84, for example, the tribunal decided that 'equal value' under S.1(2)(c) EqPA did not equate with '100 per cent parity'. The case concerned 14 women fish-packers who claimed equal pay with R, a general labourer. Upon assessment by the independent expert, nine ended up with a higher score than R while the other five scored 95, 92, 91, 86 and 79 per cent of his score. The expert decided that the five who scored lower were not employed on work of equal value. The tribunal, after hearing evidence, disagreed, finding that the scores were close enough to mean that any differences between them were not relevant, or did not make any material difference. Consequently, all the women were awarded equal pay.

By contrast, the tribunal in Brown and anor v Cearns and Brown Ltd and ors ET Case No.29411/83 and others felt that the broadbrush approach adopted in the Wells case was only appropriate to 'like work' cases for the purpose of determining whether the work is of a 'broadly similar nature'. In the context of S.1(2)(c) EqPA, however, the claimant had to show that her work was of equal, not approximately or broadly equal, value. Thus the claimant, who scored 94.7 per cent of the lower-scoring comparator's score, was not entitled to claim equal pay.

7.11 More recently, however, tribunals have favoured the broader approach adopted in the Wells case. In Southampton and District Health Authority and anor v Worsfold EAT 598 and 827/98 the claimant, a female speech therapist, submitted that her work was of equal value to that of a male clinical psychologist who worked for the same employer. An independent expert scored her job at 54 points – raised to 55 points by the tribunal following its own assessment – against her comparator's 56.5. The tribunal concluded that, notwithstanding the slight difference in scores, the jobs were of 'equal' value. In its opinion, jobs are not of equal value if there is 'an overall measurable and significant difference between the demands of the respective jobs' that is 'reflected in the real world in the terms of employment for which equality is sought'. In the claimant's case, no such difference had been shown.

The same tribunal applied identical reasoning in South Tees District Health Authority and anor v Lawson EAT 827/98, which again concerned a female speech therapist employed by a district health authority. She claimed equal pay with a male pharmacist, and an independent expert gave her a score of 154 and her comparator a score of 161. As the difference between the scores amounted to less than 5 per cent, the tribunal came to the conclusion that there was no 'overall measurable and significant difference between the demands of the respective jobs'. In other words, 'it would not expect to see the difference in demands of these two jobs reflected by a difference in the terms of employment'. As a result, the claimant was employed on work of equal value to that of her comparator notwithstanding the fact that their jobs were not given the same scores. The employers in both Worsfold and Lawson appealed, but the EAT – hearing both appeals together – refused to interfere with the tribunal's decisions.

7.12 However, tribunals must be careful only to ignore a difference in points where it is appropriate to do so. In Hovell v Ashford and St Peter's Hospital NHS Trust 2009 ICR 1545, CA, Lord Justice Elias noted that, although jobs may be equal in value even though not precisely equal in the points scored, 'equal' does not mean 'nearly equal'. He therefore rejected the claimant's submission that a tribunal could find equal value on the basis of a marginal difference in points under a job evaluation study (JES) – it was not enough for the claimant to establish that this meant the jobs were 'substantially' equal. Although Elias LJ came to this conclusion in the context of points scored under a JES, his comments apply *a fortiori* when it comes to weighing up the difference in points awarded under a specific equal value assessment of the claimant's and comparator's job. A small difference in points under a JES may be explained away, for the purpose of equal value, by the specific context of that JES. However, a small difference in points under an equal value report prepared specifically on the basis of the jobs in question is surely more significant.

An employment tribunal undertook a comprehensive analysis of this issue in Forward and anor v East Sussex Hospitals NHS Trust ET Case No.1100186/06. Having reviewed the leading case law, including Hovell, it concluded that a marginal difference in points does not mean the tribunal is obliged to find equal value. There is no obligation to apply a margin of tolerance, and a difference of even one point can negate a finding of equal value if the tribunal is satisfied that 'the difference in the relative demands is measurable and represents a real difference in the value of the jobs'. However, the points may not tell the whole story, and a tribunal may still make a finding of equal value despite a difference of more than one point. In either case, the finding must be based on the totality of the relevant evidence.

7.13 The tribunal went on to give examples of when a small difference in points might be ignored. These include where:

- a suitable methodology produces a small difference in favour of the comparator, but an equally suitable methodology produces a small difference in favour of the claimant

- borderline decisions under the separate factor headings have gone mainly in favour of the comparator

- the points difference came down to a difference in one level under one factor which, on any objective view, is of little or no significance in the context of the particular job.

7.14 **Proportionate value.** A woman is not entitled to claim a proportion of a comparator's pay equivalent to the proportionate value of her job compared to his. So, for example, a woman who is paid 60 per cent of her comparator's wage is not entitled to 90 per cent of his pay on the ground that, as a result of pursuing an equal value claim, the value of her job is shown to be 90 per cent of the value of the man's job. Subject to whatever small margin of difference the tribunal will allow in any particular case, in order to succeed in her claim the claimant must show that her job is of equal value. This is because the sex equality clause provided for in S.66 EqA only bites where the claimant and her comparator are employed on 'equal work' – defined in S.65(1) as like work, work rated as a equivalent or work of equal value.

Note, however, that a claimant in these circumstances might be able to bring a claim based on a hypothetical comparison under the limited provision in S.71 EqA – see further Chapter 4 under 'Hypothetical comparators'.

7.15 **Greater value.** 'Equal value' can mean *greater* value. This was confirmed by the ECJ in Murphy and ors v Bord Telecom Eireann 1988 ICR 445, ECJ, where it decided that the right to equal pay for work of equal value not only applied to situations where the work was of exactly the same or of very close value but also those situations where the woman was being paid less for work of greater value. The Court said that 'to adopt a contrary interpretation would be tantamount to rendering the principle of equal pay ineffective and nugatory,' and pointed out that it would allow an employer to avoid paying equal pay by the simple expedient of giving more onerous duties to members of one sex and then paying them less.

182

This decision has subsequently been followed by our domestic courts on a number of occasions, and it has been confirmed that the same principle applies where a woman claims pay parity with a man in the same employment on the basis that she is employed on 'like work' under S.65(1)(a) EqA or 'work rated as equivalent' under S.65(1)(b) – see SITA (UK) Ltd v Hope EAT 0787/04 and Redcar and Cleveland Borough Council v Bainbridge and ors 2008 ICR 238, CA.

7.16 However, a woman in these circumstances may only claim *parity* of pay with her male comparator. She cannot claim that she should be paid more. Her right is only to have her contract modified so that it is not less favourable than the man's. Thus, in order to be paid more, the woman would have to bring another claim against another comparator being paid more than the original comparator and show that her work is of, at least, equal value to his – see, for example, Evesham v North Hertfordshire Health Authority and anor 2000 ICR 612, CA.

Claim not barred by man on like work/work rated as equivalent **7.17**
An important question as to the scope of the right to claim equal value arose in Pickstone and ors v Freemans plc 1988 ICR 697, HL. That case turned on whether a woman could claim equal pay for work of equal value with men who were doing different jobs from her, when there was a man employed on the same job as her being paid the same amount. In other words, did the presence of a man doing like work prevent her claiming equal pay for work of equal value with others? The employer argued that the terms of the EqPA prevented claims for equal value being brought in these circumstances. S.1(2)(c) of that Act provided that 'where a woman is employed on work which, *not being work in relation to which paragraph (a)* [like work] *or (b)* [work rated as equivalent] *above applies*, is... of equal value to that of a man in the same employment' (our stress), she was entitled to terms and conditions not less favourable than those of the man. The employer argued that the wording of paragraph (c) meant that an equal value claim could only be brought if neither of the other two paragraphs applied. It claimed that the presence of a man on like work meant that paragraph (a) applied and this therefore prevented the women from bringing an equal value claim.

The tribunal, whose decision was upheld by the EAT, agreed with the employer and dismissed the claim. The Court of Appeal and the House of Lords, however, allowed the appeal. The House of Lords held that a woman would only be barred from bringing an equal value claim where a man was employed on like work or work rated as equivalent if that man was her chosen comparator. In order to reach this conclusion their Lordships felt it necessary to insert after the word 'applies' in S.1(2)(c) EqPA the words 'as between the woman and the man with whom she claims equality'. This meant that, so long as the men with whom the claimant claimed equality were not employed on like work or work rated as equivalent, she could bring an equal value claim regardless of whether some other man was employed on like work or work rated as equivalent to hers. Such an interpretation was necessary, in their Lordships' view, to bring the EqPA into line with European law.

7.18 The wording of the equal value provisions in S.65(1)(c) and (6) EqA differs from S.1(2)(c) EqPA, with the words at issue in the Pickstone case no longer featuring. However, the essence of the House of Lords' decision – that the existence of potential comparators doing like work or work rated as equivalent does not prevent a woman bringing an equal value claim in relation to a different comparator – would seem to apply equally to the provisions in the EqA.

Note that where a woman brings a successful equal value claim in these circumstances, there is nothing to stop the man employed on like work or work rated as equivalent from then bringing a like work/work rated as equivalent claim citing the woman, now on a higher salary given her successful equal value claim, as a comparator. Indeed, in Hartlepool Borough Council v Llewellyn and ors and other cases 2009 ICR 1426, EAT, the EAT made it clear that not only are such 'piggyback' claims possible, but they can even be lodged at the same time as the woman's equal value claim. With regard to the latter point, the EAT held that that, even if the male claimants' claims were technically premature in the sense that no cause of action could be said to have arisen until the tribunals had made awards in favour of their female comparator claimants, there were obvious conveniences in the male contingent claims being included in the equal pay proceedings from the start. The power afforded to tribunals under S.2(1A) EqPA (now S.127(3) EqA) to adjudicate claims for a declaration of the rights of the employer and worker in respect of a dispute about the effect of an equality clause provided a sufficient jurisdictional foundation for such contingent claims pending the point at which they might 'mature' into claims for substantive relief.

7.19 Equal value procedure

Initially, an equal value claim proceeds as any other employment tribunal claim would. The claimant must submit an ET1 claim form, to which the employer must reply by completing and returning the response form (ET3). The tribunal will then hold a case management discussion to identify the issues to be determined in the case and make the usual orders in respect of disclosure of evidence, witness statements, etc. It may also decide to hold a pre-hearing review to deal with any jurisdictional issues that arise, such as time limits or employment status. Both types of hearing are discussed in IDS Employment Law Handbook, 'Employment Tribunal Practice and Procedure' (2006), Chapter 8, 'Case management'.

184

Very weak cases may also be weeded out at this stage under the tribunal's general power to strike out the whole or part of a claimant's claim contained in rule 18 of the Employment Tribunal Rules of Procedure (found in Schedule 1 to the Tribunal Regulations) ('the Tribunal Rules'). Strike-outs are generally made at a pre-hearing review – either on the application of a party or on the tribunal's own initiative. In Langley and ors v Beecham Proprietaries (a division of Beecham Group plc) ET Case Nos.2321 and 2335/85 a tribunal explained that the purpose of the preliminary hearing is to sift out those cases that 'have no real merit at all; the truly absurd, the unrealistic, the obviously ill-founded. If, however, there appears to be an arguable case of any kind, then... the matter should be allowed to go forward and if, as is sometimes bound to happen, the decision is a somewhat finely balanced one, then any doubt should be resolved in favour of the [claimant].'

A claim can only be struck out on the grounds specified in the Tribunal Rules, **7.20** for instance, on the ground that the claim is scandalous, vexatious or has no reasonable prospect of success – rule 18(7)(b). So in an equal value case, what the tribunal is essentially doing at this initial stage is making its own preliminary assessment as to the value of the work of the woman and her comparator in terms of 'effort, skill and decision-making' within the meaning of S.65(6)(b) EqA. However, although the power to strike out is now more commonly used by tribunals than it used to be, it is still relatively rare in complex discrimination cases, especially those involving difficult questions surrounding the issue of equal value. Thus, the type of case that is likely to be dismissed at this early stage is one where it is patently obvious that the claimant is not employed on work of equal value with her comparator. For example, a female despatch rider can hardly claim to be doing work of equal value to that of a male managing director. Similarly, if it is obvious that the claimant and her comparator are not employed in the 'same employment' (see Chapter 4 under '"Same employment" or "single source"'), that might also be a good reason for dismissing the claim at this initial stage. The power may also be useful in cases where equal value claims are brought by claimants despite the fact that other sample claims on identical or very similar facts have already been heard and rejected.

Two cases where the power to strike out has been used:

- **Sisson v BPCC Business Magazines (Carlisle) Ltd** ET Case No.07400/91: the tribunal dismissed the equal value claim of a woman employed as a 'secretary to the directors' who was claiming equal pay with a male purchasing manager. The woman had a far less responsible job than her comparator – who had to oversee a budget of around one million pounds a year, compared with her budget of under £10,000. Similarly, he had specific skills peculiar to the printing business, while her skills and knowledge were of general business application

185

- **Ashmore v British Coal Corporation** 1990 ICR 485, CA: A persisted in her claim as one of 1,500 female catering workers claiming equal value despite the fact that 14 claimants had been selected as representative of all the others and had proceeded to a hearing at which their claims were rejected. The Court of Appeal struck out A's claim on the ground that it was 'vexatious' in that it was an abuse of process. The Court ruled that it would have been unfair to the 14 test claimants and to the respondents to permit the claimant to ask the tribunal to reach different findings of fact in her case, based on the same evidence as had been considered by the tribunal when dismissing the sample claims for equal value.

7.21 If the tribunal considers the claim to be susceptible to a strike-out, the party against whom the order is to be made must be given the opportunity of making representations as to why the order should not be made – rule 19(1) Tribunal Rules. Strike-outs are discussed in IDS Employment Law Handbook, 'Tribunal Practice and Procedure' (2006), Chapter 8.

7.22 Outline of equal value procedure

The special procedure applicable to equal value claims only kicks in once the formalities regarding the lodging of claims and any preliminary matters have been dealt with (and the parties have not reached settlement of the claim – see IDS Employment Law Handbook, 'Employment Tribunal Practice and Procedure' (2006), Chapter 9, 'Settlements, withdrawals and arbitration'). The rules of procedure relating to equal value claims were first introduced by the Employment Tribunals (Rules of Procedure) (Equal Value Amendment) Regulations 1983 but are now found in Schedule 6 to the Tribunal Regulations. These special rules applicable to equal value cases supplement the powers tribunals have by virtue of the general Tribunal Rules.

The special rules envisage either a two-stage or a three-stage procedure, depending on whether the tribunal decides to involve an independent expert in the determination of the claim. The special procedure can be summarised as follows.

7.23 All equal value claims involve a stage 1 equal value hearing. The basic purpose of this hearing is to weed out those cases that have no real prospect of success in order to save the time and cost of appointing an independent expert. The employer has an opportunity to block the claim at this stage by showing that the claimant's job is covered by a valid job evaluation study that rates it lower than that of her comparator. Alternatively, it may attempt to defeat the claim by showing, pursuant to S.69 EqA, that the variation in pay is due to a difference which is a material factor unrelated to sex (the material factor defence is discussed in detail in Chapter 8).

If the claim passes the first hurdle of the stage 1 hearing, then the tribunal must decide whether to refer the case to an independent expert for the purpose of preparing a report on whether the jobs can be said to be of equal value. If the tribunal decides to refer the matter to an expert, it will make arrangements for convening a stage 2 equal value hearing. This hearing is designed to resolve any disputed facts so that the expert can evaluate the work on the basis of the main elements of the jobs in question.

Stages 1 and 2 of the equal value procedure are essentially to resolve any **7.24** preliminary issues prior to the substantive hearing at which the tribunal considers the merits of the claim, which happens at the stage 3 equal value hearing. They are therefore very similar to pre-hearing reviews. This is reinforced by the Equal Value Rules of Procedure, in particular rules 4(1) and 7(1), which make it clear that the rules applicable to pre-hearing reviews as set out in the Tribunal Rules also apply to stage 1 and 2 equal value hearings.

Where the matter is referred to an expert, he or she will prepare the report and send it to the tribunal, which will then convene the stage 3 equal value hearing at which the report will be considered and the question of whether the jobs are of equal value will be decided. The tribunal will also consider any defence put forward by the employer under S.1(3) if that issue has not already been considered and ruled upon at the stage 1 hearing.

If the tribunal decides not to involve an independent expert (which it has a discretion to do), it will proceed from the stage 1 equal value hearing straight to a stage 3 hearing at which it will consider the issue of equal value.

Other equal pay claims pleaded as alternatives. Many equal pay claims are **7.25** pleaded in the alternative, with complainants asserting that they are employed on like work, on work rated as equivalent or on work of equal value. In such circumstances, the equal value claim will be considered last – i.e. once the claimants' alternative claims under S.65(1)(a) and (b) EqA have both failed. This is the effect of the wording of S.65(6) which provides that A's work is of equal value to B's work if it is '(a) *neither like B's work nor rated as equivalent to B's work*, but (b) nevertheless equal to B's work in terms of the demands made on A by reference to factors such as effort, skill and decision-making' (our stress).

In Redcar and Cleveland Borough Council v Bainbridge and ors 2008 ICR 238, CA, Lord Justice Kay, giving the judgment of the Court of Appeal, said: '[I]t is apparent from the terms of S.1(2)(c) that an "equal value" claim thereunder can only be advanced where a "like work" claim under section 1(2)(a) and a [work rated as equivalent] claim under section 1(2)(b) are unavailable.' So, if a woman claims that she should be paid the same as a man in the same employment on the basis that she is doing 'like work' or 'work of equal value' to that of the man, the tribunal is obliged to consider the 'like work' claim first. This has various advantages. For one, there is no equivalent to the (two- or) three-stage procedure in claims of 'like work' and 'work rated as equivalent under a job evaluation scheme': such cases proceed immediately to a main hearing. The complex, time-consuming and costly procedure applicable to equal value cases can therefore be avoided. Only if the alternative claims are rejected will it be necessary for the equal value procedure to be instituted.

7.26 The flow chart set out in Appendix 1 to this chapter illustrates the steps to be followed in an equal value claim. Each of these steps is discussed in detail below. It is worth reiterating here that the tribunal's powers conferred by the Tribunal Rules of Procedure also apply to equal value claims – rule 13(3) of the Equal Value Rules. For instance, under rule 14 of the general Tribunal Rules, the Secretary of Employment Tribunals must send notice of any hearing (other than a case management discussion) to every party not less than 14 days before the date fixed for the hearing (unless the parties agree to shorter notice) and must inform them that they have the opportunity to submit written representations and to advance oral argument.

Note that Reg 8(5) of the Tribunal Regulations enables the President of the Employment Tribunals to establish specialist panels of employment judges and lay members, and may select persons from such panels to deal with proceedings in relation to which particular specialist knowledge would be beneficial. This power could prove useful in respect of complex equal value cases where specialist knowledge would be an advantage.

7.27 Stage 1 equal value hearing

Rule 4(1) of the Equal Value Rules of Procedure requires that whenever a dispute arises as to whether any work is of equal value for the purpose of a claim under the EqA, the tribunal must hold a stage 1 equal value hearing. It used to be that a stage 1 hearing had to be conducted before a full tribunal; that is, an employment judge sitting with two lay members – rule 4(2). However, rule 4(2) was removed with effect from 6 April 2009 (subject to transitional provisions) by the Employment Tribunals (Constitution and Rules of Procedure) (Amendment) Regulations 2008 SI 2008/3240, so that an employment judge may now hear a stage 1 hearing sitting alone.

The main purpose of this hearing is for the tribunal to ascertain whether there are any reasons for the claim not to proceed beyond this stage. Effectively, there are two grounds on which the claim can be dismissed at this point. The first is where the woman's work and the man's work have been given different values following a valid job evaluation study (JES) – S.131(5) and (6) EqA and rule 4(3)(a). However, this is subject to the proviso, contained in S.131(6) EqA, that the tribunal must have no reasonable grounds for suspecting that the evaluation contained in the JES was based on a system that discriminates because of sex, or is otherwise unreliable. Where, therefore, a valid, non-discriminatory and 'otherwise reliable' JES concludes that the claimant's and comparator's jobs are *not* of equal value, that conclusion will be binding and its results can be relied upon by the employer at the stage 1 hearing to block an equal value claim. A fuller discussion of this ground can be found under 'Conclusive job evaluation studies' below.

The other ground on which an equal value claim can be blocked at this stage is **7.28** where the employer has such a clear material factor defence within the terms of S.69 EqA that it is pointless establishing equal value, since the claim would inevitably be defeated by that defence. While there is nothing specifically in S.131 or rule 4 that allows tribunals to dismiss claims at the stage 1 hearing on this ground, tribunal decisions on this point have been upheld by the EAT on a number of occasions. Furthermore, rule 4(5) specifically notes that the tribunal may, on the application of a party, hear evidence and submissions on the material factor issue before deciding whether to instruct an independent expert. The extent to which the assertion of a material factor defence at this stage may lead to an equal value claim being dismissed is discussed under 'Material factor defence' below.

Removal of 'no reasonable grounds' defence. Prior to 1 October 2004, there **7.29** was a third ground on which an employment tribunal could strike out an equal value complaint: namely where, in accordance with S.2A(1)(b) EqPA, it was satisfied that there were 'no reasonable grounds' to determine that the work of the claimant and her comparator were of equal value. However, this provision was removed by the EqPA Regulations, partly in response to criticism that it perpetuated assumptions about the value of traditionally 'female' jobs and partly because tribunals already have a general power to strike out a claim if it has no reasonable prospect of success. This power is discussed briefly under 'Equal value procedure' above and in more detail in Chapter 8 of IDS Employment Law Handbook, 'Employment Tribunal Practice and Procedure' (2006).

Procedure if claim not 'blocked' by employer. If the claim is not thrown out **7.30** at this point, rule 4 states that the tribunal must then:

- decide whether to determine the issue of equal value itself or appoint an independent expert from the Acas panel to prepare a report with respect to that issue – rule 4(3)(b)

- if appropriate, make standard orders under rule 5 – rule 4(3)(c)

- if the tribunal has decided to instruct an independent expert, require disclosure of information to the expert and fix a date for the stage 2 equal value hearing, having regard to the indicative timetable (set out in Appendix 2 below) – rule 4(3)(d) and (e)

- if no independent expert is to be appointed, fix a date for the final, stage 3, hearing – rule 4(3)(f)

- consider whether any further orders are appropriate – rule 4(3)(g).

189

Each of these steps is discussed in detail further below.

7.31 Parties attending the stage 1 equal value hearing should come prepared to discuss the many issues that can arise at this stage. If they fail to do so, they will not be allowed to plead ignorance. Rule 4(6) provides that the Secretary of Employment Tribunals, who is charged with giving parties notice of an impending hearing under rule 14 of the Tribunal Rules of Procedure, must at the same time inform the parties of the matters that the tribunal may consider at the stage 1 equal value hearing under rule 4(3) and rule 4(5) (the material factor defence). The Secretary must also give the parties notice of the standard orders in rule 5 (see under 'Case management orders' below).

7.32 Conclusive job evaluation studies

The most effective way for an employer to block an equal value claim is to point to an existing JES that rates the work of the claimant and comparator as being of unequal value. S.131(5) and (6) EqA provides that where a JES that is valid under S.80(5) ascribes different values to the work of the claimant and her male comparator, a tribunal will be obliged to determine that the jobs are not of equal value. However, this is subject to two provisos. First, the JES must not be based on a system that discriminates because of sex – S.131(6)(a). Secondly, it must not be 'otherwise unreliable' – S.131(6)(b). If the study falls foul of either of these provisos, the employer cannot rely on it to defeat the employee's claim at the initial equal value hearing. It is up to the employer to show, on the balance of probabilities, that there is a valid JES satisfying the requirements of Ss.65(6) and 80(5) and that there are no grounds for determining that the JES is tainted by sex discrimination or is otherwise unsuitable – Bromley and ors v H and J Quick Ltd 1988 ICR 623, CA.

If the employer is able to show that S.131(5) and (6) applies, and the tribunal therefore determines that the work of the claimant and the comparator is not of equal value, the tribunal must strike out the claim (or the relevant part of it) – rule 4(3)(a). This power is in addition to the general power to strike out (part of) a claim contained in rule 18(7) of the Tribunal Rules – rule 4(7). Before making the order, however, the Secretary of Employment Tribunals must send notice to the claimant giving her the opportunity to make representations to the tribunal as to whether the evaluation contained in the study falls within S.131(6)(a) or (b) because it is discriminatory or otherwise unreliable – rule 4(4). However, the Secretary is not required to send notice where the claimant has been given an opportunity to make such representations orally to the tribunal.

7.33 Section 131(6) EqA clearly obliges a tribunal to determine that two jobs are 'not of equal value' where 'the work of the woman and that of the man have been given different values' on a JES (except where there are valid reasons as to why the JES should not be relied upon). However, a gloss must be added to this section given court rulings that a comparison for the purpose of S.65(1)(c) is allowed between a claimant and a comparator whose job is of lesser value – whether on a JES or otherwise established (see 'Scope of equal value – must the work be of precisely equal value?' above).

In Redcar and Cleveland Borough Council v Bainbridge and ors 2008 ICR 238, CA, the Court of Appeal was asked to consider whether a woman's 'work rated as equivalent' claim under S.1(2)(b) EqPA could proceed despite her comparator, who earned more than her, being placed in a lower grade than her by the JES. The Council drew attention to the wording of S.1(5) EqPA, which provided that a woman is employed on work rated as equivalent to that of a man for the purpose of S.1(2)(b) 'if, but only if, her job and their job have been given an equal value' by the JES. This, the Council argued, should be read literally, thereby precluding a claim by a woman whose job had been given a higher value by the JES than that of her comparator. The Court of Appeal rejected this argument, holding that a purposive interpretation – i.e. an interpretation in line with the purpose of Article 157 of the Treaty on the Functioning of the European Union – should be adopted. As a result, it felt that it was appropriate to read S.1(5) as saying that 'a woman is to be regarded as employed on work rated as equivalent with that of any man if, but only if, her job and their job have been given an equal value *or her job has been given a higher value*' (our stress).

7.34 Applying this approach to S.65(1)(c) and (6) EqA, which implements the same EU principle into domestic law, a woman is not precluded from claiming pay parity with a man rated lower on a JES. As a result, an employer who attempts to argue that a woman's equal value claim is blocked because the comparator's job has been given a lower grading on a JES is likely to be given short shrift by a tribunal.

7.35 **Validity of a JES.** The validity of a JES is governed by Ss.65(4) and 80(5) EqA. These provisions are discussed in some detail in Chapter 6 under 'Job evaluation – general requirements'. Here we simply summarise the main points.

Effectively, a JES will be valid where:

- it is undertaken with a view to evaluating jobs done by all or any employees 'in terms of the demands made on a person by reference to factors such as effort, skill and decision-making' – S.80(5) EqA, and

- it is not overtly discriminatory, i.e. it does not set different values for men and women on the same demand under any heading – S.65(4) and (5) EqA.

7.36 In Bromley and ors v H and J Quick Ltd 1988 ICR 623, CA, the Court of Appeal held that, in order to comply with what was then S.1(5) EqPA, a JES must be 'analytical'. This means that it must evaluate the demands of the jobs in question under the various factor headings. A JES will not be valid if it simply compares the jobs of the claimant and comparator on a 'whole job' basis.

The JES must also be capable of 'impartial application' – Eaton Ltd v Nuttall 1977 ICR 272, EAT. This means that by applying the study it should be possible to arrive at the position of a particular employee at a particular point in a particular salary grade.

A JES does not have to cover every single employee employed in the undertaking concerned to be valid under the EqA. S.80(5)(a) states that a JES may evaluate the jobs of 'some or all of the workers' in an undertaking or group of undertakings. However, it will only apply to the undertaking, or group of undertakings, in respect of which it was carried out unless there is evidence showing that the JES was intended to apply to another undertaking as well. This was emphasised by the Northern Ireland Court of Appeal in McAuley and ors v Eastern Health and Social Services Board 1991 IRLR 467, NICA. In that case five domestic assistants employed at a hospital in Belfast, Northern Ireland, brought equal value claims comparing their work to that of a man employed as a domestic porter and a man employed as a groundsman. The Board sought to block their claims by relying on a JES in respect of national health ancillary workers in Great Britain, which evaluated jobs similar to those of the complainants and their comparators and which had given them different values. It argued that it should be able to rely on the JES, as the workers' remuneration and conditions of service were the same in both Great Britain and Northern Ireland.

7.37 The Northern Ireland Court of Appeal held that the JES was not binding on the workers in Northern Ireland, even though there was a policy of maintaining parity of remuneration and conditions of service between health service workers in Great Britain and Northern Ireland. The JES had not been undertaken in respect of employees employed by Northern Irish health boards, nor was there any evidence that the management and trade unions which had agreed to undertake the study in Great Britain intended that it would evaluate jobs done by employees in Northern Ireland.

7.38 **JES tainted by discriminatory factors.** Even if an existing JES is valid, an employer will be precluded from relying on it to block an equal value claim if the tribunal has reasonable grounds for suspecting that the evaluation contained in it was made on a system which discriminates because of sex – S.131(6) EqA. In Bromley and ors v H and J Quick Ltd (above) the Court of Appeal ruled that the onus is on the employer to show that a JES does *not* discriminate on the ground of sex. It is therefore up to the employer to explain how the evaluation was carried out and what factors were taken into account at every stage. The claimant is likely to point to factors that she claims indicate either direct or indirect sex discrimination. The employer should then be given the opportunity of responding to such allegations. Ultimately, however, it is for the tribunal to decide, having heard all the evidence, whether there are reasonable grounds for suspecting that the evaluation was made on a system that was discriminatory.

It is worth emphasising that, following amendments made by the EqPA Regulations in October 2004, the tribunal is precluded from relying on a JES once it has reasonable grounds for *suspecting* that it was made on a discriminatory system. This is a lower threshold than was previously in force, which required a JES's rejection where the tribunal had reasonable grounds for holding that the JES was tainted by discriminatory factors.

The question of discriminatory job evaluation exercises was considered by the European Court in Rummler v Dato-Druck GmbH 1987 ICR 774, ECJ. That case concerned the proper interpretation of Article 1 of the EU Equal Pay Directive (No.75/117) (now Article 4 of the recast EU Equal Treatment Directive (No.2006/54)), which provided that 'where a job classification system is used for determining pay, it must be based on the same criteria for both men and women and so drawn up as to exclude any discrimination on grounds of sex'. The employee complained that she should have been placed on a higher grade because she found that, as a woman, her work was physically demanding, although that was not so in the case of a man. The ECJ held that physical strength and other such criteria in respect of which men have a greater natural ability can be used as a valid component under a job evaluation system provided that: (i) the criteria in question correspond to the real requirements of the job; (ii) the evaluation system takes sufficient account of criteria in respect of which women have a special aptitude; and (iii) the system as a whole does not discriminate. This latter requirement entails that, in so far as the nature of the work allows, the criteria used must, as a whole, fairly represent the aptitudes of both sexes.

The EqA, which has to be construed consistently with the recast Equal **7.39** Treatment Directive as interpreted by the ECJ, contains two separate provisions dealing with discrimination in the context of job evaluation studies. First, S.65(4) provides that a woman is to be regarded as employed on work rated as equivalent to that of her comparator under S.65(1)(b) if her job and his have been given an equal value under an analytical JES or would have been given an equal value but for the fact that the evaluation was made on a system that set different values for men and women in respect of the same factor or heading. Secondly, S.131(6) provides that where a JES has rated the claimant's and comparator's jobs as being of different value, the tribunal must determine that the work of the woman and that of the man is not of equal value *unless* it has reasonable grounds for suspecting that the evaluation contained in the study was made on a system that discriminates because of sex (or is otherwise unreliable – see under 'JES "otherwise unreliable"' below). A system discriminates because of sex for this purpose 'if a difference (or coincidence) between values that the system sets on different demands is not justifiable regardless of the sex of the person on whom the demands are made' – S.131(7).

It is apparent that the test for discrimination under S.131(7) is wider than that laid down in S.65(4) since, whereas the latter simply prohibits overt discrimination, S.131(7) is sufficiently broadly drafted to catch more subtle (i.e. indirect) forms of discrimination. It should be noted, however, that S.131(7) speaks of the discrimination being 'not justifiable'. The test for justifiability in this context is presumably that laid down by the European Court in Bilka-Kaufhaus GmbH v Weber von Hartz 1987 ICR 110, ECJ – a case where the claimant sought to challenge indirect discrimination affecting her pay entitlements under the Equal Pay Directive. The European Court ruled that, to justify a discriminatory objective, an employer must show that 'the means chosen for achieving that objective correspond to a *real need* on the part of the undertaking, are *appropriate* with a view to achieving the objective in question and are *necessary* to that end' (our stress). Precisely what is meant by this is discussed in Chapter 8 under 'Showing objective justification'. Suffice to say here that, given the wording of S.131(7), an employer could argue that, notwithstanding the presence of subtle or indirectly discriminatory factors, any such discrimination in a JES is justified on the ground that it meets the test set out in Bilka-Kaufhaus. Clearly, however, a very heavy burden would be imposed on the employer to show that the discrimination was an appropriate means of achieving a legitimate objective and was necessary for that end. This is especially so given the ECJ's decision in Rummler and the statutory emphasis in the EqA on ensuring that a JES is free of discrimination.

7.40 In the absence of a successful argument as to justification, it would seem from the wording of S.131(6) and (7) that a claimant who seeks to challenge the results of a JES simply has to show an arguable case that the allocation of different points for the two jobs was made under a system that discriminated on the ground of sex. The tribunal would then have to proceed to appoint an independent expert or decide the question of equal value for itself.

Few cases have arisen in which an employer has sought to block an equal value claim on the ground of an existing JES. One such, however, was Neil and ors v Ford Motor Co Ltd 1984 IRLR 339, ET, where female sewing machinists claimed equal value with male cutting machinists. In that case the employer identified 28 characteristics under four headings: responsibility, working conditions, physical demands and mental demands. 56 jobs were then selected to represent the range of jobs throughout the company and to serve as a reference for all other jobs. Detailed job descriptions were produced and the demands under each characteristic assessed as low, moderate, high or exceptional. The 56 jobs were compared to the remaining 55 and a rank order established. Five characteristics were given weightings (a 'profiling scheme'). Some of the women subsequently claimed that the system undervalued aspects of their work. The company put it down to a difference of opinion, not discrimination.

The tribunal said that the relevant provisions in the then EqPA posed the **7.41** following two-part question:

- was there any reason to suppose that any of the demands or characteristics on which values had been set by the system ought in fairness to have been given a value more favourable to women?

- would the demands have been given a higher value if those undertaking the JES had not consciously or unconsciously been influenced by consideration of the sex of those on whom the demands would chiefly be made?

By a majority, the tribunal concluded that there were no specifically male attributes among the 28 characteristics valued by the JES and therefore it could not be said that a traditionally male skill or attribute had been overvalued. Accordingly, there was no discrimination.

Three further examples of where employers have sought to rely upon an existing **7.42** JES to block an equal value claim:

- **Henderson and ors v Jaguar Cars plc and ors** ET Case No.18252/90: 32 female sewing machinists employed by JC plc claimed equal pay for work of equal value to that being done by five male comparators. The employer resisted the claim on the basis that a JES had previously determined that the claimants' and comparators' jobs were not of equal value. The JES had been carried out in 1979. 60 'benchmark' (or representative) jobs had been selected and agreed job descriptions drawn up for each job under seven agreed factor headings. Using a system called 'paired comparison by direct consensus', a Central Grading Committee comprising 45 persons from management and unions compared each of the jobs, factor by factor, with every other job and then reached a judgment about the relative value of each job. This assessment was carried out by separate halves of the Grading Committee, after which each half compared their conclusions with the other. They then repeated the exercise. In both instances the level of agreement between the two halves of the Committee was very high. As a final stage, each plant established a job evaluation committee responsible for evaluating the remaining 3,600 jobs on a consensus basis. Every job was assessed on a factor-by-factor basis in order to find the benchmark job that most closely resembled it and then slotted into the grading structure established by the evaluation of the benchmark jobs. In dismissing the claimants' equal value claims, a tribunal ruled that the JES was 'a model of its kind' and was difficult to fault in terms of the requirements of S.1(5) EqPA (now S.80(5) EqA). In the tribunal's view, any risk of sex discrimination affecting the conclusions of the JES was almost entirely eliminated by the number of persons making the comparisons, the running of the exercise twice and the degree of consensus achieved

- **Inkersole and ors v Tungstone Batteries Ltd** ET Case No.21349/90: female laundry workers claimed equal pay with fork-lift truck drivers. Under an existing JES, the claimants' work had been rated as of lower value than that of their comparators. The employer contended that the JES was both valid within the meaning of S.1(5) EqPA (now S.80(5) EqA) and not discriminatory for the purposes of S.2A(3) (now S.131(7) EqA), so that it could be relied upon to prevent the claimants pursuing their claim for equal value. Rejecting that contention, the tribunal concluded that there was a real danger that sex bias had been imported into the JES. Under certain factor headings identified by the study, the men's work appeared to have been rated unduly highly. For example, they had received three points under the heading of 'training', whereas the women had received only one point. Yet the drivers needed only two days to obtain the necessary licence to drive a fork-lift truck, whereas the women spent a considerable amount of their time on skilled use of industrial sewing and patching machines. Theirs was not a skill that could be learned in a couple of days. The tribunal therefore rejected the employer's application to dismiss the equal value claim on the basis of the existing JES and referred the matter to an independent expert

- **Bateman v Hull and East Riding Community Health NHS Trust** ET Case No.1807708/00: B, a risk management adviser, claimed equal pay with three women who were employed by the Trust as training and development officers. The Trust's JES gave B's job 59.5 points, which, after the half point was removed, was converted into grade D1. The comparators' jobs were assessed at 60, and graded as D2 – which made a difference of £3,000 per annum. The tribunal refused to dismiss B's claim on the ground that the Trust's JES assessed his job as being of unequal value to the job undertaken by his comparators. In its view, the JES had not been objectively carried out. In particular, B's score had been reduced following interference by the female head of personnel, whereas she had not intervened in the assessment of the comparators' scores. This raised suspicions of sex bias in the evaluation process. B's case could therefore proceed, and the tribunal instructed an independent expert to prepare a report on the equal value question.

7.43 **JES 'otherwise unreliable'.** An employer will also be precluded from relying on an existing JES to block an equal value claim if it is shown to be 'otherwise unreliable' – S.131(6)(b) EqA. This subsection succeeds S.2A(2A)(b) EqPA, which was added by the EqPA Regulations with effect from 1 October 2004. There is a slight change of wording in the new Act – whereas S.2A(2A)(b) referred to a JES being 'otherwise unsuitable to be relied upon', S.131(6)(b) refers to a JES being 'otherwise unreliable'. However, we do not consider that there is any material difference in meaning between the two.

The broad scope of the phrase 'otherwise unreliable' appears to allow the claimant to challenge the JES for any reason not already covered by S.131(6)(a), and it is certainly arguable that the task of showing that a JES is 'unreliable' is less onerous than that of demonstrating that it is 'discriminatory'. However, there is very little case law specifically on the scope of S.131(6)(b), or its predecessor S.2A(2A)(b) EqPA. In its 'Step by step guide: equal pay for work of equal value', the EOC (now part of the EHRC) gave an example of when S.2A(2A)(b) EqPA could apply. In the EOC's view, a claimant might be able to argue that a JES was no longer suitable to be relied upon where it had not been properly maintained or reviewed. This argument is likely to succeed where the employer introduces changes to the grading structure or job content without evaluating the jobs to ensure that they remain correctly placed in the structure. In the EOC's view, given that it is rare nowadays for job content to remain constant, a JES will not be reliable unless it fully reflects an organisation's current employment practices.

7.44 In Ivanoff v City West Housing Trust Ltd ET Case No.2404804/08 a tribunal considered whether the manner in which a JES had been moderated invalidated it for the purpose of S.2A(2A) EqPA. Although the tribunal did not state that it was considering the claimant's challenge under S.2A(2A)(b) specifically, it asked whether the criticisms made by the claimant rendered the JES 'unsuitable to rely on', wording very close to that of that section. Among other things, the claimant had criticised the fact that moderation had been carried out by a single individual, rather than by a panel with trade union involvement, as had originally been envisaged. The tribunal did not consider that this departure from the planned methodology made the scheme unreliable. The fact of the matter was that, while the trade unions had initially intended to be involved at every stage of the job evaluation process, they drew back from moderation when they discovered how much work it would involve. Thus, although there had been a departure from the original methodology, the departure was agreed with the trade unions, which were content to receive notification of the results of moderation to allow them to comment at that stage.

Another ground on which it may be possible to assert that a JES is unreliable is where it is tainted by some other form of discrimination; for example, age or religious discrimination. This would apply even where the claimant herself is not in the disadvantaged group and is not being discriminated against on that ground.

7.45 **Timing of the JES.** It is clear that a valid and non-discriminatory JES which rates the claimant's and comparator's jobs as unequal, and which is in place before an equal value claim is launched, will serve to block such a claim. This is the effect of S.131(5) and (6) EqA (see above). But the question arises: until what point in the proceedings can an employer raise a JES as a potential block to such a claim? This issue arose in Avon County Council v Foxall and ors 1989 ICR 407, EAT, where the employer argued that the employees' equal value claims should be thrown out at the initial hearing on the ground that a full JES had been commissioned from an internationally recognised management consultancy, Hay/MSL. The problem was that the JES would not be completed until after the date set for the initial hearing. The employer nevertheless urged the tribunal to grant a stay of proceedings until the JES was ready, arguing that the legislation encouraged the use of job evaluation studies and that there was a major risk that the JES would be undermined if the tribunal first appointed an independent expert who reached a different conclusion from that reached by Hay/MSL.

The employment judge refused to grant the stay on the ground that he had no discretion to do so. However, on appeal, the EAT held that the employment judge did, in fact, have a power to order a stay of proceedings (a power now contained in rule 10(2)(h) of the Tribunal Rules of Procedure). However, the EAT went on to conclude that it was not appropriate in the circumstances of the particular case to grant the stay. There was no evidence that the JES would be impeded by the existence of parallel equal value proceedings and, once the JES had been properly and effectively completed, it would protect the Council completely against future claims from employees covered by the scheme. The loss to the claimants of their statutory right to pursue their claim would significantly outweigh any disadvantages to the Council arising from a refusal of the stay.

7.46 Thus it would seem that, depending on the circumstances of the case and subject to the tribunal's discretion, an employer may be able to block an equal value claim by implementing a JES after proceedings have started but before the tribunal has commissioned an expert's report. But how far does this go? Is there any deadline by which a JES must have been completed in order for it to be used to block an equal value claim under S.131(5) and (6) EqA? The answer is possibly provided by the EAT's decision in Dibro Ltd v Hore and ors 1990 ICR 370, EAT. In that case the employer commissioned a JES after an equal value pay claim had been initiated by a number of women employees. The employer then sought to introduce the JES at the tribunal's initial hearing in order to have the employees' case dismissed on the basis that, in the light of the study's results, there were no reasonable grounds for determining that the claimants' jobs were of equal value to those of their comparators. The tribunal refused to allow evidence of the JES because it had been commissioned after the initiation of the equal pay claim, and appointed an independent expert to produce a report.

However, the EAT overturned the tribunal's decision on appeal. It rejected the employees' arguments that, to be admissible, a JES must already be in existence at the time the claim for equal pay is lodged. In the EAT's view, a JES – presuming it to be valid – can be introduced as evidence at any time up to the final hearing when the decision is made as to whether the claimant's work is of equal value – even after the independent expert's report has been completed. However, this is subject to the proviso that the jobs considered under the JES are the actual jobs that were being carried out at the time the equal pay proceedings were instituted. In adding this proviso, the EAT was mindful of the fact that the issue in an equal value claim is whether, when the proceedings are initiated, the job being carried out by the claimant is of equal value to that of the comparator. If the comparison is not with the same job, the JES may still be admissible, but it will be more difficult to satisfy a tribunal that it falls within S.131(5) and (6).

It is not entirely clear whether the EAT was simply saying that a late JES is **7.47** admissible in evidence for the purpose of persuading the tribunal that the work is not of equal value or whether it was saying that a late JES is effective to block a claim under what is now S.131(5) and (6) EqA. However, it is certainly arguable that the effect of the decision is that an employer who does not agree with an independent expert's report could commission its own JES before the tribunal makes a decision on the matter and then seek to use the results to block the equal value claim at a very late stage. Against this, it could be argued that the whole scheme of the equal value procedure anticipates that once an independent expert's report has been commissioned the case should be carried through to its conclusion. Bearing in mind that once the expert's report is complete it has no special status over reports prepared by the parties' own experts (see under 'Stage 3 equal value hearing' below), it would seem strange if a JES implemented by the employer after the tribunal has appointed an expert could oust the expert's findings without the tribunal being required to consider the merits of both reports.

The practical answer to this problem may lie in the argument that, in order for a JES to be valid under Ss.65(4) and 80(5) in the first place, the scheme must be accepted by both parties. If this argument is correct, presumably an employee who wishes to avoid the employer's JES conclusively deciding the case, may refuse to accept it. The JES would then simply be treated as evidence at the final hearing along with the report of the independent expert and any report commissioned by the employee. However, it is not entirely clear whether acceptance of the JES by the employer and the employees (or employee representatives) is a necessary precondition of a JES being regarded as valid and complete. This issue is discussed in more detail in Chapter 6 in the section 'Job evaluations – general requirements' under 'When is a JES "complete"?'.

Material factor defence

7.48

The second way in which an equal value claim can collapse at the first stage is where the employer successfully raises a 'material factor' defence under S.69 EqA. This defence can also be raised at the substantive hearing of the claim – i.e. at stage 3 – if the tribunal resolves the equal value question in the claimant's favour. The scope of the material defence is considered in detail in Chapter 8. Briefly, S.69 provides that if the employer proves that the variation between the terms of the claimant's and comparator's contracts is genuinely due to a material factor, reliance on which does not involve treating the claimant less favourably because of sex and does not amount to unjustified indirect sex discrimination, there is no right to equal pay. When considering the defence the tribunal should do so on the presumption that the claimant's work is of equal value to that of her comparator and should always bear in mind that the burden of proof is on the employer to make out the defence – Financial Times Ltd v Byrne and ors (No.2) 1992 IRLR 163, EAT.

Rule 4(5) of the Equal Value Rules of Procedure allows a tribunal, on the application of a party, to hear evidence on a material factor defence before determining whether to require an independent expert to prepare a report. Whether or not the tribunal accedes to such an application is entirely a matter for it, but given the savings that can be made – both in terms of money and time – where a material factor defence is successful at this early stage, tribunals usually allow the defence to be advanced at the stage 1 equal value hearing. If the tribunal does not determine the issue at this point, the employer retains the possibility of raising it at the substantive hearing at stage 3. However, where the employer has raised the defence at the stage 1 hearing but is unsuccessful, it will be precluded from having a second bite of the cherry by raising the defence again at a later stage – see IDS Employment Law Handbook, 'Employment Tribunal Practice and Procedure' (2006), Chapter 1, under 'Limits to tribunals' jurisdiction – relitigation: the doctrine of res judicata'.

7.49 Rule 4(5) does not state expressly that the tribunal is entitled to dismiss an equal value claim at stage 1 if the employer has made out a material factor defence. In actual fact, rule 4 mentions the tribunal's power to strike out the whole or part of a claimant's claim only in the context of a valid, non-discriminatory JES assessing the claimant's and comparator's jobs as being of unequal value. Nevertheless, the EAT has held that a strike-out is the proper course of action to take where the employer has successfully made out a material factor defence at this stage – Forex Neptune (Overseas) Ltd v Miller and ors 1987 ICR 170, EAT. Furthermore, although the tribunal is not bound to start an inquiry into the defence at the first hearing stage, should it decide to do so it must either conclude that 'the matter cannot fairly be decided without the assistance of an expert and therefore must be adjourned' or it must proceed to reach a decision on the evidence – Reed Packaging Ltd v Boozer and anor 1988 ICR 391, EAT. If the tribunal adopts the second option, there must be very clear evidence that the defence is a genuine one for it to succeed – R v Secretary of State for Social Services and ors ex parte Clarke and ors 1988 IRLR 22, Div Ct.

This means that tribunals should adopt a cautious approach to dismissing equal value claims at the preliminary stage on the ground that a material factor defence has been made out. To this extent, the power of tribunals to dismiss a claim at the stage 1 hearing (which was affirmed in Forex Neptune) is circumscribed by a strict requirement that there is cogent evidence of a genuine material factor justifying the pay differentials between the claimant and her comparator. It is therefore probably accurate to say that only an unanswerable defence (which effectively means that the claim has 'no reasonable prospect of success' under rule 18(7)(b) of the Tribunal Rules of Procedure) should lead a tribunal to dismiss the claim at this point. Otherwise it should refer the case to an expert or decide the question of equal value itself before determining the merits of the defence. Such an approach is consistent with the notion of the stage 1 hearing being a filter process to get rid of hopeless cases. That said, the relevant factors to be considered are the same whether the material factor defence is raised at the initial hearing or at a later stage – McGregor and ors v General Municipal Boilermakers and Allied Trades Union 1987 ICR 505, EAT.

Decision whether to commission an independent expert's report 7.50

Section 131(2) EqA provides that where a dispute arises as to whether work is of equal value the tribunal has a discretion to take one of the following courses of action:

- to proceed to determine for itself the question of whether the claimant's and comparator's jobs are of equal value, or

- to require a member of the panel of independent experts to prepare a report with respect to that question.

This procedure is replicated in rule 4(3)(b) of the Equal Value Rules of Procedure.

Before July 1996 tribunals had no power to proceed to determine the question of equal value until they had commissioned and received the report of an independent expert. However, with a view to speeding up the adjudication of equal value claims, the EqPA and the Equal Value Rules of Procedure were amended by the Sex Discrimination and Equal Pay (Miscellaneous Amendments) Regulations 1996 SI 1996/438 to allow tribunals to determine the question of equal value for themselves without having to take the intermediary step of commissioning an independent expert's report.

Given the complexity of assessing the value of dissimilar jobs while avoiding 7.51 discrimination in the evaluation process, most tribunals will be loath to dispense with the assistance of an expert versed in the skills of evaluation. Indeed, in complex equal value cases – especially those in the public sector involving hundreds, and sometimes thousands, of complainants – there will usually be a team of independent experts evaluating the jobs in question. As a result, it is not often that tribunals make use of the power to decide the issue of equal value without calling on an independent expert. However, there are two situations in which a tribunal may prefer to dispense with an expert (and thus avoid the lengthy adjournment that inevitably follows). These are:

- where the tribunal takes the view at the stage 1 hearing that the claimant's case is well founded (perhaps on the basis of decisions in proceedings brought by other claimants)

- where both parties have commissioned their own job evaluation studies and the tribunal takes the view that there is little assistance to be gained from a third expert's opinion.

7.52 In Bragg v St Monica Home of Rest ET Case No.1400690/97 the tribunal considered the pros and cons of referring an equal value claim to an independent expert. It commented that one advantage is that 'the independent expert would be able either to agree or to decide the criteria [for evaluation] and might be able to reduce the number of comparators. In a difficult case... the presence of the independent expert would be an additional protection to ensure justice.' Against that, there was the issue of delay and the fact that the resumed hearing would inevitably take longer because the tribunal would have to take into account the evidence of three reports – that of the independent expert and those commissioned by the parties. On the facts of the particular case, the tribunal concluded that it would decide the issue of equal pay itself without commissioning an expert since that was the most expeditious and efficient way of dealing with the matter. Similarly, in Henry v University of Leeds ET Case No.6940/96 the tribunal decided to go ahead and hear the equal value claim, having obtained the parties' agreement that the question of equal value should be decided in the light of evidence submitted by one expert called by each side. In the event, after a five-day hearing, much of which was taken up by cross-examination of the expert witnesses, the tribunal rejected the equal value claim on the basis that it preferred the conclusions of the employer's expert. Unlike the claimant's expert, he had interviewed the named comparator and had shadowed both the comparator and the claimant on a typical working day.

There is nothing in S.131 EqA that prevents a tribunal that has initially decided to determine the equal value question itself without the help of an independent expert from reconsidering its position at a later date. However, where it has decided to rely on an independent expert's report, it cannot then proceed to determine the equal value question until it has received that report – S.131(4). It does, though, retain the power under S.131(3) to withdraw the requirement for a report at any stage – see 'The independent expert – withdrawing instruction for independent expert's report' below.

7.53 **Relevance of later job evaluation study.** One situation in which the tribunal may decide the question of equal value without recourse to an independent expert is where the claimant's job has been rated as equivalent to that of her comparator under a job evaluation study (JES) that was implemented *after* the period to which the equal value claim relates. For example, if a JES implemented in April 2004 places the claimant's and comparator's jobs in the same band, the claimant will be entitled to equal pay from that point forward under the 'work rated as equivalent' provisions. However, she will not be able to rely on the JES to claim back pay for the period prior to April 2004 as a JES does not have retroactive effect and so can not support a finding of 'work rated as equivalent' for any period prior to its implementation – Redcar and Cleveland Borough Council v Bainbridge and ors (No 2) and other cases 2009 ICR 133, CA. However, the claimant might be able to argue that, since she and her comparator were doing the same jobs before the JES was implemented, their work should be treated as of equal value during that period, based on the JES. The claimants in Redcar put this argument forward but the Court of Appeal refused to treat the JES as conclusive evidence of equal value for the period prior to April 2004.

The Court of Appeal revisited this issue in Hovell v Ashford and St Peter's Hospital NHS Trust 2009 ICR 1545, CA. It arose in the context of the claimant's application to withdraw the instruction for an independent expert to prepare a report. In short, her argument was that, since a JES had placed her in the same band as her comparators, her claim of equal value relating to the period before the JES was implemented had to succeed, and so an expert's report was not required. The tribunal refused to accede to her application and the EAT agreed, holding that a JES is admissible evidence of equal value in the earlier period, but does not obviate the need for an independent expert. The Court of Appeal rejected the claimant's further appeal. Although it appeared to accept that the JES was probative with regard to equal value in the period before its implementation, on the assumption that there had been no change in the relevant jobs, it rejected the argument that it could automatically lead to a conclusion of equal value.

7.54 When Hovell reached the Court of Appeal, the issue had narrowed to the question of whether, where the claimant's job has been marked lower than her comparator's in a JES (albeit within the same band), the tribunal *must* have the benefit of an independent expert's report before it can make a finding of equal value. The Court of Appeal held that the employment judge had erred in assuming that to be the case. The mere fact that the claimant scores fewer points than her comparator in a JES does not mean that a tribunal is obliged to conclude that her job is not of equal value unless there is the support of an independent expert. That was too narrow a view. However, the Court also rejected the claimant's more ambitious submission that a small difference in points under the JES would, of itself, mean that the jobs were of equal value. A tribunal may be persuaded that a very small difference in points, particularly in the context of a wide-ranging JES that has focused on benchmark jobs and has not involved a direct comparison of the jobs in issue, does not reflect a material difference in the value of the two jobs. However, it is still for the tribunal to decide whether it will be assisted by an independent expert's report.

The Court of Appeal in Hovell did not express any view on whether a tribunal would still be entitled to instruct an independent expert if a JES scored the claimant's job *higher* than that of her comparator. Given the Court's emphasis on tribunals' discretion to decide what evidence is needed to decide the question of equal value, it seems unlikely that there would be any rule against the tribunal commissioning an expert's report in this situation. However, it must be thought that a significant points difference in favour of the claimant would be strong evidence of equal (or greater) value.

7.55 Case management orders

At the end of the stage 1 hearing – and regardless of whether it has decided to commission an independent expert's report – the tribunal must make appropriate case management orders to promote the smooth running of the case. In order to avoid any unnecessary delays, the Equal Value Rules of Procedure introduce an indicative timetable for every stage of the proceedings, which the tribunal is required to have in mind when making any orders. This timetable is annexed to the 2004 Amendment Regulations and is reproduced in Appendix 2 to this chapter.

7.56 Standard orders. Under rule 4(3)(c) of the Equal Value Rules of Procedure, a tribunal must make the standard orders set out in rule 5 at the stage 1 hearing (unless it considers it inappropriate to do so – rule 5(1)). Rule 5 sets out a rigid, fast-track timetable which requires that:

- within 14 days of the stage 1 hearing, the claimant shall
  - disclose in writing to the respondent the name of the comparator or, if this is not possible, sufficient information to enable the respondent to identify the comparator, and
  - identify in writing to the respondent the relevant period for comparison – rule 5(1)(a)

- within 28 days of the stage 1 hearing
  - where the claimant has not disclosed the name of the comparator but has provided sufficient detail for the respondent to be able to identify the comparator, the respondent must disclose in writing to the claimant the name of the comparator
  - the parties shall exchange written job descriptions for the claimant and any comparator, and
  - the parties shall identify to each other in writing the facts they consider to be relevant to the question of equal value – rule 5(1)(b)

- the respondent shall grant access to the claimant and his or her representative to work premises during a period specified by the tribunal in order to interview any comparator – rule 5(1)(c)

- within 56 days of the stage 1 hearing the parties shall provide the tribunal with an agreed joint statement in writing setting out

  - job descriptions for the claimant and any comparator

  - facts which both parties consider relevant to the question of equal value, and

  - any facts on which the parties disagree (either as to the fact itself or its relevance), with a summary of reasons for their disagreement – rule 5(1)(d)

- no later than 56 days prior to the full hearing the parties shall disclose to each other, to any independent or other expert and to the tribunal written statements of any facts on which they intend to rely in evidence at the hearing – rule 5(1)(e)

- no later than 28 days prior to the full hearing the parties shall present to the tribunal a statement of facts and issues on which they are in agreement, a statement of facts and issues on which they disagree, and a summary of their reasons for disagreeing – rule 5(1)(f).

7.57 The tribunal can add to, vary or omit any of the standard orders as it considers appropriate – rule 5(2). In particular, it is free to vary the periods within which actions are to be taken by the parties – rule 3(1)(a). It is therefore free to impose a timetable that it considers appropriate given the factual matrix of the claim.

7.58 **General orders.** In addition to the standard orders that must be made at stage 1 under rule 5, tribunals have general powers under rule 3 to make orders in equal value cases to enable them to manage cases more efficiently. (These orders can also be made at stage 2 of the procedure – see below). Under rule 3 tribunals can order:

- that no new facts be admitted in evidence unless disclosed to all parties in writing by a date specified by the tribunal (unless it was not reasonably practicable for a party to have done so) – rule 3(1)(b)

- the provision of copies of documents and information to all parties and the independent expert – rule 3(1)(c)

- that the respondent grants the independent expert access to work premises during a period specified by the tribunal so that he or she can conduct interviews with relevant persons – rule 3(1)(d)

- that, where more than one expert is to give evidence, those experts present a joint statement of matters on which they agree and disagree to the tribunal – rule 3(1)(e)

- that, where proceedings have been joined, lead claimants be identified – rule 3(1)(f).

7.59 Finally, if the tribunal has decided not to appoint an independent expert, it must set a date for the full, stage 3 hearing at which the equal value question will be determined, having regard to the indicative timetable – rule 4(3)(f). Where an independent expert has been instructed, the tribunal must instruct the parties to copy to the expert all information that they are required by an order to disclose or agree between each other, and fix a date for the stage 2 equal value hearing – rule 4(3)(d) and (e).

7.60 ## Stage 2 equal value hearing

Where the tribunal has reached the conclusion that an independent expert's report on the respective values of the claimant's and the comparator's jobs is needed, it must hold a stage 2 equal value hearing – rule 7(1). Although a stage 1 equal value hearing may now be heard by an employment judge sitting alone (see under 'Stage 1 equal value hearing' above), a stage 2 hearing must be conducted before a full tribunal; that is, an employment judge sitting with two lay members – rule 7(2). According to the indicative timetable, unless a case is unusually complex, it is expected that the stage 2 hearing will take place within ten weeks of the stage 1 hearing.

The main purpose of the stage 2 hearing is to resolve facts in dispute between the parties to make it easier for the independent expert to evaluate the relevant jobs. Where the parties cannot reach agreement, the tribunal will have to make a determination of those facts – rule 7(3). Once this has been done, the tribunal will 'require the independent expert to prepare his [or her] report on the basis of the facts which have (at any stage of the proceedings) either been agreed between the parties or determined by the tribunal'. In other words, the independent expert must undertake the relevant evaluation on those facts only. Furthermore, they are the only facts that the tribunal can rely on once the issue of equal value falls to be determined by it, with the help of the independent expert's report, at the final hearing – rule 7(5).

7.61 The objective behind rule 7(3) and (5) is to define clearly the scope of the evaluation to be carried out by the expert – and later by the tribunal, when it revisits and ultimately determines the question of equal value for itself. This ensures that the expert confines the evaluation to the essential elements of the relevant jobs. It also ensures that all the parties involved in the case are placed on an equal footing, knowing exactly the factors any evaluation is based on, and thereby setting clear boundaries within which the evaluation may later be challenged before the tribunal.

Having said that, it is open to the expert to apply to the tribunal – at any stage of the proceedings – for some or all of the facts relating to the equal value question to be amended, supplemented or omitted – rule 7(6). The expert is likely to do this where he or she believes that certain crucial facts needed for preparing the report have been omitted or, alternatively, where some facts are no longer relevant and can be disregarded for the purpose of the evaluation exercise. This could occur where, for example, the expert has visited the claimant and comparator's workplace and gathered information that he or she considers to be of particular relevance to the evaluation of the jobs.

Fact-finding

7.62

A key feature of the Equal Value Rules of Procedure is the split between fact-finding and decision-making (i.e. the decision on whether jobs are of equal value). Originally, the Government intended that the independent expert would have no role to play in gathering relevant factual information. However, this was modified in light of the consultation responses. The EOC (now subsumed into the EHRC), for example, objected to the exclusion of the independent expert from the fact-finding process. In its view, 'involving the independent expert at an early stage would enable the expert to provide guidance to the employment tribunal on the issues which will be relevant to the job evaluation and allow the expert an insight into the matters in dispute between the parties and the information necessary to resolve those disputes'.

Under rule 6(1) and (2), once a tribunal has decided to commission an independent expert's report on the equal value question, the tribunal has discretion to order that expert 'at any stage of the proceedings' to assist the tribunal in establishing the facts on which he or she may rely in preparing the report. Alternatively, a party to the proceedings, or the expert him or herself, may apply under rule 11 of the Tribunal Rules of Procedure to the tribunal to make an order to call on the independent expert to help in fact-finding – rules 6(4) and 10(3) of the Equal Value Rules of Procedure.

Rule 6(3) gives a non-exhaustive list of the types of circumstances in which the **7.63** tribunal may ask for the expert's assistance in fact-finding. They cover:

- where a party is not legally represented – rule 6(3)(a)

- where the parties are unable to reach agreement as required by an order of the tribunal – rule 6(3)(b)

- where the tribunal considers that insufficient information may have been disclosed by a party which may affect the ability of the independent expert to prepare a report on the equal value question – rule 6(3)(c)

- where the tribunal considers that the expert's involvement may promote fuller compliance with the tribunal's orders – rule 6(3)(d).

Note that when the independent expert is involved in the fact-finding process, he or she has the duties and powers as specified in rule 10. Those duties are discussed under 'The independent expert – independent expert's duties and powers' below.

7.64 Case management orders

A tribunal is required to make a number of case management orders at the stage 2 equal value hearing, as set out in rules 7(4) and 8. When the Secretary of Employment Tribunals gives notice to the parties and to the independent expert of the stage 2 hearing, in accordance with rule 14(4) of the Tribunal Rules of Procedure, he or she must also give the parties notice of the standard orders in rule 8 and draw the attention of the parties to rule 7(4) (the tribunal's powers and duties at the stage 2 hearing) and 7(5) (the facts the tribunal will rely on at the hearing to determine the equal value question) – rule 7(7).

7.65 Standard orders. Under rules 7(4)(a) and 8, a tribunal must make the following standard orders set out in rule 8 at the stage 2 hearing unless it considers it inappropriate to do so:

- order the independent expert to prepare a report on the equal value question and send copies of it to the parties and to the tribunal by a date specified by the tribunal (having regard to the indicative timetable) – rule 8(1)(a); and

- order that the independent expert must prepare his or her report on the basis of the facts relating to the equal value question and no other facts that may or may not relate to that question – rule 8(1)(b).

Either of these standard orders may be added to, varied or omitted as the tribunal considers appropriate – rule 8(2). In particular, it is free to vary the periods within which actions are to be taken by the parties – rule 3(1)(a).

7.66 General orders. The tribunal may also make any other orders that it considers appropriate, or make any of the general orders that it is entitled to make at stage 1 under rule 3 (see 'Stage 1 equal value hearing – case management orders' above) – rules 3 and 7(4)(b).

Finally, the tribunal must fix a date for the full hearing (the stage 3 hearing) at which the issue of equal value will be determined – rule 7(4)(c).

7.67 The independent expert

Where the tribunal decides that it cannot itself determine the question of whether the claimant's work is of equal value to the work of a named comparator, it will require an independent expert to prepare a report on that question. The independent expert in this context is a person drawn from a panel of suitably qualified people designated by Acas – S.131(8) EqA. There are currently 29 such experts (see Acas's 'Annual Report and Accounts 2009/2010'). They are employees of neither Acas nor HM Courts and Tribunals Service, although the latter meets all the experts' fees and expenses. According to Acas's Annual Report, since the equal value rules were first introduced in 1984, experts have been appointed in 686 cases. 68 were appointed in the 2009/10 period, down from 139 the previous year (although the vast majority of the previous year's cases were NHS claims brought around the time of the introduction of Agenda for Change – see Chapter 1 under 'Growth in public sector claims').

Independent expert's duties and powers

7.68

Rule 10 sets out the duties and powers of independent experts in equal value cases. Once an independent expert has been asked to prepare a report, it falls to the Secretary of Employment Tribunals to inform him or her of these duties and powers – rule 10(1).

Under rule 10(2), the expert has a duty to the tribunal to:

- assist the tribunal in furthering the overriding objective to deal with cases justly – rule 10(2)(a)

- comply with the Equal Value Rules of Procedure and any tribunal orders made in relation to the proceedings – rule 10(2)(b)

- keep the tribunal informed of any delay in complying with any order in the proceedings, with the exception of minor or insignificant delays – rule 10(2)(c)

- comply with any timetable imposed by the tribunal in so far as is reasonably practicable – rule 10(2)(d)

- inform the tribunal, when asked, of progress with regard to the preparation of his or her report – rule 10(2)(e)

- prepare a report on the question of whether the claimant's work is of equal value to that of the comparator, based on the facts relating to that question, and send it to the tribunal and the parties (except in national security proceedings, in which case the report is only sent to the tribunal – rule 14(1)) – rule 10(2)(f) (see further 'Timescale for preparing report' below)

- make him or herself available to attend hearings – rule 10(2)(g).

The Secretary of Employment Tribunals must give notice to the independent **7.69** expert of all hearings, applications, orders or judgments in those proceedings as if he or she were a party to the proceedings – rules 10(6) and 13(1). In addition, the expert must be provided with any information that one party is required to provide to another party under the rules. The independent expert may apply for any order or hearing as if he or she were a party to the proceedings – rule 10(3).

The system replaces in its entirety the previous procedure under which the expert was required to provide cumbersome written progress reports to the tribunal at specified intervals before submitting the final report. Now, the expert is given a timescale within which to prepare the report, and is under an obligation to inform the tribunal of any delay, except minor or insignificant

209

delays, in complying with any order in the proceedings – rule 10(2)(c). The tribunal may from time to time ask the expert how far he or she has progressed with the preparation of the report.

7.70 Once the tribunal has instructed an independent expert, it is entitled to change its mind. At any stage of the proceedings the tribunal may, under rule 10(4), withdraw instructions from an independent expert and either determine the equal value issue itself or pass instructions to a new expert. This power is discussed further under 'Withdrawing instruction for independent expert's report' below.

7.71 **Independent expert's methodology**
There are no detailed statutory rules dealing with the method an expert should adopt when preparing a report. The only specific requirements are that he or she must consider the issue of equal value 'in terms of the demands made on [the employee] by reference to factors such as effort, skill and decision-making' in accordance with S.65(6)(b) EqA, and that the report must be prepared only on the basis of the relevant facts agreed by the parties or determined by the tribunal under rule 7(3).

To assist the independent expert in compiling the report, the tribunal has the power to order the respondent to grant the expert access to its premises to enable the expert to conduct interviews with any other relevant persons, and to order that the expert be sent any documents and information that is available to the parties – rule 3(1)(c) and (d). However, this is not mandatory, and the report may well be prepared based on job descriptions drawn up and agreed by the parties and/or their representatives.

7.72 **Challenges to methodology.** Two broad grounds of challenge to methodology were considered by the employment tribunal in Forward and anor v East Sussex Hospitals NHS Trust ET Case No.1100186/06. The first was whether the factor headings under which the demands of the job are assessed should be weighted. The three experts before the tribunal were all agreed that explicit weighting, such as applying a multiplier to factors deemed more important than others, is inappropriate in an equal value assessment (although permissible under a JES). However, the experts were divided on whether implicit weighting was acceptable. This kind of weighting might arise because factors are split into groups – for example, responsibility or effort – and some groups have more headings than others. Alternatively, some factors may be given more scoring levels than others, meaning that it is easier for individuals to distinguish themselves under some factors than under others. For example, if some jobs are scored on a scale of 1-8, and others on a scale of 1–5, a high score under the former category will count for more than a high score under the latter. While one of the experts thought that no kind of weighting at all is permissible, the other two took the view that all equal value assessments include some implicit

210

weighting. For example, having more than one factor under the same general heading, such as 'knowledge', is weighting, as is scoring all factors on the same level.

The tribunal preferred the majority view. It noted that not only is implicit weighting permissible, it is also desirable. A 'factor plan', designed to identify and classify each demand of the jobs under consideration, would help the tribunal compare the jobs in relation to each factor. The tribunal observed that it must be wary of making subjective judgments, or being influenced by what it knows to be the values of the particular organisation, but felt that on any objective view there will be some demands that are more relevant than others to the question of equal value. For instance, in comparing two managerial jobs, the demands under factors such as physical skill and physical effort would normally be less significant than demands under headings such as responsibility for finances or supervision. It went on to note that, if it were not satisfied that the implicit weighting given by the breakdown of factors was appropriate to the job, it could commission another expert report or (in extreme circumstances) devise its own factor plan. Alternatively, it might multiply or divide points scored under certain factors to reflect their appropriate weight, or combine or separate factors (although this would require rescoring). Furthermore, it would feel justified in adding levels under factors to separate jobs that both score highly.

The second challenge to methodology concerned the number of factors by **7.73** which jobs are evaluated. The tribunal noted the concern that having too many factors would lead to a risk of 'double counting'. By contrast, too few factors might mean that factors that deserve to be scored independently are conflated. The tribunal stated that it would feel entitled to make adjustments to the independent expert's scoring if it felt that unfairness had crept in.

Job changes during claim period. What happens where job content changes **7.74** during the period covered by the claim? This was the question the EAT had to grapple with in Potter and ors v North Cumbria Acute Hospitals NHS Trust and another case 2008 ICR 910, EAT, a case involving mass litigation against a hospital trust. The parties agreed to proceed by way of 'lead cases' and 13 claimants were selected to be compared to 12 comparators. The tribunal determined that it was appropriate to appoint two independent experts to prepare reports on the question of equal value in relation to the 13 lead claimants and the parties sought to agree 'job analysis reports' (JARs) for the jobs done by each lead claimant and each comparator, which would form the factual basis for the experts' reports. There was, however, a dispute about the date at which the JARs were intended to state the facts on which the experts could base their reports. The claimants contended that, because there had been changes in job content for some of the lead claimants over the claim period, the JARs should cover facts as existed across the whole of that period. The Trust,

211

meanwhile, took the view that the facts on which the JARs were based should be taken at the date of presentation of the claim.

The employment judge agreed with the Trust and directed that the JARs be based on the facts of the claimants' and comparators' employment as at the date of presentation of the claim. The EAT dismissed the claimants' appeal against that decision. In the course of its judgment, it set out a number of observations and general guidance for tribunals involved in similar claims. If, when approaching the question of equal value, the facts that form the basis of the JAR are not materially different throughout the claim period, then such facts can simply be provided to the independent expert. If, however, one party claims that the facts at one stage of the claim period were materially different, it will be necessary for the tribunal to find or state the different facts that existed at different times.

7.75 How a tribunal should approach a claim where there were changes in job content during the claim period will depend on the circumstances. In some instances, the difference between the facts will be sufficiently great to justify two distinct JARs, focusing on different parts of the claim period. In other circumstances, however, the parties may produce a statement of the facts at a 'base date' – usually the date of presentation of the claim, since more recent facts are more readily accessible. The variations in the facts can then be identified by tracking backwards from the base date. However, there may be occasions when it is more convenient to take a base date at the start of the period and work forward.

While a tribunal needs to decide the equal value question in respect of each part of the claim period, it does not follow that it need do so all in one go. The question of equal value is not indivisible – tribunals can and should apply ordinary case management principles, which allow for the splitting of issues to encourage the smooth and timely conduct of complex litigation. In the instant case, the judge had – by focusing on the facts at the date the claim was presented – effectively hived off the issue of changes during the claim period with the intention of returning to them in light of the independent expert's report. This, the EAT explained, was well within his case management powers and was not a decision with which it could or should interfere. It was open to the tribunal, once it had received the expert's report, either to require a second report based on the factual changes or, using the original report as a base, to decide the issue itself.

7.76 Differences between independent expert's evaluation and a JES
The exact nature of the evaluation carried out by the independent expert varies from case to case. As a general rule, the independent expert's evaluation will be different both in nature and scope to the kind of evaluation undertaken as part of a job evaluation study (JES). It is usual for a JES to cover a wide range of

different jobs, often necessitating the selection of benchmark jobs against which other jobs can be evaluated. In a typical equal value claim, however, the scope of the expert's inquiry will be much narrower, since the focus will be exclusively on the nature and respective value of the particular jobs done by the claimant and her comparator(s). Moreover, whereas a JES will be concerned to assess the value of all the jobs that are subject to the study relative to each other, an equal value claim will merely be concerned with the 'comparative value' of the particular jobs under scrutiny. This will be assessed without any reference to other jobs carried out by other employees in the employer's organisation.

There is, however, one important point of similarity between a JES and an independent expert's evaluation, dictated by the requirement that the evaluation should not be tainted by discriminatory factors. S.65(6)(b) EqA frames the relevant question to be decided by an independent expert in an equal value claim as being whether the work of the claimant, despite not being like work or work rated as equivalent, is nevertheless equal to the work of her chosen comparator 'in terms of the demands made on [the claimant] by reference to factors such as effort, skill and decision-making'. This is identical to the question to be decided where it is alleged that the claimant is employed on work rated as equivalent under a JES. In such a case, S.65(4)(a) defines 'work rated as equivalent' as meaning where the claimant's and comparator's jobs have been given an equal value in terms of the demands made on a worker. These demands are explained in S.80(5) as those 'made on a person by reference to factors such as effort, skill and decision-making'. This has been interpreted by the courts to mean that, to be valid, a JES must be 'analytical' – see Chapter 6 under 'Analytical and non-analytical evaluations' in the section entitled 'Job evaluation – general requirements'. The evaluator is accordingly expected to identify a range of factors and subfactors and to devise a fair method for allocating points to each job in accordance with the extent to which each factor features in the job. Given the identical statutory wording in S.65(6)(b), it must follow that an analytical approach should also be adopted by an independent expert for the purposes of an equal value claim.

7.77 However, as a result of the more limited inquiry involved, the range of factors to be taken into account in the case of an equal value claim is likely to be smaller than under a conventional JES. And those factors are unlikely to be decided in advance by a panel comprising representatives of employees and management (as in the case of a JES) but will normally be chosen on the basis of information gleaned by the expert from interviews with the claimants, comparators and their supervisors/managers, and from existing job descriptions and observation of the relevant jobs as they are performed in practice.

Timescale for preparing independent expert's report

7.78 The tribunal will, where appropriate, specify a date by which the independent expert must have completed the report and sent copies of it to the parties and the tribunal, having regard to the indicative timetable – see rule 8(1)(a). According to the indicative timetable, an independent expert's report should be completed within eight weeks of the stage 2 hearing. Bearing in mind rule 14(5) of the Tribunal Rules of Procedure (which governs the submission of written representations generally), the date the tribunal specifies should be not less than seven days before the hearing (although the tribunal has discretion to consider written representations submitted after that deadline – rule 14(6)).

The independent expert has a duty to keep the tribunal informed of any delay in complying with any order in the proceedings (other than minor or insignificant delays) – rule 10(2)(c). If, in giving reasons for an anticipated delay in sending the report, the expert believes that the delay has been contributed to by the action or omission of one of the parties, then he or she should give particulars of this. It is then open to the tribunal to consider whether a costs order should be made against that party. Liability for costs in respect of equal value claims is considered below under 'Stage 3 equal value hearing – costs in equal value claims'. Alternatively, the tribunal may, in extreme cases, strike out the claim or response. For example, the tribunal can strike out any claim or response (or part of one) under rule 18(7)(c) of the Tribunal Rules of Procedure on the ground that the manner in which the proceedings have been conducted by or on behalf of the claimant or the respondent (as the case may be) has been scandalous, unreasonable or vexatious.

7.79   Withdrawing instruction for independent expert's report
Section 131(3) EqA and rule 10(4) of the Equal Value Rules provide that a tribunal may withdraw an instruction given to an independent expert to prepare a report 'at any stage of the proceedings', provided it has given the expert an opportunity to make representations. Once withdrawn, the tribunal is entitled to determine the question of equal value itself. Alternatively, it can appoint another independent expert to prepare a report on the equal value question. However, instructing a second independent expert could result in further lengthy delays and might not be the most desirable course of action to take at this stage in the proceedings. For this reason, the tribunal may be inclined to determine the question for itself.

Clearly, the decision to withdraw the requirement for an independent expert to prepare a report is a drastic step. We would suggest that a tribunal might decide to make use of this power where an equal value claim has stalled owing to the expert taking an unreasonably long time to produce a report. However, we are not aware of any cases where this has happened.

7.80   Of course, a party may seek a withdrawal for tactical reasons. In Hovell v Ashford and St Peter's Hospital NHS Trust 2009 ICR 1545, CA, for example, the claimant sought a withdrawal of the requirement for an independent expert on the ground that the fact that she and her male comparators were all placed

214

in the same band under a JES constituted determinative evidence of equal value for the period prior to implementation of the JES and that, as a result, the independent expert's report could be dispensed with. The tribunal refused to accede to her application and the Court of Appeal held that it had been correct to do so (albeit for different reasons).

Whether or not the tribunal decides to withdraw the requirement and determine the question itself or instruct a different independent expert, the 'outgoing' independent expert must provide the tribunal with all documentation and work in progress relating to the proceedings by a date specified by the tribunal and in a form that the tribunal is able to use – rule 10(5). That documentation may then be used by the tribunal or any other independent expert. The tribunal can also make 'such other requests to that [expert] as are connected with the withdrawal of the requirement' – S.131(3)(b).

Use of other expert evidence

7.81

Parties often want to instruct their own experts in addition to the independent expert. However, rule 11 restricts the circumstances in which the parties can adduce their own expert evidence. Moreover, the rule emphasises that any expert's main duty is to assist the tribunal, and this overrides any duties to the paying client – rule 11(2).

According to rule 11(1) and (3), expert evidence must be restricted to that which, in the tribunal's opinion, 'is reasonably required to resolve the issues in the proceedings', and no expert evidence can be introduced without the permission of the tribunal. In general, tribunals are more likely to give permission if both parties wish to have their own experts. If only one party seeks permission to admit evidence from an expert, the tribunal may be inclined to refuse permission on the ground that allowing the evidence would be contrary to the overriding principle that parties in a case must be placed on an equal footing. In any event, no expert report may be put in evidence unless it has been disclosed to all other parties and any independent expert at least 28 days before the full hearing – rule 11(3).

Prior to the current Equal Value Rules coming into force in October 2004, 7.82 tribunals were expected to give the parties the opportunity to adduce their own expert evidence where the tribunal had decided not to refer the question to an independent expert – see Wood and ors v William Ball Ltd 2000 ICR 277, EAT. Now, however, rule 11 limits the extent to which evidence other than from an independent expert can be adduced and, in particular, gives the tribunal discretion to refuse to allow expert evidence that is not reasonably required to resolve the issues in the proceedings. That said, the tribunal must have cogent evidence enabling it to assess the respective values of the jobs in question itself before it will be inclined to refuse a party's request to adduce his or her own expert evidence on the equal value question.

Rule 11(4) deals with the circumstances in which a party may be allowed to put in his or her own expert evidence where the tribunal has required an independent expert to prepare a report. It states that the tribunal shall not admit evidence of another expert on the question of equal value unless such evidence is 'based on the facts relating to [that] question'. It then goes on to stipulate that, unless the tribunal considers it inappropriate to do so, any such expert report must be disclosed to all parties and to the tribunal on the same date as that on which the independent expert is required to send his or her report to the parties and to the tribunal. This prevents a party from holding back an expert's report until he or she has seen the independent expert's report. If an expert (other than an independent expert) does not comply with these rules or an order made by the tribunal, the tribunal may order that his or her evidence should not be admitted – rule 11(5).

7.83 The stipulation in rule 11(4) that the expert report(s) should be disclosed on the same date as the independent expert's report can cause some difficulties for the parties. As the employment tribunal noted in Forward and anor v East Sussex Hospitals NHS Trust ET Case No.1100186/06, where an independent expert has been instructed, leave to appoint a partisan expert is more likely to be given if the party raises questions as to the independent expert's methodology, rather than simply about the individual scores. However, this rather depends on the parties knowing what methodology the independent expert has adopted, which will often not be revealed until the independent expert sends out his or her final report.

This issue was considered by the EAT in Middlesbrough Borough Council v Surtees and ors (No.2) 2008 ICR 349, EAT, where an employment tribunal had appointed an independent expert to report on whether 12 female complainants were doing work of equal value with male comparators. In September 2006, the independent expert disclosed what he referred to as a 'review of job descriptions against a possible and tentative factor plan'. However, the full methodology of the assessment was not published until his final report in May 2007. That report found that 11 of the 12 claimants were doing work of equal value in respect of one comparator and four claimants were doing work of equal value in respect of the other. The Council then commissioned its own expert to prepare a report. That report sought to challenge two aspects of the independent expert's methodology that had not been indicated in the 'tentative factor plan'; namely, the weightings given to particular factors and conventions that the independent expert proposed to use to avoid double-counting.

7.84 The Council applied to the employment judge for permission to admit its own expert's report under rule 11(4). However, the employment judge refused to admit the report because of the rule's 'narrow scope', and in particular the requirement to provide the report 'on the same date' as that on which the independent expert's report was supplied. In any event, if he was wrong about the construction of the rule, he was not prepared to exercise his discretion to admit the report. The Council appealed to the EAT.

The EAT disagreed with the employment judge's opinion that rule 11(4) did not give him power to admit the expert's evidence. Rule 11(4) is a procedure allowing for admission of a party's expert's report. The rule positively envisages expert evidence being adduced but restricts its reach: the party's expert can challenge the independent expert's methodology or arithmetic provided he or she does not challenge the facts found by the tribunal or agreed to by the parties at an earlier stage in the proceedings – this, said the EAT, is the meaning of the words 'unless such evidence is based on the facts' in rule 11(4). The rule would have no meaning unless it is acknowledged that challenges can be made to methodology. The system of job evaluation is susceptible to different methodologies. Further, it is not enough that the expert's challenges can be put to the independent expert in cross-examination because, if a challenge is met by a denial, there is little basis upon which the argument can be taken further in the absence of evidence, and a refusal to allow such evidence to be admitted could deny a party the right to a fair trial. If the operation of rule 11(4) were otherwise, said the EAT, the dissatisfied party would be 'fighting with one arm behind its back', as there would be no positive evidence to support a challenge to the independent expert's methodology. In the present case the expert's report was admissible and there was power to admit it.

7.85 The EAT then considered whether the Council was nevertheless prevented from adducing its own expert's evidence by virtue of the second part of rule 11(4), which states that 'unless the tribunal considers it inappropriate to do so, any such expert report shall be disclosed to all parties and to the tribunal on the same date on which the independent expert is required to send his report to the parties and to the tribunal'. In the EAT's view, where the independent expert has disclosed in advance the full methodology used in preparing the report, the party's own expert can disclose its evidence 'on the same date'. Where the full methodology is not disclosed in advance, however, it would obviously be inappropriate for the tribunal to require disclosure of its expert's evidence challenging the independent expert's methodology on the 'same date' as that methodology is itself revealed. Accordingly, the second part of rule 11(4) did not preclude the tribunal from admitting the Council expert's evidence, because the independent expert in this case did not disclose his full methodology until he published his final report in May 2007. As a result, the employment judge should have exercised his discretion to admit the report.

The case provides useful guidance on the admissibility of reports produced by the parties' own experts. However, to avoid the delay experienced in that case, it would have been useful at the stage 2 hearing for the tribunal to have made a standard order under rule 8 for the independent expert to disclose his or her methodology prior to publishing the full report.

7.86 **Instructing a joint expert.** Under rule 11(6), where two or more parties wish to submit expert evidence on a particular issue, the tribunal has the power to insist that a single joint expert be instructed. The joint expert will be selected by the tribunal if the parties cannot agree on who it should be.

7.87 ## Written questions to experts

As a tool to manage the deluge of additional questions that may follow the disclosure of an expert's – including an independent expert's – report, rule 12 provides a standard regime for written questions from any party or expert to the expert who prepared the report. Under rule 12(2), unless the tribunal agrees otherwise, written questions:

- may only be put once – rule 12(2)(a)

- must be put within 28 days of the date the report was sent to the parties – rule 12(2)(b)

- must be for the purpose only of clarifying the factual basis of the report – rule 12(2)(c)

- must be copied to all other parties and experts involved in the proceedings at the same time as they are sent to the expert who prepared the report – rule 12(2)(d).

7.88 The expert must then respond within 28 days of receiving the questions, and all responses will be treated as part of his or her report – rule 12(3) and (4). Although this is not expressly required, we assume that the answers should be sent to the tribunal, the parties and any other expert involved.

Where one party has put a written question to an expert instructed by another party and the expert fails to answer that question, or does not do so within 28 days, the tribunal may order that the party instructing the expert may not rely on his or her evidence – rule 12(5). This regime curtails the potential for delays, tactical or otherwise.

7.89 # Stage 3 equal value hearing

At the full hearing, the tribunal must decide whether the claimant's job is of equal value to that of her named comparator. The burden of proving the claim is on the claimant – Tennants Textile Colours Ltd v Todd 1989 IRLR 3, NICA. But even if the jobs are found to be of equal value that is not necessarily the end of the matter, as the employer will be entitled to raise a 'material factor' defence, arguing that the difference between the claimant's and the comparator's pay is due to a material factor other than the difference of sex (unless the tribunal has already ruled that the employer is unable to make out this defence at the stage 1 equal value hearing). Having heard the material factor defence, the tribunal will then decide the outcome of the case, and, if appropriate, the remedy. The material factor defence is discussed in detail in Chapter 8, while the question of remedies is considered in Chapter 9 under 'Remedies'.

As mentioned above, the indicative timetable envisages that claims not involving an independent expert will take no more than 25 weeks from submitting the claim form to the final hearing, whereas claims involving an independent expert should be concluded within 37 weeks of the claim being issued – see Appendix 2 to this chapter.

Admitting independent expert's report into evidence 7.90

The first question to be decided at the stage 3 hearing is whether the independent expert's report should be admitted as evidence. Rule 9(1) contains a presumption that the report will be admitted in evidence at the hearing unless the tribunal determines that it is not based on the facts relating to the question of equal value that were determined at the stage 2 hearing (see above). A determination by the tribunal that the expert's report should not be admitted into evidence leaves the tribunal with two options: either it must decide the equal value question itself or it must start the process of commissioning another independent expert to prepare a report all over again – rule 9(2).

It is rare for a challenge to a decision to admit an independent expert's report into evidence to succeed. In Aldridge v British Telecommunications plc 1989 ICR 790, EAT, the employees failed in their attempt to have the expert's report rejected. In that case the employees had appealed against a tribunal's majority decision that the expert's report should be admitted on the grounds that the report did not adequately set out its conclusions; the expert failed to 'take no account of the difference of sex' (a requirement under the old rules); the tribunal should not have taken into account the expert's oral evidence in deciding to admit the report; and the expert's methodology was flawed. The EAT dismissed the appeal. In its view, not all of the relevant facts had to be contained in the report. Further, the tribunal was entitled to hear oral evidence from the expert and was entitled to look at all the evidence – including that of the expert – in deciding whether the report should be admitted. With regard to the expert's methodology, the EAT noted that the equal value assessment had to consider the demands made on the woman and the man by their respective work and to do so under headings such as effort, skill and decision in such a way as to avoid any influence of gender-based factors. In approaching such an assessment, the steps were: first, the choice of factors; second, the weighting of those factors; and third, ensuring that there was no bias in favour of one job over another. The EAT considered that the tribunal majority was entitled to decide that the expert's report was satisfactory in this respect.

Challenging the conclusions of the report once admitted 7.91

Either side can present arguments to the tribunal on the question of equal value upon which the independent expert has prepared his or her report. It should be noted, however, that the scope for attack on the independent expert's report is limited since no evidence may be adduced in respect of any matter of fact on which the report's conclusion is based. This is the effect of rule 11(4), which allows a party's own expert to give evidence, with the tribunal's permission, provided that evidence does not seek to challenge the facts that have already been found. If it were otherwise, the initial stages of the special procedure for equal value claims – agreeing or determining facts relevant to the equal value question – would have been in vain, and lengthy delays would again ensue. Furthermore, rule 9(3) gives tribunals the power to refuse to admit evidence of facts or hear argument as to issues that have not been disclosed to the other party as required by the Rules or any order made under them, unless it was not reasonably practicable for the party to have complied.

Although the scope for attack on the independent expert's report is therefore limited, the EAT in Middlesbrough Borough Council v Surtees and ors (No.2) 2008 ICR 349, EAT, made it clear that a party – through its own expert – is nevertheless fully entitled to challenge the independent expert's methodology in compiling the report. In the words of His Honour Judge McMullen, 'plainly an expert is there to challenge methodology given the restricted scope of challenge to facts. There is no meaning to be given to rule 11(4), unless it is acknowledged that a challenge can be made to methodology.' Parties questioning the independent expert's methodology should, however, bear in mind the requirement in rule 11(4) that an expert's report must be disclosed to all parties and to the tribunal 'on the same date' as that on which the independent expert is required to send his or her report to the parties and to the tribunal, unless the tribunal considers it inappropriate to do so. The scope of rule 11(4) and the decision in the Surtees case are discussed in greater detail under 'The independent expert – use of other expert evidence' above.

7.92 Of course, the parties are not obliged to commission their own expert reports in order to challenge the conclusions of the independent expert's report. However, as the tribunal made clear in Hayward v Cammell Laird Shipbuilders Ltd 1985 ICR 71, ET, 'the most effective (although, of course, not the only) way of mounting any attack upon the independent expert's report must be to commission and present an expert's report of one's own'. A similar point was made by a tribunal in O'Connor v The Perry Group ET Case No.10392/94. In that case the first independent expert's report took 18 months to compile and was castigated by the tribunal for failing to provide any useful assistance whatsoever. The second expert, whose report was completed within nine months, concluded that the claimant (a group personnel and training officer) and her comparator (a regional sales trainer) were employed on work of equal value. The company sought to challenge that conclusion without commissioning a professionally carried-out evaluation of its own. The tribunal observed that, although the company had attacked the independent expert's evidence by cross-examination, this merely constituted an attempt to pressure the expert into reconsidering her conclusions. In the tribunal's view, it was unreasonable, given that it had not obtained an expert opinion to support its stance, for the company not to have conceded the issue of equal value in the light of the expert's findings of fact. This amounted to unreasonable conduct and the tribunal therefore ordered the company to pay the claimant's costs from the date when it first rejected the expert's conclusions and also to reimburse the Secretary of State any costs and expenses incurred by the expert as a result of her attendance at the tribunal.

Although rule 11(4) restricts the manner in which a challenge may be made to the independent expert's report, and no question over the facts will be entertained, there is no obvious restriction on the kinds of criticism that a party may seek to make of the independent expert's methodology. Some issues that might arise in this regard are considered under 'Independent expert's methodology' above.

Status of the independent expert's report   7.93
As mentioned above, it is always open to the parties to commission their own expert reports and to place these before the tribunal as evidence. Problems can arise, however, if one (or both) of these contradicts the independent expert's report. Which report then takes precedence?

In Tennants Textile Colours Ltd v Todd 1989 IRLR 3, NICA, the Northern Ireland Court of Appeal decided that the independent expert's report does not attract any special status. In the Court's view, the Equal Value Rules of Procedure limit the introduction of new evidence to contradict the factual basis of the report. However, the parties are still free to make submissions contradicting the expert's conclusions. The Court stated that the burden of proof rests on the claimant throughout equal value proceedings and remains the same regardless of the independent expert's conclusions. It does not become any heavier if the report goes against the claimant; nor does it transfer to the employer if the report favours the claimant. Consequently, although an independent expert's report carries considerable weight, tribunals are nonetheless free to reach their own conclusions on the evidence. This may, in certain circumstances, lead them to reject the independent expert's conclusions. It could not, therefore, be said that the report of a party's own expert or, indeed, any other evidence before the tribunal necessarily has any less weight or status than the independent expert's report.

The fact that the decision as to whether the claimant's and comparator's work 7.94
is of equal value lies entirely with the tribunal and that the expert's report has no special status was re-emphasised by the EAT in Aldridge v British Telecommunications plc 1989 ICR 790, EAT. Regarding the difficulties in challenging facts contained in the expert's report, the Appeal Tribunal suggested in that case that the tribunal should hear as much evidence as

221

possible at the admission stage and then admit the report and give it such weight as is appropriate.

Obviously, at the end of the day, the weight to be attached to a report will depend on its nature and quality. If the parties do wish to put their own reports into evidence, those reports must presumably be at least as thorough and complete as the independent expert's report if they are to stand any chance of ousting his or her conclusions. In Forward and anor v East Sussex Hospitals NHS Trust ET Case No.1100186/06 the tribunal observed that 'there is no suggestion [in the authorities] that the independent expert's methodology must be preferred unless [the methodology adopted in the other report] is one which no reasonable expert could have adopted or unless it is tainted by bad faith or sex discrimination'. Thus, there may be cases where the tribunal is satisfied that an independent expert's report has been produced in good faith, does not involve discrimination, and is reasonable, but yet the findings, evidence and methodology of another report make it easier for the tribunal to decide the question of equal value. The tribunal went on to note that two different methodologies may produce two different results without either being 'wrong' in any absolute sense.

7.95 In practice, it is rare for tribunals to eschew the conclusions of the independent expert in favour of a partisan expert instructed by one or other of the parties. In the following cases, the tribunals accepted the conclusions of an independent expert in preference to those reached by job evaluators under the much-respected evaluation system deployed by Hay Management Consultants:

- **Hayes and anor v Mancunian Community Health Trust and anor** ET Case No.16977/93: the tribunal felt that the independent expert's focus on the comparative values of the jobs in question was more relevant to the particular case than the system adopted by the Hay evaluator, which relied heavily on the input of the job holders and their immediate supervisors when forming judgments and definitions. Also, the Hay system was heavily weighted in favour of factors relating to 'know-how', which gave undue emphasis to formal rather than practical qualifications. This led the tribunal to uphold the independent expert's opinion that dental surgery assistants were employed on work of equal value to that done by a technical instructor

- **Evesham v North Hertfordshire Health Authority and anor** ET Case No.17844/87: in one of the numerous cases in which NHS speech therapists claimed equal pay with clinical psychologists and pharmacists, the tribunal criticised the Hay system for failing to reflect the demands of jobs where the cure of patients was the primary function of the job. In the tribunal's words: 'The problem with the Hay scheme as used in these cases is that this essential demand is part of the overall know-how factor and is unduly constrained by its interrelation with planning and organising skills.' In the tribunal's view, a system free of such constraint (such as the evaluation method used by the independent expert in that case) was more appropriate to an equal value assessment.

However, these cases can be contrasted with two others where the independent **7.96** experts' conclusions were not followed:

- **Rippon and ors v Celtic Seafoods Ltd** ET Case No.17932/95: an expert concluded that female packers in a frozen-fish processing factory were not employed on work of equal value with a male labourer on the basis that the man knew how to drive a fork-lift truck, even though he only engaged in that activity for 2.5 per cent of his working time. The majority of the tribunal held, contradicting the expert's opinion, that the claimants' and comparator's jobs were in fact of equal value. In the view of the lay members, no reasonable employer would have allowed an unqualified and untrained employee to drive a fork-lift truck, let alone paid him extra for doing so. Had the fork-lift truck factor been left out of the equation, the claimants would have been awarded the same number of points in the evaluation exercise as the comparator. They were therefore employed on work of equal value

- **Southampton and District Health Authority and anor v Worsfold and another case** EAT 598 and 827/98: in another speech therapist case the tribunal rejected the independent expert's conclusion that the claimants were not employed on work of equal value in view of the fact that they had only scored 54 points under the evaluation exercise, whereas the comparators had scored 56.5 points. In the tribunal's view, work is not of equal value where there is 'an overall measurable and significant difference' between the demands of the respective jobs. The tribunal concluded that there was no measurable and significant difference between the jobs under consideration, and its conclusion was supported by the evidence of the independent expert who, under cross-examination, admitted that if he, as a manager, had been responsible for grading the jobs, the difference between them would not have led to any difference in grading. On appeal, the EAT upheld the decision.

What is clear from the cases discussed above is that when a tribunal finally **7.97** reaches the end of an equal value claim, after what may be many years of proceedings, the decision on whether the work is of equal value is one for the tribunal alone to make. It must take into account all the evidence and make its own assessment of it.

Costs in equal value claims   7.98

Unlike their predecessors, the current Equal Value Rules of Procedure do not contain any special provisions dealing with tribunals' powers to award costs in equal value claims. The relevant rules are therefore those governing the award of costs in employment cases generally, which are contained in the Tribunal Rules of Procedure. For example, costs may be awarded in favour of a legally represented party where a party in bringing the proceedings, or a party or his

223

or her representative in conducting the proceedings, has acted vexatiously, abusively, disruptively or otherwise unreasonably, or the bringing or conducting of the proceedings by a party has been misconceived – rule 40(2) and (3) of the Tribunal Rules. Similarly, costs may be awarded where the proceedings have been postponed or adjourned on the application of a party or a party has failed to comply with an order or direction by the tribunal – rule 40(1) and (4).

The rules relating to the making of a costs order, as well as the amount that can be awarded, are discussed in detail in IDS Employment Law Handbook, 'Employment Tribunal Practice and Procedure' (2006), Chapter 18, 'Costs and allowances'.

Appendix 1: Equal value procedure

ET1 (claim form)/ET3 (response)

Case management discussion/Pre-hearing review

Stage 1 equal value hearing

1. Is claimant employed on 'like work' or 'work rated as equivalent'?   No   Yes ⟶ Claim proceeds under normal procedure

2. Does existing JES apply to the claimant's and comparator's jobs?   Yes   No ⟶ Go to (4)

3. Is the JES discriminatory or otherwise unsuitable?   Yes   No ⟶ Equal value claim fails

4. Does the employer have a valid material factor defence?   No   Yes ⟶ Equal value claim fails

5. Does tribunal wish to appoint an independent expert?   Yes   No ⟶ Tribunal fixes date for Stage 3 equal value hearing (go to (13))

6. Tribunal fixes date for Stage 2 equal value hearing

Stage 2 equal value hearing

7. Facts agreed by parties or determined by tribunal on which expert to rely in preparing the report

8. Tribunal specifies date on which independent expert must complete report

9. Tribunal fixes date for Stage 3 equal value hearing

Independent expert's report

10. Expert interviews named comparators and any relevant persons

11. Expert submits report to parties and tribunal

12. Written questions submitted and answered

Stage 3 equal value hearing

13. Is the claimant's and comparator's work found by the tribunal to be of equal value?   Yes   No ⟶ Claim fails

14. Is difference in pay due to a material factor other than the difference in sex?   No   Yes ⟶ Claim fails

Claim succeeds

Appendix 2: Indicative timetable

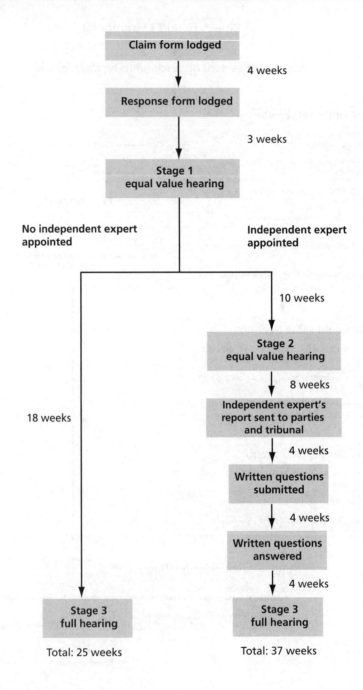

8 Material factor defence

Preliminary issues

'Material' factor

Taint of sex discrimination

Showing objective justification

Specific material factors

If a woman has shown that she is engaged on 'like work', 'work rated as **8.1** equivalent' or 'work of equal value' to that of an appropriate male comparator, then it is presumed that any difference between her salary and that of her comparator is due to the difference of sex. In the absence of a successful 'defence' on the part of the employer, this will lead to the woman's reaping the benefit of the sex equality clause deemed to be included in her contract of employment by S.66 of the Equality Act 2010 (EqA), which will modify her contractual terms so that they are in line with those of her comparator.

The employer's 'defence' is found in S.69 EqA. Under that provision, a sex equality clause will have no effect if the employer can show that the difference in pay is due to a material factor, reliance on which does not involve direct or unjustified indirect discrimination. As seen below under 'Preliminary issues', the wording of S.69 EqA is considerably different to that of its predecessor, S.1(3) EqPA. However, the substance of the provision remains the same, as S.69 in effect codifies the case law under S.1(3). Essentially, the employer, in raising a material factor 'defence', is saying: 'I know that the work of the woman and the work of her comparator are of equal value in terms of demands, skill, etc, but the man is paid more for a particular reason and that reason has nothing to do with the fact that the claimant is a woman or the comparator a man.'

In Glasgow City Council and ors v Marshall and ors 2000 ICR 196, HL, Lord **8.2** Nicholls stated that the material factor defence will succeed if the employer can show that the factor put forward as the reason for the pay differential at issue is:

- genuine and not a sham or pretence

- a material factor – i.e. is significant and relevant and caused the variation

- not due to sex discrimination, whether direct or indirect, and

- a material difference – i.e. a significant and relevant difference between the woman's case and the man's case.

227

8.3 The prevailing view (which has survived intact despite recent case law calling it into question) is that an employer who can point to a valid material factor explaining a pay differential that does not involve treating the claimant less favourably because of her sex will, in the absence of any suggestion of indirect sex discrimination, successfully bring an end to the equal pay claim: the material explanation for the differential will suffice, and there will be no need for the employer to justify his actions any further in order to avoid equal pay liability. However, where there is evidence that the material factor, or indeed the employer's pay practice generally, is in some way 'tainted' by indirect sex discrimination – for example, where statistics demonstrate that the pay practice has a disparate adverse impact on women when compared with men – the defence will not succeed unless the employer can convince the tribunal that his actions were 'objectively justified' as a proportionate means of achieving a legitimate aim.

In this chapter we explore the material factor defence in detail. We start by looking at a number of general issues, including the nature of the changes introduced by the EqA. We then examine the wording of the S.69 EqA material factor provision; what the phrase 'material factor' actually means; the circumstances in which such a factor might be 'sex-tainted' and thus require 'objective justification'; and how such justification might be demonstrated. Finally, drawing it all together, we examine the case law relating to a number of specific material factors that employers have sought to rely upon, including 'market forces', 'length of service' and 'pay protection'.

8.4 Preliminary issues

Before examining the material factor defence in detail, there are three preliminary issues of general application that need to be considered: the nature of the changes introduced by the EqA; when objective justification is required; and who, claimant or respondent, bears the burden of proving what before the tribunal. These last two issues go to the heart of how the defence works.

8.5 New statutory language

Section 1(3) EqPA, which has now been repealed, provided that no liability would arise from a difference in contractual terms between the claimant and his or her comparator that was 'genuinely due to a material factor which [was] not the difference of sex'. This wording is substantially different to that now used in S.69 EqA but despite this the defence itself has been more or less replicated in S.69, with some elaboration incorporating well-established case law.

In effect, S.69 EqA codifies the clarification of S.1(3) EqPA provided by Lord Nicholls in Glasgow City Council and ors v Marshall 2000 ICR 196, HL. In that case His Lordship pointed out that the S.1(3) requirement that the material

228

factor be something other than 'the difference of sex' did more than simply exclude gender from the list of potential differentiating factors that an employer may put forward. In fact, 'not the difference of sex' required the absence of direct discrimination and unjustified indirect discrimination.

This clarification – that a material factor must be free of both forms of **8.6** discrimination – is now clearly set out in the wording of S.69(1) EqA, which provides that:

> 'The sex equality clause in A's terms has no effect in relation to a difference between A's terms and B's terms if the responsible person shows that the difference is because of a material factor reliance on which:
>
> (a) does not involve treating A less favourably because of A's sex than the responsible person treats B, and
>
> (b) if the factor is within [S.69(2)], is a proportionate means of achieving a legitimate aim.'

The first limb above clearly covers direct discrimination. The second limb refers to S.69(2), which states that: 'A factor is within this subsection if A shows that, as a result of the factor, A and persons of the same sex doing work equal to A's are put at a particular disadvantage when compared with persons of the opposite sex doing work equal to A's'. This adopts the definition of indirect discrimination that has applied in UK discrimination law for a number of years and is now found in S.19 EqA.

It is striking that S.69(1) does not mention 'an employer' putting forward a **8.7** material factor, but instead refers to 'a responsible person'. This a partly a reflection of the more neutral statutory language adopted in the EqA, but is also attributable to the fact that S.66 can operate to imply a sex equality clause into the contract of an employee or an office holder: a 'responsible person' in the context of S.69 is either an employer or the person responsible for paying remuneration in respect of a public or private office – S.80(4).

A further noticeable difference between the S.69 EqA formulation of the material factor defence and that previously found in S.1(3) EqPA is the omission of the word 'genuinely' – thus, what was known as the 'genuine material factor defence' under the EqPA ought henceforth to be known simply as the 'material factor defence', and we must bid goodbye to the acronym 'GMF'. However, as will become apparent in the course of this chapter, this is a purely cosmetic change which makes no difference to the substance of the defence (see, in particular, 'Requirement of genuineness' below).

Finally, S.69(3) EqA makes explicit something that had previously only been **8.8** stated by the courts – that 'the long-term objective of reducing inequality between men's and women's terms of work is always to be regarded as a legitimate aim'. In Redcar and Cleveland Borough Council v Bainbridge and ors and another case; Middlesbrough Borough Council v Surtees and ors 2009 ICR 133, CA, an employer which had undertaken an equal pay review sought to implement a new 'equality-proofed' pay structure, offering pay protection to the (predominantly male) employees who would have their pay reduced under the new structure. Although this had the effect of perpetuating – albeit temporarily – past discrimination, the Court of Appeal held that phasing out discrimination by 'cushioning the blow' of sudden pay cuts may be a legitimate objective. However, the employer in the Bainbridge case had failed to consider the continuing discriminatory impact of the arrangements, and so could not establish that its arrangements were proportionate. Thus, simply because S.69(3) expressly recognises that phasing out discrimination is a legitimate aim, this does not override the further requirement in S.69(1)(b) of showing that the material factor relied upon by the employer to justify indirect discrimination was a 'proportionate means of achieving that aim'.

Note that the material factor defence in S.69(1) only applies in respect of the sex equality clause that is implied into contracts of employees and office holders by virtue of S.66 EqA. The material factor defence that applies in respect of the sex equality rule that S.67 implies into occupational pension schemes is found in S.69(4). This provides: 'A sex equality rule has no effect in relation to a difference between A and B in the effect of a relevant matter if the trustees or managers of the scheme in question show that the difference is because of a material factor which is not the difference of sex.'

8.9 Objective justification not always required
One of the most important equal pay questions that has arisen in recent years is whether an employer must *always* show objective justification for its actions whenever a woman is paid less than a man on equal work, or whether such justification is only required where evidence suggests that the employer's material factor explanation for the pay differential, or the employer's pay practice generally, is 'tainted' with sex discrimination. Why is this important? As discussed under '"Material" factor – meaning of "material"' below, a factor relied upon by the employer can be 'material' for the purposes of S.69 EqA regardless of whether it is actually a 'good' reason for a pay differential. Clearly, this presents a far easier hurdle than that of having to show that the pay differential is objectively justified as a 'proportionate means of achieving a legitimate aim'.

Thankfully for employers, it is generally accepted – as stated in the introduction to this chapter – that an employer who can explain a pay differential with reference to a material factor untainted by sex discrimination will have a valid defence to an equal pay claim; it will not, in addition, need to show objective justification for the differential. This was certainly the view taken by the House of Lords in Strathclyde Regional Council and ors v Wallace and ors 1998 ICR

205, HL, and Glasgow City Council and ors v Marshall 2000 ICR 196, HL. In the Strathclyde case, Lord Browne-Wilkinson stated: '[T]he only circumstances in which questions of "justification" can arise are those in which the employer is relying on a factor which is sexually discriminatory... Provided that there is no element of sexual discrimination the employer establishes a [material factor] defence by identifying the factors which he alleges have caused the disparity, proving that those factors are genuine and proving further that they were causally relevant to the disparity and pay complained of.'

Their Lordships' approach was queried by the EAT, however, in Sharp v **8.10** Caledonia Group Services Ltd 2006 ICR 218, EAT. There, the Appeal Tribunal was of the view that the European Court of Justice had provided clear guidelines in Brunnhofer v Bank der österreichischen Postsparkasse AG 2001 IRLR 571, ECJ, as to the need for objective justification in *all* cases where like work, work rated as equivalent or work of equal value has been demonstrated in relation to an incidence of unequal pay. In so far as there is a conflict between the ECJ decision in Brunnhofer and earlier UK decisions, the EAT continued, the ECJ's decision must be followed.

Nevertheless, more recently a number of appellate decisions – including Villalba v Merrill Lynch and Co Inc and ors 2007 ICR 469, EAT, and Armstrong and ors v Newcastle upon Tyne Hospital Trust 2006 IRLR 124, CA – have restated the pre-Sharp position. In Villalba, Mr Justice Elias, then President of the EAT, reviewed the breadth of European and UK case law on the subject before concluding that a difference in pay does not have to be objectively justified in every equal pay case. In Elias P's view, the elimination of discrimination on the ground of sex does not require objective justification for a difference in pay where the employer has satisfactorily explained the pay differential with reference to a material factor, and where there is no independent evidence of any kind to show that sex has had any influence on that differential. If justification were required in such circumstances, he explained, the EqPA would be concerned with 'fair pay' and not simply with sex discrimination.

The wording of S.69 EqA reflects the comprehensive rejection of the EAT's **8.11** decision in Sharp, since objective justification – i.e. showing that the factor is a proportionate means of achieving a legitimate aim – is only required where the factor entails indirect sex discrimination – S.69(1)(b) and (2) EqA (see further under 'Taint of sex discrimination' and 'Showing objective justification' below).

Burden of proof
8.12

Article 19 of the recast Equal Treatment Directive (No.2006/54), which covers equal pay, provides that: 'Member States shall take such measures as are necessary, in accordance with their national judicial systems, to ensure that, when persons who consider themselves wronged because the principle of equal treatment has not been applied to them establish, before a court or other competent authority, facts from which it may be presumed that there has been direct or indirect discrimination, it shall be for the respondent to prove that there has been no breach of the principle of equal treatment.' Below, we consider how this applies to the EqA.

8.13 **Material factor – burden on employer.** Article 19 of the recast Directive does not require an employer, at the outset of a discrimination claim, to prove that the complainant has not suffered discrimination. It does, however, require the burden of proof to shift to the employer once facts are established from which it might be presumed, unless the contrary is proven, that discrimination has occurred. This, in effect, is precisely what the equal pay provisions in the EqA require. Under that Act, a rebuttable presumption arises that a claimant is entitled to parity with her higher-paid male comparator if she can establish that he is engaged in like work, work rated as equivalent or work of equal value to hers. Under S.69 the burden then falls on the employer to rebut this presumption by showing three things: first, that there is a material factor; secondly, that reliance on that material factor does not involve subjecting the claimant to direct sex discrimination; and thirdly, if the factor is tainted by indirect sex discrimination, that reliance on the factor is objectively justified.

8.14 **Showing indirect discrimination – burden on employee.** Under 'Objective justification not always required' above, we explained that an employer will only be required to objectively justify a pay differential if the tribunal is satisfied that the employer's pay practice is 'tainted' with indirect sex discrimination. The question thus arises whether the employer bears the burden of showing that there is no sex taint, or the employee bears the burden of showing that there is.

Case law under S.1(3) EqPA suggested that where an employer showed a material factor accounting for a difference in pay that was not directly discriminatory, the claimant's complaint could only progress if she could show that the material factor itself, or the employer's pay practice generally, was tainted by indirect sex discrimination. The leading case on the burden of proof in this regard is Nelson v Carillion Services Ltd 2003 ICR 1256, CA. There, N's equal pay claim had failed before an employment tribunal and the EAT as a result of CS Ltd's successful material factor explanation: that N's male comparator had joined the company upon the transfer of an undertaking, meaning that his higher pay was protected by the Transfer of Undertakings (Protection of Employment) Regulations 1981 SI 1981/1794 (now SI 2006/246). Before the tribunal, N had attempted to show that her employer's pay practice was tainted by indirect sex discrimination, in that a higher proportion of men than women in the company benefited from that protection. However, the tribunal had concluded that the statistics put forward by N were not sufficient to establish 'sex taint'. On appeal to the Court of Appeal, N argued that the tribunal had erred in placing the burden on her to prove, on the balance of probabilities, that the company's pay practice was tainted by indirect sex discrimination. Rather, it should have been for the employer to show that its practice was not so tainted. The Court of Appeal, however, upheld the tribunal's decision. In doing so, it noted that the ECJ in Enderby v Frenchay Health Authority and anor 1994 ICR 112, ECJ, had established that the burden of proving 'indirect' pay discrimination lies initially on the employee: the employee must establish a 'prima facie' case of indirect discrimination by pointing to statistics which are both significant and valid suggesting that women as a group are being treated less favourably than men.

Further support for this position was given by Mr Justice Elias in Villalba v **8.15** Merrill Lynch and Co Inc and ors 2007 ICR 469, EAT. There, the claimant argued that the burden of showing that an employer's pay practice was tainted by indirect discrimination – a burden not set out in S.1(3) EqPA – 'imposed an additional hurdle on women making equal pay claims'. Elias P responded: 'We confess that we find that a curious use of language. If I make a claim for breach of contract, I must adduce evidence sufficient to show that a contract exists but it would be odd to describe this as an additional hurdle. Similarly here; if I make a claim of sex discrimination, I must adduce evidence sufficient to establish a prima facie case for saying that I have been subject to such discrimination. This is not some artificial hurdle; it is simply what is involved in establishing the claim. To dispense with this is to change the nature of the claim entirely.'

The case law above is now reflected in the wording of S.69(2) EqA, which states: 'A factor is within this subsection [and therefore the S.69(1)(b) objective justification test applies] if *A shows* that, as a result of the factor, A and persons of the same sex doing work equal to A's are put at a particular disadvantage when compared with persons of the opposite sex doing work equal to A's' (our stress). It must therefore fall to a claimant to establish 'particular disadvantage' or, to put it another way, to show a prima facie case of indirect discrimination.

Rebutting presumption of sex taint – burden on employer. The wording of **8.16** S.69 EqA would seem to suggest that once an employee has shown a prima facie case of indirect discrimination, the burden immediately shifts to the employer to show objective justification. However, it is important not to ignore a somewhat confusing line of case law under the EqPA which established that even where an equal pay claimant succeeded in showing that the employer's material factor or pay practice had a disparate adverse impact on women, this did not *automatically* mean that the employer was obliged to objectively justify the pay differential in question. Rather, before the issue of justification arose, the employer had an opportunity to argue that, regardless of the evidence adduced by the claimant, there was, in reality, no taint of indirect discrimination, or to put it another way, the employer could rebut the presumption of

233

discrimination that arose from a statistical disparity. If the employer could succeed in this endeavour, the equal pay claim would fail.

The Court of Appeal addressed the issue in Redcar and Cleveland Borough Council v Bainbridge and ors and another case; Middlesbrough Borough Council v Surtees and ors 2009 ICR 133, CA. There, Lord Justice Mummery explained that the Court of Appeal's decision in Armstrong and ors v Newcastle upon Tyne NHS Hospital Trust 2006 IRLR 124, CA, 'is authority for the proposition that, merely because it has been shown that the pay arrangements have a disparate adverse effect on women, it does not necessarily follow that the employer will have to show objective justification. Even though there is evidence of disparate adverse impact, it is still open to the employer to satisfy the tribunal that the pay differential was not due to the difference of sex, directly, or indirectly, or was not tainted by sex. If he does so, there is no obligation to justify.'

8.17 However, as the EAT (again Mr Justice Elias) had stated when the Surtees case came before it (Middlesbrough Borough Council v Surtees and ors 2007 ICR 1644, EAT), where a tribunal has decided that women as a group are adversely affected by a pay practice it will be difficult in practical terms for the employer to show that the pay disparity between the claimant and her male comparator was not, in reality, related to the difference in sex. Clearly, in the vast majority of cases where a claimant shows that women as a group are adversely affected with regard to pay, objective justification of the pay disparities will be required. Nevertheless, Elias P offered some thoughts as to the limited circumstances in which an employer might show that, regardless of a disparate adverse impact evidenced by statistics, there is in fact no 'sex taint': 'For example, it may be shown that a particular group of workers (group A) has always been paid less than another group (group B) even although the jobs are of equal value. If both groups were originally predominantly male, but group B has over time become mainly female (such as might well be the case with lawyers or academics, at least in certain fields), a tribunal might readily be satisfied that despite the current adverse effect, there is no proper basis for inferring prima facie discrimination, whether based on historical stereotyping or otherwise. The factors leading to the difference in pay may be long established but the history suggests that they do not have their roots in sex discrimination but have operated independently of the sex of the job holders.'

Mr Justice Elias's examples (above) were recently endorsed by 'obiter' (i.e. non-binding) comments of Lady Justice Smith in Gibson and ors v Sheffield City Council 2010 ICR 708, CA, where she observed that as a result of the Court of Appeal's decision in Armstrong and ors v Newcastle upon Tyne Hospital Trust 2006 IRLR 124, CA, an employer will avoid the need for objective justification if it can show that, although the pay practice in question has a statistically adverse impact on women, it is not sex-tainted. Having considered the

234

relationship between S.1(3) EqPA and the indirect discrimination provisions then found in S.1(1)(b) of the Sex Discrimination Act 1975 (now S.19 EqA), Smith LJ concluded that whether the alleged indirect discrimination arises in the field of pay or non-pay, it is always open to a defendant to demonstrate that, although the practice appears to put women at a particular disadvantage, in fact the apparent disadvantage has arisen because of factors wholly unrelated to gender.

Of course, the case law above was decided under S.1(3) EqPA, which never **8.18** explicitly mentioned indirect discrimination. By way of contrast, the material factor defence in S.69 EqA expressly raises the prospect of the material factor being tainted by indirect discrimination – see under 'Showing indirect discrimination – burden on employee' above. The question therefore arises as to whether the Armstrong decision can still be relied upon in respect of claims under the EqA.

At first glance, the language of S.69(1)(b) and (2) suggests that Armstrong has been reversed by the EqA and objective justification will always be required whenever a disparate impact has been established. In accordance with these provisions, if a claimant establishes that she and others of her sex who are performing equal work are, as a result of the material factor relied on by the employer, placed at a particular disadvantage when compared to persons of the opposite sex doing equal work (S.69(2)), then the employer *must* provide objective justification under S.69(1)(b). However, it is important to note that the EqA refers to 'particular disadvantage', whereas the gist of the Armstrong decision is that 'disparate adverse impact' will not always lead to the employer having to provide justification. Smith LJ's analysis of Armstrong in the Gibson case (above) appears to suggest that disparate adverse impact will not automatically lead to a conclusion of indirect discrimination (thus requiring justification) if the disparity in pay is due to reasons wholly unrelated to sex. Could it be the case, therefore, that showing that a material factor places a claimant at a particular disadvantage involves demonstrating both a disparate adverse impact *and* a reason for that disadvantage which is in some way related to sex?

The competing arguments in response to this question have their respective **8.19** strengths. On the one hand, introducing a 'reason why' question into a test for indirect discrimination seems to muddy the waters between direct and indirect discrimination. On the other hand, the language of S.69(2) suggests that objective justification will only be required where 'as a result of' the material factor, the claimant is placed at a particular disadvantage. This seems to leave some scope for arguing that the disadvantage is not a result of the material factor, but of some other historical, non-discriminatory factor of the type identified by Elias P in Surtees (above). There is some tacit support for the latter view in the Equality and Human Rights Commission's 'Code of Practice on

Equal Pay'. At para 85 it notes that 'statistical analysis... is one way of showing disproportionate adverse impact but it is not the only way'. Para 86 goes on to state that 'where the disadvantaged group is predominately women, and the group of advantaged comparators is predominantly men, it will be difficult for the employer to *prove an absence of sex discrimination*' (our stress). Proving an absence of sex discrimination is not the same as offering objective justification for indirect discrimination. Thus, the Code implicitly endorses the view that an employer may, at least in theory, be able to avoid having to provide justification for disparate impact shown by statistics alone, although this is likely to be very difficult to do in practice.

8.20 **Objective justification – burden on employer.** In Bilka-Kaufhaus GmbH v Weber von Hartz 1987 ICR 110, ECJ, the European Court ruled that where a pay practice is indirectly discriminatory, it is necessary for the employer to show objective justification for it in order to avoid liability. According to the ECJ, objective justification will only be made out if the employer establishes that the pay practice in question corresponds to a real need on the part of the business and that it is both appropriate and necessary for achieving that objective.

This decision is reflected by S.69(1)(b) EqA, which requires the employer to show – once the employee has established that the material factor puts her and others of her sex doing equal work at a particular disadvantage – that reliance on the factor is 'a proportionate means of achieving a legitimate aim'.

8.21 'Material' factor

A material factor defence under S.69 EqA will operate to prevent a sex equality clause from applying only if the employer can show that the variation between the claimant's contract and the comparator's contract is due to a factor that is 'material' and that reliance on that factor is neither direct sex discrimination nor unjustified indirect sex discrimination. So if, for example, an employer maintains that the comparator is being paid more than the claimant because the comparator is more flexible in the way he can perform the role, the employer will have to demonstrate not only that the comparator actually is more flexible, but also that flexibility is relevant and significant to the job in question.

In this section we consider the meaning of the word 'material' in this context. Before doing so, however, it is necessary to discuss the significance, if any, of the omission of the word 'genuine' from the S.69 defence.

8.22 Requirement of 'genuineness'

For those familiar with the old provisions under the EqPA, one of the most difficult changes to get used to is the dropping of the word 'genuine' from the material factor defence in S.69 EqA. Whereas previously the acronym GMF

236

(standing for 'genuine material factor') was ubiquitous in equal pay cases, we must now get used to the plain and simple 'material factor'.

However, the significance of this change is not as great as it might first appear – indeed, the Government, when introducing the 2010 Act, was of the view that the word 'genuine' added nothing to the defence. In Strathclyde Regional Council and ors v Wallace and ors 1998 ICR 205, HL, it was held that the word 'genuine' in S.1(3) EqPA meant the employer must satisfy the tribunal that the relevant factor is not a sham or a pretence. It would be absurd to suggest that the removal of the word means that tribunals will start to accept material factors that are not the genuine cause of a difference of treatment. To a large extent, the requirement of genuineness was part and parcel of the need for the factor to be 'material', in that it required the factor to be causally relevant to a variation in pay. The removal of the word 'genuine' can therefore be viewed in the context of simply promoting one of the key goals of the EqA – namely, to draft discrimination and equality law in such a way that it can be understood by non-lawyers.

It should also be noted that the need for the employer to satisfy the tribunal **8.23** that the relevant factor is not a sham or pretence was called into question by the President of the EAT, Mr Justice Underhill, in Bury Metropolitan Borough Council v Hamilton and ors; Sunderland City Council v Brennan and ors 2011 IRLR 358, EAT. According to Underhill P, it was not at all helpful that authorities such as Hartlepool Borough Council and anor v Dolphin and ors 2009 IRLR 168, EAT, suggested that a tribunal should consider whether the employer's explanation was dishonest or designed to conceal a different (presumably discriminatory) explanation for the difference in treatment. All that was required at the first stage of S.1(3) EqPA was for the employer to give a factual explanation, good or bad, as to how the state of affairs complained of came about. With this in mind, the EAT held that the employer did provide an explanation for the difference in treatment, i.e. that the comparators' jobs were suitable for bonuses and the claimants' jobs were not. The tribunals had been wrong to find this explanation a sham on the basis that it was no longer operative by the time of the claims. The EAT's caution against giving undue – and, in its view, misleading – attention to the word 'genuine' in S.1(3) of the 1970 Act seems entirely warranted now that the word 'genuine' has been removed by the 2010 Act, and is consistent with our suggestion above that the requirement of genuineness was part and parcel of the need for the factor to be causally relevant to a variation in pay.

As the EAT pointed out in the Bury case, few employers fail to provide an explanation for the difference in treatment – the greater challenge is showing that the explanatory material factor was not tainted by sex discrimination – see 'Taint of sex discrimination' below.

8.24 **Meaning of 'material'**

Section 69 EqA does not offer much elaboration of what is meant by 'material' in the context of the material factor defence. S.69(6) states, somewhat unhelpfully, that a factor will only be material if it is a 'material difference between A's case and B's case'. However, greater elaboration has been offered by the courts. In Rainey v Greater Glasgow Health Board 1987 ICR 129, HL, Lord Keith stated that: 'The difference [i.e. the factor explaining the pay differential] must be "material", which I would construe as meaning "significant and relevant".' What becomes clear from a scrutiny of their Lordships' decision in Rainey is that factors which can be regarded as being 'significant and relevant' go well beyond the personal qualities of the respective claimant and comparator (such as skill, experience or training) and can embrace extrinsic matters such as administrative considerations affecting the efficient operation of the employer's business or other activity.

The Rainey case concerned a female prosthetist who was recruited directly into the NHS, as a result of which she was paid NHS rates. Her comparator, a male prosthetist recruited from private practice, was permitted to retain the pay rates he enjoyed as a private practitioner. The employer contended that it was necessary to preserve the higher rates of pay of all private practitioners in order to attract a sufficient number of qualified recruits quickly enough to enable a new prosthetic service to be established. It therefore argued that market forces lay behind the different rates of pay accorded to the claimant and her comparator. This argument was accepted by the House of Lords, which held that the employer had shown that the variation in pay was genuinely caused by a material factor other than sex.

8.25 It is important to remember that in order to be 'material' (or 'significant and relevant', to use Lord Keith's phrase), the factor relied upon has to explain the difference between the particular woman's pay and the particular man's pay. In other words, simply because a factor is potentially capable of constituting a material factor for the purposes of S.69 EqA does not mean that it will always be sufficient: it must be of actual significance and relevance to the particular case. Tribunals will be expected to scrutinise any factor advanced by the employer in order to satisfy themselves that, even if it is in no way discriminatory, the factor sufficiently explains the variation between the claimant's and comparator's contracts.

That said, it seems that the employer does not have to show that the material factor amounts to a 'good' or 'objective' reason for the pay disparity in order for the factor to be regarded as material. In Glasgow City Council and ors v Marshall and ors 2000 ICR 196, HL, Lord Nicholls raised the question of what yardstick is to be used in measuring 'materiality, or significance and relevance', and answered that although the factor must have been the cause of the pay disparity, it need not be material in a justificatory sense. As explained in 'Preliminary

238

issues – objective justification not always required' above, an employer will sometimes be required to show justification for a pay differential, but only where the claimant has satisfied the tribunal that the employer's material factor or its pay practice generally is 'tainted' by indirect sex discrimination.

Relationship between material factor and assessment of equal work 8.26

There is an ongoing debate as to what kind of factors should be taken into account when considering the material factor defence. Arguably, factors relevant to the question of whether a claimant and her comparator are employed on like work, work rated as equivalent or work of equal value (for example, skills required, decision-making or physical effort) should not be taken into account when considering the S.69 defence. It would seem odd for a tribunal to find that a claimant's and a comparator's work is of equal value, only to go on to hold that the pay differential between them is genuinely due to a difference in the demands of the jobs and the skills they require. However, this is exactly what happened in the following cases (both decided under the EqPA):

● **Davies v McCartneys** 1989 ICR 705, EAT: D, a female secretary, sought pay equal to that of a man in the employer's accounts department. A tribunal rejected D's equal pay claim, finding that her comparator's higher pay was explained by a material factor – the fact that his job was more demanding than hers. On appeal, the EAT upheld the tribunal's decision. It stated that there was no limitation on the number of factors relevant to a consideration of a defence under S.1(3) EqPA (now S.69 EqA), and suggested that the same factors might be used for the purposes both of establishing whether the jobs of the claimant and comparator are of equal value and the material factor defence. In this case, 'demand' could be relevant to both the equal value assessment and the material factor defence. The EAT did, however, add the proviso that an employer could not be allowed simply to say 'I value one demand factor so highly that I pay more', unless the true reason for doing so is one that is genuine and not attributable to sex

● **Christie and ors v John E Haith Ltd** 2003 IRLR 670, EAT: C and two other female manual workers packed birdseed for JEH Ltd. They were employed in the 'packing room', dealing with the lighter part of the product range involving packages weighing up to 12kg, and were paid £4.32 per hour. The packing room employees brought equal pay claims comparing themselves with men employed in the 'bird house', who dealt with heavier packages – of up to 30kg – and were paid £4.58 per hour. The men also loaded and unloaded delivery vehicles and were required to wheel and empty rubbish trolleys. The tribunal dismissed the complaints, finding that the work of loading and unloading deliveries was more arduous and unpleasant than the packing room work. In the tribunal's view, this was a material factor accounting for the differential in pay between the bird house employees and the claimants. The claimants appealed to the EAT, arguing that the tribunal had erred in determining that the material factor which gave rise to the company's defence under S.1(3) EqPA (now S.69 EqA) had been 'the physical effort involved in loading and unloading vehicles in cold conditions', when that factor had already been taken into account in accepting that the work done by the claimants and their comparators was of equal value. The claimants argued that the effect of Davies (above) should be limited, and that a factor that has actually been taken into account in the equal value comparison should be excluded from being taken into account again in favour of the employer under the material factor defence. The approach adopted by the tribunal involved an element of 'double counting', and was wrong in principle. The EAT, however, upheld the tribunal's decision, finding no rational basis for limiting the words of S.1(3) or the principle laid down in Davies. The tribunal had made a clear finding that there was a genuine material difference accounting for the pay differential and that this was not based on the sex of the employees concerned. Accordingly, the EAT found that the tribunal had been entitled to hold that the material factor defence had been made out and that the equal pay claims could not succeed.

8.27 How many factors can be relied upon?

In Davies v McCartneys 1989 ICR 705, EAT, the Appeal Tribunal confirmed that there is no limitation on the number of factors upon which an employer is entitled to base a material factor defence. The essential requirement is for any difference between the claimant's and comparator's terms to be due to a material factor or factors.

However, where an employer relies upon more than one factor, uncertainty could arise where some of these, but not others, are found not to be 'material'. In Calder and anor v Rowntree Mackintosh Confectionery Ltd 1993 ICR 811, CA, an employer sought to rely upon two factors to explain paying a shift premium to a male employee who was required to work a rotating shift: namely, that he worked unsocial hours, and that his particular shift arrangements caused him considerable inconvenience. The claimant was able to show that one of these factors had to be discounted because it applied equally to her (i.e. she also worked unsocial hours). However, the other factor relied upon by the employer was 'material' in the sense that it was capable of explaining the difference between the claimant's and comparator's pay on a ground other than sex. But was the valid factor sufficient to defeat the equal pay claim? The Court of Appeal held that the tribunal had been entitled to conclude that it was. The variation in pay was genuinely due to, and sufficiently explained by, the fact that the comparator worked on the rotating shift, notwithstanding that some indeterminate part of his shift premium represented compensation for unsocial hours. The claimant's grievance was essentially one of unfairness – that workers on the rotating shift received compensation that included an element for working unsocial hours, whereas those on her shift also worked unsocial hours but received no such compensation. However, the Court pointed out that a tribunal's inquiry when considering the material factor defence is not directed to the fairness of an employer's system of remuneration but to whether that system is genuinely designed to differentiate between employees on some basis other than sex. In this case the tribunal had held that there was one single cause for the variation in pay – namely, the inconvenience factor resulting from the requirement to work rotating shifts – and that was a conclusion it had been entitled to reach.

Given this outcome, it was not necessary for the Court of Appeal to decide **8.28** what the position would have been had there been 'dual causation', i.e. if both factors together had been relevant in the particular case. However, the three Lords Justice of Appeal did make certain 'obiter' (i.e. non-binding) comments about this. In the views of Balcombe and Kennedy LJJ, even if the tribunal had found that the true explanation for the differential was a combination of the rotating shifts and the unsocial hours, it would not necessarily have followed that the claimant, who could show that she could comply with one of those factors, would be entitled to higher pay. Evans LJ, however, appeared to disagree. He observed: '[I]f the... tribunal had found that the variation was due to two factors... then [counsel for the claimant]'s submissions might well have persuaded me that a case for equality was made out; but I strongly suspect that in such a case there would be further findings of fact which would enable an apportionment to be made.' In the light of European case law, it is arguable that Evans LJ's approach is the correct one: had a 'dual causation' issue arisen directly for decision in Calder, it would have been necessary for the Court of Appeal to have considered the extent to which a tribunal would have been obliged to apportion different amounts of the variation between the claimant's and comparator's terms to the different factors. This issue is considered further under 'Explaining the whole differential' below.

Importance of transparency

8.29

In Handels-og Kontorfunktionaerernes Forbund i Danmark v Dansk Arbejdsgiverforening (acting for Danfoss A/S) 1991 ICR 74, ECJ, the European Court held that an employer must prove that there is no discrimination behind a pay differential where the pay system lacks transparency. Clearly, the more vague or opaque the employer's reward strategies are, the more difficult this will be to do. The importance of transparency in a pay system is illustrated by the following cases:

- **Barton v Investec Henderson Crosthwaite Securities Ltd** 2003 ICR 1205, EAT: B was employed as a media analyst by IHCS Ltd, an investment bank. In 2001 she brought an equal pay claim on the ground that H, a male colleague employed on like work, received a higher salary and better contractual benefits than her. The bank's chairman told an employment tribunal that H used to be paid the same as B, but that the latter's salary and benefits had been increased in 1999 to the highest within the organisation because of concerns that he was being head-hunted. The tribunal held that the employer had established that the difference in pay was genuinely due to a material factor that was not the difference in sex and rejected B's equal pay claim. Referring in particular to the threat of employees being head-hunted, the tribunal stated that all the increases in the comparator's pay were 'conscientious, unscientific efforts to secure the employee's services for the future by putting his benefits in line with those of other key players'. B appealed to the EAT, which overturned the tribunal's decision and remitted the case for a rehearing. In upholding the employer's material factor defence, the tribunal had (among other things) failed to take into account the lack of transparency in the employer's pay system, together with the employer's failure to respond adequately to a discrimination questionnaire which B had submitted

- **Clarke v Triton plc** ET Case No.1306157/04: C claimed equal pay with her male predecessor. The company maintained that C's comparator had been paid more because, by the time he left, he had been in the post for some years and had gained important experience. He had thus been awarded a number of merit increases on top of the normal cost of living increases. The tribunal noted that the company's argument sufficed to show the reason for the pay differential when C first took up the post in 2001. However, by the end of 2003 her performance appraisals showed that she was developing into her role. By and large, her appraisals were better than those of her predecessor, yet during the entire period up to the date of her tribunal claim she had not received a single merit increase. The company's reward strategy lacked transparency. Accordingly, in the tribunal's view, the inference of sex discrimination remained – the company had failed to persuade it on the balance of probabilities that its reward strategy was free from gender bias.

8.30　In Calder and anor v Rowntree Mackintosh Confectionery Ltd 1993 ICR 811, CA (see 'How many factors can be relied upon?' above), the claimant argued that her employer was not entitled to the benefit of the material factor defence where the lack of transparency in its pay system meant that she was unable to ascertain how much of her comparator's shift premium was paid on account of the inconvenience of working a rotating shift, and how much in respect of his having to work unsocial hours. In that case, however, the Court of Appeal decided that there was no lack of transparency because it was abundantly clear that the shift premium giving rise to the pay differential in question was payable to all employees – men and women – who worked on rotating shifts. In the words of Kennedy LJ: 'Here it is quite clear why the comparator receives his premium, and the transparency required by the decision in the Danfoss case does not mean that the employer must explain precisely how the premium figure is achieved.'

Explaining the whole differential

8.31

The point is made in Chapter 7 under 'Scope of "equal value" – must work be of precisely equal value?' that a claimant is not entitled to claim equal pay on the ground that she should be paid a certain proportion of her comparator's pay, commensurate with the proportionate value of her job vis-à-vis his. In other words, a woman is not entitled to, say, 85 per cent of her comparator's pay on the basis that a job evaluation study or investigation by an independent expert reveals that the value of her job is 85 per cent of the man's. The woman would not be regarded as being employed on like work, work rated as equivalent or work of equal value, and her equal pay claim would fail to get off the ground. However, once a woman shows that she is employed on equal work, then she is entitled to parity with her comparator to the extent that the employer is unable to account for the whole of the pay differential in terms of a material factor other than sex. So, it seems, it will not be sufficient for the factor or factors relied upon by the employer to account for some but not all of the variation between the claimant's and comparator's contractual terms.

This proposition is supported by the ECJ's decision in Enderby v Frenchay Health Authority and anor 1994 ICR 112, ECJ. In that case the question arose whether a pay differential could be 'justified' by the fact that part of that differential was attributable to a need to attract sufficient numbers of qualified employees doing the comparators' jobs by offering them higher salaries. The ECJ stated that '[I]f... the national court has been able to determine precisely what proportion of the increase in pay is attributable to market forces, it must necessarily accept that the pay differential is objectively justified to the extent of that proportion.' It went on to say that 'if that is not the case, it is for the national court to assess whether the role of market forces in determining the rate of pay was sufficiently significant to provide objective justification for part or all of the difference'.

The Enderby case was concerned with 'justifying' the whole differential, as opposed to 'explaining' the whole differential with reference to a material factor. However, there seems to be no reason why the same logic would not apply to both. Assuming that it does, the process that tribunals have to adopt can be broken down into two stages. The first requires the tribunal to consider whether all the difference in pay is explained by the material factor advanced. If not, the second stage requires it to consider what proportion of the differential is so explained. The difficulty is what a tribunal should then do if it decides that only a proportion of the differential is explained. It seems that the next logical step (though this was not actually stated by the ECJ in Enderby) would be to determine the proportion attributable to the valid defence and then award the

8.32

woman equal pay, reduced by the amount attributable to the material factor. This is the approach that was adopted by the tribunal in the following case:

- **MacDougall v Taggarts Motor Group Ltd** ET Case No.S/5598/94: M, a female management accountant employed by a motor company at its Glasgow dealership, claimed equal pay on the basis of like work with S, whose pay was £8,000 more than hers. A tribunal found that there was no significant difference between M and S in terms of qualifications, experience or workload. The only difference was that S could drive but M could not. This limited her ability to manage more than one dealership in the employer's group at any one time and so, to some extent, limited her flexibility as a dealership accountant. That factor, according to the tribunal, was not of sufficient practical importance to preclude M being regarded as employed on like work with S. Nor, with regard to the employer's material factor defence, was it sufficient to explain in full the £8,000 pay difference. In the tribunal's view, S's ability to drive explained the salary difference to the extent of around £1,000. The remainder of the difference was not based on any other material factor and was therefore presumed to arise because of the difference of sex.

8.33 Note that Mr Justice Elias seemed to accept the principle behind making a 'proportionate award' in respect of partial explanation/justification in Cumbria County Council v Dow and ors (No.1) 2008 IRLR 91, EAT. That case considered the legitimacy of productivity bonuses paid to predominantly male road sweepers, among others, but denied to the predominantly female claimants, who had established a valid equal pay comparison with the road sweepers. The tribunal had rejected the argument that the productivity scheme was a genuine material factor justifying the difference in pay, finding that there was only a tenuous link between the road sweepers' performance and their receipt of a bonus payment. The EAT upheld that decision on appeal, but Elias P acknowledged the force of the employer's arguments. Among other things, Elias P noted that the employer 'makes the legitimate point that there is no justice in the claimants obtaining the same pay as the road worker comparators in circumstances where the latter have through their own efforts made at least some productivity gains. The problem is that the employer was attempting to justify the whole of the differential on productivity grounds. *It may very well be that it would in principle be open to an employer to show that even if the full differential could not be justified on a productivity basis, a certain proportion of it could be, just as with market forces.* That might have justified differentiating between the road workers and the other comparators. However, that possible partial justification was not argued in this case, and the question will have to await another day' (our stress).

Mr Justice Elias has therefore given some support to the possibility of a proportionate pay award being made, but does not take us any further in terms of working out how such an award should be calculated. Nonetheless, an employer defending an equal pay claim ought to be aware of the possibility of such an award being made, and could feasibly argue partial explanation/justification in the alternative in case the tribunal does not accept the genuine material factor defence in its entirety.

Evaporation of historical material factor
8.34

In the discussion under 'Meaning of "material"' above, we explained that, for an employer to rely on a material factor, the factor in question must be 'the cause of the pay disparity' – Glasgow City Council and ors v Marshall and ors 2000 ICR 196, HL. But for how long can a factor that originally caused a pay disparity between a man and a woman be considered relevant? Over the years, a number of decisions have suggested that factors which genuinely triggered a variation between a claimant's and a comparator's contracts cannot amount to a material factor if they are no longer operative.

In Post Office v Page EAT 554/87 P was one of 24 employees appointed to a newly created job grade. She received less pay than some male appointees, and a year later brought an equal pay claim. The employer conceded that P was employed on 'like work' with the men, but argued that the difference in salary was due to the fact that the men, at the time of appointment, had 'direct production experience', whereas P did not. The tribunal found that although the employer had a defence at the time of appointment, this had ceased to be a defence by the time of P's equal pay claim because she had become at least as capable as any of the men. It therefore upheld her claim. On appeal, the EAT noted that the employer was afforded strong support by the earlier case of Avon and Somerset Police Authority v Emery 1981 ICR 229, EAT, where it was held that an employer's material factor defence was not invalidated where the factor initially giving rise to a pay differential had ceased to be operative. Nevertheless, the EAT in the Page case upheld the tribunal's decision that P was entitled to equal pay. It had been for the tribunal to decide, having looked at all the circumstances, whether what was a material difference other than sex at the time of recruitment continued to be so at a later date.

The move away from the EAT's position in the Emery case was effectively **8.35** confirmed by the Court of Appeal in Benveniste v University of Southampton 1989 ICR 617, CA. In that case B, who was recruited as a mathematics lecturer by the University in 1981, was paid less than the 'normal' rate as the University was subject to severe financial constraints at that time. By the end of 1981 the financial pressures had eased and over the next four years B was given incremental increases in salary. However, she remained dissatisfied with the progress she was making. Eventually, following her dismissal, she complained to a tribunal, alleging that her employer had been in breach of the EqPA. The tribunal rejected her complaint, accepting the University's material factor defence. Unlike her male comparators, B had been taken on at a time when the

245

University was enduring severe financial pressures. Although these constraints no longer applied after 1981, the material difference between her case and those of her comparators persisted. In the tribunal's view, B's case was analogous to 'red circle' cases – where the preservation of employees' pay rates, despite subsequent changes to their work, has been held to give rise to a material factor defence (see 'Specific material factors – pay protection' below).

The EAT upheld the tribunal's decision, but the Court of Appeal overturned it. The Court held that the University was unable to rely upon the defence because the material difference between the claimant's and the comparator's cases – the 1981 financial constraints – had evaporated soon after B's appointment. This was not the same as 'red-circling' cases, which, Lord Justice Neill observed, were ones 'where certain individual employees have been treated as falling into a special or different category because on humane grounds their salaries have been protected at a higher rate over a period. They remain protected employees. In the present case, however, once it is accepted that the financial constraints came to an end... the special factors which justify the lower salary disappear.'

8.36   All that leads us to the recent deluge of local authority equal pay claims, in which 'historical' material factors have often been put forward by employers to defend long-standing pay inequalities. One case in which the defence was successful was Paterson and ors v London Borough of Islington and ors EAT 0347/03 where male assistant caretakers were paid more than female cleaners and kitchen staff as a result of a historical bonus scheme, which was initiated in 1968. The scheme had been introduced as an attempt to improve performance, and was originally operated under close management supervision so that a bonus was only paid if the caretakers' performance was at an acceptable standard. However, the supervision, and indeed the caretakers' level of performance, had declined over the years but the bonus payments continued to be made as a matter of course and were eventually consolidated into normal earnings.

The employer put all this forward as a material factor accounting for the difference in pay between the comparators and the claimants (it being assumed for preliminary purposes that they were employed on work rated as equivalent). The claimants' objection was that, although the performance bonus would have been a valid material factor at the time it was introduced, now that supervision and performance were in decline it was no longer operative: by 1995 it could no longer be said that the difference in the pay rates was due to a material factor which was untainted by sex discrimination. The tribunal found in favour of the employer. In its view, the caretakers' extra pay was not only originally due to a material factor unrelated to sex, but had at all times remained so. The objective of the bonus in question was 'securing and maintaining high levels of performance and standards in the cleaning work of Assistant Caretakers', and the lapse in supervision during the post-1995 period

246

had not caused this objective to cease. On appeal, the EAT noted that Lord Nicholls' speech in Marshall (above) showed that the material factor relied upon by an employer must be the cause of the pay disparity. Furthermore, the EAT went on to state, 'the cause for the variation in pay must continue throughout the relevant period'. Thus, the suggestion was that if the bonus scheme and the performance standards attached to it had, in fact, fallen into disuse by the time the equal pay claims were brought, the Council would no longer have been able to rely on it as a material factor explaining the pay differential. However, given that the tribunal had found, as a matter of fact, that the bonus scheme was still material 30 years after its introduction, the EAT would not disturb its decision. Accordingly, the claimants' appeal was dismissed.

Local authority employers have had more difficulty, however, where the link **8.37** between bonus and incentive schemes and productivity has undeniably been severed. In Hartlepool Borough Council and anor v Dolphin and ors 2009 IRLR 168, EAT, for example, the female claimants worked for the Council in various roles, including that of care assistant and office cleaner. Unlike their male comparators (joiners, electricians, road sweepers, etc), they did not receive productivity bonuses. The Council explained that the productivity bonuses for the male-comparator roles had arisen through negotiations with trade unions in the 1970s. The tribunal found, however, that the schemes had been introduced as a result of Government pay policy, which had prevented the Council from providing pay increases to strong union-based employees except under the guise of incentive schemes. The bonuses under these schemes had no particular link with productivity, and were paid for simply turning up for work or for carrying out non-productive work, thus hardly providing any kind of incentive. Furthermore, there was little evidence of assessment and review of the schemes, and no consideration had been given as to whether any of the bonuses could have been applied to the claimants. For these reasons, the tribunal concluded that the bonus schemes were effectively a sham and could not amount to a material factor. On appeal, the EAT upheld the tribunal's decision. Furthermore, in the light of Benveniste v University of Southampton (above), the EAT stated: '[A]n explanation [for the existence of the bonus schemes] based on the history of pay freezes in the 1970s would not give a genuine reason for the continued reliance upon them in 2004.' Even if the bonuses had not been discriminatory in the 1970s, they might well have become so at a later date.

The Dolphin case came in for some criticism from the President of the EAT, Mr Justice Underhill, in Bury Metropolitan Borough Council v Hamilton and ors; Sunderland City Council v Brennan and ors 2011 IRLR 358, EAT, a conjoined appeal from two separate cases in which the tribunals had found that local authority bonus schemes, dating as far back as the 1970s, were genuine when originally introduced: they increased productivity, were self-financing, and subject to regular monitoring. The tribunals also found that the type of scheme chosen by the employers to incentivise workers, being based on

247

measured work principles, was not amenable to the claimants' jobs. For these reasons, the bonus schemes, when first introduced, were unrelated to the sex of the job holder. However, the tribunals went on to find that, by the time of the claimants' equal pay claims, the schemes had become a sham. Their nature significantly changed with the implementation of compulsory competitive tendering, whereupon the bonuses ceased to be linked to productivity, and eventually became part of pay. Owing to this, the material factor defence failed in both cases.

8.38 Although both decisions were upheld on appeal, Underhill P took the view that the approach of the tribunal in the Dolphin case (above) was not at all helpful, since 'it treated the question of whether the explanation was a sham as if it were the central question for decision'. As Underhill P noted, the terms 'sham' and 'pretence' are essentially concerned with honesty. Although in some equal pay cases the employer will try to put forward a material factor that has been fabricated and is intended to deceive the tribunal, more commonly the material factor defence hinges on the question of whether the factor is tainted by sex discrimination, and this is where tribunals should focus their attention. That said, the tribunals in the Bury and Sunderland cases had reached a decision that was plainly correct – the fact that the bonuses had ceased to be linked to productivity meant that the employer's pay practice could not be objectively justified. What this decision underlines is that the severing, over time, of the link between productivity and bonus payments is normally more relevant to the question of whether the material factor is tainted by sex discrimination, than to whether the factor put forward by the employer is 'material'.

These cases show that an employer faces an uphill struggle in seeking to rely on historical explanations to assist a material factor defence. However, the Patterson case (above) is not the only one in which an employer has been successful in this regard. In the leading case of Glasgow City Council and ors v Marshall and ors 2000 ICR 196, HL, M and several others were employed as instructors at a special school for children with learning difficulties. The staff at the school also included professionally qualified teachers who were paid substantially more than the instructors. The reason for the disparity in pay between instructors and teachers went back to the days when children with severe or profound learning disabilities were not regarded as 'educable' in mainstream schools. Until 1975, children with such learning difficulties were placed in day care centres and were cared for by instructors. After the enactment of the Education (Mentally Handicapped Children) (Scotland) Act 1974 all children were deemed to be educable. The day care centres were renamed 'schools' and began to employ professionally qualified teachers. The pay of instructors was pegged to a national 'local authority' scale, although ultimately it was for the individual local authority to decide where the instructors were placed on that scale.

M and five other female instructors applied to an employment tribunal claiming **8.39** that they were employed on like work with that of male teachers and that consequently they were entitled to the same pay. The tribunal agreed that the instructors were engaged on 'like work' to that of the teachers and found that the employer had failed to prove the material factor defence under S.1(3) EqPA (now S.69 EqA). All the employer had done was point to a 'historical basis for the disparity', which in the circumstances was not sufficient. The tribunal's decision was upheld by the EAT, but rejected by the Court of Session and the House of Lords. In their Lordships' view, the Council had identified the factor that caused the pay disparity in question: owing to historical reasons, teachers and instructors were paid according to two different nationally negotiated scales. The claimants had not questioned the genuineness of this explanation, nor had they suggested that the pay disparity was tainted by sex discrimination in that the pay practice disadvantaged women in some way. In these circumstances, the employer had done enough to make out a material factor defence.

With regard to 'historical' factors, Lord Nicholls' message was clear: they can amount to a material factor. An employer is not required at this stage of proceedings to provide a 'good' reason for the pay disparity, only a material explanation for it that is not discriminatory. However, if the historical material factor is tainted in some way by sex discrimination (see under 'Taint of sex discrimination' below) and the employer is therefore required to objectively justify the difference in pay in order to avoid liability, purely historical factors will not be sufficient. Lord Nicholls stated: 'The industrial tribunal, in the course of its self-direction on the applicable law, held that a purely historic explanation of the pay difference between sexes is insufficient. That is correct, when justification is in point. It is not correct when, as in the present case, [there is an] absence of sex discrimination.' He went on: 'The tribunal rejected the education authorities' explanation for the pay disparity not because they disbelieved the explanation but because they applied a wrong test. This is apparent from the importance the tribunal attached to the education authorities' failure to address themselves to a reassessment of the duties and responsibilities of instructors in special schools. The gist of the tribunal's reasoning was that the authorities could, and should, have done something about the pay disparity and, because they had not done so, could not bring themselves within S.1(3) [EqPA]. For the reasons stated above, I take the view that this was an erroneous approach to the application of the statute in the present case.'

So, what conclusions can be drawn from the above line of cases? We have **8.40** attempted to draw out what we believe to be the most salient points:

- an employer is not precluded from putting forward 'historical' explanations for a pay differential between a man and a woman – Glasgow City Council

249

and ors v Marshall and ors (above). If events in the past have 'caused' such a differential, these can be described as material and thus can form the basis of the employer's material factor defence – whether or not these events amount to a 'good' or 'justified' reason for the pay disparity

- however, whether a historical explanation for a pay differential can be considered to be 'material' – i.e. significant and relevant – at the time the equal pay complaint is made is a question of fact for the employment tribunal

- we suggest that, on the facts of Post Office v Page (above), where the claimant received low pay upon her recruitment because of her lack of experience yet continued to receive low pay when she was as able as her male colleagues; and on the facts of Benveniste v University of Southampton (above), where the claimant suffered low pay upon her recruitment owing to the employer's short-term financial constraints yet continued to receive low pay when those constraints no longer existed, the historical factors relied upon by the employers could no longer be considered 'material' at the time those equal pay claims were made. Put simply, the material factors relied upon by the employers no longer amounted to a material explanation for the pay disparity. Rather, they were merely a poor excuse for it

- even if a historical explanation for a pay differential is genuine and material, this does not necessarily mean that the employer's material factor defence will succeed. If evidence suggests that the employer's pay practice is tainted by sex discrimination in some way (see 'Taint of sex discrimination' below), the employer will be obliged to objectively justify the pay differentials (see 'Showing objective justification' below). And if the reasons for the differential are purely historical, showing objective justification will be an almost impossible task.

8.41 Taint of sex discrimination

One of the major criticisms of equal pay law under the EqPA was that, after three decades of judicial interpretation, the meaning of certain provisions had fundamentally departed from the statutory language. No provision highlighted this complaint better than S.1(3). This section provided that the equality clause would not operate to vary a claimant's contract if 'the employer proves that the variation is genuinely due to a material factor which is not the difference of sex'. However, while the statutory language suggested that the material factor simply had to be something other than the fact that the claimant was a woman and her comparator a man (which would amount to direct discrimination), the courts established that the material factor had to be free both of direct *and* unjustified indirect discrimination. In a welcome move towards greater clarity, the EqA now explicitly spells this out.

250

Section 69(1) EqA stipulates that:

'The sex equality clause in A's terms has no effect in relation to a difference between A's terms and B's terms if the [employer] shows that the difference is because of a material factor reliance on which:

- does not involve treating A less favourably because of A's sex than the [employer] treats B, and

- if the factor is within subsection (2), is a proportionate means of achieving a legitimate aim.'

A factor will fall within S.69(2) if 'A [the claimant] shows that, as a result of the factor, A and persons of the same sex doing work equal to A's are put at a particular disadvantage when compared with persons of the opposite sex doing work equal to A's'.

Those familiar with discrimination law will note that the first limb of S.69(1) **8.42** – less favourable treatment because of sex – closely corresponds to the definition of direct discrimination contained in S.13 EqA. It is for an employer to show that the material factor does not directly discriminate, and it must do so in every case where a woman has established that she is paid less than a male comparator doing equal work. The second limb of S.69(1) – showing that the material factor is justified – only binds an employer if the claimant has first shown a *prima facie* case of indirect discrimination, usually by means of statistics showing a disparate impact on the sexes.

Given the complexity of the topic, we begin by giving a brief overview of the different types of 'sex taint' (i.e. discrimination) that have been identified by the courts, before going on to look at them in more detail and consider how they relate to the new wording of S.69 EqA. Then, since the matter of sex taint will often be determined by reference to statistics – which may or may not suggest that women are being indirectly discriminated against as a group by an employer's pay practices – we consider the nature of the statistical analysis that tribunals may be obliged to carry out in such cases.

Overview – different types of 'sex taint' **8.43**
In Villalba v Merrill Lynch and Co Inc and ors 2007 ICR 469, EAT, Mr Justice Elias, then President of the EAT, trawled through the myriad case law – both domestic and European – concerning when a difference in pay might be tainted by sex discrimination. In an admirable attempt at simplicity, he came up with the following three 'sex tainted' scenarios:

- there is 'direct' discrimination – i.e. the claimant is paid less than her male comparator because she is a woman (now covered in S.69(1)(a) EqA – see above)

- there is 'indirect' discrimination as was then formulated by the Sex Discrimination Act 1975 (SDA) – i.e. the difference in pay between the claimant and her comparator results from the adoption of an apparently gender-neutral 'provision, criterion or practice' which, in practical terms, adversely affects women as a group. This may be because the social role which women habitually perform makes it more difficult for them to place themselves in the group of workers attracting higher pay – the classic example being where part-timers are treated less favourably than full-timers

- there are cogent, relevant and sufficiently compelling statistics demonstrating that women are adversely affected as a group with regard to pay when compared with men. Here, even though there may be no identifiable 'provision, criterion or practice' responsible for the so-called 'disparate impact', and in fact no readily forthcoming explanation for it, a presumption arises that it is a result of sex discrimination. This form of 'sex taint' arises from the ECJ's decision in Enderby v Frenchay Health Authority and anor 1994 ICR 112, ECJ.

8.44 The third of Elias P's scenarios – the 'Enderby' type of discrimination, which does not require the existence of a discriminatory 'provision, criterion or practice' – fell outside of the traditional concept of indirect sex discrimination then contained in UK discrimination law. Put simply, the Enderby case showed that the scope for 'sex taint' under the EqPA (as interpreted in the light of what is now Article 157 of the Treaty on the Functioning of the European Union (TFEU)) was wider than that under the SDA. However, as explained below under 'Indirect discrimination', the definition of indirect discrimination in S.69(2) EqA appears to encompass both indirect discrimination arising from the application of a provision, criterion or practice and Enderby discrimination. And even if on a literal construction it does not do so, it is arguable that tribunals will have to interpret it as doing so, since Enderby is a decision of the ECJ and must therefore be given effect by domestic courts and tribunals when interpreting equal pay provisions (see Chapter 1 under 'European Union law').

In Middlesbrough Borough Council v Surtees and ors 2007 ICR 1644, EAT, Elias P explained why the Enderby route of establishing sex taint in pay claims developed: 'It is important to bear in mind the purpose of the legislation and in particular the fact that there are structural reasons causing unequal pay. There has historically been much stereotyping of jobs with assumptions being made both about what work is suitable for men and women and what pay is appropriate for these jobs. This has led to much de facto job segregation (which is not to suggest that this is a deliberate or intended policy of employers, or that they have in any way formally limited women's access to the predominantly male jobs). That history continues to leave its mark on pay structures. Tribunals must be alive to the very real possibility that where there is adverse impact, identified where necessary by sufficiently cogent statistics, that may be the result of factors which are sex tainted.'

Given these comments, it is understandable that, in the Villalba case, Elias P **8.45** cautioned tribunals not to adopt too formulaic an approach to the matter of 'sex taint' in equal pay cases. In doing so, he affirmed the comments of Mrs Justice Cox in Ministry of Defence v Armstrong and ors 2004 IRLR 672, EAT, that 'in approaching these issues, technicalities should be eschewed. The fundamental question for the tribunal is whether there is a causative link between the [claimant's] sex and the fact that she is paid less than the true value of her job as reflected in the pay of her named comparator.' In fact, in Armstrong, Cox J expressly stated that it is not the case that sex taint can arise only where the rate of pay is determined by reference to characteristics which are gender-based; to factors which have the consequence in practice that the disadvantaged group is almost exclusively female; or to the application of a provision, criterion or practice that has a disparate impact on women. While pay discrimination can occur in all these circumstances, she continued, the categories of such discrimination are not closed, and a claim is not doomed to fail merely because the facts of the case do not fit precisely into one of them. So, although Elias P's summary in the Villalba case of the 'three' different types of sex taint is useful, it is not, it would seem, an exhaustive list of the situations in which such a taint might be established. Indeed, the wording of S.69(2) EqA, which refers to 'particular disadvantage', may leave some room for manoeuvre for tribunals to find that a factor requires objective justification even though it does not fit easily into the forms of indirect discrimination identified in Villalba.

Nevertheless, although a tribunal's approach to the matter of 'sex taint' should not be too formulaic, in many cases the question of whether or not such a taint is established will be considered with reference to a detailed statistical analysis. Often, it is only once such an analysis has been undertaken that the tribunal will be in a position to say that women have been placed at the requisite disadvantage. How the statistical analysis should be approached in order to obtain sensible results has often been debated, as we discuss under 'Demonstrating disparate impact' below.

Direct discrimination
8.46

The first type of 'sex taint' highlighted by Mr Justice Elias in Villalba v Merrill Lynch and Co Inc and ors 2007 ICR 469, EAT, was 'direct' sex discrimination – i.e. where a claimant is paid less than her comparator because she is a woman. This is now expressly provided for in S.69(1) EqA, which requires the employer to show that the difference in pay is due to a factor that 'does not involve treating A less favourably because of A's sex than the [employer] treats B'. This is essentially the same as the definition of direct discrimination found in S.13 of the Act, which covers, among other things, non-pay discrimination on the ground of sex.

253

8.47 **Distinction between direct and indirect discrimination.** Section 1(3) EqPA did not specifically mention direct discrimination and the inclusion of a distinct provision in S.69(1)(a) EqA prohibiting such discrimination in the application of the material factor defence represents something of a departure from the opinions of the House of Lords in North Yorkshire County Council v Ratcliffe and ors 1995 ICR 833, HL, and Strathclyde Regional Council and ors v Wallace and ors 1998 ICR 205, HL. In both cases their Lordships were of the view that the distinction between direct and indirect discrimination was less relevant in the context of equal pay under the EqA than in the context of sex discrimination under the SDA. In the Ratcliffe case Lord Slynn (with whom the other Law Lords agreed) stated that it was neither right nor helpful, when interpreting the EqPA, to import the distinction between direct and indirect discrimination then contained in the SDA. Subsequently, in Strathclyde, Lord Browne-Wilkinson (again with the full concurrence of the other Law Lords) acknowledged that there was no need to apply a strict demarcation between the two types of discrimination. He said: 'The law on [Article 157], whilst recognising that in many cases there is a de facto distinction between direct and indirect discrimination, does not draw the same firm legal demarcation between the two as does [the SDA], which permits justification of indirect discrimination but not of direct discrimination.'

We would argue, however, that S.69 EqA is arguably more in line with the recast Equal Treatment Directive (No.2006/54) than was S.1(3) EqPA. This is because Article 4 of that Directive make specific mention of direct discrimination, stating that 'for the same work or for work to which equal value is attributed, direct and indirect discrimination on grounds of sex with regard to all aspects and conditions of remuneration shall be eliminated'.

8.48 The prohibition of direct sex discrimination in the material factor defence can appear somewhat confusing at first. As explained under 'Preliminary issues – the burden of proof' above, once a claimant has shown that she is paid less than a male comparator performing like work, work rated as equivalent or work of equal value to hers, there is already a presumption that direct pay discrimination has occurred. An employer can only rebut this presumption by pointing to a material factor that does not involve direct discrimination and, if the claimant shows evidence of indirect discrimination, is objectively justified. So, why does direct discrimination need to be considered at two stages of a claim, especially if, as we saw above, there is little possibility of an employer justifying such discrimination? The answer lies in the different wording used in S.1(3) EqPA and in S.69 EqA. The old provision referred to a factor that was 'not the difference in sex', whereas S.69 EqA refers to a 'material factor, reliance on which... does not involve treating A less favourably because of A's sex'. The specific prohibition on direct discrimination spelt out in S.69 fulfils the same role as the phrase 'not the difference in sex' did under the EqPA – both make it clear that the material factor has to be something other than the difference in sex between the claimant and comparator.

Can direct pay discrimination be justified? The wording of S.69 EqA would 8.49 appear to close the door on the argument, given credence in the Strathclyde case (above), that an employer may be able to provide objective justification for a material factor which *directly* discriminates because of sex. There is now a clear demarcation between direct discrimination governed by S.69(1)(a) – the mere existence of which will invalidate a material factor – and indirect discrimination under S.69(1)(b) and (2), which, once shown by the employee, may nonetheless be objectively justified by the employer as a proportionate means of achieving a legitimate aim. It is hard to see how a tribunal could read these provisions as permitting an employer to provide objective justification for a directly discriminatory material factor. However, there is case law that suggests things might not be quite so straightforward.

As we have seen above, the material factor defence in S.69 EqA is more in keeping with the approach previously adopted under the SDA than with that adopted under the EqPA, in so far as it makes an express distinction between direct and indirect discrimination. The language of the EqPA made no such distinction, simply requiring that the factor was 'not the difference in sex'. It was case law under the 1970 Act and what is now Article 157 which established that a material factor must be free of both direct and indirect discrimination, and on more than one occasion this case law raised the prospect that direct pay discrimination could be justified. While we are of the view that the new wording in S.69 EqA has now effectively ruled this out, the fact that the appeal courts have spent so much time grappling with the issue means that it would be wise not to ignore the possibility altogether.

The first case to note is Strathclyde Regional Council and ors v Wallace and ors 8.50 1998 ICR 205, HL, where the House of Lords suggested that a justification defence is available to an employer even if the discrimination in question is direct. Lord Browne-Wilkinson summed up his understanding of how the S.1(3) EqPA defence worked as follows: '[E]ven where the variation is genuinely due to a factor which involves the difference of sex, the employer can still establish a valid defence under subsection (3) if he can justify such differentiation on the grounds of sex, whether the [discrimination] is direct or indirect.' However, Lord Browne-Wilkinson's remarks appear to run counter to the thrust of the House of Lords' previous decision in North Yorkshire County Council v Ratcliffe and ors 1995 ICR 833, HL. In that case, their Lordships accepted that importing the distinction between direct and indirect discrimination into the EqPA was not particularly helpful. However, they nonetheless concluded that if it was necessary to characterise the pay discrimination that had occurred in that case in a particular way, the discrimination was 'direct' in that the employer had paid the claimants less

255

than their male comparators because the claimants were women. Crucially, their Lordships deduced from this that the S.1(3) EqPA defence was not available to the employer. In Lord Slynn's words, '[direct discrimination] ex hypothesi cannot be shown to be justified on grounds "irrespective of the sex of the person" concerned'.

This approach was also adopted in Villalba v Merrill Lynch and Co Inc and ors 2007 ICR 469, EAT, where the argument was put to Elias P that the ECJ, in Hill and anor v Revenue Commissioners and Department of Finance 1999 ICR 48, ECJ, had suggested that direct pay discrimination could be objectively justified. In response, Elias P stated that this 'would be novel and we very much doubt that is what the Court intended'. The Court of Appeal was even firmer on this issue in Redcar and Cleveland Borough Council v Bainbridge and ors and another case; Middlesbrough Borough Council v Surtees and ors 2009 ICR 133, CA. Lord Justice Mummery, giving the judgment of the Court, commented that the treatment of the justification issue by the EAT at an earlier stage in the Bainbridge litigation had been 'slightly puzzling'. He said: 'At one stage... the EAT seemed to say that it did not matter in the context of this case whether the discrimination in question was direct or indirect because, if the arrangements were tainted by sex, the S.1(3) EqPA defence would be bound to fail. If that is what the EAT thought, it would be wrong in our view. It is always important to distinguish between direct and indirect discrimination because direct discrimination can never be justified and indirect discrimination can be justified.'

8.51 Nevertheless, uncertainty has continued to reign. Most recently, in Newcastle upon Tyne Hospitals NHS Foundation Trust v Armstrong and ors 2010 ICR 674, EAT, the Appeal Tribunal, presided over by the President, Mr Justice Underhill, proffered the view that discrimination of the type seen in Ratcliffe (above) can be justified. This view was reached despite the EAT's apparent conclusion that such discrimination is direct (the Armstrong decision is considered at length under "'Women's work" – market tainted by discrimination' below).

8.52 **'Women's work' – market tainted by discrimination.** The House of Lords' decision in North Yorkshire County Council v Ratcliffe and ors 1995 ICR 833, HL, is worthy of further discussion, in that the precise basis on which their Lordships concluded that the women in that case had been paid less 'because they were women' is somewhat obscure. To understand it, it is necessary to consider the findings made by the employment tribunal, whose decision was upheld by their Lordships.

The case concerned women employed as school dinner ladies who sought to secure equal pay with men engaged by North Yorkshire County Council as road sweepers, refuse collectors and gardeners. In 1987 the claimants' jobs had been rated as equivalent with those of their comparators under a job evaluation study, as a result of which they were accorded the same rates of pay as the men. However, the Council was then required by the Local Government Act 1988 to put certain of its activities, including the provision of school meals, out to compulsory competitive tender. In order to be able to submit an in-house tender, the Council set up a Direct Service Organisation (DSO) and hived off the school meals service into it. Under pressure from the competitive tendering exercise and with the desire to succeed with an in-house bid to retain responsibility for the school meals service, the DSO concluded that it was necessary to reduce the claimants' existing rates of pay to bring them into line with the 'market rates' payable by the private catering contractors with which it would be competing for the school meals contract. The women claimed equal pay on the ground that their work had been rated as equivalent with that of the comparators (whose pay had not been reduced). A tribunal upheld the claims, concluding that the employer had not made out a material factor defence. The need to reduce the claimants' pay in order to be competitive derived from the fact that the general market rates of pay in the catering industry were low because the particular market concerned consisted of a primarily female workforce. In the tribunal's view, the lower rates of pay arose out of 'the general perception in the United Kingdom, and certainly in North Yorkshire, that a woman should stay at home to look after the children and if she wants to work it must fit in with that domestic duty and a lack of facilities to enable her, easily, to do otherwise'.

8.53 The tribunal's decision, having been overturned by the EAT and the Court of Appeal, was restored by the House of Lords. In their Lordships' view, although the need to compete with rival tenders placed the employer in a very difficult position, the fact was that the women were paid less than men for work rated as equivalent and the tribunal was entitled to find that no defence under what was then S.1(3) EqPA had been established. In the words of Lord Slynn: 'I am satisfied that to reduce the women's wages below that of their male comparators was the very kind of discrimination in relation to pay which the Act sought to remove.' Clearly, what lay behind the tribunal's reasoning (as upheld by the House of Lords) were the social and economic factors that explained why the kind of work done by the claimants was almost exclusively women's work, and was accordingly undervalued in the marketplace. As their Lordships emphasised, the hours of work of the school dinner staff suited the women's family responsibilities and the fact that it would have been difficult for the women to find other suitable work more or less obliged them to accept the reduction in their pay that was made a condition of their continued employment. Seen in this light, the House of Lords seemed to suggest that, where the reason for reducing the wages of an exclusively female workforce was to compete in the labour market with commercial rivals, then this could not constitute a material factor defence since the women are being paid less because they are women. Any material factor explanation based on the need to pay women less in order to be competitive would be impugned for perpetuating widespread

257

discriminatory assumptions about the perceived place of women in the commercial labour market and about the value of so-called 'women's work'.

The decision in Ratcliffe stimulated a debate about whether the nature of the sex discrimination in that case was, in reality, 'direct'. Clearly, there was no 'traditional' direct discrimination since, had a man been employed in the school catering service to do the same work as the claimants, he would have been paid the same as them. Thus, the specific motivation for reducing the claimants' pay to the levels applicable to catering employees in the general marketplace was not that they were women. Yet the very fact that such employees were referred to as 'dinner ladies' was indicative of the extent to which their employment was segregated according to sex and was thus rendered vulnerable to the undervaluing associated with 'women's work'. By recognising that the marketplace pressures that led the employer to reduce the claimants' pay applied to their work but not to that of their comparators (who were all employed in traditional 'men's work'), it could be argued that the House of Lords took the opportunity of creating a wider notion of 'direct' discrimination, at least in the context of pay. Furthermore, their Lordships chose to deal strictly with such discrimination by saying that it could not be justified under S.1(3) EqPA.

8.54 The Ratcliffe decision was considered by the Court of Appeal in Armstrong and ors v Newcastle upon Tyne Hospital Trust 2006 IRLR 124, CA. Prior to 1985, the Newcastle Health Authority made bonus payments both to its domestic ancillary workers (most of whom were female) and to its porters (most of whom were male), who were employed at four hospitals, one of which was the Royal Victoria Infirmary (RVI). In that year, the domestic work at the RVI was put out to compulsory competitive tender (CCT) and an in-house tender was accepted. As a result, the domestic staff lost their right to bonuses, whereas bonus payments to porters continued. The domestic staff and the porters remained in the NHA's employ until 1991, when responsibility for the Authority's four hospitals was divided between two new hospital trusts, the RVI and Freeman. In 1998, the RVI and Freeman merged, becoming the Newcastle upon Tyne NHS Hospital Trust (the NHT). In 2001 a group of female domestic workers brought equal pay claims against the NHT. They argued that their work was of equal value to that of male porters working at the RVI, who continued to receive the bonus payments to which the domestic workers were no longer entitled.

The employment tribunal considered as a preliminary issue whether the NHT could succeed with a genuine material factor defence under S.1(3) EqPA. The employer pointed to the historical background for the difference in pay – i.e. that in 1985 the domestic work was put out to tender by the NHT, whereas the portering work was not. It put forward four reasons why the portering work was not put out to tender: it was not compulsory for it to be so; no major savings would have been made; the NHT was not aware of any companies which would have been interested in tendering; and the porters' opposition to a tendering exercise was expected to be more voluble than that of the domestic workers. The tribunal accepted that the first two reasons 'might' have been genuine at the time. It expressed concern, however, about the second two reasons. It noted, first, that the NHT had not explored the market in order to establish whether companies would have been interested in tendering for the portering work, and, secondly, that 'the male porters were in employment traditionally more heavily unionised and voluble because we know from our own experience of the local market more males tend to be full time than females and to be unionised'. The tribunal went on to find that 'these two alleged justifications amount to significant and relevant factors tainted by sex and strike at the basis of the justification claimed'. The tribunal concluded that the claims brought by the RVI claimants could proceed, and its findings were upheld on appeal to the EAT. The NHT appealed to the Court of Appeal, arguing that the tribunal had erred in its treatment of its material factor defence. In the course of their judgments, both Lady Justice Arden and Lord Justice Buxton commented on the Ratcliffe decision at some length, highlighting some reasons why the instant case might be distinguished from it.

8.55 Lady Justice Arden noted that the tribunal had found that one of the reasons why the domestic work was put out to tender was that the NHT perceived that private contractors would tender less than the cost to the NHT of continuing to employ the staff itself. This factor, she stated, could be linked to the tribunal's finding that the tenderer's staff would be almost exclusively female. If those were the only relevant factors, Arden LJ continued, 'it was open to the tribunal to find that the decision to submit domestic work to CCT was, in the words of S.1(3) [EqPA], due to "the difference in sex"'. The situation, in her view, would have been very similar to that in the Ratcliffe case, in that the lowering of women's pay would have been 'conditioned by the fact that competitors employ mainly women who are prepared to work for less pay'. Importantly, however, the tribunal in the instant case had identified other relevant factors potentially influencing the NHT's decision to put the domestic work, but not the portering work, out to tender – for example, if portering had been put out to tender the opposition from the workforce would have been greater – that could have been genuine operational reasons 'other than sex'. In the circumstances, the tribunal should have gone on to properly consider what the real reasons for the NHT's actions were, and whether those reasons were on their true analysis not tainted by sex. This it had failed to do, meaning that the case should be remitted for further consideration.

Buxton LJ was also of the opinion that the case should be remitted to the tribunal. With regard to the 'Ratcliffe issue', he stated that the House of Lords in Ratcliffe did not hold 'that to adjust wages or conditions in order to compete in a predominantly female labour market was *necessarily* discriminatory either as a matter of fact or as a matter of law'. In Ratcliffe, it was key to the finding of discrimination that, in essence, the employer had shown no material difference between the claimants and their comparators other than the difference of sex. In Buxton LJ's view, 'This is not so in our case. The complex history and effect of the introduction of CCT, fully set out by the employment tribunal, indicates that the different decisions or outcomes in relation to bonus payments were the result of a very wide range of factors.'

8.56 The Armstrong litigation – which, for a multitude of reasons, has been the source of much debate and frustration to many an employment lawyer (see under 'Preliminary issues – burden of proof' above) – did not end with the Court of Appeal's decision. Rather, the Court remitted the matter to the employment tribunal, posing three questions for the tribunal to answer: First, did the bonus arrangement have a disparate adverse impact on women? If so, was the decision to put domestic services out to tender, or to discontinue the bonus, an act of discrimination 'on grounds of gender'? And finally, if that decision was discriminatory, had the NHT established an objective justification? At the remitted hearing the tribunal answered the first two questions in favour of the claimants, and went on to find that the NHT had not established justification. It therefore rejected the material factor defence. The NHT appealed to the EAT against the tribunal's answers to the Court of Appeal's last two questions.

In Newcastle upon Tyne Hospitals NHS Foundation Trust v Armstrong and ors 2010 ICR 674, EAT, the Appeal Tribunal, presided over by its President, Mr Justice Underhill, took Buxton LJ's interpretation of Ratcliffe (see Armstrong and ors v Newcastle upon Tyne Hospital Trust above) – which he was bound to follow despite reservations as to its correctness – to mean that the NHT's decision to reduce wages to market rates would only be discriminatory if the NHT appreciated that the market rates were 'women's rates' and was willing to take advantage of this. However, although Underhill P accepted that the claim in the instant case was one of 'Enderby' discrimination (i.e. in accordance with the test laid down in Enderby v Frenchay Health Authority and anor 1994 ICR 112, ECJ – see 'Indirect discrimination' below), in that it was based on a compelling statistical disparity, he also took the view that Enderby discrimination – or at least the 'underlying' discrimination that first gave rise to statistical disparity – is capable of being direct as well as indirect. And given that in an Enderby case, such discrimination was not the immediate cause of an employer's action, Underhill P, somewhat contrary to the view of the House of Lords in Ratcliffe, saw 'no good reason' why an employer should not be able to provide objective justification for the pay disparity if it originated from historical direct discrimination. In Underhill P's opinion, the truth was that, whatever the correct reading of Ratcliffe, 'Ratcliffe discrimination' did not fit neatly into the established categories of

260

discrimination, which was why the House of Lords in that case had shied away from drawing a distinction between direct and indirect discrimination.

Applying Buxton LJ's interpretation of Ratcliffe to the facts of the case before **8.57** it, the EAT in Armstrong considered that the employment tribunal had been entitled to find that the NHT submitted the claimants' work to CCT in the knowledge that the market rate had been depressed by social and economic factors peculiar to women. The tribunal's conclusion was reached on the basis of evidence that the domestic workers were almost all women and that the labour market for domestics in the North East was almost exclusively female, and by relying on its own local knowledge. The EAT next considered whether the NHT had established objective justification for such discrimination. The tribunal had held – and the claimants had conceded – that until 1988 there was objective justification for the removal of the bonus payments; namely, the need for the NHT to put in a competitive bid and then implement it according to its terms. However, the claimants contended that from 1988 onwards the bonus scheme itself had stopped serving any legitimate business need, since the bonuses that were still paid were no longer linked to productivity.

The NHT, on the other hand, submitted that owing to cost restraints and the threat of industrial and legal action, it remained justifiable to retain the differential for a time notwithstanding the disappearance of the original rationale. However, the EAT upheld the tribunal's decision that from 1988 onwards the pattern of bonus payments was not objectively justified, concluding that the Trust had not advanced any cogent argument as to why the tribunal's decision should be overturned.

What can we conclude from this ever-growing body of case law? Perhaps that, **8.58** in narrow circumstances, there will be unjustifiable, quasi-direct pay discrimination where a group of women is paid less due to stereotypical marketplace attitudes with regard to 'women's work' – this would seem capable of fitting within the new statutory language in S.69(1)(a) EqA, which refers to a woman being treated less favourably 'because of' her sex. Where, however, there are more complicated reasons for a pay differential between a group of men and a group of women that have at their roots a degree of historical direct discrimination, but where nevertheless direct discrimination is not the 'immediate ground' of the employer's actions, the EAT in the latest Armstrong decision suggests that justification is possible. This 'grey area' is not necessarily eliminated by the new wording of S.69 EqA, since there is undoubtedly sufficient leeway for a tribunal to find either that discrimination of the type in Armstrong is direct discrimination within the terms of S.69(1)(a) and therefore unjustifiable, or that it does not have a sufficient causal connection to the claimant's sex and therefore is indirect discrimination, and so is potentially justifiable under S.69(1)(b).

8.59 Indirect discrimination

It was not originally clear whether what is now Article 157 of the TFEU extended to 'indirect' as well as 'direct' pay discrimination. However, in Bilka-Kaufhaus GmbH v Weber von Hartz 1987 ICR 110, ECJ, the European Court confirmed that Article 157 does apply in such circumstances. That case concerned the exclusion of part-timers from equal membership of an occupational pension scheme. After holding that pension benefits constituted 'pay' for the purposes of Article 157, the ECJ went on to state that, where the majority of part-time employees are women, the exclusion of such employees from the same pension benefits as full-time workers is discriminatory and in breach of Article 157 unless the employer can show that the exclusion policy was based on objectively justified factors unrelated to sex. The ECJ in Bilka-Kaufhaus did not actually use the words 'direct' and 'indirect' in its judgment. However, many of the ECJ's decisions since then have not only applied Bilka-Kaufhaus but have also used the phrase 'indirect discrimination' to describe the type of discrimination at issue – see, for example, Rinner-Kühn v FWW Spezial-Gebäudereinigung GmbH and Co KG 1989 IRLR 493, ECJ (part-timers' rights in respect of statutory sick pay); and Magorrian and anor v Eastern Health and Social Services Board and anor 1998 ICR 979, ECJ (part-timers' rights to equal access to pension scheme membership).

What is more, in Enderby v Frenchay Health Authority and anor 1994 ICR 112, ECJ, the European Court made it clear that not only does Article 157 cover 'indirect' pay discrimination as was then defined in the SDA, it also requires employers to objectively justify pay differentials in a broader set of circumstances than required by that Act (and, post-SDA, by S.19 EqA, which covers indirect discrimination in all areas other than equal pay). In order for the objective justification test to apply, all that is required is for compelling statistics to demonstrate that women as a group are being adversely affected with regard to pay when compared with men.

8.60 Below, we set out what can, in simple terms, be described as the two types of indirect discrimination that can occur in the context of an equal pay claim. First, indirect discrimination arising from the application of a provision, criterion or practice ('"PCP" indirect discrimination'); and, secondly, the broader concept of indirect discrimination arising from Enderby and subsequent case law ('"Enderby" indirect discrimination').

8.61 **'PCP' indirect discrimination.** The de facto recognition of the concept of indirect discrimination in European law was given a codified legal base when the provisions of the Burden of Proof Directive (No.97/80) came into force on 1 January 2001. That Directive has subsequently been superseded by the recast Equal Treatment Directive (No.2006/54). Article 2(1)(b) of the recast Directive defines indirect discrimination as 'where an apparently neutral provision, criterion or practice would put persons of one sex at a particular disadvantage

262

compared with persons of the other sex, unless that provision, criterion or practice is objectively justified by a legitimate aim, and the means of achieving that aim are appropriate and necessary'. Under Article 4 of the recast Directive, Member States are obliged to eliminate both direct and indirect discrimination in 'aspects and conditions of remuneration'.

The recast Directive is now given effect in the United Kingdom by means of the EqA. It is important to note here that there are two similar, but not identical, definitions of indirect discrimination in the 2010 Act. The first, found in S.19, covers indirect discrimination in all areas *other* than equal pay claims. S.19(2) provides that a 'provision, criterion or practice' (PCP) is indirectly discriminatory in relation to a 'protected characteristic' (sex, race, disability, religion or belief, sexual orientation, age, gender reassignment, and marriage or civil partnership) if: '(a) A applies, or would apply, it to persons with whom B does not share the characteristic, (b) it puts, or would put, persons with whom B shares the characteristic at a particular disadvantage when compared with persons with whom B does not share it, (c) it puts, or would put, B at that disadvantage, and (d) A cannot show it to be a proportionate means of achieving a legitimate aim.' So, for indirect discrimination to occur in areas other than equal pay, there must be a PCP applied by the employer.

8.62 Equal pay cases are covered by a separate definition found in S.69(2). This states that indirect discrimination occurs where the employer shows that the difference in treatment is because of a material factor and 'A [in this case the claimant] shows that, as a result of the factor, A and persons of the same sex doing work equal to A's are put at a particular disadvantage when compared with persons of the opposite sex doing work equal to A's'. Thus the test turns on the employer's reliance on a material factor and there is no express need for the employer to have applied a provision, criterion or practice. However, the material factor may well amount to an ostensibly gender-neutral PCP that is applied equally to all relevant employees but which nevertheless disadvantages women as a group with regard to pay. Where this is so, there will be a taint of sex discrimination, requiring the employer to objectively justify the pay disparity between the claimant and her male comparator – see Jenkins v Kingsgate (Clothing Productions) Ltd 1981 ICR 715, EAT.

In order to establish sex taint by way of the 'PCP route', the claimant must show that the employer's material factor adversely affects members of one sex more than the other, or to use the statutory language, puts them at a particular disadvantage. An example:

- **Chief Constable of West Midlands Police v Blackburn and anor** 2008 ICR 505, EAT: police officers' pay is overseen by the Police Negotiating Board (PNB). In May 2002 the PNB reached an agreement which introduced a 'special priority payments' (SPPs) scheme. Under this scheme, frontline officers in 'qualifying posts' would receive bonus payments of between £500

263

and £3,000 a year. The designation of roles as 'qualifying posts' was left to the discretion of regional forces, having regard to whether posts had a high level of responsibility, presented particular difficulties in recruitment and retention, or entailed especially demanding working conditions or working environments. 'Sector officers' in the West Midlands Police force (WMP) worked to a rotating shift pattern that included night shifts unless they were excused because of childcare responsibilities or a medical condition. Following the announcement of the PNB agreement, WMP decided that, in relation to sector officers, one of the qualifying criteria for SPPs would be '24/7 working'. This would be fulfilled, essentially, by officers who were available to be rostered for duty at any hour of the day or night. B and M, female sector officers who had been excused 24/7 working because of their childcare responsibilities, issued proceedings under the EqPA. Before the tribunal, the employer defended the claim by pointing to a genuine material factor explaining the difference in pay between the claimants and their named male comparator: the employer's desire to reward night working. The tribunal found that although this material factor explained the pay differential, it was a PCP that had a disparate adverse effect on women. Statistical evidence showed that 96.6 per cent of men could comply with the 24/7 requirement, compared to only 91.5 per cent of women, and although these figures did not show a strikingly disparate impact, they were enough to establish indirect discrimination. When the case came before the EAT, Mr Justice Elias stated that the tribunal's statistical analysis of the effect of the material factor had been correct – although he added that the analysis may not strictly have been necessary, as disparate impact might have been established in any event as 'at least in the current climate, conferring a benefit on those working throughout the night will disadvantage some women, and has disadvantaged the claimants, by virtue of the fact that they have childcare responsibilities'. (Note that the EAT nevertheless upheld the employer's defence, on the basis that the material factor was justified as a proportionate means of achieving a legitimate aim, and this decision was upheld by the Court of Appeal – see 'Showing objective justification' below).

8.63 **'Enderby' indirect discrimination.** According to the ECJ, there is no need for a discriminatory PCP to be identified in order for a taint of indirect discrimination to arise. Rather, a prima facie suspicion of indirect discrimination, potentially requiring the employer to objectively justify the pay differential, will be raised if the claimant can adduce statistical evidence relating to the pay of groups of women and men employed on like work or work of equal value that shows a sufficiently compelling discrepancy between the average pay of men and women in those groups.

This strand of indirect discrimination was first identified by the ECJ in Enderby v Frenchay Health Authority and anor 1994 ICR 112, ECJ. There, E, a senior speech therapist in the NHS, brought an equal pay claim on the basis that she was paid less than male senior pharmacists and clinical psychologists in the same employment, who performed work of equal value to hers. At the tribunal hearing, the Health Authority argued that the difference in pay was due to a material factor within the meaning of what was then S.1(3) EqPA – namely, the separate negotiating structures by which the relevant professions' pay rates were determined – and that neither the conditions of access to the respective professions nor the pay bargaining within them was tainted by sex discrimination. E, however, pointed out that the higher grades of the comparator professions comprised a greater proportion of men than women, whereas senior speech therapists were almost all women. She argued that the pay practices thus had an adverse impact on women, which amounted to indirect discrimination. The tribunal rejected E's claim, deciding that the employer had made out a defence under S.1(3) EqPA, since the differences in pay arose out of the bargaining structure and its history, and from the structures in the professions, neither of which was discriminatory.

8.64 E's appeal to the EAT was unsuccessful. In upholding the tribunal's decision, the EAT was influenced by the Secretary of State's argument that where an equal pay claimant wished to rely on indirect discrimination, she was obliged, in line with the SDA approach to such discrimination, to identify the barrier (in today's language, the PCP) that had a disparate impact on women and which placed her at a disadvantage. In this case, the EAT noted, no factor tainted by gender causing disparate impact between the sexes had been shown to exist. On further appeal, however, the Court of Appeal referred the matter to the ECJ. It wanted to know whether Article 157 required an employer to objectively justify a pay differential where there had been no identifiable discrimination in the way that the relevant collective bargaining processes had been carried out, but where those processes nevertheless had an adverse impact on a predominantly female group when compared with a predominantly male group.

In his Opinion on the matter, the Advocate General preferred E's arguments. He stated: 'In cases in which it is established that a group of women is being disadvantaged in comparison with a group of male workers (doing work which is the same or of equal value in the same plant or undertaking) no additional factor, whereby unequal treatment is applied, need be required... attention should be directed less to the existence of a requirement or a hurdle by means of which women suffer a disadvantage, and more to the discriminatory result'. The ECJ agreed. It recognised that the case before it was not the same as a standard indirect discrimination case, such as Bilka-Kaufhaus – it did not involve 'de facto discrimination arising from a particular sort of arrangement such as may apply, for example, in the case of part-time workers'. Furthermore, there was no complaint that the employer had applied a system of pay wholly lacking in transparency – the rates of pay were decided by regular collective bargaining processes in which there was no evidence of discrimination. Nevertheless, the ECJ stated: '[I]f the pay of speech therapists is significantly lower than that of pharmacists and if the former are almost exclusively women while the latter are predominantly men, there is a prima facie case of sex discrimination, at least where the two jobs in question are of equal value and the statistics describing the situation are valid.' In such circumstances, it continued, 'it is for the employer to show that there are objective reasons for the difference in pay'.

8.65 With regard to the statistical approach required (a matter we discuss further under 'Demonstrating disparate impact' below), the ECJ stated: 'It is for the national court to assess whether it may take into account [the] statistics, that is to say, whether they cover enough individuals, whether they illustrate purely fortuitous or short-term phenomena, and whether, in general, they appear to be significant.' Similarly, in Specialarbejderforbundet i Danmark v Dansk Industri 1996 ICR 51, ECJ, the European Court held that the national court must satisfy itself that the groups for comparison 'cover a relatively large number of workers in order to ensure that the differences [in the relative numbers of men and women] are not due to purely fortuitous or short-term factors'. In Villalba v Merrill Lynch and Co Inc and ors 2007 ICR 469, EAT, Mr Justice Elias put it thus: 'The statistics must at least show that it is reasonable to infer that the treatment of the disadvantaged group must have resulted from some factor or combination of factors which impinge adversely on women because of their sex, even though no obvious feature causing this disparate treatment can be identified, and indeed even though the employer has apparently demonstrated to the contrary.'

Attempts have been made to limit the ECJ's decision in Enderby to cover circumstances where the disadvantaged group comprised 'almost exclusively women' – which was the factual situation in the Enderby case. However, these attempts have been rejected, most notably by the Northern Ireland Court of Appeal in British Road Services Ltd v Loughran and ors 1997 IRLR 92, NICA. So, as Elias P stated in the Villalba cases, 'the position appears to be that a presumption of unintentional indirect sex discrimination arises even where the statistics are less stark [than those in Enderby]. Precisely how less stark is still a matter of some uncertainty.' Before turning to consider this uncertainty and the statistical approach that a tribunal should follow, we consider how Enderby discrimination relates to the new statutory language in S.69 EqA.

8.66 *Is Enderby indirect discrimination covered by S.69(2)?* On one reading of S.69(2) EqA, it is certainly arguable that the Enderby approach has been adopted in the 2010 Act. Objective justification is required where, 'as a result of the [material] factor, A and persons of the same sex doing work equal to A's are put at a particular disadvantage when compared with persons of the opposite sex doing work equal to A's'. Thus, justification is apparently required when disparate impact is shown, without any need to refer specifically to a provision, criterion or practice that the employer applies. However, it is noteworthy that objective justification is only called for where the claimant shows that the disparate impact is 'a result of' the factor that the employer seeks to rely upon. It is not entirely clear what this means. Whereas Enderby established that there is no need to say why ostensibly neutral arrangements lead to a discriminatory outcome, the wording 'as a result of' in S.69(2) implies a causal connection between the factor and the disparate impact.

At first glance, it would seem to be axiomatic that the disparate impact is a 'result' of the employer's proposed material factor – after all, it is that factor which the employer is putting forward as explaining the pay inequality. However, when an employer relies on a material factor, it is relied upon as the reason for the specific difference in treatment of the claimant and the comparator. This is not the same as accepting that the factor causes a disparate impact when looked at on a wider scale. The statistics that so troubled the ECJ in Enderby were a result of the historical pay bargaining arrangements, which the employer relied on as explaining the difference in treatment. But they were equally the result of the fact that more women than men went into speech therapy, and more men than women into pharmacy. The different pay bargaining arrangements certainly played a material role in the disparate impact revealed by the statistics. But it might be that factors entirely outside the employer's control or knowledge were equally, or even more, causative. Thus, it is arguable that under S.69(2) a reason for the disparate impact must be shown for that impact to be considered a 'result' of the proposed material factor, and so require objective justification. Without such a reason, the employer would not have to justify anything.

8.67 This new formulation of the material factor has the potential to trip up claimants bringing equal pay claims on the basis of indirect discrimination. As noted above, the burden is on the claimant to show that whatever disparate impact can be established is the result of the employer's proposed material factor. However, in practice, it will be entirely feasible for tribunals to read 'as a result of' as requiring only a loose causal connection, instead of asking whether the material factor was the true 'cause' of the disparate impact rather than just the background against which it arose. In any event, it should be remembered that Enderby discrimination is a concept derived from European union law (see above), and so potentially applies despite any obstacles that the wording of the EqA might place in its way. The Enderby case itself was determined by the ECJ with reference to what was then Article 141 of the EC Treaty (now Article 157 of the TFEU). That result then had to be read into the EqPA. There is no reason why the same process should not occur in respect of the EqA, with the result that the approach to Enderby cases as understood by the EAT and other domestic courts is carried forward into the new Act.

267

Having identified the two types of indirect discrimination covered by UK and EU equal pay law, we now turn to the tricky matter of how a claimant goes about establishing a prima facie case of indirect discrimination.

8.68 Demonstrating disparate impact

Both forms of indirect discrimination identified above – i.e. 'PCP' indirect discrimination and 'Enderby' indirect discrimination – involve women as a group being adversely affected – i.e. put at a 'particular disadvantage' – with regard to pay when compared with men. This sounds a simple enough concept, but the issue of how a tribunal should determine the matter of disparate adverse impact is far from straightforward.

In most cases, a detailed statistical analysis will be required in order for the claimant to establish that, as a result of the material factor, she and other women are being put at a disadvantage. Tribunals will thus need to determine which individuals are to be taken into account when drawing the statistics together; how the statistics should be analysed to provide a sensible result; and how great a disparity is required in order for indirect discrimination (often referred to in case law as 'sex taint') to be established. We examine these matters in turn below, and while doing so will highlight any differences in approach that might be required in Enderby cases as compared with PCP cases.

Note that a much fuller analysis of how disparate impact in PCP cases should be established can be found in IDS Employment Law Handbook, 'Sex Discrimination' (2008), Chapter 3.

8.69 **Pool for comparison.** Since both PCP cases and Enderby cases entail a comparative exercise – i.e. consideration of whether women are put at a particular disadvantage when compared with men – it will usually be necessary for the tribunal to identify an appropriate 'pool' of people in respect of whom the comparison can be made. However, S.69(2) EqA does not necessarily require a statistical comparison. There may be cases where statistical evidence is finely balanced or unavailable, but a tribunal nevertheless considers that a woman is placed at a particular disadvantage by a material factor. That said, tribunals and equal pay practitioners are attuned to the need to establish a pool for comparison, and cases under the particular disadvantage test in the discrimination enactments that preceded the EqA tended to rely on statistically-based methods.

8.70 **PCP cases.** The discriminatory impact of a PCP (in equal pay cases, the employer's material factor) is ascertained by analysing a pool comprising those who would qualify for the benefit in question (in equal pay cases, the higher rate of pay) if the PCP were not applied – University of Manchester v Jones 1993 ICR 474, CA. In the words of Lord Justice Sedley in Grundy v British Airways plc 2008 IRLR 74, CA, the comparison 'needs to include, but not be limited to, those affected by the [PCP] of which complaint is made, which can be expected to include both people who can and people who cannot comply with it'. A simple example of this exercise in an equal pay context is found in the case of Chief Constable of West Midlands Police v Blackburn and anor 2008 ICR 505, EAT. There, in assessing the impact of a '24/7' working requirement that determined whether or not an officer would receive a 'special priority payment', a tribunal identified a pool comprising all West Midlands Police officers who qualified for the payments at issue, as well as those who would have qualified if not for the 24/7 requirement. Excluded from the pool were those who would not qualify for the payments in any event because of additional service, attendance and performance criteria that were not relied upon as material factors in the case.

In Allonby v Accrington and Rossendale College and ors 2001 ICR 1189, CA, Sedley LJ characterised the identification of the pool by the tribunal as 'a matter neither of discretion nor of fact-finding but of logic... Logic may on occasion be capable of producing more than one outcome... But the choice of pool is not at large.' So, once the relevant PCP has been defined, 'there is likely to be only one pool which serves to test its effect'. That said, the ruling in Allonby does not mean that there can never be more than one appropriate pool. In the subsequent decision of the Court of Appeal in Grundy v British Airways plc (above) Sedley LJ observed: 'The correct principle, in my judgment, is that the pool must be one which suitably tests the particular discrimination complained of: but this is not the same thing as the proposition that there is a single suitable pool for every case. In fact, one of the striking things about both the race and sex discrimination legislation is that, contrary to early expectations, three decades of litigation have failed to produce any universal formula for locating the correct pool, driving tribunals and courts alike to the conclusion that there is none.'

Clearly, the make up of the pool will depend on the circumstances of the case. **8.71** For example, national demographics will be of relevance in cases where Government legislative policy is being challenged. This was so in R v Secretary of State for Employment ex parte EOC and anor 1994 ICR 317, HL (in respect of the challenge to part-time qualifying thresholds for unfair dismissal rights and redundancy pay), and in R v Secretary of State for Employment ex parte Seymour-Smith and anor 1997 ICR 371, HL (in respect of the challenge to the two-year qualifying period for unfair dismissal rights and redundancy payments). Where, however, the national population at large is not subjected to the PCP in question, a narrower pool will usually be appropriate. Sometimes this will comprise a single organisation (perhaps where the PCP applies to a company's nationwide workforce); sometimes a single workplace (where the PCP is applied at only one location); and sometimes only the employees of a particular type within an organisation (when the PCP is specific to one role, grade or category). Whatever pool is selected, it should ensure that the results are significant rather than merely fortuitous, and do not simply show a short-term phenomenon – a message that is equally relevant to Enderby-type cases, as we shall see.

8.72 Below, we set out two useful case examples (one decided under the SDA and one under the EqPA) that give a flavour of how tribunals should (and indeed should not) identify a pool for determining whether a PCP is tainted by indirect sex discrimination:

• **University of Manchester v Jones** 1993 ICR 474, CA: J was a 47-year-old female graduate who had obtained her degree as a mature student. She was turned down for a job because she fell outside the age range of 25–37 specified by the employer. The tribunal upheld her indirect sex discrimination claim on the ground that the proportion of female graduates who had obtained their degrees as mature students (i.e. at 25 years or older) and who could comply with the requirement to be aged between 25 and 37 was considerably smaller than the proportion of male graduates who had been mature students. On appeal, however, the EAT and the Court of Appeal held that the tribunal had fallen into error: the pool could not be restricted to graduates who had obtained their degrees at age 25 or older since the job advertisement was not just directed at mature graduates but at all graduates aged 25–37 who had the requisite qualifications and experience *irrespective* of when they graduated. Nor could it be correct to say that the pool should contain all female and male graduates in the national population, since the employer would have had no occasion to apply the disputed age requirement to any graduate who did not possess the other necessary qualifications and experience for the job. Nor was the pool merely those graduates in a position to comply with the requirement (i.e. those aged 25–37): in simply identifying the *numbers* of men and women who could comply with the requirement, such a choice of pool would fail to allow a comparison to be made of the relative *proportions* of men and women who could comply in relation to the total numbers of men and women to whom the requirement is or would be applied. Finally, it would not be permissible to limit the pool to graduates in a particular subject (e.g. the subject in which the claimant held a degree) since that would distort the pool by failing to include all persons – male and female – to whom the PCP is or would be applied. The appropriate pool comprised all those persons – male and female – who satisfied (or would satisfy) all the relevant criteria, apart from the PCP in question – i.e. all graduates with the relevant experience

• **Pike v Somerset County Council and anor** 2010 ICR 46, CA: the Teachers' Pension Scheme did not, generally, distinguish between part-timers and full-timers. However, it did so in respect of teachers who had retired and thereafter returned to work. It provided that retired teachers in receipt of a pension who returned to full-time work could rejoin the Scheme, but that those who returned part time could not. P, a 'part-time returner', brought a claim under the EqPA, arguing that this rule indirectly discriminated against women. The employment judge recognised that the rule in question was a PCP, and agreed with the Council that 'the correct pool is the whole of the membership of the profession to which the Pension Scheme, of which the offending requirement or provision is merely one of a number of rules, applies'. In doing so, he rejected P's contention that the pool consisted only of 'returners', both full-time and part-time. He went on to reject P's claim on the basis that the relevant statistics did not reveal a disparate adverse impact on women. P successfully appealed to the EAT. In the view of His Honour Judge McMullen, a pool for comparison which included those under retirement age and still working did not test appropriately the discrimination that P had alleged. HHJ McMullen stated that, in order to carry out the appropriate analysis, 'it is necessary in my view to choose a pool where the disadvantage could be illustrated and that did not occur if poured into the pool were all those under retirement age and working, whether full time or part time. To describe them as an advantaged group, for the purposes of juxtaposition against the disadvantaged group of part-time returners, is an abuse of the language. These people had no advantage out of the post-retirement rule favouring full-timers; it simply did not apply to them. They could only distort the view of the pool.' This analysis, HHJ McMullen noted, was in line with that of Baroness Hale in Secretary of State for Trade and Industry v Rutherford (No.2) 2006 ICR 785, HL, where she stated that those individuals who are 'uninterested' in the particular benefit in question should be removed from the statistical analysis. The EAT concluded that in this case, where the agreed disadvantaged group comprised 'part-time returners', as a matter of logic the advantaged group making up the rest of the pool would comprise 'full-time returners'. The EAT went on to note that, over a period of 13 years, 'an average proportion of 42.45 per cent of the disadvantaged pool were men and an average proportion of 57.55 per cent were women'. In these circumstances, the EAT held that P had demonstrated that the Scheme rule had a disparate adverse impact on women, and remitted the case to the tribunal for consideration of the Council's objective justification defence. That decision was subsequently upheld by the Court of Appeal.

'Enderby' cases. What approach should a tribunal take in considering a case 8.73 such as Enderby (above) – where there is no PCP as such, but a claimant argues that in any event women are adversely affected with regard to pay when compared with men? Here, a tribunal must determine whether or not there are cogent, relevant and sufficiently compelling statistics that substantiate the claimant's argument. In order to come up with cogent and relevant statistics, a pool for comparison must be identified on a logical basis.

The tribunal must be careful not to define the pool in a way that leads to a misleading result. To this end, it should satisfy itself that the two groups encompass all the workers who can be considered to be in a comparable situation and that the groups cover a relatively large number of workers. This ensures that the differences in average pay are not due to purely fortuitous or short-term factors or to differences in the individual output of the workers concerned – Specialarbejderforbundet i Danmark v Dansk Industri (acting for Royal Copenhagen A/S) 1996 ICR 51, ECJ. These matters were at the forefront of the Court of Appeal's collective mind in the following cases:

• **Nelson v Carillion Services Ltd** 2003 ICR 1256, CA: N was employed by CS Ltd in June 1998 as a steward on the Chelsea wing of the Chelsea and Westminster Hospital. She was employed on the company's standard terms and conditions, and her pay was £5 per hour. S, a man taken on a month later to do the same job, was paid the same. However, D, a man who had started work before N, was earning more than her, and received benefits that she did not receive. D received £6.11 per hour, a food allowance of £2.50, and was paid double time if he worked on bank holidays. N brought a claim under the EqPA, pointing to D as her male comparator. Before the employment tribunal the employer argued that it had a material factor defence for the difference in pay. In April 1997 the company had taken over a contract from IHS to provide services to the hospital, and had been obliged by the Transfer of Undertakings (Protection of Employment) Regulations 1981 SI 1981/1794 (TUPE) to maintain the terms and conditions of employment enjoyed by the 300 or so employees who had been servicing that contract. Six of those employees, four men (one of whom was D) and two women, worked in the Chelsea wing. In response to the employer's material factor defence, N argued that the arrangements were indirectly discriminatory against women. She identified a 'pool for comparison' comprising the six transferred employees, S and herself, noting that 80 per cent of the men in the pool had benefited from TUPE protection compared to only 66.66 per cent of the women. The tribunal, however, thought that N had chosen too small a pool for a meaningful comparison to be made, and rejected her claim – a decision upheld by the EAT and the Court of Appeal. The Court stated: 'It was highly artificial to have selected so small a pool and appears likely to have been sheer chance that the proportions between the sexes were as they were'

• **Cheshire and Wirral Partnership NHS Trust v Abbott and ors** 2006 ICR 1267, CA: a number of female domestic staff brought equal pay claims against the Trust with regard to bonus arrangements. At the date of the claims, the Trust employed 146 domestic staff, consisting of 131 females and 14 males. Of those, only one (a man) received a contractual bonus. It employed 20 porters, all male, of whom 17 received a bonus. The catering staff consisted of 13 females and 3 males. Of those, 13 received a bonus –

10 females and 3 males. The three groups, it was assumed, performed work of equal value. The claimants, in seeking to establish the type of sex taint arising in Enderby, sought to compare the predominantly female domestics group with the predominantly male porters group. The tribunal allowed them to do so, saying 'the tribunal accepts that the claimant has the right to choose the comparator'. This comparison, the tribunal concluded, gave rise to a prima facie case of sex discrimination. When the case reached the Court of Appeal, however, the Court held that the tribunal had erred in its approach. First of all, it confused a claimant's right to choose the individual with whom she seeks to compare herself for the purposes of establishing equal work (her male comparator) with the identification of the pool for comparison for the purposes of establishing indirect sex discrimination. It is not an unfettered right of a claimant to choose the pool for comparison: she is not entitled to identify an artificial comparator group so as to bolster her claim of discrimination. Rather, the tribunal must itself ensure that the group comparison exercise is valid. In this case, it was artificial and wrong 'as a matter of logic' to compare domestics and porters, while ignoring the mainly female caterers. The comparison should have been between the domestics on the one hand (the disadvantaged group) and the porters and caterers combined on the other (the advantaged group). As the employer argued, to look at the male porters alone as the comparator group 'deliberately buttresses an argument of sex discrimination'. The EAT reiterated the point made in previous case law that 'one should at least strive to include all the advantaged workers, where work is held or assumed to be of equal value, in the comparator pool'. As a matter of statistics, the larger the group of employees analysed, the more likely it is that a reliable result will be forthcoming. However, in the EAT's view the tribunal's error did not affect the result in this case. It concluded: 'The domestics are almost exclusively female and, with one male exception, do not get a bonus, whilst the porters/caterers are predominantly male and do overwhelmingly get a bonus. That is sufficient to establish a prima facie case of indirect sex discrimination.'

In the Abbott case, then, the tribunal's error with regard to the pool made no **8.74** difference to the outcome. In the following hypothetical example, however, a similar error would certainly be material. Consider an employer who employs an equal number of street cleaners (predominantly male); refuse collectors (predominantly male); school cleaners (predominantly female); and launderers (predominantly female). Let us assume that all of these roles are rated as equivalent under a job evaluation study. For historical reasons, the refuse collectors and launderers receive a contractual productivity bonus of up to 5 per cent of pay, whereas the street cleaners and school cleaners do not. A female school cleaner brings an equal pay claim, pointing to a male refuse collector as a comparator. In attempting to show that the pay differential is tainted by Enderby discrimination, she invites the tribunal to compare the

273

gender make up of the claimant (school cleaner) group and the comparator (refuse collector) group, and conclude that, statistically, women are placed at a disadvantage by the employer's pay practice. Clearly, however, this comparison would not paint a true picture. In this example, the appropriate pool should comprise all four equivalent groups – two of which (one male, one female) receive the bonus and two of which (one male, one female) do not. On this analysis, no 'sufficiently compelling' sex taint would be revealed.

8.75 **Analysing the statistics.** Once an appropriate pool has been identified, it is necessary for the tribunal to determine whether the statistics arising disclose a taint of indirect discrimination. The essence of the tribunal's task in this regard was encapsulated by Lord Justice Mummery in Secretary of State for Trade and Industry v Rutherford and anor (No.2) 2005 ICR 119, CA, as follows: 'It is a matter of applying considerations of logic, relevance and common sense to the raw material of the statistical analysis in order to determine the existence or otherwise of the objectionable state of affairs'. And as Lord Justice Buxton put it in Armstrong and ors v Newcastle upon Tyne Hospital Trust 2006 IRLR 124, CA, there should be 'a clear theoretical rationale for whatever conclusions are drawn from figures'.

Below, we discuss some key issues with regard to statistical analysis that have been thrown up in recent years. With regard to PCP cases, we consider whether tribunals are obliged to focus only on the make up of the 'advantaged' group of individuals, as some case law has suggested, or whether the make up of the 'disadvantaged' group may also be relevant; whether the statistics should only be analysed by reference to the *proportions* of men and women who are advantaged (or disadvantaged), or whether the *numbers* of women and men in the pool might also be relevant; and how great a disparity is required in order for sex taint to be established. We then go on to consider the extent to which, if at all, the approach to statistics will differ in Enderby cases, where there is no PCP at the heart of things.

8.76 **PCP cases – advantaged or disadvantaged group?** In the early indirect sex discrimination cases under the SDA, the courts tended to look only at the advantaged groups of men and women as a percentage of the whole pool and compared those figures. The reason for this was that under the original test for indirect discrimination found in that Act, there needed to be a 'requirement or condition' (now a PCP) in place and 'the proportion of women who [could] comply with it [was] considerably smaller than the proportion of men who [could] comply with it'. Hence, the focus was on who could 'comply', rather than on who could not. In later cases, however, it was accepted that it may be instructive to look at the disadvantaged groups as well (i.e. those who could not comply with a PCP). This led to a debate as to whether the focus of the comparison should be on the advantaged or disadvantaged groups.

274

This debate became central to the 'Rutherford' litigation (which culminated in the case of Rutherford and anor v Secretary of State for Trade and Industry (No.2) 2006 ICR 785, HL). In that case, two male claimants had been dismissed by their (different) employers at the ages of 67 and 73 respectively. They brought employment tribunal claims for unfair dismissal and redundancy payments, but came up against the now-repealed statutory upper age limit of 65 for bringing claims. They argued that excluding them from these payments, which constituted 'pay' for the purposes of the EqPA, amounted to discrimination contrary to what is now Article 157 of the TFEU. This was because the material reason for the difference in pay – the statutory age bar – indirectly discriminated against men. The employment tribunal, in deciding that the material factor was tainted by indirect discrimination, focused only on the 'disadvantaged' group – the 190,500 men and 115,200 women in the labour force between the ages of 65 and 79 who were unable to bring unfair dismissal and redundancy payment claims. On appeal, the EAT disagreed with the tribunal's approach. In its view, the tribunal had erred in focusing on the disadvantaged group, rather than on those under 65 who qualified for statutory unfair dismissal and redundancy rights. In Mr Justice Wall's opinion, the figures for the disadvantaged group were very small and in 'borderline country', with the result that the disadvantaged group represented an unsound basis on which to find disparate impact. Focusing on the advantaged group, there was no significant difference between the proportions of men and women in the workforce who qualified for the statutory rights in question (98.88 per cent and 99 per cent respectively), and this showed unequivocally that there was no disparate impact.

The case then went to the Court of Appeal, which rejected the claimants' **8.77** argument that the primary focus in indirect discrimination cases should be on the disadvantaged rather than on the advantaged group. The Court of Appeal explained that concentration on the disadvantaged group can lead to seriously misleading results, especially in cases where most people in the pool are advantaged. Lord Justice Mummery gave the following example: where 99.5 per cent of men and 99 per cent of women can comply with a PCP, if the focus is shifted to the proportions of men and women who cannot comply (i.e. 1 per cent of women and 0.5 per cent of men) the result would be that twice as many women as men cannot comply with the requirement. In Mummery LJ's opinion, this 'would not be a sound or sensible basis for holding that the disputed requirement, with which the vast majority of both men and women can comply, had a disparate impact on women'.

The claimants appealed further to the House of Lords, which unanimously held that the upper age exclusion on unfair dismissal and redundancy rights in the ERA was not indirectly discriminatory against men. However, their Lordships reached this conclusion on different grounds to those adopted by the EAT and the Court of Appeal and, as Lord Walker acknowledged, it was not possible to extract 'a single easily stated principle' from the speeches of his four colleagues by which employment tribunals could be guided in the future. The speeches of Lords Walker, Nicholls and Rodger do, though, lend some support to the view that in most cases the advantage-led approach to statistical comparisons should prevail. Lord Walker, whose speech was the most fully reasoned, advocated precisely this approach, while noting that there may be circumstances in which some element of 'disadvantage-led' analysis might be helpful. He stressed that the more extreme the majority of the advantaged in the relevant pool, the more difficult it will be to pay much attention to the make up of the disadvantaged group. He went on to say, however, that he could imagine some improbable cases in which a disadvantage-led approach would serve as an alert to the likelihood of objectionable discrimination: for example, if in a pool of 1,000 persons the advantaged 95 per cent were split equally between men and women, but the disadvantaged 5 per cent were all women, the very strong disparity of disadvantage would make it a special case, and the fact that the percentages of the advantaged did not differ greatly (100 per cent men and 90.5 per cent women) would not be decisive.

8.78 In Grundy v British Airways plc 2008 IRLR 74, CA, the Court of Appeal made it clear that there is no one-size-fits-all approach to assessing the disparate impact of a PCP. In that case, G began her career with BA as a member of the full-time cabin crew, but in 1987 she switched to a part-time 'Support Cabin Crew' (SCC) contract. Until 1994 this was the only way in which cabin crew could work part time, and was of particular benefit to women such as G who had childcare responsibilities. In 1994 recruitment onto SCC contracts was halted and, when the SCC scheme was wound up in 2002, G was put onto a part-time 'Cabin Crew' (CC) contract. At that point she was placed on BA's incremental pay scale but, owing to rules relating to the SCC arrangements, was credited with only five years' continuous service. She thus found herself earning nearly £4,000 less than W, a male part-time employee who was employed on 'like work' but who had never worked under an SCC contract. G claimed equal pay, and the key question for the tribunal was whether the material reason for the pay disparity – the policy that, under the SCC part-time working scheme, cabin crew would not be entitled to pay increments – was tainted by indirect sex discrimination. To answer this, it formulated a pool for comparison comprising all BA's cabin crew. Within this, it identified an 'advantaged' group, made up of full-time, part-time and job-share CC, and a 'disadvantaged' group, comprising those who had worked under the SCC scheme. It found that the percentage of female cabin crew falling into the advantaged group was 99.53, whereas the percentage of male cabin crew in that group was 99.93. Expressed in that manner, it stated, 'we consider the difference in proportions to be insignificant'. The tribunal, however, decided that 'our focus must be on the disadvantaged group'. On the basis that women in the disadvantaged group outnumbered men by 14 to one, it concluded that BA's policy of not awarding increments to SCC employees had a disproportionate,

276

disadvantageous impact on women. It therefore required BA to show objective justification for that policy – which, the tribunal concluded, it was unable to do. G's claim was therefore upheld, and BA appealed to the EAT.

The EAT overturned the tribunal's decision, citing the words of Mummery LJ from the Court of Appeal's decision in Rutherford that concentrating on the proportions of men and women in the disadvantaged group 'can produce seriously misleading results'. In the EAT's view, the tribunal in the instant case had made 'an error of law to have reversed the focus... from the advantaged group to the disadvantaged'. The tribunal should instead have focused on the advantaged group. If it had done so, it would have concluded that BA's SCC policy had no disparate impact on the sexes, and dismissed G's claim. G then appealed to the Court of Appeal, which trawled through all of the relevant case law, including Rutherford, and held that the employment tribunal had not erred, and reinstated its decision. The assessment of disparate impact, stated Lord Justice Sedley, is a question of fact for the tribunal, limited like all questions of fact by the dictates of logic. These dictates did not prevent the tribunal in the instant case from focusing on those disadvantaged by the arrangements in question: there is no legal principle that tribunals must always focus on the advantaged group.

8.79 In conclusion, in many cases, common sense will lead to the tribunal's focusing on the advantaged group. Other comparisons, however, should not be ruled out. Considering the make up of the disadvantaged group will often aid the tribunal in its attempt 'to determine the existence or otherwise of the objectionable state of affairs'. In Grundy, the Court of Appeal made it clear that, rather than seeking a magic formula, tribunals should adopt the approach that seems most sensible in the particular case in order to determine whether the reason for a difference in pay between a man and a woman is, in fact, connected with gender. As long as a tribunal has adopted a logical approach, its decision in this regard would be difficult to overturn.

8.80 **PCP cases – proportions or numbers?** The approach under the original SDA test (which was replaced in 2005) was to look at the *proportion* of women and men who could comply with the PCP, rather than at the bare number of women and men who could comply. So, if ten men and four women qualified for a particular benefit, that was not sufficient to show disparate impact. What had to be considered was the total number of people from each sex present in the pool so that the number of those able to comply with the PCP could be expressed as a proportion of that total.

However, as case law developed, it was recognised that comparing proportions was in many cases only the starting point and the courts and tribunals were encouraged to develop a more flexible approach. This approach fitted more easily with the wording of the revised test under the SDA and is reflected in the current indirect discrimination tests found in S.19 EqA (covering indirect discrimination in all areas other than equal pay) and S.69(2) EqA (covering equal pay), which focus on whether women have been placed at a 'particular disadvantage' when compared to men rather than referring to proportions. It will sometimes be appropriate, therefore, for tribunals to look behind and beyond the percentage differences between the proportions of men and women who can comply with a PCP in order to establish whether indirect discrimination has actually occurred.

8.81 For example, when very large total populations in a pool are compared, and the gender ratio of the pool is more or less equal, then small percentage differences between the proportions of men and women that can comply with a PCP can mask considerable differences in the absolute numbers of men who can comply compared with women. If 2 per cent of men can comply and 1 per cent of women, then that means that twice as many men as women can comply (assuming the total number of men and women in the pool to be roughly equal). If the pool is a large one – say, the economically active national population – then a difference of just 1 per cent of a total population of 15 million men would mean 150,000 more men being able to comply than women. By contrast, if the total pool is small – say, comprising only 16 persons equally divided between men and women – then if 62.5 per cent of the men can comply with the PCP in question but only 37.5 per cent of the women, this means that in actual figures five men and three women can comply. The 25 per cent difference between the proportions of men and women who can comply may seem substantial, yet it would only have taken one of the men who could comply to leave and one woman who was capable of complying to be recruited for the differential impact to be entirely eradicated.

So, it all comes back to Lord Justice Mummery's plea in Rutherford and anor v Secretary of State for Trade and Industry (No.2) (above) for tribunals to apply 'logic, relevance and common sense'. In general, tribunals may find the guidance given by the EAT in Harvest Town Circle Ltd v Rutherford 2001 ICR 123, EAT, of some assistance in this regard. According to Mr Justice Lindsay in that case, there will be some cases where, on the statistics, a disparate impact is so obvious that a look at numbers alone or proportions alone will suffice. However, it will never be wrong for a tribunal to look at more than one form of comparison, if only to confirm that the case remains as obvious as it had first appeared. Moreover, if there is any doubt as to the obviousness of the case, the tendency should always be to look at a second or further form of comparison. Thus in less obvious cases it will be proper for the tribunal to look not merely at proportions, as proportions alone can be misleading, but also at numbers, and to look at both disadvantaged and non-disadvantaged groups, and even to the respective proportions in the disadvantaged groups expressed as a ratio of each other. Finally, after looking in detail at such figures, the tribunal in less obvious cases must then stand back and, assimilating *all* the figures, judge

278

whether the apparently neutral PCP in issue has a disparate impact that could fairly be described as considerable or substantial.

PCP cases – how great must the disparity be? There is no simple equation **8.82** that can determine whether a disparity is sufficient to show that a PCP is tainted by sex discrimination. Principles such as the 'four fifths' rule adopted by the US Equal Employment Opportunity Commission have not been favoured in UK or European courts – see McCausland v Dungannon District Council 1993 IRLR 583, NICA. So, the question of disparate impact must always be determined with reference to the circumstances of the case. It is a question of fact for the tribunal to decide and, provided no error of law has been made and the decision is not perverse, it is not readily interfered with on appeal – see Wetstein v Misprestige Management Services Ltd and anor EAT 523/91 and London Underground Ltd v Edwards (No.2) 1999 ICR 494, CA. In the latter case, Lord Justice Potter said that the wide variety of different situations applicable in the employment field made it impossible to come up with a figure which could be applied in all situations. 'If a figure were to be selected... it would be likely to vary according to the context, and in particular as between a case where the [PCP] is applied on a national scale in respect of which reliable supporting statistics are available and those where it is applied in relation to a small firm or an unbalanced workforce where the decision may have to be made on far less certain evidence and to a large degree upon the basis of the... tribunal's own experience and assessment as applied to such figures as are available.' In Potter LJ's view, while a percentage difference of no more than 5 per cent or thereabouts is not inherently likely to amount to a considerable disparity, such a conclusion need not inevitably follow in every case.

In some cases where the bare statistics might suggest that an employer's PCP does not have a significant disparate impact between the sexes, a tribunal might nevertheless conclude that a taint of discrimination is present. This was made clear by the Court of Appeal in the Edwards case. There, the claimant was one of only 21 women in a total pool comprising 2,044 train operators. All 2,023 men were able to comply with a requirement for flexible working hours, as were all the women save for the claimant herself. A tribunal held that, regardless of the statistics, there was a taint of sex discrimination. Given the disparity in numbers between male and female train operators, it ruled that it was appropriate to go beyond the specifics of the pool in question and take account of common knowledge that women are more likely to be single parents and have primary responsibility for childcare. The tribunal accordingly held that the requirement for flexible working was one with which the proportion of women who could comply was considerably smaller than the proportion of men. Both the EAT and the Court of Appeal upheld the tribunal's decision in this regard. In doing so, they specifically sanctioned the right of tribunals to use their general knowledge and expertise to look outside the pool for comparison and take into account national statistics showing that ten times as many women

279

as men are single parents or look after children. In the words of Potter LJ: '[T]he comparatively small size of the female component [in the pool] indicated... without the need for specific evidence, both that it was either difficult or unattractive for women to work as train operators... and that the figure of 95.2 per cent of women [able] to comply was likely to be a [maximum] rather than a [minimum] figure.' Rejecting the employer's contention that the tribunal should have confined itself to a consideration of the evidence of adverse effect on the members of the particular pool in question, Potter LJ remarked: '[A] tribunal does not sit in blinkers. Its members are selected in order to have a degree of knowledge and expertise in the industrial field generally. The high preponderance of single mothers having care of a child is a matter of common knowledge.'

8.83 Two other cases – one an equal pay case and one a sex discrimination case – where tribunals looked beyond the bare statistics to conclude that a taint of indirect discrimination was present:

- **Chief Constable of West Midlands Police v Blackburn and anor** 2008 ICR 505, EAT: as discussed at greater length under 'Indirect discrimination' above, this case involved police constables who were available for '24/7' working receiving 'special priority payments' that were not made to constables who were unable to work at night. Two female constables, who had been excused 24/7 working because of their childcare responsibilities and hence did not receive the additional payments, brought equal pay claims. In the EAT, Mr Justice Elias accepted the tribunal's findings that the employer's material factor – its desire to reward night working – explained the differential between the claimants and their male comparators, but was tainted by sex discrimination as it had a disparate adverse effect on women. The EAT upheld the tribunal's finding that where 96.6 per cent of men could comply with the 24/7 requirement, compared to only 91.5 per cent of women, this was sufficient to establish indirect discrimination. Interestingly, Elias P went on to say that, on the facts of the case, the statistical analysis may not strictly have been necessary, as disparate impact might have been established in any event as 'at least in the current climate, conferring a benefit on those working throughout the night will disadvantage some women, and has disadvantaged the claimants, by virtue of the fact that they have childcare responsibilities'. (This aspect of the tribunal's decision was not before the Court of Appeal when it upheld the EAT's finding that the payments were objectively justified – see below under 'Showing objective justification')
- **Chief Constable of Avon and Somerset Constabulary v Chew** EAT 503/00: of 2,581 men and 453 women, all except one man and ten women could comply with the shift pattern imposed by the employer – in other words, 99.96 per cent of men and 97.7 per cent of women could comply, a difference of 2.26 per cent. A tribunal nevertheless held that the shift

pattern had a sufficiently disparate impact on women to amount to indirect sex discrimination, and the EAT refused to intervene. In so doing, the EAT accepted that the percentage difference of 2.26 did not amount, on the face of it, to a sufficiently disparate effect. However, it held that the tribunal had been correct to adopt a flexible approach and to have regard to factors other than the identified percentage difference. The tribunal had been entitled to conclude that an inherently likely effect of the condition was that it would disadvantage officers with childcare responsibilities, and to note that the overwhelming burden of such responsibilities falls on women.

Enderby cases. The ECJ in the Enderby case said that there would be a prima **8.84** facie case of sex discrimination, even in the absence of a discriminatory PCP, 'if the pay of speech therapists is significantly lower than that of pharmacists and if the former are almost exclusively women while the latter are predominantly men... at least where the two jobs in question are of equal value and the statistics describing the situation are valid'. Since that ruling, the courts and tribunals have had to determine whether such Enderby discrimination can only occur where the disadvantaged group are 'almost exclusively women' and the advantaged group are 'predominantly men', or whether it can cover a wider range of circumstances.

An important decision in this regard is that of the Northern Ireland Court of Appeal in British Road Services Ltd v Loughran and ors 1997 IRLR 92, NICA. There, the employer sought to advance a material factor defence, explaining that the claimants (clerical officers) and their comparators (warehouse operatives) belonged to separate bargaining groups. The employer argued that, in order for the claimants to establish a 'sex taint', it was necessary for the workers in the claimants' group to be 'almost exclusively' female, given that that was the phrase used by the ECJ in Enderby. The Appeal Court rejected that argument. It held that where a 'significant majority' of the disadvantaged claimant group are women, an employer cannot merely rely upon separate bargaining processes as material factor defence, but must go on to show an objective justification for the pay differential. The ECJ in Enderby, in using the words 'almost exclusively' to refer to the claimant group, had been merely reflecting the factual situation in that particular case (where 98 per cent of the claimant group were women). The European Court had not intended to propound the principle that, unless the disadvantaged group could be described as consisting 'almost exclusively' of females, a presumption of discrimination could not arise. Rather, the presumption of discrimination arises if the evidence shows that the relative number of women in a group is sufficiently representative to identify it as a female group. A significant majority of women within a group may be as reliable an indicator of a history of unequal treatment as is a group composed virtually exclusively of women. The Court concluded that it had been open to the tribunal to hold that a group comprising 75 per cent females and 25 per cent males was sufficiently representative to provide a reliable

— 281

indication of unequal treatment. Accordingly, it rejected the employer's argument that the history of the separate pay structures (without more) could satisfactorily explain away the pay disparity between the claimant and comparator groups.

8.85 The Loughran case is only of persuasive authority outside Northern Ireland, but was followed by the EAT in England in Paterson and ors v London Borough of Islington and ors EAT 0347/03. There the EAT stated: 'Enderby cannot be understood as a case whose principle only applies in circumstances in which the disadvantaged group is made up "almost exclusively" of women... we consider that the broader underlying principle of Enderby must be, and is, that there will be cases in which, having regard to the relative sizes of the proportions of women in the disadvantaged group and men in the advantaged group, a prima facie case of direct sex discrimination in relation to pay will be regarded as arising that is sufficient to cast on to the employer the burden of proving that the pay difference is objectively justifiable. We consider that is the only rational basis upon which the decision can have been founded.'

More recently, in Home Office v Bailey and ors 2005 ICR 1057, CA, the Court of Appeal went even further, holding that the appropriate approach to statistics in Enderby cases is no different to that adopted in PCP cases (discussed above). The facts of Bailey were that some 2,000 female administrative, executive, secretarial and support staff within the Prison Service brought claims comparing their pay to that of employees in other grades predominantly occupied by men. One group of claimants worked as higher executive officers (HEOs) and were paid less than male comparators employed in the grades of governor and principal officer. An employment tribunal heard a lead case in respect of this group brought by two women HEOs. The employer argued that it did not have to raise the claimants' pay because there was a non-sex material factor explaining the pay disparity; namely, the separate pay bargaining arrangements for the claimant and comparator groups that had been in place for years. The claimants argued, however, that the pay arrangements were tainted by sex discrimination. The tribunal found that the employer had imposed a requirement or condition (the forerunner to a PCP) to the effect that, in order to obtain the advantages enjoyed by the comparator group, a claimant had to belong to that group. In March 2000, the disadvantaged group consisted of men and women in approximately equal numbers, whereas the advantaged, comparator group was predominantly male. With reference to a pool for comparison comprising the HEOs and the comparator grades, the tribunal found that the proportion of women within that pool who were disadvantaged was considerably greater than the proportion of disadvantaged men. It concluded that there was a prima facie case of indirect discrimination, obliging the employer objectively to justify the difference in pay.

282

On appeal, however, the tribunal's decision on 'sex taint' was overturned. The **8.86** EAT held that it was wholly artificial to erect as a 'requirement or condition' of being a member of the advantaged group the fact that one is a member of that group. In other words, this was not a PCP case, but an Enderby-type case. Furthermore, there was a clear difference, in the EAT's view, between assessing the disparate impact of a PCP that presents a barrier to women becoming a member of a particular work group, and considering whether a disparity of pay that has arisen by reason of a history of different arrangements for collective bargaining evidences sex discrimination. In the former case it was sensible to compare the extent to which men and women across a pool could satisfy the PCP in order to become a member of that working group, thus measuring the disparate impact of the PCP. In the latter case it made sense, as in Enderby, to conclude that if the advantaged group was predominantly male and the disadvantaged group predominantly female, there was a prima facie case of discrimination. Where, however, the advantaged group was predominantly male and the composition of the disadvantaged group was neutral in gender terms, as in the instant case, the EAT took the view that while the situation may not be fair, it was not prima facie discriminatory on the ground of sex as envisaged by the ECJ in Enderby. The claimants appealed to the Court of Appeal.

The Court agreed with the EAT that this was an Enderby case rather than a PCP case, but it nevertheless reinstated the tribunal's decision that the statistics demonstrated prima facie sex discrimination, requiring the employer to show objective justification. In the Court's view it could not be right that, if a case could be categorised as involving the application of a PCP, a valid statistical approach could lead to a conclusion of prima facie discrimination whereas, if it were categorised as an Enderby-type case involving disparity of pay between two work groups, prima facie discrimination could only be found if the disadvantaged group was predominantly of one gender and the advantaged group predominantly of the other. Lord Justice Peter Gibson stated that, in each type of case, the task for the tribunal is 'to determine whether what on its face is a gender-neutral practice may be disguising the fact that female employees are being disadvantaged as compared with male employees to an extent that signifies that the disparity is prima facie attributable to a difference of sex.' Furthermore, 'a common approach to the two types of case has the merit of ensuring that the 1970 Act is applied consistently to all forms of indirect discrimination'. Turning to the facts of the instant case, he stated: 'Where, as here, there is one group of employees of an employer which contains a significant number, even though not a clear majority, of female workers whose work is evaluated as equal to that of another group of employees of the employer who are predominantly male and who receive greater pay, it would be very surprising if [a tribunal] were to be precluded by the presence in the disadvantaged group of a significant number of men from holding that that disparity in favour of

283

men required justification by the employer.' Given this, the tribunal had been entitled to conclude that there was a prima facie case of indirect sex discrimination in this case, and its decision in this regard was reinstated.

8.87 The Court of Appeal's conclusion in Bailey – that the same statistical approach is required in both PCP and Enderby cases – has not been universally embraced, however. In Villalba v Merrill Lynch and Co Inc and ors 2007 ICR 469, EAT, Mr Justice Elias stated: '[T]here is a real issue as to whether the statistics which would be sufficient to establish the [PCP] form of indirect discrimination will also be sufficient to establish the Enderby form, or whether the latter, where there is no apparent reason why women have been adversely affected, should require more striking statistics.' Elias P noted that the Court of Appeal in Bailey thought that there was no difference in the statistical requirement for both forms of discrimination. He mused, however: 'It is far from obvious that the evidence sufficient to justify a finding that a particular criterion or practice adopted by the employer adversely affects women is the same as the statistical evidence required to justify an inference that there must be prima facie discrimination where none apparently exists.' If it were the case that disparate adverse impact could just as easily be shown without the presence of a PCP, he continued, then the concept of a PCP in indirect discrimination law becomes effectively redundant.

And in the following case the EAT seemed to take a similar view to that of Elias P in Villalba:

- **Tyne and Wear Passenger Transport Executive (trading as Nexus) v Best and ors** 2007 ICR 523, EAT: the EAT considered whether there was indirect discrimination inherent in Metro train drivers ('drivers') being paid more than Metro Operators ('MOPs'), who, it was accepted, were employed on like work. As no PCP had been identified, the tribunal relied primarily on a statistical comparison of men and women in each group in order to decide whether or not a prima facie case of sex discrimination could be inferred. The correct 'pool for comparison' was all the drivers who received the higher pay (the 'advantaged group') plus the MOPs, who did like work but at a lower rate of pay (the 'disadvantaged group'). Comparing the proportion of men, as a group, who were advantaged with the proportion of women, as a group, who were advantaged, the respective proportions were 63.5 per cent and 50 per cent. This comparison provided the basis for the tribunal's conclusion that there was disparate adverse impact on women, meaning that the employer would be required to show objective justification. The EAT, however, overturned the tribunal's decision. In its view, in the absence of a PCP, where the only evidence of disparate impact that can be relied upon comprises statistics, 'those statistics must be so clear as to speak for themselves'. In this case, the EAT pointed out, the *disadvantaged* group as a whole was overwhelmingly male, comprising almost 12 times as many men as women. In such circumstances, the statistics could not be said to be 'sufficiently compelling' to give rise to a prima facie case of 'Enderby' discrimination. The EAT stated: 'We find it difficult to conceive of a situation in which it would be correct to make a finding that a pay disparity is tainted by sex and discriminatory against women, where there is no direct discrimination and no provision, criterion or practice that might lead to a disparate impact on women, even if the overall proportion of women in the disadvantaged group is higher than that of men *but where the overwhelming majority of the disadvantaged group is male*' (EAT's emphasis).

It is difficult to reach any clear conclusions from these cases. From the Court of **8.88** Appeal's decision in Bailey, it would seem that, in essence, the same statistical approach is required for both PCP and Enderby cases. Indeed, the difference between the two types of case should not be overestimated. In fact, Peter Gibson LJ went so far as to say that 'the difference between a formal requirement or condition for obtaining a benefit which divides two groups of workers and a division by reference to jobs for which different amounts are paid is one of form rather than substance'. The tribunal's job in every case is 'to determine whether what on its face is a gender-neutral practice may be disguising the fact that female employees are being disadvantaged as compared with male employees to an extent that signifies that the disparity is prima facie attributable to a difference of sex'.

Nevertheless, as the EAT noted in the Best case, where there is no PCP – meaning that 'pure' statistics are the only evidence of disparate impact – 'those statistics must be so clear as to speak for themselves': they must, as Elias P put it in Villalba, be 'striking'. Clearly, such striking statistics are not always required in PCP cases. For example, in London Underground Ltd v Edwards (No.2) 1999 ICR 494, CA, and Chief Constable of West Midlands Police v Blackburn and anor 2008 ICR 505, EAT, the statistical evidence did not demonstrate a significant disparity, but in each case a taint of indirect discrimination was identified: the courts were entitled to take into account the fact that, regardless of the statistics, the PCPs in those cases – requirements of flexible and night working – would be more likely to place women at a disadvantage than men. If Edwards and Blackburn had been Enderby cases rather than PCP cases, we suggest that the statistics thrown up would have failed to reach the threshold required to show a taint of sex discrimination.

Showing objective justification
8.89

As previously explained, if an employer puts forward a material factor to explain a pay differential between a claimant and her comparator that is not directly sex discriminatory, but the claimant convinces the tribunal that, as a result of that factor, she and other women doing equal work are put at a particular disadvantage when compared to men doing equal work, the employer will have to show 'objective justification' for its actions in order to defeat an equal pay claim. So what is 'objective justification'? According to the ECJ in Bilka-Kaufhaus GmbH v Weber von Hartz 1987 ICR 110, ECJ, an employer can show such justification for the purposes of what is now Article 157 of the TFEU where a pay practice:

(i) corresponds to a real need on the part of the employer

(ii) is appropriate with a view to achieving the objective pursued; and

(iii) is necessary to achieve that objective.

Soon afterwards, the House of Lords in Rainey v Greater Glasgow Health Board 1987 ICR 129, HL, confirmed that the Bilka-Kaufhaus test as laid down in respect of Article 157 applied equally to S.1(3) EqPA (and indeed to the SDA).

8.90 In the subsequent Court of Appeal decision of Hampson v Department of Education and Science 1989 ICR 179, CA (a race discrimination case), Lord Justice Balcombe, after setting out the Bilka-Kaufhaus test, offered a formulation which he said accurately encapsulated what that test requires: that is, 'an objective balance between the discriminatory effect of the condition and the reasonable needs of the party who applies the condition'. This formulation – which has become known as the 'principle of proportionality' – was endorsed by the House of Lords in Webb v EMO Air Cargo (UK) Ltd 1993 ICR 175, HL (a sex discrimination case) and Barry v Midland Bank plc 1999 ICR 859, HL (an equal pay case). Now the principle of proportionality is expressly incorporated into the EqA and requires an employer attempting to show objective justification to demonstrate that its actions were a 'proportionate means of achieving a legitimate aim' – S.69(2) EqA.

Below we briefly examine the key concepts of objective justification. A more detailed analysis can be found in IDS Employment Law Handbook, 'Sex Discrimination' (2008), Chapter 3.

8.91 Legitimate aims

As outlined immediately above, under S.69(2) EqA an employer's reliance on a material factor will be objectively justified only if it is a proportionate means of achieving a 'legitimate aim'. So, unless the aim behind a 'sex tainted' pay differential between a claimant and her comparator can be regarded as 'legitimate', the employer's attempt to show objective justification will be bound to fail.

While the meaning of 'legitimate aim' is largely to be discerned from a consideration of the case law, S.69(3) EqA provides that 'the long-term objective of reducing inequality between men's and women's terms of work is always to be regarded as a legitimate aim'. Thus, where the purpose behind the material factor is an attempt by the employer to achieve equal pay for equal work across the workforce, the sole question will be whether that factor is a proportionate means of achieving such equality (see under 'Proportionality', below).

Clearly, if the aim behind a pay practice is itself sex discriminatory, then it can **8.92** never be legitimate – see R v Secretary of State for Employment ex parte EOC and anor 1994 ICR 317, HL, and Allonby v Accrington and Rossendale College and ors 2001 ICR 1189, CA. Furthermore, it is not enough for an employer simply to show that an indirectly discriminatory measure was imposed in pursuance of an intrinsically laudable and otherwise reasonable policy – Greater Manchester Police Authority v Lea 1990 IRLR 372, EAT (a sex discrimination case). Rather, there has to be a nexus established between the functional needs of the employer and the imposition of the pay practice at issue. Without showing this connection or nexus, it would be impossible to carry out the objective balancing exercise entailed in applying the principle of proportionality.

Whether or not an employer's discriminatory pay practice pursues a legitimate aim will clearly depend on the facts of the case: what might be a legitimate aim for one employer might not be for another. Nevertheless, in an equal pay context it is clear that there is a broad range of material factors, many of which will be legitimate – such as the need to recruit able staff; the wish to reward loyalty; and the desire to reward good performance – see further 'Specific material factors' below.

Cost as a legitimate aim. Where a pay differential is tainted by indirect **8.93** discrimination, it is unclear whether the employer's financial constraints will amount to objective justification for that differential. Certainly, it would be foolhardy for an employer to attempt to show justification by explaining to a tribunal that the reason for discriminating was simply that it was cheaper to do so. However, it seems that cost may be *one of* the factors to put into the balance when considering justification – see Cross and ors v British Airways plc 2005 IRLR 423, EAT, which is authority for this view in the context of sex discrimination. This suggestion that cost can be a valid consideration was backed by Mr Justice Elias in Redcar and Cleveland Borough Council v Bainbridge and ors 2008 ICR 249, EAT. In his view, although it is not legitimate to discriminate where the sole aim or purpose is to save costs, the question of cost will not always be irrelevant to the question of objective justification. Where a benefit is introduced and costs determine the scope and size of that benefit, then it is unlawful to allocate the benefit on a discriminatory basis, and in that sense it would not be open for an employer to say that the restriction on cost prevented the benefit from being conferred on the disadvantaged group. But the issue of cost may become material when an employer is being asked to put right some alleged continuing discrimination. In those circumstances, although the employer cannot defeat the right to equality by pointing to financial burdens alone, it can pray the financial burdens in aid as some support for a decision which is objectively justified on other grounds.

The general view of the EAT, therefore, seems to be that while costs can be a relevant factor, they are not sufficient on their own. However, that view is not universal and in Woodcock v Cumbria Primary Care Trust 2011 ICR 143, EAT (a sex discrimination case), the President of the EAT, Mr Justice Underhill, stated that contrary to the EAT in Cross (above) he saw no principled basis for a rule that cost considerations can never by themselves constitute sufficient justification for discrimination. Underhill P noted that the adoption of such a rule would tend to involve parties and tribunals in an artificial game of 'find the other factor', producing arbitrary and complicated reasoning. Moreover, he considered that deciding where 'cost' stops and other factors start is not straightforward.

This matter is likely to come before the Court of Appeal in due course. Until then, it would seem prudent for employers – particularly in equal pay cases – to adopt a cautious approach and continue to follow the Cross decision by identifying another justifying factor in addition to cost.

8.94 Proportionality

In many cases, it will be fairly straightforward for an employer to show that its 'discriminatory' pay practice is pursuing a legitimate aim. The question of whether the practice is a 'proportionate means' of achieving such an aim, however, is likely to give rise to much more argument.

8.95 Reasonably necessary. At first glance, the test set out by the ECJ in Bilka-Kaufhaus GmbH v Weber von Hartz 1987 ICR 110, ECJ (see under 'Showing objective justification' above), seems to present a formidable hurdle for an employer seeking to justify indirect discrimination: the employer is required to show to the satisfaction of the tribunal that the 'discriminatory' policy corresponds to a real need on the part of the employer; that the policy is appropriate with a view to achieving the employer's objective; and – on its face the most difficult of all – that the policy is 'necessary' for this purpose.

However, the word 'necessary' in this context has not been given its strictest possible interpretation: an employer is not required to prove that there was no other way of achieving its business objectives. In Hardys and Hansons plc v Lax 2005 ICR 1565, CA (a race discrimination case), Lord Justice Pill stated: 'I accept that the word "necessary" used in *Bilka* is to be qualified by the word "reasonably"... The presence of the word "reasonably" reflects the presence and applicability of the principle of proportionality. The employer does not have to demonstrate that no other proposal is possible. The employer has to show that the proposal, in this case for a full-time appointment, is justified objectively notwithstanding its discriminatory effect.' Nevertheless, Pill LJ went on to state that this 'reasonably necessary' test is much stricter than the 'range of reasonable responses' test applicable in unfair dismissal law. He accepted that the principle of proportionality requires a tribunal to take into account the reasonable needs of the employer's business. However, that was not to suggest that the tribunal is confined to considering whether the employer's views on those needs fell within the band of reasonable responses available. Instead, the tribunal has to make its own judgment, upon a fair and detailed analysis of the working practices and business considerations involved, as to whether the discriminatory proposal or measure is reasonably necessary.

Balancing exercise. The principle of proportionality requires a tribunal to **8.96** carry out a balancing exercise between the discriminatory effects of an employer's pay practice and the reasonable needs of the employer in applying that practice – Hampson v Department of Education and Science 1989 ICR 179, CA (a race discrimination case). So, it would seem, the greater the degree of discrimination, the greater the burden on the employer to show that the practice corresponds to a real commercial objective and is appropriate for achieving that objective. The House of Lords in Barry v Midland Bank plc 1999 ICR 859, HL, noting that the ECJ in Enderby v Frenchay Health Authority and anor 1994 ICR 112, ECJ, drew attention to the need for national courts to apply 'the principle of proportionality', explained the principle thus: '[T]he ground relied upon as justification must be of sufficient importance for the national court to regard this as overriding the disparate impact of the difference in treatment, either in whole or in part. The more serious the disparate impact on women, or men as the case may be, the more cogent must be the objective justification.' In other words, the degree of justification required is 'proportionate' to the degree of disparate impact caused by the employer's practice or policy.

It follows from Barry that stringent scrutiny of the justification defence is appropriate where the discrimination, although indirect in form, is very closely related in substance to the direct form of the discrimination – R (on the application of Elias) v Secretary of State for Defence 2006 IRLR 934, CA (a race case involving a successful challenge to the Government's non-statutory compensation scheme for British civilians who were interned by the Japanese during World War II). In that case, the dispute centred on birth-related criteria that needed to be satisfied in order for former prisoners of war to be eligible for compensation. In holding that the eligibility criteria were not proportionate, the Court of Appeal stated that the trial judge had correctly adopted a rigorous standard in scrutinising the reasons advanced by the Secretary of State in justifying the criteria. A stringent standard of scrutiny of the justification was appropriate because the discrimination, though indirect in form, was closely related in substance to the direct form of race discrimination on the ground of national origins. In that particular case, the right to compensation was confined to 'British civilians', who for these purposes were defined as those born in the United Kingdom or who had a parent or grandparent who was born in the United Kingdom. The same argument about a more stringent standard of proof was deployed (unsuccessfully) by the claimants in Blackburn and anor v Chief Constable of West Midlands Police 2009 IRLR 135, CA. There, the claimants failed to convince either the EAT or the Court of Appeal that the form of discrimination they had suffered – where they could not qualify for special '24/7' working payments owing to their childcare responsibilities – was 'closely related' to direct discrimination and that the task of establishing objective justification was therefore particularly onerous.

8.97 Before moving on, we should note that the House of Lords' explanation of the 'principle of proportionality' in the Barry case – in essence, that justification must be proportionate to the seriousness of the disparate impact – was questioned by Lord Justice Sedley in British Airways plc v Grundy (No.2) 2008 IRLR 815, CA. Sedley LJ indicated that he had found it impossible to know how to gauge the seriousness of the disparate impact of a particular practice or term, and concluded that such an exercise was not necessary in any event. He stated: 'Ex hypothesi the disparity is substantial, not marginal, otherwise justification would not be needed. It cannot matter that it affects a relatively small number of employees, for the right which it invades is a personal contractual right. Nor can it matter that the amount involved is small: for an employee who is unlawfully underpaid 50p an hour, the difference may be between subsistence and poverty.' This analysis enabled the Court to uphold a tribunal's decision that an employer's pay practice had not been objectively justified, despite the tribunal's failure to follow the Barry proportionality test to the letter. Sedley LJ concluded: 'If... the tribunal have not tried to measure the disparate impact which they have found, it seems to me, with respect, that they have avoided an elephant trap rather than committed an error of law.' It remains to be seen what effect these words will have on future cases. However, to the extent that they conflict with the test laid down by the House of Lords in the Barry case, that established test should be preferred.

8.98 **Assessing the alternatives available.** As noted above, in Hardys and Hansons plc v Lax 2005 ICR 1565, CA, the Court of Appeal stated that the employer, in showing objective justification, does not have to demonstrate that there was no route other than the discriminatory practice by which the legitimate aim could have been achieved. However, if a claimant puts forward a non-discriminatory alternative for achieving the same objective a tribunal may well decide that the alternative ought reasonably to have been adopted and find that, because it was ignored, justification has not been made out – Cobb and ors v Secretary of State for Employment and Manpower Services Commission 1989 ICR 506, EAT. A similar stance was taken by the ECJ in Kutz-Bauer v Freie und Hansestadt Hamburg 2003 IRLR 368, ECJ, where it held that national courts should take into account the possibility of achieving by other means the aims pursued by the provisions in question. And in its 'Coming of Age' consultation document concerning the Employment Equality (Age) Regulations 2006 SI 2006/1031 (now replaced by the age discrimination provisions in the EqA), the Government summed matters up thus: where a legitimate aim can be achieved equally well by a measure that has a big discriminatory effect and one that has a small discriminatory effect (or that does not discriminate at all), the latter should be used.

When considering less-discriminatory alternatives that might have been **8.99** available, tribunals need to keep in mind the aim that the employer was seeking to achieve in the first place. Two cases that illustrate this point:

- **Barry v Midland Bank plc** 1999 ICR 859, HL: the issue in this case was whether an employer was discriminating against women in the way redundancy payments were calculated. This was done in the same way as under the statutory redundancy scheme, by focusing on their salary at the time of dismissal. Some women who had earlier worked full time but who, at the time of their dismissal, were working part time contended that this meant that they were not getting the full reward for their service. It was accepted that the reason for fixing the payment by reference to final salary was in part to cushion the redundant workers from the loss of income that would flow from their being made redundant. To give effect to that objective, the focus necessarily had to be not on past service but on future loss. In the House of Lords, four of their Lordships held that there was no discrimination at all on these facts. Lord Nicholls, on the other hand, considered that there was prima facie indirect discrimination but concluded that the method of determining pay was objectively justified. Once the aim of cushioning against future loss was seen as legitimate, relating compensation to the actual pay received at the date of termination was inevitable. The way in which the women said the pay should be calculated – namely, by reference to the service over the whole period of employment – would have involved adopting a different scheme and would have undermined that particular objective. In so deciding, Lord Nicholls agreed with the Court of Appeal that to compel the employer to abandon its scheme and substitute a scheme where severance pay was treated and calculated not as compensation for loss of a job but as additional pay for past work would not be right

- **Chief Constable of West Midlands Police v Blackburn and anor** 2009 IRLR 135, CA: the West Midlands Police force (WMP) introduced special priority payments (SPPs) to reward police officers working unsocial hours. One of the qualifying criteria for SPPs was 24/7 working. This scheme had a disparate adverse effect on women. Although the tribunal accepted that the employer's material factor – a wish to reward night-time work – was a legitimate aim, it thought that the same objective could have been achieved by less discriminatory means – for example, by simply paying the female claimants as if they had worked at night. The tribunal therefore concluded that the pay disparity at issue in this case was not objectively justified. Allowing WMP's appeal, the EAT held that the tribunal had failed to engage with WMP's actual aim behind the scheme. Its purpose was to single out and reward those working nights – an objective that would not be achieved if those who were not working nights were paid the same amount as those who were. Furthermore, the fact that WMP could afford to pay the bonus to those who could not work 24/7 was irrelevant. It was no answer to a defence of justification for a difference in pay to say that there was no need for the difference in the first place. The EAT pointed out that, if this was followed to its logical conclusion, there would be no reason in principle why a woman whose childcare commitments were specifically accommodated by being allowed to work part time should not be paid as if she worked full-time hours. The Court of Appeal dismissed the appeal. It found the issue 'straightforward', agreeing with the EAT that if the objective of the scheme was to reward 24/7 working it was difficult to see how that objective would be achieved if those who did not work it were paid the same amount.

8.100 **Justification required at date of 'discrimination'**
As discussed under '"Material" factor – evaporation of historical material factor' above, there is a degree of uncertainty as to whether a historical explanation for a pay differential can amount to a material factor giving rise to a S.69 EqA defence. There is, however, no such debate with regard to justification. The justification put forward by the employer for an indirectly discriminatory pay practice falls to be judged *at the time when the claimant was affected*: not at the time when the pay practice was introduced. Accordingly, employers should periodically monitor their employment policies and practices, as a pay practice can start off life as being justified, only for this to change (see further Chapter 10, 'Equal pay audits').

However, it should be noted that in the context of the justification of an indirectly discriminatory pay policy based on a 'length of service' criterion, the Court of Appeal has held that an employer must justify both the adoption of the criterion in the first place and its continued use – Wilson v Health and Safety Executive 2010 ICR 302, CA (see further under 'Specific material factors – length of service' below).

8.101 **Specific material factors**

Up to this point in this chapter we have been concerned with the legal principles relevant to an employer's material factor defence to an equal pay claim. Now we turn to look at how those principles have been applied in practice, examining a number of material factors that employers have relied, or attempted to rely, upon.

8.102 **Market forces and related factors**
The so-called 'market forces' material factor covers various situations that may arise in the particular labour market in which the employer's enterprise operates.

These could include, for example, a shortage of the type of skills that the male comparator has; the fact that the claimant and comparator are being paid the 'going' (or 'market') rate; the need to pay a higher rate to the comparator in order to reduce labour turnover in respect of the particular job he is doing, or in order to recruit him in the first place; and the fact that, because of the weak bargaining power of the group of workers to which the claimant belongs, the claimant needs only to be paid the lowest rate necessary to attract workers such as herself.

In Clay Cross (Quarry Services) Ltd v Fletcher 1979 ICR 1, CA, Lord Denning MR stated: 'An employer cannot avoid his obligations under the [EqA] by saying: "I paid him more because he asked for more", or "I paid her less because she was willing to come for less". If any such excuse were permitted, the Act would be a dead letter.' However, the Clay Cross decision was overruled by the House of Lords in Rainey v Greater Glasgow Health Board 1987 ICR 129, HL, in so far as it prevented an employer from raising any factor that was extraneous to the personal circumstances of the claimant and comparator (such as market forces or administrative efficiency). The Rainey case concerned the setting up of a prosthetic service within the NHS in Scotland and the continuing payment of private sector rates of pay to prosthetists who came in a 'block transfer' from private practice to set up the new service. In contrast, those recruited directly into the NHS once the service was established were paid ordinary NHS Whitley Council rates. The House of Lords held that the need to attract a sufficient number of recruits within a short period of time constituted a material factor justifying the higher rate of pay paid to the comparator (who was recruited from private practice). There was also a good and justified reason for paying a lower rate to the direct recruits such as the claimant: it would have been administratively anomalous and inconvenient if prosthetists recruited directly into the NHS were subject to a different salary structure and negotiating mechanism than other NHS employees.

8.103 The availability of a 'market forces' defence was affirmed in Enderby v Frenchay Health Authority and anor 1994 ICR 112, ECJ, with regard to what is now Article 157 of the TFEU. There, the European Court said that 'the state of the employment market, which may lead an employer to increase the pay of a particular job in order to attract candidates, may constitute an objectively justified economic ground'.

8.104 **Case examples.** Below, we consider a number of cases in which 'market forces' and related material factors have been relied upon successfully by employers to defeat equal pay claims:

- **Lee v Wakefield College** ET Case No.1805044/04: F was an agency worker lecturing at the College. The College initiated a drive to persuade agency staff to convert to being College employees, and F was offered a post at the same point on the incremental scale as an existing employee, L. F had an offer from another employer that was more attractive, and thus would not accept the College's offer unless it could be improved. The College needed to secure F's services for the beginning of the term – this was only one-and-a-half weeks away and it would have been difficult for the College to conduct the term's teaching without him – and therefore offered him the post two increments higher on the scale. F accepted, and in response L brought an equal pay claim. The College mounted a 'market forces' material factor defence before the tribunal. The tribunal recognised that 'it should never be sufficient for an employer simply to allege market forces without advancing proof of the market forces on which it relies'. However, in its view the College had satisfied the burden of showing the market forces element in this case. It had been vital for the College to secure F's services on the higher rate of pay. Furthermore, the tribunal accepted that the market forces defence continued to protect the College in respect of the ongoing pay disparity between L and F, given that under the College's incremental pay structure lecturers were put on to the next increment at the beginning of each academic year. F would continue to be paid at a higher rate than L until L reached the top of the incremental scale, at which point her salary would catch up with his

- **McHale v HHG Services Ltd** ET Case No.1900269/04: McH, HHG Ltd's Head of Facilities Management, brought a tribunal claim seeking pay equal to that of two male comparators – H, the Director of UK Procurement, and B, Head of IT Strategy and Planning. An independent expert concluded that McH's work was of equal value to that of her comparators, but the company argued that this conclusion was flawed. In addition, it put forward a material factor defence that the reason for the pay differentials in question was 'market forces' – persons engaged in the financial sector in facilities management are not able to command the salary levels that are paid to those engaged in procurement or IT. The tribunal accepted the company's arguments and dismissed C's claims. With regard to the material factor defence, the tribunal agreed with the company that the salaries in question were in accordance with those paid within the relevant marked sectors. Hence, the pay differentials existed by reason of market forces – a material factor unrelated to the difference in sex

- **Cunningham v Pama and Co Ltd** ET Case No.2409804/03: C was employed by P Ltd as a 'pre-packer' at its Kingsway site, earning £4.50 an hour. P Ltd needed to recruit employees for another site at Bredbury and, since it was unable to do so at the rate of £4.50 an hour, it decided to pay them £5 an hour. Two men were recruited at the new rate to do essentially the same work as C. She brought an equal pay claim before an employment tribunal, but her claim was dismissed. The tribunal accepted P Ltd's argument that there was a material difference between the circumstances of C and those of her male comparators, in that, in order to recruit new staff (male or female) to the Bredbury site at the time in question, it had needed to pay a higher rate. The tribunal made it clear, however, that had the pay differential continued for any length of time, P Ltd would have had more difficulty in explaining it away. A material difference at the time of recruitment will not necessarily remain so throughout the life of the contract. In this case, however, C's pay rate, and that of other employees engaged on pre-packing work, had been increased to £5 an hour prior to the hearing

- **Grafton v Arriva Trains Northern** ET Case No.1803776/03: G worked as HR Manager for ATN, earning £22,500 per annum. He claimed pay equal to that of female Finance and Passenger Managers, who were paid more than £30,000 per annum. Although the jobs were rated as equivalent under a job evaluation study, an employment tribunal dismissed G's claim. He had worked for the employer and its predecessors since 1972, beginning in a clerical post. The comparators, on the other hand, were recruited externally in 2000/01 at the prevailing market rates for the jobs in question. With regard to the Finance Manager, recruitment consultants had advised that a salary in excess of £30,000 would be necessary to attract suitably qualified applicants; and the Passenger Manager had been recruited from a competitor and, in the circumstances, had to be paid more than her salary in her previous job. Furthermore, the tribunal noted, G had two HR colleagues on the same grade as him, and he was the highest paid of the three. In the tribunal's view, the employer had demonstrated that the explanations for the differences in pay were both genuine and material

- **Denham v Health and Safety Executive** ET Case No.2103091/02: D joined the HSE as a Band 3 Inspector, based in Bootle, in 1997. The post had been advertised at a salary between £20,000 and £38,000 per annum, and he was paid £33,000. By 2002 he was earning just over £39,000. His comparator joined the HSE in 2002, also as a Band 3 Inspector. Based in Aberdeen, she was offered a starting salary of £45,000 and, after further negotiation, joined the HSE on a salary of £46,500. The employer maintained that the pay differential resulted from market forces, and the tribunal agreed. There was substantial evidence to establish that the HSE genuinely believed that a higher salary would have to be paid to attract applicants to perform the job in Aberdeen at that time. The variation in salaries was thus genuinely due to a material factor which was not the difference of sex, and D's equal pay claim was dismissed

- **Spencer v Jakubowski and anor** ET Case No.1700414/01: S worked as nurse in charge of the night shift at Oakridge Nursing Home. He was paid £7.50 per hour. On 31 March 2000 his employer recruited a woman to work as nurse in charge of the day shift. She was paid £8 per hour. S learnt of the discrepancy in pay in February 2001 and complained to his employer. He was offered an increase to £8 an hour, but refused to accept it unless it was backdated to March 2000. He brought an equal pay claim, but this was rejected by the tribunal. The tribunal noted that two nurses – as it happens, one male and one female – were paid £8 an hour. These were both recent recruits, and the tribunal was satisfied on the evidence that neither would have agreed to work for less than that salary. The fact was that the employer, which was obliged to compete in the open market at a time when there was a national shortage of nurses, could not recruit staff for less than £8 an hour. The tribunal also noted that there were four female nurses who were paid the same as or less than S. There was no evidence of the College's seeking to employ staff of only one sex at the higher rate and, in the circumstances, the material factor defence had been made out

- **Broadbent v Bridgefords Ltd ET** Case No.2100298/99: B was manager of a branch of an estate agency. She sought equal pay with a male comparator, S, who was employed on like work to hers. The employer contended that there was a material factor explaining the difference in pay. S had been head-hunted to take over a branch that was performing badly, he had been poached from another estate agency, and had been employed on relatively generous terms because he simply would not come for less. The tribunal upheld the employer's material factor defence, and dismissed B's claim. In its view, the employer's contract with S 'was a freely negotiated agreement entered into between its parties that reflected their respective bargaining power at the time. It may or may [not] be appropriate to consider this an agreement dictated by "market forces", but we saw no reasons why this should not amount to a genuine material factor. Certainly, it was a material difference between his case and [B's].'

8.105 By way of contrast, four cases in which employers failed to make out a 'market forces' material factor, largely because the reasons for the pay differentials were not fully transparent:

- **Barton v Investec Henderson Crosthwaite Securities Ltd** 2003 ICR 1205, EAT: B was employed as a media analyst by IHCS Ltd, an investment bank. In 2001 she brought an equal pay claim on the ground that H, a male colleague employed on 'like work', received a higher salary and better contractual benefits. Prior to this B had served a questionnaire on the employer under S.74 SDA (now S.138 EqA) asking the bank for reasons for the differences in pay, but had not received a proper reply. The bank's chairman, C, told the employment tribunal that H used to be paid the same as B, but the latter's salary and benefits had been increased in 1999 to the highest within the organisation because of concerns that he was being head-hunted. The tribunal held that the bank had established that the difference in pay was genuinely due to a material factor which was not the difference in sex within the meaning of S.1(3) EqPA (now S.69 EqA). Referring in particular to the threat of employees being head-hunted, the tribunal stated that all the increases in the comparator's pay were 'conscientious, unscientific efforts to secure the employee's services for the future by putting his benefits in line with those of other key players'. On appeal, the EAT overturned the tribunal's decision. In its view, in assessing whether the bank had a material factor defence the tribunal had failed to take into account the lack of transparency in its pay system and its serious failure adequately to respond to the questionnaire. The EAT commented that 'no tribunal should be seen to condone a City bonus culture involving secrecy and/or a lack of transparency because of the potentially large amounts involved, as a reason for avoiding equal pay obligations'. The EAT allowed B's appeal and directed a rehearing before a different tribunal

- **Smith v Atex Media Command Ltd** ET Case No.2601163/05: S was employed by AMC Ltd in 1999 on a salary of £13,500 per annum. J was engaged with effect from January 2001 on an annual salary of £22,000, and thereafter received annual increments that were seen as cost of living increases. AMC Ltd maintained that the pay discrepancy between S and J was due to market forces, but was unable to provide evidence to support this contention. The tribunal upheld S's equal pay claim, and in doing so stated that it is incumbent on an employer who seeks to explain a higher salary as the product of market forces to put forward some evidence of the dictates of the market on the relevant date

- **Mezzotero v BNP Paribas SA** ET Case Nos.2201221 and 2203101/03: M, a female banker, was paid a lower contractual bonus than those paid to eight male colleagues who were employed on 'like work'. She brought an equal pay claim before an employment tribunal. The tribunal accepted that BNP's reason for paying different amounts was genuine – it was concerned that another employer was trying to poach staff at the time, and paid staff the level of bonus thought necessary to retain them. Furthermore, the tribunal accepted that the lower amount paid to M reflected the value that the employer placed on retaining her. However, the tribunal did not accept that BNP's reasons were not gender-related. The system for setting the bonus payments lacked transparency: the system was not explained to the tribunal, it was not clear who made the decisions, and no documents were provided. Furthermore, the employer had been unwilling to answer the relevant questions in the statutory questionnaire, and there was a lack of compliance with the Equal Opportunities Commission's *Code of Practice on Equal Pay* (replaced by the Equality and Human Rights Commission's *Code of Practice on Equal Pay* from October 2011: see Chapter 1 under 'Codes of Practice')

- **Chamberlain v North West Leicestershire District Council** ET Case No.1902503/08: in April 2007 C successfully applied for a post as a civil enforcement officer, for which the salary range was £15,459 to £17,352. She started at the bottom of the grade, having been told that this was not

297

negotiable. Her comparator joined in July 2008, but started at a higher salary point on the grade. Before the tribunal, the Council relied on market forces as the non-discriminatory reason for the difference in pay. The tribunal found that the Council had not made out the material factor defence: it had been unable to demonstrate that there was a recruitment or retention problem in 2008 that necessitated paying above the grade minimum. The simple fact was that, unlike C, the comparator was given the opportunity to negotiate his pay.

8.106 **Market rates that discriminate between women's and men's work.** Even where an employer's decision on pay is transparent, the scope for using market forces as a basis for explaining the variation between a claimant's and her comparator's contractual terms is not limitless. Where a market forces argument is itself dependent on practices which, historically, socially or economically, discriminate against women, then it will not necessarily be a viable basis for a S.69 defence – see North Yorkshire County Council v Ratcliffe and ors 1995 ICR 833, HL. Certainly, an employer putting forward going rates as a material factor would do well to enquire as to any underlying discriminatory reasons for the applicable pay levels and whether objective justification can be shown for those levels. This topic is discussed at length under 'Taint of sex discrimination – direct discrimination' above.

Note that in at least one exceptional area of employment, market forces may dictate that women's pay is *higher* than men's. In the field of security and protection services, earnings statistics have shown that full-time female security guards have, in fact, been paid more than their male counterparts. This is presumably because, although the vast majority of such employees are men, it is sometimes necessary or desirable to employ a woman to undertake body frisking and other similar tasks. The perceived risks of such work and the unsocial working hours involved combine to make recruiting women in this area more difficult than is the case with men. Women are therefore in a position to command higher rates of pay. However, this did not prevent a tribunal in McGlary v Burton International plc ET Case No.7549/96 from concluding that an employer who relied upon such market forces to justify paying a woman £1 an hour more than the male claimant had not made out a material factor defence. In somewhat terse reasoning, the tribunal concluded that the employer's explanation for the pay differential was invalid because it related to gender: 'the need to pay females more may well have been a commercial reality but it is not a factor which we can within the regime of the EqPA accept as excusing the difference in pay between a man and a woman in this employment'. The tribunal's decision makes a degree of sense. The employer would clearly have paid any suitably qualified woman a higher rate because she was a woman and paid any similarly qualified man the lower rate because he was a man. It is

298

difficult to escape the conclusion that, market forces notwithstanding, the claimant and comparator were being treated differently on the ground of their sex – i.e. there was direct sex discrimination.

Geographical differences   8.107

The fact that a male comparator is employed in a different part of the country can constitute a material difference between the man's and the woman's cases. The most obvious example of a material factor relating to geographical location which could give rise to a defence under S.69 EqA would be the payment of a London supplement or weighting allowance to compensate for the higher cost of living in the capital.

In Navy, Army and Air Force Institutes v Varley 1977 ICR 11, EAT, V, who was employed by the NAAFI in Nottingham, pointed out that her contractual hours (37 per week) were less favourable than those of a man employed on like work in London (36½ per week). The EAT, overturning the tribunal decision that her equal pay claim had been made out, held that the difference was not due to sex, but to the custom that employees in London worked shorter hours than those in Nottingham.

Skills, qualifications and vocational training   8.108

The different skill levels of a claimant and her comparator can explain and justify a pay difference (or other contractual variation) between them; and the same can be said of different formal qualifications: see Hawker Fusegear Ltd v Allen EAT 794/94 and Glasgow City Council and ors v Marshall and ors 2000 ICR 196, HL. An example:

- **Leacock v Association of MBAs** ET Case No.2204564/03: L began working for the Association as assistant database administrator, deputising for U. When U finally left altogether, L took over his job. She claimed she should have received equal pay with U after taking over his role. U had been appointed in 2000 on a salary of £18,000; L, on the other hand, was being paid only £16,000 in respect of the same role in 2002. In summer 2003 the Association sought advice on salaries from independent consultants and were advised that database administrators such as L earned between £18,000 and £22,000 per annum. L's salary was increased to £17,430. Before the tribunal, the Association maintained that U had been paid more than L because he was a graduate, because of his particular skills and abilities (including the fact that he was socially adept), and because of his previous experience as a manager. The tribunal, however, upheld L's equal pay claim. In its view, the qualities that the Association put forward as explaining why it had paid U more than L were not relevant to the job at hand, and there was no evidence of any appraisal system. There was a lack of transparency in the pay structure, and decisions about pay were often the subjective and unstructured judgements of individual managers. In the absence of any adequate explanation for the difference in pay, L's equal pay claim succeeded.

8.109 In Handels-og Kontorfunktionaerernes Forbund i Danmark v Dansk Arbejdsgiverforening (acting for Danfoss A/S) 1991 ICR 74, ECJ, the European Court stated that applying a criterion of vocational training as a factor for rewarding employees with higher pay could systematically disadvantage women, in so far as they have fewer opportunities to obtain such training or to exploit the rewards of such training. If so, the employer must justify the use of such a criterion. The ECJ made it clear that, as with other similar criteria, the employer will show justification only if the training in question specifically improves the performance of employees in respect of the duties with which they are entrusted.

8.110 **Experience**

'Experience', when used as a basis for the material factor defence, can have different meanings. One is the experience an employee gains over a period of time in terms of familiarity with his or her job. This is closely connected to length of service, which we discuss separately below. Another relates to more specific types of 'experience', whether garnered inside or outside the workplace, that have given rise to particular skills or know-how. Such experience can justify a pay differential provided it is not simply used as a smokescreen to conceal gender inequality. In Payne v Brindley Twist Tafft and James, Solicitors ET Case Nos.1300092/08 P was appointed assistant employment solicitor on a salary of £24,000 per annum upon qualifying. The department was run by another employment solicitor, M, who had started up the department in October 2004 on a salary of £40,000 a year, which rose to £42,000 in July 2005. M left the firm in April 2006 and P effectively took over the running of the department. The case load was managed with the help of locums and, between March and September 2007, a legal executive, S, who earned £33,000 a year. P's salary increased to £27,500 in July 2006 and to £32,000 in July 2007. P left the firm in October 2007 and brought an equal pay claim, citing M and S as her comparators. The tribunal rejected her claim to be paid the same as M – he was employed on a higher salary because of his post-qualification experience, which gave him the necessary skill and knowledge to carry out his role, and his salary was further increased because of his success in building up the department. However, her claim to be paid the same as S succeeded because the firm failed to show that S's previous employment experience or any other factor explained his higher salary in a less responsible role.

Difficulties can arise where the employer submits that the comparator's higher starting salary was to reflect greater prior experience than the claimant, as this factor is likely to fall away once the claimant has 'caught up'. In Hastings v Davisons Solicitors ET Case No.1305947/08 the tribunal found that it took

300

the claimant – a trainee conveyancing solicitor – nine months' training in the job to match the greater experience that her comparator – a paralegal in the mortgages department – had upon his appointment. The tribunal held that once that nine-month period had elapsed, the difference in experience no longer amounted to a material factor and the claimant was entitled to pay equal to that of her comparator.

8.111 Even where it is appropriate to reward experience, it is important that the employer ensures that a higher value is not placed (without good cause) on the kind of experience men habitually acquire compared with women. Two contrasting examples:

- **Baker and ors v Rochdale Health Authority** unreported 14.1.94, CA: female nurses claimed equal pay with a male community nurse. A tribunal found that the difference in their pay was due to the comparator's special expertise in the area of male catheters. The employer had operated a policy whereby male catheters would be fitted by male nurses and female catheters by female nurses. Since the comparator was the only male nurse working in the community, this meant he fitted as many catheters as all the female nurses put together. Consequently, he developed a great deal of expertise in this area and was consulted throughout the district on the problems of male catheterisation. Indeed, his expertise was such that he became involved in training other nurses in the techniques involved. The tribunal held that these factors meant that the man's extra pay was due to a material factor other than the difference in sex. An appeal by the claimants to the EAT was unsuccessful, and on further appeal the Court of Appeal also upheld the tribunal's finding. The Court ruled that, while it was true that there was a gender-related reason why the comparator obtained the expertise that led to his training duties, the tribunal had been entitled to find that the training function was an independent factor and that he was entitled to be specially rewarded for it. He had developed his expertise through his own skill, and not through any discriminatory policy operated by his employer

- **Charles v Pembrokeshire County Council and anor** ET Case No.25695/96: the rules governing teachers' pay provided for increments to be awarded in respect of 'years of experience other than employment as a teacher [which is] of value to the performance of the classroom teacher's duties'. As a result of this, the Council awarded a male teacher incremental pay points in view of his 'relevant experience' as an assistant in a physical education department. C, who accordingly earned less than the male teacher, brought an equal pay claim, in the course of which she contended that her experience of bringing up two children before entering the teaching profession should similarly be rewarded. The tribunal upheld her claim. In rejecting the employer's 'experience' material factor defence, it commented that parenthood should not, in the context of the pay scheme, be disregarded as being merely part of 'the common fund of universal human experience' but as useful and relevant experience that better equipped employees for teaching in a primary school. It was therefore appropriate to accord C's experience monetary recognition in the same way as the comparator's experience had been recognised.

8.112 Length of service

It is not in dispute that length of service can count as a material factor explaining a pay disparity. However, it is also clear that a pay structure that takes length of service into account can have a disparate adverse effect on women, who are statistically less likely than men to attain long service.

As explained under 'Taint of sex discrimination' above, an employer whose material factor has a disparate impact as between men and women will be required to objectively justify the pay differential between the claimant and her comparator if it is to avoid liability under the EqA or Article 157 of the TFEU. However, there has been much debate about whether a length of service criterion is deserving of special treatment; that is, whether it is *intrinsically* justified, meaning that employers will not be required to show justification for it on the facts of each individual case.

8.113 The starting point for discussion of this issue is the ECJ's decision in Handels-og Kontorfunktionaerernes Forbund i Danmark v Dansk Arbejdsgiverforening (acting for Danfoss A/S) 1991 ICR 74, ECJ. There, the European Court recognised that application of a length of service criterion may well result in the less favourable treatment of female employees, given that many women will have entered the labour market more recently than men and are subject to more frequent interruptions in their career. Crucially, however, the ECJ ruled that it is permissible for an employer to reward seniority because this goes hand in hand with experience, which generally places a worker in a better position to carry out his or her duties. The upshot was that employers would not be required to provide special justification for using the criterion of length of service when determining pay; there was no need to show its importance for the performance of the specific duties entrusted to the employee concerned.

In subsequent cases, however, the ECJ appeared to resile somewhat from the position adopted in Danfoss:

* **Nimz v Freie und Hansestadt Hamburg** 1991 IRLR 222, ECJ: this case concerned a provision in a collective agreement that rewarded length of service (the calculation of which differed depending on whether the employee was full time or part time) by means of increased pay. The ECJ held that the use of such a pay criterion, which has the effect of indirectly discriminating against predominantly female employees, has to be objectively justified with regard to the circumstances of each case. It was thus necessary for the national court to examine the relationship between the nature of the duties performed, and the experience gained by working over a longer period of time

- **Gerster v Freistaat Bayern** 1998 ICR 327, ECJ: the provisions of German national law made promotion in the Civil Service partly dependent upon length of service, and provided for part-timers' length of service to be assessed on a pro rata basis according to the number of hours worked. The case, as it turned out, fell within the scope of the Equal Treatment Directive (No.76/207) rather than the Equal Pay Directive (No.75/117) (both of which have subsequently been consolidated into separate provisions in the recast Equal Treatment Directive (No.2006/54)), but it is clear that the general principles laid down by the ECJ are also applicable in a pay context. The ECJ ruled that the statutory provisions in question were indirectly discriminatory unless they could be justified on an objective basis. In this regard, it would be necessary for the employer to establish that part-time employees are generally slower than full-time employees in acquiring job-related skills and abilities, and that, in the light of this, the measures for calculating their accrual of service for the purposes of promotion were adopted because they reflected a legitimate social policy aim, were an appropriate means of achieving that aim, and were necessary in order to achieve it. If there is no special link between the length of service and the acquisition of a certain level of knowledge or experience, then the requirement that part-time employees complete longer periods of service in order to be eligible for the same chances of promotion as full-time employees could not be justified.

All of which brings us to the more recent high-profile case of Cadman v Health **8.114** and Safety Executive 2006 ICR 1623, ECJ, in which the ECJ was given the opportunity to consider the issue of length of service and justification once more. In that case C, a Principal Inspector for the HSE, was paid at a lower level than four male colleagues on the basis that her length of service was shorter than theirs. When she brought an equal pay claim before an employment tribunal, the HSE accepted that she was doing work rated as equivalent to that of her comparators, and that the length of service criterion (the HSE's material factor explaining the pay differential) had a disproportionate adverse impact on women and was therefore potentially indirectly discriminatory. It submitted, however, that the length of service criterion was, by its very nature, objectively justified. In this regard, the HSE sought to rely on the ECJ's decision in Handels-og Kontorfunktionaerernes Forbund i Danmark v Dansk Arbejdsgiverforening (acting for Danfoss A/S) (above) that it is permissible for an employer to reward length of service without the need to show the importance of such service for the performance of the specific duties concerned. C countered by arguing that equal pay law has developed at a great pace since Danfoss was decided, with nearly all of the subsequent decisions having a common message: that if the factor relied upon by an employer to explain a difference in pay is tainted by discrimination, then the employer has to show specific objective justification for adopting that measure. There was no reason, in C's view, why the adoption of length of service criteria should provide some kind of blanket

303

justification that did not require consideration of whether a difference in pay based on such criteria corresponded to a genuine business need on the part of the employer.

The tribunal agreed with C, taking the view that the Danfoss decision had been watered down by subsequent decisions, such as that in Nimz. Given this, the onus was on the HSE to demonstrate specific justification for its reliance on seniority as a factor explaining the pay differentials. This, the tribunal concluded, it could not do. Accordingly, the long service requirement did not give rise to a valid material factor defence, and C's claim would be upheld. On appeal, however, the EAT overturned the tribunal's decision, concluding that the Danfoss decision remained good law. In its view, where groups of full-time workers are treated differently from each other according to their length of service, there is no requirement on an employer to provide special justification. C appealed to the Court of Appeal, which referred the matter to the ECJ so that it could determine whether subsequent European case law had altered the principle laid down in Danfoss, and if so to what extent. The Court of Appeal asked the ECJ whether, where a length of service criterion with regard to pay has a disparate adverse effect on women, Article 157 requires the employer to provide special justification for recourse to that criterion; and if the answer to this depends on the circumstances, what are those circumstances? Furthermore, the Court asked whether there is any relevant distinction to be drawn between the use of a length of service criterion in cases involving part-time workers and the use of that criterion in cases only involving full-time workers.

8.115 With regard to the main point at issue, the European Court, contrary to the Advocate General's Opinion, concluded in line with Danfoss that employers do not need to provide specific justification for a length of service criterion in every case. However, the ECJ added an important caveat, noting that Danfoss did not exclude the possibility that there may be situations in which recourse to the criterion of length of service must be specifically justified by the employer. In the ECJ's view, specific justification on the facts *will* be required where the claimant provides evidence capable of giving rise to 'serious doubts' as to whether recourse to the criterion of length of service is, in the circumstances, appropriate. According to the ECJ: '[S]ince, as a general rule, recourse to that criterion is appropriate to attain the legitimate objective of rewarding experience acquired which enables the worker to perform his or her duties better, the employer does not have to establish specifically that recourse to that criterion is appropriate to attain that objective as regards a particular job, unless the worker provides evidence capable of raising serious doubts in that regard.'

Unfortunately, the ECJ did not go on to give any indication of what sort of evidence would suffice to raise 'serious doubts' as to the validity of a length of service criterion. In its statement on the Cadman ruling, the Equal Opportunities Commission (now incorporated into the Equality and Human Rights

Commission) attempted to fill the gap, surmising as follows: '[L]ong pay scales in jobs which can be effectively mastered within a few months/years of starting, such as unskilled and semi-skilled work, will be open to challenge and will have to be justified in detail. Also, employees will now be able to challenge the use of very long pay scales in more complex jobs where the scale goes beyond the point where the tasks are effectively mastered.'

The uncertainties created by the ECJ's decision in Cadman were addressed by the Court of Appeal in a subsequent case that also involved the HSE. In Wilson v Health and Safety Executive 2010 ICR 302, CA, W claimed equal pay with three male colleagues who were paid substantially more than her because of their longer service. The HSE admitted that she and her comparators were employed on work rated as equivalent under a job evaluation study. However, it put forward a material factor defence that the pay disparity was due to the use of length of service as a criterion in the incremental pay system, which had a disparate impact on women but was objectively justifiable. The tribunal initially addressed the matter prior to the date of the ECJ's ruling in Cadman. At that stage, taking its cue from the EAT's decision in Cadman (2004 ICR 378, EAT), the tribunal held that it was obliged to follow Danfoss and find that any difference in pay that resulted from a length of service criterion was objectively justified. However, the tribunal observed that, had it not been so bound, it would have found that the period of time over which length of service was rewarded in W's case – ten years – was not objectively justified. The tribunal stated that it was persuaded, albeit on 'sparse and anecdotal' evidence, that five years was sufficient. **8.116**

W's appeal was stayed pending the ECJ's decision in Cadman, following which the EAT remitted W's case to the tribunal to determine whether W had provided evidence capable of raising 'serious doubts' that would require justification of the length of service criterion in the particular circumstances of the case. The tribunal analysed the ECJ's decision in Cadman, and recorded its surprise that 'the reasoning is disappointingly sparse'. Nevertheless, it concluded that, once it had been accepted that a length of service criterion was appropriate, it was not open to it to scrutinise the way in which it had been *applied*. W's claim was again dismissed and she appealed once more to the EAT.

The Appeal Tribunal held, after some admitted difficulty, that the Cadman 'serious doubts' exception *did* extend to the application of a service-related pay criterion (including the period over which it operates). It indicated, however, that a claimant has a high hurdle to clear in establishing serious doubts as to whether a length of service criterion is appropriate. As to the procedure for such claims, the EAT directed that the tribunal should address the issue of 'serious doubts' before hearing all the evidence on justification. It therefore remitted W's claim to another tribunal to consider whether she had raised **8.117** serious doubts regarding the appropriateness of a service-related pay structure that covered a ten-year period. The HSE appealed to the Court of Appeal and W cross-appealed.

In Lady Justice Arden's view (a view shared by the rest of the Court of Appeal) the language of the ECJ's judgment in Cadman, while undoubtedly opaque, was capable of applying to both the adoption and the use of a length of service criterion, and indeed both adoption and application were in issue in that case. Arden LJ saw no reason to distinguish between 'adoption' of a service-related criterion, in the sense of the initial act of an employer in establishing pay scales which incorporate a service-related criterion, and 'use' or application, in the sense of the employer's implementation of such a criterion in the operation of those pay scales.

8.118 Turning to the 'serious doubts' test, Arden LJ considered that the ECJ was putting forward this test as a preliminary 'filter' on claims. The requirement of establishing 'serious doubts' was merely the counterpart of the proposition that a length of service pay criterion does not, in the usual case, require justification; it could not be interpreted as imposing a further burden of proof on the employee. In essence, the 'serious doubts' requirement was merely a sensible evidential requirement to ensure that the complaint has some prospect of success. The employee has to show that there is evidence from which, if established at trial, it can properly be found that the general rule – i.e. that service-related pay does not require justification – does not apply. The employee does not necessarily have to flesh this contention out in minute detail, although there would have to be some basis for inferring that the adoption or use of the length of service criterion was disproportionate. It followed from Arden LJ's analysis of the Cadman decision that the original decision of the employment tribunal in W's case – that rewarding length of service for a period of ten years was not justified – should be restored.

So, where does this leave us? In effect, the Court of Appeal has done away with much of the confusion emanating from the ECJ's decisions in Cadman and Danfoss, treating the 'serious doubts' test as no more than a preliminary filter on hopeless claims. Since, as Arden LJ acknowledged, it is a general rule that length of service goes hand-in-hand with experience, a claimant will have to provide some evidence to show that she has an arguable case that the employer's reliance on length of service to explain a pay difference is not proportionate, but this is a very low hurdle for the claimant to pass and certainly does not amount to any shift in the burden of proof.

8.119 It follows that employers who adopt a length of service criterion in their pay scales will need to review their policies to ensure that their use of length of service as a pay criterion genuinely serves a purpose (i.e. a 'legitimate aim') in respect of, for example, the skills and experience that the job in question requires, or the need to reward or encourage loyalty, and that the discriminatory effect of applying such a criterion is proportional. In the Wilson case, even though the claimant accepted that the employer's desire to reward length of service justified some initial difference in pay, the tribunal found that the employer could not justify rewarding length of service over a ten-year period.

Before moving on, there are two further points worth mentioning from the ECJ's decision in Cadman v Health and Safety Executive (above). First, after upholding Danfoss and adding its musings about the 'serious doubts' issue, the ECJ stated: '[I]t should be added that where a job classification system based on an evaluation of the work to be carried out is used for determining pay, it is not necessary for the justification for recourse to a certain criterion to relate on an individual basis to the situation of the workers concerned. Therefore, if the objective pursued by recourse to the criterion of length of service is to recognise experience acquired, there is no need to show in the context of such a system that an individual worker has acquired experience during the relevant period which has enabled him to perform his duties better.' We quote at length, because it is not entirely clear what the ECJ is saying here. We should point out, though, that Mrs Cadman and her four male comparators were employed on work rated as equivalent under a job evaluation study. Does the ECJ's ruling provide the HSE with a blanket defence because her job had been evaluated, regardless of consideration of the 'serious doubts' issue? Possibly so, although any form of blanket defence should be treated with caution in light of the Court of Appeal's decision in the Wilson case (above).

8.120 Secondly, we return to the question posed by the Court of Appeal to the ECJ in Cadman with regard to part-timers: whether there is any relevant distinction to be drawn between the use of a length of service criterion in the case of part-time workers (such as in the Nimz case) and the use of that criterion in the case of full-time workers (such as in the Danfoss case). Unfortunately, despite the apparent discord between the Nimz and Danfoss cases, the ECJ declined to answer this question. The tribunal in the Wilson case summed things up neatly, stating: '[A]lthough [the ECJ] mentioned... the cases of Nimz... and Gerster, the Court undertook no analysis of those cases and did not comment on the distinction between part-time and full-time working... In the final analysis, this tribunal is not at all clear why no comment on Nimz etc was necessary. The authority and logic of those cases is now left in some doubt.'

Responsibility and potential

8.121 The greater responsibility that comes with work experience may constitute a material factor justifying a pay differential. A trainee for a job (even assuming that he or she is doing like work to the permanent employees) will not usually be entitled to equal pay – De Brito v Standard Chartered Bank Ltd 1978 ICR 650, EAT. Also, an employee's future potential may be a relevant factor. In this regard, although the question of whether the claimant and comparator are employed on 'like work' must be determined solely by what they are actually doing at the present time, an employer may, it seems, seek to explain a difference in pay on the ground that the comparator's higher pay is due to the fact that the employee is being groomed for a much more responsible job – Guest v Ferro (Great Britain) Ltd EAT 287/77. We would advise, however, that employers be wary of making such a factor a basis for their defence. It is preferable that employees are paid on a fair and transparent basis for what they are doing rather than for what they might be doing at some point in the future.

8.122 **Pay protection**

When jobs are regraded, or when employees are moved from higher-paid to lower-paid work, perhaps because of physical incapacity, it is common practice to allow those adversely affected to retain the higher salary, on either a temporary or a permanent basis. This practice is known as 'pay protection' or, traditionally, as 'red-circling'. On one level, pay protection is desirable, not only to protect an individual employee from the hardship of an immediate salary reduction, but also because such a reduction could amount to a breach of contract. On the other hand, where a man's pay has been protected, a woman employed on like work or work of equal value who falls outside the protected group will be earning less, potentially giving rise to an equal pay claim.

In Audit Commission v Haq EAT 0123/10 two roles within the employer's organisation were amalgamated into one but the 11 affected employees were allowed to retain their existing points on the pay scale. This resulted in the two highest-paid occupants of the new role being male and the lower-paid women sought to claim equal pay. A tribunal found that the statistical disparity raised a prima facie case of indirect discrimination, and that the discrimination could not be objectively justified. On appeal, the EAT took a different view. It noted that the case could not be one of Enderby discrimination since there was no suggestion that the roles of the men and women prior to the amalgamation had been subject to gender stereotyping. Nor did the EAT consider that a prima facie case of PCP discrimination had been raised. The employer applied a practice of pay protection, but that practice did not put women at a particular disadvantage; it merely advantaged anyone who had been previously been on a higher pay grade, including a number of the female claimants. Furthermore, the EAT held that had there been, contrary to its findings, any indirect discrimination, it was justified – a pay protection policy, being introduced to achieve fairness to an employee, or group of employees, who have been downgraded through no fault of their own, will be a proportionate means of achieving a legitimate aim, provided that, as was agreed by the parties in the instant case, it did not incorporate past discrimination.

8.123 By and large, where pay protection is confined to individuals, any cause for grievance is unlikely to be acute, especially where the protection has been imposed on 'humane' grounds. This is also likely to be the case where small groups are affected and the pay protection does not incorporate any past

308

discrimination (as in the Haq case). Equal pay claims are much more likely to arise where the pay of whole groups of employees has been protected following the downgrading of their work – particularly where the purpose of the regrading exercise was to resolve pay inequalities. In such circumstances, pay protection might simply prolong the pre-existing pay discrimination that the regrading exercise was intended to remove. This point is writ large by the volume of high-profile equal pay litigation that has flowed from the implementation of the 'single status' agreement in local government, the background to which we discuss in Chapter 1 under 'Growth in public sector claims'.

Below, we look in some detail at the difficulties arising from pay protection in the context of the 'single status' agreement. In particular, we examine the critical questions of whether, and if so in what circumstances, a local authority can found a material factor defence on the existence of pay protection where such protection has been introduced in order to implement 'single status' effectively. We then move away from the problems in local government to consider more general issues around the use of pay protection as a material factor.

'Single status' – pay protection resulting in continuing inequality. One of 8.124
the main aims of the 'single status' agreement, reached in 1997, was to iron out inequality in pay and conditions in local government. The terms and collective bargaining structures of manual and white collar workers, previously separate, were to be unified under the umbrella of the 'Green Book', and to this end job evaluation studies were carried out. Once these were completed, and the Green Book implemented, employees placed on the same grade would be 'rated as equivalent', regardless of the nature of their work.

However, not everyone who was rated as equivalent under the new system was on the same terms and conditions, and this inequality then had to be rectified. Owing to a lack of central funding, the approach of most local authorities was to 'equalise down' rather than raise the wages of the 'underpaid' staff. In many cases, this was achieved by simply ending bonus schemes that, in the past, had advantaged predominantly male groups. However, in order to avoid industrial relations problems, authorities reached agreements with trade unions to grant periods of 'pay protection' to those employees previously in receipt of higher pay or bonuses, so that the blow of the wage reductions would be cushioned, at least for a few years. This meant that, even after the implementation of the single status agreement, certain predominantly male groups whose jobs had been rated as equivalent to those of predominantly female groups were still, for a period of time, receiving higher pay. This led a number of female employees – with the encouragement of 'no win, no fee' lawyers – to bring equal pay claims. In response, the local authorities argued that the pay protection arrangements in the context of 'single status' negotiations amounted to a material factor explaining (and, indeed, objectively justifying) the ongoing pay inequality.

8.125 A number of these cases eventually came before the Court of Appeal in Redcar and Cleveland Borough Council v Bainbridge and ors and another case; Middlesbrough Borough Council v Surtees and ors 2009 ICR 133, CA. The Court's conclusion – to the consternation of local authorities – was that the pay protection arrangements in these cases were unlawful as they perpetuated historical indirect sex discrimination against women with regard to pay. Since this decision is extremely important, both in legal and practical terms, we examine it below at some length.

In April 2004 Redcar and Cleveland Borough Council implemented the Green Book, bringing manual workers and administrative, professional, technical and clerical (APTC) workers under the same pay structure. Previously, these workers were covered by the 'White Book' and 'Purple Book' respectively. In April 2005, Middlesbrough Borough Council did the same for its manual and APTC workers. The backdrop to this was that both Councils had, from the summer of 2003, been the subject of large numbers of equal pay claims relating to the pre-Green Book era. Redcar had received claims from female White Book employees, and conceded liability in respect of many of these. Middlesbrough, for its part, had received claims from both White Book and Purple Book employees. It had refused to concede liability in any of those claims and advanced material factor defences. The White Book hearings took place in February and March 2005, and the decision was promulgated on 25 May, after Middlesbrough had implemented the Green Book. The White Book claimants succeeded, and Middlesbrough did not appeal. In a later decision, promulgated on 3 January 2006, the Purple Book claimants succeeded in their claims and Middlesbrough's appeal to the EAT against that decision was unsuccessful.

8.126 Additionally, and more importantly for the purposes of this discussion, a number of female employees of both Redcar and Middlesbrough brought equal pay claims post-April 2005 relating to the way in which the Green Book had been implemented. Both Councils, following negotiations with unions, had introduced pay protection arrangements, so that employees who would eventually end up on a lower salary under the new structure had their pay reduced gradually – normally over a period of three or four years. This meant, for example, that male gardeners and street cleaners, who under the Councils' policy of 'equalising down' lost their entitlement to bonuses and allowances, received pay protection; whereas female care workers, who were rated as equivalent to the gardeners and street cleaners on the new Green Book scale, did not receive pay protection as they were not receiving a drop in pay. The female claimants pointed out that they had been historically underpaid by comparison with their male comparators – a fact evidenced by the outcome of the pre-April 2005 claims. The claimants went on to argue that, had they not been underpaid in the past, they too would have been receiving the bonuses and allowances that the men were receiving at the time of the Green Book's implementation and as a result they would have qualified for pay protection upon their regrading. In their view, this meant that their exclusion from the pay protection scheme perpetuated historical pay discrimination and could not be objectively justified.

Separate tribunals allowed these 'pay protection' claims against both Redcar **8.127** and Middlesbrough. On Redcar's appeal, the EAT upheld the tribunal's decision, holding that the female claimants' exclusion from pay protection came about because of Redcar's failure to implement pay equality in the past, and that Redcar could not pray in aid that failure as a justification for defeating a claim for equal pay. However, a different division of the EAT (albeit presided over by the same judge, Mr Justice Elias, then President of the EAT) allowed Middlesbrough's appeal. It held that although the pay protection arrangements in question were tainted with indirect discrimination, they were objectively justified. The EAT was influenced by the fact that when it put the pay protection arrangements in place, Middlesbrough, unlike Redcar, had neither conceded liability nor lost a tribunal claim for equal pay in respect of the pre-Green Book period. In other words, Middlesbrough had not actually known that the pay protection arrangements would be perpetuating pre-existing indirect sex discrimination. Redcar Council and the Middlesbrough claimants appealed to the Court of Appeal against the EAT's decisions.

The Court dealt first with the Redcar case. There, the tribunal had considered the reason why the female claimants were excluded from the pay protection arrangements, and found it to be because they were not receiving higher pay on the day of transition to the Green Book. It had then looked to the underlying reason for that, and decided that it was because the women had been unlawfully discriminated against prior to that date. It had therefore concluded that the reason for the post-Green Book pay differential was causally related to historical indirect discrimination, and so looked to the employer for justification. The EAT had endorsed that approach and the Court held that it had been right to do so. As to justification, the Court observed that the tribunal had approved 'cushioning the blow' to downgraded employees as a legitimate aim. It had then, correctly, weighed up the appropriateness and necessity of the means used to achieve that objective. The tribunal had stated that the temporary nature of the pay protection and the fact that it was limited to existing employees were both in the Council's favour. However, it had noted, the Council had given no thought to the discriminatory nature of the scheme, and there was no evidence that it had taken the claimants' views into account or considered the cost of including them. Given all this, the Court of Appeal held that there had been an adequate and proper basis for the tribunal's conclusion that the Council's pay protection scheme – which excluded female employees who had already been successful with equal pay claims in respect of the Council's pre-pay-protection pay arrangements – was not objectively justified. The Court approved the observation of the EAT that there will be circumstances in which an employer will be able to justify a discriminatory pay protection scheme if, when it implemented it, it had no reason to think that it would be discriminatory. But that was not the case here. Accordingly, the Council's appeal failed.

8.128 As to the situation in the Middlesbrough litigation, the Court of Appeal began by noting that, for exactly the same reasons as applied in Redcar, the pay protection arrangements were prima facie indirectly discriminatory. The Court rejected the Council's argument that, as no pre-Green Book equal pay claims had succeeded or been conceded before the pay protection was put in place, the Council had not known for certain that it had been guilty of past discrimination, meaning that it had not discriminated in making the pay protection arrangements. In the Court's view, the employer's knowledge of discrimination, while something to be taken into account when considering whether its actions were objectively justified, has no relevance to the issue of whether there was a taint of discrimination in the first place: this has to be determined objectively on the facts. Turning to the issue of justification, the Court noted the tribunal's conclusion that Middlesbrough should have known that there was a real risk of the pre-Green Book claims against it succeeding. The tribunal had identified the 'intrinsic difficulty' of speculating on the outcome of pending claims, but had not thought it as problematic as the EAT had done. Furthermore, the Court of Appeal added, it would be 'most unattractive' if an employer who turns a blind eye to the potential for discrimination should be in a better position to justify its pay practices than one who investigated and discovered the potential for inequality. The Court went on to note that the question of justification is one of fact, and so a very high hurdle must be cleared if the EAT is to interfere with a tribunal's decision. Here, there was no error of law in the present tribunal's approach, and its decision – that the discriminatory effect of excluding female claimants from Middlesbrough's pay protection scheme was not objectively justified – would be restored.

Although it was not necessary to go any further than this for the purpose of the appeal, the Court of Appeal went on to make observations on some remarks of the EAT in the Middlesbrough case with regard to justifying pay protection schemes. The Court noted that the EAT had been sympathetic to the Council, recognising the strict budgetary pressures that exist on public employers. However, the Court could not agree with the EAT's statement that, in such circumstances, the employer will always be entitled to say that it must continue to discriminate for another three or four years (albeit on a decreasing scale) because it cannot afford to bring female claimants into line with men at the time of a reorganisation. The Court found that 'a very surprising and undesirable general conclusion'. Although an employer might be able to demonstrate that the constraints on finances were so pressing that it could not do other than it did, and that it was justified in putting the need to cushion the men's pay reduction ahead of the need to give parity to the women, that result should not be a foregone conclusion.

312

The Court of Appeal's judgment is something of a mixed bag for those involved **8.129** in equal pay litigation. On the one hand, employers will be buoyed by the Court's confirmation that discriminatory pay protection arrangements can, in principle, be justified. On the other, employees will welcome the Court's rejection of the justification defence in both cases, setting as it does a high hurdle for employers to overcome. The Court had some words of caution for those who might think the Councils had been hard done by in this decision. Although it acknowledged the difficult times councils such as Redcar and Middlesbrough are going through, it could not accept that such councils were blameless. Employers have been under a duty to reorganise their pay structures so as to root out inequality and prevent discrimination from creeping back in since equal pay provisions first came into force in 1975. It could not be right that employers who allowed their pay practices to fall out of compliance with the law could then assert the right to take a further three or four years to comply. That will only be possible where the justification test is satisfied.

Pay protection resulting from direct discrimination. If pay protection comes **8.130** about as a result of direct sex discrimination, a material factor defence pointing to such protection will inevitably fail. Two cases neatly illustrate this point:

● **Snoxell and anor v Vauxhall Motors Ltd** 1977 ICR 700, EAT: S and D were long-serving female inspectors who worked alongside male inspectors. Before 1970 the male and female inspectors were graded differently under the employer's wage scale. In 1970 the wage scale was revised by agreement with unions, and it was recognised that certain male inspector jobs, which were graded X2 in the old scale, should be regraded as H3, a lower grade, in the new scale. In order to protect their wages the former X2 male inspectors were 'red-circled' and put into a special grade known as OX. As X2 had been an all-male grade there were no women in the OX grade. It was further agreed that red-circling of men in the OX grade would continue until they ceased to be employed in those jobs for any reason. In 1975, upon the implementation of the EqPA, the employer offered to transfer women employed on like work with men to the appropriate male grades. S and D took advantage of the offer and were regraded H3. Thereafter they were paid the same as their male colleagues in the H3 grade, except for those who had been placed in the OX grade in 1970. They applied to a tribunal for equal pay with the red-circled inspectors in the OX grade. The tribunal, however, upheld the employer's defence that the red-circling of the men in the OX grade constituted a genuine material factor other than sex. S and D appealed successfully to the EAT. The EAT held that the red-circling of grades which, prior to the implementation of the EqPA, were considered to be 'men only' or 'women only' could not give rise to a valid material factor defence, because at the root of the difference in pay lay direct sex

313

discrimination. Had the employer not discriminated against women in the past, when the red-circling took place those women too would have been entitled to the protected rate

- **SITA (UK) Ltd v Hope** EAT 0787/04: H was made redundant and a man was redeployed into her old role. He was paid at a higher rate in order to preserve his previous salary. The EAT held that a tribunal had been correct to reject the employer's material factor defence based on pay protection. In this case, the appointment of the man to the claimant's old role had itself been an act of sex discrimination, which tainted the red-circling of his salary. (Note that the EAT has since held that a claimant is not, in fact, permitted to pursue an equal pay claim, either under the EqA or EU law, based on a 'successor' comparator – see Walton Centre for Neurology and Neuro Surgery NHS Trust v Bewley 2008 ICR 1047, EAT, considered in Chapter 4 under 'Predecessors and successors'.)

8.131 **Reason for pay protection must apply to every protected employee.** An employer wishing to raise pay protection as a material factor explaining a pay differential must do so in respect of every employee who falls within the protected ring. Two cases:

- **Honeywell Ltd v Farquhar** EAT 554/77: a 'red circle' had been devised to protect the pay of employees whose old jobs as security officers had become redundant and whose new jobs as clerical officers would, in the ordinary course of events, have been accorded a lower rate of pay. After the red circle had come into operation, a man was recruited as a clerical officer. Originally he was placed on the pay rate applicable to clerical officer grades, along with the female claimant. However, he protested about earning a lower rate of pay than those colleagues who enjoyed the benefit of the red circle, and the employer duly raised his pay. This, however, had the effect of destroying the basis for a material factor defence based solely on the pay protection arrangement. Since the new male recruit did not qualify as a special case, the EAT held that his promotion deprived the employer of the protection afforded by S.1(3) EqPA (now S.69 EqA) with effect from the date of that promotion. Thus, the claimant was entitled to equal pay as from that date

- **United Biscuits Ltd v Young** 1978 IRLR 15, EAT: Y, who worked as a packaging supervisor on the day-shift, sought equal pay with five male supervisors on the night-shift. At the time when the original rate for the night-shift had been fixed it had contained an element for extra responsibility, which had since declined, although the pay rate stayed at the higher level. As two of the men had entered the 'red circle' after it was set, the employer had to show that the responsibility element had not disappeared before the men entered the protected wage group. The employer failed to do this, so Y's claim for equal pay succeeded.

314

Could pay protection have been extended to claimants? As we saw under **8.132** 'Showing objective justification – proportionality' above, one of the questions a tribunal must ask when considering objective justification is whether the legitimate aim pursued by the employer could have been achieved by less discriminatory means. Given this, and the fact that the burden of showing justification for a prima facie indirectly discriminatory material factor falls on the employer, it follows that employers seeking to run a pay protection material factor defence will have to provide detailed proof that they cannot afford to extend pay protection to women claimants.

This was confirmed by the EAT in Bury Metropolitan Borough Council v Hamilton and ors; Sunderland City Council v Brennan and ors 2011 IRLR 358, EAT. There, in circumstances similar to those in Redcar and Cleveland Borough Council v Bainbridge and ors and another case; Middlesbrough Borough Council v Surtees and ors 2009 ICR 133, CA (see '"Single status" – pay protection resulting in continuing inequality' above), pay protection arrangements had been put in place as part of Bury Council's move towards 'single status'. These were applied to largely male groups of workers (including gardeners, refuse collectors and drivers) whose productivity bonuses were withdrawn. The Council had considered extending the benefit of the pay protection to the claimants – female council workers including caterers, cleaners and carers – but decided against it on grounds of cost and uncertainty. The tribunal accepted the pay protection material factor defence, finding that it was not possible to identify with any degree of precision which of the claimants would have been eligible for the bonuses, and thus pay protection.

Overturning that decision in the EAT, the President, Mr Justice Underhill, **8.133** accepted the difficulty the Council faced, in advance of the determination of the claimants' claims, in deciding who would be entitled to pay protection and to what amount. However, whether such a payment was practically ascertainable was not a material consideration when showing objective justification. Otherwise, no cases of this kind would succeed. While Underhill P accepted that it was not ideal for an employer to be faced with an unquantifiable contingent liability, this was far from an uncommon situation and was normally dealt with by making prudent provisions and, if appropriate, by setting money aside. Moreover, while costs could be a legitimate reason for not extending pay protection to the claimant groups, the tribunal had not been entitled to accept this argument in the absence of sufficiently detailed evidence of the costs themselves and the financial context – a local authority cannot prove unaffordability by mere assertion. In the EAT's opinion, the Council could have produced illustrative calculations that would have enabled the tribunal to assess the scale of the costs. That it did not meant that it could not avail itself of the material factor defence.

8.134 **Duration of pay protection defence.** Although there may be perfectly good reasons for introducing pay protection for certain groups of employees, there are strong arguments for saying that their salaries should not remain artificially inflated indefinitely. In Snoxell and anor v Vauxhall Motors Ltd 1977 ICR 700, EAT, the Appeal Tribunal recognised this, stating: '[I]t seems to us to be desirable where possible for red circles to be phased out and eliminated, for they are bound to give rise to confusion and misunderstanding. One of the difficulties seems to be that although understood and accepted as fair when first introduced, with the passage of time memory dims, the reason for their institution is forgotten, and they are seen as examples of discrimination.' The EAT, while giving this statement of 'good industrial relations practice', thought, however, that there was nothing in the terms of the EqPA to say that a red circle could not continue indefinitely.

In Outlook Supplies Ltd v Parry 1978 ICR 388, EAT, a claimant sought equal pay with a man who did 'like work' to her but was paid some £228 a year more, reflecting the higher wage he was getting in a previous job which he had to leave because of his ill health. The tribunal rejected the employer's defence because the differential had continued for two-and-a-half years. In its view, this was too long. On appeal, the EAT thought that two-and-a-half years was a relatively short period of time for the maintenance of a red circle and remitted the case to the tribunal for reconsideration. Nevertheless, the EAT stated that, in principle, it was relevant for a tribunal to consider the length of time that had elapsed since the introduction of the red circle when considering whether the employer had discharged the burden in showing that a S.1(3) EqPA (now S.69 EqA) defence applied to the case.

8.135 In general terms, then, the longer pay protection lasts, the more chance there is of a tribunal concluding that it is no longer a material factor explaining a pay differential. Furthermore, as touched upon in the discussion of Redcar and Cleveland Borough Council v Bainbridge and ors and another case; Middlesbrough Borough Council v Surtees and ors 2009 ICR 133, CA (see '"Single status" – pay protection resulting in continuing inequality' above), the passage of time is likely to have even greater relevance where a pay protection practice might be said to be tainted by sex discrimination. At this point the employer will be called upon to objectively justify its actions, and the longer the pay protection has lasted without the lower paid group 'catching up', the less likely it is that a justification argument will stand up to scrutiny.

8.136 **TUPE protection**
When a transfer of an undertaking occurs – for example, where a company purchases a business or takes over a service provision contract following a successful tender – the Transfer of Undertakings (Protection of Employment) Regulations 2006 SI 2006/246 (TUPE) will apply to safeguard the terms and conditions of transferring employees. Under Reg 4, the transferee employer is

316

obliged to take over the transferring employees' contracts and becomes bound by their terms and conditions as if it were the original employer. What is more, Reg 4(4) provides that any detrimental changes to these terms and conditions made by the transferee – whether or not with the consent of the employees concerned – will in certain circumstances be void. It states: '[I]n respect of a contract of employment that is, or will be, transferred by [Reg 4(1)], any purported variation of the contract shall be void if the sole or principal reason for the variation is – (a) the transfer itself; or (b) a reason connected to the transfer that is not an economic, technical or organisational reason entailing changes in the workforce.'

These provisions are discussed at length in IDS Employment Law Handbook, 'Transfer of Undertakings' (2011), Chapters 2 and 4. For our purposes, suffice it to say that where, shortly after a relevant transfer, a transferee employer seeks to harmonise the terms or conditions of its pre-existing and newly-acquired workforces, this exercise will be considered 'transfer-connected', and will not be for an 'economic, technical or organisational reason entailing changes in the workforce'. Hence, any detrimental changes to an employee's terms and conditions will be void. For example, in Lansing Linde Severnside Ltd v Spiers EAT 1490/01 a transferee purported to alter enhanced redundancy terms as part of a post-transfer harmonisation exercise. An employment tribunal found the purported variation to be void because the reason that prompted it was intimately linked to the transfer. Upholding this decision, the EAT stated that not only was it open to the tribunal to reasonably conclude that the principal reason for the variation was connected to the transfer, but that in the circumstances this conclusion was 'inescapable'.

There is every chance that, upon a transfer of an undertaking, an employer will **8.137** acquire employees whose contracts are, in some respects, more favourable than those of members of its existing workforce who are performing work equal to that of the newcomers. Such circumstances are ripe for an equal pay claim but the employer may be able to use the fact that its hands are tied to an extent by TUPE to found a material factor defence, as the following case demonstrates:

- **Nelson v Carillion Services Ltd** 2003 ICR 1256, CA: N was employed by CS Ltd in June 1998 as a steward on the Chelsea wing of the Chelsea and Westminster Hospital. She was employed on the company's standard terms and conditions and was paid £5 per hour. S, a man taken on a month later to do the same job, was paid the same. However, D, a man who had started work before N, was earning more than her, and received benefits that she did not receive. D received £6.11 per hour, a food allowance of £2.50, and was paid double time if he worked on bank holidays. N brought a claim under the EqPA, pointing to D as her male comparator. Before the employment tribunal, CS Ltd argued that it had a material factor defence because the difference in pay was the result of a transfer to which the 1981

TUPE Regulations (the precursor to the 2006 Regulations) applied. In April 1997 the company had taken over a contract from IHS to provide services to the hospital, and had been obliged by TUPE to maintain the terms and conditions of employment enjoyed by the 300 or so employees who had been servicing that contract. Six of those employees, four men and two women, worked in the Chelsea wing. After the transfer, five had either been promoted or left the company, and by the date of N's complaint, D was the only one of the original IHS employees who was doing the same job as N and being paid at a higher rate than her. The tribunal was satisfied that the employer's explanation for the difference in pay revealed a genuine material factor, and held that the pay differential was not remotely tainted by sex discrimination. It therefore rejected N's claim, and the EAT and Court of Appeal upheld this decision.

8.138 **Duration of TUPE defence.** How long after a TUPE transfer will an employer be able to rely upon the Regulations to explain, and potentially justify, a pay differential between a man and a woman performing equal work? Many of the pertinent considerations here will be similar to those discussed in respect of 'Pay protection' above: in short, if a differential has lasted for many years, a tribunal might be disinclined to find that the TUPE 'excuse' still constitutes a material factor explaining the pay differential; and, even if the TUPE material factor remains 'material', the ongoing pay differential will need to be objectively justified if for some reason it is tainted by sex discrimination – perhaps favouring a predominantly male group over a predominantly female one.

There is, however, another issue to throw into the pot here – that is, the question of how long after a TUPE transfer will the transferred employees' terms and conditions remain protected or, to put it another way, how long after the transfer will a harmonisation exercise be 'transfer-connected'? Clearly, the longer an employer's hands are tied to an extent by TUPE, the longer a differential is likely to be material and indeed justifiable.

8.139 In Lansing Linde Severnside Ltd v Spiers EAT 1490/01 the EAT specifically pointed to the proximity in time between the date of the variation and the date of the transfer as evidence of the fact that the reason for the variation was connected with the transfer. This suggests that the greater the time lag between the two, the less likely it is that the requisite causal link will be established, and harmonisation of terms will no longer be impermissible. Certainly, this was the view taken by Lord Slynn in (1) British Fuels Ltd v Baxendale and anor (2) Wilson and ors v St Helens Borough Council 1998 ICR 1141, HL, when he said: 'I do not accept the argument that the variation is only invalid if it is agreed on as a part of the transfer itself. The variation may still be due to the transfer and for no other reason even if it comes later. However, it seems that there must, or at least may, come a time when the link with the transfer is broken or can be treated as no longer effective.'

Unfortunately, however, assessing the length of TUPE protection is not an exact science. There is no definitive 'safe' date after which it can be guaranteed that the nexus between the variation and the transfer will be broken. The Department for Business, Innovation and Skills (BIS) guide to TUPE, 'Employment rights on the Transfer of an Undertaking' (March 2007), recognises this, stating: 'There is likely to come a time when the link with the transfer can be treated as no longer effective. However, this must be assessed in the light of all the circumstances of the individual case, and will vary from case to case. There is no "rule of thumb" used by the courts or specified in the Regulations to define a period of time after which it is safe to assume that the transfer did not impact directly or indirectly on the employer's actions.' This guidance is, in part, a nod towards the EAT's decision in Taylor v Connex South Eastern Ltd EAT 1243/99 where the Appeal Tribunal held that the fact that a claimant's dismissal for refusing to accept contractual variations took place two years after a TUPE transfer was not enough to negate the connection between the two events. It said: '[T]he mere passage of time without anything happening does not in itself constitute a weakening to the point of dissolution of the chain of causation.'

8.140 Clearly, the more time that passes after a TUPE transfer, the more chance there is that an intervening event will have broken the chain of causation between the TUPE transfer and the materiality of the pay disparity. This is precisely what an employment tribunal found had occurred in the following case (although its decision was overturned by the EAT on the facts):

- **King's College London v Clark** EAT 1049/02: the employment of C, a woman, and T, a higher-paid man, transferred in 1998 to KCL under the 1981 TUPE Regulations. Owing to the operation of TUPE, C's and T's pre-transfer terms and conditions transferred to KCL, and the pay disparity between them remained. In time, C brought an equal pay claim pointing to T as her comparator. The tribunal accepted that T and C were employed on 'like work', meaning that KCL was obliged to mount a material factor defence in order to avoid liability. It claimed that the TUPE protection enjoyed by T amounted to a material factor explaining the pay differential. The tribunal disagreed. It was not persuaded that TUPE protection was genuinely the reason why T was paid more than C. It noted that KCL had reviewed C's grading in July 1999 and had concluded that her post was correctly graded. That regrading exercise was an opportunity for the employer to decide whether C's terms and conditions should be altered to bring them into line with T's terms. In deciding not to do this, the employer was, in effect, taking a decision that the differential was justified by factors other than the fact that the employees had transferred under TUPE on different terms and conditions. Given this, the tribunal was not satisfied that the pay differential was genuinely due to the reason put forward by the employer. Rather, the reason for the differential was the employer's mistaken view that T and C were not doing like work. Thus, the employer fell at the first hurdle:

its reason put forward for the variation in pay, TUPE protection, was not a genuine reason. Hence, the material factor defence failed. On appeal, the EAT overturned the tribunal's decision. In its view, the present case was no different to that of Glasgow City Council and ors v Marshall and ors 2000 ICR 196, HL, where the House of Lords declined to find that a 'historical' explanation for a pay disparity could no longer be a material factor simply because the respondent employer could have chosen, at some point, to pay the claimants more. The EAT concluded: '[T]he grading review in July 1999 did not break the causative chain stretching back to the historical difference in pay due to the protection afforded by TUPE to [T's] terms and conditions of employment. Further, even if the respondent mistakenly concluded that the [claimant] was correctly graded, at a level lower than that of [T]... such mistaken, if genuine belief, is itself capable of amounting to a material factor for the purposes of the S.1(3) defence.'

8.141 The employer ran a similar line of defence to that used in the King's College case in Buchanan and anor v Skills Development Scotland Co Ltd ET Case Nos.113105–6/08. In that case B and H claimed equal pay with a comparator, S, who like them had transferred from various predecessor bodies to Careers Scotland (CS) in 2002, and then transferred again to the employer in 2008. Prior to the transfer, S contractually agreed future pay increases to take place on 1 April 2002, 1 January 2003 and 1 August 2003. His contract further provided that 'on the expiry of 2003, your salary will be reviewed on an annual basis as per normal arrangements applying from April 2004'. Neither B nor H had a similar clause in their contracts. A pay audit by CS in 2003 revealed a concentration of men in the senior roles and at the top of the senior pay scales, and a performance-related pay scheme was introduced, with provision for 'red-circling' (i.e. freezing) the pay of employees who were overpaid for their current provision. However, S's salary was not frozen, and he continued to receive pay increases. This had the effect of not only continuing but increasing the pay disparity between the women and S.

In response to B and H's equal pay claims, the employer raised a material factor defence, arguing that the differential was due to the protection of S's contractual rights as a result of TUPE. The employment tribunal was satisfied that the transfer explained the pay differential up to April 2004, since CS had been obliged to enact the pay increases agreed to by the transferor. However, the tribunal considered that the transfer did not offer a material explanation for CS's decision not to red-circle S's pay after April 2004 and instead to award him pay increases and bonuses that had the effect of increasing the disparity.

8.142 Even if TUPE protection remains a material reason for a pay disparity, this does not mean that a pay disparity between two groups of employees will necessarily lead to a successful material factor defence – particularly where women as a group are being adversely affected. For one thing, the obligation under TUPE is to *maintain* rather than improve the transferred employees' terms and conditions. So, the employer might be able to honour those terms, but freeze them – declining to pay annual increases until such time as the terms of the existing workforce have caught up (as the tribunal thought the transferee could have done in the Buchanan case above). This option, however, is only available where the transferred employees' contracts do not provide for a guaranteed annual pay increase or uplift of financial benefits (as S's did for the first two years post-transfer in the Buchanan case). Another obvious point to make here is that there is nothing (financial considerations aside) preventing the employer from improving the terms and conditions of its existing workforce to bring them into line with those of the transferred workforce. In some circumstances, where the disparity in pay is seen to be tainted by sex discrimination, a tribunal might rule that the employer was not justified in failing to do precisely this.

Grading schemes and incremental pay scales

8.143

In a number of early equal pay cases, placements on different grades, or at different levels within the same grade, that resulted in pay variations were held to amount to a material factor. This was so whether they were the result 'of the fine adjustment of a job evaluation scheme' – O'Brien and ors v Sim-Chem Ltd 1980 ICR 573, HL; in accordance with nationally, or widely, negotiated wage scales – Waddington v Leicester Council for Voluntary Service 1977 ICR 266, EAT; or because of a company's own evaluation scheme based on its own subjective judgment – National Vulcan Engineering Insurance Group Ltd v Wade 1978 ICR 800, CA.

However, in all cases the evaluation had to be undertaken on a non-discriminatory basis – Snoxell and anor v Vauxhall Motors Ltd 1977 ICR 700, EAT. Employers may struggle to convince a tribunal of the non-discriminatory nature of their evaluation where the criteria used for determining where on a scale employees should be placed are complicated or unclear, or where the employer used its own discretion as to where employees should be placed. In such circumstances, the evidence could lead a tribunal to find that the employer had failed to show a genuine, transparent reason for the pay differential, or that the employer's material factor was tainted by sex discrimination in some way.

In the following case, the employer failed to convince a tribunal that the 8.144 fact that claimants and comparators were on different grades was due to a material factor:

- **Bulman and anor v Carlisle City Council** ET Case Nos.6404624 and 6204629/00: the Council provided accommodation for homeless and vulnerable people. B worked at the London Road Hostel, where the staff was exclusively female. She, along with the majority of her colleagues, was on 'Grade 3'. She sought to compare her pay with that of a male employee working at John Street Hostel, where the staff was predominantly male and on 'Grade 4'. A tribunal hearing centred on whether or not the Council could mount a material factor defence to B's complaint. The Council explained that the John Street Hostel employees had been upgraded to Grade 4 on appeal to an independent panel because of alleged additional duties and responsibilities. Accordingly, the Council had been obliged to pay them at the higher grade. The London Road Hostel employees, on the other hand, had not obtained an upgrade, meaning that the Council had been under no obligation to pay them at Grade 4. The tribunal rejected the Council's defence, concluding that the proffered reason for the pay differential 'was not genuine'. The tribunal noted that the job descriptions of the claimants and the comparators were virtually identical, and that the independent panel's decision in respect of the John Street Hostel employees had put the Council on notice that its basic assumption that the London Road Hostel employees should be on Grade 3 might be wrong. Yet, the Council had not addressed this issue. Put another way, it did not honour its normal practice of applying the decision of the independent panel to all of those with the same job description. The tribunal concluded that the Council had failed to establish any reason other than sex for the pay differential in question, and upheld B's claim.

8.145 **Performance-related pay**
There is nothing wrong in principle with paying better performers a higher wage. A performance-related pay scheme, for example, which will almost inevitably lead to differences in levels of pay between employees doing similar jobs, is capable of providing a valid material factor. However, the implementation of such a scheme, or a system of merit increases, by line managers – for example, where performance is rated by individual managers on an essentially subjective basis – can inadvertently let in discriminatory considerations that might leave the system open to challenge. The risk of unconscious discrimination in performance rating can be lessened with effective diversity and equality training.

A case example where an employer failed to convince a tribunal that a performance-related pay scheme amounted to a material factor explaining a pay differential:

• **Latham v Eastern Counties Newspapers Ltd** ET Case No.32453/93: in 1992 E Ltd decided to introduce a performance-related pay scheme under which assessors were required to determine the aptitude of all employees in the department in which L worked. However, they were given no guidance or benchmarks for their awards, nor were parameters set within which to make their assessments. Under the scheme, L was placed on grade B5 and paid £12,300 per annum with an overtime rate of £6.44 per hour, whereas her three male comparators, who were employed on like work, were put on grade B2, with annual pay of £13,000 and an hourly overtime rate of

£6.85. The employer sought to defend L's equal pay claim on the basis that the results of the performance-related pay scheme constituted a material factor that was not the difference of sex. The tribunal, however, rejected this on the grounds that there was confusion, double-counting and an absence of transparency in the system. It particularly criticised the fact that no parameters had been laid down to define the areas to be considered in the various aptitude tests. Overall, the employer had failed to satisfy the tribunal on the balance of probabilities that difference of sex was not the reason for the differential in pay between L and her comparators.

Note that in Brunnhofer v Bank der österreichischen Postsparkasse AG 2001 **8.146** IRLR 571, ECJ, the European Court made it clear that a difference in pay between two employees of different genders that is instituted at the time of their appointment to the same work or to work of equal value cannot be justified by reference to the quality of work performed. Whereas professional training, for example, can be a valid justification for a difference in pay because it is a factor that is objectively known at the time the employee is appointed, work performance can be assessed only after appointment and cannot therefore constitute a proper ground for unequal treatment right from the start of employment.

Productivity bonuses **8.147**

A number of public sector equal pay claims in recent years have concerned the payment, in some cases for historical reasons, of 'productivity bonuses' to some (often predominantly male) groups of employees but not to other (often predominantly female) groups. In Gibson v Sheffield City Council 2010 ICR 708, CA (considered under 'Preliminary issues – burden of proof' above), for example, the claimants – women who had been employed as carers – sought to compare themselves with male street cleaners and gardeners who, as a result of historical productivity bonuses that were incorporated into basic pay, were paid 33.3 per cent and 38 per cent higher respectively. The Council argued that the productivity bonuses had been necessary to ensure efficient working practices in the gardening and street cleaning roles, while the nature of care work was such that productivity bonuses were not necessary or appropriate, and so the pay differential was due to a reason other than sex. The employment tribunal and the EAT accepted this argument, but the Court of Appeal considered the decision perverse. The Court referred to Cumbria County Council v Dow and ors (No.1) 2008 IRLR 91, EAT, and Coventry City Council v Nicholls and ors 2009 IRLR 345, EAT, in which Mr Justice Elias (then President of the EAT) had suggested that if bonuses are paid only to male-dominated groups of employees because of particular features of their jobs not shared by the female claimants, that necessarily gives rise to indirect sex discrimination requiring objective justification. There was clear evidence in the

323

instant case that the disparity had an adverse effect on women, and so the case was remitted for the tribunal to consider whether it could be justified.

Objective justification was found to exist in Redcar and Cleveland Borough Council v Bainbridge and ors 2008 ICR 249, EAT, where a number of female council workers (including caterers) sought to compare themselves for equal pay purposes with 'equal' male council workers (including refuse collectors). Although the claimants received the same basic pay as their comparators, their overall pay was significantly less because of bonuses paid to their comparators under productivity schemes. Before the tribunal, the Council put forward a material factor defence, pointing out that a productivity scheme was applied to the refuse collectors for genuine reasons. The Council accepted that the lack of availability of such a scheme for certain groups of employees had a disparate adverse impact on women, but argued that the pay differentials could be objectively justified. The tribunal disagreed, finding that while the bonus payments paid to refuse collectors were genuinely related to productivity, the Council's defence nevertheless failed. Although evidence showed that it would not have been possible for the Council to adopt a similar productivity scheme for the caterers, it would have been possible for it to construct a different bonus scheme for them and thereby equalise pay. On appeal, however, the EAT overturned the tribunal's decision on this point. In its view, the tribunal had erred in concluding that the Council had failed to objectively justify the difference in pay between the claimants and the refuse workers – which was genuinely due to a valid bonus incentive scheme that it could not feasibly have applied to the claimants – simply because the Council had failed to consider the possibility of adopting some other kind of bonus scheme that could have achieved pay equality. On the tribunal's own findings of fact there was an obvious and vital difference between the situation of the claimants and that of their comparators, in that the latter were employed in work which enabled a productivity scheme to be adopted and which as a consequence brought savings and greater efficiency to the work being carried out. Once the tribunal had concluded that the higher bonus was justified because of that arrangement, it should not have found that the employer's defence was not made out because of the failure to apply a wholly different kind of scheme to the claimant groups.

8.148 The central issue is whether the reason for awarding the bonus is tainted by sex discrimination, not whether it is a good or fair reason. In Hartlepool Borough Council and anor v Dolphin and ors 2009 IRLR 168, EAT, the employer's material factor defence failed since the 'productivity' bonus schemes giving rise to the pay disparities at issue had, in reality, no link with productivity at all. The schemes had simply been introduced to get round a Government pay policy that had prevented the Council from providing pay increases to strong union-based employees except under the guise of incentive schemes. However, the Dolphin decision was stated to be 'unhelpful' in Bury Metropolitan Borough Council v Hamilton and ors; Sunderland City Council v Brennan and ors 2011

IRLR 358, EAT, since it suggested that the central focus of a tribunal should be whether the employer's explanation is dishonest or designed to conceal a different (presumably discriminatory) explanation for the difference in treatment, rather than the question of whether the factual explanation – be it good or bad – is tainted by sex discrimination.

Case law suggests that even if a productivity bonus scheme was initially introduced for non-discriminatory reasons, it will not provide the employer with a material factor defence if those reasons have ceased to apply. This is what occurred in the Bury case (above), where a productivity bonus scheme had been introduced for predominantly male gardeners, refuse collectors and drivers, but was legitimately considered not to be suitable for predominantly female caterers, cleaners and carers. Given that the bonuses had, in time, ceased to be linked to productivity, the material factor was tainted by unjustified indirect sex discrimination. Note that the questions of whether, and if so to what extent, an employer can base a material factor on historical reasons are discussed at length under '"Material" factor – evaporation of historical material factor' above.

Different pay structures and collective bargaining 8.149
It has long been accepted that the provisions of a collective agreement, or the fact that the pay of a claimant and her comparator is determined by different collective agreements, can provide an explanation for a pay differential amounting to a material factor. As far back as the 1970s, Mr Justice Phillips said that where pay is fixed by widely negotiated wage scales there would be a strong case for saying that a material factor explanation is present – see Waddington v Leicester Council for Voluntary Service 1977 ICR 266, EAT.

Nevertheless, a tribunal should not simply accept a 'collective bargaining' material factor at face value. It may well need to examine the reasons why the pay disparity came into being – perhaps by looking at the negotiations that gave rise to the collective agreement or agreements – to ensure that sex discrimination in some shape or form was not at the heart of it.

Even if the material factor is accepted by the tribunal, difficulties for the 8.150 employer could arise where women as a group are adversely affected by the collectively agreed terms as compared with men as a group. As discussed at length under 'Taint of sex discrimination – indirect discrimination' above, in such circumstances the collective agreement(s) might be said to be 'tainted' with sex discrimination (under the test set down by the ECJ in Enderby v Frenchay Health Authority and anor 1994 ICR 112, ECJ), meaning that the employer will be obliged to show that the pay differential is objectively justified. If justification is required, then, as the ECJ in Enderby made clear, an employer's simple reliance on the existence of a collective agreement or separate bargaining structures will not be sufficient. The ECJ's ruling in this regard in effect

325

overturned the decision of the EAT in that same case (Enderby v Frenchay Health Authority and anor 1991 ICR 382, EAT). There, the EAT had been prepared to accept separate collective bargaining and collective agreements as a complete answer to any disparity in pay between a claimant and her comparator so long as there was no overt discrimination in the way the collectively bargained rates of pay were achieved.

The principles laid down by the ECJ in Enderby were clearly in the mind of the Court of Appeal in British Airways plc v Grundy (No.2) 2008 IRLR 815, CA, which provides a useful case example. As touched on elsewhere in this chapter, the Grundy case involved G, who began working for BA as a member of the full-time cabin crew but in 1987 switched to a part-time 'Support Cabin Crew' (SCC) contract. Until 1994 this flexible SCC contract was the only way in which cabin crew could work part time, and was of particular benefit to women such as G who had childcare responsibilities. When the SCC category had been introduced by collective agreement in 1985, the relevant employees were given different, less favourable terms and conditions than other employees in order to address the concerns of full-time cabin crew that SCC employees might have an advantage over them. Crucially for this case, they were not entitled to pay increments. When the SCC scheme was wound up in 2002, G was given a part-time 'Cabin Crew' (CC) contract and was placed on BA's incremental pay scale. However, as a result of the collectively agreed rules relating to the SCC arrangements, she was only credited with five years' continuous service. This meant she was earning nearly £4,000 less than W, a male part-time employee who was employed on 'like work' but who had never worked under an SCC contract. G brought an equal pay claim before an employment tribunal. The tribunal concluded that the material reason for the disparity – that, under the SCC working scheme, cabin crew would not be entitled to pay increments – was tainted by indirect sex discrimination, in that it had a disparate adverse impact on women. This finding was eventually upheld by the Court of Appeal, which then turned its mind to whether the pay disparity was nevertheless objectively justified.

8.151 The Court rejected BA's argument that the fact that the terms and conditions had been agreed through collective bargaining amounted to justification. There may be many reasons why, in the give and take of collective bargaining, one group does worse than another. But one of the important principles laid down by the EqPA (and now by the EqA) is that attention must be paid by negotiators to the possibility that such differentials will have a disparate impact on employees of one gender. If this is overlooked, with a consequent breach of one group's equality clauses, the oversight cannot be justified by reference to the agreement which resulted in the breach. Accordingly, the tribunal had been right not to be overly influenced by the fact that the SCC terms had been collectively agreed. Endorsing comments made by the EAT, the Court held that because the purpose of the parties to the agreement was to achieve less

326

favourable terms for predominantly female SCC staff, that agreement could not amount to an objective justification for the pay disparity.

The Grundy approach was followed in Clark v Metropolitan Police Authority and anor, The Mayor's and City of London Court, Case No.0MY00263, a case which turned on the fact that the Met did not pay inspectors for overtime. This meant that C, a part-time Sector Inspector who was paid an hourly rate for a 32-hour week, received no additional pay for any extra hours she worked. Full-time Sector Inspectors were paid for the equivalent of 40 hours a week, even if they worked longer hours. Thus, if C and a full time Inspector both worked the same number of hours in excess of 32, the full-time Inspector received a higher hourly rate of pay than the claimant. The Court found that the practice of not paying for hours worked over and above normal working hours was tainted by indirect sex discrimination as it was less favourable to part-time workers who were overwhelmingly women. The fact that the practice came about as a result of national collective bargaining did not constitute objective justification as no consideration had been given, at the time of the negotiations, to its impact on women.

Union 'intransigence' is not a material factor. A novel argument raised by the 8.152 employer in Coventry City Council v Nicholls 2009 IRLR 345, EAT, was that so-called trade union 'intransigence', which hampered negotiations and delayed agreement on equal pay, amounted to a material factor explaining the disparity in pay between the claimants and their male comparators. The Council had sought to introduce a 'single status' pay agreement, and had carried out a job evaluation study (JES) to that end. However, it was unable to reach agreement with the relevant trade unions on implementing the result of the JES and ultimately imposed single status without agreement. When a group of female employees claimed equal pay with refuse collectors, the Council advanced a number of material factors to explain the pay differential, among which was the argument that, even if the difference in pay had originally been sex-tainted, it had been overtaken by a separate and distinct cause – namely, union intransigence. Had the unions been more cooperative, an agreement on single status would inevitably have been reached much sooner and any inequality resulting from the different pay arrangements removed. By the time the claims were lodged, it was the unions' intransigence, the Council submitted, that caused the difference in pay.

In upholding the tribunal's decision to reject the Council's argument, the EAT stated that it could not be said that the unions' stance had negated sex as a cause of the difference in pay. While it might explain why the discrimination was not removed earlier, it did not replace the original discriminatory explanation for the difference. In effect, the alleged material factor defence amounted to a plea in mitigation. The Appeal Tribunal did not in any event accept the premise that the Council was impeded from putting the situation right because of the unions' attitude. Ultimately, the ability to remedy unequal pay was always in the Council's own hands. It could at any time have chosen to impose equality against the wishes of the unions if need be. It was not compelled to accept that it could do nothing in the light of the unions' hostile opposition.

8.153 **Flexibility and working hours**

Certain characteristics and qualities relating to the way in which employees carry out their work are often prized by employers. These have less to do with the innate skills or aptitude of particular individuals than with their relative preparedness to work in ways that suit the modern business environment. Can an employer rely upon such factors to found a material factor defence?

8.154 **Adaptability.** Any link between pay and criteria such as willingness to be flexible, whether in terms of working hours, work arrangements, mobility or job duties, is likely to result in lower pay for women, since more women than men carry the primary burden of childcare and other domestic responsibilities and are therefore less able to be flexible. Thus, while flexible working might amount to a material factor explaining a pay differential, that differential is likely to be tainted with indirect discrimination and must be objectively justified if the employer is to avoid equal pay liability.

The issue of 'flexibility' as a basis for justifying a variation between a claimant's and her comparator's contractual terms was considered by the ECJ in Handels-og Kontorfunktionaerernes Forbund i Danmark v Dansk Arbejdsgiverforening (acting for Danfoss A/S) 1991 ICR 74, ECJ. In that case, a collective agreement enabled employers to increase the remuneration payable to different categories of employees covered by the agreement on account of a number of factors, including flexibility. The claimants contended that it was not open to an employer to differentiate in respect of pay by reference to non-measurable criteria such as flexibility. The ECJ obviously thought that this argument went too far. It ruled that it was necessary to draw a distinction according to whether the criterion of flexibility is used to reward the quality of work carried out by the employee or to reward the employee's adaptability to variable work schedules and places of work. With regard to rewarding quality of work, the criterion of flexibility was, in the view of the Court, totally neutral from the point of view of sex. Where its application results in systematic unfairness to female employees, that can only be because the employer has misapplied it and there can be no scope for justifying it, since it is inconceivable that the work carried out by female employees would be generally of a lower quality. Where flexibility refers to the adaptability of the employee to various work schedules and places of work, the application of such a criterion may also operate to the disadvantage of women because, as a result of household and childcare duties, they may face greater difficulty than men in organising their working time in a flexible manner. However, in the case of a pay practice that rewards the adaptability of employees, the employer may justify the higher rate of pay by showing that adaptability is of importance in the performance of the specific duties entrusted to the employee concerned.

Unsocial working hours. It has been established by case law that the time at **8.155** which work is carried out may constitute a material factor giving rise to pay differentials. An employer may thus be entitled to pay a shift premium or a sum to represent the fact that an employee has the inconvenience of working unsocial hours – see, for example, National Coal Board v Sherwin and anor 1978 ICR 700, EAT. However, any such premium must be specifically related to the unsocial hours worked, and the ordinary basic rates of pay of those doing like work should remain the same.

There is a strong danger, though, that unsocial hours premiums can indirectly discriminate against women as a group, in which case they will require objective justification – see, for example, Blackburn and anor v Chief Constable of West Midlands Police 2009 IRLR 135, CA. In that case, which is discussed at greater length under 'Showing objective justification – proportionality' above, the Court of Appeal upheld the EAT's decision that although a bonus scheme designed to reward police officers who were available to work at night did adversely affect women as a group, it was nevertheless justified as a proportionate means of achieving a legitimate aim.

Part-time work   8.156
In most cases where a part-time employee is paid less (pro rata) than a full-time employee, the aggrieved individual will be able to bring a claim under the Part-time Workers (Prevention of Less Favourable Treatment) Regulations 2000 SI 2000/1551. These Regulations, which are outside the scope of this Handbook, require an employer to show objective justification for such a pay differential, without the rigmarole of the material factor defence.

However, if, for some reason, a claimant cannot rely on those Regulations – for instance, where she is not engaged on 'the same or broadly similar work' as her comparator (but is nevertheless employed on work of equal value), or where she falls foul of the Regulations' stringent time limit provisions – she may be able to bring an equal pay claim instead.

It is well established that a pay practice that is biased against part-timers is likely to be indirectly discriminatory against women, since more women than men work part time. An employer will therefore be required to objectively justify any such practice in order to avoid equal pay liability.

Hourly rate. Although it is clear that the difference between full- and part-time **8.157** working will not itself be sufficient to justify a discriminatory pay practice, it is also clear that, by definition, a woman working part time is unlikely to be earning the same as a male full-timer employed on comparable work. To the

329

extent that a full-timer works longer hours, it is inevitable that his take-home pay will be greater. What is important is that both the man and the woman are employed on the same basic rates for the job in respect of the hours they work. It will be extremely difficult for an employer to justify a different basic hourly rate for part- and full-timers.

8.158   **Overtime.** Access to overtime rates, however, is a different matter. An employer is perfectly at liberty to define 'overtime' in terms of normal full-time working hours as opposed to hours in excess of the normal working hours of the individual employee concerned. In Stadt Lengerich v Helmig 1996 ICR 35, ECJ, the European Court ruled that it was permissible for a collective agreement to exclude overtime supplements for part-time employees who, although they worked in excess of their individual working hours, did not work in excess of the number of hours normally worked by full-time employees. According to the ECJ, there would only be unequal treatment contrary to Article 157 if the overall pay of full-time employees was higher than that of part-time employees in respect of the same number of hours worked. In that particular case, a part-time employee whose contractual hours were 18 per week received, in any week where she worked 19 hours per week (i.e. one hour above her normal hours), the same overall pay as any full-time employee who worked 19 hours in a particular week. Similarly, part-time employees also received the same overall pay as any full-time employee if they worked more than the normal working hours for full-time employees since, on doing so, they (like full-timers) would become entitled to overtime supplements. This pay practice was found to be permissible under Article 157.

As noted above, the ECJ in the Helmig case suggested that there would be a breach of Article 157 if the overall pay of full-time employees was higher than that of part-time employees in respect of the same number of hours worked. This was the point at issue in Voß v Land Berlin 2008 1 CMLR 49, ECJ. In that case, V was a teacher employed by Land Berlin on standard terms dictated by various federal statutes. She was contracted to work part time for 23 teaching hours a week, in comparison with the full-time employees' standard week of 26.5 teaching hours. From 11 January to 23 May 2000, V worked four to six teaching hours a month in addition to her normal hours. The combined effect of the relevant pieces of federal legislation was that civil servants, including teachers, were required to work additional hours where the job demanded it, either for no extra remuneration or at a reduced rate. This principle applied equally to both part-time and full-time employees in respect of hours worked over and above their respective normal working hours. However, the effect was that over a period of (for example) 24 hours of paid work, V received less pay than a comparable full-time employee would receive for working the same number of hours. V's 24th hour would be at the reduced rate because it would, for her, constitute overtime – whereas the full-time employee would be paid at the full rate for all 24 hours because all of that period would constitute his or her normal working hours. V complained to her local administrative court that the overtime hours she worked – up to a ceiling of 26.5 teaching hours a week – should have been paid at the standard hourly rate. The Federal Administrative Court referred the matter to the ECJ. The ECJ noted that for the legislation in question to be indirectly discriminatory under Article 157, three elements had to be satisfied. First, there must be a difference in treatment between part-time and full-time workers; secondly, that difference must affect a considerably higher number of women than men; and finally, there must be no objective factors wholly unrelated to sex which can justify the difference found. There would be unequal treatment, the ECJ stated, wherever the overall pay of full-time employees was higher than that of part-time employees for the same number of hours worked, as it was in this case. Accordingly, if, of the workforce affected by the legislation in question, the percentage of part-time workers who are women is considerably greater than the percentage who are men, the difference in treatment between full-timers and part-timers caused by the legislation will be contrary to Article 157 of the EC Treaty, unless it can be objectively justified. In this case, it was not clear to the ECJ exactly which legislative provisions the national court considered caused the unequal treatment; and nor was it clear whether the discrimination was objectively justified. These questions would therefore need to be considered by the national court.

Similar facts arose in Clark v Metropolitan Police Authority and anor, The Mayor's and City of London Court, Case No.0MY00263. That case turned on the fact that the Met did not pay inspectors for overtime. This meant that C, a part-time Sector Inspector who was paid an hourly rate for a 32-hour week, received no additional pay for any extra hours she worked. Full-time Sector Inspectors were paid for the equivalent of 40 hours a week, even if they worked longer hours. Thus, if C and a full-time Inspector both worked the same number of hours in excess of 32, the full-time Inspector received a higher hourly rate of pay than the claimant. The Court found that the practice of not paying for hours worked over and above normal working hours was tainted by indirect sex discrimination as it was less favourable to part-time workers who were overwhelmingly women. The fact that the practice came about as a result of national collective bargaining did not constitute objective justification as no consideration had been given, at the time of the negotiations, to its impact on women. **8.159**

Shift patterns. It is clear that if, as a result of working full time, employees are required to work on rotating shifts that cause a proportion of their working time to be done at inconvenient and unsocial hours, that may be a valid reason for conferring upon them benefits denied to part-timers. In Montgomery v Lowfield Distribution Ltd EAT 932/95 the EAT upheld a tribunal's finding that the employer had been justified in conferring on full-time employees (who were almost exclusively men) entitlement to double time and a day off in lieu of **8.160**

Bank Holidays worked (or an option of triple time if no day off in lieu was taken) in circumstances where the same benefit was withheld from the exclusively female part-time workforce. The full-time workers were employed on rotating shifts whereas the part-time workers were employed on fixed hours. The EAT was satisfied that it had been open to the tribunal to conclude that the contractual difference between the claimants and comparators was one that was genuinely due to a material factor which was not the difference in sex.

8.161 **Holidays**

The amount of holiday an employee is entitled to will sometimes be taken into account when assessing his or her pay. Where this happens, the question arises whether a difference in pay between a claimant and comparator can be accounted for in terms of their respective holiday entitlements. This was one of the issues that arose in Leverton v Clwyd County Council 1989 ICR 33, HL. In that case the claimant (a nursery nurse) worked 32.5 hours a week and was entitled to 70 days' annual leave in contrast to her comparators, who worked between 37 and 39 hours a week and were entitled to only 20 days' holiday (plus increments after five years' service). A pro rata calculation of notional hourly income yielded figures of £4.42 for the claimant and £4.40 for the comparator. On this basis, the House of Lords ruled that a 'causal connection' existed between the differences in hours of work and holiday entitlement between a female school nursery nurse and her comparators such as to comprise a material factor justifying the pay differential between them. Their Lordships held that, as a general rule, where a woman's and a man's regular annual working hours, unaffected by any significant additional hours of work, can be translated into a notional hourly rate of pay that yields no significant difference between them, it is a legitimate if not a necessary inference that the difference in their annual salary is both due to, and justified by, the difference in the hours they work over the course of a year and has nothing to do with the difference of sex.

8.162 **Offsetting other contractual terms**

As a result of the House of Lords' decision in Hayward v Cammell Laird Shipbuilders Ltd 1988 ICR 464, HL, a woman has a right to claim equality of treatment in respect of each individual term of her contract. The House of Lords held that an employer would not have a S.1(3) EqPA (now S.69 EqA) defence to a claim for equal pay based on inequality with regard to one particular term of the contract simply by showing that another term of the contract is more favourable. At the very least, it would have to be shown that the difference in the claimant's pay is actually due to her more favourable treatment with regard to the other term. Further, the employer would have to show that the difference in treatment was not in any way due to the reason of sex. This issue has been discussed in some detail in Chapter 2 under 'The sex equality clause – term-by-term comparison'. For the reasons mentioned there, it is questionable whether, in the light of European law as interpreted by the ECJ, any material factor defence would, in fact, be available to an employer who seeks to justify a less favourable term in a claimant's contract by counter-balancing it against a more favourable term (see, though, Leverton v Clwyd County Council 1989 ICR 33, HL, above, in respect of additional holiday entitlement).

Mistake and administrative error 8.163

In Young v University of Edinburgh EAT 244/93 the EAT held that reasons that can be broadly described as administrative in character may, in appropriate circumstances, constitute a material factor defence, but that the employer must do more than merely explain historically how the difference in remuneration came about. Administrative explanations must not be allowed to become a cloak for discrimination. Accordingly, in any case where the employer points to an administrative error as explaining the difference in pay between a claimant and her comparator, the circumstances must be scrutinised in order to ensure that the error was a genuine one.

In the Young case the employer established that the difference in pay between the claimant and her comparator arose because the latter had been placed on the higher pay scale by mistake. The employer had further established that the difference in treatment could not have been eliminated without departing from the normal basis of remuneration and so creating further anomalies. Accordingly, the tribunal had been right, in the EAT's view, to hold that the employer had made out a genuine material factor defence. Two further examples:

- **Yorkshire Blood Transfusion Service v Plaskitt** 1994 ICR 74, EAT: P was employed as a medical laboratory scientific officer grade 1 under Whitley Council Rules. She claimed equality of pay with a male comparator, also a scientific officer grade 1, who had previously been in different employment on a higher grade and salary and whose salary had been maintained on engagement by the employers. The employer argued that a pay difference was due to its own mistake in employing the comparator on the wrong grade under the Whitley Council rules. The EAT, overturning the tribunal's decision that that was not a sufficient basis for a material factor defence, held that the employer was not required to do anything other than to show that the mistake had genuinely caused the pay differential and that no gender-discriminatory factors had influenced it

- **Assefa Abraha v Home Office** ET Case No.2300774/04: A, a female security guard, was paid less than two male security guards employed on 'like work'. In response to A's equal pay claim, her employer explained that the reason for the pay differential was that a mistake had been made in calculating the pay to which the comparators (and indeed two other security guards, including one woman) were entitled. The majority of the security guards (men and women), it pointed out, received the same pay as A. The tribunal accepted the employer's material factor defence. It was satisfied on the evidence that the employer's mistake (relating to shift allowances) accounting for the pay differential was genuine. Furthermore, given the gender make up of the higher and lower paid groups, the tribunal was satisfied that the employer's mistake was not tainted by sex discrimination. Accordingly, no objective justification of the pay differential was required in order for the employer's defence to succeed.

9 Enforcement

In this chapter we consider the issues involved in enforcing the right to equal **9.1** pay. We begin by examining the jurisdiction of employment tribunals and the way in which claims under the Equality Act 2010 (EqA) and Article 157 of the Treaty on the Functioning of the European Union (TFEU) are put. We then look at the procedural aspects of equal pay cases, considering, among other things, time limits and the statutory questionnaire procedure. Finally, we consider the issues of remedies and costs, and the role of the Equalities and Human Rights Commission.

With regard to procedure, we focus on the questions that have particular application in the field of equal pay. The more general procedural issues that apply to all tribunal claims are explained in depth in IDS Employment Law Handbook, 'Employment Tribunal Practice and Procedure' (2006).

Note that there is one aspect of equal pay procedure not covered in this chapter; **9.2** namely, the specific rules for determining 'equal value' claims. These rules, which among other things provide for the appointment of an independent expert to report to the tribunal, are dealt with separately in Chapter 7 under 'Equal value procedure'.

9.3 **Jurisdiction of tribunals**

Although, following the advent of the EqA, the provisions relating to equal pay and sex discrimination are no longer contained in different statutes as was the case with the EqPA and the SDA, the enforcement regime for equal pay remains separate from the other equality strands covered by the 2010 Act.

The basic jurisdiction for employment tribunals in respect of a complaint under Part 5 of the EqA – this Part is entitled 'Work' and includes both the discrimination in employment provisions (Chapter 1 of Part 5) and the equality of terms provisions (Chapter 3 of Part 5) – derives from S.120 EqA and, strictly speaking, a claim of equal pay is a claim under S.120. However, specific jurisdiction in respect of equal pay is conferred upon employment tribunals by S.127(1) and (2) EqA, which provide that tribunals may hear claims relating to, or arising out of, a breach of an equality clause or rule. This replaces Ss.2(1) and (1A) EqPA, which conferred jurisdiction in 'respect of the contravention of a term modified or included by virtue of an equality clause'. Note that the jurisdiction under S.127(1) and (2) EqA covers not only breaches of sex equality clauses in contracts of employment, but also sex equality rules in occupational pension schemes (see Chapter 2, 'Right to equal pay', under 'Occupational pension schemes'). It also applies to breaches of maternity equality clauses and rules – see Chapter 2 under 'Maternity'.

9.4 In addition to a claim brought by an individual in respect of his or her own terms, an employment tribunal also has jurisdiction to determine an application by a 'responsible person' for a declaration as to the rights of that person and a worker in relation to a dispute about the effect of a sex equality clause or rule – S.127(3) EqA. A responsible person for these purposes is an employer or someone responsible for paying an office holder, as defined by S.80(4).

An employment tribunal may also determine an application by the trustees or managers of an occupational pension scheme for a declaration as to their rights and those of a member in relation to a dispute about the effect of any equality rule – S.127(4) EqA. An employer is entitled to be treated as a party to proceedings in an employment tribunal that relate to a breach of an equality rule, and to take part in those proceedings – S.127(8).

9.5 **Power to transfer claims to a tribunal.** Although the EqA does not set this out expressly, since equal pay is a cause of action rooted in the terms of the employment contract, an employee has the option of bringing an equal pay claim in the county court or High Court by way of an action for breach of contract. S.127(5) confers jurisdiction on an employment tribunal to determine any question in relation to an equality clause or equality rule that has been referred to it by a court in accordance with S.128 EqA. This allows for court proceedings relating to an equality clause or rule to be transferred to an employment tribunal. Accordingly, when proceedings in a court are pending and it appears to the court that a claim or counterclaim relating to an equality clause or rule could more conveniently be determined by an employment tribunal, the court may strike out the claim or counterclaim – S.128(1). If a question about an equality clause or rule arises during court proceedings the court may refer the question to an employment tribunal for determination and stay or sist the proceedings in the meantime – S.128(2). Both these possibilities are discussed in more detail under 'Choice of forum' below.

By giving employment tribunals the power to hear references from other courts, it is clear that the law assumes the former will be the usual proper forum for determining equal pay matters. Since the employment tribunal is the forum with the requisite expertise and specialised procedure for determining equal pay issues, even where an equal pay claim is brought as a breach of contract in the civil courts, it will almost always be more convenient for the matter to be dealt with by the employment tribunal. However, an issue may arise where the time limit for presenting a claim in the tribunal has passed, but the time limit for presenting a contract claim in the High Court or county courts has not. In that case, it may be that the claimant has the option to proceed in the civil courts – again, see under 'Choice of forum' below.

Jurisdiction in respect of the armed forces. Members of the armed forces who **9.6** wish to enforce the EqA provisions relating to equality of terms must bring a complaint under service complaints procedures before they can bring a claim to an employment tribunal (S.127(6) EqA). That provision makes it clear that the tribunal will be entitled to entertain such a complaint only if the claimant has made a complaint and it has not been withdrawn. Furthermore, if the claim relates to an act done when the claimant was serving as a member of the armed forces the tribunal does not have jurisdiction to hear it unless the individual has complied with the same criteria as apply in respect of discrimination claims set out in S.121 – S.127(7) EqA. These provide that a complaint is treated as withdrawn if it has not been referred to the Defence Council – S.121(2) and (3). But the fact that a member of the armed forces subsequently makes a complaint to an employment tribunal does not affect the continuation of his or her service complaint or service redress procedure – S.121(5).

Choice of forum
9.7

As noted above, a breach of the 'equality clause' set out in S.66 EqA is a breach of contract capable, at least in principle, of being remedied in the civil courts. This is subject to two powers provided to the civil courts by virtue of S.128 EqA, which are broadly the same as those previously provided for in S.2(3) EqPA. First, under S.128(1) a court may strike out a claim or counterclaim that relates to an equality clause or rule if the court considers that the matter 'could more conveniently be determined by an employment tribunal'. Secondly, S.128(2) allows a civil court, when a question arises about an equality clause or rule, to refer the question to an employment tribunal for determination, and stay or sist proceedings in the meantime.

One reason why a claimant might bring an equal pay claim in the civil courts is to attempt to avoid the more stringent time limits that apply in the employment tribunal. As we explain under 'Time limits' below, an equal pay claim must generally be brought within six months of the end of the woman's employment – S.129 EqA. The EqA gives tribunals no discretion to extend this time limit, and so would-be claimants who do not act swiftly may lose out on their right to recover back pay in the employment tribunal. By contrast, the EqA does not lay down any specific limits on bringing a breach of contract claim based on the equality clause in the civil courts. Thus, the standard civil time limit in breach of contract cases of six years from the date on which the cause of action accrues should arguably apply, with the court free to make a reference to an employment tribunal for determination of the question of equal pay. It might therefore be possible for a claimant who is willing to face the procedural hurdles and cost of bringing a claim in the ordinary courts to do so in respect of an equal pay claim going back up to six years. If so, and there has been a breach of the equality clause, then the claimant can expect to recover damages up to the limit normally available in the civil courts. The limit on damages in civil actions is six years from the date that the claim is instituted, and so no back pay could be awarded in respect of a period more than six years before the claimant brought the civil claim.

9.8 It should be noted, however, that the bringing of a civil claim is subject to the power of the Civil Courts under S.128(1) EqA to strike out a claim that could 'more conveniently be determined by an employment tribunal'. The purpose and scope of this power are open to interpretation. On the one hand, it could be that the power is designed only to be used where an employment tribunal would be able to hear the claim instead of the civil courts – if so, this would only be where the claimant is still within the six-month time limit for bringing a tribunal claim. If this is the case, it is hard to see this power ever being used, as no claimant who has the opportunity to have his or her claim determined under the tribunal system would prefer to undergo the travails of the civil court system instead. On the other, it could be that the power is designed to prevent abuse of the time limits rules, so that any claim that should have been brought under the employment tribunal regime will be struck out in the civil court if out of time under the tribunal rules.

For many years, this was a purely theoretical point for employment lawyers, as all equal pay claims were brought in tribunals. Recently however, the scope of a court's power to strike out equal pay claims has been the subject of two – not entirely consistent – decisions in the High Court. In Abdulla v Birmingham City Council 2011 IRLR 309, QBD, the Council sought to have the High Court claims of 174 former employees, all of whom were out of time for bringing an equal pay claim in the employment tribunal, struck out under S.2(3) EqPA, which, in similar terms to S.128(1) EqA, afforded the civil courts a power to strike out claims where the claim 'could more conveniently be disposed of separately by an employment tribunal'. Rejecting the application to strike out the claim, Mr Colin Edelman QC considered that the statute was contemplating the situation where the case could be disposed of by the tribunal after a full consideration of its merits. He rejected the notion that a case could 'more conveniently' be disposed of by a tribunal where the tribunal would immediately have to dismiss the case on the basis that it is out of time. This view was supported by the fact that S.2(3) does not mandate that a tribunal must strike out any claim that could more conveniently be disposed of by a tribunal; it merely provides the court with the unfettered discretion to do so. Mr Edelman QC further pointed to the second half of S.2(3) EqPA, which is now found in S.128(2) EqA: a court has a power to refer a question about an equality clause or rule to an employment tribunal for determination, and may stay or sist proceedings in the meantime. This, he reasoned, means that a civil court hearing an equal pay claim can refer those questions in relation to which it lacks the necessary expertise to address – such as whether the claimant and comparator are employed on equal work, or whether there is a valid material factor defence – to a tribunal, but retain the case under its jurisdiction and reach a decision on remedies and costs once the other questions have been determined by the tribunal.

The second case, Ashby and ors v Birmingham City Council 2011 IRLR 473, **9.9** QBD, was not a first instance decision like Abdulla, but an appeal from the Birmingham County Court. There, the equal pay claims of 14 claimants, all of whom were out of time for bringing a claim in a tribunal, had been struck out under S.2(3) EqPA on the basis that such claims were generally more conveniently disposed of by a tribunal, and that the claimants were attempting an abuse of process by seeking to litigate them in the civil courts after the tribunal time limit had expired. Mrs Justice Slade – who also sits in the EAT and is thus no stranger to equal pay law – considered that the county court's decision on the strike-out could not stand, as it was wrong to rely on the generalisation that claims are more conveniently disposed of by a tribunal without exposing the individual circumstances of the case to scrutiny.

However, contrary to the view of Mr Edelman QC in Abdulla on the scope of S.2(3), Slade J held that a claim can be 'more conveniently' disposed of by a tribunal in circumstances where a tribunal would have to reject the claim as out of time. This conclusion was reached in the light of a shipping case, Spiliada Maritime Corp v Cansulex Ltd (The Spiliada) 1987 AC 460, HL, where Lord Goff had stated that a stay for *forum non conveniens* (a legal doctrine that allows a court to refuse to take jurisdiction over matters where there is a more appropriate forum available to the parties) could be granted even where the claim would be out of time in the alternative, more appropriate forum. This,

Slade J reasoned, provided useful guidance as to the meaning of the word 'conveniently' in S.2(3) EqPA, as did the fact that Lord Goff had referred to the need for 'practical justice' to be done. With that in mind, she concluded that in determining whether a claim could be disposed of more conveniently by a tribunal, a court should ask whether it could be dealt with 'more suitably in the employment tribunal in the interests of the parties and the ends of justice'. In remitting the matter to the county court for reconsideration of that issue, Slade J made it clear that the court should consider the facts and circumstances surrounding the case, including the reasonableness of the claimant's actions in failing to bring the claim within the employment tribunal time limit.

9.10 It seems certain that, sooner or later, the Court of Appeal will come to consider the meaning of S.2(3) EqPA or its successor provision in S.128(1) EqA. For the time being, however, the High Court decisions discussed above form the sole jurisprudence in this area. That raises the question of which approach is to be preferred: Mr Edelman QC's view in Abdulla that a claim could never be dealt with more conveniently by a tribunal if that tribunal would have to reject the claim as out-of-time; or Slade J's view in Ashby that behind the word 'conveniently' lies a test of practical justice and reasonableness? In our view, the approach in Ashby seems more in keeping with the nature of the discretionary power the legislation vests in a court confronted with an equal pay claim, in that it identifies factors that a judge should take into account when deciding whether to exercise the discretion to strike out a claim. Abdulla, by contrast, fetters a court's discretion by saying that it cannot be exercised where a claim is out of time in an employment tribunal.

Should Slade J's approach be favoured, the further question arises as to just how high a hurdle the test of reasonableness and practical justice will present to equal pay claimants. One factor to consider here is the influence of EU law – in particular the principle of equivalence – which dictates that national rules that give effect to EU rights must not be less favourable than those governing similar domestic actions. (The parameters of this principle were considered and applied by the European Court in Levez v TH Jennings (Harlow Pools) Ltd 1999 ICR 521, ECJ – a case specifically concerned with equal pay issues.) In Abdulla, Mr Edelman QC held that the construction of S.2(3) EqA advanced by the defendant in that case – namely, that a claim in the civil courts must be struck out if it would be out of time in an employment tribunal – would offend the principle of equivalence as it would present an additional hurdle to a claimant that would not exist in a contract action in domestic law. If he was correct on this point, but wrong that a claim cannot be disposed of more conveniently when out of time in a tribunal, then the hurdle presented by Slade J's test in Ashby must, it would logically follow, be a low one.

Article 157 claims

9.11

We noted in Chapter 1 that there are differences between the EqA and the European legislation which the Act is designed to implement into UK law. This might confuse the way in which a claim is put before an employment tribunal. The right to equal pay derives from Article 157 TFEU (previously Article 141 of the EC Treaty), which requires Member States to ensure that 'the principle of equal pay for male and female workers for equal work or work of equal value is applied' – Article 157(1). Article 157(2) goes on to define 'pay' as 'the ordinary basic or minimum wage or salary and any other consideration, whether in cash or in kind, which the worker receives directly or indirectly, in respect of his employment, from his employer'.

These provisions create a slightly different regime for establishing equal pay than does the EqA. Three significant differences are worth noting. First, Article 157 restricts the right to equality to pay and consideration in kind and so, on the face of it, excludes employment benefits such as holiday entitlement, which are covered by the equal pay provisions in the EqA so long as they are contractual in nature (non-contractual rights being covered instead by the provisions on discrimination in employment in Chapter 1 of Part 5 of the 2010 Act). Secondly, and conversely, Article 157 does not restrict the right to 'pay' equality to contractual terms, as the EqA does. Thirdly, the European Court of Justice's interpretation of the term 'employer' in Article 157 has developed a wider scope for comparison than is ostensibly permitted under S.79 EqA (see Chapter 4, 'Comparators'). It follows that employees in particular circumstances might find that they have a valid claim under Article 157 but not on a strict reading of the EqA. The question then arises whether, and if so by what authority, the employment tribunal is competent to hear claims arising directly under (or relying directly upon) the Treaty.

It is well established, in a line of cases beginning with Defrenne v Sabena 1976 **9.12** ICR 547, ECJ, that the right to equal pay for equal work enshrined in what is now Article 157 has 'direct effect'. This means that it is capable of being relied upon directly in national courts even without further implementing measures (i.e. domestic legislation) being put in place. In other words, the Article confers a right to equal pay for equal work directly on individuals. What is more, Article 157 has both 'vertical' and 'horizontal' direct effect: 'vertical' meaning it is capable of being enforced against the state and emanations of the state; 'horizontal' meaning that it can be enforced against private individuals. As the Court in Defrenne noted, 'since Article [157] is mandatory in nature, the prohibition on discrimination between men and women applies not only to the action of public authorities, but also extends to all agreements which are intended to regulate paid labour collectively, as well as to contracts between individuals'. However, it is all very well asserting that Article 157 can be enforced by individuals directly, but without any specific mechanism for that enforcement how do employment tribunals acquire jurisdiction? Employment

341

tribunals are creatures of statute, having competence only in matters expressly placed under their jurisdiction by the relevant legislation – S.2 Employment Tribunals Act 1996. While the EqA confers jurisdiction upon employment tribunals to hear complaints arising out of the operation of the equality clause created by S.65 of that Act, nothing in the EqA or any other piece of domestic or European legislation confers jurisdiction on tribunals to hear claims based directly on Article 157. So, while there is no doubt that Article 157 can be relied upon without reference to the EqA, it is far from clear that an employment tribunal is the appropriate forum for this to be done.

The decision of the European Court of Justice in Impact v Minister for Agriculture and Food and ors 2008 IRLR 552, ECJ, gives some clue as to how tribunals might acquire jurisdiction. There, Irish civil servants sought to rely on the direct effect of provisions of the EU Fixed-term Work Directive (No.1999/70) based on facts occurring after the deadline for transposition of the Directive had passed in July 2001 but before the implementing provisions of Irish law came into force in July 2003. They brought their complaints before a Rights Commissioner, whose jurisdiction was established under the domestic provisions from July 2003 but who enjoyed no express jurisdiction to hear claims based directly on the Directive. The employer challenged the Rights Commissioner's jurisdiction to hear claims based on facts occurring before 2003 and, after an appeal to the Labour Court, a reference was made to the ECJ. The ECJ held that a specialised court (in this instance, the Rights Commissioner) which is granted jurisdiction in matters relating to transposing legislation must also have jurisdiction to hear claims arising directly from the Directive thereby transposed, in respect of the period between the deadline for transposing the Directive and the date on which the transposing legislation entered into force. This is so provided that it is established that the obligation on the claimant to bring, at the same time, a separate claim based directly on the Directive before an ordinary court would involve procedural disadvantages liable to render excessively difficult the exercise of the rights conferred on him by Community law.

9.13 What relevance does this have to equal pay claims? Like the Irish civil servants' claims based directly on the Fixed-term Work Directive, a claim based directly on Article 157 would, in the absence of effective implementing measures, rely on its direct effect: for example, the claimant might wish to compare herself with an employee who is a valid comparator under Article 157 but not under the EqA. Thus, the principle in the Impact case – that such a claim should be able to be heard by the court or tribunal with jurisdiction under the implementing legislation – should apply to give the employment tribunal jurisdiction to hear the Article 157 claim, so long as the alternative (pursuing the employer in the civil courts) would be procedurally less favourable.

342

Putting the Impact case to one side, the EAT has in any event suggested that the procedural rules of domestic legislation can be used for claims brought by virtue of the direct effect of Community law where the Member State has failed to make provision for the enforcement of such rights before the national courts. In Livingstone v Hepworth Refractories Ltd 1992 ICR 287, EAT, the Appeal Tribunal held that the procedures of the Sex Discrimination Act 1975 could cover claims of sex discrimination based on the direct effect of what was then the EU Equal Treatment Directive (No.76/207), where the Directive had not been fully transposed. By extension, the same argument might persuade a tribunal to deal with a claim based on the full effect of Article 157 within the mechanism laid down by the EqA.

Given that direct reliance on Article 157 is more straightforward in theory than **9.14** in practice, many practitioners prefer to see Article 157 in terms of influencing the interpretation of provisions of the EqPA (and now the EqA) rather than in terms of its direct effect. It is a long-established principle of EU law that courts and tribunals must so far as possible interpret domestic legislation in conformity with the provision of EU law it is intended to implement – see Marleasing SA v La Comercial Internacional de Alimentacion SA 1992 1 CMLR 305, ECJ. This is certainly true of equal pay, having been restated on several occasions. Mr. Justice Burton, sitting in the EAT in Department for Environment, Food and Rural Affairs v Robertson and ors 2004 ICR 1289, EAT, summed up the effect of Article 157 on domestic legislation as being that Article 157 'can... be relied upon in addition to the provisions of [the EqA], and so as to supplement or fill any lacuna in it'. So, even where a claim does not appear possible based on a literal reading of the EqA, the claimant can still bring his or her claim under the Act and rely on Article 157 to fill in the gaps.

Estoppel

9.15

In this Handbook we consider separately the three bases on which a woman can establish a claim for equal pay: like work (Chapter 5), work rated as equivalent (Chapter 6), and work of equal value (Chapter 7). Whichever of these the claimant relies upon, she is seeking to establish the same thing: that the employer is in breach of the equality clause inserted by S.66 EqA into every contract of employment. One of the several issues on appeal in Redcar and Cleveland Borough Council v Bainbridge and ors and another case; Middlesbrough Borough Council v Surtees and ors 2009 ICR 133, CA, was whether this means that an equal value claim, for example, amounted to the same 'cause of action' as a work rated as equivalent (RAE) claim for the same pay period. If so, the doctrine of 'res judicata' might 'estop' (that is, prevent) a claimant who has already brought a claim on the basis of equal value bringing another on the basis of work RAE, or like work, in respect of the same period.

Redcar Council argued that this should be the case, submitting that where claimants had received final judgment in their claims for equal pay based on

RAE, they could not then claim on the basis of equal value in respect of the same period. It submitted that there can only be one entitlement to an amount of pay under the contract for a particular period, and only one cause of action for breach of the contractual entitlement to receive pay at the particular level. While it accepted that the equal value claims involved different facts and different comparators to the RAE claims, the Council argued that this did not make them different causes of action, and so the doctrines of res judicata and/or merger could provide an absolute defence to the claimants' equal value claims. The Council also argued that the doctrine of election – by which a claimant must choose only one remedy for his or her particular cause of action – prevented the second claims. It contended that the claimants had elected for the remedy of RAE pay and were therefore barred from seeking the remedy of equal value pay in respect of the same period.

9.16 The employment tribunal, EAT and Court of Appeal all rejected these arguments. The Court of Appeal pointed out that it would be wrong to characterise equal pay as a remedy. It is a substantive right for the infringement of which remedies, in the form of back pay and declaratory relief, are available. Furthermore, it would be wrong to see the failure to give equal pay as comprising a simple breach of contract, thus giving rise only to one possible cause of action. Although the equality clause mechanism is rooted in the contract of employment, the clause operates only within the context of what is now Chapter 3 of Part 5 of the EqA, which by virtue of S.65(1) accords three different legal bases for a claim. There is nothing mutually inconsistent in these three different bases. Nothing in the EqA expressly or implicitly confines the claimant to one of the three ways of putting her claim; nor do the doctrines of res judicata or merger, or any other general principle of law, require the claimant to make an irrevocable choice between the three ways of establishing a breach of the equality clause.

9.17 Time limits

The time limit provisions now found in Ss.129 and 130 EqA have their origins in the Equal Pay Act 1970 (Amendment) Regulations 2003 SI 2003/1656, which amended the time limit provisions of the EqPA in response to the ECJ's decisions in Levez v TH Jennings (Harlow Pools) Ltd 1999 ICR 521, ECJ, and Preston and ors v Wolverhampton Healthcare NHS Trust and ors (No.1) and another case 2000 ICR 961, ECJ. In those cases, the ECJ had to consider whether the requirement in old S.2(4) EqPA that all claims be brought within six months of the end of employment, and the rule in old S.2(5) EqPA restricting arrears of remuneration to two years in the event of a successful claim, were compatible with EU law. While upholding Member States' right to impose procedural rules limiting the period within which civil actions may be brought and the extent to which damages may be recovered, the ECJ raised concerns over whether the limits set down by the EqPA were less favourable than those applying to comparable actions in domestic law for breach of contract. If so, there might be a breach of the principle of 'equivalence', under which rules governing the enforcement of rights derived from EU law should be no less favourable than those governing the enforcement of purely domestic rights. Following further litigation in the Preston case the UK Government, having weighed up these concerns, decided to make changes. In this section we consider the time limit rules under the EqA, which are broadly the same as those that appeared in the EqPA post-2003. The provisions limiting the amount of arrears of remuneration that a successful equal pay claimant can recover, which the 2003 amendments also addressed, are considered under 'Remedies' below.

An equal pay claim made by an individual, an employer or the relevant Minister 'may not be brought in an employment tribunal after the end of the qualifying period'– S.129(2) EqA. The duration of the qualifying period depends on what type of case it is, as defined in S.130. This specifies four classifications of case, which are the same in principle as those formerly listed in S.2ZA EqPA, although two of the names have changed slightly. They are:

- a 'standard case'

- a 'stable work case' (previously 'stable employment case')

- a 'concealment case'

- an 'incapacity case' (previously a 'disability case').

We consider each of these in turn below, before turning to the particular problems that arise in the context of equal pay claims brought following a transfer of an undertaking.

Standard case

9.18

The default is the 'standard case', which is a claim not falling into any of the three other categories (stable work, concealment and incapacity). In a standard case, the qualifying period is 'the period of 6 months beginning with the last day of the employment or appointment' – S.129(3). So, time starts running not on the date on which the equality clause is breached, but when the 'employment' (or 'appointment' in the case of office-holders) in respect of which the breach occurred comes to an end. An employee who claims equal pay in a standard case during the currency of his or her employment will not, therefore, face any difficulty with regard to time limits.

There is, however, no provision in the EqA for the standard time limit to be extended in equal pay claims. Under most other employment legislation, tribunal complaints can be heard out of time where there is good reason for doing so – for example, under the discrimination provisions in the EqA a claimant who has missed the deadline for presenting a claim can nonetheless have the claim heard if he or she can persuade the tribunal that, in all the circumstances of the case, it is 'just and equitable' to hear it – S.123(1)(b). Thus, the only possible avenue for a claimant who has missed the time limit in a standard case is to pursue the matter in the High Court or county court (or Sheriff's Court in Scotland) – see under 'Jurisdiction – choice of forum' above for a discussion of the issues involved in bringing such a claim.

9.19 **Variation of terms.** It is important to distinguish between the end of 'employment', which sets time under the EqA running, and a variation in terms and conditions, that generally will not.

In Newcastle upon Tyne City Council v Allan and ors and another case 2005 ICR 1170, EAT, four of the claimants had changed positions within the Council more than six months before their equal pay claims were presented. The Council successfully argued before the tribunal that this made them out of time to claim except in respect of their current posts, the six-month time limit for their previous positions having already expired. The EAT overturned this decision in respect of three of the four claimants on the basis that the tribunal had failed to give full reasons for these conclusions. In so holding, the EAT emphasised the difference between a variation of contractual terms, which does not set time running, and a termination of a particular contract of employment, which does. It took the view that for a variation to amount to a termination, it must be such a significant change that it can no longer be said that the original contract survives. The EAT was influenced in its decision by the Court of Appeal's judgment in Young v National Power plc 2001 ICR 328, CA. There, the Court accepted that there was a distinction between 'work', for the purpose of determining whether a claimant is performing 'equal' work to that of her comparator, and 'employment' for the purpose of the time limit. The Court held that the reference to 'employment' is a reference to the contract of employment and so, even if the claimant's job function (work) has changed over the course of her employment, the time limit does not begin to run so long as the original contract is still in place.

9.20 The difference between a variation in terms and a termination of employment is not an area of law that makes for hard and fast rules. Much turns on a tribunal's appreciation of the facts before it. This is well illustrated by the EAT's decision in Winder v Aston University and anor EAT 0025/07. That case involved two female employees of the same University, both of whom wanted to bring equal pay claims based on their historical exclusion from the occupational pension scheme. The jobs of both women had changed over time as described immediately below:

- C was employed in 1972 as a part-time Data Preparation Officer. In 1984 she accepted a secondment to work in a secretarial capacity for a manager, which was initially for 12 months, but was extended for a further 12 months. This involved a change in office location within the same building and training in additional skills. However, the secondment brought no change in her salary apart from a £200 'honorarium' in addition to her normal pay. On 1 September 1986 she was formally given the job title of full-time secretary to reflect current working practice. On 23 August 1990 she was placed on the secretarial salary scale at grade 3. She later brought a claim for pension access based on her employment between 1976 and 1986

- W began continuous employment as a part-time secretary in the Business School on 3 December 1984 on clerical salary grade 2. In July 1990 she applied for and, after interview, was appointed to the position of Research Secretary Information Assistant in the same Business School, moving up to clerical grade 3. While the exact nature of the work done before and after July 1990 was rather different, W took the view that both roles were largely secretarial. In January 1993, again after application and interview, she accepted a new role for which she resigned from her existing position with one month's notice. Her work location changed, although she was still within the Business School, and her role became more academic and involved more contact with students, although she remained on the clerical grade 3 salary scale. After six months in the new role W changed to full-time working. She later brought an equal access claim based on the whole period of her employment.

An employment tribunal allowed C's claim to proceed, finding that there were **9.21** no changes of sufficient substance to terminate her employment prior to her move to full-time employment in 1986. However, the tribunal held that W's claim could not proceed in respect of any period before the start of 1993. On appeal, the EAT saw no reason to interfere with the tribunal's decisions. The circumstances of C's case were a 'paradigm' of a long-serving employee's job evolving over time. While the tribunal had correctly noted that C's job was very different at the end to what it was in 1972, it had been entitled to find that each incremental change was simply a variation of contract. It is often the case that changes occur by the addition of new duties in exchange for new money, as in the circumstances surrounding C's secondment. At no point was there a change such as to evince an intention by the parties to give up one job and start another. By contrast, in W's case there was clear evidence before the tribunal that the intention of the parties was to create a new relationship at each change of role. This was particularly so on the second occasion in January 1993, when W resigned with notice before changing to her new role. The tribunal had also been influenced by the fact that, on each occasion, W's move to a new role followed an application and interview. While the EAT noted that it might have reached a different conclusion itself, the tribunal's decision was properly reasoned and so there were no grounds on which to interfere with it.

It is clear that in attempting to distinguish between variations of contract and terminations of employment, the focus of the tribunal must be on the intentions of the parties, viewed objectively, at the time of each change. The EAT reaffirmed this in Cumbria County Council v Dow and ors and other cases (No.2) 2008 IRLR 109, EAT, where various claimants' jobs had altered in status, hours or duties. The EAT held that, in practice, where parties had signed what was stated on its face to be a new contract superseding all previous contracts, this could be taken as conclusive evidence that they had chosen to end the previous agreement. On the other hand, where a new contract was only issued after the alterations had been brought into effect – and was not signed or returned by the employee – this could not recharacterise a previously effective variation as a termination of employment. The EAT recognised that there is a degree of artificiality in distinguishing between claimants on the basis of whether or not they signed written contracts at the time of the change, given the probability that, subjectively, none of them would have given any thought as to whether there was a new contract or a variation of the old one. However, in the interests of legal certainty, the EAT considered that traditional objective tests must apply.

9.22 In Slack and ors v Cumbria County Council and ors 2009 ICR 1217, CA, the employer argued that the contractual changes to the claimant employees' contracts had been effected by the termination of the original contracts of employment and their replacement by new contracts. Accordingly, any part of the employees' claim that related to their employment under their old contracts was out of time. The employees, on the other hand, argued that they had always been employed under a single contract that had simply been varied and that they were accordingly entitled to bring a claim in respect of the whole period of their employment with the employer.

The matter went to the Court of Appeal, which held that the changes in the employee's contractual terms had been effected by the introduction of a new contract of employment rather than a variation of contract. Each claimant had signed a document containing detailed terms and conditions of employment, which included terms different from their previous terms and which expressly stated that it superseded any previous contract. These documents were not alleged to be shams or to have been obtained by improper pressure or to offend public policy. Nor did they contain terms that were so unusual or onerous that it could be argued that the employer was under a positive duty to draw them specifically to the employees' attention. The claimants had signed up to and agreed express wording rescinding the previous contracts of employment and replacing them with new contracts. The unambiguous, express and comprehensive contractual document recording the parties' intentions left no room for an argument that the parties should not be taken to have intended to exercise their freedom to contract in the way that they did. The signed documents were new contracts that were valid and binding, even though the employees may not have appreciated the effect that the documents would have on the triggering of the time limits for bringing equal pay claims. All this said, however, although the case had been put to the employment tribunal and the EAT below on the basis of a 'standard' case, the EHRC intervened before the

Court of Appeal to successfully argue that the claim was in fact a 'stable employment' case (now a 'stable work' case under the EqA), with the result that the claims were, in fact, in time. This aspect of the decision is considered further under 'Stable work case' below.

Concealment case   9.23

As the name implies, a concealment case covers the situation where the facts giving rise to a potential equal pay claim are hidden from the would-be claimant. S.130 EqA explains that a concealment case arises where:

- the employer deliberately concealed from the woman any fact (a 'qualifying fact') which is relevant to the alleged breach of the equality clause and without knowledge of which the woman could not reasonably be expected to bring the proceedings; and

- the woman did not discover the qualifying fact (or could not with reasonable diligence have discovered it) until after the last day on which she was employed in the employment, or the day on which the 'stable employment relationship' ended (see below).

In any concealment case that is not also an incapacity case (see under 'Incapacity case', below), the qualifying period is '6 months beginning with the day on which the worker discovered (or could with reasonable diligence have discovered) the qualifying fact' – S.129(3) EqA.

Although the concept of a 'concealment case' was added to the EqPA in 2003, **9.24** there is scant appellate guidance on what amounts to such a case. The leading precedent is still Levez v TH Jennings (Harlow Pools) Ltd 1999 ICR 521, ECJ – being the European Court's judgment which first suggested the need for the 2003 amendments to the EqPA, the successor provisions to which are now found in Ss.129 and 130 EqA. In that case, L, a woman, was recruited in February 1991 as manager of a betting shop on a salary of £10,000. In December, she moved to another shop where she replaced a man who, from the start of his employment, had earned £11,400. L's pay rose to £10,800 at the end of December, THJ Ltd falsely declaring to her that this was what her predecessor had been paid. Her salary did not rise to £11,400 until April of the following year and she did not discover the truth about her predecessor's salary until after she left her job in March 1993. L brought an equal pay claim in September 1993 and was initially successful, the employment tribunal deciding that she was entitled to a salary of £11,400 from the start of her employment in February 1991 and ordering THJ Ltd to pay arrears. However, following a review held at the request of THJ Ltd, the employment judge acknowledged that S.2(5) EqPA – as it then was – applied to the claim, barring the claimant from obtaining pay arrears in respect of any period more than two years before the date on which her complaint was presented. The tribunal had no discretion to extend that period and so L was not entitled to arrears in respect of unequal pay before September 1991, despite her employer's deception. On L's appeal, the EAT decided to refer the issue to the ECJ to deal with L's contention that this was contrary to European law.

The ECJ held that the two-year limit on pay arrears prescribed by old S.2(5) EqPA was precluded by European law in a case where the woman's delay in bringing the claim was attributable to the employer's deliberate misrepresentation as to the level of remuneration of a male employee performing like work. Furthermore, while nothing in EU law prohibits the imposition of reasonable limitation periods for bringing proceedings in the interests of legal certainty, such limitations, as they apply to rights derived from EU law, must not be less favourable than those governing domestic rights (the principle of 'equivalence'). Nor must they render virtually impossible or excessively difficult the exercise of EU-derived rights (the principle of 'effectiveness'). These principles were analysed and developed in the later ruling of the European Court in Preston and ors v Wolverhampton Healthcare NHS Trust and ors (No.1) and another case 2000 ICR 961, ECJ – see under 'Stable work case' below.

9.25 At first glance, the reference in Levez to 'deliberate misrepresentation' suggests that the employer must have given a false assurance that a woman was being paid the same as a male comparator in order for a concealment case to be made out. However, in Thacker and anor v Secretary of State for Education and Skills and anor EAT 0039/05 the EAT appeared to accept that a lower threshold of deceit applied. There, T was initially employed part time in a college from 1989 until 1995, when she became a permanent employee and entitled to join the pension scheme. She was assured by the college's HR department that her continuity of employment for pension purposes would nevertheless begin in 1989, and a number of other similar representations were made thereafter, along with reassurances that she did not need to make a tribunal claim to enforce her rights. When she commenced equal pay proceedings relating to her pension entitlement in 2004, the college argued that any stable employment relationship relating to T's period of part-time employment ended in 1995 when T became permanent, and so the pre-1995 part of her claim was out of time. T accepted that she had no arguable 'stable employment' case (see below), but instead argued that there had been concealment. An employment judge struck out the claim but, on appeal, the EAT held that the concealment point was at least arguable. In the EAT's view, the repeated assurances from the HR department to the claimant to the effect that her continuity of employment was preserved from 1989 and that she did not need to present a claim to an employment tribunal might amount to a concealment requiring the standard time limit under the EqPA (now EqA) to be disapplied.

It seems that tribunals might well be prepared to take a broad approach to deciding what amounts to concealment, as the following case demonstrates:

- **Smith v Morgan Lovell plc** ET Case No.1301736/06: S's letter of appointment stated that it was a condition of her employment that her individual terms of employment remained confidential between her and the company. ML plc pursued a positive policy of not revealing details of salary to anyone other than the recipient of the salary. In April 2004, ML plc appointed a man, B, to a comparable job to S. S was assured that B was coming into the company at the same level as her and that he was being employed as her equal. B was later promoted, which caused S to bring a claim of sex discrimination in November 2005. As part of the disclosure process in that claim, S discovered that B, when recruited, was put on a salary that was over £10,000 higher than hers. S brought an equal pay claim, seeking to rely on the concealment provisions as her claim was otherwise out of time. The employment tribunal found that ML plc's deliberate policy of not revealing salary details meant that it had deliberately concealed from S the fact that her comparator's salary exceeded hers. The tribunal felt able to depart from the principle set out in leading authorities that 'deliberate concealment' must mean more than deliberately not telling. The cases to which the tribunal had been referred addressed the provisions contained in the Limitation Act 1980, not the EqPA. To decide otherwise would enable employers to avoid litigation under the EqPA (and now the EqA) by the simple expedient of a policy of silence on pay. Furthermore, adopting a higher standard for 'concealment' would be likely to render the exercise of S's right to equal pay excessively difficult, contrary to the principles set down in the Levez case (above).

(Note that contractual 'pay secrecy' clauses of the type seen in the Smith case may now be caught by S.77 EqA and so rendered unenforceable. See under 'Pay secrecy clauses' below for further details.)

Incapacity case 9.26

An incapacity case under the EqA is broadly the same as what was previously termed a 'disability case' under the EqPA. However, given that the EqA has extensive provisions on disability discrimination (see IDS Employment Law Handbook, 'Disability Discrimination' (2010) for details), which use a wider definition of the term 'disability' than was used for the purposes of the EqPA, the Government opted to change the label for such cases to 'incapacity'. The incapacity case time limit provisions are designed to cover the situation where incapacity has prevented a claimant from bringing an equal pay claim in time.

An incapacity case is defined in S.130(7) EqA as a case where the worker had an incapacity during the period of six months beginning with the later of –

- the relevant day – S.130(7)(a), or

- the day on which the worker discovered (or could with reasonable diligence have discovered) the qualifying fact deliberately concealed from the worker by the employer – S.130(7)(b).

9.27 The 'relevant day' for the purposes of S.130(7)(a) is either the last day of the employment or appointment, or the day on which the stable working relationship between the worker and the responsible person ended – S.130(10) EqA.

Section 129(3) provides that the qualifying period for an incapacity case which is not also a concealment case is the period of six months beginning with the day on which the worker ceased to have the incapacity. Where, however, an incapacity case is also a concealment case, the qualifying period is the period of six months beginning with the later of the days on which the period would begin if the case were merely a concealment or incapacity case.

9.28 **Definition of incapacity.** The EqA provides differing definitions on incapacity for the two jurisdictions covered by the Act. S.141(6) provides that in England and Wales, a person has an incapacity if he or she has not attained the age of 18, or lacks capacity within the meaning of the Mental Health Act 2005. While a detailed discussion of the 2005 Act is obviously outside the scope of this Handbook, suffice it to say that S.2(1) provides that 'a person lacks capacity in relation to a matter if at the material time he is unable to make a decision for himself in relation to the matter because of an impairment of, or a disturbance in the functioning of, the mind or brain'. S.141(7) EqA provides that in Scotland, a person has an incapacity if he or she has not reached the age of 16, or is 'incapable' within the meaning of the Adults with Incapacity (Scotland) Act 2000. A person is incapable for the purposes of that Act if he or she is not capable of acting or making, communicating or understanding decisions, or of retaining the memory of such decisions, by reason of mental disorder or of inability to communicate because of physical disability.

9.29 Stable work case

Formerly known under the EqPA as a 'stable employment case', this final category covers a situation where there have been breaks in what would otherwise have been continuous employment with a single employer. S.130(3) EqA defines a stable work case as 'a case where the proceedings relate to a period during which there was a stable working relationship between the worker and the responsible person (including any time after the terms of work had expired)'. A responsible person is an employer or someone responsible for paying an office holder, as defined by S.80(4) EqA.

In a stable work case that is not also a concealment or incapacity case (or both), the qualifying period within which an equal pay claim must be presented is 'six months beginning with the day on which the stable working relationship ended' – S.129(3) EqA.

352

In order to define the kinds of situation that the 'stable work relationship' **9.30** provision that is now found in S.129(3) EqA is intended to cover, it is necessary to set out some of the case history that led to the 2003 amendments to the EqPA and, in particular, the insertion of the stable employment relationship provision into that Act. The amendments responded, in part, to judgments in the 'Preston litigation', which involved around 60,000 claims submitted to employment tribunals by part-time employees complaining of unlawful exclusion from membership of occupational pension schemes. The first major decision in the Preston litigation was a ruling of the ECJ, Preston and ors v Wolverhampton Healthcare NHS Trust and ors (No.1) and another case 2000 ICR 961, ECJ (Preston No.1). There, the European Court had to consider a question referred to it by the House of Lords asking whether the six-month time limit under the EqPA, which then made no provision for the stable employment case, was contrary to EU law. Many of the claimants had been employed on successive part-time contracts before being taken on permanently, and the question arose of how the six-month time limit should be applied. The ECJ held that in circumstances where there has been a stable employment relationship resulting from a succession of short-term contracts concluded at regular intervals in respect of the same employment to which the same pension scheme applies, it would be contrary to EU law for a procedural rule to require such claims to be brought within six months of the end of each contract of employment.

When the case returned to the House of Lords for it to consider the position of UK law in the light of the ECJ's ruling, their Lordships established the need for stable employment relationships to be given special treatment in the EqPA – Preston v Wolverhampton Healthcare NHS Trust and ors (No.2) and another case 2001 ICR 217, HL (Preston No.2). The clearest analysis of what amounts to a stable employment relationship can be found in the EAT's judgment in Preston and ors v Wolverhampton Healthcare NHS Trust and ors (No.3) and another case 2004 ICR 993, EAT (Preston No.3). (Although one aspect of the EAT's decision, the effect of TUPE on the time limit in such cases, was successfully appealed to the House of Lords, the rest of the EAT's judgment remains good law.) There, His Honour Judge McMullen endorsed an employment judge's application of the ECJ's ruling in Preston No.1 to a number of test cases. The employment judge had stated that:

'1. A stable employment relationship arises (and only arises) when an employee is employed – by the same employer – on a succession of contracts – punctuated by intervals without a contract – on the same or broadly similar terms – to perform essentially the same work – under the same pension scheme – provided that the sequence of contracts and the pattern of intervals between them is dictated either by the nature of the work itself or the employer's requirements for employees to perform it – and (subject to 2 below) the contracts and the intervals between them are sufficiently regular for it to be apparent without the benefit of hindsight to determine when the sequence is broken, that being the moment from which time begins to run.

2. Where the sequence is intermittent rather than regular, the intention of the parties, both as to the inception and the cessation of the working arrangement which is said to give rise to the stable employment relationship, outweighs the absence of a pattern of strict regularity. Where a stable employment relationship has arisen in such circumstances it remains in being until the parties intend otherwise, notwithstanding changes in the frequency of the work, provided that any such changes arise exclusively from the nature of the work.'

9.31 This analysis led the employment judge to dismiss three of the claims before him. In one of the dismissed claims, he found that where a supply teacher had undertaken 14 assignments of varying duration over two years, the periods of employment had been 'far too brief and the work was far too spasmodic to be capable of creating a stable employment relationship'. In another, he concluded that, where a succession of short-term contracts had been superseded by a full-time, permanent contract, the time limit under old S.2(4) EqPA had started to run, meaning that, on the facts, the employee's claim had been out of time.

The judge did, however, remit a fourth test case to a tribunal for further findings. That case involved a home tutor who had entered into a new contract with a home tuition centre in respect of each child in need of tuition. The judge thought that this was 'a fairly rare instance of a pattern of intermittent working which is capable of being a stable employment relationship', and so remitted it to a tribunal to consider whether the employee and employer 'had the necessary expectations of each other to create a stable employment relationship'.

9.32 In the interests of clarity, the judge went on to set out five events that would bring to an end a stable employment relationship and so set time running:

- a party indicates that further contracts will either not be offered or not be accepted if offered

- a party acts inconsistently with the continuation of the relationship

- a further contract is not offered when the periodicity of the preceding cycle of contracts indicates that it should have been offered

- a party ceases to intend to treat an intermittent relationship as stable

- the terms of the contract or the work to be done under it alters radically, e.g. a succession of short-term contracts is superseded by a permanent contract.

9.33 **Succession of short-term contracts followed by permanent contract.** The last of the above criteria cited by HHJ McMullen in Preston (No.3) has attracted a fair amount of attention in subsequent cases. In Thatcher v Middlesex University and anor EAT 0134/05, the claimant worked as a teacher under regular contracts of between six months' and a year's duration until 1992. Her hours and her pay varied under each of the contracts, but all contracts covered broadly the same teaching, administrative and research duties. These duties were then replicated in a two-year fixed-term contract covering the period 1992 to 1994. However, unlike the short-term contracts, the fixed-term contract provided for fractional pay and entitled the claimant to join a pension scheme. HHJ McMullen had to consider whether the two-year fixed-term contract was radically different from the preceding contracts and concluded that it was not. This was not a case of a short-term contract being replaced by a permanent contract, which the same judge had said was excluded from the stable employment relationship category in Preston (No.3). Although the final contract was for two years, compared to previous contracts of no more than a year, HHJ McMullen took the view that two years was still 'short-term' in this instance, as the first year was probationary. It was also clear from the parties' conduct that they intended to be engaged with each other for the performance of a succession of substantially unchanged contracts. The conversion under the later contract of the claimant's method of payment from part-time hours into fractional pay, and her entitlement to join a pension scheme, did not amount to radical differences in the contract or the work done under it in the absence of any change of duties before and after 1992.

However, in Jeffery and ors v Secretary of State for Education and anor 2006 ICR 1062, EAT, the Appeal Tribunal was specifically required to consider whether the claimants remained in a stable employment relationship where, following their employment on a series of short-term contracts, they were placed on permanent, open-ended contracts. The claimants were teachers employed on temporary contracts for a succession of academic years (roughly from September to June). In each case, the claimants had had their most recent temporary contract converted into a permanent contract while the temporary contract was still running. They tried to distinguish their circumstances from those in Preston (No.1) on the basis that Preston dealt specifically with a series of short-term contracts, each of which was terminated and eventually replaced with a new, permanent contract. The claimants argued that the fact that their temporary contracts had been converted into permanent contracts, instead of being terminated and replaced by new contracts, meant that the final temporary (now permanent) contract was still part of the stable employment relationship. The tribunal rejected that argument and Mr Justice Elias, then President of the EAT, dismissed the claimants' appeal. Elias P acknowledged that it might be said that entry into a permanent job did not destroy a stable employment relationship. But he accepted that it was not apt to describe the succession of short-term contracts followed by a permanent contract as a 'succession of short-term contracts' – which is how the ECJ defined a stable relationship in the Preston (No.1) case – and, accordingly, it could not be said that there was a continuation of the stable relationship into a new permanent contract.

Furthermore, Elias P held there is inevitably a fundamental change when a temporary contract is made indefinite such that there is effectively a termination of the fixed-term contract to be replaced by a new indefinite one. For these reasons, the stable employment relationship was to be taken to have ended, and time began to run at the point that each claimant became a permanent employee.

9.34 We would respectfully suggest that the EAT's decision in the Jeffrey case is counterintuitive: after all, what could logically be a better indicator of a 'stable employment relationship' than that the employee is finally given permanent status, having been previously engaged on a series of short-term contracts? It seems odd that the time limit for bringing an equal pay claim must be viewed as run as soon as the employee becomes permanent even where there is no significant alteration to the terms and conditions that pertained under the last of the short-term contracts. Furthermore, the EAT's decision does not square with subsequent decisions of the Court of Appeal, which have emphasised that the lack of any break in the work done by an employee across a series of contracts is a paradigm example of a stable employment relationship – see Slack and ors v Cumbria County Council and ors 2009 ICR 1217, CA, and North Cumbria University NHS Hospitals Trust v Fox 2010 IRLR 804, CA. In the latter case, the Court of Appeal pointed out that the ECJ's ruling in Preston (No.1) had adopted the concept of 'stable employment relationship' by reference to the factors of that particular case, which involved a succession of short-term contracts. However, the language of the actual ruling should not be confined to this factual situation. On the contrary, if stability of the relationship was the guiding principle, it would be perverse to hold that a succession of long-term contracts could not achieve the same result. The ECJ had adopted a broad, non-technical test, looking at the character of the work and the employment relationship in practical terms. In particular the word 'employment' in the phrase 'stable employment relationship' was intended to refer to the nature of the work rather than the legal terms under which it was carried out. Thus, in stipulating that a succession of contracts had to be in respect of the same employment the ECJ could not have intended to use the word employment in the legal sense of a contract of employment.

9.35 **No need for break between contracts.** In Slack and ors v Cumbria County Council (see above), three claimants – women employed by the Council who had signed new contracts of employment – had put forward their claims to an employment tribunal and the EAT as 'standard' cases. The Court of Appeal held that if the claims were to be so regarded, they were time-barred in respect of the period of employment before the new contracts took effect, since the new contracts had brought an end to the previous employment, thus triggering the six-month time limit from that point – this aspect of the decision is considered under 'Standard case' above. However, this was not the end of the matter, since the Equality and Human Rights Commission (EHRC) intervened in the case, submitting to the Court of Appeal that the claims were, in reality, 'stable employment' cases. The EHRC contended that where there has been, as here, a termination of a contract of employment and a continuation of employment under another contract for substantially the same work with the same employer, this comprises a 'stable employment' (not a 'standard') case, with the consequence that the time limit is not triggered until the expiry of the final contract in the succession of contracts.

Prior to this intervention, it had generally been assumed that the stable employment provision then found in S.2ZA(2) EqPA (now Ss.129(3) and 130(3) EqA) simply covered situations similar to the one that arose in Preston (No.1), where employees have worked regularly but intermittently for the same employer under a succession of short-term contracts. Consistent with this assumption, the Council argued before the Court of Appeal that a stable employment case could not arise where there was an unbroken succession of contracts. The Court disagreed, holding that the irresistible logic of the ECJ's reasoning in Preston (No.1) and of the purpose behind the subsequent EqPA amendments was that stable employment was established even more strongly by an uninterrupted succession of contracts. In the light of this, two of the three claimants' equal pay claims were held to have been presented within six months of the termination of the last of their contracts (i.e. the date on which the stable relationship ended) and so were in time. In respect of one of the claimants, the Court ruled that the facts as found by the tribunal were not sufficiently clear to establish whether or nor the 'stable relationship' case applied, and the matter was therefore remitted to the tribunal for clarification of that issue.

The decision in Slack was resoundingly endorsed by the further decision of the **9.36** Court of Appeal in North Cumbria University NHS Hospitals Trust v Fox (see above). In that case it was held that claimant nurses whose terms of employment had changed following the implementation of a Job Evaluation Scheme (JES) remained in a stable employment relationship for the purposes of S.2ZA EqPA. Accordingly, in determining whether their claims were in time, it was not necessary to decide whether the claimants' contracts had been terminated or merely varied by the contractual changes. There was no suggestion that the nature of their jobs as nurses changed materially following the implementation of the JES, nor that there was any other practical break in their employment relationships. In so holding, the Court of Appeal confirmed, in the light of the decision in Slack, that the concept of a 'stable employment relationship is not confined to cases in which there are breaks in a succession of employment contracts. An uninterrupted succession of contracts is an *a fortiori* case of a stable employment relationship.

Conversion from part time to full time. In Kolesnik v Swindon College ET **9.37** Case No.1401598/09 the claimant began working for the employer in 1975 as a part-time Further Education teacher on a series of short-term contracts that required her to set class and home work, examine and mark the work and set

357

and mark end-of-term exams. She did not confine herself to contractual duties, but involved herself in the work of the department, attending all departmental meetings and acting as a tutor to students. By 1983 she was working as many hours as a full-time lecturer and, following a recruitment process and interview, was appointed full-time lecturer on a new contract with significantly different terms and conditions. With regard to her equal pay claim and whether this had been brought in time, an employment tribunal held that the claimant was employed in a stable employment relationship from 1975 until her retirement in 2009. In this case she was in such a relationship from an early stage in her part-time employment and this continued after she became full time.

9.38 Effect of TUPE

As we have seen, the six-month period within which a standard equal pay case must be brought is expressed to run from the last day the woman is 'employed in the employment' – S.129(3) EqA. Below, we consider the tricky matter of whether 'the employment' for this purpose might continue where an employee transfers automatically from one employer (the transferor) to another (the transferee) under the Transfer of Undertakings (Protection of Employment) Regulations 2006 SI 2006/246 (TUPE).

The relevant rules of TUPE are discussed at length in IDS Employment Law Handbook, 'Transfer of Undertakings' (2011). For present purposes, it is important to note that when a 'relevant transfer' takes place from one employer to another – essentially, when there is a sale of a business or a change of service provider – the transfer does not operate so as to terminate the employment contract of any person employed by the 'transferor' employer in the transferring entity. Rather, any such contract will have effect after the transfer as if originally made between the employee and the 'transferee' employer. Furthermore, owing to Reg 4(2), all the transferor's rights, powers, duties and liabilities under or in connection with any such contract will transfer to the transferee. There is, however, an added complication with regard to pension rights. Reg 10(1) provides that an employee's rights in connection with an occupational pension scheme do not transfer to the transferee. Thus, any liability for a failure to allow an employee access to the pension scheme – a liability that may arise under equal pay law – remains with the transferor employer.

9.39 The questions to be considered, then, are as follows:

- does TUPE have the effect of extending the 'employment' in which the woman is employed, meaning that the S.129(3) qualifying period in respect of a claim based on her employment with the transferor does not start to run until the end of her employment with the transferee? And

- is the situation any different where the claim in question relates to non-transferable pension rights?

358

Pensions cases. The House of Lords considered the pension claims issue in 9.40 Preston and ors v Wolverhampton Healthcare NHS Trust and ors (No.3) and another case 2006 ICR 606, HL – a case also known as Powerhouse Retail Ltd and ors v Burroughs and ors (and which we shall refer to as 'Powerhouse' in order to distinguish it from other aspects of the Preston litigation). In Powerhouse, the claimants were employed for many years within the nationalised electricity industry. Until 1988, they were excluded from their occupational pension scheme on account of their being part-time workers. On 1 April 1988 the ban on part-time workers belonging to the pension scheme was removed and the claimants became members of the scheme. Following the privatisation of the electricity industry, the claimants' contracts of employment transferred under TUPE to PR Ltd. They brought equal pay claims against the transferor (i.e. their original employer) in relation to their exclusion from the occupational pension scheme. However, these claims were presented to the employment tribunal substantially more than six months after the date of the transfer of their employment to PR Ltd. The tribunal held that the claims were out of time under S.2(4) EqPA, as it then was. In the tribunal's view, S.2(4) meant that the claims needed to have been brought within six months of the date of the transfer. In other words, the transfer brought about the end of the 'employment' for equal pay purposes. The claimants appealed, arguing that, since under TUPE their contracts of employment continued as if originally made with the transferee, time did not begin to run under S.2(4) for the purposes of their claims until the date of the cessation of their employment with the transferee.

The EAT allowed the claimants' appeal, but its decision was then overturned by the Court of Appeal. When the case finally reached the House of Lords, their Lordships upheld the tribunal's decision. In their view, the plain and natural meaning of S.2(4) when read as a whole was that a claim must be brought within six months of the end of the employment to which the claim relates. In the instant case, since TUPE did not transfer liabilities connected with occupational pension schemes, the claim related only to the claimants' employment with the transferor. According to the House of Lords, the best way of achieving the purpose of the time limit is to link it as closely as possible to the liability which is the subject of the claim so that, with a claim relating to the operation of an equality clause with regard to an occupational pension scheme provided by the transferor, the period of six months runs from the end of the claimant's employment with the transferor, to whom the liability belongs, rather than the end of the employment with the transferee.

Note that although Powerhouse was decided on the basis of S.2(4) EqPA – 9.41 before the 2003 amendments took effect – the definition in S.129(3) EqA of the 'qualifying period' before the end of which a claim in a 'standard case' must be brought is substantively the same as the 'qualifying date' by which a 'standard' equal pay claim had to be presented under S.2(4), and subsequently S.2ZA,

EqPA. Hence, their Lordships' reasoning in Powerhouse is equally applicable under both the post-2003 EqPA and the EqA.

9.42 **Non-pensions cases.** At first glance it might be assumed that the principle in Powerhouse applies only to pensions cases. The fact that pension liabilities do not transfer under TUPE seemed central to their Lordships' reasoning, allowing them to arrive at the conclusion that 'the employment' to which old S.2(4) EqPA (now S.129(3) EqA) referred meant only that with the transferor employer. Recent case law has suggested, however, that their Lordships' decision – that the 'employment' for equal pay purposes is terminated by a TUPE transfer – applies to all equal pay claims, and not just pension-related ones.

Like Powerhouse, the case of Unison v Allen and ors 2008 ICR 114, EAT, involved claims of unlawful exclusion from an occupational pension scheme brought many years after a TUPE transfer. There, the EAT held that, following Powerhouse, the pensions claims were out of time. Importantly, it went on to note that its decision in this regard did not depend on the exclusion of pension liabilities from the TUPE Regulations. In the EAT's view, the House of Lords in Powerhouse was enunciating a broader principle that applied regardless of whether the relevant liabilities had transferred. In essence, Lord Hope in Powerhouse had treated the periods of employment pre- and post-transfer as separate employments for the purposes of the EqPA time limit provisions: TUPE did not artificially extend 'employment' within the meaning of S.2ZA(3) EqPA (now S.129(3) EqA).

9.43 Mr Justice Elias, then President of the EAT, presided in the Allen case. He had another opportunity to consider the meaning of Powerhouse in the later case Sodexo Ltd v Gutridge and ors 2009 ICR 70, EAT. While in Sodexo Elias P acknowledged the strength of some arguments against his interpretation of Lord Hope's reasoning, he nonetheless maintained that it was correct. In his view, Lord Hope had rejected the basis on which the Court of Appeal in Powerhouse had reached the conclusion that the claims in question were out of time, that basis being the exclusion of pension liabilities from TUPE transfers. Rather, Lord Hope was saying that the concept of 'employment' in the EqPA (and now the equal pay provisions in the EqA) must be treated the same in the face of TUPE as it would have been in the absence of TUPE. In summary, Elias P's considered view on the effect of TUPE on the time limit for equal pay claims was that 'the six-month time limit runs from the date of transfer itself for all equal pay claims which derive from the equality clause with the transferor, at least with respect to alleged breaches by the transferor. This is so whether liability for breach transfers pursuant to TUPE or not.'

Elias P's interpretation of Powerhouse was subsequently approved by a majority of the Court of Appeal (Lord Justices Pill and Wall) in Sodexo Ltd v Gutridge 2009 ICR 1486, CA, and is therefore unquestionably binding on tribunals.

Lady Justice Smith's dissenting judgment, however, took the view that Powerhouse was restricted to the transfer of occupational pension rights and did not provide authority for the proposition that claims in respect of pre-transfer breaches had to be brought within six months of the date of the transfer. Furthermore, she thought that the EqPA's 'most unusual limitation provision' (now replicated in the EqA) was not designed to provide the usual form of protection from 'stale' cases. In an ordinary equal pay case, she pointed out, the employer is exposed to claims for as long as the woman's employment continues, even though the comparator may have left the employment years ago and the reasons why they were paid differently may have been lost in the mists of time.

Equal pay as an ongoing breach of contract. While the Sodexo judgments in 9.44 the EAT and Court of Appeal cleared up some of the uncertainty surrounding the Powerhouse decision, they introduced a new complexity into TUPE-related equal pay claims. The claimants in Sodexo were cleaners and domestic staff employed by North Tees and Hartlepool NHS Trust until 1 July 2001, on which date they transferred under TUPE to S Ltd. Over five years later, in December 2006, G and several of her colleagues brought pay claims against S Ltd. They based their claims on a comparison, not with any of S Ltd's employees, but with maintenance workers who had been employed by the Trust at the same time as them, and who had not transferred under TUPE. The employment tribunal held a pre-hearing review to determine whether the claims were misconceived or out of time, and decided that they were not. S Ltd appealed to the EAT, where Elias P identified two aspects to the claimants' case.

The first was their attempt to claim in respect of their employment with the Trust. With regard to this, Elias P's interpretation of Powerhouse (set out above) led him to conclude that time for bringing these complaints began to run at the date of the transfer, meaning that they were out of time. This aspect of the decision was upheld by the Court of Appeal (see above). The second aspect was the claimants' attempt to claim against S Ltd – the transferee employer – in respect of the post-transfer period. This, Elias P accepted that they could do. The claimants' argument in this regard, with which Elias P agreed, was that the equality clause implied into every contract of employment 'does not simply hover over the employment relationship... it bites once the conditions for its application are met'. So, as soon as there is a case of unequal pay – as there was assumed, for the sake of argument, to have been during the claimants' employment with the Trust – the claimants' rights under the EqPA crystallised. The claimants therefore had a contractual right, at the date of the transfer, to be paid at the same rate as their comparators. This right could then transfer to S Ltd under TUPE. Thus, G and her co-claimants could enforce against S Ltd their ongoing right to the terms that would have been enforceable before the transfer against the Trust.

9.45 The effect of Sodexo is complicated to say the least. Elias P summarised the position as being that, after the transfer, 'the claimant is enforcing a contractual right which is derived from the equality clause operating with respect to the transferor'. The effect of TUPE is that the contractual liability derived from the equality clause is transferred and the claimants must be entitled to enforce that right as if it had arisen under an equality clause with the transferee. The claimants therefore benefit from a continuing liability on the part of the transferee to honour the contractual terms they were entitled to at the date of the transfer, i.e. terms no less favourable than those enjoyed by their comparators when employed by the transferor. This aspect of Elias P's reasoning was unanimously upheld by the Court of Appeal (Sodexo Ltd v Gutridge 2009 ICR 1486, CA).

Unfortunately, neither Elias P nor the Court of Appeal explained exactly how the claims should proceed in these circumstances. The mechanism of the equal pay provisions does not allow the claimants to claim against the transferee on the basis of a comparator whom the transferee has never employed and, as was comprehensively established, the six-month time limit prevents any claim being brought directly against the transferor. Elias P stated that the claimants can 'enforce their equal pay claims in so far as they relate to the failure by the transferee to honour their contracts', which might suggest that he had in mind either a breach of contract or an unlawful deduction from wages claim against the transferee. But the claimants will nonetheless have to rely on the tenets of the EqPA/EqA to establish the pay inequality by reference to the claimants' chosen comparators, and thus the extent of the transferee's liability.

9.46 It also appears that, even if the claimants succeed in their claims against the transferee, they will not be able to recover back pay in respect of the period of their employment with the transferor. While stating that the claimants' equal pay claims can be enforced on the basis of the transferee's failure to honour their contracts, Elias P went on to note that 'it is now too late to claim with respect to the liability incurred by the transferor before the transfer'. It appears, then, that the liability incurred by the transferor before the transfer is not part of the transferee's ongoing liability; at least, not after the six-month time limit for bringing the claim against the transferor has expired. However, there are two possible avenues for an employee once that time limit has expired. First, as we note under 'Jurisdiction of tribunals – choice of forum' above, there is (in theory at least) nothing to stop an employee bringing an equal pay claim in the civil courts up to six years after they have left employment. So, while they are out of time in the employment tribunal with regard to the transferor's liability, there is the possibility that they could bring proceedings in the county court or the High Court to recover back pay from the transferor directly. This is subject to the fact that in the civil courts no damages may be recovered in respect of any breach of contract occurring more than six years before the claim was instituted.

The second option is procedural: if the claimant has brought an equal pay claim against the transferor to recover payment, then in exceptional circumstances it may be possible to apply to the tribunal to amend the claim in order to join the transferee as a respondent. This is so even if the application for joinder is made more than six months after the date of the transfer. This is precisely what happened in Walsall MBC and anor v Birch and ors EAT 0376/10. In that case 103 claimants sought equal pay following a TUPE transfer in respect of the failure by the transferor (Walsall Metropolitan Borough Council) to pay them in accordance with the equality clause. The transfer took place on 2 April 2008. The claims were presented on 29 April 2008, but at that time the claims named the transferor as the sole respondent. One year later, the claimants' solicitors applied to have the transferee (H Ltd) joined as a respondent. It was accepted by the parties, the tribunal and subsequently by the EAT that, in view of Reg 4(2) of TUPE, all the Council's duties and liabilities under or in connection with the claimants' contracts of employment were transferred to H Ltd and that any act or omission committed by the Council before the transfer was completed was deemed to have been an act or omission in relation to H Ltd. Accordingly, even if the Council was in breach of the equality clause prior to the transfer, that liability could not be enforced by the transferred employees against it after the transfer, but instead had to be enforced against H Ltd as the transferee. However, as the EAT pointed out – relying upon the majority decision of the Court of Appeal in Sodexo Ltd v Gutridge – once the claimants had transferred to H Ltd, the six-month time limit specified in S.2(2) EqPA (now S.129(3) EqA) for bringing a standard equal pay claim began to run from the date of the transfer. This meant that by the time the application to amend the claim and join H Ltd to the proceedings was made, the six-month time limit for bringing a claim had well and truly expired.

Even so, the EAT upheld an employment judge's decision to grant the joinder. **9.47** Applying the principles set out in by the EAT in Selkent Bus Co Ltd v Moore 1996 ICR 836, EAT, the judge had concluded that the balance of hardship came down in favour of granting the claimants' application. On appeal, His Honour Judge Richardson presiding at the EAT accepted a concession made by H Ltd's counsel that, on the state of the authorities at present, an employment tribunal has discretion to allow an amendment that introduces a new claim out of time and that there is no rule of law that such an amendment cannot be allowed simply because it would, if presented as a fresh claim, be time-barred. The EAT further rejected H Ltd's contention that the employment judge's decision circumvented the decision in Sodexo Ltd v Gutridge to the effect that the limitation period for bringing an equal pay claim in respect of pre-transfer arrears of pay was six months from the date of the transfer. In HHJ Richardson's view, while it was an important consideration that the relevant limitation period had already expired prior to the joinder of a new party, equal pay claims were not in a special category simply because they are subject to immutable time limits, whether as to the commencement of the claim or the period of time over which arrears may be claimed. It was clear that, in the instant case, the employment judge had taken into account that the limitation period had expired and had accorded sufficient weight to that factor when deciding, nevertheless, to allow the amendment.

9.48   Time limits in armed forces cases

The time limit provisions outlined under 'Standard case', 'Concealment case', 'Incapacity case' and 'Stable work case' above are mirrored in the provisions relating to complaints by members of the armed forces relating to the terms of service, except that the time limit is nine months instead of six – S.129(4) EqA. Note that civilians working for the armed forces are covered by the standard rules and not those related to terms of service in the armed forces (see para 144 of the EHRC Code of Practice on Equal Pay).

9.49   Time limit for response

It is not only the claimant who has to comply with strict time limits. Once the complainant's claim form (ET1) has been received and accepted, the employment tribunal will send a letter to the employer, together with a copy of the ET1 and a response form (ET3). The employer should then 'present a response' by completing and returning the ET3 to the tribunal within 28 days of the date on which he was sent a copy of the ET1 – rule 4 of the Rules of Procedure set out in Schedule 1 to the Employment Tribunals (Constitution and Rules of Procedure) Regulations 2004 SI 2004/1861. Where the employer fails to return the ET3 on time, he will be barred from taking any further part in the proceedings except for some very limited purposes – rule 9. Furthermore, the employer's default will entitle the tribunal, at its discretion, to issue a default judgment, which will effectively determine the claim in favour of the claimant without the need for a hearing – rule 8. This situation is explained in detail in IDS Employment Law Handbook, 'Employment Tribunal Practice and Procedure' (2006), Chapter 4.

9.50   Repeal of the statutory dispute resolution procedures

The Employment Act 2002 and the Employment Act 2002 (Dispute Resolution) Regulations 2004 SI 2004/752 (the statutory disciplinary, dismissal and grievance procedures) prevented employment tribunals from hearing an equal pay complaint where the employee had failed to follow the statutory grievance procedures. These procedures were abolished in April 2009, but the sheer volume of equal pay claims currently in the tribunal system, coupled with transitional provisions, mean that there may still be some cases where they still apply. For details of the transitional provisions, see IDS Employment Law Supplement, 'Disciplinary and Grievance Procedures' (2009), Chapter 1.

Statutory questionnaire procedure 9.51

Although the mechanism for establishing a claim under the discrimination provisions in the EqA is different to that laid down by the equal pay provisions in the same Act, there are broad similarities. Under the discrimination provisions generally, the complainant must establish a 'prima facie' case from which the employment tribunal could conclude, in the absence of an adequate explanation, that discrimination has occurred. A prima facie case might be made out where, for example, a woman is passed over for promotion in favour of a less-qualified man, or a black man is denied benefits afforded to all his white colleagues. Absent an adequate explanation, there is good reason to suppose that the reason for the difference in treatment is sex or race, and so the burden of proof passes to the employer to discharge the presumption of discrimination.

The equal pay provisions can be seen as taking a similar approach. In order to get a claim off the ground, a female claimant must point to a man in the same employment who is engaged on like work, work rated as equivalent or work of equal value and who is being paid more than her. That done, a presumption of unequal pay arises and it is for the employer to prove the absence of discrimination, either by challenging the validity of the claimant's proposed comparison or by establishing a material factor explaining the difference in pay (see Chapter 8, 'Material factor defence').

The key for an equal pay claimant, then, is to establish a valid male comparator who is paid more than her. Clearly, her ability to do so relies on her knowing what her co-workers are paid. While this information might be freely available as a published pay structure in some organisations, and through word-of-mouth in others, relative pay levels are clouded in secrecy in many workplaces, with salary and bonus details jealously guarded by individual employees (see under 'Pay secrecy clauses' below for details of the EqA's limited measures to counter such secrecy). In these circumstances, the statutory questionnaire procedure will be enormously useful.

The same questionnaire procedure applies to discrimination and equal pay 9.52 claims by virtue of S.138 EqA (subsection (6) confirming that the procedure applies to a breach of an equality clause or rule). The procedure contained in S.138 enables an employee who believes that she may be receiving unequal pay to seek the key facts from her employer before deciding whether or not to pursue a case before a tribunal.

365

9.53 **Prescribed forms**

Section 138(2) EqA requires a Minister to prescribe question and response forms for the purpose of allowing a person who suspects they may have been a victim of a contravention of the EqA to question the alleged perpetrator over a relevant matter, although the questions and answers do not have to be in a prescribed form in order to be admissible as evidence in proceedings – S.138(3). Pursuant to this requirement, the Equality Act 2010 (Obtaining Information) Order 2010 SI 2010/2194 ('the Order') prescribes the relevant forms by which persons who believe they have been subject to contraventions of the EqA can obtain information from the putative respondent. Although, as mentioned above, the procedure is the same for equal pay claims as for discrimination claims, the forms to be used are different. Article 3 of the Order provides that the forms to be used for equality of terms cases are those contained in Parts 1 and 2 of Schedule 2 to the Order. These are broadly similar to those which were previously prescribed under the Equal Pay (Questions and Replies) Order 2003 SI 2003/722. One form is for the complainant to question the employer on any matter that is or may be relevant to an equal pay claim; the other is for the respondent to reply, if it so wishes.

Although these forms are not compulsory, they provide a useful framework, especially for a complainant acting without legal advice. In summary, the forms direct the complainant to state the names or job titles of the person or persons with whom equal pay is claimed; to ask whether the employer agrees that the complainant is paid less than the comparator; to ask the reasons for the difference in pay, if the difference is conceded; and if it is not conceded, to ask for reasons why. The form also includes a section for the complainant to ask if the employer agrees that the comparator is employed on like work, work rated as equivalent or work of equal value and, if not, to ask for reasons why the employer disagrees.

9.54 While an employer and employee are not obliged to use these forms, many claimants will use the questions listed as general headings to pose more specific questions, such as asking for general salary information broken down by gender and for individual-specific information in relation to proposed comparators. Questions and replies may be used in evidence before any tribunal hearing, whether or not they are asked or answered in the prescribed form, provided the claimant served the questions within a prescribed period (see under 'Time period of questions' below) – S.138(3) EqA.

Previously, S.7B(5) and (7) EqPA provided that where the question of whether or not an equality clause was breached by an employer was referred to a tribunal by a Minister under the provisions of S.2(2) EqPA, a similar questionnaire procedure to that above applied in respect of the questions the Minister could ask of the employer. Under the EqA, however, a tribunal no longer has the jurisdiction to hear a reference from a Minister (see 'Jurisdiction

366

of tribunals' above), and accordingly the provisions of S.7B(5) and (7) EqPA have not been recreated in S.138 EqA.

Time period for questions

9.55

The questionnaire procedure is normally used before employment tribunal proceedings are started, but it can also be used once they have begun. Article 4 of the Equality Act 2010 (Obtaining Information) Order 2010 SI 2010/2194 specifies that questions must be served on an employer either:

- before proceedings under the EqA have been commenced, or

- where proceedings under the Act relating to the contravention have been commenced, before – (i) the end of the period of 28 days beginning on the day on which proceedings were commenced, or (ii) such later time as the court or tribunal specifies.

In Williams v Greater London Citizens Advice Bureaux Service 1989 ICR 545, EAT, the EAT held that the terms of the Race Relations (Questions and Replies) Order 1977 SI 1977/842 (a precursor of S.138 EqA and the 2010 Order) clearly contemplated that tribunals should be given control over matters relating to discrimination questionnaires after a certain stage and it was not for the EAT to interfere when a tribunal refused to extend time where there had been no satisfactory explanation for the delay. There is no reason to assume that the same reasoning would not apply in respect of the current provisions.

Drawing inferences

9.56

If the employer fails to respond to the questionnaire within eight weeks, or answers the questions in an evasive or equivocal fashion, an employment tribunal may draw an inference from this – S.138(4) EqA. There are limited circumstances in which a tribunal may not draw an inference from a failure to respond or the nature of the employer's response, and these include where the answers might prejudice a criminal matter – S.138(5).

The tribunal's power to draw inferences on the basis of an evasive or equivocal reply, or a failure to reply, will be used differently in claims brought under the equal pay provisions compared with how it is used in respect of complaints under the discrimination provisions. As noted above, the questionnaire procedure was originally drawn from the legislation outlawing discrimination in employment generally on the grounds of sex, race, disability, religion or belief, sexual orientation and age, where it is for the complainant to establish facts raising a 'prima facie' case of discrimination. An employer's failure to respond to a statutory questionnaire can, in certain circumstances, do the complainant's job for him or her, as the tribunal is entitled to draw an inference of discrimination and, in the absence of an adequate explanation, find for the complainant. In equal pay claims, by contrast, an employer's failure to reply, or an equivocal or evasive reply, cannot of itself raise a presumption of pay discrimination if the claimant has not also satisfied the requirement of showing a better-paid comparator of the opposite sex. The absence of a timely, non-evasive and unequivocal reply to a questionnaire is therefore more likely to be used to cast doubt on the material factor defence should such a defence be advanced by the employer (as to which, see Chapter 8).

9.57 By virtue of S.138(8) EqA, the questionnaire provisions take effect subject to existing rules regarding the admissibility of evidence and other interlocutory and preliminary matters in the tribunals. For example, the powers of a tribunal to request further particulars from either party, or to rule certain matters inadmissible in evidence, are unaffected.

9.58 Confidential information

One of the most difficult issues connected with equal pay questionnaires concerns information relating to a potential comparator that the employer or comparator is unwilling to disclose. Information about salaries may be a sensitive issue and it is often organisations with the least transparent pay systems that are the most susceptible to equal pay claims.

The Data Protection Act 1998 is likely to be relevant in this context in that it allows employers to process 'personal data' (such as a particular employee's salary details) only in certain circumstances. If the employee in question consents to having the details revealed, then there is no breach of the DPA. In order to process personal data without consent, however, one of the conditions specified in Schedule 2 to the Act must be satisfied. These include:

- that the processing is necessary for compliance with a legal obligation to which the employer is subject – para 3

- that the disclosure is needed for the administration of justice – para 5(a), or

- that the disclosure is necessary for the purposes of legitimate interests pursued by the data controller or by the third party to whom the data is disclosed, except where the processing is unwarranted by reason of prejudice to the rights, freedoms or interests of the data subject – para 6(1).

9.59 It is the third of these categories that is most likely to allow disclosure in response to an employee's equal pay questionnaire. However, the nature of the third category is that it requires some degree of balancing between the legitimate interest being pursued – the answering of the questionnaire to facilitate the equal pay claim – and the rights, freedoms and interests of the 'data subject' (the comparator). This would tend to suggest that it may be more difficult to disclose detailed information about salaries than to provide a simple answer to the question proposed in the statutory questionnaire; namely, 'does the comparator earn more than me?' This yes/no answer is clearly less detrimental to a potential comparator than divulging their previously unknown salary details.

However, even if the disclosure does fall within the third category, that is not the end of the matter. The employer still has to process the data in a manner consistent with the broad data protection principles, one of which is that the processing should be fair and lawful. The problem here is that the common law on breach of confidence may come into play. Some commentators have suggested that the information discussed above could be confidential in a common law sense and, if it is, then regardless of the fact that the DPA at first glance appears to allow disclosure, such disclosure would not be lawful and would, therefore, in fact be prohibited by the Act.

The Government, recognising some of these difficulties, produced guidance **9.60** with regard to the equal pay questionnaire entitled 'Equal Pay Act 1970: The Questionnaire'. The guidance, which conformed to the Code of Practice on equal pay published by the Equal Opportunities Commission (now replaced by the Equality and Human Rights Commission, which has issued its own Code (see under 'Equality and Human Rights Commission – Codes of Practice' below)), noted: 'In many cases employers will be able to answer detailed questions in general terms whilst still preserving the anonymity and confidence of their workers. For example, they could describe groupings on a pay scale, or confirm that a comparator's pay is above a certain rate. Where more than one comparator is named, information could be provided in an anonymised way. If only one comparator is named, employers could provide some of the information being sought in a generalised fashion – for example, by explaining more fully how the pay system operates. Much of the information requested will not be confidential. For example, it could include details of pay schemes and job grading systems, job descriptions, or how skills and experience are reflected in the employer's pay system. In some cases employers may not feel able to disclose specific information that they believe is confidential. If the case proceeds to a tribunal complaint, tribunals may order disclosure of relevant information if they believe it is in the interests of justice to do so.'

Pay secrecy clauses

9.61

One of the key intentions announced in the White Paper that accompanied the publication of the Equality Bill – 'A Fairer Future – The Equality Bill and other action to make equality a reality' – was to 'ban pay secrecy or "gagging" clauses which stop employees discussing their pay with their colleagues'. The White Paper went on to state that where colleagues work closely together but are paid different amounts, they should be able to compare those amounts if they wish. At first glance, then, the intention was to outlaw pay confidentiality clauses altogether. However, the actual prohibition set out in the Equality Act 2010 is not nearly so wide-ranging.

369

Under the heading 'Discussions about pay', S.77(1) EqA renders unenforceable any term that purports to prevent or restrict a person from disclosing or seeking to disclose information about the terms of his or her work, 'in so far as [that person] makes or seeks to make a relevant pay disclosure'. Furthermore, S.77(2) provides that a term of a person's work that purports to prevent him or her from seeking disclosure of information from a colleague about the terms of the colleague's work is unenforceable against that person in so far as he or she seeks a 'relevant pay disclosure' from the colleague. A 'colleague', for this purpose, includes a former colleague in relation to the work in question. Note that subsection (1) is not as limited as subsection (2): whereas the latter protects the seeking of relevant pay information only from a colleague (or former colleague), the former protects the making of a relevant pay disclosure to anyone. As originally drafted, S.77(1) would only have protected pay disclosures between colleagues, but the clause was widened by amendment made at the Lords Committee stage, motivated by a desire to protect discussions with trade union representatives. Thus, as the Explanatory Notes point out, disclosures made to a trade union official are potentially protected, but then so are disclosures to any third party, provided that the other conditions specified in S.77 are satisfied.

9.62 A 'relevant pay disclosure' is one made for the purpose of enabling the person who makes it, or the person to whom it is made, to find out whether or to what extent there is, in relation to the work in question, a connection between pay and having (or not having) a protected characteristic – S.77(3). Thus, S.77 is concerned with more than discrimination in pay because of sex – a suspicion of pay inequality linked to race or disability, for example, would also be covered. However, S.77 is clear that some protected characteristic must be at the heart of the pay discussion. This means that there is no general prohibition on clauses that hinder pay discussions: only clauses that hinder those pay discussions aimed at establishing the existence of discrimination.

The Explanatory Notes illustrate what is and is not protected, as follows:

'A female employee thinks she is underpaid compared with a male colleague. She asks him what he is paid, and he tells her. The employer takes disciplinary action against the man as a result. The man can bring a claim for victimisation against the employer for disciplining him.

A female employee who discloses her pay to one of her employer's competitors with a view to getting a better offer could be in breach of a confidentiality clause in her contract. The employer could take action against her in relation to that breach.'

9.63 Some commentators have criticised the narrowness of the statutory drafting of S.77, noting that it misses the point of why confidentiality clauses are such a hindrance to pay equality – it is not so much that they prevent employees following up their suspicions about inequality, but that by prohibiting any discussion of pay at all, they have the effect that such inequalities are highly unlikely to become apparent in the first place. In practice, any employee faced with action for breach of a confidentiality clause in a workplace pay discussion is free to claim that the discussion was aimed at uncovering pay discrimination, which it may be difficult for the employer to disprove. In contrast, where the disclosure is made outside the workplace, it might be more obvious that the employee is not following up a suspicion of pay discrimination – for example, where an employee discloses her pay to one of her employer's competitors with a view to negotiating a job offer on better terms.

By virtue of S.77(4) and (5) EqA, seeking or making a relevant pay disclosure or receiving information disclosed therein is also a 'protected act' covered by the victimisation provisions (see Chapter 11, under 'Victimisation – protected acts'). Thus, an employee potentially has a remedy if his or her employer imposes sanctions for having discussed pay inequality. As with the restrictions on secrecy clauses, this only applies where the employer seeks to punish 'relevant pay disclosures' – salary discussions between colleagues unrelated to discrimination are not covered.

Burden of proof

9.64

Under the EqPA, there was no specific provision concerning the burden of proof. In practice, however, employment tribunals followed the same approach as applied under the SDA and other discrimination enactments. Thus, the claimant was required to establish a difference in pay between her or himself and a comparable worker of the opposite sex, and it was for the employer to then prove that the difference in pay was genuinely due to a material factor which was not the difference of sex.

Although, as stated at the outset of this chapter, much of the enforcement regime for the equal pay provisions in the EqA is separate to that of the discrimination provisions, S.136 EqA, which concerns the burden of proof in claims under the 2010 Act, applies to both sets of provisions. This should not be viewed as a significant change but instead as the mere formalisation of the approach (outlined above) that tribunals have taken in equal pay cases for many years. S.136(2) and (3) provides that, if there are facts from which the court could decide, in the absence of any other explanation, that a person (A) contravened the provision concerned, the court *must* hold that the contravention occurred, *unless* A shows that he or she did not contravene the provision. The reference to a 'contravention of the Act' includes a reference to a breach of an equality clause or rule – S.136(4). Further, the reference to a 'court' includes a reference to an employment tribunal – S.136(6)(a).

9.65 Remedies

Employment tribunals have the same powers under the EqA as they had under the EqPA in relation to remedying breaches of an equality clause. They also have some further additional powers in relation to breaches of an equality rule in occupational pension schemes cases.

As most equal pay cases are brought by individuals complaining about discriminatory pay and benefits, the most common remedy will be an award of arrears of remuneration or damages. Any claim for breach of a term modified or included by virtue of an equality clause may include a claim for arrears of remuneration (in respect of terms relating to pay) or damages (in respect of non-pay terms) – S.132(2) EqA (replacing S.2(1) EqPA).

Where proceedings have been instigated by the employer or person responsible for paying an office holder under S.127(3) (see under 'Jurisdiction of tribunals' above) with the aim of establishing the effect of an equality clause, the tribunal has the power to make an order declaring the rights of the employer and the employee. By virtue of S.124(2)(c) EqA, a tribunal that finds a contravention of the discrimination provisions in the EqA may make an 'appropriate recommendation' to the employer for the purposes of taking steps to eliminate discrimination. However, no such equivalent power exists in S.132 EqA, which governs the remedies available in equal pay claims, with the result that a tribunal will only be able to make recommendations if the claimant has also brought a successful sex discrimination claim alongside her successful equal pay claim.

9.66 Modification of terms

If a woman is successful with her equal pay claim, the equality clause that is deemed to be included in her contract by virtue of S.66(1) EqA will have the effect of modifying the disputed term in her contract so that it is no longer less favourable than the comparable term in the man's contract – S.66(2)(a). If the woman's contract does not include a term corresponding to a term benefiting the man, it is deemed to do so – S.66(2)(b). These provisions apply to all contractual terms including 'non-pay' terms covering, for example, holiday entitlement, cheap mortgages, etc. As explained in Chapter 2 under 'The sex equality clause – term-by-term comparison', it is established that women are entitled to equal pay with men on a term-by-term basis, and that it is no defence for an employer to argue that the woman's package is overall no less favourable – Hayward v Cammell Laird Shipbuilders Ltd 1988 ICR 464, HL.

9.67 Arrears of remuneration

In addition to establishing a claimant's right to higher pay for the future, a successful equal pay claim will generally result in back-payment of the pay the claimant should have been receiving. S.132(3) EqA provides that pay can be backdated no further than the 'arrears day', which depends on the type of case at issue – for the three relevant types of case (standard, incapacity, and concealment), see under 'Time limits' above. S.132(4) identifies the arrears date for proceedings in England and Wales as :

- in a standard case, the day falling six years before the day on which the proceedings were instituted

- in a concealment case, or an incapacity case (or a case which is both), the day on which the breach (of the equality clause) first occurred.

9.68 In Scotland, in a standard case arrears are limited to the period of five years ending on the day on which proceedings were commenced – S.132(5)(a) EqA. If, however, the case involves a relevant incapacity or a relevant fraud or error, the arrears day is to be determined in accordance with S.136(6) and (7) – S.132(5)(b). The effect of these provisions is that the five-year period shall not be regarded as running during any time when, by reason of the employer's fraud or the woman's error based on the employer's words or conduct, the woman is induced to refrain from instituting proceedings, unless she could with reasonable diligence have discovered the fraud or error. Nor shall the five-year period be regarded as running during any time when the woman had an incapacity. This is subject to an overall maximum of 20 years once the periods of incapacity and/or concealment have been taken into account.

Note that there is an important exception to the application of the six-year cap on arrears of pay. A successful claim for access to an occupational pension scheme can result in the granting of retrospective access in respect of any period going back to 1976 – see under 'Pension scheme cases' below.

9.69 **Effect of amendment to claim on 'arrears day'.** The question posed to the EAT in Prest and ors v Mouchel Business Services Ltd and anor EAT 0604/10 was how the arrears day in a standard case is affected by a claimant amending her claim in order to change the comparator – does the six-year period have to be calculated by reference to the presentation of the original ET1 or the subsequent amendment? Mr Justice Underhill, President of the EAT, concluded that the answer to that question depends on 'whether the work said to be being done by the new comparator is different from that said to be being done by the comparators originally named'. It is only if a substantially new claim is being advanced that the arrears day will be calculated by reference to the date the claim was amended. In the instant case, the claimants' amendments had sought to substitute different comparators who nevertheless fell within the same category of worker – in one case street sweepers and in the other refuse drivers. As a consequence, Underhill P considered that the claimants were not advancing a new claim and the arrears day was six years prior to the presentation of the ET1.

9.70 **Lawfulness of limiting arrears of remuneration.** The provisions in S.132 EqA governing the calculation of the arrears date are essentially the same as those which were inserted into the EqPA with effect from 19 July 2003. Previously, S.2(5) EqPA had limited arrears of remuneration to the two-year period before the claim was presented. This provision was the subject of a reference to the European Court in Levez v TH Jennings (Harlow Pools) Ltd 1999 ICR 521, ECJ, where the Court held that, although there is nothing in principle that prohibits the imposition of limits on arrears, such limits must not be less favourable than those governing similar domestic actions (the principle of 'equivalence').

When the case returned to the EAT, which had made the reference, it held that comparable domestic claims included breach of contract, arrears of pay, unlawful deductions from wages or race or disability discrimination, in respect of which claimants can receive compensation covering losses dating back six years by virtue of the Limitation Act 1980. The two-year limit on back pay in equal pay claims was, therefore, less favourable, in breach of the 'equivalence' rule. These decisions gave rise to the Equal Pay Act 1970 (Amendment) Regulations 2003 SI 2003/1656, which inserted the more favourable provisions into the EqPA. That more favourable position is now identically reflected in S.132 EqA.

9.71 **No limit on period of comparison.** Note that the six-year period under S.132 EqA is relevant only to the arrears of remuneration that may be recovered, not to the period during which an equal pay comparison may be made. In Kells v Pilkington plc 2002 IRLR 693, EAT, the respondent employer sought to defend an equal pay claim based on a comparison with an employee who had left the respondent's employment over six years previously. The employment tribunal accepted the employer's argument that the six-year limit on arrears should prevent an equal pay claim based on a comparator who had not, within a period of six years prior to the lodging of the claim, done like work, work rated as equivalent or work of equal value to that of the claimant. On appeal, the EAT overturned that decision as being unsupported by any authority. It acknowledged that evidential problems may arise where there has been a lengthy period of time between the employment of the comparator and the claim and that, if the nature of the work, pay scales or working or economic conditions changed over the years, it would be difficult to prove that any difference in pay was due to gender alone. However, the EAT considered that these were evidential matters for the tribunal to determine, rather than any good reason to prevent such historical comparisons being made.

9.72 **Pension scheme cases**
Historically, changes to equal pay law regarding remedies became necessary following judgments of the ECJ and the House of Lords in the 'Preston litigation' – Preston and ors v Wolverhampton Healthcare NHS Trust and ors

(No.1) and another case 2000 ICR 961, ECJ, and Preston v Wolverhampton Healthcare NHS Trust and ors (No.2) and another case 2001 ICR 217, HL. That long-running legal saga arose in the context of part-time workers challenging their historical exclusion from occupational pension schemes. The part-time workers argued that, being predominantly female, their exclusion from the pension scheme breached Article 157 as it had a disproportionate adverse effect on women, and so amounted to indirect sex discrimination. That argument was accepted a long time ago by the European Court, in Bilka-Kaufhaus GmbH v Weber von Hartz 1987 ICR 110, ECJ, where it held that in so far as such exclusion affects a greater number of women than men, it requires objective justification on grounds unrelated to sex in order to be lawful. However, that principle gives rise to problems of application when one considers what actually amounts to 'exclusion' from a pension scheme, and this was one of the issues that the Preston litigation went on to address.

The part-time workers involved in the Preston litigation found themselves in **9.73** various different circumstances. Some had simply been refused access by reason of their part-time status. Others had the option of joining, while full-time workers were compulsorily enrolled. Still others were entitled to join but were not told of their entitlement. Thus, it was unclear whether each category of claimant had actually suffered a detriment and, if so, when. The EAT analysed these issues in Preston and ors v Wolverhampton Healthcare NHS Trust and ors (No.3) and another case 2004 ICR 993, EAT. A basic outline of the EAT's conclusions is essential to understanding the ruling's effect on the available remedies, and so the key points from the EAT's decision are summarised below:

- *Blanket exclusion of part-timers from pension scheme.* The EAT in Preston No.3 held that exclusion of an employee from an occupational pension scheme on account of her part-time status constitutes a breach of the EqPA (and, therefore, the equal pay provisions in the EqA), without any need to enquire whether the employee suffered less favourable treatment as a result of her exclusion. The EAT thought it clear from previous decisions of the ECJ that, subject to the question of justification, mere exclusion from an occupational scheme on discriminatory grounds is unlawful and that no further examination of any particular employee's personal circumstances is necessary. Accordingly, it was irrelevant to enquire whether the employee would have joined the pension scheme had she been eligible to do so. In such circumstances, the exclusion constitutes an ongoing breach of the equality clause and the claimant may claim a remedy in respect of the employer's failure to grant access throughout the whole of the period that that failure continued

- *Optional access to pension scheme for part-timers.* The EAT also decided that there is no breach of a woman's right to equal pay where scheme membership is compulsory for full-time staff and optional for part-time

375

staff. It pointed out that there was nothing in the case law of the ECJ to suggest that there is a breach of the equal pay legislation when a woman is offered voluntary membership of a pension scheme. Indeed, having such a choice offers the possibility of membership where it is advantageous without the burden of membership where it is disadvantageous. So, no question of remedy arose

- *Failure to inform part-timers of right to access.* According to the EAT, there was no continuing breach of the equal pay provisions where an employee's failure to join a pension scheme is attributable to her employer's failure to inform her that, having previously been unlawfully excluded from the scheme, she has become eligible for membership. Once the inequality in relation to scheme access was removed, the failure to notify the employee about it was not a continuing inequality in breach of the equality clause, unless it could be shown that an employer had in place a discriminatory policy or practice of not informing part-timers of their contractual rights. So, in these circumstances, although the time limit for claiming a remedy does not begin to run until the end of the employment to which the pension scheme relates (see under 'Time limits' above), the claimant's right to a remedy is limited to the period during which the claimant was actually refused access. Only if there was a discriminatory policy in place, preventing the claimant from enforcing his or her right to equal treatment thereafter, will a remedy be possible in respect of any period after the bar to access was removed.

9.74 The remedy for an unlawful failure to grant access to a pension scheme is to grant access retrospectively, requiring the employer to make up the contributions that it would have had to make into the scheme on the claimant's behalf during the period that the claimant was unlawfully excluded. The cost to an employer of back-paying contributions to the scheme can be huge. While claims for arrears of pay are limited to six years, any claim for equal access can be backdated to cover all periods of pensionable service since 8 April 1976 (the date on which the European Court of Justice first ruled in Defrenne v Sabena 1976 ICR 547, ECJ, that what is now Article 157 of the Treaty on the Functioning of the European Union – but was then Article 119 of the Treaty of Rome – has direct effect), or the commencement of the employee's employment, whichever is later – Preston v Wolverhampton Healthcare NHS Trust and ors (No.2) and another case 2001 ICR 217, HL. The House of Lords so held on the basis that applying a limit on the backdating period for pension membership would make it impossible for claimants fully to enforce their right, under Article 157, to equal access. If there were a limit on the period in respect of which membership of the scheme could retroactively be granted, the claimants could not hope to secure a comparable level of future benefits under the scheme. However, it should be noted that employers' pension scheme contributions are generally contingent on the employee making contributions as well. In such

376

cases, the successful claimant will also have to make catch-up payments in order to have his or her rights recognised retrospectively.

Given the complexity of part-time workers' pension claims, the Tribunals Service has devoted a section of its website to answering questions about them – see www.employmenttribunals.gov.uk.

Pension scheme remedies under the EqA. Remedies in pensions cases are **9.75** contained in Ss.133–134 EqA. S.133 applies to claims relating to breach of an equality rule or of an equality clause with respect to membership of, or rights under, an occupational pension scheme, unless the claimant is already receiving payment from a pension scheme, in which case S.134 applies. These provisions replace those previously inserted into the EqPA by the Occupational Pension Schemes (Equal Treatment) Regulations 1995 SI 1995/3183.

Unless the claimant is a pensioner in the scheme (i.e. already drawing a pension), an employment tribunal cannot award arrears of pay or damages – S.133(2)(b) EqA.

Non-pensioners. Under S.133 EqA an employment tribunal may make a **9.76** declaration as to the rights of the parties in respect of the matters to which the proceedings relate, but (as noted above) it must not order arrears of benefits or damages or any other amount – S.133(2). Nevertheless, it can declare that the claimant is entitled to be admitted to the scheme with effect from a specified date, and thus his or her membership can be backdated – S.133(4). However, this date must not be before 8 April 1976, i.e. the date on which the ECJ ruled in the Defrenne case that Article 157 has direct effect (see above) – S.133(5).

If the breach of the equality rule or clause relates to the terms on which members of the scheme are to be treated, a tribunal may declare that the claimant is entitled, in respect of a specified period, to rights that would have accrued to him or her if the breach had not occurred – S.133(6) EqA. The specified period cannot begin before 17 May 1990 – S.133(7). This is the date of the European Court's judgment in Barber v Guardian Royal Exchange Assurance Group 1990 ICR 616, ECJ, which established that occupational pensions were 'pay' for the purposes of Article 157. If the tribunal makes a declaration under S.133(6), the employer must provide such resources to the scheme as are necessary to secure those rights for the claimant without any further contribution by him or her or other members – S.133(8).

Pensioners. Where a claim is brought by a 'pensioner member' of an occupational **9.77** pension scheme about a breach of an equality clause or rule, the tribunal can award arrears of benefits or damages in addition to a declaration of the claimant's and respondent's respective rights – S.134(2) EqA. Any such award is limited by S.134(3) to six years for standard cases, and to the day on which the breach first occurred for concealment or incapacity cases (or a case which is both) – S.134(5). (For an explanation of these different categories of case, see under 'Time limits' above.) A 'pensioner member' is defined for the above purposes as including 'a person who is entitled to the present payment of pension or other benefits derived through a member'. This would presumably include a surviving spouse, dependant or other nominated beneficiary. In Scotland the corresponding periods in respect of which arrears can be awarded are five years or a period as determined in accordance with S.135(6) and (7) – S.134(6), as amended by the Equality Act 2010 (Consequential Amendments, Saving and Supplementary Provisions) Order 2010 SI 2010/2279. This provides that the maximum period of damages is five years before proceedings were commenced unless the case involves a 'relevant incapacity', 'relevant fraud' or 'error' (as defined in S.135(8)). If the case does involve such incapacity, fraud or error the period is determined in accordance with Ss.135(6) and (7), as amended, and may be up to a maximum of 20 years.

If the tribunal makes such an award, the employer must provide such resources to the occupational pension scheme as are necessary to secure the amount of the award for the claimant without him or her or other scheme members making any further contribution – S.134(4).

9.78 Non-pay terms

Where a woman successfully demonstrates that she is entitled to equality with regard to a non-pay term, the tribunal will have to calculate the damages to which she is entitled as a result of the employer's breach of contract. Clearly, this will depend on the nature of the term that has allegedly been breached and the assessment of its value. For example, if a woman succeeds in claiming entitlement to a company car, damages in respect of her loss could be assessed by reference to the amount of the company car allowance that her chosen comparator receives.

9.79 Injury to feelings

Awards for injury to feelings were not available under the EqPA. In Newcastle upon Tyne City Council v Allan and ors and another case 2005 ICR 1170, EAT, the Appeal Tribunal contrasted the compensation regime under the EqPA with that under other (now-repealed) discrimination statutes, such as the Sex Discrimination Act 1975 and the Race Relations Act 1976. Actions under the latter were clearly statutory torts. Actions under the EqPA, on the other hand, were contractual in nature. According to the EAT, while awards for injury to feelings are routinely available in actions in tort, this is only exceptionally the case in respect of claims for breach of contract.

Although both discrimination and equal pay claims are now to be brought under the EqA, the distinction that the EAT drew between the two types of claim is still surely relevant. There is no provision within Chapter 4 of Part 9 of the Act – the Chapter that deals with remedies in equal pay cases – which confers upon a tribunal the power to award a sum for injury to feelings, and in the absence of any express indication to the contrary, it appears fair to assume that the status quo under the EqPA continues to apply under the EqA.

Interest   9.80
Like all tribunal awards in respect of discrimination, equal pay compensation can attract interest. Previously, employment tribunals had the power to award interest on awards in equal pay cases in accordance with the Employment Tribunals (Interest on Awards in Discrimination Cases) Regulations 1996 SI 1996/2803. S.139 EqA similarly provides for regulations to be made, or modified, enabling a tribunal to include interest in its award and specifying the manner, periods and rate by reference to which such interest is to be determined. In this regard, the 1996 Regulations are expressly saved by provisions of the Equality Act 2010 (Commencement No.4, Savings, Consequential, Transitional, Transitory and Incidental Provisions and Revocation) Order 2010 SI 2010/2317. Article 21(1) of that Order states that: 'Subordinate legislation specified in the first column of the table in Schedule 7, in so far as made under the provision of a previous enactment specified in the second column, is to be treated as made under the provision of the 2010 Act specified in the third column.' Suffice it to say that the 1996 Regulations are one of the items of subordinate legislation in column one of Schedule 7, and that S.183 EqA is specified in column three. The effect is that those Regulations are now regarded as having been passed pursuant to S.139, with the consequence that they continue to govern the award of interest in respect of claims successfully brought under the EqA.

Under the 1996 Regulations, employment tribunals are required to consider whether to make an award of interest without the need for any application by any party in the proceedings – Reg 2(1). Reg 3(1) provides that interest shall be calculated as simple interest accruing from day to day, at a rate set under rule 27(1) of the Court Funds Rules 1987 SI 1987/821 – the rate for England and Wales has remained unchanged at 6 per cent since 1 March 2002.

Interest on arrears of remuneration, rather than accruing over the whole period **9.81** in respect of which arrears are awarded, only begins to accrue from the 'mid-point' date – Reg 6(1)(b). This is the date halfway between the date of contravention of the equality clause and the date on which the tribunal calculates the interest (in most cases, the date of the remedies judgment) – Reg 4. Thus, an award of back pay under the EqPA/EqA typically only attracts interest in respect of half the period of the award. The tribunal may, however, award interest in respect of a different period if it considers that 'serious injustice' would be caused if it followed the rules set out above – Reg 6(3).

Taxation of compensatory awards   9.82
Section 62 of the Income Tax (Earnings and Pensions) Act 2003 defines 'earnings' as that term is used to impose liability for tax and national insurance contributions (NICs) on employment income. 'Earnings' includes any salary,

379

wages or fee, any gratuity, profit or incidental benefit, and anything else that constitutes an emolument of the employment. HMRC's Employment Income Manual addresses the implications of this definition for equal pay awards at 'EIM02530 – Employment Income: arrears of pay and awards under the Equal Pay Act 1970'. The Manual – which has not been reissued since the repeal of the EqPA and its re-enactment in the EqA – makes it clear that awards made under the EqPA are awards of arrears of pay and, as such, are to be treated as earnings falling within this section. This means that, even though the arrears are paid in a lump sum, sometimes more than six years after they became due, the tax liability is treated as arising in the year of entitlement (i.e. each year represented in the award of compensation). The Manual notes that the employer should operate a special PAYE procedure to calculate tax arising in each year covered by the award.

Given that the nature of an equal pay award under the EqA is the same as it was under the EqPA, it seems fair to assume that HMRC will continue to apply the same approach under the new Act.

9.83 Declarations

Where there is a dispute about the effect of an equality clause, the employer can seek an order from an employment tribunal declaring its rights and those of its employees – S.127(3) EqA. The employer may do this to clarify and settle matters where appropriate, although in practice such orders may be of limited practical use. In Trico Folberth Ltd v Groves and anor 1976 IRLR 327, ET, for instance, the employer successfully sought a declaration that the claimants were not entitled to equal pay, yet the women continued their action all the same. A declaration will be of most practical use when there is an application by an employer in conjunction with a union to settle a matter in dispute. For example, in Tremlett v Freemans (London SW9) Ltd 1976 IRLR 292, ET, a declaration that male employees were entitled to the same rest periods as women served its purpose as the union had consented to the application.

With specific reference to a claim for breach of the implied equality clause in the context of a failure to grant equal access to a non-compulsory occupational pension scheme during a period when membership was closed, a claimant will not be entitled to a declaration of her rights unless she adduces evidence to show that she would have joined the scheme during the closed period had this been available to her – Copple and ors v Littlewoods plc and ors 2011 ICR 296, EAT. His Honour Judge McMullen pointed out in the Copple case that the only remedy available in respect of denial of membership is a declaration and an accompanying order requiring the employer to provide the necessary funding of the scheme: an award of arrears of damages or remuneration is not an option. As a declaration is a discretionary remedy, a tribunal should consider evidence regarding what the claimant did in fact do during any open period when she was entitled to have joined the scheme and, if she did not join the scheme, evidence as to her reasons for not doing so. That evidence is likely to inform the tribunal as to what the claimant would have done had membership of the scheme been open to her during the closed period. HHJ McMullen also observed that a claimant who succeeded in obtaining such a declaration would not, in any event, be entitled to a declaration of rights in respect of any period during which membership was open and available. Once a claimant had equal access to membership, there was an express term in her contract that she could join the scheme and there was no scope or need to imply such a term to the same effect.

Costs 9.84

The 2004 Employment Tribunals Rules of Procedure (contained in Schedule 1 to the Employment Tribunals (Constitution and Rules of Procedure) Regulations 2004 SI 2004/1861) made significant changes to the costs regime in the employment tribunal. Historically, costs have rarely been awarded in employment tribunals. When the 2001 version of the Rules came into force, rule 14(3) increased the maximum sum of unassessed costs that a tribunal has power to award from £500 to £10,000. That limit is maintained in the 2004 Rules at rule 41(1). This change has inevitably led to an increase in the average level of costs awards made by tribunals.

Tribunals have a discretion, under rule 40, to award costs in whole or in part in any of the following circumstances:

- where a party has caused a hearing or a pre-hearing review to be postponed or adjourned

- where a party has failed to comply with an order or a practice direction

- where a party has acted 'vexatiously, abusively, disruptively or otherwise unreasonably' in bringing the proceedings

- where a party or a party's representative has acted 'vexatiously, abusively, disruptively or otherwise unreasonably' in conducting the proceedings

- where the bringing or conducting of the proceedings by a party has been misconceived.

The 2004 Rules introduced a power for tribunals to take into account the **9.85** parties' ability to pay when making an award under any of the above heads – rule 41(2). They also gave tribunals a new power to make 'preparation time' orders in favour of unrepresented litigants in respect of their preparation time for a hearing. The calculation of such orders is based on evidence provided by the receiving party and the tribunal's assessment of what is a reasonable and proportionate amount of time to spend on preparatory work, having regard to matters such as the complexity of the proceedings and the number of witnesses and documentation required. That time is multiplied by an hourly rate set by rule 45(2), which increases by £1 on 6 April each year – as of 6 April 2011, the rate is £31.

The rules operating in the EAT are more or less in line with those in the employment tribunals. The costs regime in both the tribunals and the EAT is discussed in detail in IDS Employment Law Handbook, 'Employment Tribunal Practice and Procedure' (2006), Chapter 18.

9.86 Settlements

Generally speaking, any term in an agreement that attempts to limit the operation of the employment provisions of the EqA or prevents a person from presenting a complaint to an employment tribunal under those provisions is unenforceable – S.144(1) EqA. There are two exceptions to this general rule, either of which allow parties to reach a binding agreement to settle a dispute. The first is where a contractual settlement has been made with the assistance of an Acas conciliator (commonly known as a 'COT3 agreement' or 'conciliated settlement') – S.144(4)(a) EqA. The second exception is where the conditions for reaching a 'qualifying compromise agreement' have been fulfilled – S.144(4)(b). In this chapter we give a brief overview of the rules governing Acas-conciliated settlements and compromise agreements. For an in-depth analysis, see IDS Employment Law Handbook, 'Employment Tribunal Practice and Procedure' (2006), Chapter 9, 'Settlements, withdrawals and arbitration'.

9.87 Acas-conciliated settlements

The Employment Tribunals Act 1996 (ETA) seeks to encourage the use of the conciliation service provided by Acas in order to avoid litigation wherever possible. Whenever an equal pay complaint under S.127 EqA is presented to a tribunal, a copy is automatically sent to an Acas conciliator – S.19(1)(a) ETA and rule 21 of the Rules of Procedure. The conciliator is then under a duty to promote settlement of the dispute if he or she is requested to do so by both parties or, in the absence of such a request, if he or she thinks that there is a reasonable prospect of achieving a settlement – S.18(2) ETA. The conciliator may also be called in by either party before a complaint has been lodged with a tribunal. The same duty to promote a settlement then applies – S.18(3) ETA.

The conciliator can recommend the use of existing grievance procedures where appropriate – S.18(6) ETA. Anything said to a conciliator who is trying to bring about a settlement is privileged and may not be used in evidence before a tribunal without the consent of the person who said it – S.18(7).

9.88 Scope of settlement.
Where a COT3 agreement has been concluded, the complainant will lose his or her right to complain to a tribunal about the act in respect of which settlement has been reached. By virtue of S.144(4) EqA, such

a COT3 settlement will only be effective if it settles a complaint over which a tribunal has jurisdiction as provided for in S.120. That section refers to a 'complaint relating to a contravention of Part 5 (work)'. Although, clearly, equal pay claims fall within Part 5, rather oddly the specific jurisdiction in respect of complaints relating to breach of a sex equality clause or rule is set out in S.127. It is not immediately apparent why S.127 separately and specifically provides for tribunals to have jurisdiction in respect of such complaints when S.120 has already given them jurisdiction to deal with complaints relating to a contravention of Part 5 in general. Be that as it may, it would seem that S.144(4) effectively allows equal pay claims to be compromised by an Acas-conciliated settlement. That is certainly the view taken in the Explanatory Notes to the Act, which include a complaint of a breach of an equality rule or clause in the matters that can be settled in this way. If no such complaint or potential complaint has been identified, the agreement will not be effective in this regard. This point is illustrated by Livingstone v Hepworth Refractories Ltd 1992 ICR 287, EAT, in which L – on leaving the company after 38 years' service – did not raise any complaint of sex discrimination when a COT3 agreement was made. As a result, that agreement could not bar his subsequent claim under the SDA that the rules of the company pension scheme were discriminatory and should be altered so that he could receive higher benefits.

Settling future claims. It is perfectly possible for the terms of an Acas- **9.89** conciliated settlement to purport to bar not only present claims but also future claims. However, in order for the claimant to effectively release claims or rights that he or she has not even contemplated it is necessary that the COT3 agreement expressly state that this is the employee's intention. This point is illustrated in Royal National Orthopaedic Hospital Trust v Howard 2002 IRLR 849, EAT, where the EAT considered whether a COT3 barred a claim that arose from an employer's future act not contemplated by the parties at the time of the agreement. In that case, H brought claims of sex discrimination, marital discrimination and constructive dismissal, each of which was settled after Acas conciliation. The COT3 stated that the employer's payment was made 'in full and final settlement of these proceedings and of all claims which the claimant has or may have against the respondent' under a number of listed statutory provisions, including the Sex Discrimination Act 1975. Subsequently, the hospital prevented H from carrying out a day's work at the hospital in a private capacity. H complained of victimisation contrary to the SDA – a claim, the hospital argued, that was barred by the compromise agreement. The EAT held that 'the law does not decline to allow parties to contract that all and any claims, whether known or not, shall be released'. The question is whether, looking objectively at the settlement agreement, this was the intention of the parties, or whether some limitation has to be placed on the agreement's scope. Looking at the COT3 in H's case, the EAT concluded that the COT3's reference to claims which the claimant 'has or may have' could cover claims existing at the time of the agreement (whether or not they were known to the employee), but it was not sufficient to cover possible future claims. H's victimisation claim could therefore proceed.

9.90 Compromise agreements
In order to be effective in excluding tribunal jurisdiction in an equal pay claim, a compromise agreement must meet the following strict conditions set out in S.147(3) EqA:

- the agreement must be in writing and relate to the particular complaint – S.147(3)(a) and (b)

- the complainant must, before entering into the contract, have received advice from a 'relevant independent adviser' covering the terms and effect of the proposed compromise agreement and, in particular, its effect on the employee's ability to pursue complaints before an employment tribunal – S.147(3)(c)

- when the adviser gives the advice he or she must be covered by a contract of insurance or a professional indemnity covering the risk of a claim by the employee in respect of loss arising in consequence of the advice – S.147(3)(d)

- the agreement must identify the adviser and state that the conditions in subsections (c) and (d), above, have been met – S.147(3)(e) and (f).

9.91 Section 147(4) EqA defines an independent adviser as one of the following:

- a qualified lawyer – i.e. a barrister (advocate in Scotland) in private practice or employed to give legal advice, a solicitor who holds a practising certificate or a person other than a barrister or solicitor who is an authorised advocate or litigator within the meaning of the Courts and Legal Services Act 1990 – S.147(4)(a)

- an officer, official, employee or member of an independent trade union who has been certified in writing by the trade union as competent to give legal advice and as authorised to do so on behalf of the trade union – S.147(4)(b)

- an advice centre worker (whether an employee or a volunteer) who has been certified in writing by the centre as competent to give advice and as authorised to do so on behalf of the centre – S.147(4)(c)

- a person so specified in an order made by the Secretary of State – S.147(4)(d).

The Equality Act 2010 (Qualifying Compromise Contract Specified Person) Order 2010 SI 2010/2192 provides that Fellows of the Institute of Legal Executives practising in a solicitor's practice also qualify as independent advisers for these purposes.

384

A person is not a relevant independent adviser in relation to a compromise **9.92** agreement if he or she is a party to, or connected to a party to, the contract or the complaint – S.147(5)(a) and (b) EqA. A person is also not an independent adviser if he or she is employed by or is acting in the matter for a party to the contract or the complaint or a person connected with a party to the contract or the complaint – S.147(5)(c) and (d); if the trade union or advice centre referred to in S.147(4)(c) (see above) is the other party or a person connected with the other party – S.147(5)(e); or if, in the case of an advice centre worker, the employee pays for the advice – S.147(5)(f).

Any two persons are treated as connected if one is a company of which the other (directly or indirectly) has control, or both are companies of which a third person (directly or indirectly) has control – S.147(8). Further, two persons are also connected for the purposes of S.147(5) in so far as a connection between them gives rise to a conflict of interest, in relation to either the contract or the complaint – S.147(9).

Apart from a rather serious drafting problem (see below), these exclusions are **9.93** broadly the same (though worded slightly differently) as those that applied under the EqPA.

The drafting problem mentioned above concerns S.147(5)(d), which stipulates that 'a person who is acting for a person within paragraph (a) or (b) in relation to the contract or the complaint' is not an independent adviser for the purposes of drawing up compromise agreements. S.147(5)(a) and (b) refer to 'a person who is a party to the contract or the complaint' and 'a person who is connected to' such a person. On a literal interpretation, this has the bizarre effect of precluding a solicitor instructed by the complainant from advising on the effect of the compromise agreement or from signing off the agreement. Such an interpretation would drive a coach and horses through the compromise agreements provisions in the EqA and was clearly never Parliament's intention.

The problem would not have occurred had the word 'other' been retained in **9.94** the relevant provisions of the EqA. In view of the difficulty, it is hard to conceive of tribunals – while they await an amendment to the Act – being prepared to adopt a literal interpretation that leads to so absurd or impracticable a result. Therefore, it is likely that they will resort to the standard rule of statutory interpretation that Parliament is presumed not to have intended a construction of an enactment that produces an unworkable or impracticable result – see *Bennion on Statutory Interpretation*, 5th ed (2008), p.971 – to get round the problem. In this regard, it is significant that the 'FAQs on commencement of the Equality Act', published on the website of the Government Equalities Office (www.equalities.gov.uk), specifically state that S.147(5)(d) does not prevent a complainant's legal representative from acting as the qualified adviser for the purpose of a compromise agreement. This result is achieved by the somewhat tortuous route of reading S.147(4) and (5) – which are concerned with who can and cannot be an independent adviser – as not referring to the complainant at all, since it is clear from the scheme of S.147 that the complainant and the independent adviser are separate people. The result, according to the GEO, is that S.147(5)(d) cannot be referring to a person acting for the complainant. Considerable concern has been raised about the impact of S.147(5)(d), not least by the Law Society. However, while some other drafting errors identified in the EqA were addressed in the Equality Act 2010 (Public Authorities and Consequential and Supplementary Amendments) Order 2011 SI 2011/1060, no action was taken over S.147(5)(d) and there is no sign that the Government has any immediate intention of amending this provision. This means that parties who have signed compromise agreements under the EqA are left in the unsatisfactory position of waiting for a case to reach the EAT and confirm that such agreements are valid.

Previously, under the Sex Discrimination Act 1975 (which covered contracting out of the EqPA) a compromise agreement had to contain a statement that all the conditions under the statute had been met. For example, in the Disability Discrimination Act 1995 the conditions regulating compromise agreements were dealt with in para 2(2) of Schedule 3A to the Act, and para 2(2)(f) stated 'the contract must state that the conditions regulating compromise contracts under this Schedule are satisfied'. However, the EqA simply requires a statement that two specific conditions have been met – the fact that the complainant has received independent advice and that, on the date when that advice was given, an insurance contract or insurance indemnity was in force covering the risk should the complainant seek to recover loss arising from the advice – see S.147(3)(f) EqA.

9.95 No doubt this change addresses the quirks that would otherwise be thrown up as a result of all the discrimination strands now being housed under a single Act. Previously, a claimant who sought to compromise different claims brought under one or more statutes – for example, where he or she alleged that his or her dismissal was both unfair and discriminatory on grounds of sex and race – would have to include a declaration that the requirements of a valid compromise agreement had been fulfilled under each Act. It is certainly arguable that a compromise agreement that meets the validity requirements of, say, the Employment Rights Act 1996 may also serve to compromise claims made under the EqA without a further statement of compliance or specific reference to the EqA, so long as the compromise agreement makes mention of the discrimination claim. This is necessary because one of the conditions that must be complied with in order to effect a valid compromise agreement is that the agreement 'relates to the particular complaint' – S.147(3)(b) EqA. In Palihakkara v British Telecommunications plc EAT 0167/09 the claimant was allowed to continue with claims of race and sex discrimination despite having signed a compromise agreement settling 'all claims'. This was because the agreement stated that the conditions of S.203 ERA had been satisfied but there was no similar statement in respect of the SDA or the Race Relations Act 1976. Arguably, the position is now different, and a similarly worded agreement would be held to have effectively compromised all the complainant's claims.

Scope of settlement. Like a COT3 agreement, a properly constituted **9.96** compromise agreement will bar the employee from taking a claim any further. However, unlike COT3 agreements, there is a requirement that compromise agreements 'relate to the particular complaint' – S.147(3)(b) EqA. This does not mean that each claim or potential claim must be settled by a separate agreement. As with COT3 agreements, a single compromise agreement is capable of settling all the matters in dispute between the parties – Lunt v Merseyside TEC Ltd 1999 ICR 17, EAT.

In Hinton v University of East London 2005 ICR 1260, CA, the Court of Appeal considered what is required for an agreement to 'relate to the particular proceedings' for the purposes of S.203(3)(b) ERA. This provision relates to contracting out of the rights conferred by the ERA, but the principles established in that case apply equally to claims compromised under discrimination law. There, H, a lecturer, took voluntary redundancy. In June 2003 he signed a compromise agreement expressed to be 'in full and final settlement of all claims in all jurisdictions', attached to which was a lengthy list of possible claims to be compromised (although H had not, in fact, raised most of them). The list did not include claims under S.47B ERA, which protects employees from being subjected to a detriment because they have made a protected disclosure. This was despite the fact that H had in the past complained to his employer that he had suffered such detriments. In October 2003 H brought tribunal proceedings on the basis of these alleged detriments. The employment tribunal held that the compromise agreement did not prevent H from bringing the proceedings, because it did not specifically cover H's complaint. The EAT, however, allowed the employer's appeal. In its view, H's S.47B allegations did not have to be particularised in the agreement to be compromised. The list of claims expressly excluded by the agreement was not intended to be exhaustive, but was merely illustrative of the type of claim covered, and the claim under S.47B was compromised by the general 'full and final settlement of all claims' wording. H appealed to the Court of Appeal.

The Court of Appeal held that, contractually, the compromise agreement was **9.97** wide enough to cover H's S.47B claim. However, it did not comply with the S.203 requirement that it relate to 'particular proceedings'. The 'particular proceedings' intended to be compromised had to be clearly identified, either by a generic description such as 'unfair dismissal' or by reference to the section of the statute giving rise to the claim. It was not sufficient for a compromise agreement to use 'a rolled-up expression such as "all statutory rights"', nor even to identify the proceedings only by reference to the statute under which they arose. In H's case, although from a contractual point of view the wording of the agreement was wide enough to cover his potential S.47B claim, the agreement had not specifically referred to S.47B, and thus did not 'relate to the particular proceedings' within the meaning of S.203(3)(b). H could therefore proceed with his claim.

There is, however, no requirement that proceedings have been lodged at the time the compromise agreement is entered into, nor that the complaint has been articulated at some earlier stage before it can be compromised – McWilliam and ors v Glasgow City Council EAT 0036/10. The EAT in that case made the point that it would be absurd to insist that the time, trouble and expense of presenting a claim to a tribunal be incurred before a valid compromise agreement can be entered into. Furthermore, it does not matter whether or not there has been a history of communication or dialogue about the complaint. What matters is that both parties know to which particular complaint the compromise agreement relates. The EAT went on to uphold the validity of compromise agreements preventing a group of Council employees bringing equal pay claims. The McWilliam case is considered further under 'Nature and form of advice' and 'Independent adviser must not be acting for employer' below.

9.98 **Compromising future claims.** In Lunt v Merseyside TEC Ltd (above) the EAT stated that Parliament did not intend to permit a blanket compromise agreement compromising claims that had never been raised. Accordingly, a compromise agreement cannot exclude complaints that have not yet arisen – unlike a negotiated settlement arising by way of Acas conciliation (see under 'Acas conciliation' above); nor can such an agreement be used to sign away all the employee's rights to bring tribunal claims. It would seem, then, that compromise agreements will be valid only in so far as they settle those complaints that have been raised – as a potential tribunal claim, if not in actual proceedings – by the date of the agreement.

In Hilton UK Hotels Ltd v McNaughton EAT 0059/04 the EAT stated that the Lunt case was not authority for the proposition that a party cannot contractually compromise a future claim of which he or she has no knowledge. It went on to refer to the case of Royal National Orthopaedic Hospital Trust v Howard 2002 IRLR 849, EAT, which suggested that future claims can be compromised, but must be so 'in language which is absolutely clear and leaves no room for doubt as to what it is [the parties] are contracting for'. However, whether this interpretation of the Lunt case is correct is open to debate, particularly as the Howard case to which the EAT referred was concerned with the scope of COT3 agreements (see under 'Acas conciliation' above) and not with compromise agreements.

9.99 In any event, in the context of equal pay, it will be rare for an agreement to seek to settle a claim that has not yet arisen. Such agreements are most commonly concluded on the termination of employment, by which time the essential ingredients of an equal pay claim – a comparator being paid more for equal work – will either exist or not. Unlike the Employment Rights Act 1996 or the discrimination provisions in the EqA, for example, the equality of terms provisions in Chapter 3 of Part 5 of the EqA do not create any causes of action that can arise once employment has ended. There are only two conceivable circumstances in which a claim related to equal pay might arise after the employment has been terminated. The first is if the woman is allowed to compare herself with her successor in the job – but as we note in Chapter 4 under 'Predecessors and successors – successors' such claims are not currently permitted under the EqA or Article 157. The second is if the woman, having brought a claim, is later subjected to a detriment amounting to victimisation under S.27 EqA. Such claims are considered in Chapter 11.

Nature and form of advice. Section 147(3)(c) EqA provides that the employee **9.100** must receive 'advice... covering the terms and effect' of the compromise agreement. The nature and form of the advice required to be given was considered by the EAT in McWilliam and ors v Glasgow City Council (above), where the Council wished to compromise the potential equal pay claims of over 10,000 employees. The Council agreed to settle what it called its 'apparent equal pay liability', and made £40m available. It engaged a panel of six law firms to act as independent advisers to the employees involved. The Council negotiated a draft compromise agreement with the panel solicitors. The solicitors then held group sessions with the employees, at which they made PowerPoint presentations detailing the compromise agreement on offer. Employees were then able to meet a solicitor individually. At these individual meetings, many employees signed letters of engagement and the compromise agreement on offer. Some then sought to bring equal pay claims in the employment tribunal but were prevented from doing so when the tribunal decided that the claims had been validly compromised under S.77 SDA (the precursor to S.147 EqA). The employees appealed against that decision.

The EAT rejected the employees' argument that they had not received 'advice' on the terms and effect of the agreement. Taking together the information presented at the group presentations and the advice given at the individual meetings, there was enough to satisfy S.77. The EAT noted that the presentations had been carefully put together by six leading independent law firms which specialised in employment law. The solicitors involved in the individual meetings knew exactly what was in the presentations, referred to them specifically in the meetings and provided each employee with her own copy of the relevant slides. The presentations were therefore part of the overall advice given. It would, said the EAT, have been 'ludicrous' to expect each individual solicitor to give the presentation again at the one-to-one meetings. In effect, the thrust of the employees' challenge was that the solicitors had not told each employee whether the deal on offer was a good one for them personally. However, the EAT noted that this is not required by S.77 SDA (and therefore by extension S.147 EqA).

9.101 **Independent adviser must not be acting for employer.** An individual cannot be a relevant independent adviser if he or she is 'acting in the matter' for 'a person who is a party to the contract or the complaint'. As noted above, this is not intended to include a solicitor instructed by the complainant, although on a literal interpretation it could be construed as doing so. Clearly, however, a solicitor 'acting in the matter' for the employer is precluded from being a relevant independent adviser to the employee. In McWilliam and ors v Glasgow City Council (above) the EAT held that the solicitors were not 'acting in the matter' for the Council, and thus were not barred from advising the employees. Although the solicitors could not properly be said to have been acting for the employees until the individual meetings, they were all prior to that acting to protect the employees' interests as a group. Furthermore, while it was true that the scope of the advice the solicitors gave was dictated by the information provided by the Council, that could be the case in any consultation on a compromise agreement. In the EAT's view, the Council gave the impression that it was at pains to see to it that the employees were provided with advice that was truly independent.

9.102 ## Legal advice and financial assistance

Potential claimants may obtain legal help and advice from a trade union, law centre or a Citizens Advice Bureau. General advice on individuals' legal rights under the EqA, as well as the basic procedural aspects of bringing an employment tribunal claim, is also available from the Equality and Human Rights Commission (which replaced the Equal Opportunities Commission on 1 October 2007).

Complainants on a low income or in receipt of social security benefits may apply to the Community Legal Service (CLS) for financial assistance – formerly known as legal aid. The CLS can give assistance, under the Legal Help scheme, so that claimants receive free advice and preparatory work from a solicitor or legal adviser up to the tribunal hearing. However, legal aid is not available in respect of legal representation before an employment tribunal. In Scotland, legal aid – which is, again, means tested – may be obtained through the Scottish Legal Aid Board. However, legal aid in Scotland is only provided where the case is arguable; it is reasonable in the particular circumstances of the case that assistance by way of representation be made available; and the case is too complex to allow the claimant to present it to a minimum standard of effectiveness in person – Regs 3(m) and 13(2) Advice and Assistance (Assistance by Way of Representation) (Scotland) Regulations SSI 2003/179.

9.103 Would-be claimants seeking tribunal representation might also apply to the Equality and Human Rights Commission, which has a statutory discretion under S.28 of the Equality Act 2006 to grant assistance in equal pay claims. For an outline of the circumstances in which the EHRC may exercise this

390

discretion, see under 'Equality and Human Rights Commission' below. Finally, claimants who are unable to obtain assistance – financial or otherwise – in any of the ways discussed above may turn to one of the organisations providing free legal advice, case preparation and tribunal advocacy services such as the Bar Pro Bono Unit and the Free Representation Unit (although these organisations generally only accept referrals through solicitors, law centres and advice agencies).

Equality and Human Rights Commission

9.104

The Equality and Human Rights Commission (EHRC) was established by the Equality Act 2006 (EqA 2006) as the first single equality commission in Great Britain. The Commission assumed overall responsibility for combating unlawful discrimination in employment and other fields and promoting equality of opportunity. It opened its doors on 1 October 2007, when it took over the role and functions of the three existing equality Commissions – the Equal Opportunities Commission (EOC), the Commission for Racial Equality (CRE) and the Disability Rights Commission (DRC) – and assumed responsibility for promoting equality and combating unlawful discrimination in the 'new' discrimination strands of sexual orientation, religion or belief, and age, as well as for the promotion of human rights – see Article 3 of the Equality Act 2006 (Dissolution of Commissions and Consequential and Transitional Provisions) Order 2007 SI 2007/2602. According to the previous Government's White Paper, 'Fairness for All: A New Commission for Equality and Human Rights', published in May 2004, the rationale for establishing the EHRC was to have 'a strong and authoritative champion for equality and human rights' to benefit individuals and organisations alike by providing a single access point on all discrimination issues.

The EHRC has not been without controversy during its four years of operation, and the Coalition Government that came to power in May 2010 has recently set out plans to reform the institution. The thrust of the proposed reforms is to scale back the EHRC's activities in promoting equality of opportunity, and focus instead on providing advice and assistance in relation to discrimination, equality and human rights law. It is therefore likely that there will be few if any changes to the EHRC's powers in so far as they relate specifically to equal pay. These include powers to provide assistance or intervene in equal pay cases and to issue Codes of Practice, both of which are considered further below. The EHRC's wider powers and duties in respect of sex discrimination in employment generally are covered in depth in IDS Employment Law Handbook, 'Sex Discrimination' (2008), Chapter 16. The EHRC's powers and duties in respect of disability discrimination are covered in depth in IDS Employment Law Handbook, 'Disability Discrimination' (2010), Chapter 11.

391

9.105 Help for complainants

The EHRC has the power to provide assistance to an individual who is or may become party to legal proceedings if the proceedings relate or may relate (wholly or partly) to a provision of the EqA 2010, and the individual alleges that he or she has been the victim of behaviour contrary to a provision of the 2010 Act – S.28(1) EqA 2006.

The criteria according to which the legal assistance is granted are determined by the Commission. Furthermore, there is no express duty on the EHRC to consider every application it receives. By way of contrast, the EOC was under an obligation to consider every application for assistance against set criteria. Having said that, the previous Government took the view that in practice the EHRC will have to consider all applications. According to Baroness Ashton, 'the intention is that the Commission will use its power to assist an individual in bringing proceedings in an effective and strategic way... So we have taken away the statutory criteria for supporting cases that feature almost identically in each of the Commissions. The purpose behind that is to allow the Commission to use its power in the way it considers most effective... We do not see any need to put an express obligation on the Commission to consider applications. In practice, it has to consider all the applications if it is to identify which, if any, it wishes to support. As a public body, it has an implicit obligation to not act unreasonably and could be challenged if it ignored applications it received' (Hansard (HL) 11.7.05, col.947). The current Government, though committed to reforming the EHRC, has indicated that it views 'bringing or supporting individuals to bring strategic test cases to clarify and enforce the law' as one of the EHRC's core functions (see the consultation paper 'Reform of the Equality and Human Rights Commission', published in March 2011).

9.106 The EHRC may provide or arrange legal advice, legal representation, facilities for the resolution of a dispute, or any other form of assistance for an individual – S.28(4) EqA 2006. Assistance may only be given to an individual who has become party to legal proceedings relating, wholly or partly, to the 'equality enactments', which include the EqA 2010 as well as relevant provisions of European Union law – Ss.28(12) and 33(1) EqA 2006.

In general, the cases granted legal advice or representation by the Commission will be those likely to produce changes, either in law or in practice, which will promote equality of opportunity for men and women. Unusually, the last major equal pay case in which the EHRC was involved was one from which it ended up withdrawing financial support. The EHRC originally offered backing to the claimants in their appeal to the Court of Appeal in the case of Redcar and Cleveland Borough Council v Bainbridge and ors and another case; Middlesbrough Borough Council v Surtees and ors 2009 ICR 133, CA. However, in January 2008, shortly before the Court of Appeal was due to hear the case, the EHRC announced that it would not be directly funding the claimants. The EHRC was concerned that the Court's ruling on the lawfulness of pay protection arrangements put in place by respondents while they tried to remove inequality from their pay systems would restrict the freedom of unions, employers and employees to negotiate workable solutions to long-standing pay inequality. The EHRC instead acted as an intervenor, submitting to the Court that such arrangements should be held to be lawful, even if they prolong inequality for a short time, provided the method chosen disadvantages women as little, and for as short a period, as possible. For further details of the Court's ruling on this aspect of the claim, see Chapter 8 under 'Specific material factors – pay protection'.

Power to intervene

9.107

Section 30 EqA 2006 gives the EHRC capacity to institute or intervene in judicial review or other legal proceedings where the proceedings are relevant to any of its functions, subject to any limitations imposed under legislation or by rules of court – S.30(1) and (4)(b). By virtue of S.30(2) EqA 2006 the EHRC also has the necessary title and interest in relation to any such legal proceedings in Scotland.

This power of intervention is essentially the same as that held by the EOC before the EHRC came into being. In its last full annual report, covering April 2006 to March 2007, the EOC named some of the high-profile equal pay cases in which it had intervened, including Derbyshire and ors v St Helens Metropolitan Borough Council and ors 2007 ICR 841, HL (victimisation claims) and Cadman v Health and Safety Executive 2006 ICR 1623, ECJ (objective justification in equal pay claims). More recently, the EHRC acted as intervenor in the Redcar v Bainbridge litigation (see above) and in Slack and ors v Cumbria County Council and anor 2009 ICR 1217, CA (see under 'Time limits – stable work cases' above).

Codes of Practice

9.108

Apart from providing assistance and advice, probably the EHRC's most important role with regard to equal pay is the issuing of Codes of Practice. S.14 EqA 2006 allows the EHRC to issue a Code in connection with a matter addressed by the EqA 2010. Under S.15(4) EqA 2006, while a failure to comply with a provision of any such Code will not give rise to criminal or civil liability, the Code shall be admissible in evidence in equal pay claims, and shall be taken into account by the tribunal in any case in which it appears relevant.

The EHRC Code of Practice on Equal Pay was issued on 11 October 2010, but officially came into force on 6 April 2011 – the Equality Act 2010 Codes of Practice (Services, Public Functions and Associations, Employment, and Equal Pay) Order 2011 SI 2011/587. (Note that Northern Ireland has its own equivalent Code – the 'Code of Practice on equal pay'.)

9.109 The EHRC Code sets out the requirements of the law, its implications for employers, and the process of a pay review, and identifies discriminatory elements in pay systems. Guidance is provided on drawing up an equal pay policy and a model equal pay policy is included. The Code's recommendations on undertaking equal pay reviews are examined at length in Chapter 10, 'Equal pay audits'.

Note that the EHRC Code of Practice on Employment, also issued on 11 October 2010, may be relevant where a claimant brings a claim of victimisation – see Chapter 11 for more details.

9.110 Representative actions

We have so far considered the bringing of an equal pay claim from the point of view of an individual bringing a claim alone. In reality, equal pay claims are often brought by groups of (usually) women doing similar jobs. This is particularly so in local government and the public sector, where pay levels are more likely to be set by workplace agreements than on an individual basis. However, there was no provision for any kind of group or representative action under the EqPA, and the Government did not introduce such a provision into the EqA 2010. This decision came despite the fact that the Equality and Human Rights Commission, since its establishment in October 2007, has called for the introduction of representative actions in equal pay, where a representative of a group of claimants raises proceedings on their behalf against a particular respondent. In this regard, the EHRC has continued the long-running campaign of the Equal Opportunities Commission, which it replaced. The call was echoed by several other respondents to the consultation on Government proposals for a Single Equality Bill, which ultimately led to the EqA 2010. Unfortunately for the EHRC and other respondents of like mind, the previous Government, in its response to the consultation published in July 2008, ruled out providing for representative actions. The current Government has shown no imminent intention of abandoning this stance.

Although representative actions are not currently possible under the EqA equal pay regime, employment tribunals have adopted procedures for dealing with mass equal pay litigation. A common procedure is for tribunals to take as test cases a handful of claims typical of the issues being litigated, with all the claimants party to the proceedings. However, this still requires all individuals with potential equal pay complaints to lodge tribunal claims individually. Such procedures have become increasingly necessary in light of the tens of thousands of equal pay claims being brought by local government employees, particularly in the North East – for further details, see Chapter 1 under 'Growth in public sector claims – local government "single status" litigation'.

10 Equal pay audits

An equal pay audit (EPA) – sometimes known as an equal pay review – involves **10.1** comparing the pay of women and men doing equal work, investigating the causes of any gender pay gaps that are identified, and closing those gaps that cannot be satisfactorily explained on grounds other than sex.

In Chapter 1 we outlined some of the reasons why there continues to be inequality between men's and women's pay in this country. The gender pay gap is essentially explicable in terms of the historical and ongoing undervaluing of women's work compared to men's. But this is not just a UK phenomenon, as is made clear in the EU Code of Practice on the implementation of equal pay for work of equal value for women and men (COM (96) 336) ('the EU Pay Code'), published by the European Commission in 1996. This Code acknowledges that, despite many years of EU law measures dealing with equal pay, substantial pay differentials between men and women persist across all EU Member States.

According to the EU Pay Code, the difference between men's and women's **10.2** incomes is due to many factors but in particular to:

- the segregation of jobs held by women both across the general workforce and internally within specific organisations, resulting in so-called 'women's jobs' being less well paid

- the numerous sectors of the economy where mainly men work that offer extra pay and bonuses that serve to widen the pay disparities between these sectors and those where women are more commonly employed

- the differentiation of pay resulting from collective agreements linked to the recognition of skills and to the type of business or industry; and

- collective agreements that allow salary structures to reflect the negotiating power of different groups of employees.

Clearly, given these structural reasons for unequal pay, there is a limit to what the law can achieve to eradicate inequality while job segregation within and across workplaces remains a fact of life. However, to the extent that change can be achieved by eliminating discrimination in the pay practices of individual establishments, EPAs provide the best means of doing this.

10 Equal pay audits

10.3 The task of carrying out pay reviews is made easier by the Equality and Human Rights Commission (EHRC)'s Code of Practice on Equal Pay (published in October 2010) ('the Code of Practice'), which, like the EU Pay Code, is designed to assist employers in the process of reviewing their own pay systems for bias. The EHRC has also issued an equal pay audit toolkit ('the EPA toolkit'), which is available on its website (www.equalityhumanrights.com), along with a number of 'equal pay in practice' checklists addressing specific issues that may arise during an equal pay audit. In addition, the EHRC publishes a separate equal pay audit toolkit for small businesses (of up to 50 employees).

Under S.15(4)(b) of the Equality Act 2006 (EqA), an employment tribunal hearing a sex discrimination or equal pay case is obliged to take into account any provision in a Code of Practice that the tribunal deems relevant to the proceedings before it. The EU Pay Code and EPA toolkit can, of course, be referred to by a tribunal for guidance.

10.4 In this chapter we discuss the reasons for carrying out EPAs. We then examine the recommendations regarding EPAs that are set out in the Code of Practice, the EPA toolkit (and accompanying checklists), and the EU Pay Code. Finally, we consider those aspects of pay systems that are most susceptible to discrimination and which will therefore need to be checked with particular care by an employer carrying out an EPA.

10.5 Why carry out equal pay audits?

There is currently no legal obligation to carry out an EPA, although local authorities are under a general statutory duty when exercising their functions to 'have due regard to the need: (a) to eliminate unlawful sex discrimination and harassment, and (b) to promote equality of opportunity between men and women' – see IDS Employment Law Handbook, 'Sex Discrimination' (2008), Chapter 16, under 'Duty to promote gender equality'. However, the EU Pay Code encourages employers and unions to examine pay systems with a view to detecting and eliminating sex discrimination in matters of pay. Moreover, EPAs are recommended by the Code of Practice as 'the most effective method of ensuring that a pay system is free from unlawful bias'.

There have been calls from bodies such as the former Equal Opportunities Commission (now absorbed into the EHRC) and various trade unions for EPAs to be made mandatory, given that only a relatively small proportion of companies undertake them voluntarily. Indeed, there was speculation that the EqA would make provision for this, but the then Government made it clear that it did 'not want to make equal pay job evaluation audits mandatory'. It did, however, express a desire 'to examine in more detail the impact equal pay job evaluation audits have had' and stated that it would 'work with the CBI, unions and others to gather evidence on the effectiveness of equal pay job

396

IDS Handbook • Equal Pay

evaluation audits in narrowing the pay gap and spreading best practice' – see 'The Equality Bill – Government response to the Consultation' (Cm 7454), published in July 2008. Subsequently, while shying away from introducing mandatory equal pay audits, the Government did introduce provisions into the 2010 Act that, when brought into force, will require larger employers to publish information on their gender pay gaps (see Chapter 1 under 'UK gender equality legislation'). This is a considerably less arduous task than carrying out an EPA. Future reforms to equal pay could, however, see EPAs become compulsory in certain circumstances – the present Government's consultation paper, 'Modern Workplaces', published in May 2011, includes a proposal to impose mandatory equal pay audits on employers who lose equal pay claims.

10.6 In their present, non-mandatory form, EPAs can be used by an employer to identify and examine those aspects of its pay system that are particularly susceptible to discrimination and remove any discrimination that is detected. They can also be used to identify and remove any glaring inconsistencies or errors. As discussed under 'Potentially discriminatory features of pay systems' below, many pay systems contain features that potentially give rise to equal pay claims. However, under S.69 EqA an employer can rebut the presumption of discrimination by showing that the pay differential between the claimant and her comparator is due to a material factor, reliance on which does not entail direct sex discrimination nor unjustified indirect sex discrimination. An EPA should help employers determine whether such a factor exists.

A pay review is also a chance for employers to make their pay systems more structured and transparent. In essence, a pay system is transparent if it is capable of being easily understood. Carrying out a thorough pay audit will, in itself, help to ensure that employees understand how their pay is made up. From the employer's perspective, the more vague or opaque the pay system, the more difficult it will be to prove that there is no discrimination behind a pay differential. The importance of transparency in pay systems is discussed in more detail in Chapter 8 under '"Material" factor – importance of transparency'.

10.7 **Job evaluation studies.** It is worth pointing out that job evaluation studies (which are discussed in Chapter 6 under 'What is job evaluation?') can play an important part in EPAs by helping to determine whether men and women are doing equal work (see under 'A model equal pay review – Step two: Determining where men and women are doing equal work', below). To that extent, therefore, job evaluation studies and EPAs are complementary. However, EPAs do not have to include job evaluation and, unlike job evaluation studies, EPAs cannot be used specifically to support or defend equal pay claims. A job evaluation study tends to be a time-consuming exercise involving the allocation of points to specific jobs and needs to satisfy a number of quite stringent conditions before it can be used by an employer to defend an equal pay claim – see Chapter 7 under 'Stage 1 equal value hearing – conclusive job evaluation studies'. EPAs, by contrast, can be carried out more quickly and informally by employers who wish to assess on a more general basis the risk and cost of equal pay claims being made against them. However, it should be borne in mind that the Code of Practice emphasises that a proper EPA entails 'eliminating those pay inequalities that cannot be explained on non-discriminatory grounds' – para 167. Furthermore, the EPA toolkit and the Code of Practice set out a five-step model EPA (see 'A model equal pay audit' below) that is both comprehensive and time-consuming.

10.8 A model equal pay audit

The Code of Practice explains how a model EPA should be carried out, recommending a five-step process to be followed. We analyse each of these steps in turn below, drawing on the additional suggestions made in the EPA toolkit (which expands upon the five-step formula) and on guidance given in the EU Pay Code, where relevant.

The Code of Practice states that whatever EPA process is used, it should include:

- comparing the pay of men and women doing equal work – ensuring that this considers work that is the same or broadly similar ('like work'), work rated as equivalent, and work that can be shown to be of equal value or worth

- identifying and explaining any pay differences, and

- eliminating those pay inequalities that cannot be explained on non-discriminatory grounds – para 167.

10.9 The Code goes on to recommend at para 171 a five-step equal pay review model. The EPA toolkit states that for practical reasons the employer may decide to carry out the review in stages. However, it points out that this could increase the risk of an equal pay claim being brought so it would be advisable for employers to agree a timetable and set out targets for progress in order to minimise this risk.

10.10 Step 1: Deciding scope of review and identifying data required

The employer first needs to decide which employees to include in the review. According to the Code of Practice, it is advisable to include all employees who are deemed to be in the same employment or whose pay can be attributed to a single source (see Chapter 4 under '"Same employment" or "single source"') – para 172. The EU Pay Code backs this up, stating that information should be collected across the whole of the organisation's workforce, since problems of sex discrimination may well arise between employees who work at the same or separate establishments, across grading structures or in different bargaining units – see Part II, para A. However, it is worth bearing in mind that in the context of job evaluation, Acas has made the point that if all jobs in the organisation are included, this may cause employee unrest where none currently exists (see Acas Advisory booklet, 'Job Evaluation: considerations and risks').

The employer also needs to decide who will carry out the audit. The Code of Practice emphasises that the review must have the involvement and support of managers with the authority to deliver the necessary changes (see para 169). It goes on to state that carrying out an EPA requires different types of input from people with different perspectives; in particular, people with knowledge and understanding of:

- the pay and grading arrangements

- any job evaluation schemes

- the payroll and human resource systems, and

- key equality issues, such as occupational segregation and the systemic tendency to undervalue work done by women – para 175.

10.11 The validity of the audit and success of any subsequent action will be enhanced if the pay system is accepted not only by the managers who are operating it but also by the employees and their unions. Employers should, therefore, aim to secure the involvement of employees and, where possible, trade union representatives – para 170. The EPA toolkit makes the point that employees and their representatives may be able to contribute valuable information and that employees who are involved will have more opportunity to understand the new system and the reasons for any changes, thereby contributing towards transparency and reducing the risk of disagreement at a later stage.

Although the Code of Practice is concerned with one aspect of discrimination (i.e. the pay of women compared to men doing equal work), as a matter of good practice employers may also want to look at other types of discrimination, such as ethnicity, disability or age when carrying out an audit – see para 161 of the Code of Practice. Indeed, public sector organisations carrying out equal pay audits will need to ensure that they cover pay gaps across the full range of 'relevant protected characteristics' provided for in S.149(7) EqA (age, disability, gender reassignment, pregnancy and maternity, race, religion or belief, sex, and sexual orientation) in accordance with the public sector equality duty. For further information on the public sector equality duty, see IDS Employment Law Guide, 'The Equality Act 2010', Chapter 7.

10.12 **Data required.** Once the employer has decided on the scope of the review, it will need to collect the following types of information:

- all the various elements of pay, including pensions and other benefits

- the personal characteristics of each employee (that is, gender, whether full time or part time, qualifications relevant to the job, hours worked (and

399

when and where they are worked), length of service, role and time in grade, and performance-related pay ratings)

- any relevant bargaining unit or collective agreement, and

- pay arrangements and practices.

Difficulty in getting the necessary information together may itself be an indication that the pay system is not sufficiently transparent.

10.13 **Step 2: Determining where men and women are doing equal work**
This stage of an equal pay audit involves checking whether men and women are doing like work, work rated as equivalent or work of equal value.

'Like work' is where men and women are doing the same or broadly similar work – see Chapter 5. Men and women are likely to be doing like work where they have the same job title and/or job description. Therefore, a straightforward way of checking like work is by reference to job title. However, as the EHRC points out in the EPA toolkit, job titles can be misleading and employers will need to look at what the employees actually do. Minor differences can be ignored.

10.14 Work is rated as equivalent where men and women have had their jobs rated as such under an analytical, non-discriminatory job evaluation scheme – see Chapter 6. Men and women are likely to be doing work rated as equivalent where they have similar, but not necessarily the same, job evaluation scores and are in the same grade.

Work is of equal value where, although the work done by a woman and a man is different, it can be shown to be of equal worth. This can be measured by comparing the jobs under headings such as effort, skill and decision-making – see Chapter 7.

10.15 The EPA toolkit states that the most reliable way of assessing whether jobs are of equal value is to use an analytical job evaluation scheme. Employers who use such schemes (for work rated as equivalent and work of equal value purposes) need to check that their schemes have been designed and implemented in such a way and at all times so as not to discriminate on the ground of sex (para 176 of the Code of Practice) – see Chapter 6 under 'Discrimination in the evaluation exercise'. To this end, the EPA toolkit includes extensive guidance at step 2.1, 'Job Evaluation Check: Job evaluation schemes free of sex bias'.

However, employers which do not have analytical job evaluation schemes designed with equal value in mind will need to find an alternative means of assessing whether men and women are doing work of equal value – para 176 of the Code. At step 2.3 of the EPA toolkit, 'Assessing equal value', there are suggestions as to how this can be done. For example:

400

- using grades based on job profiles or a classification system (for organisations with a single grading or banding structure based on a single set of criteria)

- using levels in a 'competence framework' (for organisations with no formal grading structure or more than one formal structure)

- matching those in equivalent positions in different job families or occupational hierarchies (for organisations with clear job families or other occupational group hierarchies)

- identifying a number of male and female employees' jobs within the organisation (which appear susceptible to discrimination) for equal value 'spot checks' (for any organisations for which none of the above checks are appropriate).

Step 3: Collecting pay data to identify equal pay gaps   10.16
Once the employer has established which men and women are doing equal work, it needs to collate and compare pay information for the men and women in question – para 177 of the Code of Practice. This is done by:

- calculating average basic pay and total earnings, and

- comparing access to and amounts received of each element of the pay package.

Calculating average basic pay and total earnings. This should be calculated   10.17 separately for men and women. To ensure consistency, employers should calculate either on an hourly basis or on a full-time salary basis (grossing up or down for those who work fewer, or more, hours – excluding overtime – per week than the norm) – para 178 of the Code of Practice. The EPA toolkit warns against over-reliance on averages, stating that while they are a useful step in identifying pay gaps, averages can conceal important differences between individuals and in certain circumstances can become unrepresentative.

It is advisable to record all the significant or patterned pay gaps that have been identified – para 179 of the Code.

Comparing access to and amounts received of each element of the pay   10.18 **package.** The EPA toolkit recommends that for each element of pay received by men or women doing equal work, employers should calculate:

- the proportion of men and women who receive this element

- the average amount of each pay element received by men and women.

This analysis will show:

- if men and women have differential access to the various pay elements

- if men and women receive unequal pay in respect of any of the pay elements.

401

10.19 Employers need to review the pay comparisons to identify any gender pay gaps and decide if any are significant enough to warrant further investigation – para 179 of the Code. The EPA toolkit provides that, as a general guide, further investigation is needed if any of the checks reveal either:

- significant differences (i.e. differences of 5 per cent or more) between the basic pay or total earnings of men and women performing equal work, or

- patterns of basic pay difference (of 3 per cent or more), e.g. women consistently earning less than men for equal work at most or all grades or levels in the organisation.

10.20 **Examples of key indicators of potential sex bias.** The EU Pay Code (in Part II, para B) lists a number of factors that could indicate potential sex bias and therefore require further investigation. These include:

- women having lower average earnings than men with the same job title

- women having lower average earnings than men in the same grade

- women in female-dominated unskilled jobs being paid less than the lowest male-dominated unskilled job

- jobs predominantly occupied by women being graded or evaluated lower than jobs predominantly occupied by men at similar levels of effort, skill or responsibility

- women being paid less than men with equivalent entry qualifications and length of service

- where separate bargaining arrangements prevail within one organisation, those dominated by men receiving higher pay than other bargaining groups dominated by women

- the majority of men and women being segregated by different grading, classification and evaluation systems

- part-time or temporary workers, who are mainly women, having lower average hourly earnings than full-time or permanent employees in the same job or grade

- holiday entitlements varying between jobs in the same grade disproportionately affecting one gender.

10.21 As stated in the EU Pay Code, while the above factors do not in themselves mean that there is unlawful sex discrimination in the pay system, they all merit further investigation to ensure that there is an objective justification which is not affected by the sex of the workers that explains the differences in pay.

Step 4: Establishing causes of any significant pay gaps and 10.22
assessing reasons for these
The Code of Practice states that employers need to:

- find out if there is a real, material reason for the difference in pay that has nothing to do with the sex of the jobholders. This 'material factor defence' is discussed in detail in Chapter 8

- examine their pay systems to find out which pay policies and practices may have caused or may be contributing to any gender pay inequalities – para 181.

All aspects of the pay system – policies, practices and pay elements (such as starting pay, pay progression, performance pay, bonuses, shift pay) – need to be checked from a variety of standpoints (design, implementation, differential impact on men and women) – para 182. Typical discriminatory factors (and how to check them) are discussed under 'Potentially discriminatory features of pay systems' below.

Once the fourth step has been completed, the employer should be in a position to decide whether:

- the pay policies and practices are operating free of sex bias

- the pay policies and practices are causing sex-based pay

- there is a need to close any pay gaps.

Step 5: Developing an equal pay action plan and/or reviewing 10.23
and monitoring
What happens at this stage depends upon what findings the employer has made following step 4 of the audit. If there are gaps between men's and women's pay for which there is no satisfactory explanation, the employer should develop an 'equal pay action plan' (see below).

Employers who find no gaps between men's and women's pay, or who find gaps for which there are genuinely non-discriminatory reasons (bearing in mind the full range of possible discrimination on the basis of all the protected characteristics under the EqA), should nevertheless keep their pay systems under review by introducing regular monitoring, undertaken jointly with trade unions or employee representatives, to ensure that the pay system remains free of sex bias – para 185 of the Code of Practice.

Developing an equal pay action plan. Where the reason for the pay difference 10.24
is connected with gender, employers will need to close the pay gap for current and future employees doing equal work. Employers seeking to avoid equal pay claims will also need to change any pay policies and practices that contribute to unequal pay. To achieve these goals they should develop an 'equal pay action

403

plan'. The EPA toolkit acknowledges that it may not be possible to introduce equal pay for equal work immediately, although employers need to be aware that in the meantime they are vulnerable to equal pay claims. To minimise this risk, the action plan should make clear what timescale the organisation has in mind and how it is going to compensate employees who may be entitled to equal pay. Employers may also need to consider how to manage the possible dissatisfaction of employees who perceive a loss of status.

Obviously, part of the action plan will be to eliminate the discriminatory elements from the particular components of the pay system affected. Typical discriminatory factors are discussed under 'Potentially discriminatory features of pay systems' below. The EU Code also suggests other ways of remedying more general, structural discrimination in pay systems and recommends the following:

- merging jobs that are gender-specific in terms of the workers who carry them out and applying the higher rate of pay received by men

- making efforts to harmonise pay systems that create barriers between different types of job (e.g. office jobs and production jobs)

- redefining and re-evaluating formal qualifications – for example, certain skills that women are likely to acquire in an informal manner could be taken into account and put on an equal footing with formal skills traditionally associated with men

- organising active training measures to allow employees of one sex to access jobs done predominantly by the opposite sex

- extending to part-time employees the benefits and other advantages currently enjoyed by full-time employees – see Part III, para B.

10.25 **Reviewing and monitoring.** Even if a pay system is currently free from sex bias, an employer should keep it under review by introducing regular monitoring (undertaken jointly with trade union or employee representatives) to ensure it remains free of sex bias – para 185, EHRC Code. Partial reviews are, in any event, advisable whenever there are major changes that affect the pay system, e.g. where downsizing or redundancies occur, where there is a reduction or merger of job grades, or where performance-related pay is introduced.

10.26 Potentially discriminatory features of pay systems

The following are some of the most common features found in pay systems that are the most susceptible to discrimination, particularly indirect discrimination. These are relevant to the fourth and fifth steps of the model EPA, where an employer is required to establish the causes and reasons for any pay gaps and to take action to close any pay gaps that are not objectively justified. Note that some of these features can also form the basis of a material factor defence and are therefore dealt with in some detail in Chapter 8, with reference to the relevant case law, under 'Specific material factors'.

Basic pay   10.27

Practices relating to the payment of basic pay can be discriminatory, especially where pay is determined according to grade. The EU Pay Code suggests that where women are consistently appointed at lower points on a pay scale than men, employers should examine their recruitment and promotion records to check whether the different treatment is objectively justified (irrespective of sex) – Part III, para C1.

Where a formula is used to assess the 'entry' rate of pay on joining a job or pay grade, the impact of the formula should be tested to ensure that its operation is not favouring one gender over another. Where there is managerial discretion over the entry rate of pay or how staff are graded, the impact of decisions should also be checked by gender – see EHRC Checklist 4, 'Grading and Equal Pay'.

Where men are paid more by reason of additional supplements or higher **10.28** grading because of recruitment or retention problems, the employer should attempt to adopt non-discriminatory measures to deal with these problems. Such measures might include more extensive in-house training of existing staff and expanding the pool from which recruits are normally drawn; for example, clerical and non-manual staff might be considered for management training and apprenticeships through positive action programmes – Part II, para C1, EU Pay Code. It should be borne in mind that positive discrimination is, to some degree, permissible under UK law in a training context – see IDS Employment Law Handbook, 'Sex Discrimination' (2008), Chapter 13.

Where women are paid less than male predecessors in the same job, the employer should satisfy itself that the job duties have since changed and that the changes justify the lower pay rates – Part III, para C1, EU Pay Code.

The EPA checklists suggest that an employer should ask the following questions **10.29** when reviewing pay:

- do the grade boundaries reflect distinct differences in the relative value of jobs?

- are men and women performing equal work receiving equal average basic pay and equal average total earnings?

- does a statistical analysis confirm that neither men nor women predominate at the tops and bottoms of grades?

- are there clear rules governing pay on entry, pay progression and pay protection?

- were those involved in the design of the rules trained in equal pay principles?

- do the rules apply consistently to all employees?

- are the rules applied consistently and even-handedly in practice?

- where managerial discretion applies, are there clear guidelines on the exercise of that discretion? (See Checklists 4, 5 and 6 ('Grading and Equal Pay', 'Starting Pay' and 'Pay Progression'.)

10.30 Seniority and service-related benefits

The use of seniority (in terms of length of service) as a basis for rewarding pay increases or additional benefits is one means by which employers seek to reduce labour turnover and reward loyalty. However, women often find it more difficult to meet a seniority criterion owing to the breaks that can occur in their careers on account of childbearing and related responsibilities. As explained in Chapter 8 under 'Specific material factors – length of service', it appears that as the law currently stands employers are not required to provide objective justification for using the criterion of length of service when determining pay unless the claimant raises some evidence capable of instilling 'serious doubts' over its validity. However, employers should still check how any length of service criterion is applied to ensure that no discrimination has crept in.

Employers should verify that any period of employment (including part-time employment) is included in the reckonable service when assessing eligibility for, and the amount of, service-related benefits. Careful consideration should also be paid to how maternity absence is treated for these purposes. Provided that the contract continues during maternity leave, any maternity absence should be included in the equation.

Where there is evidence that women progress more slowly through incremental salary scales and seldom reach the higher points on those scales, the employer should investigate the criteria applicable for progression – Part II, para C1, EU Pay Code.

10.31 Competence-based pay

Competence-based pay systems link grading and rewards to the achievement of defined levels of competence. Competence-based pay is usually based on descriptions of expected or desired skills, qualifications and behaviour that are used to indicate to employees what is expected of them to perform satisfactorily in their jobs. It is, of course, closely linked to performance-related pay, which is considered under 'Performance-related pay' immediately below. However, the EHRC checklists deal with the two issues separately. Checklist 7,

'Competence pay', sets out the following questions an employer should ask when reviewing a competence-based pay system:

- are all groups of employees included in the competence based pay system? In particular, are part-timers, temporary or casual staff, those on maternity or career breaks, or any group that is likely to be predominantly of one sex included?

- does the same competence-based pay system apply to different groups of employees doing equal work?

- do all employees have equal access to opportunities to develop the desired competencies?

- does the distribution of competence assessments and payments show that there may be gender bias between male and female employees?

- are competence criteria which may favour attributes and roles perceived to be 'male' (e.g. assertiveness, leadership, decision making skills) or 'female' (e.g. cooperation, consultation, nurturing) included in a balanced way?

- do the competence criteria avoid any which could be indirectly discriminatory; for example, those related to attendance or flexibility in hours of work?

- where there are differences in the competence-based payments made to male and female employees doing equal work, can those differences be objectively justified?

Performance-related pay   10.32

Many pay systems apply pay rates that are related to the production output of individual employees. Piece-work is a classic example. Tips in restaurants, bonuses for work in excess of a specified amount during a specified time, and shared bonuses to pools of employees are other examples.

There is nothing wrong in principle with paying better performers a higher wage; such a system does not, of itself, involve unlawful pay discrimination. A performance-related pay system, which will almost inevitably lead to differences in levels of pay between employees doing similar jobs, is capable of providing the employer with a valid material factor explaining the differential in pay – see Chapter 8 under 'Specific material factors – performance-related pay'. However, the implementation of such a scheme by line managers – for example, where performance is rated by individual managers on an essentially subjective basis – can inadvertently let in discriminatory considerations, which might leave the system open to challenge on the basis that it is tainted by sex discrimination. The risk of unconscious discrimination in performance rating can be lessened with effective diversity and equality training. The EHRC, in Checklist 8, 'Performance pay', suggests that asking a group of managers to reach a consensus on performance assessments is one way to filter out potentially discriminatory considerations.

10.33 Employers should check that women are given equal access to performance-related pay, particularly where their work is easily assessable in terms of output. Any differences must be objectively justifiable as a proportionate means of achieving a legitimate aim. For example, does the different availability of bonuses reflect a real difference in productivity or in the value of the work? – Part II, para C2, EU Pay Code.

Clearly, the questions posed in the EHRC Checklist 7 (see under 'Competence-based pay' above) are also relevant when an employer comes to review performance-based pay systems.

10.34 Other contractual fringe benefits

Eligibility for pay benefits such as occupational pensions, low interest loans, sick pay, company cars and share options should be reviewed if a smaller percentage of women than men are in receipt of such benefits – Part II, para C3, EU Pay Code. The areas of particular concern in respect of such benefits are likely to be unequal access to benefits for men and women, providing different levels of benefit to different categories of employee, and providing different levels of benefit according to length of service.

The EHRC Checklist 13, 'Benefits and equal pay', suggests that where there are differences in access to, or the level of, benefits, an employer should ask the following questions in order to ascertain the reason for those differences:

- is 'status' within the organisation a factor in determining access to benefits such as company cars and share options?

- how are benefits allocated? Does it depend on what the employee asks for? Or on what his or her manager thinks he or she deserves? What safeguards are there against the inappropriate use of managerial discretion?

- are there variations in the levels of benefits provided? What determines these variations?

- is length of service used to determine access to benefits?

- are market comparisons – which run the risk of importing discrimination from outside the organisation – used to determine access to benefits?

10.35 Flexibility

Rewards in terms of pay and fringe benefits based on criteria such as willingness to be flexible – for example, in respect of working hours, work arrangements, mobility or job duties – have a potentially indirectly discriminatory effect because women, with their typically more burdensome domestic responsibilities, find it more difficult than men to be flexible. Therefore, employers should check that such criteria are objectively justifiable by ensuring that adaptability is of importance in the performance of the

408

specific duties entrusted to the employee concerned – see further Chapter 8 under 'Specific material factors – flexibility and working hours'.

Skills and training   10.36
Where pay increases or other benefits are based on additional skills or training, the employer should be prepared to justify the use of these criteria if it is shown that fewer women than men satisfy them. For example, the application of a criterion of vocational training as a factor for awarding employees higher pay can systematically disadvantage women in so far as they have fewer opportunities to obtain such training. As with other similar criteria, the employer will only be able to show justification if the training in question specifically improves the performance of employees in respect of the duties with which they are entrusted – see Chapter 8 under 'Specific material factors – skills, qualifications and vocational training'.

Working time payments   10.37
It is probably true to say that rewarding overtime is less likely to be discriminatory than other additional payments. So long as basic payments are equal, it is usually acceptable for employers to pay employees who work overtime a special hourly rate. The same is true of shift or on-call premiums to take into account unsocial working hours. The fact that many women find it impracticable to work at night and are less able to take advantage of overtime (at least to the same degree as men) makes it inevitable that, on average, their relative total pay is likely to be lower than that of their male counterparts. But unless there is evidence to show that male jobs are structured in such a way as to encourage overtime and female jobs structured in such a way as to encourage part-time working (where there may be no question of overtime payments), then special overtime rates are likely to be justifiable.

But it is still important for employers to check that *access* to overtime and premiums for unsocial hours and weekend and shift working are provided on an equal basis. Equal pay problems in this context primarily arise from unequal access; for example, where:

• predominantly female jobs are excluded from the premium payments or have restricted access to them

• overtime is restricted to certain grades or jobs or allocated on a discretionary basis

• working conditions allowances are paid to those in male-dominated jobs as a result of past collective agreements or 'industrial muscle'.

The EHRC Checklist 11, 'Working time payments', suggests the following **10.38** questions an employer should ask when reviewing working time payments:

- are the payments still relevant and necessary, or do they reward people for a practice that died out some time ago?

- are there differences between the payments received by men and women doing equal work?

- what is the approach to working time payments made to part-time workers – do they receive such payments whenever they exceed their normal working hours, or only when they exceed normal full-time working hours? (See further Chapter 8 in the section on 'Specific material factors' under 'Part-time work – overtime'.)

10.39 Part-time working

The possible discriminatory consequences of treating part-time workers less favourably in terms of pay and other benefits than full-time workers are examined in Chapter 8 under 'Specific material factors – part-time work'. There has been a widespread tendency in the past for payment systems to be designed to reward work patterns traditionally associated with men's employment. These fail to recognise the different working patterns applicable to women's work, in particular part-time working, job sharing and casual employment. The denial of pro rata and/or service-related benefits and lower rates of basic pay are the types of differential treatment that part-time employees frequently suffer. Since considerably more women than men work part time, it is inevitable that to discriminate against part-timers is to discriminate indirectly against women. Unless a clear and objective explanation is provided, the discriminatory treatment of part-time workers is therefore likely to amount to a breach of the principle of equal pay for equal work – Part II, para C4, EU Pay Code. (It is also likely to be in breach of the Part-time Workers (Prevention of Less Favourable Treatment) Regulations 2000 SI 2000/1551.)

By definition, a woman working part time is unlikely to be earning the same as a male full-time worker employed on comparable work. To the extent that a full-time worker works longer hours, it is inevitable that his take-home pay will be greater. What is important is that both the man and the woman are employed on the same basic rates for the job in respect of the hours they work.

10.40 Until fairly recently, courts and tribunals were generally happy to accept the argument that part-time workers were less committed than, and took longer to acquire the same level of skills, experience and know-how as, full-time workers as justification for pay differentials. But such sweeping generalisations are no longer tolerated, as the case law discussed in Chapter 8, 'Material factor defence', confirms. An employer will be expected to fully demonstrate that such arguments have validity in relation to the particular organisation and the particular jobs under consideration if it wishes to justify unequal pay.

11 Victimisation

Scope of provisions

Prohibited circumstances

Protected acts

Detriment

Detriment 'because of' protected act

Proving victimisation

Individuals wishing to bring an equal pay claim may be deterred from doing so **11.1** by fear of reprisals. To address this concern, the Sex Discrimination Act 1975 (SDA) introduced special protection against victimisation. This protection was designed to prevent workers from being penalised for taking action under, or in relation to, either the SDA or the Equal Pay Act 1970 (EqPA). This protection is now found in the Equality Act 2010 (EqA), albeit with some changes to the statutory language.

Victimisation was defined by S.4(1) SDA as occurring when an employer treated an individual less favourably than the employer treated or would treat other persons in the same circumstances, and did so by reason that the individual had done or intended to do a 'protected act' (i.e. action under, or related to, the SDA or EqPA). The EqA takes a slightly different approach. S.27(1) states that:

'A person (A) victimises another person (B) if A subjects B to a detriment because (a) B does a protected act, or (b) A believes that B has done, or may do, a protected act.'

This provision only applies 'where the person subjected to a detriment is an individual' – S.27(4).

It follows from S.27(1) that a claimant seeking to establish that he or she has **11.2** been victimised must show two things: first, that he or she has been subjected to a detriment; and secondly, that he or she was subjected to that detriment because of a protected act. There is no longer any need, as there was under the SDA, for the claimant to show that his or her treatment was *less favourable* than that which would have been afforded to a comparator who had not done a protected act. The significance of this change is considered in detail under 'Detriment because of protected act' below.

The following are 'protected acts' for the purpose of S.27(1):

• bringing proceedings under the EqA

411

- giving evidence or information in connection with proceedings under the EqA

- doing any other thing for the purposes of or in connection with the EqA, and

- making an allegation (whether or not express) that A or another person has contravened the EqA – S.27(2).

11.3 In addition, S.77 treats as protected acts certain things done in relation to pay secrecy clauses in employment contracts (see Chapter 9 under 'Pay secrecy clauses'). This provision – which is an innovation in the 2010 Act, having no equivalent in the EqPA – is designed to stop employers covering up unlawful pay inequality by means of confidentiality clauses. In short, any attempt by an employee to discover whether there is pay discrimination at work will be protected, even if the employee thereby breaches or solicits a breach of a pay secrecy clause.

In this chapter we examine the scope of the victimisation provisions in the EqA, before looking at the relevant circumstances in which victimisation by an employer can arise. We then consider the acts protected by the victimisation provisions, before discussing the meaning of 'detriment' and how this differs from the previous requirement to establish 'less favourable treatment'. Finally, we address the burden of proof in victimisation claims.

11.4 Scope of provisions

The victimisation provisions give wide protection to employees who have been penalised for bringing, or involving themselves in almost any way with, an equal pay complaint. It is not necessary for a tribunal claim to have been brought – the victimisation provisions cover a wide range of conduct related to the EqA, such as alleging a breach of the Act or doing anything 'in connection with' the Act – see 'Protected acts', below. That said, in most cases the issue of victimisation is linked to a previous or concurrent tribunal claim by the claimant.

Where the complaint of victimisation does relate to litigation, the success or otherwise of the main equal pay claim is not a relevant factor in the success or otherwise of the victimisation claim. It may be that the claimant's original claim fails but a subsequent victimisation action leads to a large award of compensation. This is because, in a victimisation claim, the focus is not on the sex of the complainant but on his or her actions in alleging a breach or bringing a claim or in assisting in someone else's claim. Anyone whose conduct amounts to a 'protected act' can seek to rely on the statutory protection from victimisation – Cornelius v University College of Swansea 1987 IRLR 141, CA. An example:

- **Brown v Department for Education and Skills** ET Case Nos.2304579/00 and 2302776/01: B failed in his equal pay claim, based on comparison with F, a female employee, because the DES was able to make out the 'genuine material factor' defence under S.1(3) EqPA (now S.69 EqA) – F had not been prepared to accept a lower salary and the DES had only paid what was necessary to secure her services. Some time after B had brought his claim, the men's toilets in the premises where he worked were deliberately flooded. CCTV footage showed B leaving the toilets shortly before the flood was discovered, and he was suspended from duty. He was later exonerated. B brought a victimisation claim under S.4 SDA (now S.27 EqA). The tribunal held that he had been unlawfully victimised. Consciously or subconsciously, the person who had investigated the flooding incident formed the view that B was a troublemaker and, as such, a likely culprit. Had the investigator been unaware of the fact that B had brought an equal pay claim, he would not have taken this view.

11.5 The protection from victimisation provisions can even come into play in respect of the employer's conduct during the main proceedings. For example, in Lorde v Eden Brown Ltd ET Case No.2201996/09 the employer's defence of L's sex discrimination claim gave rise to victimisation. The employer had approached witnesses who were due to give evidence for L and frightened them off by telling them that, if they did so, compromise agreements they had concluded with the employer would not be honoured. The tribunal found that this caused stress and anxiety to L, since it meant she had to apply for witness orders to ensure the attendance of her witnesses. The tribunal awarded £8,000 for injury to feelings and £6,000 aggravated damages, noting that the employer had tried to subvert the course of justice, undermine L's right to a fair trial and damage her credibility.

The Court of Appeal has also indicated that failure to pay the compensation awarded by a tribunal in respect of the main claim may amount to unlawful victimisation, so long as the failure to pay was itself motivated by the fact of the employee having brought tribunal proceedings. In Coutinho v Rank Nemo (DMS) Ltd 2009 ICR 1296, CA, C won a claim of race discrimination and was awarded over £70,000 in compensation. He did not receive any money from RN Ltd, despite obtaining a county court order for payment, and he then claimed that the failure to pay was itself an act of victimisation under the Race Relations Act 1976 (RRA). The Court allowed the claim to proceed, rejecting RN Ltd's argument that the claim was an illegitimate attempt to enforce the award in the tribunal. The Court held that, even if RN Ltd paid the award immediately, the victimisation claim could still continue, with C seeking to recover damages for any loss of benefit or detriment suffered in consequence of RN Ltd's reluctance to pay.

11.6 In some cases, the complaint of victimisation will hang on a tribunal claim brought by *another* person, in which the person victimised is or has been involved. An example:

- **Laidlaw v South Durham Social Club** ET Case No.2500971/04: L was due to give evidence for his girlfriend in a sex discrimination claim against his employer. After taking two weeks' holiday, he did not turn up to work the next day because he was attending the tribunal as a witness. The employer knew this, as witness statements had been exchanged. L was disciplined for unauthorised absence and subjected to other less favourable treatment in his working arrangements. The tribunal held that he was victimised contrary to S.4 SDA (now S.27 EqA) because the employer knew he would be attending the tribunal and must have known he would not be attending work. He was subjected to a detriment for carrying out a protected act.

11.7 Belief and suspicion

Protection under S.27(1) clearly applies where the discriminator *believes* that the person victimised has done or may do a protected act. For example, in France v Chief Constable of Hertfordshire Constabulary ET Case No.1200783/98 the claimant succeeded with a victimisation claim when, following his internal complaints of sex discrimination, the employer transferred him to a different unit in the knowledge that he intended to bring sex discrimination claims.

Under the pre-EqA legislation, such as the SDA, protection against victimisation extended to situations where the employer *suspected* that the person victimised *intended* to do a protected act. This was emphasised in Miller v Crime Concern Trust Ltd EAT 0758/04 where the EAT held that a tribunal had erred in failing to consider whether the alleged discriminator had suspected that the claimant was going to make an allegation of race or sex discrimination. S.27(1) imposes a slightly different test: it applies where the employee does a protected act or where the employer '*believes* that [the employee] has done, or *may do*, a protected act' (our stress). It is unclear whether a *suspicion* that a person *intends* to do a protected act (under the old test) is the same as a *belief* that a person *may* do such an act (under S.27(1)). Strictly speaking, 'belief' suggests a higher level of credence than 'suspicion', but the fact that a person 'may do' an act suggests something less than that he or she 'intends' to do it. The new terms may, therefore, achieve the same balance as the previous legislation. The Explanatory Notes to the Act do not highlight this change of wording, which implies (by omission) that no substantive change to the law was intended. In any event, it seems unlikely that tribunals will adopt a construction of the new Act that amounts to a regression in protection for employees so, since suspicions were covered by the old law, they are likely to be covered by the new provisions.

11.8 Three-stage victimisation test

Baroness Hale in Derbyshire and ors v St Helens Metropolitan Borough Council and ors 2007 ICR 841, HL, and Lord Nicholls in Chief Constable of West Yorkshire Police v Khan 2001 ICR 1065, HL, endorsed a three-stage test for establishing victimisation under the pre-EqA discrimination legislation. Their approach called for answers to the following questions:

- did the employer discriminate against the claimant in any of the *circumstances* covered by the SDA?

- in doing so, did the employer treat him or her *less favourably* than others in those circumstances?

- was the *reason for the less favourable treatment* the fact that the claimant had done a protected act; or that the employer knew that he or she intended to do a protected act, or suspected that he or she had done, or intended to do, a protected act?

As previously mentioned, the new definition of victimisation in S.27 EqA uses **11.9** somewhat different wording to that used in S.4 SDA. It provides that:

'A person (A) victimises another person (B) if A subjects B to a detriment because (a) B does a protected act, or (b) A believes that B has done, or may do, a protected act.'

In light of the new wording, we would submit that the above three-stage test can be adapted as follows:

- did the alleged victimisation arise in any of the prohibited *circumstances* covered by the EqA? (See 'Prohibited circumstances' below)

- if so, did the employer subject the claimant to a *detriment*? (See 'Detriment' below)

- if so, was the claimant subjected to that detriment *because he or she had done a protected act*, or because the employer believed that he or she had done, or might do, a protected act? (See 'Protected acts' and 'Detriment "because of" protected act' below).

The explanation for the change of wording given in the Explanatory Notes is **11.10** that victimisation is no longer treated as a form of discrimination. Under the SDA and the other discrimination legislation before 1 October 2010, one provision would make it unlawful for an employer to discriminate in employment, while other sections would define 'discrimination' for that purpose. One of these sections would define victimisation as a form of discrimination. So, for example, S.4 SDA set out the definition of victimisation and stated that it amounted to discrimination, while S.6 stated that discrimination in employment was unlawful. In the EqA, by contrast, S.27 sets out the definition of victimisation and S.39(3) and (4) states that victimisation in employment is unlawful. Thus, there is no need to treat victimisation as a form of discrimination – it is unlawful per se – and so the need to define it in the same way as discrimination falls away.

In the next section we set out the circumstances in which victimisation is prohibited under the EqA. We then examine the nature of the protected acts covered by the victimisation provisions and discuss the meaning of 'detriment', before turning to consider the relationship between the two; i.e. what it means for a detriment to be 'because of' a protected act. It should be borne in mind, however, that the stages of analysis overlap to some extent.

11.11 Prohibited circumstances

The circumstances in which discrimination by way of victimisation is prohibited in the employment field are set out in S.39(3) and (4) EqA. S.39(3) provides that an employer (A) must not victimise a person (B):

- in the arrangements A makes for deciding to whom to offer employment – S.39(3)(a)

- as to the terms on which A offers B employment – S.39(3)(b), or

- by not offering B employment – S.39(3)(c).

Section 39(4) provides that an employer (A) must not victimise an employee of A's (B):

- as to B's terms of employment – S.39(4)(a)

- in the way A affords B access, or by not affording B access, to opportunities for promotion, transfer or training, or for any other benefit, facility or service – S.39(4)(b)

- by dismissing B – S.39(4)(c), or

- by subjecting B to any other detriment – S.39(4)(d).

11.12 Similar protection from victimisation is afforded to contract workers, office holders, partners, and barristers, etc – see Ss.41–58 EqA. Note that this protection is wider than the right to claim equal pay. As noted in Chapter 2 under 'Who is covered?', the right to claim equal pay applies to 'employment', as broadly defined, and also to various specified categories of worker, such as crown employees, armed forces personnel and office holders. However, contract workers, partners and barristers are not expressly covered and so do not necessarily have the right to equal pay. But given that protection from victimisation is not limited to those who seek to enforce rights on their *own* behalf it is entirely possible that a worker who is not covered by the equal pay provisions may be afforded protection from victimisation suffered as a result of being involved in someone else's equal pay claim or allegation.

In practice it is the catch-all 'detriment' provision in S.39(4)(d) that is most frequently cited in victimisation claims. For the meaning of 'detriment' in the context of both S.27 and S.39(4)(d) EqA, see 'Detriment' below.

Post-employment victimisation. The wording of S.27(1) is capable of covering **11.13**
the situation where a former employee is subjected to a detriment by his or her
former employer because of a protected act. However, victimisation by
employers is not actually prohibited by S.27, which is simply a definition
provision. As noted above, it is S.39(3) and (4) that specifically prohibits
victimisation in employment, but this does not expressly apply to post-
employment victimisation. S.108 prohibits *discrimination* and *harassment* that
arises out of and is closely connected to a relationship which has ended (such
as an employment relationship). However, this extension is expressly stated not
to apply to victimisation – S.108(7).

Thus, on the fact of it, the EqA would appear not to cover victimisation of
former employees by their former employers (unless it arises in the context of
recruitment, which is covered by S.39(3)). However, such a literal interpretation
of the statutory provisions would amount to a serious degradation of the
protection afforded to employees, not to mention contrary to the House of
Lords' decision in Rhys-Harper v Relaxion Group plc 2003 ICR 867, HL. In
that case their Lordships ruled that the wording of the SDA, RRA and Disability
Discrimination Act 1995, which referred to employment relationships in the
present tense, had to be given an interpretation that extended protection to
conduct following termination of employment, provided the discrimination
(including victimisation) arose out of the employment relationship. We would
therefore contend that S.39(4)(d) must similarly be interpreted as applying not
only to current but also to former employees, and that the familiar scenario
where a former employee is victimised by his or her former employer's refusal
to provide a reference is covered by S.39.

The Equality and Human Rights Commission (EHRC)'s Code of Practice on **11.14**
Employment gives some support for this view, albeit without citing any
authority for it. Para 9.4 simply states that: 'Former workers are also protected
from victimisation', while para 10.62 explains that: 'If the conduct or treatment
which an individual receives after a relationship has ended amounts to
victimisation, this will be covered by the victimisation provisions.'

Protected acts
11.15

The acts protected by the victimisation provisions are set out in S.27(2).
They are:

- bringing proceedings under the EqA – S.27(2)(a)

- giving evidence or information in connection with proceedings under the
EqA – S.27(2)(b)

- doing any other thing for the purposes of or in connection with the EqA –
S.27(2)(c)

- making an allegation (whether or not express) that A or another person has contravened the EqA – S.27(2)(d).

11.16 These are substantially the same as those listed in S.4(1) SDA. There is also a new category of protected act introduced by S.77 EqA, a provision which bans certain forms of pay secrecy clauses in employment contracts (see Chapter 9 under 'Pay secrecy clauses'). S.77(4) states that seeking, making, seeking to make, or receiving a 'relevant pay disclosure' are all to be treated as protected acts. A 'relevant pay disclosure' for these purposes is a disclosure 'made for the purpose of enabling the person who makes it, or the person to whom it is made, to find out whether or to what extent there is, in relation to the work in question, a connection between pay and having (or not having) a particular protected characteristic' – S.77(3). In other words, an attempt to uncover the existence of pay inequality is also a protected act.

11.17 **Transitional provisions.** In the period between the EqA receiving Royal Assent on 8 April 2010 and coming into force on 1 October 2010, it became apparent that there was a loophole in the wording of S.27(2). Subsections (a) to (d) of that provision all refer to something done in respect of 'this Act', i.e. the EqA. Since the EqA repealed the previous discrimination legislation, this would have meant that a claimant bringing a claim of victimisation that was alleged to have occurred after 1 October 2010, but which arose from protected acts that occurred when the EqPA was still in force, would have been left without legal redress. Article 8 of the Equality Act 2010 (Commencement No.4, Savings, Consequential, Transitional, Transitory and Incidental Provisions and Revocation) Order 2010 SI 2010/2317 closed this loophole by making clear that references in S.27(2) to 'this Act' are to be read as also applying to the previous discrimination and equality enactments, including the EqPA.

11.18 **Bringing proceedings**

Bringing any legal proceedings under the EqA will fall within S.27(2)(a) and therefore be protected. Most victimisation claims relate to reprisals suffered because of earlier proceedings brought by the claimant against the alleged victimiser, although concurrent proceedings are also covered (including the initial act of presenting a claim form to an employment tribunal – Northamptonshire County Council v Dattani EAT 314 and others). Note that subsection (a) covers *any kind* of proceedings against *any person*. Suppose, for example, that an employee brings proceedings in an employment tribunal claiming equal pay with a male colleague. Some time later, she applies for a job with another company, which refuses to offer her employment because it knows that she brought an equal pay claim against her old employer. She could claim victimisation under S.39(3)(c) EqA (victimisation by not offering employment) against that company.

Giving evidence or information in connection with proceedings 11.19

Subsection 27(2)(b) clearly protects giving evidence at a tribunal hearing. Giving evidence prior to a hearing will also be covered, but only if proceedings have already been instigated. In Kirby v Manpower Services Commission 1980 ICR 420, EAT, K was demoted after he gave information to his local Community Relations Council that eventually led to race discrimination proceedings against his employer. The EAT held that K's claim that his demotion amounted to victimisation could not be brought under S.2(1)(b) RRA (equivalent to S.27(2)(b) EqA) because the incidents that gave rise to the demotion occurred three months before the proceedings were actually commenced. However, his claim did succeed under S.2(1)(c) RRA – see 'Acts done for the purposes of or in connection with the EqA' below.

False evidence or information. Giving false evidence or information is not a 11.20 protected act if it is done in bad faith – S.27(3). This is not, however, the same as saying that the evidence or information must be true. If a claimant provides evidence or information in good faith that turns out to be inaccurate, he or she will still enjoy protection under S.27(2)(b) in respect of the provision of that evidence or information. For more detail on the meaning of 'bad faith' in a victimisation context, see under 'Allegations of a contravention of the EqA' below.

Acts done 'for the purposes of or in connection with' the EqA 11.21

Subsection (c) is generally seen as a sweep-up clause for actions not specifically covered by S.27(2)(a) and (b). The statutory wording has been simplified somewhat from that found in the original discrimination statutes. Previously, S.4(1)(c) SDA referred to acts done 'under or by reference to' the EqPA. The other discrimination legislation, such as the RRA, contained similar wording. Now, all acts done 'for the purposes of or in connection with' the EqA are covered. The ambit of the original wording came in for scrutiny by the EAT in Kirby v Manpower Services Commission 1980 ICR 420, EAT, which took a restrictive view of what constitutes action 'under' an Act. The EAT held that such action must be done under a specific statutory provision. On the facts, a report to the local Community Relations Council was not made under any specific provision. The phrase 'by reference to' was given a much wider interpretation, however. The EAT was prepared to assume that it was wide enough to cover the report to the Community Relations Council because the purpose of the report was to inform the Council that facts were available which ought to be investigated and which indicated a possible breach of the RRA. The Court of Appeal confirmed this interpretation in Aziz v Trinity Street Taxis Ltd and ors 1988 ICR 534, CA, where it stated that an act could properly be said to be done 'by reference to' the RRA if it were done by reference to the legislation 'in the broad sense, even though the doer does not focus his mind specifically on any provision of the Act'.

419

If an identical case were to be heard today under S.27(2)(c), the report would almost certainly be taken to have been made 'in connection with' the EqA. Indeed, it is arguable that it might also be viewed as having been made 'for the purposes of' the Act, a test that would appear to be wider than the previous 'under' test.

11.22 Allegations of a contravention of the EqA

Subsection (d) covers allegations, whether or not express, made by the claimant that the employer or another person has contravened the EqA. S.27(5) states expressly that this includes a contravention by way of breach of an equality clause or rule. Thus, employees and members of occupational pension schemes enjoy protection from victimisation from the moment they make an allegation that they are not receiving equal pay, terms or access to a pension scheme – it is not necessary for an individual to have brought an equal pay claim in a tribunal to be protected by the victimisation provisions.

It is not necessary that the EqA actually be mentioned in the allegation or even envisaged as coming into play. However, the asserted facts must, if verified, be capable of amounting to a breach of the EqA. Two examples:

- **Beneviste v Kingston University** EAT 0393/05: B claimed that she had been victimised because she had raised various grievances. She admitted that she had not at the time complained that her treatment was on the grounds of sex or race but thought this did not matter. The EAT upheld the tribunal's decision that the grievances could not amount to protected acts, saying that a claim does not identify a protected act in the true legal sense 'merely by making a reference to a criticism, grievance or complaint without suggesting that the criticism, grievance or complaint was in some sense an allegation of discrimination or otherwise a contravention of the legislation'

- **Waters v Commissioner of Police of the Metropolis** 1997 ICR 1073, CA: a woman police officer accused a male colleague of sexually assaulting her. Following this accusation, she was subjected to various forms of harassment and other unfair treatment at work. The Court of Appeal held that, on the officer's own version of events, her colleague had not committed the assault 'in the course of his employment', and so the Commissioner of Police could not be held liable. It followed that she was not entitled to rely on her allegation of assault for the purpose of a victimisation claim as she had not alleged that her employer had committed an act which would amount to a contravention of the SDA.

11.23

The result of the Waters case seems somewhat harsh, as claimants are unlikely to know, without the benefit of legal advice, whether the facts they are alleging could theoretically give rise to a successful claim in law. However, the effect of the narrow interpretation of subsection (d) may be less of a problem than might first appear: in many cases where subsection (d) is inapplicable, it may be possible to argue that the case falls within subsection (c) if the allegation can be said to have been made in connection with the EqA 'in the broad sense' – see Aziz v Trinity Street Taxis Ltd and ors 1988 ICR 534, CA.

Subsection (d) imposes no restrictions as to whom the allegations must relate to or to whom they must be made. For example, in Davey v Aldam t/a John Charles Associates ET Case No.3101781/98 D complained to her employer's son about her employer's treatment of her. He said that he would speak to his father. The next day she was dismissed. A tribunal found that her dismissal amounted to victimisation. The allegations do not even have to be against the same person in respect of whom the claimant subsequently alleges victimisation – although it may arguably be harder for a claimant to demonstrate that an employer treated him or her less favourably because of a protected act where that act did not directly concern the employer.

Note that S.27(2)(d) covers allegations made about A (the alleged victimiser) or 'another person', so it is quite possible for an employer to victimise an employee because the employee has made allegations about an entirely unrelated person.

False allegations. Protection from victimisation under S.27(2)(d) is still **11.24** available if the allegation turns out to be untrue. However, S.27(3) EqA provides that making a false allegation will not be protected if it is done in 'bad faith'.

This provision is the successor to S.4(2) SDA, which provided that an allegation would not amount to a protected act if it was 'false and not made in good faith'. S.4(2) was considered by the EAT in GMB Union v Fenton EAT 0798/02 and others. In that case, F, an educational assistant at the GMB National College, was frustrated at being excluded from a GMB pension scheme and brought a claim under the EqPA against the union. However, as he admitted, his exclusion was in fact on the ground of his employment status, not gender, so his claim was held to be misconceived. He made a further claim of victimisation and the union claimed that there was no protected act because F's first claim, on which he relied, was false and made in bad faith. The EAT said that the test in S.4(2) has two limbs: first, whether an allegation is false, and secondly, whether the person making the allegation knew it was false at the time it was made. The EAT said that if a claimant 'has a belief that he has a good claim, but perhaps one that is not terribly likely to succeed, and he brings that claim with some collateral purpose, it appears to us that that does not necessarily make the bringing of that claim in bad faith. The issue is not the purpose, but the belief in the claim.' So the fact that a person is being opportunistic in making an allegation does not necessarily mean that the allegation is not made in good faith. However, according to the EAT, an allegation made in bad faith does not necessarily have to be 'treacherous'.

421

11.25 **Pay disclosure protected acts**
As explained in Chapter 9 under 'Pay secrecy clauses', S.77 EqA is a new provision designed to protect employees who discuss their pay with colleagues with a view to finding out whether there is a connection between pay and any of the protected characteristics covered by the Act (i.e. age, disability, gender reassignment, marriage and civil partnership, pregnancy and maternity, race, religion or belief, sex, or sexual orientation). S.77(1) and (2) provides that terms in employment contracts that purport to restrict or prevent a person from seeking disclosure of, or disclosing or seeking to disclose, information about pay will be unenforceable to the extent that they prevent or restrict a disclosure made for the purpose of discovering whether there is such a connection.

Section 77(4) supports these provisions by providing that the following are protected acts for the purpose of S.27 EqA:

- seeking a disclosure that would be a relevant pay disclosure – S.77(4)(a)

- making or seeking to make a relevant pay disclosure – S.77(4)(b)

- receiving information disclosed in a relevant pay disclosure – S.77(4)(c).

11.26 A pay disclosure is 'relevant' for these purposes if it is 'made for the purpose of enabling the person who makes it, or the person to whom it is made, to find out whether or to what extent there is, in relation to the work in question, a connection between pay and having (or not having) a particular protected characteristic' – S.77(3). In other words, the exchange of information must be motivated by a desire to uncover pay discrimination, rather than simple curiosity.

11.27 # Detriment

Under the SDA, in order to make out a complaint of victimisation, it was not enough for the claimant to show that he or she had suffered a disadvantage. Victimisation occurred only where the employee, having done a protected act, was treated *less favourably* by the employer *than another person was or would have been treated*. Indeed, many of the difficulties that arose in victimisation cases under the old legislation concerned the appropriate comparison that needed to be made to establish less favourable treatment.

It is apparent from the wording of S.27(1) EqA, which refers to detriment 'because of' a protected act, that the EqA has removed the absolute need for a tribunal to construct an appropriate comparator in victimisation claims. As the EHRC's Code of Practice on Employment states: 'The worker need only show that they have experienced a detriment because they have done a protected act or because the employer believes (rightly or wrongly) that they have done or intend to do a protected act' (para 9.11). In this respect the victimisation provisions in the EqA are similar to the provisions in Part V of the Employment

Rights Act 1996 (ERA), which afford protection from detriment on specified grounds covered by that Act. For example, S.47B ERA makes it unlawful for an employer to subject a worker to a detriment 'on the ground that the worker has made a protected disclosure'. Assuming that 'because of' and 'on the ground of' are equivalent formulations of causation (which case law suggests they are), it can be said that victimisation under the EqA and protection from detriment under the ERA are now very similar in scope.

In its response to the Consultation on the Equality Bill, the Government stated **11.28** that the removal of the requirement for a comparator 'offers a more effective, workable system – not one in which it would necessarily be easier to win a case, but one where attention [is] rightly focused on considering whether the "victim" suffered an absolute harm, irrespective of how others were being treated in the same circumstances' (para 7.35 of the 'The Equality Bill – Government response to the Consultation', July 2008 (Cm 7454)). In practice, however, a comparison of the claimant's treatment with that of an appropriate comparator will often be an effective way of establishing whether the treatment was 'because of' the protected act.

Below we consider, by reference to case law under the SDA, the ERA and other legislation, what can amount to a 'detriment' for the purposes of S.27 EqA.

What amounts to 'detriment'?
11.29

It was established under the victimisation provisions in the SDA and other discrimination legislation that preceded the EqA that 'less favourable treatment' could take many forms, ranging from general hostility to dismissal. The same is undoubtedly true of 'detriment' and so even the more subtle forms of victimisation will not necessarily escape the law. As Lord Hope observed in Derbyshire and ors v St Helens Metropolitan Borough Council and ors 2007 ICR 841, HL, 'fear of public odium or the reproaches of colleagues is just as likely to deter an employee from enforcing her claim as a direct threat'. His Lordship made those comments with regard to a local authority that had written to a group of school canteen employees, warning of the potential consequences for the school meals service if employees who were bringing equal pay claims were to win.

A similar conclusion was reached in GMB v Allen and ors 2007 IRLR 752, EAT. There, the respondent union had persuaded several female members to settle their equal pay claims for about 25 per cent of their potential value while negotiating the implementation of a new single pay structure with the local authority. The tribunal found that the union had victimised the women when it reminded the local authority of its agreement that all members should be treated the same whether or not they had brought litigation, as this meant that the payments which might otherwise be made to the claimants would have to be reduced in order to accommodate the other union members who had not lodged claims. On appeal, the EAT disagreed, holding that there was no less favourable treatment and the union was simply seeking to ensure that all were treated equally favourably by the local authority. However, it noted that the tribunal's finding that the union portrayed the claimants to other union members and to the local authority as 'self-centred money grabbers' was in principle capable of constituting detrimental treatment in the context of victimisation discrimination, but that this allegation had not been put to the tribunal. (Although the case subsequently went to the Court of Appeal – see Allen and ors v GMB 2008 ICR 1407, CA – the victimisation finding was not appealed.)

11.30 It is clear, then, that indirect pressure on employees to abandon their equal pay complaints can amount to a detriment. In Parker v Chancery (UK) Ltd ET Case No.1201764/07, for example, P was victimised when the employer tried to dissuade her from raising a grievance about unequal pay. When P had queried her pay relative to a male colleague whom she asserted was employed on equal work, she was told that if she raised a grievance it would create a difficult work environment and that she would be better off leaving and seeking alternative employment. The tribunal awarded £3,000 for injury to feelings, among other heads of compensation, having regard to the fact that the incident was one among several factors that led her to leave C Ltd's employment.

The House of Lords in Chief Constable of West Yorkshire Police v Khan 2001 ICR 1065, HL, established that an *omission* to act – such as a refusal to provide a reference – may constitute detrimental treatment. The House of Lords also stated that, although less favourable treatment involved some kind of disadvantage, it did not have to have damaging consequences. In that case, West Yorkshire Police refused to supply a reference for a serving police officer (who had applied to another force for a post) while that officer's race discrimination claim against West Yorkshire Police was pending. West Yorkshire Police argued that K had not been treated less favourably because he would have been worse off had the reference been supplied – he would not even have reached the interview stage, as he had done without having the reference. The House of Lords decided that K had clearly been treated less favourably because he had been refused a reference, whereas any other officer who did not have a race discrimination complaint pending before a tribunal would have been given one. However, it is not enough merely to show that the employee has been treated differently to others. Lord Scott made it clear that 'there must also be a quality in the treatment that enables the complainant reasonably to complain about it. I do not think, however, that it is appropriate to pursue the treatment and its consequences down to an end result in order to try and demonstrate that the complainant is, in the end, better off, or at least no worse off, than he would have been if he had not been treated differently. I think it suffices if the complainant can reasonably say that he would have preferred not to have been treated differently.'

Lord Scott's final point – looking at the treatment from the employee's point of view – encapsulates the concept of 'detriment' rather neatly, and later cases have taken a similar approach. Shamoon v Chief Constable of the Royal Ulster Constabulary 2003 ICR 337, HL, which concerned the meaning of 'detriment' in Article 8(2)(b) of the Sex Discrimination (Northern Ireland) Order 1976 SR 1976/1042, established that a detriment exists if a reasonable worker would or might take the view that the treatment was in all the circumstances to his or her disadvantage. The House of Lords took the view that an unjustified sense of grievance could not amount to a detriment, but did emphasise that whether or not a claimant has been disadvantaged is to be viewed subjectively. **11.31**

The EHRC's Code of Practice on Employment offers the following explanation of 'detriment', which accords with the case law: 'Generally, a detriment is anything which the individual concerned might reasonably consider changed their position for the worse or put them at a disadvantage. This could include being rejected for promotion, denied an opportunity to represent the organisation at external events, excluded from opportunities to train, or overlooked in the allocation of discretionary bonuses or performance-related awards. A detriment might also include a threat made to the complainant which they take seriously and it is reasonable for them to take it seriously. There is no need to demonstrate physical or economic consequences. However, an unjustified sense of grievance alone would not be enough to establish detriment.'

Thus, it is clear that 'detriment' does not necessarily require financial loss, loss of an opportunity, or even a very specific form of disadvantage. In Popa v PriceWaterhouseCoopers LLP ET Case No.2201667/09, for example, a tribunal found that P had suffered a detriment sufficient to amount to victimisation in the way her employer drew up her reference. The company had a prescriptive reference procedure, under which former employees were coded as to the type of reference they would receive. P's code was changed after she brought tribunal proceedings, and a passage relating to honesty and integrity was omitted from the next reference the employer gave her. She did not lose the employment in question as a result of the reference, and nor was she caused any significant distress. Nonetheless, the tribunal found that she had been victimised under the RRA and awarded her £750 for injury to feelings. **11.32**

Detriment 'because of' protected act   **11.33**

To succeed in a claim of victimisation the claimant must show that he or she was subjected to the detriment *because* he or she did a protected act or *because* the employer believed he or she had done or might do a protected act. Where there has been a detriment and a protected act, but the detrimental treatment was due to another reason, e.g. absenteeism or misconduct, no claim of victimisation will succeed.

425

It is not always easy to determine whether detriment was meted out 'because of' a protected act. In Chief Constable of West Yorkshire Police v Khan 2001 ICR 1065, HL, the Chief Constable maintained that he had refused to give a reference to the police force to which K had applied for a post because he did not want to prejudice his position in K's pending race discrimination claim against West Yorkshire Police. The Court of Appeal held that the refusal was by reason of the fact that K had brought proceedings in the sense that, had K not brought the proceedings, he would have been provided with a reference. However, the House of Lords rejected this 'but for' approach to victimisation. While it was true that the reference was withheld by reason that K had brought the race discrimination claim in the strict causative sense, Lord Scott said that the language used in S.2(1) RRA was not the language of strict causation. Rather, it required the tribunal to identify 'the real reason, the core reason, the causa causans, the motive' for the treatment complained of. Lord Scott concluded that the real reason for the refusal to provide the reference was that the provision of a reference might compromise the Chief Constable's handling of the case being brought against the West Yorkshire Police, which was a legitimate reason for refusing to accede to the request. Their Lordships were unanimous in their conclusion that K had not been refused a reference because he had done a protected act.

11.34 The House of Lords in Khan was considering victimisation under the RRA, which was defined in S.2(1) of that Act as less favourable treatment 'by reason that' the individual has done a protected act. The change in statutory wording to 'because' under S.27 EqA is unlikely to herald a substantive change to the test of causation. In Amnesty International v Ahmed 2009 ICR 1450, EAT (a race discrimination case), Mr Justice Underhill, then President of the EAT, noted that authorities interpreting the statutory language 'on grounds of' equated that phrase with 'by reason of'. He went on: 'Some of the authorities use a third phrase, asking whether the treatment in question was "because of" the proscribed factor. There can be no objection to this as a synonym for the statutory language'. On this basis, it seems safe to assume that 'on grounds of', 'by reason that' and 'because of' all mean much the same thing.

However, recent case law has raised doubts over the distinction drawn by their Lordships in Khan between lawful and unlawful conduct relating to discrimination litigation. In that case, Lord Hoffmann observed that employers who act 'honestly and reasonably' ought to be able to take steps to preserve their position in pending discrimination proceedings without laying themselves open to a charge of victimisation. The House characterised the Chief Constable's refusal of a reference as a reasonable act done to protect his position in litigation, rather than retaliation for K having brought the proceedings in the first place, and decided that this was the real reason for the refusal. Unfortunately, this approach is not without difficulties. For example, the House of Lords seemed to be advocating a test of reasonableness to decide whether or not there has been victimisation, whereas no such test exists (or existed) in the legislation. Furthermore, employees could find themselves in a situation where they were unable to obtain a reference until outstanding proceedings were concluded, making it potentially difficult to obtain another job.

The approach in Khan was reconsidered by the House of Lords in the context **11.35** of equal pay claims in Derbyshire and ors v St Helens Metropolitan Borough Council and ors 2007 ICR 841, HL. In that case, the Council employed D and her colleagues to provide school meals. In 1998 510 catering staff brought equal pay claims, most of which the Council settled. However, the claimants did not accept the settlement terms and continued with their claims. Two months before the hearing, the Council wrote to all the catering staff spelling out the likely consequences if the claims were successful – in particular, that the price of school meals would rise by such an amount as to make the service 'wholly unviable' and that the service would have to be reduced, requiring only 'a very small proportion of the existing workforce'. The Council also wrote to each of the claimants individually, stating that it could not afford any immediate increase in pay and urging them to reconsider the offer of settlement. It added that it was impossible to overstate 'the impact that the current course of action will have on the service and everyone employed within it'. The claimants said that the letters had caused them distress and reproaches from colleagues. This, they argued, amounted to detriment for the purpose of establishing victimisation under S.4(1) SDA. A tribunal upheld their claims and the EAT dismissed the Council's appeal. However, the majority of the Court of Appeal (Lord Justice Mummery dissenting) held that, although the Council's motive in sending the letters was to persuade the claimants to settle their claims, it did not follow that the Council had discriminated against them. The crucial question was whether the employer's conduct had been part of an honest and reasonable attempt to compromise the proceedings. The appeal was allowed and the case was remitted to the tribunal for determination of that question.

The employees appealed to the House of Lords, which unanimously allowed the appeal. Lord Hope noted that while the test adopted by their Lordships in Khan of whether the employer's conduct was 'honest and reasonable' could be 'a convenient way of determining whether the statutory test is satisfied', it was no substitute for the statutory test then contained in S.4(1)(a) – whether the employer's conduct was 'by reason that' the employee was insisting on her equal pay claim. Lord Neuberger of Abbotsbury, who gave the leading judgment, observed that a difficulty with the Lords' reasoning in Khan is that it suggested that whether or not a particular act can be said to amount to victimisation must be judged from the point of view of the alleged *discriminator*. According to his Lordship, it was true that the words 'by reason that' in S.4(1)(a) SDA required consideration of why the employer had performed the particular act (in this case, the sending of the two letters), and to that extent it was necessary to assess the alleged act of victimisation from the employer's

427

point of view. However, Lord Neuberger suggested that a more satisfactory approach involved focusing on the concept of 'detriment' – the basis upon which discrimination in St Helens was claimed – rather than on the words 'by reason that'. If, in the course of equal pay proceedings, the employer's solicitor were to write to the employee's solicitor setting out, in appropriately measured and accurate terms, the financial or employment consequences of the claim succeeding, or the risks to the employee if the claim fails, or terms of settlement which are unattractive to the employee, any distress thereby induced in the employee could not possibly be said to constitute 'detriment' under the test formulated by Lord Justice Brightman in Ministry of Defence v Jeremiah 1980 ICR 13, CA. An alleged victim cannot establish 'detriment' merely by exhibiting mental distress: before he or she could succeed, it would have to be objectively reasonable in all the circumstances. Distress and worry induced by the employer's honest and reasonable conduct in the course of its defence or in the conduct of any settlement negotiations cannot (save in the most unusual circumstances) constitute 'detriment' for the purposes of the SDA (or, by analogy, the EqA).

11.36 In support of his argument for adopting the detriment test, Lord Neuberger pointed to Coote v Granada Hospitality Ltd 1999 ICR 100, ECJ – not cited in Khan – where the European Court of Justice focused on the effect of the relevant act on the alleged victim, rather than on the purpose of the alleged discriminator in carrying out the act. If Coote had been before the Lords in Khan, they might, in Lord Neuberger's opinion, have adopted a different juridical basis for their conclusion. Nevertheless, Lord Neuberger considered that his preferred approach would in practice produce the same result to that achieved following the reasoning adopted in Khan. It was hard to imagine circumstances where an 'honest and reasonable' action by an employer, in the context of an employee's equal pay claim, could lead to 'detriment' on the part of the employee.

On the facts, their Lordships concluded, the tribunal had made no error of law as it had correctly considered whether the two letters had given rise to detriment. The Council went further than was reasonable to protect its interests in the litigation and the reason for its doing so was that the claimants had brought the equal pay claims and were pursuing them. On the meaning of the words 'by reason that' a person has 'brought proceedings' in S.4(1)(a) SDA, Baroness Hale held that the tribunal had correctly pointed out that the reason for the adverse treatment could be the *continuation* as well as the commencement of proceedings. It would make no sense to prevent an employer from treating an employee badly because he or she had brought proceedings but not to prevent him from treating the employee badly if he or she refused to abandon them.

11.37 It is worth noting here that there were important differences between the facts in the Khan case and those in the St Helens case which may go some way to explaining the different outcomes. In both cases, the claimants' bringing proceedings was the context (to put it neutrally) for the employer's actions. However, the degree to which those actions were linked to the proceedings was different. The bringing (and the continuance) of equal pay proceedings in St Helens was unarguably the motive for the Council's letters to the claimants – the tribunal found that the claimants' equal pay case 'was not simply the setting for the detriment: its continuance was the efficient cause'. The Council wanted to stop the equal pay claims, and so the claims were the core reason for the Council's actions. By contrast, the employer in Khan refused to do something (provide a reference) for fear of prejudicing its position in litigation. Had there been a finding in Khan that the employer had refused to provide the reference in order to persuade the claimant to give up his claim, the result would undoubtedly have been different.

Following the St Helens case, even 'honest and reasonable' attempts by an employer to protect its position in litigation are not *automatically* exempted from the scope of S.27 EqA, but employers still have room for manoeuvre in this regard. In British Medical Association v Chaudhary 2007 IRLR 800, CA, the Court of Appeal held that the BMA did not victimise C when it refused to reconsider its decision not to offer him support in his complaint of race discrimination against the Royal College of Surgeons. C had warned the BMA that its refusal to assist him could also be viewed as race discrimination, and he asserted that the BMA's refusal to reconsider its earlier decision was a response to that allegation. However, the Court noted that, when deciding not to reconsider the decision not to offer support, the BMA was in the position of a potential respondent to a discrimination claim by C. That claim would have been out of time (the original refusal having taken place eight months previously), and the only way to give rise to a fresh claim would have been for the BMA to reconsider and once more to refuse. In those circumstances, by refusing to reconsider, the BMA was seeking to protect its position in respect of potential litigation, which was a legitimate response. The Court of Appeal acknowledged that St Helens had criticised the basis on which Khan had been decided. However, according to Lord Justice Mummery, giving the judgment of all the members of the Court, St Helens 'reaffirmed the essential statement of law that a person does not discriminate if he takes the impugned decision in order to protect himself in litigation'. (It is worth noting that Mummery LJ's dissenting judgment in the Court of Appeal in St Helens was expressly approved by the House of Lords' judgment in that case, and so his opinion in Chaudhary carries substantial weight.)

Accordingly, employers are still entitled to take reasonable steps to defend **11.38** themselves in litigation, but they must give thought to the effect of their actions on the employee concerned. If their actions, from the employee's point of view, could be regarded as undue pressure to give up his or her claim, then, on the basis of the analysis in the St Helens case, those actions may be viewed as

429

amounting to detrimental treatment of the employee 'because' he or she brought a claim, and therefore potentially amount to victimisation. Two examples:

- **Commissioners of Inland Revenue and anor v Morgan** 2002 IRLR 776, EAT: the Appeal Tribunal upheld a tribunal's decision that the employer had victimised M when a memorandum had been circulated to M's colleagues, informing them that M had brought a race discrimination claim and warning them that some of their personal details might be revealed as a result of the disclosure process. This had an adverse effect on the attitude of M's colleagues towards her. The EAT considered that the sending of the memorandum was not a reasonable step taken to protect the employer's position. The circulation of the memorandum did not materially advance the employer's position in the proceedings and the employer's interests would not have been harmed had it not been done. It might have been different if the memorandum had simply been asking for witnesses to come forward, for example. The tribunal had not erred in concluding that the memorandum had been sent 'by reason that' M had brought a race claim, within the language of the RRA. (Although this case was decided before St Helens, its rationale seems to accord with the current understanding of victimisation in the context of litigation)

- **Aziz v First Division Association** ET Case No.2330314/10: a tribunal struck out a claim of victimisation based on FDA's response to A's claim of race discrimination against it for failing to support her in litigation against her employer. FDA had denied A's claim by letter and had gone on to state that, if A did not withdraw her claim, it reserved the right to seek costs against her. The tribunal found that the letter was written in a measured tone and was not intimidatory in any way – there was nothing improper in warning A that a costs application would be made if her claim failed.

11.39 **Significant influence.** It was clear under the pre-EqA discrimination provisions that a person claiming victimisation need not show that less favourable treatment was meted out *solely* by reason of the protected act. As Lord Nicholls indicated in Nagarajan v London Regional Transport 1999 ICR 877, HL (a race discrimination claim), if protected acts have a 'significant influence' on the employer's decision-making, discrimination will be made out. Nagarajan was considered by the Court of Appeal in Igen Ltd (formerly Leeds Career Guidance) and ors v Wong and other cases 2005 ICR 931, CA, in the context of sex discrimination. In that case Lord Justice Peter Gibson clarified that for an influence to be 'significant' it does not have to be of great importance. A significant influence is rather 'an influence which is more than trivial. We find it hard to believe that the principle of equal treatment would be breached by the merely trivial.'

These decisions are capable of applying equally to S.27(1) – the requirement that the detriment be 'because of' the protected act would seem to allow for multiple causes. This view is supported by the EHRC's Code of Practice on Employment, which notes at para 9.10 that the protected act need not be the only reason for detrimental treatment for victimisation to be established.

Length of time between protected act and detriment. A considerable length **11.40** of time may elapse between the protected act being done and the detriment being suffered. However, the longer the period between the protected act and the detriment, the harder it is likely to be to show a nexus between the two, particularly where the relationship is ongoing.

Subconscious motivation. For many years the rule was that not only must **11.41** there be a causal link between the protected act and the unfavourable treatment (now detriment), but it must also be shown that the discriminator acted from a motive which was consciously connected with the discrimination legislation – see Aziz v Trinity Street Taxis Ltd and ors 1988 ICR 534, CA. This was in direct contrast to the test in direct discrimination claims, where conscious motivation is not required. However, the need for a conscious motive in victimisation claims was rejected by the House of Lords in Nagarajan v London Regional Transport (above). It is not necessary, therefore, for a tribunal to distinguish between 'conscious' and 'subconscious' motivation when determining whether a complainant has been victimised. The House of Lords ruled that victimisation may be 'by reason of' an earlier protected act if the discriminator subconsciously permitted that act to determine or influence his treatment of the complainant.

That said, a discriminator cannot be even subconsciously influenced by a protected act of which he or she was not, directly or indirectly, aware. In Chief Constable of Cumbria v McGlennon 2002 ICR 1156, EAT, M claimed that he had been victimised for submitting a sex discrimination questionnaire. The EAT criticised the tribunal's decision for failing to properly address the issue of whether M's superiors were aware of the fact that M had submitted the questionnaire or that their decisions were induced in some way by a person who was so aware.

Manner of carrying out protected act. Employees may lose the protection of **11.42** the anti-victimisation provisions because of the *manner* in which they carry out the protected act. In In re York Truck Equipment Ltd EAT 109/88, for example, X, a cleaner, alleged that she had been the victim of an attempted rape by one of her employer's tenants. She became dissatisfied at what she perceived as her employer's failure to investigate the incident adequately or to take appropriate measures against the alleged culprit. Eventually her persistence, and the manner in which she pursued her grievance, led to X being dismissed. She claimed sex discrimination because of the failure to act on her allegations and victimisation because of her dismissal in relation to those allegations. Both claims failed. The victimisation claim failed because the EAT upheld the tribunal's conclusion that

X's dismissal was not by reason of the allegation which constituted a protected act but was due entirely to the manner in which she had made the allegation.

Similarly, in London Borough of Hackney and anor v Odedra EAT 253/96 O had brought a discrimination claim against the Council but then withdrawn it when the tribunal told her that her case had little prospect of success. The employer thought that this was an end to the matter and when, sometime later, O resurrected the same issues, she was told to stop complaining. The tribunal hearing the ensuing victimisation claim found that O had been treated less favourably on account of the earlier proceedings, but the EAT overturned this decision because the tribunal had made no finding as to causation. In particular, it had not considered whether the Council's view that the manner in which O pursued her old complaints was unreasonable and vexatious was correct and whether this, and not the earlier proceedings, was the reason for it not dealing with those complaints. The case was remitted to a different tribunal.

1.43 The approach taken in these cases can be criticised for the rather artificial way in which the *protected act* and the *manner of doing that act* have been separated. It should also be noted that these cases pre-date the House of Lords' decision in Nagarajan v London Regional Transport (above) and must therefore be treated with some caution. It is hard to see how the complainant's doing of the protected act in no way *influenced* the employer when deciding to dismiss. However, there is still case authority for distinguishing between something an employer does *because* litigation has been brought, and something the employer does *in the context of* that litigation – see, for example, Chief Constable of West Yorkshire Police v Khan 2001 ICR 1065, HL. Furthermore, it makes sense that not every act done by an employee that can be pegged to an allegation of discrimination is protected. Imagine that an employee suspects that his or her employer's pay structure is indirectly discriminatory. It would clearly be unlawful to subject that employee to a detriment for suggesting as much. But if the employee very publicly exaggerated the suspected unlawfulness – for example, by stating on a social networking site or in a letter to a national newspaper that the employer is knowingly sexist in its employment practices – then the employer might have legitimate grounds for taking action. The employer could argue that it did not act *because* the employee had made an allegation of sex discrimination, but *because* the employee had brought the company into disrepute. Of course, such behaviour might also fall outside S.27 EqA on the ground that it contains an element of bad faith, but that is difficult to establish – see under 'Protected acts – allegations of a contravention of the EqA' above.

An approach that distinguishes between a protected act and the manner of doing that act has been endorsed with regard to the whistleblowing provisions contained in the Employment Rights Act 1996 (ERA). S.103A ERA makes it automatically unfair to dismiss an employee for having made a 'protected disclosure'. Protected disclosures are defined at Ss.43A–43H ERA, and include disclosure of information tending to show that the employer is likely to be in breach of legal obligations. In Bolton School v Evans 2007 ICR 641, CA, the Court of Appeal held that an employee who was dismissed for hacking into the school's computer system to demonstrate its vulnerability to attack was not dismissed for having made a protected disclosure. The hacking was misconduct, for which dismissal was a potentially fair response. Even if the act of hacking could amount to a disclosure, the employee was dismissed for misconduct and not because of the potential legal breach he had highlighted. A similar distinction might be acceptable under S.27 EqA.

Proving victimisation   11.44

Victimisation claims under the EqA are subject to the 'shifting burden of proof', which is set out in S.136 of that Act. This section provides that the initial burden is on the claimant to prove facts from which the tribunal could decide, in the absence of any other explanation, that the respondent has contravened a provision of the Act (a 'prima facie case'). The burden then passes or 'shifts' to the respondent to prove that discrimination did not occur. If the respondent is unable to do so, the tribunal is obliged to uphold the discrimination claim.

The shifting burden of proof is designed to help claimants get the claim off the ground, since discrimination is notoriously hard to prove. However, the claimant must still show some prima facie evidence before there will be a case for the respondent to answer and tribunals will be alert to weed out baseless claims. For example, in Hill v Arriva Southern Counties Ltd ET Case No.1101308/10 the employer had referred to H's complaints of discrimination in the letter it sent dismissing her for gross misconduct. It noted, 'you are not a victim of harassment, victimisation or discrimination as you claim and these accusations are raised by you whenever the management team have a need to speak to you over work-related issues'. The tribunal concluded that this did not indicate victimisation. H had genuinely been dismissed for her unreasonable refusal to comply with management instructions. The reference to her allegations of discrimination arose only because H raised them orally and in writing before and during the disciplinary hearing.

One of the essential elements of the prima facie case that a claimant must make 11.45 out is that the employer actually knew about the protected act on which the claimant bases his or her claim. In Scott v London Borough of Hillingdon 2001 EWCA Civ 2005, CA, the Court of Appeal upheld the EAT's decision that an unsuccessful job applicant had not been victimised for bringing a race discrimination complaint against a former employer. The Court ruled that knowledge of a protected act is a precondition of a finding of victimisation and that as there was no positive evidence that the respondent knew of the claimant's previous complaint, there had been no proper basis for the tribunal to infer that the claimant had been victimised.

433

Case list

(Note that employment tribunal cases are not included in this list.)

A

Abdoulaye and ors v Régie Nationale des Usines Renault SA 2001 ICR 527, ECJ   2.59
Abdulla and ors v Birmingham City Council 2011 IRLR 309, QBD   2.48, 9.8
Adamson and Hatchett Ltd v Cartlidge EAT 126/77   5.8
Ainsworth v Glass Tubes and Components Ltd 1977 ICR 347, EAT   4.60
Alabaster v Barclays Bank plc (formerly Woolwich plc) and anor 2005 ICR
  1246, CA; 2005 ICR 695, ECJ   2.60, 3.16, 4.58
Aldridge v British Telecommunications plc 1989 ICR 790, EAT   7.90, 7.94
Allen and ors v GMB 2008 ICR 1407, CA   11.29
Allonby v Accrington and Rossendale College and ors 2001 ICR 1189, CA;
  2004 ICR 1328, ECJ   2.19, 4.32, 4.57, 8.70, 8.92
Amnesty International v Ahmed 2009 ICR 1450, EAT   11.34
Angestelltenbetriebsrat v Wiener Gebietskrankenkasse 2000 ICR 1134, ECJ   5.21
Arbeiterwohlfahrt der Stadt Berlin eV v Bötel 1992 IRLR 423, ECJ   3.19, 3.20
Armstrong and ors v Newcastle upon Tyne Hospital Trust 2006
  IRLR 124, CA   4.33, 8.10, 8.16, 8.17, 8.54, 8.56, 8.75
Arnold v Beecham Group Ltd 1982 ICR 744, EAT   2.68, 6.18, 6.26, 6.36
Ashby and ors v Birmingham City Council 2011 IRLR 473, QBD   9.9
Ashmore v British Coal Corporation 1990 ICR 485, CA   7.20
Audit Commission v Haq EAT 0123/10   8.122
Avon and Somerset Police Authority v Emery 1981 ICR 229, EAT   8.34
Avon County Council v Foxall and ors 1989 ICR 407, EAT   7.45
Aziz v Trinity Street Taxis Ltd and ors 1988 ICR 534, CA   11.21, 11.23, 11.41

B

Bainbridge and ors v Redcar and Cleveland Borough Council (No.2) 2007
  IRLR 494, EAT   4.64
Baker and ors v Rochdale Health Authority EAT 295/91;
  unreported 14.1.94, CA   5.3, 8.111
Barber v Guardian Royal Exchange Assurance Group
  1990 ICR 616, ECJ   1.64, 2.33, 2.51, 2.53, 3.23, 3.31, 9.76
Barry v Midland Bank plc 1997 ICR 192, EAT; 1999 ICR 859, HL   1.45, 8.90, 8.96, 8.99
Barton v Investec Henderson Crosthwaite Securities Ltd 2003 ICR 1205, EAT   8.29, 8.105
Beddoes and ors v Birmingham City Council and other cases EAT
  0037–43/10 and others   4.35
Beneviste v Kingston University EAT 0393/05   11.22
Benveniste v University of Southampton 1989 ICR 617, CA   8.35, 8.37, 8.40
Bestuur van het Algemeen Burgerlijk Pensioenfonds v Beune 1995
  IRLR 103, ECJ   3.26, 3.38
Biggs v Somerset County Council 1995 ICR 811, EAT; 1996 ICR 364, CA   1.44, 1.45
Bilka-Kaufhaus GmbH v Weber von Hartz 1987
  ICR 110, ECJ   1.54, 3.29, 3.31, 7.39, 8.20, 8.59, 8.89, 8.95, 9.72
Blackburn and anor v Chief Constable of West Midlands Police 2009
  IRLR 135, CA   5.16, 8.96, 8.155

C

441

442

Staffordshire County Council v Barber 1996 ICR 379, CA   1.45
Strathclyde Regional Council and ors v Wallace and ors 1998
   ICR 205, HL   8.9, 8.22, 8.47, 8.50

T
Taylor v Connex South Eastern Ltd EAT 1243/99   8.139
Tennants Textile Colours Ltd v Todd 1989 IRLR 3, NICA   7.89, 7.93
Ten Oever v Stichting Bedrijfspensioenfonds voor het Glazenwassers-en
   Schoonmaakbedrijf 1995 ICR 74, ECJ   3.37
Thacker and anor v Secretary of State for Education and Skills and anor
   EAT 0039/05   9.25
Thatcher v Middlesex University and anor EAT 0134/05   9.33
Thomas and ors v National Coal Board 1987 ICR 757, EAT   4.62, 5.14, 5.17
Tyne and Wear Passenger Transport Executive (trading as Nexus) v Best
   and ors 2007 ICR 523, EAT   8.87

U
Unison and anor v Brennan and ors 2008 ICR 955, EAT   1.50
Unison v Allen and ors 2008 ICR 114, EAT   9.42
United Biscuits Ltd v Young 1978 IRLR 15, EAT   8.131
University of Manchester v Jones 1993 ICR 474, CA   8.70, 8.72

V
Vakante v Addey and Stanhope School (No.2) 2005 ICR 231, CA   2.16
Van Duyn v Home Office 1975 Ch 358, ECJ   1.48
Van Gend en Loos v Nederlandse Administratie der Belastingen 1963
   ECR 1, ECJ   1.41, 1.42, 1.43, 1.47
Villalba v Merrill Lynch and Co Inc and ors 2007
   ICR 469, EAT   1.69, 8.10, 8.15, 8.43, 8.46, 8.50, 8.65, 8.87
Von Colson and Kamann v Land Nordrhein-Westfalen 1984 ECR 1891, ECJ   1.49
Voß v Land Berlin 2008 1 CMLR 49, ECJ   8.158

W
Waddington v Leicester Council for Voluntary Service 1977
   ICR 266, EAT   5.3, 5.17, 8.143, 8.149
Walsall MBC and anor v Birch and ors EAT 0376/10   9.46
Walton Centre for Neurology and Neuro Surgery NHS Trust v
   Bewley 2008 ICR 1047, EAT   4.41, 4.47, 4.52, 4.53, 8.130
Waters v Commissioner of Police of the Metropolis 1997 ICR 1073, CA   11.22
Webb v EMO Air Cargo (UK) Ltd 1993 ICR 175, HL   1.50, 8.90
Webb v EMO Air Cargo UK Ltd (No.2) 1995 ICR 1021, HL   1.50
Wetstein v Misprestige Management Services Ltd and anor EAT 523/91   8.82
Williams v Greater London Citizens Advice Bureaux Service 1989 ICR 545, EAT   9.55
Wilson v Health and Safety Executive 2010 ICR 302, CA   8.100, 8.116
Winder v Aston University and anor EAT 0025/07   9.19
Wood and ors v William Ball Ltd 2000 ICR 277, EAT   7.82
Woodcock v Cumbria Primary Care Trust 2011 ICR 143, EAT   8.93

443

Y

Index

A

Acas
  Codes of Practice
    job evaluations, 6.40
  independent experts, 7.67
  settlements, 9.86–9.89
Adaptability
  material factor defence, 8.154
Additional duties
  like work, 5.12–5.13
Additional voluntary contributions
  occupational pensions, 3.40
Administrative errors
  material factor defence, 8.163
Admissibility
  independent expert's report, 7.85
  statutory questionnaire procedure, 9.57
Advice
  compromise agreements, 9.91–9.94,
    9.100–9.101
  Equality and Human Rights
    Commission, 9.102–9.103
Advisory, Conciliation and Arbitration
Service
  see Acas
Age
  gender pay gap, 1.11–1.12
Allowances
  pay, 3.19–3.22
Anti-social hours
  material factor defence, 8.27–8.28,
    8.155
  working time payments, 10.37–10.38
Armed forces personnel
  enforcement
    jurisdiction of tribunals, 9.6
    time limits, 9.48
  right to equal pay, 2.28
Arrears of pay
  remedies, 9.67–9.71
  time limits, 4.68, 9.17, 9.47
Article 157 TFEU
  Equal Treatment Directive
    direct effect, 1.69
  gender equality, 1.53–1.55

  jurisdiction of tribunals, 9.11–9.14
  pay, meaning of, 3.5–3.7
  workers under, 2.19–2.20
Associated employers
  comparators, 4.26–4.27

B

Basic pay
  equal pay audits, 10.17
Benchmark jobs
  job evaluation studies, 6.20
Benefits
  occupational pensions, 3.31–3.37
Bonuses
  pay, 3.9–3.11
Broadly similar work
  meaning, 5.4–5.6
Burden of proof
  enforcement, 9.64
  Equal Treatment Directive, 1.66
  equivalent work, 6.11
  job evaluation studies, 6.11
  material factor defence, 8.12–8.20
  sex discrimination claims, 1.58
  statutory questionnaire procedure, 9.51
  victimisation, 11.44–11.45

C

Case management orders
  equal value work hearings
    stage 1, 7.55–7.59
    stage 2, 7.64–7.66
    stage 3, 7.89
Choice of forum
  jurisdiction of tribunals, 9.7–9.10
Claims for equal pay
  collective claims, 2.6–2.7
  in combination with sex discrimination
    claims, 1.36
  individual claims, 2.4–2.5
  introduction, 2.2–2.3
Classification of jobs
  job evaluation studies, 6.5
Codes of Practice
  employment, 1.39

445